G. Washington.

THE HISTORY OF NATIONS
HENRY CABOT LODGE, Ph. D., LL. D. · EDITOR-IN-CHIEF

THE
UNITED STATES
(VOLUME I)
BY JAMES WILFORD GARNER, Ph. D.,

AND

HENRY CABOT LODGE, Ph. D., LL. D.

WITH A HISTORICAL REVIEW

BY JOHN BACH McMASTER, Litt. D., LL. D.

VOLUME XXIII

ILLUSTRATED

P · F · COLLIER & SON COMPANY
PUBLISHERS ∴ NEW YORK

Copyright, 1907, by
JOHN D. MORRIS & COMPANY

Copyright, 1910, by
THE H. W. SNOW & SON COMPANY

Copyright, 1913, by
P. F. COLLIER & SON

Copyright, 1916, by
P. F. COLLIER & SON

Copyright, 1920, by
P. F. COLLIER & SON COMPANY

Copyright, 1928, by
P. F. COLLIER & SON COMPANY

Copyright, 1932, by
P. F. COLLIER & SON COMPANY

MANUFACTURED IN U. S. A.

THE HISTORY OF NATIONS

EDITOR-IN-CHIEF

HENRY CABOT LODGE, Ph.D., LL.D.

Associate Editors and Authors

ARCHIBALD HENRY SAYCE, LL.D.
Professor of Assyriology, Oxford University,
England

SIR ROBERT K. DOUGLAS,
Professor of Chinese, King's College,
London

CHRISTOPHER JOHNSTON, M.D., Ph.D.
Professor, Syriac Language, Johns Hopkins
University, Baltimore

JEREMIAH WHIPPLE JENKS, Ph.D., LL.D.
Professor of Political Economy and Politics,
Cornell University

KANICHI ASAKAWA, Ph.D.

D. W. C. OMAN.
Professor of History, Oxford University

THEODOR MOMMSEN.
Late Professor of Ancient History, University
of Berlin

WILFRED HAROLD MUNRO, LL.D.

ARTHUR C. HOWLAND, Ph.D.

C. MERCER ADAM.

CHARLES MERIVALE, LL.D.

FRED MORROW FLING, Ph.D.

FRANÇOIS AUGUSTE MARIE MIGNET.

S. HIGGINSON CABOT, Ph.D.

JAMES WESTFALL THOMPSON, Ph.D.

SIR WILLIAM W. HUNTER, F.R.S.

SAMUEL RAWSON GARDINER, LL.D.

GEORGE M. DUTCHER, Ph.D.

P. W. JOYCE, LL.D.

THE HISTORY OF NATIONS

EDITOR-IN-CHIEF

HENRY CABOT LODGE, Ph.D., LL.D.

Associate Editors and Authors

ARCHIBALD HENRY SAYCE, LL.D.,
Professor of Assyriology, Oxford University

CHRISTOPHER JOHNSTON, M.D., Ph.D.,
Associate Professor of Oriental History and Archaeology, Johns Hopkins University

C. W. C. OMAN,
Professor of History, Oxford University

THEODOR MOMMSEN,
Late Professor of Ancient History, University of Berlin

ARTHUR C. HOWLAND, Ph.D.,
Department of History, University of Pennsylvania

CHARLES MERIVALE, LL.D.,
Late Dean of Ely, formerly Lecturer in History, Cambridge University

J. HIGGINSON CABOT, Ph.D.,
Department of History, Wellesley College

SIR WILLIAM W. HUNTER, F.R.S.,
Late Director-General of Statistics in India

GEORGE M. DUTCHER, Ph.D.,
Professor of History, Wesleyan University

SIR ROBERT K. DOUGLAS,
Professor of Chinese, King's College, London

JEREMIAH WHIPPLE JENKS, Ph.D., LL.D.
Professor of Political Economy and Politics, Cornell University

KANICHI ASAKAWA, Ph.D.,
Instructor in the History of Japanese Civilization, Yale University

WILFRED HAROLD MUNRO, L.H.D.,
Professor of European History, Brown University

G. MERCER ADAM,
Historian and Editor

FRED MORROW FLING, Ph.D.,
Professor of European History, University of Nebraska

FRANÇOIS AUGUSTE MARIE MIGNET,
Late Member of the French Academy

JAMES WESTFALL THOMPSON, Ph.D.,
Department of History, University of Chicago

SAMUEL RAWSON GARDINER, LL.D.,
Professor of Modern History, King's College, London

P. W. JOYCE, LL.D.,
Commissioner for the Publication of the Ancient Laws of Ireland

ASSOCIATE EDITORS AND AUTHORS—Continued

JUSTIN McCARTHY, LL.D.,
Author and Historian

AUGUSTUS HUNT SHEARER, Ph.D.,
Instructor in History, Trinity College, Hartford

W. HAROLD CLAFLIN, B.A.,
Department of History, Harvard University

CHARLES DANDLIKER, LL.D.,
President of Zurich University

ELBERT JAY BENTON, Ph.D.,
Department of History, Western Reserve University

SIR EDWARD S. CREASY,
Late Professor of History, University College, London

ARCHIBALD CARY COOLIDGE, Ph.D.,
Assistant Professor of History, Harvard University

WILLIAM RICHARD MORFILL, M.A.,
Professor of Russian and other Slavonic Languages, Oxford University

CHARLES EDMUND FRYER, Ph.D.,
Department of History, McGill University

E. C. OTTE,
Specialist on Scandinavian History

EDWARD S. CORWIN, Ph.D.,
Instructor in History, Princeton University

PAUL LOUIS LEGER,
Professor of Slav Languages, College de France

WILLIAM E. LINGELBACH, Ph.D.,
Assistant Professor of European History, University of Pennsylvania

BAYARD TAYLOR,
Former United States Minister to Germany

SIDNEY B. FAY, Ph.D.,
Professor of History, Dartmouth College.

J. SCOTT KELTIE, LL.D.,
President Royal Geographical Society

ALBERT GALLOWAY KELLER, Ph.D.,
Assistant Professor of the Science of Society, Yale University

EDWARD JAMES PAYNE, M.A.,
Fellow of University College, Oxford

PHILIP PATTERSON WELLS, Ph.D.,
Lecturer in History and Librarian of the Law School, Yale University

FREDERICK ALBION OBER,
Historian, Author and Traveler

JAMES WILFORD GARNER, Ph.D.,
Professor of Political Science, University of Illinois

JOHN BACH McMASTER, Litt.D., LL.D.,
Professor of History, University of Pennsylvania

JAMES LAMONT PERKINS, Managing Editor

The editors and publishers desire to express their appreciation for valuable advice and suggestions received from the following: Hon. Andrew D. White, LL.D., Alfred Thayer Mahan, D.C.L., LL.D., Hon. Charles Emory Smith, LL.D., Professor Edward Gaylord Bourne, Ph.D., Charles F. Thwing, LL.D., Dr. Emil Reich, William Elliot Griffis, LL.D., Professor John Martin Vincent, Ph.D., LL.D., Melvil Dewey, LL.D., Alston Ellis, LL.D., Professor Charles H. McCarthy, Ph.D., Professor Herman V. Ames, Ph.D., Professor Walter L. Fleming, Ph.D., Professor David Y. Thomas, Ph.D., Mr. Otto Reich and Mr. Francis J. Reynolds.

ASSOCIATE EDITORS AND AUTHORS—Continued

JUSTIN McCARTHY LL.D.

AUGUSTUS HUNT SHEARER Ph.D.

W. HAROLD CLAFIN B.A.

CHARLES PANDUKER LL.D.

ELBERT JAY BENTON Ph.D.

SIR EDWARD S. CREASY.

ARCHIBALD CARY COOLIDGE Ph.D.

WILLIAM RICHARD MORFILL M.A.

CHARLES EDMUND FAYER Ph.D.

E. C. OTTEY.

EDWARD S. CORWIN Ph.D.

PAUL LOUIS LEGER.

WILLIAM E. LINGELBACH Ph.D.

BAYARD TAYLOR.

SIDNEY B. FAY Ph.D.

J. SCOTT KELTIE LL.D.

ALBERT GALLOWAY KELLER Ph.D.

EDWARD JAMES PAYNE M.A.

PHILIP PATTERSON WELLS Ph.D.

FREDERICK ALISON OBER.

JAMES WILFORD GARNER Ph.D.

JOHN BACH McMASTER Litt.D., LL.D.

JAMES LAMONT PERKINS, Managing Editor

The editors and publishers desire to express their appreciation for valuable advice and suggestions received from the following: Hon. Andrew D. White, LL.D., Alfred Thayer Mahan, D.C.L., LL.D., Hon. Charles Emory Smith, LL.D., Professor Edward Gaylord Bourne, Ph.D., Charles F. Thwing, LL.D., Dr. Emil Reich, William Elliot Griffis, LL.D., Professor John Martin Vincent, Ph.D., LL.D., Melvil Dewey, LL.D., Alston Ellis, LL.D., Professor Charles H. McCarthy, Ph.D., Professor Herman V. Ames, Ph.D., Professor Walter L. Fleming, Ph.D., Professor David Y. Thomas, Ph.D., Mr. Otto Reich and Mr. Francis J. Reynolds.

vii

PREFACE

In the preparation of this work, written expressly for THE HISTORY OF NATIONS, it has been the purpose of the authors to write for the general reader a simple narrative of the rise and growth of the United States from the discovery to the present time. In doing so, they have striven to avoid unnecessary and uninteresting details and have endeavored to give prominence only to those characters who have been conspicuous in determining our national destiny and to those measures and events which may be said to constitute the landmarks of our progress from insignificant colonies to our present position as one of the great powers of the world.

In the limited compass of the work, it is obviously difficult to describe thoroughly all the forces and movements which have entered into our unparalleled growth, and, hence, much has necessarily been omitted which would have a proper place in a more elaborate historical treatise. What is here offered has been written with an honest effort at judicial fairness and historical accuracy. No pretense is made that this work is based on investigation of primary sources; on the contrary, it rests mainly on the standard and authoritative treatises of others who have made extended studies of special fields.

Grateful acknowledgment is hereby made to Professors Herman V. Ames, University of Pennsylvania; Charles H. McCarthy, Catholic University of America; Walter L. Fleming, University of West Virginia; David Y. Thomas, University of Florida, and Mr. O. M. Dickerson for important services rendered in the preparation of this work.

PREFACE

In the preparation of this work, written expressly for THE HISTORY OF NATIONS, it has been the purpose of the authors to write for the general reader a simple narrative of the rise and growth of the United States from the discovery to the present time. In doing so, they have striven to avoid unnecessary and uninteresting details and have endeavored to give prominence only to those characters who have been conspicuous in determining our national destiny and to those measures and events which may be said to constitute the landmarks of our progress from insignificant colonies to our present position as one of the great powers of the world.

In the limited compass of the work, it is obviously difficult to describe thoroughly all the forces and movements which have entered into our unparalleled growth, and, hence, much has necessarily been omitted which would have a proper place in a more elaborate historical treatment. What is here offered has been written with an honest effort at judicial fairness and historical accuracy. No pretense is made that this work is based on investigation of primary sources; on the contrary, it rests mainly on the standard and authoritative treatises of others who have made extended studies of special fields.

Grateful acknowledgment is hereby made to Professors Herman V. Ames, University of Pennsylvania; Charles H. McCarthy, Catholic University of America; Walter L. Fleming, University of West Virginia; David Y. Thomas, University of Florida, and Mr. O. M. Dickerson for important services rendered in the preparation of this work.

INTRODUCTION

THE history of the United States covers only three hundred years, a brief space even in the short period for which we possess written records of man's deeds and movements on earth. But the importance of a country's history is not to be measured merely by length of days. The place which a nation occupies in the world, the influence which it exercises in the present, and the future of which it gives promise, make a right understanding of its origin and meaning as important as that of any gift which can be bestowed by the slow passing of the centuries. The position of the United States to-day in world politics, the economic effect of the vast industrial and commercial system built up by the American people, as well as the moral, intellectual and material influence which they exert, make the country's history of the utmost importance, especially in connection with the study of the larger subject of Western civilization, of which America is the latest development. At the present moment, when in a single year we are promised half-a-dozen elaborate and general histories of the United States, the statement just made reads like a rather tiresome truism which it is needless to repeat. But it is well to remember that this widespread interest in American history is of very recent growth, and it therefore may not be amiss, when adding another work to the already long list, briefly to review the past and note the process by which the present condition, wherein there is to be found far more than a merely literary interest, has been reached.

A little more than thirty years ago* it was possible for a boy to enter Harvard College and after four years of study graduate with the highest honors without knowing of the existence of the Declaration of Independence or when the Constitution of the United States was framed. What was true of Harvard was true of other universities and colleges. American history, although occasionally taught, was not included in the scheme of the higher education. Boys entering college were required to know something of the " glory that was Greece and the grandeur that was Rome," but they were permitted to remain in complete ignorance of all that related

* Written in 1904. xi

to the history of their own country. During the four years of the college course they had modest opportunity to study the history of England and Europe, but none to learn aught of the United States. This condition of education, which seems so melancholy now, was really the result of a general attitude of mind then passing away, but which had once been predominant. The usual opinion during the first half of the nineteenth century seems to have been that there was no American history worth telling, apart from the adventures of the earliest settlers and the events of the Revolution, which were both connected so closely with the history of Europe that they might fairly be deemed of some importance. Among the most highly educated portion of the community the ignorance was, comparatively speaking, densest, and for the very obvious reason that the history of democracy, then a new thing in the world, was entirely different in its attributes and conditions from the history with which everybody had been familiar during many centuries. To conceive of a history destitute of kings and nobles and aristocratic traditions, unillumined by the splendor of a court, without the lights and shades which the contrast of ranks alone can give, was very difficult, because it involved a new idea. It always takes time for people to grasp the proposition that because a thing is different from that to which they have been accustomed it is not necessarily inferior. Habit and prescription, although in their very nature never fully realized nor perfectly understood, are forces of enormous power among men and nations.

American history had also to contend with feminine indifference, and women influence largely the success of historic writings, as they do that of other books. Macaulay knew precisely the test of popularity and wide circulation when he said that he wanted his history to take the place of the novel on every young lady's table. To suppose, therefore, that women would easily or at once take interest in the seemingly stern, gray story of state building and war, of law-making and constitutions, stripped, as it was in America, of all the glitter and romance and refinement which clung about the history of monarchies and empires to which they had always been accustomed, would have been to expect too much. " Fishers and choppers and ploughmen," constituting a state in Emerson's noble verse, were very fine, but they seemed unlikely to have a history as interesting or leave memoirs as entertaining as those of the Courts of St. James or of Versailles, which educated Americans were wont to read. The truth was that the higher education to which I have alluded to was defective in regard to the history of the United States simply because that history during the first half of the nineteenth century had neither audience nor demand either at home or abroad. Here and there a state historical society, local antiquarians or the descendants of some of the great men who fought in the Revolution and made the Constitution, collected material, gathered traditions or edited letters and memoirs, but these efforts were commonly regarded as amiable idiosyncrasies, quite harmless but not designed for general use. Nothing indeed illustrates better this attitude of mind toward American history at that time than that Prescott and Motley devoted their brilliant talents to Spain and Holland at a period which had no connection, or at best a very slight one, with the vast region which was one day to be the United States. The fact was that educated people did not think, as a rule, that the United States had any history worth consideration, just as they likewise thought that while we undoubtedly had public men they were not to be seriously considered as statesmen in the sense of European ministers or English Parliamentary leaders. They were unable to realize that the organization of a nation and the development of a new country by a great democracy demanded power, ability and statesmanship of a very high and strong variety. It was all different, it was new, and it was not therefore really important tried by the fashions of the Old World. The colonial habit of mind died hard in regard to American history, as it did in many other ways.

Yet even then there were men who saw what a field was open to the historian in the story of the United States and of the colonies out of which the United States had been developed. Richard Hildreth, working only on public documents, newspapers, printed books and pamphlets and Congressional debates, produced his history of the United States from the earliest settlements down to his own time. The volumes are dry, without literary quality or charm, almost unreadable indeed as literature, and yet Hildreth's work, considering his material, is very accurate and remains as a comprehensive book of reference more valuable than many which have succeeded it. Mr. Bancroft attained to much wider success and to greater fame. He had the advantage of an unoccupied field to cultivate and a smaller world to appeal to, so that his labors achieved a success impossible now to much better work. He brought to this task the best education and training which the universities of the United States and Germany could afford, a keen mind, vigorous abilities, an intense love of country and an unwearied industry. But withal his history is diffuse; there is an inordinate space given to the affairs of contemporary Europe, and in the earliest edition there was some rather turgid writing in praise of the principles of democracy and the rights of man, as expounded by democracy, and the rights of man, as expounded by Rousseau and Jefferson. But Mr. Bancroft rendered, nevertheless, an incalculable service to American history by the vast mass of original matter which he brought to light and use and by the manner in which he gave unity and coördination to the history of the colonies. So wide were his researches and so extensive was his material that even his long and industrious life did not enable him to get beyond the period of the Confederation. To the same time we owe Mr. Palfrey's history of New England, a work of the highest and most admirable scholarship, of the best type of historical work, but somewhat dry in narration and necessarily covering only one group of the colonies which were to become the future United States.

In Francis Parkman, of a later generation than Bancroft or Palfrey, American literature found its first really great historian, one fairly entitled to a place in the small group where Thucydides, Tacitus, and Gibbon stand apart as the great and hitherto unrivaled exemplars. Mr. Parkman not only had untiring industry and the capacity for sifting evidence and marshaling facts drawn in many cases from the dark corners of forgotten manuscripts, but he possessed also the power of compression, the reserved but vigorous style, and above all the imagination, which enabled him to make history live and have a meaning, without which life and meaning it will surely die and be buried among incoherent animals and scientific catalogues of facts. In a series of volumes he gradually drew a noble picture of the mighty struggle of races which ended in giving North America to the English-speaking people. The drama spread over a continent, the actors who flitted across the vast stage were Indians and Jesuits, courtiers of Louis XIV., and sober Puritans of New England, French adventurers and sturdy Dutch traders from the Mohawk and the Hudson, all with the wilderness as a background and a future beyond imagination as a prize for which they blindly strove. Parkman made the world comprehend not only that American history was important, but that if it did not have the precise kind of picturesqueness to which that of Europe had accustomed us, it had a picturesqueness of its own, a light and color and a dramatic force not less impressive because they differed in kind from what had gone before.

Parkman began his work under the old conditions of indifference and inattention. When he brought his brilliant volumes to an end those conditions had utterly and entirely changed. The strong Departments of American History which have grown up at some of our leading universities in the last thirty years of the century is merely a sign of the complete alteration in opinion and feeling which had taken place not only in the universities and in the schools, but in the public mind after the close of the Civil War. Nothing in our earlier days, for example, showed more conclusively the national indifference to the past than the reckless destruction of landmarks and historic buildings. Now every effort is made to preserve all that remains which gives to past events a local habitation. Americans have learned, too late unfortunately in many instances, that the buildings and streets, the forests and the fields, which have been the scenes of memorable events, have not only inestimable worth historically and sentimentally, but that they are also pecuniarily valuable, to take a highly practical view, to any community lucky enough to possess them.

In the same way books ranging from the most extensive histories to antiquarian monographs, rich in minute learning upon some single incident, have multiplied almost beyond belief. Biographies, compilations of essays by specialists, general histories and manuals of all sorts have been duplicated and reduplicated until we seem in danger almost of losing sight of the city on account of the number of houses which cut off our view. The whole of our history, from the first voyage of Columbus to the last administration at Washington, has been examined and written about in some fashion. In the old days the period between the landings at Plymouth and Jamestown and the Declaration of Independence, and that which stretched forward from the surrender at Yorktown might have been labeled, like portions of the maps so familiar a generation ago, the "Great American Desert." And people dwelt contented with their "Desert" and their ignorance. But the settlements have spread and, as they spread, have subdued and conquered. "The Great American Desert" is no more; irrigation threatens its last stronghold, and the unopened tracts of the history of the United States have all been roamed over and explored. Most of the exploration and examination has resulted merely in what is so dear to the purely scientific historian, vast masses of catalogued facts where literature is excluded, and one fact is just as good and important as any other, simply because it is a fact. These heaps of information, some of it valueless, much of it undigested, still only partly assorted, are the necessary conditions for real history written by one capable and understanding man as distinct from the huge aggregations of special articles, immensely valuable as books of reference, but having the same relation to history in its highest sense that the English dictionary bears to the plays of Shakespeare or the verse of Milton. Out of this mass of material thus fervently and indiscriminately collected in the last forty years have come two histories of the highest type in scholarship, research and original thought — Mr. Henry Adams's " History of the United States during the Administrations of Jefferson and Madison," and that of Mr. James Ford Rhodes covering the period subsequent to the Compromise of 1850. In addition to these we have many excellent biographies and monographs, as well as some admirable presentations and brilliant pictures of certain epochs and movements, like those of Mr. Fiske and Mr. McMaster, which are read by everyone and which are even more necessary than the highly scientific catalogues, stripped according to rule of all beauty of style and all human interest, and which are read by no one. To have brought so much pure gold as this out of the incalculable mass of " huddling silver little worth " is highly creditable to American letters and American history. It is an excellent record, not to be bettered elsewhere in the same period either in form or in the net contributing to human knowledge, and to the comprehension of the meaning of man upon earth.

Historians and learned societies, antiquarians and biographers, however, cannot create history unless the material for it exists, nor can they by their efforts alone develop from nothing a real interest in it among the people at large. The popular feeling which arouses the interest and manifests itself, not merely in the sale of histories and biographies, but by the enthusiasm shown in the celebration of local anniversaries, in numberless addresses, usually forgotten at once, except in the town or village commemorated, in the passion for genealogies and family histories, in the preservation and erection of monuments, springs from causes deep down among the people themselves. This activity and this earnestness in all things pertaining to the past are sound and wholesome, and also full of meaning. It is a commonplace to say that a people which cares nothing for its past has no present and deserves no future. But it is not quite so obvious that widespread interest in history is a proof of national consciousness and of the abiding sense that a nation has come to its place in the world.

While we looked to Europe for all our inspiration in art and letters, in thought and in politics, it was not to be expected that we should consider our own doings of much consequence or worthy of a serious place in history. Nor were those doings in themselves of much importance, for colonies are mere appendages, and what chiefly concerns mankind is the tree, not the dependent shoots which push up from spreading roots. The history of the American colonies intrinsically was not very important nor, apart from a certain air of adventure and rude picturesqueness, very generally interesting. But when the colonies became an independent state the case altered at once. It then became highly important to know and understand the origin and the past of the new nation in all its details. The ways of life, the habits and customs, of the tribes which wandered in the forests of Scandinavia and Germany are not in themselves very valuable, and are certainly not entertaining. But research exhausts itself, and wisely, too, in the effort to find the minutest facts which shall throw light upon the origin and history of the people from whom have come not only the dominant races of Western Europe, but the Western civilization which has crossed oceans and subjugated continents. To take another example, the island of Jamaica, now and always a dependent colony, is historically negligible, but the little State of Rhode Island deserves the careful attention of the historian because of her part and influence in founding, making and guiding a nation.

Many years passed before we emerged wholly from the colonial condition. Long after we had become independent politically, the old colonial habits of thought, as strong as they were impalpable, clung fast about us. Only step by step did we shake off the provincial spirit and rid ourselves of the bated breath of the colonist. We did not come to a full national consciousness until we had passed through the awful trial of the Civil War. Then we realized what we were, and the trembling deference to foreign opinion, the sensitive outcry against foreign criticism, as well as the uneasy self-assertion and boasting which accompanied them, fell from us as the burden fell from the shoulders of Christian. There was still much to do, but the old colonial habit of mind was shattered beyond recovery. It lingered on here and there; it dies hard, but it is dying, and now is nearly dead.

With the coming of a true national consciousness came the interest in the past and in history. It was apparent that the United States was one of the most considerable facts of the age when its consolidation had once been effected and all peril of dissolution had departed with the crushing out of the powers which aimed at separation. Anything which helped to explain this great fact became, therefore, of intense interest. As the years passed on the fact has grown larger. In due time a not very serious war revealed the fact to the world, and it appeared that this fact known as the United States had, and was destined to have, a strong and increasing influence upon all the other facts generally spoken of as the nations of the earth. Thus did it become more than ever obvious that the explanation of the United States to be found in the history of the past four centuries was worthy of the best efforts of the historian. The pride in what the country is spurs men on to pride in all who shared in making the nation. From the abortive attempts of the earliest adventurers, from the feeble settlements clinging to the Atlantic seaboard, through the confused and seemingly petty history of the colonies, and of the scattered people and small states struggling out of revolution and dissension to a larger national life, onward, to those who saved the Union from disintegration, and still on to those who have carried her power forward to the Pacific, and from first to last made a great nation where there was none before, all alike have come to possess deep meaning and importance. Hence the rise of American history, and, what is more important, of the general interest in that history, which may be trusted to separate the wheat from the chaff, and give us not only knowledge, but also something worthy to take a place in literature by the manner in which the knowledge is communicated to men.

Indeed, signs are not wanting that the inhabitants of England and Europe are beginning to think that the history of a people who have made a great and powerful nation to whom the future in large measure belongs is worthy of consideration, and that it may not be amiss to know something of the men who have led and guided that people in the past, and who lead and guide them now. There is evident, even on the other side of the Atlantic, a dawning idea that this knowledge may be as useful and even as illuminating as to trace the fortunes of some petty and wholly effaced Italian city despot or the personal intrigues of forgotten courtiers.

H. C. Lodge

James W. Garner.

CONTENTS

CHAPTER I

ABORIGINAL AMERICA

CHAPTER II

DISCOVERIES AND EXPLORATIONS. 1000–1606

CHAPTER III

THE PLANTING OF THE SOUTHERN COLONIES. 1606–1776

CHAPTER IV

THE PLANTING OF THE NORTHERN COLONIES. 1620–1776

CONTENTS

CHAPTER IX

RUPTURE WITH THE MOTHER COUNTRY. 1763–1775

CHAPTER X

REVOLUTION AND INDEPENDENCE. 1775–1776

CHAPTER XI

THE WAR IN THE MIDDLE COLONIES. 1776–1778

CHAPTER XII

THE WAR IN THE SOUTHERN COLONIES. 1778–1782

CONTENTS

CHAPTER XIII

TRANSITION FROM COLONIES TO STATES. 1781–1789

CHAPTER XIV

ESTABLISHMENT OF THE REPUBLIC. 1785–1789

CHAPTER XV

THE FIRST EIGHT YEARS OF THE CONSTITUTION.

CHAPTER XVI

THE FEDERALIST SUPREMACY. 1796–1801

CHAPTER XVII

JEFFERSONIAN REPUBLICANISM. 1801–1809

CONTENTS

CHAPTER XVIII

THE SECOND WAR WITH GREAT BRITAIN. 1809–1815

CHAPTER XIX

THE ERA OF GOOD FEELING AND INDUSTRIAL DEVELOPMENT. 1816–1824

CHAPTER XX

RISE OF THE DEMOCRATIC PARTY. 1824–1828

CHAPTER XXI

THE JACKSONIAN EPOCH. 1828–1841.

LIST OF ILLUSTRATIONS

GEORGE WASHINGTON (Van Dyck Photogravure in color) *Frontispiece*

TEXT MAPS

THE HISTORY OF
THE UNITED STATES

HISTORY OF
THE UNITED STATES

Chapter I

ABORIGINAL AMERICA

I

ORIGIN OF THE FIRST AMERICANS

"Many an æon moulded earth before her highest, man, was born."—
Tennyson

THE origin of the race which first peopled America is obscure in the darkness of prehistoric times, that is, prehistoric in America. The earliest man everywhere was a savage and has left few records of his life save in the implements of his daily use. His period is commonly designated as the Palæolithic (Unground Stone) Age, and that of his successors, the Neolithic (Ground Stone). The resemblance in the relics of all prehistoric races is very strong; indeed, the resemblance between the relics of the remotest tribes and the races of to-day is so striking that an expert is sometimes puzzled to distinguish an arrowhead of a modern Indian from one used by prehistoric man. In spite of this, however, Humboldt holds that the monument methods of computing time, systems of cosmogony, and many myths of America offer analogies with the ideas of eastern Asia too strong to admit of any explanation save that of an ancient connection. The natives of the extreme northwestern part of North America undoubtedly belong to the same family as the natives of northeastern Asia. For these and other reasons Hubert Howe Bancroft,[1] who has made an extended study of the Indians of the Pacific coast, inclines to the view that America was peopled from Asia. He acknowledges, however, that the migration may have been in the opposite direction, Asia being peopled by a race autocthonous in America.[2]

[1] Bancroft, "Native Races of the Pacific States," vol. i. pp. 16-19.
[2] A notable effort has recently been made under the auspices of Morris K. Jesup, President of the American Museum of Natural History, to settle more

Other theories have been advanced of racial connection, such as that the aboriginals of America were of Celtic, Egyptian, Phœnician, or even Jewish origin. But all of these belong to the realm of wild speculation or pure myth along with the lost Atlantis, over which some of them are reputed to have made the migration. The only conservative and defensible position is one of frank ignorance. The thorough ethnological studies now being undertaken may in the future throw light on the question, but it is extremely doubtful whether the results will be convincing.[3]

The theory of autocthonic origin is deserving of more respect. Certain fossil remains have been discovered which seem to give it at least a shadow of support. After the earthquakes of 1811-1812 a fragment of a human bone was found in a fissure near Natchez, Mississippi, along with the bones of a mastodon and other extinct animals. In 1852 a skeleton was dug up in New Orleans beneath four successive buried forests of cypress.[4] Similar discoveries have been made in the shafts of mines in California, but the authenticity of none of these is beyond dispute. But if this is the oldest continent, it certainly is not unreasonable to suppose that man first made his appearance here. Aside from the evidence just mentioned, there is abundant proof that the continent has been inhabited a long time, probably several thousand years.

definitely the question of the origin of the American Indians. Mr. Jesup, in consultation with a number of eminent anthropologists, came to the conclusion that the only satisfactory way to discover if there were any evidences of contact between the early settlers of America and Asia was to make a thorough investigation of the oldest remaining tribes of both countries. With this end in view the "Jesup North American Expedition of the American Museum of Natural History" was organized in 1897, and for seven years it has studied the characteristics, customs, traditions, and languages of the Indian tribes in America, from the Columbia River to northern Alaska, and in Asia as far south as the line of civilization. By studying how long the tribes had been on the Pacific Coast, what changes had taken place in the tribal physical characteristics, and what relation the various tribes bore to one another, it was possible to trace the relationship between the Asiatic and American tribes, and probably the cause of emigration in prehistoric times. The results of the expedition point to the existence of intimate relationship between the Asiatic and American Indians, and the conclusion of the members of the expedition is that the Indian originated in America and spread into Asia.

[3] Farrand, "Basis of American History," p. 87.

[4] Winsor, "The Antiquity of Man in America" in Winsor, "Narrative and Critical History," vol. i. p. 389; also Haynes, "Prehistoric Archæology of North America," vol. i. ch. vi.

Back of the Indians of historic times were the Mound Builders. The theory that they were a distinct race which disappeared before the Indian ever came, or were driven out by him, is no longer regarded as tenable. The Indian is now regarded as the descendant of the Mound Builders — degenerate, perhaps, in some respects.[5] The mounds, which constitute the only monuments of the existence of this race, are scattered throughout the Ohio and Mississippi valleys and are of varying size and shape. The purpose of some of them is beyond conjecture; others have been designated as mounds of observation, worship, or sepulture. In shape they are of four distinct classes, conical, elongate, pyramidal, and effigial. The first were used for sepulture. The purpose of the second, which consist of walls about four feet high, ten to twenty broad, and fifty to nine hundred long, is unknown. The pyramidal probably were used for worship, since mounds of similar construction have been found in Mexico with temples on them. The "Serpent Mound" in Adams County, Ohio, is a good specimen of the last class. Some occur in lowlands, indicating that they probably were used for refuge from high water. The defensive character of others is apparent, such as the walls of earth and stone constructed in such a manner as to reveal evidence of no little military skill.

The twenty miles of embankment at the mouth of the Scioto may have belonged to this class, but other similar works are difficult to explain. Sometimes graded roads lead from terrace to terrace, possibly to secure access to streams; others "begin nowhere and lead nowhere." In places there are perfect squares, in others, perfect circles, some of them a mile in circuit. In different parts of Ohio is found the curious arrangement of a square with two circles. In all cases the dimensions are the same, each side of the square measuring one thousand and eighty feet and the circles seventeen hundred and eight hundred feet in circumference. Sometimes moats are found inside these walls. Rings of from five to fifteen feet in diameter have been denominated "hut rings." The square house site may be found in Arkansas. In Michigan and Wisconsin appear mounds from four to six feet high, which evidently were intended to represent animals (the elephant for one), birds, fishes and implements. So-called "garden

[5] Farrand, "Basis of American History," p. 73.

mounds," which are but six or eight inches high, are found in Michigan and Wisconsin.

Excavations have brought to light many implements of war and the chase, fine specimens of pottery and other implements of domestic life. Pipes may be found in one, arrow-heads in another and copper tools in a third. The last named relics indicate that they were approaching the Metal Age, though they still belonged to the Stone Age. There is no evidence that metals were ever smelted above Mexico. In the north it was simply beaten out, but a great deal was done in this way. A mass of copper weighing six tons, raised upon a scaffold five feet high, probably in preparation for removal, was found in the Minnesota Mine eighteen feet below the surface. So long ago was the mining done that even the tradition of it was lost among the Indians whom the Europeans found there.[6]

The number and extent of the mounds are conclusive proof that the people who made them were numerous and industrious. Did they abandon them and move to the far southwest, or were they driven out by a hostile foe, or did they remain there and degenerate into the savages of historic times? One does not like to take the last alternative, yet he can adduce no conclusive proof for either of the others. This much is certain, however, that the culture of the Mound Builders was improved upon in Mexico, and in Central and South America.[7]

An account of the Indians of Mexico does not properly belong to a history of the United States, but the temptation to say a word concerning them as affording a high type of Indian civilization is irresistible. However, not all the Indians of Mexico were of this kind; all types were found there, from the beastly Yuman stock of Lower California to the Aztecs of the plateau. According to tradition the best Mexican stock had migrated from the north. Of these the Aztecs may be taken as a type, though the Tarascos and the Tapotecs were not far behind them, and the Mayas were, in some respects, their superiors.

The traditional history of the Aztecs, who centered about the

[6] Farrand, "Basis of American History," ch. v.
[7] The most valuable literature on the subject of the Indian mounds is to be found in the "Annual Reports" of the Smithsonian Institution. Hardly a year has passed since 1861 but these "Reports" have had in them contributions on the subject. The "Annual Reports of the U. S. Bureau of Ethnology" likewise frequently contain valuable papers on the Indian races and related subjects.

City of Mexico dates back to the fifth century. Some stone implements were still used by them, but they were, nevertheless, in the metal-agricultural age. They reckoned descent in the male line, though land was still held in common and marriage was regulated by gentile law. The achievements in architecture and public works were really marvelous, and revealed evidence of great engineering skill. Their cities were adorned with temples, but they practiced human sacrifice in a most revolting manner. Schools were maintained where the boys were taught history, religion and military science, while the girls learned domestic science and textile work. Much attention was given to the moral training of both sexes — the teachers were priests and priestesses — but one can not commend the basis of instruction, which was terror, not respect or love. Their writing was hieroglyphic, but far inferior to that of the Egyptians. They had preserved a great number of manuscripts, but the Spaniards destroyed the most of them.[8] In Central and South America were several tribes of equal, if not higher, attainments, especially the Incas in Peru. The civilization of the Incas, in fact, represented the highest development among the native races of America.[9]

The more exact method of classifying the Indians is by their physical and lingual characteristics. Most writers, however, following the lines of least resistance, classify them according to their culture and geographical location. A very satisfactory classification on the basis of language has been made by the Bureau of Ethnology in Washington. It recognizes fifty-nine independent families north of Mexico, the most important of which are the Algonquian, Athapascan, Eskimauan, Iroquoian, Muskhogean, and Siouan.[10]

A study of a map showing the location of the various families raises some interesting questions. While it indicates comparative stability of location at the time when the Europeans appeared, it speaks in unmistakable terms of great migrations in earlier times. One cannot but compare them with the great migrations of the time when the barbarians were sweeping over Europe. There is an Athapascan stock in the far northwest between Hud-

[8] Prescott, "Conquest of Mexico" (ed. Kirk), vol. i. pp. 72, 97.
[9] Sir C. R. Markham, "The Inca Civilization in Peru," in Winsor, "Narrative and Critical History," vol. i. p. 209.
[10] Farrand, "Basis of American History," pp. 92–96.

son Bay and the Pacific, and another on the Mexican border. So long ago was the separation, however, that their dialects and culture reveal few things in common. Some of the other widely scattered races have more in common. The movement of the Algonquian family evidently was from the north Atlantic region westward and southward, a few being found so far south as South Carolina. The Siouan family seems to have moved westward from the Carolinas and Virginia through Ohio, where they probably came in conflict with the Algonquian and Iroquoian. This was near the home of the latter, who centered about Lake Erie and Lake Ontario, forming the famous Five Nations, which gave Hiawatha to romance. Some of them were found in the southern Appalachian region. The best known tribes of the Sioux found by Europeans in the east and south were the Catawba of Carolina, and the Biloxi of Mississippi. Of the Algonquian stock, Delaware, Massachusetts, Pequot, Narraganset, and Shawnee, who gave Tecumseh to history, are familiar names of the colonial era in the east; also the Powhatan confederacy in Virginia. The Cheyenne, Illinois, Fox, Kickapoo and Pottawattomie belong farther west. The Muskhogean seem to have remained east of the Mississippi, and south of the Cumberland. The well-known tribes of these were the Alabama, Chickasaw, Choctaw, Creek and Seminole. These, with the Iroquoian Cherokee, constitute the civilized tribes of the present-day Oklahoma.

II

INDIAN CHARACTERISTICS AND RELIGION

Certain physical characteristics are common to the Indians of America, at least when we omit the Aleuts and Eskimos, though they differ among themselves as much as the people of Europe. Popularly called the " Red Man," his characteristic color is in reality brown with varying tints, from comparatively dark to light yellow. " Red Indian " probably arose from the sight of Indians painted red when on the war-path, as few really had the reddish tint. The hair is raven black, glossy and nearly always straight, and baldness is uncommon, as is also the presence of hair on the face. A common practice was to pluck the beard to prevent its growth. One of the most marked characteristics of the Indian is the high cheek bone, together with a large nose, generally aquiline. In some tribes the shape of the forehead was influenced by the custom of head-flattening. In stature he stood from five and a half to six feet, though many went beyond this — the Patagonians being reputed the tallest race in the world. The females were slightly under-sized and showed a tendency toward obesity.

In physical endurance the Indians were inferior to both the white man and the negro. True in all climes, this was especially so in the tropics, though by exception the Florida Indians were noted for their fine physical qualities. When parceled out as slaves by the Spanish in the West Indies and South America and forced to labor, they speedily perished and whole tribes became extinct. In mental capacity they were superior to the negro, but somewhat inferior to the white man in most things; even in fields particularly his own, knowledge of the forests and the habits of its denizens, the Indian often had to confess the superior skill of the whites.

A child of the forest and the plain, the "Red Man" felt his kinship with nature and bowed to her as his god.[11] He dwelt in a land of spirits and dreamed of "ampler hunting-grounds beyond the night," where his spirit would join in the chase with those of his companions gone before. The Great Spirit was worshiped, generally in the person of the sun. This was especially true in Mexico and South America. But all nature about the Indian was peopled with spirits, and it is doubtful if he ever venerated one great overruling spirit until taught by the white man. On the plains the spirit-buffalo was of prime importance; in agricultural realms, the rain-god. There were evil spirits as well as good, both of which he implored, and appeased the former with charms, sacrifices and fastings.[12] Even the conception of good and bad spirits shows the influences of the forces of nature. The Cherokees, for example, looked to the Sunland, or east, for the red gods of victory; out of the cold north came the blue spirit of disaster. Human sacrifices were not common north of Mexico, though some tribes made a feast of the slain after a notable victory. Though the Indian worshiped the myriad spirits of nature, he seldom bowed to gods of wood and stone made with his own hand. Some tribes, however, had palladiums which were the centers of great

[11] Grinnell, "The Story of the Indian," p. 163.
[12] Frederick Starr, "The American Indian," p. 80.

ceremonials and with which their prosperity was inseparably bound up. The Indian religion was peculiar in that the idea of personal sin was almost wholly absent. If the god had been offended, the tribe, not an individual, was guilty, and entrance to the happy hunting ground did not depend upon an upright life in this world. The Indian often tortured himself, but this was to win the favor of his god, not to appease him. Each tribe had a reputed founder whose good-will must always be kept. Often he was said to have been a great trickster, sometimes an anthropomorphic animal. The prophet or priest was also a medicine man, who effected his cures by charms and incantations. From the ghost dance, which originated in Nevada about twenty years ago, and took the place of the plains ceremonials, we learn that the religion of a tribe was not cast in a fixed mold, but was subject to decay or to development.[13]

Burial customs varied in detail, but inhumation was commonly practiced. The Hurons exposed their dead on scaffolds for a season, until the " Feast of the Dead," and then gathered their bones into a common sepulcher. Those who buried their dead often placed them in a sitting posture, facing the east, and put into the grave the implements of war and the chase belonging to the deceased and food enough for the journey of one of his spirits to the happy hunting ground. Another spirit, for each individual was believed to have several, haunted the body and the village.[14]

North of New Mexico on the plains and in the east, the prevailing plan for a house or wigwam, as it was called, was conical. It was constructed by setting several poles in the ground and bringing them together at the top. Splits, poles, bark, brush and reeds were used for covering. Smoke escaped through a hole at the top. The wigwams were grouped in villages and sometimes they were surrounded by palisades. The " long houses " of the Iroquois, from fifty to one hundred feet long, were well constructed with a stout framework. Small compartments provided with sleeping bunks ranged around the walls. Great communal houses were found in the Columbia region. In California the dugout and dome-shaped houses built of clay, and entered from the top, were the general type. In New Mexico the Spaniards found

[13] Starr, " First Steps in Human Progress," pp. 205–215.
[14] Farrand, " Basis of American History," p. 251; Brinton, " The Myths of the New World," p. 60.

aggregations of continuous rooms which they called "pueblos," and which were several storeys high. Entrance was made through the flat roofs by means of ladders, the walls often being made without gates for the sake of protection. For the same reason the so-called "cliff-dwellers" constructed their rooms on the sides of cliffs difficult of access.[15]

III

INDUSTRIES, LIFE, AND RECREATIONS OF THE INDIANS

Aside from war, the pursuits of the Indian depended largely on his locality and environment. Most of the tribes depended mainly on agriculture for their subsistence. Especially was this true on the Atlantic slope, while hunting was more common in the north and west. Corn stood first in importance among the agricultural products, but vegetables were not unknown. The products of the farm were supplemented by hunting and fishing, and by gathering the edible products of the forest. The Indians of the plains lived almost wholly by the chase. Strange to say, they would not eat birds or fish, but sometimes partook of the flesh of horses and dogs, along with dried grasshoppers, snakes and other like delicacies. The "Digger" Indian of the Columbia region lived mainly upon roots, and the acorn was a staple food in California.[16] Since the coming of the Spanish the Navajos have depended mainly on their herds of sheep and goats, but often have raised them only to see them driven away by the predatory Apaches. The horse and dog were the domestic animals of common use. The Indian pony of to-day is descended from a stock brought by the Spanish, though the Indian of the plains claims to have had horses before the Spanish ever came.

The prevailing dress was made of skins, heavy in the cold regions for warmth and decreasing in weight and importance toward the south. The men wore a skirt, a breech-clout, leggings, and moccasins. The women wore a tunic with short sleeves, a sort of apron, a belt, leggings and moccasins. When the weather permitted the men stripped to the breech-clout. Their head-dress, especially in the war dance, was very ornate, consisting of a sort

[15] Read Morgan, "Houses and House-life of the American Aborigines."
[16] Read Wilson, "Prehistoric Man," chs. ii.–iii.

of cap covered with long feathers, with a long streamer of feathers hanging down the back. The children wore no clothing in warm weather. The age of ten was a sort of "coming out" period for the boys, when they assumed the breech-clout and were allowed to accompany their elders in the chase or war. The hair was worn long and on the plains it was plaited in two braids and hung down on each side; in the east the head was shaved except for a crest along the top, which was left for a scalp-lock. In war the victor cut this from the head of his slain foe and hung it to his belt as a trophy. Paint was used freely before going on the warpath. Tattooing was practiced to some extent in various tribes. Necklaces, of shells, turquoise, and pearls, and nose and ear pendants were in common use.[17]

The languages of the Indians were polysynthetic; that is, "much putting together," though some tribes showed a different class. Some of the dialects were pleasing to the ear, while others were harsh and grating. North of Mexico there was no written language except a rude sort of picture-writing; consequently the Indians have left no literature. John Eliot, missionary to the Indians of Massachusetts, succeeded in reducing the Algonquin tongue to writing and translated the Bible into it. At a much later period (1824) the Cherokees invented a sort of syllabic system of writing. The Indian of poetry and romance is credited with expressing himself in language of poetic beauty. The total number of languages for the two Americas is put by some authorities as high as 760, which means that few tribes spoke the same language. The necessity of intercommunication, however, compelled them to know something of the language of their neighbors. In the absence of this, resort was had to sign language — the bundle of arrows tied with a snakeskin and sent to the English was a declaration of war. Treaties were recorded by means of wampum belts. Time was reckoned by moons, but the length of its passage was lost in the haze of years.

The social and political organization was based upon the gentile or clan system. It is uncertain whether the clan is an enlarged family or the family a new formation within the clan. Descent was reckoned in the female line and intermarriage within a clan, several of which made a tribe, was forbidden. When a warrior

[17] See Starr, "First Steps in Human Progress," ch. xiv.

married he passed over to his wife's clan and the children belonged to her clan.[18] Some argue from this an existing or previously existing sexual promiscuity, the children being assigned to the mother because their paternity was uncertain. This reasoning, however, is unsafe, for examples may be found of transition from the paternal system to the maternal, such as among the Kwakiutl of Vancouver Island. " Blood revenge " was a clan matter, the clan demanding satisfaction for the loss of a member. When murder was committed within a clan by one of its members, the act was either overlooked, as to kill the offender would only be a new act of sacrilege, or he was first expelled and then hunted down.[19]

The principal clan officers were the sachem, the leading man in times of peace, and the chief or leader in war. The office of sachem was loosely hereditary within the clan, vacancies being filled by election. Immediate blood-relations, such as a brother or a sister's son, were generally chosen, but any male member of the clan was eligible, and he could be deposed for cause. Personal fitness was the test for leadership — in most places ability to lead in war, but in the northwest, wealth and social rank. The number of chiefs varied: among the Iroquois there was one to every seventy-five or one hundred persons. The Indians were essentially democratic, equality and independence being at the basis of their political institutions, and hence the choice of chiefs, like that of sachems, belonged to the clan. In a few cases, perhaps, the term king was not inaptly applied, as in the case of Philip, commonly called King of the Wampanoags, but in general the title was a misnomer. The chief's preëminence depended mainly on the condition of war, but he was also a member ex-officio of the tribal council. This was natural, however, since the principal matters of discussion in the council related to war and foreign relations. In these councils the women were allowed to be heard by proxy.

Strangely enough, among the Iroquois the women had the sole right to declare war. They also had the right of adoption; that is, to decide the fate of captives in war. Female chiefs were met with a few times by Europeans, but usually woman held a position popularly regarded as inferior. The task of tilling the soil fell to her lot, partly because the braves were engaged in the

[18] Starr, "First Steps in Human Progress," pp. 196–203.
[19] Farrand, "Basis of American History," p. 198 et seq.

more arduous duties of war and the chase, partly because they considered it beneath their dignity to perform such labor. But that does not necessarily mean that woman was a drudge; in reality there was a more or less equitable division of labor, and being mistress of her wigwam she there did as she pleased. With the changes wrought by later development, the cessation of war and decrease in importance of the chase, the task of the brave became less arduous, that of the squaw more so, in comparison at least.

When the clan system prevailed land was held in common and the right of inheritance rested with the clan. Individual ownership is said to have existed among certain tribes in California and the northwest. Such of an individual's personal effects as were not buried with him went to his nearest of kin within the clan. Hospitality was so free that almost anything might be taken by anyone who wanted it, and the niggard was classed along with the coward. Regular slavery existed in the west, a mild form of it in the east, and after the coming of the white man the Indians imitated him in the ownership of negro slaves.

In the simple life of the Indian few things were needed to supply his daily wants, hence there was but little industrial activity. Stone, bone, shells and wood furnished the material for his tools. From the first he made his tomahawk or battle-ax, his arrow-points, many of which may still be found in various parts of the country, his knife and his pipe. Bowls, pots, mortars and pestles for pounding grain also were made of stone. Great care was bestowed upon the tomahawk and the pipe, the latter an important adjunct on state occasions. The Haidas were famous for their slate carving and Navajos and Pueblos for their necklaces and ear-pendants. Fishing-hooks, sewing-awls, knives and sometimes arrow-heads were made of bone. The Pueblos carved their mythological characters out of wood and gave them to their children for dolls. The huge totem poles of the northwest, used to designate the clans, were elaborately carved and painted. Navajos and Pueblos had attained no little skill in textile work, the material being cotton at first and later wool. Feather weaving was practiced by the Gulf tribes, where the subtropical birds furnished them with beautiful material. Every squaw had at the door of her wigwam a mat woven of the native grasses and rushes and stained with the beautiful native dyes. Woven baskets were found everywhere, except on the plains, where boxes made of rawhide took their place. The baskets of California were famous for their beauty of design and closeness of weaving. Pottery also was of almost universal use; the vessels of the east are inferior to those of the Pueblos, who understood how to paint figures and fix them by burning. All of this work fell to the women, who also dressed the skins and made thread of sinew. But in all this they have made no distinctive contribution, with a few exceptions. We admire their handiwork as that of Indians, not because of any intrinsic merit, but in a sort of patronizing way.

War and the chase were the only occupations worthy of an Indian brave. His weapons consisted of the knife, club, lance, bow and arrow and tomahawk or hatchet. The lance and shield were used only by the horsemen of the plains where there were no trees and underbrush to interfere with them. Like the German leaders described by Tacitus, the chief commanded not so much because of his authority as by his personal qualities. If he could recount many deeds of valor in battle and wore many scalps in his belt, the young braves were ready and willing to follow him. When the decision for war had been made, the braves were invited to take part. The preparation for war often lasted some time, the object being to assemble a sufficient number of braves and arouse their fury to an uncontrollable pitch. This latter was done by recounting the story of their wrongs and how their ancestors, or how on previous occasions they themselves, had avenged their insults and won glory.

The Indian battle was something very different from the battle of the Europeans, who several times learned this to their sorrow. It was a surprise, or a skirmish from ambush, or a hand-to-hand encounter. The brave was in reality a man of courage, yet he would not fight in the open so long as he could help it or unless he could gain an advantage by the surprise. He preferred to lurk in the shadow and fell his enemy from behind, springing upon him with a yell which in itself struck terror into the mind of his unsuspecting victim. The ordinary rule was neither to ask nor give quarter, but prisoners were often taken and were either tortured to death or enslaved or adopted. Women and children shared the fate of the warriors. The wars were wars of extermination, and to kill a child or a squaw was to decrease the number of future enemies.

If a campaign proved a failure, the braves shrunk back and

moped in silence with a feeling of disgrace, often taunted by the squaws for their lack of valor. If successful the return was celebrated with a grand scalp-dance, the women now singing the praise of the braves as they flourished the scalps about. Captives were made to run the gauntlet or were tied to trees so that the braves might amuse themselves by tossing their tomahawks at them to see them dodge. They were either killed in this way or burned at the stake. Sometimes they feasted upon one of the slain, or made a pretense of doing so. Real cannibalism, of which this possibly was a survival, cannot be said to have existed north of Mexico. Though the condition of war was almost chronic, there were tribes which buried the hatchet; that is, made peace and enjoyed long periods of repose.

The savage wars waged against the white colonists were horrible indeed, but hardly more so than those waged by Indians against Indians. In the former the "Red Man" was fighting for his native heath; he saw slowly but surely his lands taken from him, while he was being pushed backward, backward, ever backward into the forest and toward the setting sun. Ofttimes, too, he was mistreated by knavish whites and he judged the race by his opinion of the meanest individual.

Peace had her victories as well as war, this time in athletic contests, games, dances, feasts and story-telling. Foot-racing and horse-racing were common, but ball was the chief sport. It was played with sticks and netted sticks resembling rackets. Shinny and football were indulged in by women, not, however, according to Rugby rules. Music charmed the savage, whether made by the drum, the flageolet, whistle, or in songs of lullaby or work, love or war.

IV

PRESENT CONDITION AND FUTURE OUTLOOK

Popular misconceptions regarding the Indians are common. These have arisen from the romance writers and from the accounts left by the colonists, who often did not know the Indian as he really was. The Indian was by training and nature deliberate and dignified on state occasions, and it was at just such times that the colonists received their strongest impressions of him. In consequence, they described him as taciturn, often morose and sullen. On the contrary, those who have known him in his home and observed his life there declare that he is cheerful and talkative. The "noble red man" was largely a creation of the romantic imagination. His much-vaunted stoical indifference to pain was, indeed, a remarkable characteristic; but even this was a sort of dress put on for show in public. In private life he was nervous, hysterical, often manifesting a childish dread of pain. As for honor, some of the colonists looked upon the Indian very much as the Romans did the Carthaginian, but often without just cause. In most cases the Indian kept faith when dealt with fairly, even when being gradually pushed backward from his hunting grounds. But at best he was a dirty savage, dwelling in squalor and filth, and content therewith. In consequence epidemic diseases have often decimated the tribes.

No reliable statistics are to be had regarding the number of Indians in America at the time of the discovery, but conservative estimates place the number east of the Mississippi at 200,000. West of the river were many more. In 1900 there were 260,000 in the United States, 129,815 of whom were "Indians not taxed." Whole tribes have become extinct. Out of sixteen tribes met with on a journey from Charleston to Albemarle Sound in 1701, only the famous Tuscaroras and Catawbas remain. The most marked decrease has occurred on the plains. The Pawnees have fallen from 12,000 in 1834 to 650 in 1900. The Navajos have been almost undisturbed and are holding their own; but the native Californians, numerous at the time of the discovery of gold, have almost become extinct. A century ago the Aleuts were estimated at 25,000, now at about 2,000.

For this destruction the coming of the white man is chiefly responsible. Neither in war nor in peace has the Indian been able to stand against or beside him. Sentimentalists have inveighed against the whites for this; but history teaches that inferior people must yield to a superior civilization in one way or another. They must take on civilization or pass out. The negro was able to endure slavery while learning the rudiments of civilization; the Indian could not endure slavery, and, for centuries at least, he refused to be taught. He is at last going to school, but his graduation probably will only hasten his extinction as a race. An intense race feeling has preserved the negro from amalgama·

tion, but this feeling does not exist so strongly among the whites against the Indians, nor between the Indians and negroes.

It is not meant by this to convey the idea that the day will soon come when there will be no Indians in the United States, much less in America. Nearly all the Indians are now west of the Mississippi, practically all of whom retain a real tribal organization. The disappearance of the separate organization does not seem to be far distant, but communities of distinctly Indian blood probably will be met with centuries hence. And no doubt they will make good citizens, taking part in the teeming life all around them instead of standing aloof, like the Basques in the mountain fastnesses of the Pyrenees.

Chapter II

DISCOVERIES AND EXPLORATIONS. 1000–1606

I

PRECURSORS OF COLUMBUS

SO far as man can see now, Christopher Columbus will be honored throughout all time as the discoverer of America; yet there is good historical evidence that Europeans visited our shores many years before he was born. This evidence is found in the "sagas" or writings of the Northmen. These sagas were put into written form two or three hundred years after the events they describe, but their credibility is not thereby destroyed, for students of the classics know well that the Homeric poems were handed down by word of mouth for centuries. The sum and substance of the report of the sagas is that Leif Ericson sailed away from Norway about the year 1000 A. D., and that he discovered an unknown land while on a missionary voyage from Iceland to Greenland.[1] The precise whereabouts of the new land thus discovered is not known, but from the several accounts contained in the "*Codex Flatoensis*," or the "Flatey Book," as the compilation is called in English, it is impossible to believe that the shores touched were other than those of America, probably Nova Scotia or New England.

Subsequently the Northmen conducted several voyages to Vinland the Good, as the new land was called, and made a few attempts at settlement. One party seems to have visited a southern latitude where they passed the winter without seeing snow and where their cattle were supported by grazing. According to their story, they also found a wonderful birdland where the eggs were so thick that it was hardly possible to step between them. Self-sown wheat fields were also there, and in the hollows were vines heavy with grapes. The natives, whom the Northmen called

[1] Channing, "History of the United States," vol. i. p. 3.

Skrellings (inferiors), were said to have come in skin boats and exchanged perfect unsullied skins for a red stuff (cloth) a span in length, which they bound about their heads.[2]   The Skrellings were very fond of cow's milk, and we are told in the Icelandic writings that the outcome of their trading was that they carried away their stomachs.   The Northmen made many voyages to this goodly land and carried away timber, peltries, grapes and all kinds of game and fish, " and other good things," but after a while they ceased to come, and the memory of it was lost save to a few scholars who read about it in old manuscripts.   While, therefore, Leif Ericson and his followers were probably the first Europeans to visit America, their discovery had no permanent result and the history of the country would have been what it has been had they never left their native shores.[3]

Omitting the stories of the very ancient empires of Babylon and upper Egypt, practically all interest in the history of civilization down to the close of the middle ages centers about the Mediterranean Sea.   The Greeks and Romans really knew very little of any countries not bordering upon it, and much that they knew was forgotten after their splendid civilizations ceased to be a living force.   When the Saracen invaders occupied northern Africa and Spain they so threatened the commerce of Europe with Asia that Constantinople alone kept up a considerable trade with the East. Then came the Seljukian Turks, a nomadic tribe from central Asia, whose conversion to Mohammedanism seemed only to increase their barbarism.   Not content with desecrating the Holy Land and sweeping away the civilization of Asia Minor, they began to threaten the very center of the Byzantine Empire, Constantinople, and even Europe itself.   This danger aroused the leading minds in Christendom to a realization of the necessity of self-defense, and the result was the Crusades.

To many people the Crusades mean simply a series of expeditions based on religious zeal to rescue the tomb of the Savior from the impious hands of the infidel.   While this was the ostensible object, it is probable that mixed motives never entered more largely into any expedition.   Kings went to extend their borders and found empires; nobles, in the hope of gaining power and be-

    [2] Reeves, " Wineland," p. 174.
    [3] Winsor, " Pre-Columbian Explorations " in " Narrative and Critical History," vol. i. ch. 2; also Fiske, " Discovery of America," vol. i. pp. 149–255.

coming kings; knights, in search of adventure; serfs, to gain their freedom. As a spiritual reward all who went on the first Crusade were to receive plenary indulgences.[4] In all was the instinct of self-defense. These expeditions accomplished no permanent results in rescuing the tomb or in founding empires, but they stimulated men's minds and aroused in western Europe a deeper interest in the eastern shores of the Mediterranean, an interest which was never wholly lost, and although the West again sank into comparative inactivity after the failure of their romantic adventures, the trade with the East went on by way of Constantinople, Alexandria and Venice. Rulers in Europe, both petty and great, were kept busy at home in maintaining their security against usurping vassals and jealous neighbors, until in the latter half of the fifteenth century the movement toward absolute monarchies may be said to have begun. The nations began to feel the throb of a new life under its touch and to look abroad in anticipation of the strength which would come with their unification.

At the same time that kings were building up their power the mind of man was being set free. The literatures of Greece and Rome were rediscovered and the bonds of ignorance were breaking. Printing from movable type, recently discovered, was paving the way for a more general diffusion of knowledge. Sculpture and painting were cultivated as never before — and while science was still groping in darkness there were on every hand signs of a coming dawn. This great period was known as the Renaissance, and it began in Italy.

But Italy was not at this time wholly absorbed in literature, art and architecture. Capital was abundant, agriculture and manufacturing were flourishing and commerce was in a thriving condi-

---

[4] These terms are used in a sense strictly technical. Precisely what was said by Pope Urban II., who presided at the Council of Clermont, it is now impossible to determine; but from extant versions of his addresses we know that he spoke of the Saracen attack upon Spain, the victories of the Turks and the appeal from Constantinople for aid. The desecration of holy places, the oppression of Eastern Christians, and the suffering of pilgrims were also discussed. The necessity of ceasing combats at home and aiding fellow Christians in the East required little emphasis. These were the chief considerations which prompted the Pope to preach the First Crusade. Though some authorities believe that there was on the part of the Crusaders an expectation of enjoying the spoils of the enemy, it is by no means certain that they were promised any temporal power beyond the advantages of checking the career of the Turks. See Munro in *American Historical Review*, January, 1906.

tion. Perhaps the chief permanent result of the Crusades was the stimulus given to commerce with the East, or Indies, as the southeastern part of Asia, with its adjacent islands, was known. The leader of the Italian states in this respect was Venice, though Genoa became no mean rival. Of the two important trade routes to India the Venetians took the one by Cairo and the Red Sea, that is, the water route; the Genoese allied themselves with Constantinople and took the northern route by the Black Sea and thence overland by caravans. This trade consisted mainly in the exchange of glass vessels, wine, linen and light woolen goods for silks, ivory, precious stones, and the much coveted spices. It contributed largely to the wealth and importance of these diminutive states, whose increasing power was viewed with jealous eyes by the states of the West, which naturally became restless at their dependence on the Italians for these wares. Could they not find a route to India and secure them directly? This question had been pondered for some time when one of the great events of history, the capture of Constantinople (1453) by the Turks, which cut off the route used by the Genoese and threatened that of the Venetians, made it more imperative than ever to find an answer. But how? In spite of the fact that this commerce had lasted many years and had been considerable in amount, not even the Italians knew much of the countries whence it came. The traffic had not been carried on directly, but through the Mohammedans, and few Europeans had ever seen India or Cathay (China). By what other than the well-known routes could those lands be reached?

The commerce of India was controlled through the Black and the Caspian Seas. The Venetian mariner, Da Gama, had not yet discovered the long maritime route down the coast of the continent to the south of the Mediterranean Sea. Only the trackless ocean stretched away to the west. It was the claim of some philosophers that the earth was round, and, if the Italian geographer, Toscanelli, could be believed, so small that sailing westward a few thousand miles would bring the mariner to the coveted shores of Cipango (as Marco Polo had called Japan) and Cathay.

Nearly six hundred years before Christ, Pythagoras announced his belief that the earth was a sphere, and his teaching was accepted by Plato and Aristotle. Aristotle in the fourth century B.C. demonstrated his theory with remarkable accuracy by observing that the earth's shadow on the moon at the time of eclipse was circular in form, and by noticing that certain stars which were visible in southerly latitudes could not be seen farther north.[5] How men could walk in the antipodal world with their " heads down " was a problem that puzzled even the philosophers, but they held on to a vague belief in some such world. Strabo, the Roman geographer (40 B.C.–60 A.D.), quoted with approval the belief of Eratosthenes (third centry B.C.) in the feasibility of a sea voyage from Iberia (Spain) to India on the same parallel of latitude.[6] But no mariner was found bold enough to pass beyond the Pillars of Hercules and tempt the Sea of Darkness, as the Atlantic was then called, and which popular belief had peopled with dreadful monsters. There was also the fear that a ship having once passed down the slope of the globe could never return even if it escaped the fiery zone at the middle belt of the earth where the vertical rays of the sun caused the sea to boil with fury. A popular belief was that the outer or unknown world was composed chiefly of water. In the second century A.D. Claudius Ptolemy propounded the theory that Asia extended indefinitely to the north and east, that Africa likewise extended indefinitely to the south and east, and that the two met and inclosed the Indian Ocean.[7]

Such were the inherited beliefs of the middle ages, but the globular theory of the form of the earth does not appear ever to have been entirely forgotten. It was easily preserved among the Arabs, who were devoted students of Aristotle. Whether derived from the same source or not, for Christians, especially the schoolmen, were also students of Aristotle — we find the same theory referred to by Christian writers, such as Roger Bacon in his " *Opus Majus* " in the thirteenth century A.D., and by D'Ailly in his " *Imago Mundi*," written in the following century. The revival of the study of the Greek writers in the fifteenth century greatly strengthened the hold of the theory, but even before that time men's minds had been prepared to accept it. There was first of all the desire to find a western or southern route to India. In the thirteenth century certain travelers who had returned from the East declared that Ptolemy was mistaken in supposing Asia to be

[5] See Aristotle, " *De Cælo*," Taylor's translation.
[6] See Strabo, " Geography," ch. iv.
[7] See Tillinghast, " Geographical Knowledge of the Ancients Considered in Relation to the Discovery of America," in Winsor, vol. i. ch. i.

of indefinite extent, for it was bounded on the east by an ocean. Some years later this report was confirmed by the book of a remarkable man, Marco Polo.

Marco Polo, a Venetian, the son of a wealthy merchant, accompanied his father on a trading journey to the far-away Orient, where he won the favor of the famous Kublai Khan. After an absence of twenty-four years he returned to Venice in 1295, only to be cast into prison by the Genoese, with whom the Venetians were at war. While in prison he dictated " The Book of Ser Marco Polo the Venetian concerning the Kingdom and Marvels of the East," in which he described his wondrous travels through Thibet, Burmah, Hindoostan, Siam, Cathay and even made mention of Cipango (Japan). While the marvels received their due share of attention, the book, first circulated in the early fourteenth century, made a real contribution to the geographical knowledge of Europe, perhaps the greatest made by any one man to the geographical knowledge of the middle ages.[8] It helped to confirm the belief that there was an ocean east of Asia. Together with " The Voyage and Travels of Sir John Mandeville," which appeared toward the last of the fifteenth century, it also helped to whet men's greed for the wealth of the East and to keep alive their interest in its fabled stone bridges, pillars of gold, large precious stones, and a fountain whose waters possessed the remarkable power of bestowing perpetual youth.

In spite of all these incentives, however, and notwithstanding the fact that men now had the mariner's compass as a guide, the Sea of Darkness still remained untried. The Portuguese resolved to make the attempt, and their first ship set out in 1419 and discovered an island (probably known to the Portuguese before this) which they called Madeira. The island was set on fire and is said to have burned seven years, after which they planted it with grapes from Greece and sugar from Sicily and Cyprus, the first of which are still there. It was the policy of the Portuguese to establish factories or trading posts in newly discovered lands, and it was Prince Henry, surnamed the Navigator, who led the voyagers that blazed the way for these. The clergy were his hearty coadjutors, and each ship carried a priest, and a church arose in each factory. Prince Henry died in 1463, but his suc-

[8] Channing, "History of the United States," vol. i. p. 9.

EXPLORATIONS

cessor, John II., inspired by him, continued the work. In 1484 Diogo Cam passed down the west coast of Africa to a point far below the equator, and in 1487, Bartholomew Diaz, accompanied by Bartholomew Columbus, a brother of the future discoverer of America, sailed around the southern point of Africa, called the Cape of Storms, and proceeded several hundred miles into the Indian Ocean before returning to Portugal. The name of the cape, King John, with good sense and true insight, changed to that of Good Hope.

Shortly after this, Columbus, the greatest navigator of his time, if not of all times, made his famous voyage; but it is proper to break the chronology here and follow the fortunes of the Portuguese a little farther. July 8, 1497, Vasco da Gama left Lisbon with four ships and one hundred and sixty men. May 20, 1498, he rode at anchor before the city of Calicut, India, where was founded the first European factory in the Orient. Albuquerque, by the capture of Socotora on the Red Sea and Ormuzon on the Persian Gulf (1507), closed to the Mussulmans and Venetians their former routes to the "wealth of Ormus and of Ind." In 1510 he conquered Goa, which, with its fine harbor, became the center of a vast colonial empire. Four thousand leagues of coast line, from Lisbon to the Cape of Good Hope, from there to Hindoostan, thence on to Malacca, Indo-China, and even Cipango, were dominated by Portuguese fortresses. Patriotic and religious zeal, combined with love of gain, had inspired the heroic work. None of these hardy Portuguese seamen had ever reached American shores, but it may be said that their voyages constituted a school of navigation for the future American voyagers.

The western coast of Africa was of no importance until after the introduction of the slave trade. From eastern Africa came gold dust and ivory. Ormus poured out the wealth of central Asia, while Malacca opened up the commerce of Indo-China. From Macao, near Canton, the hardy traders reached out to Japan.[9] This good fortune of Portugal proved the ruin of Venice. In desperation she freed everything coming through Egypt and taxed heavily everything coming via the cape, but all in vain. The currents of commerce had set to other shores, never to return to hers with the old strength.

[9] Cheney, "European Background of American History," ch. iv.

II

THE VOYAGES OF COLUMBUS

The voyages of the Portuguese had been watched with no little interest by an Italian navigator, Christopher Columbus, who took up his residence in Lisbon about 1470, and who, there is good reason to believe, had actually participated in some of the Portuguese maritime adventures.[10] The exact date of the birth of Christopher Columbus, or Colon, as he preferred to call himself, is not known, but many writers have given 1436 as the year, though some favor a later date, some an earlier one.[11] Seven cities claimed the honor of being the birthplace of Homer; not less than eighteen Italian towns have claimed a similar honor for Columbus, but he always referred to Genoa as the place of his nativity, and nearly all scholars have agreed in awarding the honor to Genoa. Little is known of his boyhood, but it probably was spent in helping his father, who was a wool comber. While not possessed of wealth, his father was able to give him a respectable education. Beyond the common studies he learned something of Latin, the higher mathematics and astronomy, while cosmography and nautical science were objects of study with him all his life, and he knew as much about them as any man of his age.

Genoa, like her rival, Venice, was a seafaring state, and it was only natural that Columbus should take to the Mediterranean. His first voyage was made when he was but a lad of fourteen; as he grew older he was much at sea, sometimes in commercial adventures, sometimes in the service of his native city in her naval struggles with her Italian rivals. Doubtless the fame of Lisbon as the center of nautical science and marine adventures attracted him to that place. Here he took to the sea again and visited the Cape Verde Islands, the Azores, and tradition says touched the coast of Iceland. When not at sea he spent his time in study and in making maps and charts. A few years after reaching Lisbon he married, a step which promoted his ambition, his wife's father having been a great navigator and having left many maps and charts.

[10] Channing, "History of the United States," vol. i. p. 12.

[11] Harrisse and Winsor agree upon 1436 as the year; Henry Vignaud thinks 1451 more nearly correct; while Bourne makes no attempt to settle the question.

Until recently historians have accepted the statement that Columbus corresponded with the great Florentine astronomer Toscanelli, who sent him a map of the world on which Europe and Asia were represented as separated only by an ocean, and expressed the belief that India could be reached by sailing westward from Europe. But lately this story has been attacked and rendered more than doubtful. Whether he ever received a letter and map from Toscanelli or not, it is only reasonable to suppose that he was familiar with the teachings of a man so well known, although

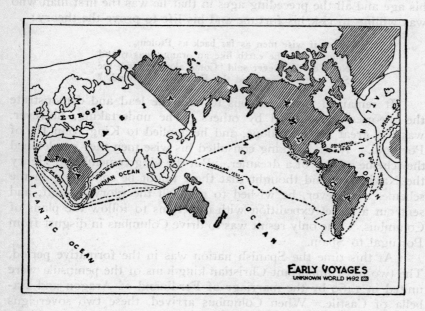

EARLY VOYAGES
UNKNOWN WORLD 1492

he nowhere makes mention of him.[12] Certain it is that he was familiar with the geographical writings of Ptolemy, Roger Bacon, Marco Polo, whose book made a lasting impression on his mind. Æneas Sylvius, later Pope Pius II., and also with Pierre d'Ailly's

[12] For a scholarly discussion of the controversy concerning the Toscanelli map see E. G. Bourne, "Spain in America," pp. 12–15. This author does not, as does Henry Vignaud, deny the authenticity of the correspondence between Columbus and the astronomer, but insists that even if the letters were genuine they contained no information which was not already known to Columbus. Channing, vol. i. p. 17, inclines to the same view, while Sir C. R. Markham in his "Journal of Columbus," pp. 1–10, goes to the other extreme.

"*Imago Mundi,*" an encyclopædic compilation printed between 1480 and 1483, and on a copy of which at Seville one may still read marginal notes of a highly critical character in what appears to be the handwritng of Columbus.[13] If, as these books taught, the world was round, why could not India, only about three thousand miles away to the west, as Toscanelli and he believed, be found by sailing westward?

The idea that India could be reached by sailing to the west was not original with Columbus, but he towers above the men of his age and all the preceding ages in that he was the first man who was willing to risk his fortune and his life to prove the theory:

> "What if wise men as far back as Ptolemy,
> Judged that the earth like an orange was round.
> None of them ever said 'Come along, follow me,
> Sail to the West, and the East will be found.'"

It remained for Columbus to take the lead and demonstrate the theories propounded by others. The undertaking, however, was too great for him alone, and he applied to King John II., of Portugal. When the king consulted his wise men they condemned the scheme as that of a dreamer. But the king remembered Henry the Navigator, and thought that there might be something in the scheme. However, he wished to gain all the glory himself, and sent out a secret expedition with directions to follow the plans of Columbus. The only result was to drive Columbus in disgust from Portugal to Spain.

At this time the Spanish nation was in the formative period. The two most important Christian kingdoms of the peninsula were united in 1469 by the marriage of Ferdinand of Aragon and Isabella of Castile. When Columbus arrived, these two sovereigns were busily engaged in carrying out their determination to add the Moorish kingdom to their own; consequently it was difficult for him to reach the royal ears. But as they pursued the enemy Columbus pursued them from Cordova to Salamanca, to Malaga, and back again to Cordova. Here, as in Portugal, the wise men were consulted; some favored, others condemned the project. Powerful

---

[13] E. G. Bourne, "Spain in America," p. 10. Channing, "History of the United States," vol. i. p. 15, is disposed to minimize the influence of the ancient theories on Columbus, and asserts that he had already reached his conclusions with regard to the sphericity of the earth before reading D'Ailly's "*Imago Mundi.*"

friends at the royal court took up his cause. The sovereigns expressed a real interest in it, but their answer was always the same, —To-morrow, when the war is over. After six or seven years of fruitless effort, Columbus at last despaired of securing aid in that quarter and decided to leave Spain, although he never for once wavered in his belief and purpose. His brother Bartholomew had already gone to England to seek the needed help from Henry VII.

But at last the sovereigns of Spain were moved to action. Weary and footsore with the journey afoot, Columbus stopped at the monastery of La Rabida to ask for bread and water for his child, whom he had taken with him on leaving the rest of his family behind in Portugal.[14] The prior, Father Juan Perez, formerly confessor to the queen, heard his story and believed it. At the entreaties of these and other influential personages at court she agreed to hear the story once more and sent the Genoese adventurer a sum of money with which to array himself properly before coming into her presence. Shortly after his arrival he witnessed the fall of Granada (January 2, 1492), and saw Boabdil pass out the gates and pause to weep over the city while his mother upbraided him with the loss of an empire which the Moslem had conquered for him eight centuries before.

The Moorish war over at last, Ferdinand and Isabella had realized their dream of a united Spain and were ready to hear this dreamer tell of rich realms beyond the Sea of Darkness, which should also be theirs. But Columbus would exact hard conditions. First of all he must be a grandee and admiral of the ocean and viceroy of all the heathen lands he might discover. One-eighth of the gold and silver from such lands should be his, as also one-tenth of the profits by trade or conquest. In return he would bear one-eighth of the expense. The conditions were rejected and Columbus again turned his face toward foreign lands, but the Marchioness de Moya, at the time a confidential friend of the queen, appealed to her in his behalf, and she at length consented to give the aid desired.

Three vessels of the caravel class were finally fitted out, the *Santa Maria,* the *Pinta,* and the *Nina,* all of them very small, so small, indeed, that one would be considered foolhardy should he venture to cross the ocean in such craft to-day. Securing a crew

[14] Winsor, "Columbus and His Discoveries" in "Narrative and Critical History," vol. ii. p. 5.

was no easy task, and for a time it looked as if the government would be compelled to use force by impressing seamen and releasing criminals for that purpose; but through the influence of the powerful Pinzon family a crew was finally obtained without resorting to conscription or emptying the jails. The expense of the voyage was borne by the queen, Luis Santangel, and Columbus himself, the total amount aggregating according to careful estimates about $100,000.[15] A metallurgist was taken along to test the gold they felt sure of finding. In all there were ninety souls.[16] Friday morning, August 3, 1492, they weighed anchor at Palos and set out on a voyage from which few of those who either went or remained behind believed they would ever return. For more than a month the fleet was delayed at one of the Canary Islands by an accident to the rudder of the *Pinta*, which necessitated repairs. Something was known of the volcanoes of the Mediterranean, especially of Mt. Ætna, yet the eruption of Mt. Teneriffe on one of the Canaries threw them into consternation. The deflection of the needle from the north star alarmed the pilots; they were unacquainted with the trade winds, and the constant blowing of these from one direction brought on the fear that they would never change.

But no terror could shake the purpose of the admiral, and he kept on his way undisturbed. The strain gradually became greater, and soon there were grumblings and plottings to throw the admiral overboard or otherwise dispose of him. But they were quieted by the soothing promises of their captain, who reminded them of their rewards in case of success. Week after week passed with no sight of land, though tropical birds flying overhead and floating seaweed raised the hope that it was not far off. On September 25, Pinzon, who commanded the *Pinta*, raised the cry, "Land, land!" The night was spent in rejoicing and giving thanks to God, but the next morning the land had disappeared — it was only a mirage. The crew became more and more convinced that they were venturing into a world of enchantment. Columbus himself was puzzled. He had supposed that twenty-five hundred miles of sailing would bring him to Cipango, yet he had sailed twenty-seven hundred miles only to find himself still on the Sea

[15] Thatcher, "Christopher Columbus," vol. i. p. 490.

[16] This is the number given by Las Casas; Oviedo says the number was 120; among the crew were the three Pinzon brothers, Juan de la Cosa, a Jewish inter-

of Darkness. October 7 Pinzon induced him to change his course to the southwest. The many small birds flying in that direction held out the hope that land was to be found in that quarter. Four days later the signs of land were so unmistakable that not even the mutinous crew could doubt any longer. That night not an eye was closed in sleep, but everyone was steadily gazing forward in the hope of descrying land. About ten o'clock the admiral, standing on the top of the castle of the *Santa Maria* and eagerly peering into the darkness, saw a light in the distance describing a waving line as though carried by someone walking. When the dawn came, October 12, 1492 (old style), it revealed a coast line covered with trees, only a few miles distant.

Many natives, " as naked as when their mother bore them," had gathered on the shore to watch the caravels, which they took to be white-winged birds. As Columbus, clad in scarlet and carrying the standard of Spain, made for the shore accompanied by Pinzon and a few others, they fled in terror. On reaching the land the admiral burst into tears, kissed the ground and gave thanks to God for the supposed realization of his long cherished dream. Drawing his sword, he took possession in the name of the sovereigns of Spain. The natives called the island Guanahani; Columbus called it San Salvador (Holy Savior). It was one of the Bahama group, probably Watling Island.[17]

Columbus supposed that he was in the Indies, not far from some of the great cities of the Grand Khan. The naked savages did not correspond to the descriptions of Marco Polo, nevertheless he called them " Indians," a name which the aboriginal inhabitants of America have ever since borne. Cathay could not be far away, still he would not trust to them for delivering his letter to the Grand Khan. " Directly I reached the Indies in the first isle I discovered," says Columbus, " I took by force some of the natives that from them we might gain some information of what there was in these parts; and so it was that we understood each other, either by words or signs." When asked where gold was to be found they always pointed to the south.

Leaving San Salvador, Columbus cruised about for several

preter, two Englishmen, and one Irishman. In addition to the complement of sailors some authorities state that thirty adventurers accompanied the expedition.

[17] Markham, "Life of Columbus," p. 100 *et seq.* For contrary views see biographies of Columbus by Harrisse and Winsor.

weeks and discovered Cuba and Hayti; the latter he named Hispaniola. On the shoals of this island his largest vessel, the *Santa
Maria,* was wrecked. Columbus then bethought himself of home
and the wonderful story he had to relate to his sovereign. The
material of the wrecked vessel was used to construct a rude building in which forty-four men, supplied with food, seed and tools,
agreed to remain and await the return of the admiral; the rest
embarked for Spain, January 4, taking ten of the natives, a quantity
of gold and other trophies with them.[18] The return voyage was
stormy and eventful. The two vessels were driven apart to meet
no more until they sailed into the harbor of Palos on the same day,
March 15, 1493, only a few hours apart. Thus was completed
the most momentous voyage in all history. Had Columbus reached
India and opened up a new route to the ancient civilization of
Cathay, it would have been a great accomplishment; but he had
done more than this; he had discovered a new world without
knowing it, one where civilization was to gain a new foothold, take
on new life and advance by leaps and bounds such as it had never
known before.

Columbus soon informed the king and queen of his return,
and, after having given due notice of his discovery to the Pope,
they at once commanded his presence at Barcelona. The news of
his return rapidly spread; the country was wild with enthusiasm,
the whole population turned out to greet him, and his journey
hither was a triumphal march. His reception by the king and
queen was made a great state occasion, perhaps the greatest Spain
had even known, and Columbus was accorded the highest distinction that could be shown to a Spanish subject; yet he is said
to have borne these honors with all due modesty.

As Spain was now becoming the rival of Portugal as a
claimant for lands hitherto unknown, something had to be done
to prevent disputes from arising. A very simple solution was
found by appealing to Pope Alexander VI., who issued two bulls,
May 3 and 4, 1493, establishing a " Line of Demarcation," or, in
modern phrase, creating two spheres of influence in which the right
of discovery would give unquestioned title. At first this imaginary
line was drawn from pole to pole one hundred leagues west of
the Azores and Cape Verde Islands; Portugal to have all the lands
east of the line, and Spain those to the west. There was dissat-

[18] E. G. Bourne, " Spain in America," p. 27.

EXPLORATIONS

isfaction with the arrangement, however, and in consequence it was agreed by the Treaty of Tordesillas between Spain and Portugal, June 7, 1494, that the line of demarcation should be changed to 370 leagues west of the Cape Verde Islands.[19] This gave Spain all the New World except the eastern part of Brazil, assigned to Portugal — a very simple arrangement if only the rest of the world would acquiesce.

Columbus was now eager for a second voyage, and Ferdinand and Isabella were no less eager to have him go, for he had promised them all the gold, spices, cotton, mastic and lignaloe they desired and as many slaves as they cared to send for, all heathens. On September 25, 1493, the admiral, accompanied by his brother Bartholomew and Ponce de Leon, of later fame, set out from Cadiz with seventeen vessels and 1500 men, soldiers, missionaries, artisans, etc., and once more turned his face to the west. Brood mares, sheep, cattle, farm implements, tools, seed and all the paraphernalia of colony planting were taken along with the evident intention of making a permanent settlement in the New World. He first sought out the little colony of forty-four men left behind on his first voyage, but found no record of them save their bones, which lay bleaching in the tropical sun. Not a man had survived. But the undaunted admiral founded another colony, this time in San Domingo, December, 1493, and spent three years in cruising about and exploring the islands of the West Indies, as they later came to be called. He returned to Spain in December, 1496, leaving his brother Bartholomew in control of the colony at Española. On a third voyage (1498) he discovered Trinidad and anchored in the mouth of the Orinoco, where he first beheld the mainland of the, as yet, unnamed continent. The magnitude of the river and the luxuriant growth of the tropical forest led him to think that this might be one of the great rivers of the Garden of Eden mentioned in the Bible.

The great explorer had tasted of adversity and had drunk of the cup of the highest success, but his last days were to be like unto his first. Malice, hatred, and envy had done their work at home, where jealous enemies had belittled his discoveries and represented to the king and queen that he was a tyrant incapable of governing colonies. A viceroy was sent out to investigate. He exceeded his instructions and sent Columbus home in irons. The story of his

[19] Thatcher, "Life of Columbus," vol. ii. pp. 124 *et seq.*

wrongs and the sight of his sufferings moved the queen to tears. He was released and restored to royal favor, but was not reinstated in his position as governor of the colony, and, if the truth must be told, he was ill-fitted for the position. A fourth voyage, in the course of which he discovered the coast of Honduras, added little to his fame. With indomitable spirit he kept planning still greater things for the country which repaid him only with neglect; but old age, anxiety and exposure had broken his strength. May 20, 1506, he breathed his last at Valladolid, without knowing that he had discovered a New World, and before he had realized how utter was the wreck of his hope and ambitions.[20]

The simple arrangement of Spain and Portugal by which the choicest domains of the world were parceled out between them was not acquiesced in by the rest of Europe. Henry VII. of England, in particular, was chagrined at having let the prize slip from his grasp by refusing the aid which Columbus had asked, and now when John Cabot, a naturalized citizen from Venice of the Jersey Norman race, and, like the great discoverer, born in Genoa, applied for permission to search for the all-sea route to India, the request was readily granted. The permit, dated March 5, 1496, granted to the patentees and their assigns forever the exclusive right of frequenting all the countries they might discover, in return for which the king was to receive one-fifth of all their gains and Bristol was to be their only port of entry. Thus was begun the system of commercial restriction which ended only with the revolution, nearly three hundred years later.

The voyage was delayed over a year, but finally in May, 1497, Cabot, with a single vessel and eighteen men, set sail from Bristol on his perilous quest. The patent included Cabot's three sons, but it is not definitely known whether any of them sailed with him or not, although it is probable that Sebastian went. In June, 1497, Cabot landed somewhere on the coast of Labrador or about the mouth of the St. Lawrence River, possibly on Cape Breton Island or Newfoundland, believing, of course, that he had reached the shores of the territory of the Grand Khan. After an absence of only three months, during which time he sailed along the coast for some 300 leagues without seeing an inhabitant or attempting to land,[21] he returned to England, where he was given a popular

20 Channing, "History of the United States," vol. i. p. 25.
21 Weare, "Cabot's Discovery," p. 143 et seq.

reception very much like that accorded to Columbus in Spain, and was, moreover, rewarded with a pension of £20 per year. The following year (1498) he made a second voyage and coasted down the shore of the United States as far as Cape Hatteras, some say to Florida, again believing that he was on the shore of Cipango or Cathay.[22] These voyages were the basis of the English claim to North America.

Such is the story now generally accepted by historians. For many years the credit for these voyages, or at least the second, was accorded to Sebastian Cabot, but it now seems certain that his father commanded both.[23] Sebastian was a great navigator, later became chief hydrographer to the King of Spain, and probably began that fruitless search for a northwest passage to India in which so many fortunes and lives were lost; but the glory of discovering North America belongs to his father, John Cabot. These voyages created a good deal of excitement in England, but brought no gold and the excitement soon died down.

As mariner after mariner sailed into the west, it at last dawned upon Europe that a new world had been found. The first to use this term was Amerigo Vespucci, or Americus Vespucius, another Italian, a native of Florence, but resident at Seville, who had made at least four voyages across the Atlantic between 1499 and 1503. His account of the "New World" ("*Mundus Novus*"), published in a pamphlet and translated into many languages, created something of a sensation in Europe, for he asserted that the new continent was more populous and more desirable as a place in which to live than either Europe, Asia, or Africa. The fame of Columbus was already in eclipse. In 1507 a German professor, Waldseemüller, in a little college of St. Dié in Lorraine, the same place at which Cardinal d'Ailly had written his "*Imago Mundi*," published a pamphlet entitled "Cosmographic Introductions," in which he suggested that this New World be called America, in honor of its discoverer, Americus Vespucius. The same year he used the name on a map which is still to be seen at Würtemberg. Gradually the name found favor, and though applied only to Brazil at first, was at last applied to all the western world.

[22] Bancroft, "History of the United States," vol. i. pp. 10-14; Channing "History of the United States," vol. i. p. 34; Fiske, "Discovery of America," vol. ii. ch. vii.

[23] Winsor, "Narrative and Critical Hist.," vol. iii. p. 31; Bourne, "Spain in America," pp. 60-61; Harrisse, "American Historical Review," vol. iii. p. 448.

There is no evidence that either the professor or Vespucius had any thought of depriving Columbus of honors justly due to him, and the latter in fact was a friend of the admiral.[24]

III

SPANISH EXPLORATIONS

Natives of Italy under the patronage of Spain had begun the work of exploration in the west; the Spanish and Portuguese now took it up and carried it on with vigor. The chief motive back of this activity was the " cursed thirst for gold." Marlowe, in " Dr. Faustus," well expressed the spirit of the age. On learning that he has power to command spirits, Faustus exclaims:

> " I'll have them fly to India for gold,
> Ransack the ocean for orient pearl,
> And search all corners of the new-found world
> For pleasant fruits and princely delicates."

The love of adventure was a powerful motive force, as was the sincere desire to convert the heathen, but gold, gold, gold was always the cry.

The year 1513 saw Vasco Nuñez de Balboa, a bankrupt in both fortune and patriotism, searching the Isthmus of Panama (probably within the canal zone acquired in 1904 by the United States) for gold with which to satisfy his creditors, from whom he was a fugitive, and a discovery that would atone for his treason. Accompanied by one hundred and ninety-five picked Spaniards, besides several hundred Indian porters and dogs, he set out, September 1, on what is now regarded as a wonderful expedition, made as it was through well-nigh impenetrable thickets, tangled swamps and marshes reeking with deadly malaria. Led on by the report of an Indian that the yellow metal abounded beyond the mountains in the lands bordering upon a great sea, in such quantities that the commonest utensils were made of it, he climbed a lofty peak, and, on the morning of September 25, 1513, while

[24] Winsor, "Amerigo Vespucci," in "Narrative and Critical Hist.," vol. ii. ch. 2. For scholarly discussions of the controversy concerning the naming of America, see Bourne, "Spain in America," ch. vii. and Fiske, "Discovery of America," pp. 130–170.

straining his eyes to the south, beheld a broad expanse of water, which he called the South Sea, and which, together with the adjacent coasts and islands, he took possession of in the name of his master, the King of Spain. This was the most important discovery since that of Columbus, and aroused intense interest in Spain. Balboa's career, however, had a sad ending, for four years later he was put to death by a jealous and suspicious governor, Pedrarias d'Avila.

Six years later Ferdinand Magellan, a native of Portugal, but sailing under the banner of Spain, his adopted country, set out with five old, half-rotten vessels and about two hundred and fifty men, a considerable portion of whom were worthless adventurers, if not downright rascals, to find a water passage to the South Sea. Sailing from Spain in the autumn of 1519 (September 20), he reached the straits which now bear his name thirteen months later, after having long suffered the pangs of hunger on account of short rations, and after experiencing a mutiny of the crew which was put down in cold blood. Leaving the straits he entered the boundless ocean — the *Mar Pacifico* — and steering northwestward struck out boldly in search of new lands. Days, weeks, and months passed with nothing in sight but the prospects of starvation. Soon the crew had to be put on half rations and presently the few rats that infested the ships were luxuries at half a ducat each. Living on wormy crumbs and soaked ox leather they managed to keep alive until the island of Guam was reached. Finally, in April, 1521, they sighted the now familiar island of Samar, belonging to the Philippine group; but a month later Magellan was killed in a fight with the natives. One of the ships, the *Victoria,* finally succeeded in rounding the Cape of Good Hope, and, after an absence of three years, reached Spain with thirty-one survivors. At last the earth had been circumnavigated and the globular theory proved forever beyond further question. The voyage thus ended, says Fiske,[25] was doubtless the greatest feat of navigation that has ever been performed, and nothing can be imagined that would surpass it except a journey to some other planet.[26]

In the case of Ponce de Leon, another Spanish explorer, to the thirst for gold was added the thirst for eternal youth.

---

[25] Fiske, "Discovery of America," vol. ii. pp. 184–210.
[26] Bourne, "Spain in America," ch. ix.

Ponce de Leon was an intrepid warrior and explorer, who had come out with Columbus on his second voyage in 1493. Learning of an Indian tradition concerning a wonderful fountain situated on an island called Bimini, somewhere to the north of San Domingo, whose waters, if drunk, restored the drinker to eternal youth, he secured permission from the king to go in quest of it, and, in March, 1513, he sailed from Porto Rico for the north. On the 27th of the same month, it being Easter Sunday (Spanish, *Pascual Florida*), he came in sight of land and anchored off the site of the future city of St. Augustine. In honor of the day he named the country Florida. In vain did he search for the fabled fountain and treasures of gold. After coasting around the peninsula in his futile quest, he returned to Porto Rico. Eight years later he returned and tried to make a settlement, the first attempt within the borders of the present United States; but the effort resulted in failure, and, being attacked and seriously wounded by the Indians, he sailed back to Cuba, where he died after prolonged suffering.

In 1520 Vasquez de Ayllon set out from San Domingo with two vessels in search of slaves to work the plantations and mines. He landed on the coast of South Carolina and by the basest treachery kidnaped a number of the natives. One of his ships foundered, while the captives on the other sickened and died. He returned to Spain and as a reward for this expedition was appointed (1525) to conquer Chicora, as he called Carolina. Accordingly, in June, 1526, with three vessels and some five or six hundred men, De Ayllon set out on his voyage of conquest and settlement, and in due course reached the coast of what is now North Carolina or Virginia. Here they established the settlement of San Miguel, on the site of the future Jamestown as some historians contend. The colony, however, soon succumbed from a variety of causes, De Ayllon died, and the survivors, numbering about one hundred and fifty persons, returned to San Domingo.

The greatest, however, and judged by modern standards, the most infamous of the Spanish expeditions in the New World was that of Cortes. A native of Spain, Cortes was destined for the law by his parents, but he was born an adventurer in an age of adventure. At 19 he left Spain for the New World. He learned the art of Indian warfare under Velasquez in the conquest of Cuba (1511), and when Grijalva discovered Mexico in 1518

EXPLORATIONS

Cortes was eager to possess its cities of fabulous wealth. The Mexicans were far in advance of the Indians on the islands and on the continent to the north of them. Their god, Quetzalcoatl, so their tradition said, had taught them the arts of civilization, but had been forced to depart because he incurred the wrath of a higher divinity. On leaving, he promised that he and his descendants would revisit the Mexicans in after years. The belief was now prevalent that the time for his return was near, and when the white man came, bearing thunder and lightning in his hand, many were convinced that the " fair god " had returned. Montezuma, the emperor of the Mexicans, taking counsel of his fears, adopted a half-hearted policy marked by friendliness and suspicion. His fate probably would not have been very different had he displayed full confidence in the invaders or adopted a policy of open hostility.

Early in March, 1519, Cortes, with a force consisting of about 500 Spaniards, several cannon, and fifteen horses, landed on the east coast of Mexico, and at once sent messengers bearing gifts to Montezuma. The expedition then set out for the capital city of Montezuma's dominion. In the course of an interview Cortes told the ambassador that "the Spaniards were troubled with a disease of the heart, for which gold was a specific remedy." That gold, which the capital was reputed to contain, he had determined to secure; also to convert the heathen, either by the mouth of the priest or that of the cannon. With our modern notions of Christianity this sounds very strange; but with many of the conquerors religion was often a matter of faith rather than of morals. By diplomacy, by aid of the natives, who turned against the Mexican emperor, and by deceit and treachery, he at last gained the capital and got Montezuma in his power. By profaning the temples in setting up Christian worship he turned the Aztecs against him, and they stirred up a revolt against the tame submission of Montezuma. Cortes left the capital in fear, but soon returned, and in August, 1521, captured it after a long siege. The number of lives lost, mainly Mexicans, is estimated at from 120,000 to 240,000. The Spanish loss was small, as was their gain in booty.[27]

The enemies of Cortes, meantime, were busy both at home

[27] Winsor, "Cortes and His Companions," in "Narrative and Critical Hist.," vol. ii. ch. vi.; Prescott, "Conquest of Mexico."

and in America, but Charles V. confirmed his acts and appointed him Captain General and Chief Justice of New Spain, as that part of the world was called. The City of Mexico was rebuilt on a grand scale, and the system of repartimientos was adopted by which the Indians were assigned in lots for work on the plantations or in the mines; in other words, reduced to slavery. To the credit of the crown, be it said, that a decree was issued annulling this, but the colonists managed to evade it, and the conversion of the heathen went on at a rapid rate, 9,000,000, as it was enthusiastically asserted, in twenty years.

But it would be unfair to judge Cortes by the standards of to-day. Prescott, who wrote the story of his conquest, says that he used no more cruelty than was common at home and shed no more blood than was necessary to effect the conquest. The conversion of the heathen was considered in that day a sufficient justification for the conquest itself, and there can be little doubt, as Fiske points out, that after making all allowances, the Spaniards did introduce a better state of society into Mexico than they found there, while Bourne adds that Cortes devoted his every energy to the restoration of the country to peaceful prosperity.

Pamfilo de Narvaez, who had been sent from Cuba by Velasquez to overtake and arrest the insubordinate Cortes, but who had himself been captured, now determined to look farther north for fields of conquest, and in 1527 secured from the king a grant of all the gulf coast from Mexico to the cape of Florida. In June of the same year, with five ships and about six hundred persons, he set out on the voyage and landed at Tampa Bay in April, 1528. Directing his ships to meet him elsewhere, he foolishly pushed inland through swamps and jungles in search of the gold which unfortunately was always just a little farther on. The fleet being unable to find the ports in accordance with Narvaez's instructions, and, after vainly searching for him, returned to Spain a year later. The remnant of his army, three hundred in number, pushed their way along the coast through forest and swamps, harassed by the Indians and tortured by hunger and thirst. Near St. Marks they constructed five rude boats in which the survivors (two hundred and forty) embarked in September and painfully threaded their way along the coast, one after another of their frail vessels succumbing to the winter storms. About eighty of their number, destitute and enfeebled, finally succeeded in reaching an island off the coast of Texas. In the course of the winter the little band was reduced by cold and hunger to fifteen. Cabeza de Vaca, the treasurer of the expedition and a former officer under Cortes, with three others, soon formed the sole remnant of Narvaez's band. After eight years of wandering over the inhospitable country between the Mississippi River and California, beaten by the Indians, suffering the tortures of hunger and thirst, at times acting as "medicine men," they finally reached the City of Mexico in July, 1536. The whole story of their hardships and triumphs, of their perseverance and courage, constitutes one of the most thrilling narratives in the history of Spanish America.[28]

The cupidity of the settlers in Mexico had been aroused by rumors of wealthy cities in what is now Arizona and New Mexico, called the "Seven Cities of Cibola," and several expeditions pushed out in that direction. In 1528 Cortes sent out one which coasted up the Pacific for three hundred miles. In 1530 another entered the Gulf of California and a few years later his lieutenants were claiming the peninsula of Lower California for Cortes. There is a tradition that Spanish vessels passed northward beyond the mouth of the Columbia, but there is no authentic record of their discoveries.

The arrival at Mexico of De Vaca and his companions aroused a new interest in the "Seven Cities of Cibola," for they declared that they had seen them with their own eyes. The inhabitants were said to be so wealthy that their household utensils were made of gold and silver and their doorways studded with precious gems. Once more the gold-hunters set out, this time led by Vasquez de Coronado, governor of the northwest province of New Spain. With a small but picked band he set out in April, 1540, and, after a long and perilous march, in the course of which many of his number perished by the wayside, Coronado reached the first of the fabled "Cities," only to find a village of thatched Indian pueblos, interesting to the archæologist and ethnologist of to-day, but very disappointing to Coronado, because they contained neither gold nor silver. That was a little farther on, and so he pushed northward on the track of the will-o'-the-wisp, but always with the same sense of disillusionment. For three years Coronado and his companions thirsted in the mountains or toiled

[28] Read Woodbury Lowery, "Spanish Settlements in America," pp. 170 *et seq.* Also Smith, "Cabeza de Vaca."

over trackless deserts only to descend into valleys of hunger and despair. Northward, still northward, they pressed, sometimes over plains " as full of crookback oxen as the mountain Sierra in Spain is of sheep." Coronado at last, after having discovered the Grand Cañon of Colorado, reached a great river, probably the Platte or Missouri, and turned back satisfied that the gold was to be found only at the end of the rainbow.[29] At length, in the spring of 1542, he returned to Mexico greatly chagrined at having found no cities of gold and to find himself deposed as governor for his failure.

One more Spanish exploration of consequence deserves to be mentioned, that of Hernando de Soto. De Soto's career was one of the most romantic of that romantic period. At thirty-one (1531) he found himself second in command to Pizarro in the conquest of Peru, an exploit even more infamous than the conquest of Mexico. He indeed denounced Pizarro for some of his acts, but he remained with the band and carried away, not half a million dollars in spoils, as is generally asserted, but hardly more, as Channing says, than a paltry hundred thousand ducats.[30] While governor of Cuba in 1538 he heard of Florida, and wished for an opportunity to search that land for more treasures. With nine vessels carrying about six hundred men and over two hundred horses he set sail from Havana in May, 1539, and in due course landed on the coast of Florida, but instead of gold, found only hostile Indians, who harassed him at every turn. Proceeding northward to the Savannah River, De Soto then turned westward and southward to the fortified Indian town of Mauvilla, near the junction of the Alabama and Tombigbee rivers, where he was attacked and a fourth or fifth of his men killed in the course of the desperate battle which ensued. Thousands of the Indians, if we may believe the chroniclers, were in turn killed by the Spaniards, while the rest were put to flight and their houses burned. From Mauvilla De Soto marched in a northwesterly direction across Alabama and Mississippi, fighting his way as he went, finally reaching the Mississippi River, near the present site of Memphis, in May, 1541. Crossing the river, he turned southward, and after wandering far to the west in the vain quest for signs of the

[29] Read Bourne, " Travels of Coronado," 2 vols., in the " Trail Makers Series "; also Haynes in Winsor's " Narrative and Critical History," vol. ii. ch. 7.
[30] Channing, " History of the United States," vol. i. p. 67.

new El Dorado, he died May 21, 1542, and his body was buried in the great river which he is said to have discovered, but which we know De Vaca must have seen some ten years previous. It was altogether, says Professor Bourne, the most remarkable expedition in the history of North America, though closely challenged by the contemporary enterprise of Coronado, which did for the southwest what De Soto did for the eastern and central belt.[31]

What had this half century of unparalleled activity given to Spain? In South America she claimed practically everything in view except Guiana and Brazil, the latter of which Cabral had discovered for Portugal in 1500. In Mexico and the West Indies her sway was undisputed save by the savages, but as yet she had no settlements within the present limits of continental United States. Even at the close of the sixteenth century she had only a few, the chief being St. Augustine (1565), Santa Fé (1598), and a chain of missions reaching to the Gulf of California.[32] Such in brief, were the results of Spanish achievement in North America.

Spain was at her zenith at home as well as abroad. At the beginning of this activity in exploration she was being unified into a national state by Ferdinand and Isabella. Ferdinand was succeeded by his grandson, Charles I., who, on becoming German emperor in 1519, took the title of Charles V. Actual ruler of Spain, Austria, the Netherlands, and the two Sicilies, and titular head of all the Germans, he yet took as his motto, "*Plus ultra.*"

For the government of the Spanish-American colonies there was a Council of the Indies, through which the king made all laws relating to them. Every colonial officer was subordinate to it. Under the direction of the king it exercised supreme legislative and judicial control of Spanish America. It served also as an advisory or nominating board in regard to all civil or ecclesiastical appointments in America, somewhat after the manner of the English Board of Trade and Plantations. The colonies themselves were divided into two great provinces: Mexico or New Spain, including Venezuela; and Peru comprising the rest of South Amer-

[31] Read Bourne, "Spain in America," p. 168; also King, "De Soto in Florida"; Winship, "The Journey of De Soto," in the "Trail Makers Series"; Lowery, "Spanish Settlements in America," pp. 235 *et seq.;* and Bandelier, "Contributions to Southwestern History."

[32] Bancroft, "History of the United States," vol. i. ch. ii.

ica except Brazil. Legally, they did not belong to Spain, but were a part of the hereditary domains of the sovereigns of Castile as heirs of Queen Isabella, and the Spanish Parliament had little or nothing to do with them.

Each was governed by a viceroy, who acted as the personal representative of the king, and each was subdivided for administrative purposes into a number of *audiencias* or Supreme Court districts. At the expiration of their terms of office the viceroys were compelled to submit to an inquest into their official conduct. They were further checked by councils or *audiencias,* which at the same time served as the highest colonial courts of appeal. Jealousy of the power of these viceroys caused their removal every few years, hence they sought to make their fortunes quickly. The cities were allowed town councils, the only measure of local self-government recognized in America. The councils consisted of *regidores* or aldermen, and a number of *alcaldes* or justices, the latter elected by the former. The public offices were generally sold for cash and this was one of the regular sources of government revenue. No Spaniard born in the colony was eligible to any office. The population was a superposition of castes. The colonists were forbidden to cultivate European products, to manufacture goods, or construct ships, and all commerce was monopolized by a few opulent houses at Seville. At first an effort was made to use the Indians as laborers, but it was found to mean their destruction. Hispaniola is reputed to have had 1,000,000 inhabitants in 1492; nineteen years later 14,000. From the beginning the conversion of the Indians to Christianity was one of the dominant motives of Spanish policy. Following upon the heels of conquest came an army of indefatigable friars who devoted themselves assiduously to preaching, baptizing and learning the native tongue.

Every village, whether Indian or Spanish, was required by law to maintain a church, hospital, and school for the instruction of native children in the Spanish language and religion. Converted Indians were gathered together in villages called missions, where, under the direction of the friars, they were taught to live industrious, peaceful, religious lives. Every mission thus became an industrial school and in time the whole of Spanish-America was dotted with such institutions, where tens of thousands of Indians went through a process of schooling which ended only

with their lives. The government was apparently extremely so-
licitous for the education of the natives and it is the opinion of
careful investigators that the efforts made by Spain for its promotion greatly exceeded anything attempted by the English government in its American colonies. Indian boys were taught to
read and write the Spanish language and to become tailors, carpenters, blacksmiths, and shoemakers. Higher institutions of
learning were established in various places, and in number, range
of studies and standard of attainments they probably surpassed
anything of the kind in English-America before the nineteenth century. Especially in Mexico were the achievements in medicine,
surgery, linguistics, anthropology and history of a notable character. Dictionaries, grammars, and histories of Mexican institutions testify to the intellectual activity and industry of the Spanish
scholars. In Peru the University of Lima had at one time over
two thousand students and some two hundred doctors of theology,
law and medicine.

In spite of the restrictions upon foreign trade, Spanish manufactures formed hardly one tenth of the importations into the
colonies — the rest were smuggled. The population of Spain was
decimated by continual wars and by immigration to the colonies.
Military adventurers and the idleness of the aristocracy suspended
labor. Spain ceased to produce her own necessities and bought
them of other countries with the gold and silver poured into her
lap by her American mines. Humboldt estimated the average
annual output of the mines at 6,000,000 pesos during the seventeenth century, and at 33,000,000 during the latter half of the
eighteenth, while the total yield from 1493 to 1803 he put at
5,706,700,000 pesos, or about ten times the known production of
the rest of the world. Spanish galleons laden with the precious
metals were naturally the envy of other nations and were constantly preyed upon by their daring corsairs, even when the nations
were not at war on land. But those which reached her ports only
contributed to her downfall by teaching her people to put their
trust in gold, then thought to be true wealth, instead of in the
fruits of industry.

It is generally asserted by historians that the Spanish colonies
were oppressed and exploited by the mother country, but according
to Professor E. G. Bourne, a careful investigator and writer on
Spanish rule in America, these facts have been greatly exag-

gerated. This writer's conclusions are substantially as follows: Justice was slow and uncertain; the evidence of financial corruption, especially of judicial bribery, is abundant, but all things considered, Spanish-America was quite as well governed as was Spain, and was on the whole more prosperous, and at no time in the history of Mexico, up to within the last quarter of a century, has the government been so good as her people enjoyed under the able viceroys sent over by the kings of Spain.[33]

IV

EXPLORATIONS OF THE FRENCH

The King of France declared that he would not respect the Papal "Line of Demarcation" unless authority for it could be traced back to Adam's will, and attracted by the hope of fish and furs Frenchmen soon began to frequent the coasts of northeastern America. The French king also entertained the belief that the passage to Cathay and India lay in this direction, and so in 1524 he sent out Giovanni Verrazano, a native of Florence and a daring corsair and explorer, to find the coveted route. Verrazano crossed the Atlantic, sighted the shores of what is now North Carolina and explored the coast as far north as New England, after which he disappeared from view, how or where no one knows. In 1534 another Frenchman, Jacques Cartier, explored the coasts and islands about the Gulf of St. Lawrence and the following year sailed up the St. Lawrence River as far as the rapids, where he named the hill on the northern bank Mount Royal (Montreal), near which was situated the Indian village of Hochelaga. Six years later he and Roberval, a nobleman of France, attempted to plant a colony on this river, but they did not work together harmoniously and the attempt ended in disaster. Other Frenchmen came to these northern regions to engage in the fish and pelt industry, but the sixteenth century ended without any successful colonization. The French next turned south in search of a more hospitable clime.

Here they might have succeeded but for the criminal neglect

[33] See Bourne, "Spain in America," chs. xix–xx., from which the facts above stated are mainly drawn.

of their government. In 1562 Admiral Coligny, the leader of the Huguenots, as the French Protestants were called, sent out an expedition under Jean Ribaut, a seaman of renown in his day, who discovered St. John's River and sailed northward, naming the country Carolina, in honor of Charles IX., King of France. A colony of twenty-six persons was established at Port Royal, near the modern Beaufort, but the following year, after an experience marked by hunger, mutiny and bloodshed, the settlers followed their leader home, only to be captured by an English cruiser. Laudonière then (1564), under the patronage of the king, sought the Carolina coast with a company of Protestants, who established themselves on the St. John's River. The colonists were a dissolute set, many of them European jail-birds, who were then thought to be good material for colonists, and they gave the governor no little trouble. A piratical expedition which some of them organized against the Spanish betrayed the presence of the little colony. Those who escaped the Spanish sword and the governor's gibbet were soon reduced to dire straits by their own improvidence and by their bad treatment of the Indians, who had at first received them kindly. August, 1565, Sir John Hawkins, an English slave trader, entered the St. John's River, and sold the Frenchmen one of the vessels in exchange for their heavy guns. They had intended returning home, but before they started Ribaut arrived with fresh supplies.

The Spanish had not succeeded in colonizing Florida, but they were determined not to give it up, and Pedro Menendez de Aviles, " the bloodiest Spaniard who ever cursed American soil," says Channing, " and one of the ablest," [34] was commissioned to destroy the French colony on the St. John's, and for this purpose a fleet of nineteen vessels and fifteen hundred men was placed at his command. After founding a colony to the south of them as a base of operations he proceeded to " gibbet and behead all the Protestants " in that region, with the savage cruelty characteristic of the Spaniards in that age.[35] Philip II. approved the action of Menendez, and wrote the following endorsement on one of the latter's dispatches: " Say to him, that as to those he has killed, he has done well, and as to those he has saved, they shall be sent to the galleys." Thus did Spain make good her claim

[34] Channing, " History of the United States," vol. i. p. 98.
[35] Read Parkman, " Pioneers of France in the New World," chs. vii.-viii.

to North America and crush the first attempt of the French to gain a foothold in Florida.

The town which Menendez founded in this region was named St. Augustine (1565) and was the first permanent settlement within the limits of continental United States. But it came near being wiped out of existence two years later in a terrible retribution which Dominic de Gourgues, a daring soldier of Gascony, sought to inflict in revenge for the massacre of his fellow countrymen. He destroyed all the settlements left by Menendez, except St. Augustine, hanged his prisoners to a tree and sailed back to France in triumph. The King of France, as already stated, did not even protest against this cruel act of Menendez, although the blood of hundreds of loyal Frenchmen had cried from the ground for retribution. But the victims of Menendez's ferocity were to his Catholic majesty only despised Huguenots, intruders in his realm and followers of the hated Coligny, and so they were left to their fate by an unnatural sovereign. But at last they had found a powerful avenger, and although the king could and did disavow his acts, he could not undo them. The chivalrous annals of France, says Parkman, may be searched in vain for a deed of more romantic daring than the vengeance of Dominic de Gourgues.[36]

Later in the century exploration and colonization were again taken up at the north, for here seemed to lie the hope of French colonization. The fur trade was found very lucrative and received no little attention, while the fisheries grew steadily in importance. In 1578 there were not less than one hundred and fifty French fishing vessels at Newfoundland, besides two hundred of other nations. Rude huts were springing up along the shores of Anti Costi, and were becoming centers of the far more lucrative trade in bear skins and beaver skins. French merchants and adventurers were turning their eyes toward these regions, not like the Spaniards seeking gold and silver, but the more modest gains of fish, oil and peltries.

In 1603 Samuel de Champlain, one of the most remarkable

[36] Parkman, "Pioneers of France in the New World," p. 139. Lossing says that De Gourgues was himself a Catholic. It appears that during the Italian wars he was taken prisoner by the Spaniards and condemned to the galleys. This humiliation gave him for that nation an implacable hatred. In equipping his expedition, however, the personal resentment was concealed. Those who knew his intentions regarded him as serving his king and country. Though his head was demanded by the Spanish ambassador, he escaped the fate of Raleigh.

Frenchmen of his day, says John Fiske, and a French explorer of
indomitable perseverance and great merit, who years before had
gone on a voyage to the West Indies, sailed up the St. Lawrence
past Mount Royal; but being unable to ascend the rapids, turned
back and recrossed the Atlantic to France. His curiosity still
unsated, he came out again next year with Sieur de Monts, who
had secured from the king an appointment as Lieutenant-General
or Viceroy of Acadia, as the English called the country from the
fortieth to the forty-sixth parallel of north latitude. At the same

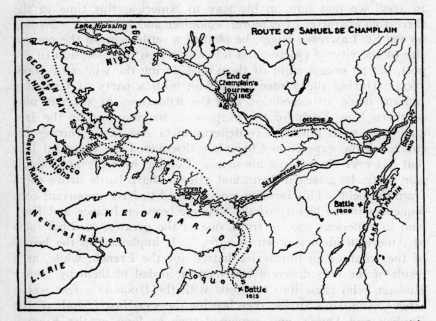

time De Monts was given a monopoly of the fur trade in all this
vast region.[37]

In April, 1604, De Monts and Champlain sailed from Havre
de Grace with two ships, carrying the material for the proposed
colony, which consisted of a curious mixture of gentlemen, thieves,
and vagabonds mainly impressed from the streets of French cities.
The voyagers proceeded to the Bay of Fundy, thence to the Passa-
maquoddy Bay and finally to the mouth of the St. Croix River,
where they made a settlement which was identified nearly two

[37] See H. P. Biggar, "Early Trading Companies of New France," ch. iv.

hundred years later at the time of the dispute between Great Britain and the United States over the northeastern boundary. The colonists soon abandoned this cold, inhospitable site, or rather the remnant of them who were left after pestilence had carried off a considerable portion of their number, crossed the Bay of Fundy and settled Port Royal, now Annapolis, which proved to be the first permanent French settlement in America.

After several unimportant exploring expeditions along the northeastern shores, Champlain returned to France. But again in 1608 we find him on his way to America, this time in the three-fold character of explorer, colonizer and fur trader. Sailing up the St. Lawrence River, he planted a settlement on the present site of the city of Quebec and left a garrison in possession of the post, but all except eight of them died during the winter of 1608-1609. During the winter Champlain with a party of Canadian Indians made an expedition into the wilderness of what is now northern New York for the purpose of making war on the Iroquois, the most powerful confederation in America. During the course of the expedition Champlain discovered the beautiful lake that has ever since borne his name. Coming up with an Iroquois war party, he attacked them, and after a sharp battle drove them from the field. This incident was destined to have important consequences in the history of the struggle between France and England in America; was, in truth, one of the greatest cardinal facts of American history down to 1763.[38] It implanted in the hearts of the Iroquois an implacable hatred for the French, while, as a result of the very different treatment accorded to them by Henry Hudson, who came into relations with the Iroquois a few weeks after Champlain's attack, they became the steadfast friends of the English and Dutch, and remained such as long as the English supremacy in America lasted. Several years after this incident Champlain made an expedition against the Indians in western New York, which ended his career of exploring and fighting. The remaining years of his life were devoted mainly to promoting the progress of his lifeless settlement at Quebec, which as late as 1628 had a population of only one hundred persons.[39] During the

[38] John Fiske, "Discovery of America," vol. ii. p. 530.
[39] For good accounts of Champlain's explorations see Parkman's "Pioneers of France in the New World," chs. ix.-xvii.; Winsor, "Cartier to Frontenac," chs v.-viii, and Kingford's "History of Canada," vol. i. chs. ii.-vii.

latter half of the same century La Salle and Hennepin traversed the Mississippi Valley and the region of the Great Lakes, and Marquette and other missionary explorers were sent out from France by the Society of Jesus.

As the search for gold and silver was the dominating motive back of Spanish explorations in America, so the fish and peltry industries constituted the chief stimulus to French adventure. Added to the economic stimulus also was the desire to convert the heathen to the Catholic faith. Along with every fur trader went a black-robed priest, and while the one bartered with the dusky savage for his skins, the other talked to him of salvation and grace. Manifesting a genuine sympathy for the Indian customs and fraternizing with them on terms of social equality, the French pioneers gained an ascendancy over the savages (except, of course, the Iroquois, who were alienated by the conduct of Champlain) which neither the Englishman nor the Spaniard was able to rival.

As in New Spain, so in New France trade and commerce were greatly hampered by royal grants of exclusive privileges, but during the time of Richelieu notable reforms in this regard were introduced. The French, unlike the Spaniards who came before them, as well as the English who followed, were not successful colonizers. Their settlements always languished and signs of material progress were seldom seen. Half a century after the founding of Quebec there were not above three thousand white settlers in all New France and Acadia put together.[40] The successful colonization of America was left for another race, who sent over families without priests and missionaries, whose dominating motive was not the quest for gold and silver, and about whose history there lingers none of the romance of the *courier de bois* or the *conquestador*.

V

EARLY ENGLISH ATTEMPTS AT COLONIZATION.

After the voyages of the Cabots, under Henry VII., English fishermen continued to frequent the Grand Banks of Newfoundland, and slave merchants traded with the Spanish colonies in the south, but it was not until Elizabeth ascended the throne and

[40] Channing, "History of the United States," vol. i. p. 109.

England had broken forever with Catholicism that she began to contest in earnest the claims of Spain to the land and treasures of the New World. The Elizabethans were as famous upon the sea as upon the stage; the chief actors there were Hawkins, Sir Humphrey Gilbert and his half brother, Sir Walter Raleigh, Gosnold, Newport, Frobisher, and Francis Drake, and to these hardy seamen England owes her colonial empire, and the United States its existence.

Drake in particular had a special grudge against the Spaniards, and he wreaked his vengeance upon them in such a way as to go down in the Spanish annals as "The Dragon." In 1557 he set out with four vessels on a buccaneering tour without a commission from the queen, but three of the ships were lost by mutiny, desertion and cowardice. Drake, however, kept on in the *Pelican* and entered the Pacific in October, 1578. He then proceeded to harry the unprotected settlements on the western coast of America and to relieve homeward bound Spanish galleons of their burdens of silver and gold wherever he could find them. He sailed northward as far as California and then turned west, returning to England by way of the Cape of Good Hope. The amount of spoil which Drake gathered in during the course of his piratical cruise was enormous, and stirred to the highest pitch the wrath of the Spaniards. The queen graciously overlooked his conduct, however, rewarded him and his men handsomely with a share of the spoil and knighted the daring admiral in person on board the *Pelican*.[41] Frobisher and Gilbert each made three voyages, the former to the Arctic regions, the latter to Labrador and the Gulf of the St. Lawrence. But each accomplished little beyond interesting others in that part of the country and inducing them to attempt colonization there.

The first serious effort was made farther south. Gilbert had been lost at sea on the return trip of his third voyage, and the patent which had been issued to him was transferred to Raleigh. It authorized him and his heirs and assigns " to have and to hold, to occupy and enjoy " all the lands not possessed by any Christian prince, the lands referred to doubtless being those of northeastern America. Raleigh was one of Elizabeth's favorites, was the friend of statesmen, men of letters, courtiers,

[41] " Hale, Hawkins and Drake " in Winsor, " Narrative and Critical History," vol. vii. ch. ii.

soldiers and mariners, and himself a leader in all those fields of activity. In 1584 he sent out two vessels under command of Philip Amadas and Arthur Barlow, who landed at Roanoke Island in Albermarle Sound and carried back a glowing description of the country, which, he asserted, was "the most plentiful, sweet, fruitful and wholesome of all the world." As a reward really for what Amadas and Barlow had only described, Raleigh was knighted and his claim was confirmed. He named the country Virginia, in honor of the Virgin Queen, and by her help sent seven vessels with one hundred and eight colonists the next year. A piratical detour was made around by the Canaries in order, it was said, to force the Spanish to help pay the expenses.

The colonists, one hundred in number, were landed on Roanoke Island under the leadership of Ralph Lane as governor, but they too "spun out their days in cursed thirst for gold," and starvation soon stared them in the face. At this juncture Drake happened to pass that way while returning from a cruise in the West Indies, and carried them home just a few weeks before another expedition under Grenville arrived with supplies and recruits, of whom fifteen were left behind to hold the deserted post, while Grenville proceeded to the West Indies to collect the expenses of his voyage from the Spaniards. Raleigh, whose fortune had been depleted by these repeated efforts, now secured help from certain merchants and men of influence and fitted out another expedition of three vessels destined this time for Chesapeake Bay. In July, 1587, they touched at Roanoke for the purpose of taking on board Grenville's men, but found not one of them. The governor, John White, set ashore the colonists, among them his wife, his daughter and grand-daughter, Virginia Dare, the first English child born in America, and returned to England to hurry forward needed supplies. When he reached Roanoke again, three years later, not a trace of the colonists was to be found, although the houses which they had occupied were still standing. From then until now the fate of White's "lost colony" has been a fruitful theme of speculation among historians. Most of them probably perished; some of them may have been adopted by the Indians, for at a much later time people with light hair and eyes were found among the Indians. Some such people may be found in North Carolina to-day, and some have been led to believe that they were the descendants of the lost colonists, but it seems very improbable.[42] With undaunted courage Raleigh tried still another expedition in 1602, but again failed. James I. imprisoned him for twelve years, and later, after Raleigh's voyage to Guiana, basely executed him on an old and false charge of treason.

The cause of White's failure to return sooner was the war with Spain. The English buccaneers were becoming more and more daring, robbing Spain of her treasure ships and even harrying the Spanish Main. Her very existence seemed to depend upon free communication with her colonies, which was now threatened, and for this and other reasons she determined upon one supreme effort to crush her maritime rival. For this purpose Philip II. fitted out his " Invincible Armada," consisting of one hundred and thirty ships, carrying thirty thousand soldiers and three thousand heavy guns. In May, 1588, this gigantic fleet appeared off the coast of England. The English vessels were smaller in size and fewer in number than the Spanish, but much faster; and manned by such masterly seamen as Hawkins, Frobisher and Drake, they proved irresistible. What the English left the winds destroyed, and the two together dealt Spain a blow from which she never recovered.[43] The destruction of her colonial empire, begun at this time by England, was completed just three hundred and ten years later, almost to a day, by the United States.

Bartholomew Gosnold deserves mention among the English navigators as being one of the first to sail directly for America from England, instead of passing down by the West Indies, thereby shortening the route by nearly a thousand miles. Cape Cod was named by him in 1602 while exploring the coast of Massachusetts and New Hampshire. In the following year Martin Pring was sent out with two vessels by certain British merchants to explore the New England coast, and in 1604 he was followed by George Weymouth, who explored some of the same coast. The report of the abundance of good harbors in this region fixed still more firmly the attention of the English upon it as better suited for colonization than the country farther south; but the honor of receiving the first English colony was reserved for Virginia.

Such, in brief, was the experience of the Europeans in

[42] Read Brown's " Genesis of the United States," vol. i. p. 20 et seq., and S. B. Weeks in " American Historical Papers," vol. v. p. 4.
[43] Read Corbett's " Drake and the Tudor Navy."

America in the sixteenth century. Of the nations most active and
destined to play leading roles, Spain seemed to have the firmest
hold. But she had fallen upon the indolent south, where nature
saps the very energies her luxuries promise to sustain. France
turned to the frozen north, but wasted by dissensions at home
and constant wars abroad, she had a slender hold on the extensive
region to the north and south of the St. Lawrence to which she
laid claim. The English, whether from choice or necessity, had
taken the safer middle ground and claimed all from Newfoundland to Florida, though nobody knew where the dividing lines
were. But at the dawn of the seventeenth century not a single
permanent settlement had yet been effected by the power destined
to dominate the New World.

Chapter III

THE PLANTING OF THE SOUTHERN COLONIES
1606-1776

I

VIRGINIA

AFTER the failure of Raleigh no single individual was found to risk his fame and fortune in efforts at colonization, but the work was soon taken up by corporate companies. The success attending the Muscovy and East India Companies, which had been founded to trade with Russia and India respectively, led a few venturesome merchants and traders to inquire if similar results could not be obtained by corporate action in America. The conditions were indeed vastly different, but the venture was made and a charter secured from King James I. in 1606 for a company with two subdivisions, the London Company and the Plymouth Company, so called from the names of the towns which became the headquarters of the two companies respectively. The first was granted permission to plant a colony anywhere on the coast of Virginia (the name applied to all the English claims in America at this time) between the thirty-fourth and thirty-eighth degrees of north latitude; the second was given the same privilege between the forty-first and forty-fifth, neither company to plant a colony within one hundred miles of a settlement already made by the other. The announcement of a new colonial policy such as had not yet been introduced in America was contained in the clause which declared that the colonists and their posterity should enjoy all " liberties, franchises and immunities " as though they were abiding in the realm — that is, they were to enjoy the benefits of the common law equally with the inhabitants of England. This declaration really deserves to be called an epoch in the history of colonization.[1]

The government of the colony was to be nominally in the

[1] Channing, "History of the United States," vol. i. p. 162.

hands of two councils, one resident in England, the other in the colony; but as one was appointed directly, and the other indirectly, by the king, all power was virtually in his hands. The council in America was to administer affairs according to instructions issued by the king, but any laws or ordinances which it might make were subject to repeal by the crown or by the home council. The form of government thus provided was absurdly cumbrous and soon had to be abandoned. The first instructions ordered that the land tenure should be the same as in England; that trial by jury should be preserved, and the supremacy of the king and of the Church of England maintained.[2]

The colony itself was to be started on a system of communism. In the words of Doyle, it was to be a " vast joint-stock farm, or collection of farms, worked by servants who were to receive, in return for their labor, all their necessaries and a share in the proceeds of the undertaking." All trade was to be in the hands of a treasurer or cape merchant, and was to be public. The patentees were given the right to exact a duty of two and a half per cent. from all English subjects, and five per cent. from all foreigners trading with the colony. For twenty years the proceeds were to accrue to the company, after that to the crown.[3] Among the first councilors appointed by the king were Sir Ferdinando Gorges, Sir Edwin Sandys, Sir Thomas Smythe and Sir Francis Popham, all able and well-known men of their time. These preliminaries being completed, preparations were made to send out the first colony to take possession of the company's lands.

On December 19, 1606, three puny vessels, with an aggregate tonnage of not over one hundred and sixty tons, sailed from England on what was perhaps, for Englishmen at least, the most important voyage in its results since Columbus had sailed out of Palos with his three caravels more than a hundred years previous. The three ships were called the *Susan Constant,* the *Godspeed* and the *Discovery,* all belonging to the Muscovy Company, and they carried one hundred and four settlers to the coast of Virginia under the command of Christopher Newport, a well-known seaman of the time. The voyage was long and stormy and spring was well advanced when they entered Chesapeake Bay (May, 1607). The two capes at the entrance of this bay were named Charles and

[2] Fiske, "Old Virginia and Her Neighbors," vol. i. p. 64.
[3] Doyle, "English Colonies in America," vol. i. p. 128.

Henry, in honor of the king's sons,[4] and one of the largest rivers flowing into the bay they called James, in honor of their king. Sailing up this for fifty miles they selected a place for settlement and called it Jamestown.

An inventory of the settlers shows that they were ill-fitted for the task which they had undertaken. Fifty-five, more than half the entire number, were ranked as " gentlemen," that is, men disdaining labor, and out for adventure : a London tailor, a barber and a perfumer were sent along to look after the wants of these gentlemen. Twelve laborers and a few artisans were expected to furnish the necessary brawn and sinew. There was not a woman in the company. The place selected for the town, a malarial peninsula, chosen in flat contradiction to the instructions of the Virginia council, was no better suited to colony-building than the men who settled there.

However, the company contained a few men of worth, among them John Smith, whose life, says Fiske, reads like a chapter from " The Cloister and the Hearth," and but for whose presence and foresight the colony would have met the fate of Raleigh's earlier experiment. The thirst for gold was still strong, and the settlers were instructed to find this and also a way to India. So that while others were engaged in erecting huts or stretching tents, Captains Newport and Smith went up the river on this quest, but after a conference with the Indian chief, Powhatan, the supreme ruler in these parts, turned back at the falls where Richmond now stands and returned to Jamestown.[5]

Shortly thereafter Newport sailed for England with a batch of cheerful reports and a quantity of ore which proved to have been " taken from the wrong heap." It was hardly reasonable to expect that such a company would be harmonious. Dissensions had broken out on shipboard, where Smith was kept in irons for a month mainly on account of jealousy, and was actually excluded from the council, of which he had been appointed a member, for another month after landing. After the departure of Newport in July the dissensions increased and the troubles of the colonists grew apace. To internal trouble was added the haunting fear of

[4] Bancroft, " History of the United States," vol. i. p. 124; Brown, " Genesis of the United States," vol. i. pp. 151 *et seq.*
[5] Eggleston, " Beginners of a Nation," pp. 32–38; Fiske, " Old Virginia and Her Neighbors," vol. i. pp. 82–85.

Indian attacks, for, in spite of special instructions to that end, some of the red men had not been well treated by the newcomers. Heat, famine, and fever made deadly work, and by the end of September about half the colonists had succumbed.

Fortunately for the colonists Smith was among the survivors. Several of his enemies had perished and this made it all the easier for him to gain the ascendency. The story of his career for the next two years forms one of the most romantic pages in American history. He has left us an account of a still more remarkable career preceding this in Europe and Asia Minor, so remarkable, indeed, that its credibility has been seriously doubted by careful critics. There is no question that he was a vain fellow, a sort of "braggart captain"; but neither is there any doubt that he was a remarkable man, a true Elizabethan Englishman, and that there is a considerable element of truth in his narrative of his own exploits.

The first incident of consequence was his capture by the Indians while he was searching for the Pacific. The story of his release by the chief Powhatan at the intercession of Pocahontas is familiar to every American schoolboy. The Pocahontas part is now generally discredited, but there is no reason to doubt the story of Smith's capture. Certain it is that he rendered invaluable aid to the colonists by keeping the peace with the Indians and by securing from them corn sufficient to preserve the life of the thirty-eight settlers still alive when Newport returned in January, 1608. He ruled like a military despot, but nothing else would have saved the colony. He set the "gentlemen" to work, declaring that "he who will not work shall not eat." Before leaving Virginia he had thoroughly explored the Chesapeake Bay and its environs and made an excellent map of it. His enemies at last gained the ascendency, and he was practically driven out of the colony in the fall of 1609, never to return. Nevertheless he afterwards made several visits to America, explored the New England coast and published accounts of his explorations.

The year 1609 was notable to Virginia in that it brought a new and more liberal charter for the colonists. The council in England was originally distinct from the company, but it now became a part of it. A governor took the place of the council resident in the colony and the whole government of the corporation and its colony was placed in the hands of the stockholders. The boundaries were vaguely defined as extending two hundred miles each way from Old Point Comfort, and " up into the land throughout from sea to sea, west and northwest." Here was a basis for the future Virginia claim to the Northwest Territory.

Lord de la Warr, or Delaware, became the governor under the new charter and embarked with five hundred men and women, but was delayed many months by terrible storms. Meantime there came, in 1609–1610, the awful " starving time " for Virginia. Men were so crazed by hunger that some were driven to dig up and eat the putrid remains of their own dead after they had consumed all their brood hogs, their horses and dogs, and every rat, mouse or adder that could be found. Some died while wandering about in the woods in search of food; others in sheer desperation threw themselves upon the tender mercies of the Indians and were slain. Of the five hundred settlers in the colony when Smith left only sixty half-starved wretches were alive in the spring of 1610, and these would probably have succumbed within a few days had not help soon arrived. In their despair they determined to abandon the colony, and crowding themselves with their few remaining provisions into four pinnaces, two of them improvised for the purpose, they sailed down the river for England, but near the mouth met Delaware with recruits and supplies and returned to Jamestown to face again the horrors of life in this pestilential Virginia swamp.

Delaware next went up the James to chase the ever-receding rainbow which marked the site of the gold-fields, only to be driven back by men of copper hue.[6] Under his management conditions improved a little, however, but he left in less than a year and was succeeded by Sir Thomas Dale (1611), a soldier who had served against the Spanish in the Netherlands. Dale came out clothed with authority to rule by martial law, and he appears to have stretched his authority to the uttermost. He inflicted the death penalty for blasphemy, disrespect to the public authorities and many other offenses that would now go unnoticed. Under his pitiless rule the colony became half military camp and half penal colony. His little finger proved to be heavier than the loins of his predecessors. Whether the rod of iron was necessary to the

[6] For an interesting account of the illusions of the colonists in this respect, see Eggleston, " Beginners of a Nation," ch. iii.; see also Fiske, " Old Virginia and Her Neighbors," vol. i. pp. 122–123.

life of the colony or not, it is certain that at the end of five years Dale left the settlement in a better condition than he found it,[7] even though the settlers always alluded to the period as " five years of slavery." He also established other settlements along the James.

One of his best services to the colony was the termination of the communal system, under which the fruits of each man's labor went to the common stock and the settlers were fed and clothed from a common store-house. It had been limited to five years as an experiment, but Dale began its extinction before the expiration of that time by assigning to each settler three acres, the proceeds of which were to be his own, though he was still to labor for the community. Even this three acres of private right put so much more life in the colony that private ownership was destined to become the rule. Another event of importance which occurred during Dale's administration was the introduction of the cultivation of tobacco. At first the Virginia product was unsuited to the English market on account of its bitter taste, but through the aid of John Rolfe the settlers were taught how to cure it for export. The use of this weed had spread so rapidly after its discovery, and its cultivation in Virginia was so easy, that the economic success of the colony was now assured.[8] As early as 1620 40,000 pounds were annually being shipped to England.

The year 1619 is remarkable in the history, not only of Virginia, but also of America, for the introduction of two systems diametrically opposed — slavery and democracy. Both made a profound impression on the future life of a great nation, and more than two hundred years later the former perished at the hands of the latter. There were indeed servants in the colony before this, but this year marked the coming of negro slaves in a Dutch ship, which arrived at Jamestown, bringing several for the use of the settlers. The number of negroes increased slowly, for the demand was inconsiderable, and as late as 1661 there were only two thousand in the colony, while the indented white servants numbered eight thousand.[9]

The charter of 1609 had been followed by one still more liberal in 1612. On November 13, 1618, the Virginia Company is-

[7] Read Bruce, "Economic History of Virginia," vol. i. pp. 215 *et seq.*
[8] Read Bruce. "Economic History of Virginia," vol. i. ch. vi.
[9] Doyle, "English Colonies in America," vol. i. p. 385.

sued to the colonists a " Great Charter or Commissions of Privileges, Orders and Laws," which limited the power of the governor and established a legislature representing the " cities," " plantations," and " hundreds." The first legislature, or " House of Burgesses," as it was called in Virginia, that ever assembled in America met at Jamestown in July, 1619. It consisted of the governor, the councilors and twenty-two burgesses popularly elected from eleven plantations or hundreds. Such was the beginning of the present American system of an executive and a bicameral legislature, though in Virginia the council and the burgesses, together with the governor, continued to sit as one body for a number of years. A little more than a year later the principle of democracy gained more recruits in the New England Pilgrims. In 1621 the Virginia colony was given a sort of written pledge guaranteeing these privileges. It even provided that no order of the London Company should bind the settlers unless ratified by their general assembly of the Company. Thus was Virginia made the nursery of freemen in the very beginning of colonization.[10]

Another event of importance in the year 1619 was the coming to Virginia of ninety women, " young, handsome and well recommended," to be wooed and won by the bachelor planters; for, according to the quaint phrase of the time, " a plantation can never flourish till families be planted and the respects of wives and children fix the people in the soyle." [11] The first shipload of maidens did not prove a drug on the market; the cost of their transportation was quickly defrayed by the anxious bachelors of Jamestown, and after the necessary consent was gained, marriages promptly followed. The supply was not equal to the demand, and soon other shiploads arrived in the colony, and were easily disposed of to the eager suitors who gathered about the wharf on such occasions. With wives, mothers and children in the colony the rude huts of the settlers became happy homes, and soon no one any longer dreamed of returning to England. Three years later the first great Indian massacre occurred, which was a great blow to the progress of the colony. Powhatan, the Indian potentate of this region, who had been friendly to the English, had recently died. His brother and successor, Opechancanough, had never

---

[10] Bancroft, "History of the United States," vol. i. p. 118; Fiske, "Old Virginia and Her Neighbors," vol. i. pp. 243-245.

[11] Eggleston, "Beginners of a Nation," p. 57.

shared Powhatan's friendship for the settlers, and now led an attack in which three hundred and forty-seven of them perished; but the whites soon returned the blow with even more deadly effect. There were now only about twelve hundred persons in the colony out of more than six thousand that had landed in Virginia since 1607. Four-fifths of the early comers had perished; but if we may believe the writers of the time the high mortality was largely good riddance of bad rubbish.

The massacre was one of the reasons given by the crown for annulling the charter of the Virginia Company in 1624, and the reduction of the colony to the position of a royal province. A stronger reason, probably, was that the Puritan element, which was so troublesome in Parliament, had gained the ascendency in the Company. When threatened with the loss of their liberties and the reëstablishment of the old tyranny the previous year, the colonists petitioned the king, saying: " Rather than be reduced to live under such a government, we desire his majesty that commissioners may be sent over to hang us." However, the colonists were hardly any the worse off for the change. If James had any designs on Virgina he was unable to carry them out, for he died shortly afterward. Charles soon had enough at home to keep him busy, and government in Virginia went on very much as it had done before. One result of the change from a corporate to a royal province was that the public officers were now dependent on the crown, and the colonists were thus deprived of any control over their conduct and also over the public expenditures. This soon became a grievance, and remained a cause of complaint until the Revolution.

Among the Virginia executives Sir George Yeardley, who was governor when the first assembly met, deserves at least to be mentioned by name. He was a judicious executive and the colony prospered under his rule. He was followed by a number of governors of varying temper and ability until Sir William Berkeley, a rough old cavalier, was sent over in 1642. With the exception of a few years during the Commonwealth he held office until 1677, during all of which time he ruled the colony with a strong and masterful hand. Soon after his arrival occurred a second great Indian uprising (1644), which he put down with vigor, among the Indians slain being the aged chief, Opechancanough, who had led the first attack against the settlers in 1622. The Puritans were becoming stronger and stronger in England, and in 1649 they compassed the death of King Charles I. His son was invited to Virginia by Berkeley, who, with most of the Virginians, sympathized with the Cavaliers, but he never came. Commissioners from Parliament, however, arrived in 1652 and reorganized the colonial government with the Puritan element in charge. But the change of masters from king to Parliament was probably to the advantage of the colonists, since they were allowed greater freedom in the management of their own affairs and an era of prosperity soon set in.

The period of the Commonwealth in England was also a period of Commonwealth in Virginia. In addition to their burgesses the colonists now elected their governor and council. Another important effect of the Puritan ascendency in England was the exodus of Cavaliers by the thousand to Virginia. In 1649 the population of the colony was estimated at 15,000 English and 300 negro slaves.[12] By 1670 the population had risen to 40,000. The Cavaliers who came over at this time were of a better class than the " gentlemen " who came in the earlier years of the colony. Some of the most famous names in the history of Virginia and of the United States, such as Washington, Madison, Monroe, Marshall and others, then first became known in America.

The restoration of the Stuarts in 1660 brought only ill to the colonists, although they might reasonably have expected fair treatment at the hands of Charles II. The offices were given to profligate favorites of the king; dissenters, who had flocked to Virginia as a place of refuge, were repressed by harsh measures, and the Navigation Act, which is described elsewhere, was enforced with rigor. These and other acts of repression finally led to a rebellion (1663), but this was soon put down and the leaders were hanged. In 1673, with a reckless disregard of vested rights, Charles granted the whole of Virginia to two of his favorites, Lords Arlington and Culpeper. But the colonists resisted and the patentees surrendered their rights, except the quit-rents and escheats, taking in lieu thereof a duty of three half-pence per pound on tobacco.

With the restoration of the Stuarts came also the restoration of Berkeley. Though of a narrow mind and hot temper, his

[12] Doyle, " English Colonies in America," vol. i. p. 207; Fiske, " Old Virginia and Her Neighbors," vol. ii. ch. xi.

personal qualities had been such as to make him popular with a large party in Virginia and tolerable to all. But the sufferings of his party during the Commonwealth seem to have embittered him, and in his later years he was little better than a rapacious tyrant. The assembly which recalled him sought to impose a condition that he should call the legislature together every two years. Soon after his return he secured the election of an assembly of decidedly royalist tendencies, and refused to order another election for fifteen years. The fires of discontent smoldered under these and other grievances, among them the disfranchisement of all except landholders and householders, and certain oppressive measures of taxation, but they finally broke out over the Indian question.

The Virginians had been on friendly terms with the Indians for many years, and the assembly had passed several laws to protect the red men, but these relations were disturbed in 1675. Acts of reprisal and retaliation followed one another, until the situation became unbearable. Still the governor remained inactive. A young lawyer of wealth and popularity, by the name of Nathaniel Bacon, then raised a company and asked the governor for a commission to chastise the Indians, but this Berkeley refused, because, as some thought, this would disturb the fur trade, in which he had a pecuniary interest. Bacon then marched out in defiance of the governor, and the governor promptly marched after him. Finding that the temper of the colonists was against him, Berkeley returned to Jamestown, dissolved the old assembly, and ordered a new election (1676). The new assembly passed a number of reform measures, voted to carry on the war with the Indians, nominated Bacon to command the expedition, and passed an act of indemnity. The governor was now brought to bay by Bacon with an armed force; but a reconciliation was patched up, the commission granted, and Bacon marched off to fight the Indians. Berkeley then proclaimed Bacon a rebel and a traitor, and called out the militia, but they were in no mood to support him, whereupon Bacon summoned a convention to meet at Williamsburg. Most of the planters in that neighborhood answered the summons and loyally supported Bacon, except in his project for independence of the crown. The leader now chastised the Indians, returned and disbanded most of his troops before learning that the governor was still after him. Bacon then laid siege to Jamestown, captured and burned it, but died of malarial fever soon after. With the death of Bacon the backbone of the insurrection was broken. Twenty-three of his followers were executed in cold blood by the vindictive old governor. On hearing of his tyrannical course Charles exclaimed, " That old fool has hanged more men in that naked country than I have done for the murder of my father." He was immediately recalled, and died not long afterwards (1677).

Soon after these events, Culpepper, one of the men to whom Charles had granted the whole province, came out as governor (1679). He was a tyrant even more rapacious than Berkeley, and brought on a rebellion among the tobacco planters because of the ruin wrought on their industry by his attempt to regulate prices and establish ports of shipment. The rebellion was suppressed and a number of the leaders were hanged. Some of Culpepper's successors were better men, but none of them could be described as really excellent until the coming of Alexander Spottswood, who was governor from 1710 to 1722. He was one of the best of a long line of colonial governors and his name is revered in Virginia even to this day. By this time it had become customary for the nominal governor to reside in England, where he could spend his salary in a way more to his liking and send out lieutenants to perform his duties.

The limits of this work do not allow an extended discussion of the policy of imperial control, but a word must be added in regard to the commercial policy of the mother country in its dealings with the colonists.[13]   This was one of restriction, but was not adopted through any premeditated tyranny or extortion; it was a part of the accepted political economy of the day. A statute of Richard II. had restricted exportation to " ships of the king's ligeance." Under Henry VII. and Elizabeth other restrictions were added, and these were imposed upon the colonists. The cultivation of tobacco in England was forbidden for the benefit of the Virginia Company, but a limit was soon put upon the amount they might import. The colonists then sought a market in Holland, only to be forbidden to sell anywhere except in England. In 1621 the limitation on the amount imported was removed. The colonists had evaded the Navigation Acts, but as the contest between the English and the Dutch for supremacy in the carrying trade became sharper more stringent measures were adopted.

13 On the subject of Imperial Control, see Greene, " Provincial America," ch. iii.

SOUTHERN COLONIES 67

In 1651, during the Commonwealth, a Navigation Act was passed, which is frequently referred to as the beginning of the coercive trade measures which finally led to the Revolution, but very similar acts, only less stringent, had been passed in 1645–1646. By the Act of 1651 the carrying trade to and from the colonies was restricted to English ships. It had been provided at the start that the colonists were to remain Englishmen. Likewise their vessels were " English built," within the meaning of this act, but they were required to land their goods in English ports. The law was reënacted by the Cavaliers after the Restoration (1660), and three years later it was so amended as practically to force the colonists to buy all their wares in England. In 1673 a blow was dealt at inter-colonial trade by levying heavy duties on all articles which could be supplied in England. And so the work went on until stopped forever by the Revolution. Justice to the mother country compels admission that the acts were not as a rule rigidly enforced against the colonists. Indeed, they were not enforced at all during the period of the Commonwealth.[14]

Taken all in all, Virginia cannot be said to have had smooth sailing during the latter part of the seventeenth century. In consequence immigration fell off, but the population still numbered nearly one hundred thousand at the close of the century, and nearly all were English. In 1700 the colony received an infusion of Huguenot blood, and in 1730 the Scotch-Irish opened up the Shenandoah Valley. These peoples brought with them new ideas of religion and new modes of life, but Virginia society always remained predominantly English.

Religion and education were not wholly neglected in Virginia. Indeed, the former, for a time, received very minute attention. Services were held under a tent soon after the colonists landed, and conformity to the Church of England was required. Dale's famous (or infamous) martial code required attendance at the daily services and imposed the penalty of death for failure to attend on Sunday, but this severity was soon relaxed.[15] Non-conformists were persecuted, but the Scotch Presbyterians finally secured toleration.

[14] Bancroft, " History of the United States," vol. i. 150.
[15] Doyle, " English Colonies in America," vol. i. 139.

II

MARYLAND

The founding of Maryland marked a new departure in the form of colonial government, for the plantation and government of the colony were both entrusted to an individual called a lord proprietor. In previous cases the founding had been done by corporations. The model for the proprietary colony was found in the great Palatinate of Durham.[16] In mediæval times kings often found it convenient, especially on the continent, to grant powers of government that were almost regal in extent to some feudal lord in a border province, such territories being called palatinates. The object of this was to erect a sort of buffer state to serve as a protection to the kingdom from invasion. The county of Durham, on the Scotch border, had been erected into such a state by William the Conqueror, and still retained much of its old-time independence at this time.[17] This was now taken as a model for the proprietary province and was closely followed in the charter of Maryland.

George Calvert, whom King James had raised to an Irish peerage with the title of Lord Baltimore, was a member of the London Company and was very much interested in colonization, his first two attempts having failed, one in Newfoundland because of the inhospitable climate and the opposition of the French, the other in Virginia because of religious intolerance. Calvert, having become a Catholic, now asked for a slice of that same Virginia territory from which he had been driven out on account of his religious views. He was granted the land between the Potomac River and the fortieth parallel of latitude, which was the southern boundary of New England, and asked that the province be named Maryland in honor of his queen, Henrietta Maria. Together with the grant he also acquired a boundary dispute which lasted many years, for the western limits of the colony were very imperfectly described. Calvert had in view a two-fold object: To found a great state, of which he should be the ruler and from which he could secure a revenue, and to provide a refuge for his

[16] Fiske, "Old Virginia and Her Neighbors," vol. i. ch. viii.
[17] See Lapsley, "The Palatinate of Durham," in "Harvard Historical Studies," No. viii.

persecuted fellow Roman Catholics. Upon the death of the elder Calvert, which occurred before the grant had passed the Great Seal, his plans were immediately taken up by his son Cecilius, to whom the patent was now issued. He was an astute, able, and tactful individual, and like his father was a Roman Catholic in religion. Never visiting Maryland, he was, says Channing, the most successful absentee landlord of his day.[18]

The terms of the charter showed clearly that an attempt was being made to transplant feudalism, including the manorial system, to America. It defined the relations of the proprietor to the king and to his subjects. He was to send the king two Indian arrows each year and one-fifth of all the gold and silver mined in the province; but with this exception he was to be practically a king himself with independent powers. He was given the right to declare war, make peace, appoint all officers, from the lowest to the highest, proclaim martial law, confer titles, grant pardons, etc. But this despotism was mixed with a little democracy, which soon leavened the whole lump for the proprietor, for he was to summon the freemen to assist him in making laws, and was forbidden to tax them without their consent. Lord Baltimore attempted to initiate legislation himself, leaving to the colonists only the right of assent, but they resisted at the outset and soon won.

Baltimore was a tolerant man, but it is not wholly due to this fact that Maryland became the first colony where religious toleration was practiced. The Catholic minority, represented by the proprietors, were in control, but still a minority, and a minority can always be trusted to be tolerant when they are at the mercy of a majority. Moreover, the charter itself provided that all churches should be consecrated according to the laws of the Church of England, although this probably was intended merely to guard against making Catholicism an established religion. Had Calvert attempted to exclude Protestants, he would only have raised a storm of opposition both in Maryland and in England, which would have been fatal to his whole project. It was all these reasons combined which for a time made Maryland, in practice, a colony of religious freedom.

In March, 1634, Leonard Calvert, brother to the proprietor, arrived in Maryland, bringing about two hundred settlers on two

[18] "History of the United States," vol. i. p. 250; see also Bernard Steiner, "Beginnings of Maryland," in "Johns Hopkins University Studies," vol. xxi. p. 368.

small vessels, the *Ark* and the *Dove*. The material for the new colony consisted of some twenty gentlemen; the rest were laboring men and artisans. Most of the gentlemen were Roman Catholics, while a majority of the laborers were probably Protestants.[19] They gained the friendship of the Indians at the outset by purchasing their land and by treating them kindly, a relation which was not seriously disturbed for many years. Soon after his arrival, Governor Calvert paid a visit to the "Emperor of Pascatacacy," as the Indian chief who exercised sovereignty over the adjacent forests was called, and received a hospitable welcome from this dusky potentate. He not only gave the newcomers permission to settle on his lands, but placed at their disposal one-half the huts of the village and did all in his power to make them comfortable and happy. The first settlement was made on an island at the mouth of the Potomac, where they proceeded to lay out a town, which they called St. Mary's, in allusion to the queen, and the colonists being thrifty and aided by very favorable auspices, prospered, at least for a time.

The remarkable friendliness of the Indians was exemplified in many ways. The missionaries who had accompanied the colonists from England began at once on their labors and found the natives favorable subjects for conversion. Many readily accepted Christianity, and the chief himself asked to be baptized and married according to the Christian rites, and brought his little daughter to be educated in the settlement.

With the Indians of the region thus well disposed, it would seem that the peace of the colony was thereby assured; but the inevitable affliction of the colonists from hostility from without was soon to overtake them.

This disturbing element was found in a trading post of Virginians nearby, who refused to be placated. These good churchmen were not pleased with the prospect of having "Papists" for neighbors. Besides, the country now called Maryland had been

[19] Browne, "History of Maryland," p. 23. "The statement that the policy of toleration was unavoidable," says Dr. George Park Fisher, "is only a fraction of the truth. It fails to do full justice to the spirit of the founders of Maryland. There is no reason to think that Cecilius Calvert, any more than his father, would have yielded to any demand, had it been made, to deprive their fellow disciples of the Roman Church of religious liberty; nor can it be shown that under any circumstances they would have felt disposed to withhold an equal toleration from Protestants."—"*The Colonial Era*," p. 65. See also C. C. Hall, "The Lords Baltimore and the Maryland Palatinate," Lecture iii.

included in the grant made to them by the charter of 1609. By the annulment of their charter in 1624 the province had indeed reverted to the Crown, but the Virginians still felt that this territory was rightfully theirs. More than a year before the grant was made to Calvert, one of their number, William Claiborne, originally a surveyor of Jamestown, later treasurer of the colony, had settled on Kent Island, in the upper Chesapeake, within the bounds of Maryland. Baltimore's attempt to subject him to his government was resisted and brought on a chronic state of trouble which lasted for more than ten years. Sometimes it broke out into open war, in the course of which men on both sides were killed or wounded and others were hanged as pirates. In 1645 Claiborne succeeded in driving out Calvert and attempted to take the government of Maryland in charge, but the latter found refuge in Virginia — a fact which shows that neither the government of Virginia nor the people as a whole was very hostile to him — and soon after recovered his own, permanently subjecting Kent Island to his control. Claiborne was attainted by the Maryland assembly and his property declared forfeited. The controversy ultimately was carried to the English courts, and a decision followed in due course establishing Baltimore's title to Kent Island, at least to the satisfaction of the lawyers.[20]

The evolution of the Maryland legislature had a curious history. At first it was a primary assembly in which every freeman might be represented by proxy. As a result of this practice, the governor and his secretary, both of whom were appointees of the proprietor, sometimes held enough proxies from absent freemen to outvote all those present. On one occasion a freeman held seventy-odd proxies, which gave him control of the assembly. Later representation became the rule, but freemen might, and actually did, claim the right to sit in person. In 1647 the purely representative system was adopted, and three years later the legislature was made bicameral.[21]

The Protestant party grew apace in Maryland as the religious troubles became more acute in England. The toleration practiced by the proprietor from the first was now enacted by statute. This famous " Toleration Act," passed in 1649, provided that no one professing Christianity should " in any ways be molested or dis-

[20] Channing, "History of the United States," vol. i. p. 258.
[21] See Mereness, "Maryland as a Proprietary Province," p. 196.

countenanced for or in respect of his or her religion nor in the free exercise thereof." But one was required to be a Christian of some sort, or keep a bridle on his tongue, for there were severe laws against blasphemers and profaners and gossipers, and, indeed, Jews, Unitarians and others were excepted from its benefits. This seems to have been a sort of a compromise between the Catholics and Protestants, but during the period of the Commonwealth the dissensions between them became so violent that civil war broke out. The Puritans rejected the Toleration Act and passed one tolerating everybody, says Fiske, "except Catholics, Episcopalians, and anybody else who disagreed with them." In a pitched battle they defeated the Catholics and imprisoned the governor, Stone, Leonard Calvert's successor, who, though a Protestant, sided with the proprietor. Cromwell now appears to have thought that the Parliamentary Commissioners had gone too far, and the province was restored to Lord Baltimore (1657), who thereupon promised never to repeal the law granting to the people freedom of worship.

This marked the beginning of another era of prosperity for the colony. In 1661 Charles Calvert, son of the proprietor, came out as governor and served ably for fourteen years, or until the death of his father (1675), when he himself became the proprietor. Maryland became widely known for her religious freedom and this attracted to her borders many Quakers, Dutch, Germans, and Huguenots, who were seeking homes from religious persecution. Still the colonists were not without cause for complaint. Among their grievances were the imposition of a property qualification for suffrage, the boundary dispute with William Penn, and the enforcement of the Navigation Act. The last in particular was galling to the Marylanders, as they originally enjoyed freedom of trade.

The reign of James II. was marked by the revocation of many charters and Lord Baltimore's came near suffering a like fate, but was saved by the expulsion of James himself from England (1688). The new sovereigns, William and Mary, seemed not to have been favorably impressed with Lord Baltimore and revoked his charter in 1691, reducing Maryland to the position of a royal province. Soon after this the Church of England was established by law and the persecution of dissenters, especially Catholics, was begun. In consequence the prosperity of the colony suffered a de-

LANDING OF THE PILGRIM FATHERS AT PLYMOUTH
Painting by A. Gisbert

—page 84

cline until 1715, when it was restored to the fourth Lord Baltimore, who had become a Protestant. It remained in the hands of the family from that time until the Revolution.[22]

III

THE CAROLINAS

The attempts of Raleigh and of the French Huguenots to settle Carolina have already been described. Not many years elapsed after the planting of Virginia before the adventurous hunters of that colony were familiar with the country to the south of them as far as the Chowan River. In 1653 a company of Virginia dissenters, led by Roger Green, went south in search of religious freedom and settled on the Chowan and Roanoke Rivers. This settlement, called Albemarle, was the first permanent colony within the limits of the present State of North Carolina. Shortly afterwards other victims of religious persecution from New England settled on the Cape Fear River, but they were not so careful to preserve their history as those whom they left behind, and we know very little about them. By some act they incurred the hostility of the Indians and in a few years the survivors abandoned the colony or were absorbed by a company of settlers from the Barbadoes (1665) led by Sir John Yeamans.

By means of two charters, (1663, 1665) Charles II. conveyed to a coterie of his favorites the vast domain lying between Virginia and Florida, that is, between thirty-six degrees thirty minutes and the twenty-ninth degree north latitude, westward to the " South Sea," or Pacific Ocean. This grant insured a boundary dispute with the Spanish, for they had settled north of the latter line one hundred years before. Among the proprietors were Sir John Berkeley, the Duke of Albemarle and Lord Ashley-Cooper, afterwards known as the Earl of Shaftesbury, the Earl of Clarendon, and Sir George Carteret.[23] At their request John Locke, the English philosopher, drew up what was perhaps the most elaborate and complicated scheme of government ever devised for

[22] Read Brantly, " The English in Maryland," in Winsor, " Nar. and Crit. Hist." vol. iii. ch. xiii.; also Eggleston, " Beginners of a Nation," pp. 220-257.

[23] McCrady, " History of South Carolina under Proprietary Government, pp. 61-65.

any colony. It was called the "Fundamental Constitution," or "Grand Model." The colonists were to be divided into four estates known as proprietaries, land-graves, caciques and leet-men or commons. Corresponding to these the province was to be divided into seigniories, baronies, precincts and colonies. The leet-men were to be practically serfs bound to the soil. The object was to establish " the interests of the lords proprietors " and a government " most agreeable to monarchy — and that we may avoid erecting a numerous democracy." But the forest is inevitably the home of liberty, and this mental creation of the philosopher fell of its own weight. The several attempts made to put it in force only irritated the colonists and it was finally abandoned.[24]

One William Drummond, a Scotch Presbyterian clergyman, became the first governor of Albemarle, as the colony was called, and summoned an assembly in 1667, which enacted several laws for the purpose of attracting settlers, among them one containing an exemption from taxation for a year and release for five years from liability for debts contracted elsewhere. In derision the Virginians named the colony " Rogue's Harbor," from the character of the newcomers who were thus attracted. The planting of a more promising colony in what is now South Carolina, by which the Cape Fear settlement was soon absorbed, caused the proprietors to neglect Albemarle. Owing to incapable and dishonest governors of the Seth Sothel type, the prosperity, contentment and good order of the colony were greatly retarded during the rest of the century; population diminished instead of increased, and many of those remaining moved back into the forests to secure their freedom.

The two settlements thus established gradually came to be known as North and South Carolina, but their governments were united for a time in 1695, when John Archdale, a good Quaker and one of the proprietors, came out as governor of both colonies. During the next fifteen years North Carolina received many new settlers, who were not rogues, but sturdy Germans and honest Huguenots. This expansion necessitated encroachment upon the lands of the red man and brought with it a train of Indian troubles. In 1711 the Tuscaroras and other Indians fell upon the settlers on the Roanoke and at New Berne and slaughtered over two

[24] Fiske, "Old Virginia and Her Neighbors," vol. ii, pp. 271–273; McCrady, "History of South Carolina Under Proprietary Government," ch. iv.

hundred of them in cold blood.[25]   But a stinging blow was inflicted on them by a body of militia under John Barnwell and James More near the Neuse, where four hundred braves were killed.   At last the Tuscaroras returned to New York, whence their fathers had emigrated, and joined the Iroquois, or Five Nations, thus making them the Six Nations.

One of the governors of North Carolina, Charles Eden, deserves mention because of his excellent rule (1714-1722), but after his death in 1729, the proprietors meantime having sold out to the Crown, the colonists were divided into North and South Carolina, and each thenceforth became a royal province.   After that the governors were of varying ability and morality.   Some were good, but many were incompetent and rapacious.   Still the colony waxed stronger with every passing year.   Germans and Scotch-Irish came down from Pennsylvania and were followed by a few " poor whites " from Virginia.[26]   They settled in the foothills of the Blue Ridge Mountains and gradually pushed westward until the summit was passed.   There was at least one marked difference between the eastern and western settlements.   The former were slaveholding, while the latter had very few slaves, a difference partly due to physical conditions.   Neither was noted for commercial activity, though the eastern settlements carried on a considerable trade with the New England smugglers.   The principal industries of the colony were rice and tobacco growing; the manufacture of naval stores, particularly tar, pitch, and turpentine from the pine forests, and the raising of cattle and swine.

The first permanent colony in South Carolina was planted on the bank of the Ashley River in 1670 by William Sayle, who brought over three shiploads of emigrants from the Barbadoes, a hundred years after Ribaut's disastrous attempt to plant a French settlement in these parts.   The next year Sir John Yeamans joined the colony with two hundred slaves, and the same year witnessed the coming of two shiploads of Dutch emigrants from New York. It was the policy of the proprietors to attract settlers from other colonies, and they also wished to have them grouped about some urban center.   A place more suitable for this than the point first settled was found near by, and the seat of government, together

[25] Rivers, " The Carolinas," in Winsor, " Nar. and Crit. Hist." vol. iv. p. 298.
[26] See McCrady, " South Carolina under Royal Government," vol. ii. pp. 623-625.

with the name, Charleston, was transferred hither in 1680. Within two years the town was regularly laid off with wide and uniform streets. Such was the beginning of the Charleston of the present day.[27]

The one redeeming feature of the "Fundamental Constitution," was its promise of religious freedom. Even before the revocation of the Edict of Nantes in 1685 French Huguenots had begun to arrive in South Carolina. After the revocation they came in large numbers and had no little influence for good upon the character of the colony, for they were an industrious, intelligent, and virtuous people. Denied political rights for a time, and looked upon with suspicion by the English settlers in Carolina, they soon came to be admired and were accorded full political rights. A small company of Presbyterians from Scotland planted themselves at the ill-starred Port Royal, but the settlement was soon wiped out of existence by Spaniards from St. Augustine (1686).

The Spanish were jealous of these encroaching settlements and also irritated because pirates, whom they believed to be sheltered in Charleston, preyed upon their commerce. The English settlers, on the other hand, were much aggrieved when the proprietors forbade them to take revenge upon the colony of a nation with which England was at peace. In 1715 some Irish settled in the region of Port Royal, which had been devastated by the Spaniards thirty years previous. All the settlements at this time were still on the seaboard; indeed, the back country was held by the Indians until 1755. After that date many emigrants from the other colonies as far north as Pennsylvania moved into this region. By 1760 South Carolina contained about one hundred and fifty thousand souls, three-fourths of whom were slaves.

That South Carolina was so distinctly a slave State was due to two causes: First, her early settlers were from the Barbadoes and were thoroughly imbued with belief in the slave system; and, second, it was due to the climate and the physical features of the country, which largely determined the character of its industries. Rice and indigo were the chief products. Both, especially the former, grew best in marshy ground, and the white man could not endure so well as the negro the heat and the malarial atmosphere of the swamps which were adapted to rice culture. But for him their reclamation would probably have been delayed many years.

[27] Bancroft, "History of the United States," vol. ii. ch. xiii.

As the negro showed very little disposition to labor without a master, there seemed to be no alternative for slavery, if a rice growing colony was to be built up in South Carolina.

Unfortunately the settlers from the Barbadoes were only too familiar with the Spanish custom of enslaving the Indians, and they introduced it in their new home. So late as the beginning of the eighteenth century Indians made up one-fourth of the slave population,[28] a condition which could have had only an irritating effect on the relations subsisting between the settlers and the natives. But the wily Spaniard knew how to make the simple red man his tool, and, with a shameless disregard of the Treaty of Utrecht, proceeded to do so for the purpose of destroying the English settlements. The war began in 1715, when the Yamassees fell upon the scattered farmers with savage fury and slew nearly one hundred in a day.[29] The contest lasted ten months, but the Indians were finally defeated and driven into Florida. Charles Craven, who was governor at the time, played a conspicuous part in the war and has had a thread of romance woven about his name by the novelist, William Gilmore Simms.

Like her nearest neighbor on the north, South Carolina had a varied experience with her governors. Among those of merit were Archdale, already mentioned, and Joseph Blake, a nephew of Admiral Blake, who swept the Dutch from the sea in the war between England and Holland. The advent of Sir Nathaniel Johnson in 1703 marked the beginning of a chronic state of turbulence lasting for some time.[30] But the colonists showed themselves in every way capable of coping with their would-be oppressors. The very foundations of the colony were based on liberty, and it was maintained by a popular assembly which met a short time after the first settlers arrived. Here, as in North Carolina, the " Grand Model " was suspended at first as unsuited to an infant colony. In 1687 an effort was made by the proprietors to put it in operation, but the people resisted and based their resistance on that clause of the charter which declared that the proprietors should make laws only " by and with the advice, assent and approbation of the freemen." The contest lasted several years, but the popular cause won and the " Grand Model " was overthrown.

[28] Doyle, "English Colonies in America," vol. i. p. 359.
[29] Fiske, "Old Virginia and Her Neighbors," vol. ii. p. 306.
[30] See W. Roy Smith, "South Carolina as a Royal Province," p. 9.

The early years of the colony were marked by a conflict over the religious question. Dissenters, except Catholics, had been tolerated in the absence of legislation against them. About this time Lord Granville, a High Churchman, gained the ascendency among the proprietors and sought to enforce conformity among the colonists. The dissenters had shown their liberality by voting money to support the Church of England, but this was not enough. By packing the council and by frauds in the election of the representatives, Governor Johnson secured the passage of an Act in 1704 excluding dissenters from the assembly. Several members had been absent when the Act was passed, but they took their seats at the autumn session of 1706 and voted to repeal the obnoxious measure. The governor and council opposed it, whereupon the colonists sent an agent to appeal to the proprietors. Meeting with no success, they turned to the House of Lords, who recommended the veto of the measure by the queen. The Board of Trade even favored the forfeiture of the charter, but only the Act was declared void.[31] However, the Church of England was established by law, although the dissenters appear to have been in the majority — they claimed to make up two-thirds of the population and continued to enjoy this advantage until the Revolution.

Hardly had another decade passed before the proprietors had forgotten the lesson of this contest and were again exasperating the settlers. The expense of the war with the Yamassees bore heavily upon the colonists and they, with full justice, called upon the proprietors to share the burden. But this the proprietors refused to do, although they derived a large income from the quit-rents; nor would they allow the assembly to levy import duties or sell the public lands for this purpose. Another cause of irritation was the fact that there was only one polling place in the colony, namely, at Charleston. Not only was this a source of great inconvenience to the settlers of the outlying districts, but it also gave the official party an undue weight of influence. At length a law was passed substituting local representation for the existing method of election. The law was put in force at once and a new assembly was elected under it, but the proprietors vetoed the law as soon as it reached them and ordered the governor to dissolve the assembly. Remonstrance produced no effect. In 1719 a new assembly was called, but it was no more ready to submit than its predecessor.

[31] Doyle, " English Colonies in America," vol. i. p. 369.

It drew up a list of grievances and declared that the rights of the people had been violated, especially in the packing of the council, which made it an illegal body. There being no redress through constitutional forms, it assumed constituent powers, deposed the governor, chose another, and asked the Crown to make the colony a royal province (1719). The request was granted, the political rights of the proprietors were annulled, and their territorial rights were brought up under an act of Parliament.

From this time on the growth of the colony was rapid and continuous, although it was not wholly free from political unrest. Indeed, the colonists showed no more fear of the royal governors than they had of the proprietors, and steadily encroached upon their powers. In 1748 Governor Glenn reported that the people, by means of the assembly, " had the whole of the administration in their hands, and the governor, and thereby the Crown, is stripped of its power." But there was one thing for which the assembly cannot be commended — its passion for cheap money. The repeated issues of paper money had here the same blighting effect as in New England.

The student of the history of liberty will find no more interesting pages than the story of its struggles in the Carolinas. The avowed object of the proprietors was to found a monarchial system, which even then was beginning to break down in England. If the Anglo-Saxon at home was steadily carrying out his determination to control his own political fortunes, what would he do when given the forest and three thousand miles of water as allies? Yet here was exhibited one of those curious contradictions in which history abounds. New England was founded by men seeking religious freedom for themselves, yet they manifested a spirit of intolerance such as was found nowhere else in America. South Carolina was building up a splendid aristocracy on a basis of slavery, yet nowhere was the spirit of liberty stronger. If this spirit often manifested itself in turbulence, especially in North Carolina, this was due to oppression and not to any noteworthy lack of popular morality or to a spirit of unrest such as may be seen in South America to-day. Most of the bad governors were endured as one of the ills of life; those who could not be endured were imprisoned or banished. Long before the final break with England the Carolinas were well trained in the art of revolution.[32]

[32] The most comprehensive history of South Carolina during the colonial

IV

GEORGIA

The last of the southern, and of the thirteen colonies, to be founded was Georgia. It also was a proprietary colony, and its chief proprietor was General James Oglethorpe, who had served in the European wars under the great Marlborough and Prince Eugene. At home, as a member of Parliament, he became a social reformer and was particularly interested in the debtor class, whose condition at that time was particularly unfortunate in view of the severe laws against insolvents. Oglethorpe made an examination of the debtors' prisons and found their condition so bad that he determined to offer the inmates a home in the forests of America, where they might retrieve their fortunes. He entertained no thought of personal gain, no ambition of a sordid character; his entire project was open, disinterested, charitable, loyal, and patriotic.[33]

The territory south of the Savannah River was included in the Carolina grant, but it had never been occupied by settlement, and with the revocation of the charter it reverted to the Crown. Oglethorpe now formed a company and prayed the Crown for a grant of this territory for the purpose mentioned above, as also to form a sort of military barrier between Carolina and the Spaniards in Florida. The grant, which was named Georgia in honor of the king, included the country between the Savannah and Altamaha Rivers, and extended westward to the " South Sea." The government of the colony was committed to a company of twenty-one trustees, by whom all officers were to be appointed for the first four years, and after that by the Crown. Slavery and traffic in rum were prohibited, no one could own more than five hundred acres of land, and this must descend in the male line. Foreigners were to have equal rights with Englishmen, and all religions except the Roman Catholic were to be tolerated.[34]

The first settlers, consisting of thirty-five families, sailed up

period is McCrady, "South Carolina under Proprietary Government," in two volumes; see also W. R. Smith, "History of South Carolina as a Royal Colony."
[33] Jones, "History of Georgia," vol. i. p. 86.
[34] Jones, "The English Colonization of Georgia," in Winsor, "Nar. and Crit. Hist.," vol. v. ch. vi.; also Fiske, "Old Virginia and Her Neighbors," vol. ii. pp. 334-335.

the Savannah River in February, 1733, under the personal leadership of Oglethorpe, and founded the city of Savannah, one hundred and twenty-six years after the settlement of Jamestown. It was soon discovered that the debtors were not likely to prosper much more in their new home than they had done in England, but a more thrifty class came out the following year — a ship load of Protestant refugees from Salzburg, and these were followed shortly thereafter by Moravians and Highlanders. Among the early immigrants were three men whose names are forever linked with the social and religious history of the time — Charles and John Wesley and George Whitefield — who came as missionaries to the Indians. The first mentioned served as secretary to Oglethorpe, the two latter were the most powerful preachers of the time. The magnificent live oak under which John Wesley sometimes preached is still pointed out to the traveler. Whitefield founded an orphan school and established a slave farm across the river in South Carolina to support it.

Oglethorpe served the colony well for twelve years as governor. He established friendly relations with the Cherokees, with whom a thriving fur trade was carried on in rivalry with the Spanish and French settlers, Augusta (1734) being the center of this traffic. When the War of the Spanish Succession broke out Oglethorpe led an army of invasion against St. Augustine, but failed to capture that well-fortified town.[35] A few years later he exhibited no little skill in repulsing a Spanish invasion (1742). In 1748 General Oglethorpe left Georgia never to return. Soon after his arrival in England he was promoted to the position of a full general in the British army, at the same time retaining his seat in Parliament. He died in 1785 in his ninetieth year, the only one of the colonial founders who lived to see the colonies independent.

Up to the departure of Oglethorpe the progress of the colony was steady, if somewhat slow, but after that the settlers found causes of complaint. Chief of these was the prohibition of slavery. Slavery had been prohibited, not so much on moral as on economic grounds, it being feared that it would interfere with free white labor. The settlers looked across the river at their more prosperous neighbors where slavery flourished, and straightway desired it for themselves. After years of importunity they finally

[35] Jones, "History of Georgia," vol. i. ch. xxi.

secured it in 1749, when by act of Parliament Georgia became a slave colony. The colonists also wanted rum, at least they wanted to trade with the West Indies, and they declared that this trade was driven away by the prohibition on the rum traffic. This restriction was removed, as also that upon the size of an estate which an individual might own. The colonists again looked across at their neighbors and saw that they enjoyed many liberties which the Georgians were denied, and were consequently not content until they themselves were given a government similar to that of South Carolina. This came in 1752, when the charter was surrendered and Georgia became a royal province with a legislative assembly elected by the freemen of the colony, Catholics excepted, and a governor appointed by the king.

After these changes the colony advanced more rapidly, but at the outbreak of the Revolution it was little better than a frontier settlement. The chief industries were the growing of rice and indigo, the manufacture of lumber, and the peltry trade with the Indians. Experiments were made with the silkworm with a view to the production of silk, but the business did not prosper and was soon abandoned. Life in the colony was of the rudest and simplest sort. Except Savannah, which was little more than a wooden village, there were no towns, and the only roads were Indian trails. The school facilities were very poor, and the few ships which carried away their rice, indigo, lumber and peltries brought to the Georgians but little contact with the stronger forces of civilization.

Chapter IV

PLANTING OF THE NORTHERN COLONIES
1620-1776

I

PLYMOUTH

THE men of the age of discovery and exploration and of the early part of the age of colonization were animated mainly by the desire of adventure and the thirst for gold. It is pleasant now to turn to the study of a people who came into the forest to seek not gold but God and the right to worship Him in their own way. If we find that they were not inclined to allow others the same privilege, we must remember they lived in an age of intolerance. To say that they sought the right to worship God in their own way does not mean that they sought religious freedom. They wished to make their own ideas dominant in England; failing in that they sought the forest where they could make them dominant.[1]

The reign of Henry VIII. is commonly given as the date of the Protestant Reformation in England, though little more was done then than to substitute the supremacy of the king for that of the Pope in matters of religion. As the years passed by the divergence between the Church of England and the Catholic Church increased; but a large party within the former, the Puritans, desired still further to eliminate Roman creeds and forms. Some of these went so far in their dissent as to withdraw from the Established Church, and became known as Independents or Separatists. The Presbyterian tendency among the latter contributed its part in securing the hostility of James I. His experience in Scotland had convinced him that Presbyterianism in the church meant growing republicanism in the state. It had already limited his royal power in Scotland; he was determined it should not do so in England. The church was a part of the state, consequently he could, with some

---

[1] "The Religious Element in the Settlement of New England," by G. E. Ellis, in Winsor, "Nar. and Crit. Hist., vol. iii. ch. vii.

show of reason, regard an attack upon the former as an attack upon the latter. Thus he felt justified in considering the dissenters inimical to his government; and so he determined, as he announced at the Hampton Court Conference, to compel them to conform or to " harry them out of the land." [2]

Some conformed, but others were harried out of the land. A number of the latter under the leadership of John Robinson, their pastor, and William Brewster, a ruling layman, found a refuge at Leyden in Holland; but they never became really contented there among an alien people. They longed for the English ways and the English laws, and, not being able to enjoy these upon their native heath or in Holland, determined to transplant them to the forests of the New World. This project was not wholly at one with the objects of the London Company, but they managed to obtain a grant and by promising obedience to the king, " if the thing commanded be not against God's Word," secured his promise not to interfere with them if they lived peaceably. To secure the necessary funds they formed a sort of stock partnership with a company of London merchants, who owned about three fourths of the shares. The communal system was to obtain for seven years, at the end of which time the corporation was to disband and the assets were to be distributed.

The Pilgrims, as by this time they had come to be called, sailed from Southampton. Thither members of the Leyden congregation had been brought by the *Speedwell,* a vessel of sixty tons bought for the purpose. The final voyage was to be made in the *Mayflower,* a larger vessel which they had hired. The smaller vessel was to accompany them; but it proved unseaworthy, and only the *Mayflower* made the voyage. It carried one hundred and one Pilgrims and entered Cape Cod harbor (Provincetown) November 11, 1620 (old style). On that day the adult males, forty-one in number, drew up a paper which posterity has named the Mayflower Compact. It was simply an agreement to form a body politic and a promise to give " all due submission and obedience " to the laws it might enact. They then elected John Carver governor and sent out an exploring party. Finally a landing was made at a place which they called Plymouth, and the work of building cabins was soon begun. The winter was not so severe as it often is, but nearly

[2] Eggleston, " Beginners of a Nation," p. 162; also Gardiner, " History of England," vol. i. pp. 153-157.

half the company perished, among them Governor Carver. William Bradford was chosen as his successor, and for many years proved an able leader of his people. The loss of the first winter was made up the following November by the arrival of fifty more from Leyden, but the colony had many difficulties to contend with and its growth was slow. Ten years after the first company landed it contained only about three hundred inhabitants.[3]

The Pilgrims were very fortunate in their relations with the Indians. Pestilence had decimated their number, and those who remained felt grateful to the English for the restitution of some of their companions who had been kidnaped. The story of Samoset's entrance into their settlement crying " Welcome, Englishmen! " has been told many times. He and another Indian named Squanto, who became the agricultural instructor of the colony, were instrumental in bringing about a treaty with their chief, Massasoit, which was faithfully observed until his death.

But if comparatively free from trouble with the Indians, the Pilgrims were not so fortunate in their relations with men of their own color. Certain " lewd fellows of the baser sort," who were settled on Massachusetts Bay in 1622 by Thomas Weston as a commercial venture, gave them no little trouble, but the settlement was abandoned the next year. In 1625 another settlement of a similar kind was made in the same neighborhood by Captain Wollaston. The settlers, mostly indented servants, under the leadership of Thomas Morton, soon drove out Wollaston's agent and renamed the place Merrymount. The famous Maypole at Merrymount and its sequel make one of the most serio-comic episodes in New England history. When they tossed off ten pounds' worth of strong liquor in a morning and then set up a Maypole round which, says Bradford, they " frisked like fairies, or rather furies," in the good old English style, it was too much for the Puritans of Salem and Boston, and in 1630 they proceeded under Endicott to break up the settlement, shipping Morton off to England. Some justification for this action is to be found in the fact that the merrymakers were debauching the Indians, and also teaching them the use of firearms. In later years the Pilgrims had many disputes with Massachusetts, especially in regard to boundaries.

The fact that the colonists had settled outside the territory of the Virginia boundary rendered their grant of no value. They

[3] Channing, " History of the United States," vol. i. ch. xi.

were mere squatters upon the soil of the old Plymouth Company, which was reorganized in 1620 as the Council for New England, and from this company they now sought a grant. One of doubtful legality was secured in 1621, but their rights to the soil were not made secure until a patent issued in 1630.

The communal system proved as great a failure in Plymouth as it had done in Virginia. In 1623 it was partially abandoned, each family being given one acre of ground. Plenty followed, as it had in Virginia. In 1627 further increase in private ownership was allowed. Each household was then given twenty acres as a private holding. Thus the communal system was finally abandoned, although the system of " commons " and of pasture and wood rights on the land of the community remained in places almost to the present day.[4] About the same time that the communal system was given up, the colonists purchased the shares held by the London merchants, and thus obtained complete control of their affairs.

At first Plymouth was in government a pure democracy, where all the freemen (those who had signed the compact or who had been made freemen by the governing body) met in primary assembly; but as the colony expanded it became more and more inconvenient for all the freemen to assemble in one body, and the representative system was introduced. The General Court, as the body of representatives was called, was not, however, given law-making powers, and for several years longer the primary assembly could still meet and undo the work of the deputies. Though the Pilgrims enjoyed these privileges of government, they never felt secure in them because they were not a vested right. They had them simply through neglect. This feeling of insecurity caused them to try several times to secure a charter from the king, but never with success. Finally their separate existence was lost by the incorporation of the colony with that of Massachusetts in 1691.[5]

II

MASSACHUSETTS BAY

Before the coming of the Pilgrims the Plymouth Company had made several efforts at colonization, all of them unsuccessful.

---

[4] Channing, " History of the United States," vol. i. ch. xi.
[5] See Dexter, " The Pilgrim Church and Plymouth Colony," in Winsor, " Nar. and Crit. History," vol. iii. ch. viii.

Captain John Smith, in 1614–1615, explored the coast of North Virginia, as this company's territory was called, made a map of it, and changed the name to New England. He also wrote pamphlets setting forth the attractions of New England for colonists. The fishing industry there, he declared, was more profitable than the Spanish mines. Upon the reorganization of the company in 1620, as the Council for New England, a new charter was secured and also a new grant, this time to the lands lying between the fortieth and the forty-eighth degree north latitude.

The failure of the efforts at colonization does not appear to have been due to any lack of liberality on the part of the company with its lands. Indeed, it granted them away in a kingly fashion, having little regard to-day for the rights granted yesterday. The conflicting claims thus created were a source of vexation for many years. Perhaps the most important of these grants was one made in 1628. It comprised the strip of territory between the Merrimac and the Charles Rivers, with three miles on the farther side of each, and extended westward to the Pacific Ocean. It was made to a company composed of John Endicott and five associates. In September of that year Endicott came over with a company of sixty and joined the settlers who had come out to Gloucester under the auspices of the Dorchester Company, and had later removed to Naumkeag, afterwards Salem. Such was the prelude to the great Puritan exodus. The following year, March, 1629, a royal charter was secured from Charles I. for a legal corporation styled the Governor and Company of the Massachusetts Bay in New England.

The membership of the company was now enlarged. The charter provided that it should be directed by a governor, deputy governor, and eighteen assistants chosen by the freemen, that is, the members of the company. The patentees strenuously resisted the efforts of the advisers of the Crown to have the government of the company fixed in England. This omission really was as important as anything which the charter contained, for it made possible the removal of the corporation, together with its charter, to Massachusetts.[6] This was done in 1630, when the corporation and colony were merged into one self-governing body. And this was the distinguishing characteristic of the corporate colony, the thing which contrasts it most sharply with the provincial colonies south of the Hudson.

[6] Doyle, "English Colonies in America," vol. i. p. 90.

The reasons for the formation of the Company and for the transfer of its charter to the New World are to be found in the condition of affairs in England. The Petition of Right, the closing of Parliament in 1629, and the imprisonment of John Eliot had given the opponents of the government fair warning that they could expect no half-way measures. Ecclesiastical affairs took on an ominous aspect. William Laud was the practical ruler of the Established Church. He set about securing conformity with a thoroughness that meant ruin to all non-conformists. The Puritan element had fallen upon evil days in both church and state. The wiser heads turned naturally to America as a safe retreat until the storm should blow over. It was under these circumstances that the project of a trading charter was conceived and carried out.[7]

The situation was becoming more and more unbearable to the Puritan party in England, whether Separatists or not; and in 1630 a number of them made the transfer of the charter the condition of their crossing the Atlantic. The great exodus had begun. Eleven ships with more than a thousand passengers made the voyage. With them came their new governor, John Winthrop, and the deputy governor, Thomas Dudley. Winthrop decided that Salem was not a suitable location, and so removed to Boston Harbor as the most satisfactory site. Many of those who came were men of education, some had held high stations at home, membership in Parliament or preferment in the Church of England, while all were " wise in their day and generation." The original patent was to a trading company. Some disavowed any project to establish a community of Separatists, nor for a time did they want their independence at Salem; but at the very first they were bold enough to reject the Anglican ritual and shipped off to England John and Samuel Browne for no other offense than using it. Their churches were organized on what is known to-day as the congregational plan.

The government of the colony was not a real theocracy, as it is sometimes called; neither was it a pure democracy; it was a mixture of the two. Mention has been made of the fusing of the corporation and the colony. This fusion was not complete for many years, for no one could become a free man who could not stand the religious test. But within the corporation the government was democratic, though Winthrop and the assistants endeavored to

[7] Channing, " History of the United States," vol. i. p. 323.

make it oligarchic. The first rebuke to this spirit came in a dispute over taxation, when the freemen resumed the right to impose taxes and sent representatives or deputies to advise the governor and assistants in such matters. All these together made up the General Court, which exercised both legislative and judicial powers, but the freemen still met to elect the governor and assistants. In 1644 a trivial lawsuit over a lost pig led to the establishment of a bicameral legislature. The Bible and the common law of England were the law of the land until 1641, when the " Body of Liberties " was adopted. The main object of this instrument was to limit the discretionary power of the executive.

When religious disputes were the chief concern of men it would not have been reasonable to expect a colony with a distinctly religious aim to be free from troubles of that nature. The expulsion of the Episcopalian Browne has already been mentioned, and scarcely was the colony freed from the danger of prelacy when another disturbing factor arose in the person of Roger Williams, who landed at Boston in 1631, went to Plymouth, and came to Salem in 1633. The freemen had provided for an oath of allegiance to the colony, but Williams refused to take this and denied the right of the government to require it. He declared for the separation of church and state and for voluntary attendance at services and voluntary contributions for the support of the church. More than this, he pronounced the king's patent void and declared that valid patents could be secured only from the Indians, who were the rightful owners of the soil. Much of this sounds very modern, and his theories in regard to the church have been adopted in every American commonwealth. But Williams was not only far in advance of the time, but was also an impractical extremist. His preaching was nothing short of an attack upon the state, and there was nothing to do but deal with him as a public enemy. Salem sided with her pastor for a while, but was brought to terms by being disfranchised. Williams would neither amend his preaching nor keep silence, and was finally banished (1635). On account of his illness the decree was not carried out for some months; but as Williams could not keep still it was finally decided to ship him back to England. To avoid this fate he fled from the colony in the dead of winter (1636).[8]

Another religious disturber was Mrs. Anne Hutchinson, who

[8] Bancroft, " History of the United States," vol. i. p. 378.

landed at Boston in 1634. She appears to have had a fondness for notoriety and did not like to be excluded from the meeting where the men came together to discuss theological and political questions. As a counter movement she held meetings for the women, where similar questions were discussed. Soon it was discovered that her teachings were heretical, and that she was gaining a following among men of consequence. The heresy consisted in her declaration that she and her followers were under a " covenant of grace," while the others were under a " covenant of works." Among her followers were her brother, the Rev. John Wheelright, the Rev. John Cotton, and the young governor, Henry Vane. The Boston church, indeed all Massachusetts society, was shaken to its very foundations by the agitation of this question of " grace " and " works." In September, 1637, a synod of divines drew up and condemned ninety-one erroneous opinions said to have been held by members of the community. The heretics were asked to subscribe to this condemnation, but refused. Wheelright was banished, while others were fined or disfranchised. Mrs. Hutchinson was then brought to trial, if such a travesty on justice may be dignified by the name of trial. The witnesses against her were not sworn; she was not allowed an attorney; and she and her witnesses were browbeaten with shameless disregard of justice. But in some inexplicable way, dim now, but clear and real then, her teachings were believed to endanger the theocratic state, and she was found guilty. Banishment was the penalty (1637), and she fled to Rhode Island, and later went to New York, where she was murdered by the Indians four years afterwards. This the divines considered God's vindication of their judgment.

Comparative religious quiet now appears to have reigned for a number of years, only to be broken by what is commonly regarded as the most inoffensive of all sects, the Quakers. At that time, however, a few of them practiced certain fanatical customs which would not be tolerated in any civilized community to-day, such as walking through the streets and entering the churches naked. Persecution in England drove some of them to Massachusetts in 1656. When they refused to take the oath of allegiance, they were suspected of being Jesuits in disguise. They were banished, and the penalty of death was imposed upon any who returned. To the surprise of the authorities some returned and demanded the repeal of the law. Four were hanged, but the law had to be repealed in response to public opinion. In the seventeenth century belief in witchcraft was common throughout the world. The "Body of Liberties" made it a capital offense for one to be a witch. In the last decade of the century this law was invoked against many suspected persons, and nineteen actually paid the penalty on the gallows. Because this delusion as to witches centered around Salem, this is popularly known as the Salem Witchcraft.

In the midst of the religious persecution one beam of light breaks out which is still growing brighter with every passing day. The year following the banishment of Roger Williams, and the year preceding that of Mrs. Hutchinson, witnessed the birth of Harvard College. This was founded by the Commonwealth at Newtowne. The latter name was soon changed to Cambridge in honor of the Alma Mater of most of the college men of the community. Two years later John Harvard, a young clergyman, died, leaving his library and an estate valued at £800 to the college. The new institution was named Harvard in grateful recognition of its first great benefactor.

III

CONNECTICUT AND RHODE ISLAND

The settlement of Connecticut, in being an offshoot of other colonies, marks a new stage in colonial development. The Dutch at New York had looked upon the fertile Connecticut Valley and saw that it was good, especially for trading. With unusual magnanimity they reported this to the settlers at Plymouth, who immediately made a treaty with the Mohicans and established a trading post at Windsor (1633) to check the Dutch, who had settled at Hartford. Certain men of Massachusetts, who also desired this goodly country, came into the valley and, with a shameless disregard of the rights of the Plymouth squatters, took possession of the "Lord's waste" on which they had already settled. This migration was at first opposed by Massachusetts, but in 1635 the legislature gave its formal sanction, furnished the settlers with a commission, with ammunition and cannon, and provided that they should be subject to its jurisdiction.

This new exodus was led by the Rev. Thomas Hooker. This divine appears to have been the rival of the Rev. John Cotton, but was of a less aggressive disposition and wished to seek a new field, where his light would be more conspicuous. He was also opposed to the close connection between church and state which obtained in Massachusetts. He was democratic in his ideas and wished a wider franchise than one based on church membership. A third consideration probably had more weight with the ordinary emigrants. The settlers were in search of more fertile soil, and public policy demanded the checking of the Dutch. Before the end of 1636 about eight hundred people had settled in the valley in the three towns of Hartford, Windsor, and Wethersfield. The establishment of Saybrook (1635), at the mouth of the river, by John Winthrop, Jr., son of the governor of Massachusetts, served to protect them from the Dutch. This was done under the authority of Lord Brooke and Lord Saye and Sele, to whom, with ten others, that part of the country had been granted by the Council for New England.[9]

Much has been made of the Fundamental Orders under which the colonists governed themselves. Fiske calls it " the first written constitution known to history that created a government "; but it was too closely modeled on that of Massachusetts to deserve any extended analysis. One important difference was that there was no religious test for citizenship. Neither was there any mention of allegiance to the British King, though there probably was no intention to deny it.

New Haven was founded as a separate colony in 1638, by Theophilus Eaton and the Rev. John Davenport.[10] This colony is noteworthy for the thorough-going way in which it carried out the ideas on which the others had been founded, but from which they deviated as political expediency dictated. For a year their only constitution was a simple agreement to obey the Scriptures. In June, 1639, they adopted a constitution closely modeled upon the Bible, and agreed among themselves that " the word of God shall be the only rule attended unto in ordering the affairs of government." It was another of those governments founded on the closest union between church and state. Other towns sprang up about New Haven, and maintained an independent existence until 1643, when they united with it under the title of the New Haven Colony. They were troubled by the Dutch, but managed to maintain their position against all encroachments.

[9] Channing, " History of the United States," vol. i. pp. 398-401.
[10] Eggleston, " Beginners of a Nation," p. 343.

The very life of Connecticut was threatened in 1636-1637 by the Pequot Indians. The war concerned all the colonies, but the brunt of it was borne by Connecticut. While Massachusetts and Plymouth were disputing about what each should do, John Mason, an interpid soldier who had served in the Netherlands, organized a company and marched against the enemy. Reinforcements arrived from outside in time to take part in the annihilation of the power of the Pequots by the destruction of their last stronghold.

Until after the restoration of the Stuarts the people of Connecticut, excepting the military station at Saybrook, were mere squatters, with no title to the land except such as had been secured in some cases from the Indians. When the news of the Restoration was received, Connecticut proclaimed the new king and sent over the courtly Winthrop as its agent. With the help of Lord Saye and Sele, now a member of the king's council, he secured a very liberal charter (1662). The colonists were made a self-governing corporation and were practically independent in everything but name. Not even their laws had to be sent over for the inspection of the king.[11] New Haven, to her intense disgust, found that she was included in this charter. For a time she resisted incorporation, but finally yielded when threatened with absorption by New York. With the exception of the reign of Andros, Connecticut retained her full independence. One other attempt, however, was made to bring her into partial subjection to New York. During the first of the Inter-Colonial Wars, Fletcher was made commander of the Connecticut and New Jersey militia. William III. did this to secure some sort of military unity in the war against the French. Fletcher visited Hartford in October, 1693, and attempted to carry out his commission. The Assembly of Connecticut refused to recognize his authority. It is very doubtful whether his little episode with Captain Wadsworth, in which his attempt to read his commission was drowned by the beating of drums, and the doughty captain threatened " to make the sun shine through " him, ever occurred. But it is evident from his own statement that he met with a decided rebuff.[12]

The history of the early years of Rhode Island reads like

[11] Bancroft, " History of the United States," vol. ii. pp. 54-55.
[12] Fiske, " Dutch and Quaker Colonies," vol. ii. pp. 218-219.

the story of a mild form of anarchy.[13]   Like Connecticut, this colony was an offshoot of Massachusetts, but one of which the parent colony was not very proud.   When Roger Williams fled from her borders, he turned southward to Narragansett Bay, where he and five associates founded the town of Providence on a tract of land secured from Canonicus and Miantonomi.   In 1637 some of Mrs. Hutchinson's followers, among them William Coddington and John Clarke, found life in Massachusetts uncomfortable and sought a cooler climate in Maine, but one winter there satisfied them.   Turning south they settled on Aquidneck (Rhode Island), where Mrs. Hutchinson soon joined them.[14]   Coddington presently fell out with Mrs. Hutchinson and gracefully withdrew from Portsmouth and founded Newport (1639), but the towns were reunited the following year.   The machinery of government was set in motion by thirteen in Providence and by about twenty on Aquidneck.   Through the exertions of Williams the settlements, together with the new town of Warwick, were united in 1643 as the Providence Plantations, and a charter was secured from the Parliamentary Committee on the Colonies.   In 1663 John Clarke, the agent for Rhode Island, secured another charter from Charles II.   This charter was so liberal that it was used as the constitution of government until 1842.   A method of legislation, seldom found now outside of Switzerland, was introduced here in 1647, the referendum, by which any one town could defeat an objectionable measure.

From the first Rhode Island was a country of " soul liberty." The right of freedom in doctrinal belief was assured by statutes in 1641, and was included in the charter of 1663, though subsequently Roman Catholics were denied the right of franchise.   As a consequence the colony became a sort of haven of refuge for all sorts of heretics who had found other places, especially Massachusetts, uncomfortable.   The result of the mixture of such heterogeneous elements was that Rhode Island itself became uncomfortable to all except those who delighted in turmoil and turbulence. But democracy was in training, and there were no very serious results.

[13] See Richman, " Rhode Island, Its Making and Its Meaning," vol. ii chs. i.–iii.
[14] Eggleston, " Beginners of a Nation," p. 340.

IV

NEW HAMPSHIRE AND MAINE

Two of the New England colonies, New Hampshire and Maine, were not unlike the southern colonies in origin. Sir Ferdinando Gorges, one of the chief moving spirits in the Council for New England, succeeded in 1622, with John Mason (not the conqueror of the Pequots), in obtaining a patent to the country between the Merrimac and the Kennebec rivers. Later (1629) this territory was divided between them, Mason taking that lying bebetween the Merrimac and Piscataqua, Gorges that between the Piscataqua and Kenebec.[15]

The first settlement in New Hampshire appears to have been made by David Thompson and a few associates near the mouth of the Piscataqua in 1623. Dover was founded by some Puritan fish-mongers from London, Exeter and Hampton by Antinomians (adherents of Mrs. Hutchinson) from Massachusetts. By this time Mason began to take an interest in his territory, though he does not appear ever to have secured a patent as proprietary governor. In 1629 he and Gorges formed the Laconia Company, which sent out a few colonists the next year and founded Portsmouth. They were Anglicans, and it may be readily inferred that these settlements of Puritans, Antinomians and Anglicans had little in common. They quarreled among themselves and invited the interference of Massachusetts, who was watching for an opportunity to make good her claims to jurisdiction over them. This she did in 1641, in a comparatively liberal way, giving the towns the right of representation. In 1691 New Hampshire was separated from Massachusetts and became a royal province. For a hundred years the progress of the colony was retarded by the insecurity of land titles. This was due to the fact that the Mason heirs constantly asserted their claims to the land. Finally this source of vexation was removed by the purchase of the Mason claims. Vermont was an offshoot of this colony. For many years it was a bone of contention between New Hampshire and New York, but finally the king decided in favor of the latter. The

---

[15] Bancroft, "History of the United States," vol. ii. p. 114; Thwaites, "The Colonies," p. 150.

attempt, however, to disregard the land titles based on the New Hampshire grants led to the revolt of the Green Mountain boys and the formation of a new commonwealth.

Gorges was not content with a simple patent to the land, but secured a charter from the king in 1639, which made him a pala-tine. He drafted a very cumbersome form of government, which reminds one of Locke's Constitution, but was never able to put it in operation, because there were hardly more than enough settlers in Maine to hold the numerous offices. Gorges gave much time, thought, and money to his colony, but never lived to see any great returns. After his death the colonists wrote to his heirs repeatedly, but could get no reply. Massachusetts then discovered that the country belonged to her, and proceeded to absorb it (1652–1656). In 1677 the heirs of Gorges made a virtue of necessity, and sold out their claims to Massachusetts.

V

THE NEW ENGLAND CONFEDERATION

The formation of the New England Confederation in 1643 gives a sort of unity to the history of this region for a time. Connecticut had made overtures for such a union as early as 1637. Only four of the colonies were included, Connecticut, New Haven, Plymouth and Massachusetts, and they agreed upon twelve articles for a " firm and perpetual league of friendship and amity for offense, mutual advice and succor." Rhode Island was not deemed worthy to be a member and therefore was not invited to join. Eight federal commissioners, two from each colony, regardless of population, were empowered to " determine all affairs of war or peace, leagues, aids, charges and numbers of men for war, division of spoils and whatsoever was gotten by conquest." The spoils as well as the expenses of war were to be divided according to the military population. One article provided for the rendition of fugitives from justice and runaway slaves. Within its own limits each colony was to preserve its own " peculiar jurisdiction and government " free from any intermeddling by the Confederation. The commissioners were to meet in the various colonies in rotation. A three-fourths vote (the vote being by individuals, not by colonies) was necessary for any measure;

failing in this it was to be referred to the legislature of the different members of the Confederation.

Although the population of Massachusetts was greater than that of all the other members combined, she stood on an equality with each of them in the federal council. Her only remedy lay in assuming a domineering attitude, or in actually violating the terms of the compact, which she sometimes did. However, the Confederation served a useful purpose, especially in dealing with the Indians. It declined after the Restoration and was finally dissolved in 1684.[16]

As in the south, so in New England, the colonists desired to convert the heathen Indian. The most famous of all the workers among the red men was the Rev. John Eliot, who was known as the Apostle to the Indians. He labored among them many years and translated the Bible into the Algonquin language. Those who accepted his teachings were known as "praying Indians," and a goodly number were gathered into the fold. But the great majority were true to the faith of their fathers, and the chief of the Pokanokets even tried to insert in a treaty a stipulation that no effort should be made to convert any of his warriors. With jealous eye the Indian saw his hunting grounds vanishing with each advance of the English, and the number of warriors diminished by the increase of "praying Indians." He could draw but little distinction between the cheating trader and the pious missionary, and he hated all. He knew but little of the sacred nature of treaties, such as the English made with him, and frequently broke them. The summons to the settlement to answer for this, as also to be arraigned before a jury of white men for some offense, humiliated his pride and excited his wrath. At last the smoldering fires of hostility were fanned into a flame by Philip, son of and successor to Massasoit. There is no evidence of a widespread conspiracy, but Philip was under suspicion in 1674, and was summoned to an examination. The informer against him was murdered, the murderers were tried by jury and hanged, and the war at once broke out.

Philip succeeded in winning over the powerful Narragansetts, and soon all New England was ablaze. Several towns, among them Brookfield, Deerfield and Northfield, were burned. An attack on Hadley, according to tradition, was repelled under the

[16] Frothingham, "Rise of the Republic," ch. ii.

leadership of an aged man commonly believed to have been Goffe, one of the regicides who had found a refuge in America. During the winter of 1675–1676 the war was prosecuted with vigor by the whites. The Indians were unused to continuous fighting and

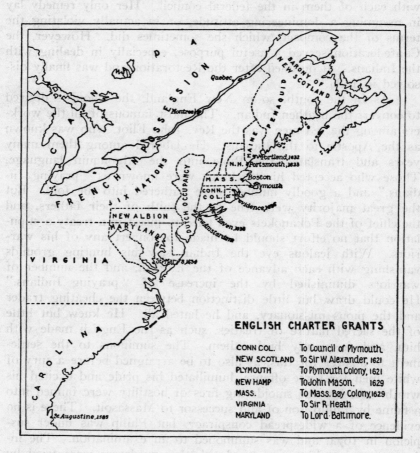

ENGLISH CHARTER GRANTS

CONN COL.	To Council of Plymouth.
NEW SCOTLAND	To Sir W Alexander, 1621
PLYMOUTH	To Plymouth Colony, 1621
NEW HAMP	To John Mason. 1629
MASS.	To Mass. Bay Colony, 1629
VIRGINIA	To Sir R Heath
MARYLAND	To Lord Baltimore.

were gradually exhausted. Philip's allies sued for grace and Philip himself became a fugitive, only to be overtaken by Captain Church in a swamp, where he was slain by one of his own race. The loss in blood and treasure was very great. More than 600 men fell in the struggle and almost as many houses, including thirteen towns, went up in smoke. Bancroft estimates the disbursements and losses at half a million dollars.[17]

The Restoration in England marked a turn in the tide of affairs in the Confederation. We have already seen that one of the members, New Haven, was absorbed by Connecticut in her new charter. Rhode Island, too, despised and rejected of the Confederation because of her heterodoxy, received the royal favor, much to the disgust of Massachusetts, which was ordered to accord better treatment to the Quakers, to tolerate the Anglicans, and to administer justice in the name of the king. Still another factor contributed to the decline of the Confederation. The early settlers were thoroughly imbued with the spirit of independence. They probably never aimed at complete separation from the mother country, but they wished to have as little to do with her as possible. But by this time a new generation had grown up, one which knew not the tyrannies from which their fathers had fled. They were becoming tired of the austere rule of the Puritan divines. Men of wealth who engaged in commerce were unwilling to offend across the sea for fear of damaging trade. They also knew something of life in Old England and strove to imitate it.

All these facts made it possible for Edward Randolph, who came over in 1676, to look after the enforcement of the Navigation Acts, to build up a small following; but he was bitterly hated by the majority for his tyranny and for his malicious reports about the colony.

Soon after the Restoration New England affairs were entrusted to a committee of twelve members of the privy council. In 1664 they sent over a commission, but they were unable to get much satisfaction out of Massachusetts in their efforts to have her mend her ways. They detached Maine from her the following year, but three years later she quietly took it back, and in 1677 bought up the Gorges claim which Charles himself was intending to buy. The Puritans were as skillful as the Spanish in evasion and delay, but finally the blow fell. The insult in the purchase of Maine, the constant evasion of the Navigation Acts, the coining of money, and the disfranchisement of Anglicans were deemed a sufficient pretext for the destruction of her liberties, and her charter was annulled in 1684, by a writ of *quo warranto*. The same year witnessed the end of the Confederation.

[17] Bancroft, "History of the United States," vol. ii. p. 92.

In 1686 Sir Edmund Andros came to Boston with a commission as governor of New England, and two years later New York and New Jersey, where he had already made a reputation, were added to his jurisdiction. Some modern historians are inclined to think that he was hardly as black as he has been painted, and the colors used by his contemporary colonists were certainly very dark. He was not carrying out a policy of arbitrary government for the sake of being despotic. Conditions in the colonies had occupied the serious attention of the home government. The evident solution of the problem of administration was to consolidate and unify the various colonial governments. James II. determined to do this. In order to accomplish such a result it was necessary to confiscate existing charters and abolish the independent governments in the various colonies. In executing such a policy Andros certainly could not have won the love and gratitude of the colonists and at the same time been faithful to his instructions. He chose the latter and governed despotically. He suspended the writ of *habeas corpus* and instituted a rigorous censorship of the press. He annulled land grants and divided up the common lands among his friends. He abolished the General Court and himself levied the taxes. And finally he set up the Anglican worship, sometimes seizing Congregational churches for that purpose. He demanded the charter of Rhode Island. This was refused, but the colony yielded to his sway. At Hartford he demanded the Charter of Connecticut in person. The story goes that the assembly was prolonged far into the night, when the lights were suddenly put out and the precious charter was spirited away and concealed in an oak. The Charter Oak, as the tree was ever afterwards known, was carefully preserved for a time, but was blown down in August, 1856.[18]

At last relief came in news from over the sea. As soon as it was known that William of Orange had landed in England, and before the result could be ascertained, the colonists imprisoned Andros and quietly shipped him back home. Connecticut and Rhode Island then brought their old charters out of hiding and went on as before. Massachusetts made strenuous efforts to get back her old rights, but there was no way of avoiding the fact that her charter had been legally declared void. Increase Mather was sent to England to secure a restoration of the old charter, but

[18] Read Andrews, " Self Government in America," chs. xvi.-xvii.

failed. William III. would have preferred to see all of New England united under one strong government, as he foresaw the coming struggle with the French. He was compelled, however, to yield to the dissatisfaction created by the Andros régime. It was intimated that a proposition for a new charter would be favorably received. This was at once drawn up, probably under the personal direction of Mather, and received the royal assent in 1691. Even in this the unifying policy of the British Government was manifest, for the bounds of Massachusetts were enlarged so as to include Plymouth, Maine and Nova Scotia. Her legislature was restored, but every law it passed had to receive the royal sanction, while the governor was appointed by the Crown. Congregationalism was still the state religion, but the absolute domination of the Puritan clergy was at an end, for the religious test for citizenship was now replaced by a property qualification.[19]

During the first half of the eighteenth century the charters were threatened several times, but were never again revoked, and the colonies continued their development with only such serious interruptions as the wars waged against the French and the Indians, which were but an echo of the great contest in the Old World. A source of perennial dispute was the governor's salary, in which the Crown tried to dictate, but finally had to yield, and the matter was left to legislative discretion. With the passing years more and more emigrants, mostly English, came over, and the settlements spread to the west. Connecticut remained almost purely an agricultural community, but Massachusetts and Rhode Island developed a large carrying trade. Their industrial and social life will be described in another chapter.

VI

NEW YORK

The Dutch were bold navigators, and after the defeat of the Spanish Armada their rise was so rapid that they soon rivaled the power which had defeated their old-time enemy. It was an Englishman, Henry Hudson, who in September, 1609, while in the employ of the Dutch East India Company, sailed up the river

[19] Bancroft, "History of the United States," vol. iii. pp. 78-82; Greene, "Provincial America," ch. ii.

which bears his name and gave them a claim to "as fair a land as ever was trodden by the foot of man." The country between the Hudson and Delaware Bay, which the navigator also entered, was named New Netherlands, but no settlements were made in it for several years, except a few trading posts.

In 1621 the Dutch West India Company was chartered by the States General and given large commercial and political powers in all the Dutch possessions between the straits of Magellan and Newfoundland.[20] Three years later they sent over thirty families of Walloons (Protestant refugees), some of whom settled on the Delaware River, others on the Connecticut, and a few on Long Island. Eight stopped on Manhattan, but the greater part went up the Hudson to the present site of Albany, which they called Fort Orange. We have already seen that the English claimed all this country, and had even granted it away more than once. However, they were allied with the Dutch at this time against their common enemy, Spain, and preferred their friendship to the track-less forests which they were occupying.

Cornelius May, whose name is perpetuated by a county and cape in New Jersey, was the first director or governor. In 1626 he was succeeded by Peter Minuit, who, upon his arrival, bought the whole of Manhattan Island from the Indians for trinkets worth about twenty-four dollars. He built a fort on the island and called it New Amsterdam.[21] But immigrants were few in number, and in 1629, by the charter of "privileges and exemptions," an effort was made to attract men of wealth and station. It was simply an effort to establish the feudal system in America, antedating that in Maryland by several years. Members of the company were privileged to plant colonies on lands purchased by them from the Indians. Each one who established as many as fifty persons over fifteen years of age was given a perpetual grant of a tract extending sixteen miles along the river or eight miles on each side, and indefinitely into the interior.[22] The tenants were practically the serfs for ten years of the patroons, as the proprietors were called, who collected the rents and exercised feudal rights of government. Some of these patroons became the

[20] Fiske, "Dutch and Quaker Colonies," vol. i. p. 3.
[21] Bancroft, "History of the United States," vol. ii. p. 279; Fiske, "Dutch and Quaker Colonies," vol. i. p. 116.
[22] Fiske, "Dutch and Quaker Colonies," vol. i. p. 134.

founders of families still well known in New York. Remnants of the feudal system prevailed far into the nineteenth century, but the attempt to collect rents long in arrears on the great Van Rensselaer estate led to riots (1839–1846) which finally caused the State to abolish all such rights.

Still the colony did not thrive. The patroons were great landlords and their tenants were but litttle better than serfs. Traders were not attracted, because the company had a monopoly of commerce. As a further inducement to settlers, the patroon system was curtailed and trade and the cultivation of the soil were opened to all. The effect was not all that could have been desired. A few more settlers came in, but the growth was slow, for in 1653 the province numbered only about two thousand souls. Yet even before this it had attained a somewhat cosmopolitan character, about eighteen languages being spoken within its bounds.[23]

Minuit was succeeded by Van Twiller in 1632, who soon gave place to Kieft, an autocrat who made things lively in and about the colony for ten years. In response to public opinion he was forced to call a council (1641) representing the different settlements, but he quarreled with this and with a later one (1644), and was finally removed on petition of the colonists. He was succeeded by Peter Stuyvesant (1647), the last and best of the Dutch governors. Although he was better than his predecessors, the people were not satisfied and demanded still more liberties, for the leaven of democracy was at work here as well as in the English colonies. He was forced to call a council (the nine men), but the body was made self-perpetuating. However, in a contest over excise taxes (1651) the people won, and in 1652 a measure of municipal government was granted the colony. In the matter of religion Stuyvesant sought to enforce conformity to the Dutch Reformed Church, and persecuted dissenters without mercy until the pressure of public opinion forced him to stop. After a long dispute with New England he agreed to give up all claims to the Connecticut Valley and to place the western boundary of Connecticut about where it now is. In 1655 he forced the South Sea Company of Sweden to abandon its settlement on the Delaware, which had been made under the leadership of Minuit, Usselinx and Blommaert, and annexed them to his realm.

[23] Read Schuyler, "Colonial New York," vol. i.

But the time soon came for the Dutch to yield. For centuries the English and Dutch had been firm friends; but the rapid rise of the Netherlands as a sea power after humbling Spain caused England to become jealous of the increasing maritime supremacy of the Dutch. The policy of Charles II. was vacillating; sometimes he was the pensioner of the French king, sometimes the ally of the Stadtholder. Pretexts for interference in America were not hard to find. There was the constant friction between the English and Dutch settlers and the evasion of the Navigation Acts by the Dutch. Then, too, the finest harbor on the continent separated the English colonies, a harbor which, with its environs, England now claimed by right of discovery. All the country from the Connecticut to the Delaware must be made English, and in 1664 Charles granted it to his brother, James, Duke of York.

Richard Nicolls was sent over with some of the king's troops to make good this claim. He landed in Boston, and sought help there, but obtained none, and turned to Connecticut, who sent her militia. When he arrived before New Amsterdam Stuyvesant rushed about as fast as his wooden leg would carry him and summoned the people to defend the fort; but they contrasted the liberties of the English colonists with their own, and refused to support him loyally, in consequence of which he was forced to surrender.[24] He went to Holland, but returned to the colony, where he and Nicolls drank many a bumper of ale together. His memory is still preserved in the names of certain localities in New York City.[25]

At the time of the conquest the colony contained about ten thousand inhabitants, of whom about fifteen hundred were on Manhattan Island. Nicolls became governor and at once took up the work of Anglicizing the colony. The name of the province, as also that of the town of Manhattan, was charged to New York, and Fort Orange became Albany. However, few immediate changes were made in the political system beyond the introduction of trial by jury, the granting of equality in the matter of taxation, and the promulgation of the Duke's Laws. The latter, drawn by Nicolls and a convention of the settlers, provided

[24] Bancroft, "History of the United States," vol. ii. p. 313; Fiske, "Dutch and Quaker Colonies," vol. i. p. 299.

[25] Stevens, "The English in New York," in Winsor, "Nar. and Crit. Hist.," vol. iii. ch. x.

a system of town government whereby a constable and eight over-seers were elected by the people and vested with judicial and legis-lative power. Several towns were combined into a " riding," pre-sided over by a sheriff. In 1683 these ridings developed into counties; afterwards (1703) it was arranged that supervisors should be elected by each town. Thus the whole system of local government was a sort of compromise between the town system of New England and the county system of the south, and gave rise to the mixed system now prevalent in most of the States. Religious liberty was guaranteed to all.

Outside the towns the people had no share in their own gov-ernment, for the sheriff was appointed by the governor and the laws were made by the duke. The English settlers clamored for more liberties. No man can be contented without security of prop-erty. The Dutch were vexed by an order that all land grants must be confirmed by the new governor, for which he was al-lowed to exact a fee. In consequence they welcomed the Dutch fleet when it appeared before the city in 1673, but their joy was shortlived, for the English were again in possession the following year. Edmund Andros then came out as governor. His rule was vigorous and on the whole wise, but the agitation for more liberties was kept up. In 1680 he was recalled and Thomas Dongan sent in his place. Three years later Dongan yielded to the demands of the people and called an assembly. This body drew up a char-ter of liberties, to which the king gave his assent. This provided that the assembly should be coördinate with the governor and council in legislation; that no taxes should be levied without the consent of the assembly; that the franchise should be extended to all freemen and free-holders, and that religious toleration should be given to all Christians.[26] But their liberties were not enjoyed long; James hated popular government even more than Charles, and when he came to the throne he abolished the charter of liber-ties (1686), annexed New York to New England, and appointed Andros to govern the whole as a royal province.

But relief soon came in the enforced abdication of the king and the imprisonment of Andros (1688–1689). Jacob Leisler, a German shopkeeper, headed the revolution in New York and pro-claimed William and Mary as the lawful sovereigns. He gov-erned the colony with energy, and took active measures to defend

[26] Thwaites, " The Colonies," p. 205.

it against the French and Indians. At his call the first Colonial
Congress met at Albany in 1690 to take counsel for measures
of defense and offense against the French and their Indian allies.
But Leisler was rash, and many of his arbitrary acts offended the
so-called conservative element. This element was, in the main, the
Andros party, and the members were known to be sympathizers of
the Stuarts.

In 1691 Colonel Henry Sloughter came out as governor.
Leisler was arrested on the charge of treason and imprisoned.
The anti-Leisler party acquired the ascendency with the new governor. Leisler was convicted, and Sloughter, while intoxicated,
placed his signature to the death warrant. This judicial murder
of Leisler profoundly affected New York politics. For many
years the two parties in the colony kept up a bitter controversy,
and each governor found it necessary to ally himself with one or
the other of them.[27] Sloughter's successor, Benjamin Fletcher,
was an unprincipled scoundrel and caused the colony much distress. It was during his administration that New York became
a center for the illegal trade of the pirates that infested the Indies.
It is not at all certain that Fletcher himself was not personally interested in this traffic. Many efforts were made to suppress the
sea robbers. Among other schemes, a hardy mariner, named
William Kidd, was sent out to prey upon them. But the chance
for gain was too tempting for him and his men, and he turned
pirate and became the most famous of them all. After about two
and a half years of this life, Kidd appeared on the American
coast in 1699. In the meantime Fletcher had been succeeded by
Bellomont. It had been under the latter's advice that Kidd had
been sent out. Kidd hoped to secure immunity through his wealth
and his acquaintance with Bellomont. In this he was mistaken,
and in an effort to convince Bellomont of his innocence he landed
in Boston, was arrested, sent to England for trial, and finally executed. Where he disposed of his fabulous wealth is one of the mys-
teries men are still trying to solve.[28]

The next governor, the Earl of Bellomont (1698-1701), was
perhaps the best the colony ever had.[29] He was also the first governor sent out under the new Board of Trade and Plantations. He

[27] Fiske, " Dutch and Quaker Colonies," vol. ii. pp. 183-208.
[28] *Ibid.*, vol. ii. pp. 226-235.
[29] *Ibid.*, vol. ii. pp. 228.

allied himself with the old Leisler party and managed to carry on the government in a most vigorous manner.

Bellomont was succeeded by Cornbury, who proved himself one of the most rapacious governors that ever plundered the colony. It was due to his mismanagement that the assembly appointed a treasurer of its own and took full charge of expenditures for war purposes (1706). The movement thus begun could not be stopped. The assembly constantly enlarged its scope of activity. The council was denied any voice in the framing of money bills, all taxes were lodged with the treasurer appointed by the assembly, committees were appointed to carry out its orders, and in 1739 the assembly proceeded to appropriate salaries by name and for specific offices, so that the governor and council lost all practical control over appointments. Thus New York furnishes a good illustration of what was going on in all the colonies during the first half of the eighteenth century. In all of them the assemblies were slowly but surely acquiring practically all control of government, executive as well as legislative.

A trial which occurred in 1735 deserves notice here, because of its bearing upon the history of liberty. Governor Cosby brought suit in the Supreme Court to secure a sum of money, but the case went against him. Thereupon he removed the judge and appointed one of his partisans. Peter Zenger, editor of the New York *Weekly Journal,* then criticised the governor unmercifully in his paper. In retaliation the governor ordered the paper to be burned and prosecuted Zenger for libel, but again lost. This was an important victory for the freedom of the press which has never been forgotten.

In spite of a succession of bad governors, New York enjoyed a steady growth. Its cosmopolitan character was maintained by the arrival of immigrants from the various countries of Europe, but the English and Dutch predominated. New York City became a center of trade, but the commercial preëminence which it now enjoys was not attained in Colonial times.

VII

DELAWARE AND NEW JERSEY

Three different nations, the Dutch, the Swedes and the English, laid claim to Delaware It also had three different individuals as proprietors, Lord Baltimore, the Duke of York and William Penn. The Dutch made the first settlement within the present bounds of the State (near Lewes) in 1631; but the little colony was destroyed by the Indians. Next came some Englishmen from New Haven, only to be taken prisoners by the Dutch. The third attempt was made by the South Sea Company of Sweden, which was chartered by the great soldier-statesman, Gustavus Adolphus, in 1624. In 1638 Peter Minuit, whom we have already met as governor of New Amsterdam, led out the first company from Sweden and built Fort Christina where Wilmington now stands. Governor Kieft protested against this invasion of Dutch territory, and no doubt his ire was raised all the more because it was done under the leadership of one of his predecessors. But the Swedes paid no attention to Kieft except to build another fort to checkmate his rebuilding of Fort Nassau. Then came more English from New Haven, but the Dutch and Swedes forgot their own animosities long enough to unite in driving out the race whose thirst for land was becoming as insatiable as that of the Spanish for gold. New Sweden, as the colony was called, prospered for a while, but as already related, was captured by the Dutch in 1655.[30] A part, and later the rest of it, was sold to the city of Amsterdam, under whose government there was a period of retrogression. With the conquest of New Amsterdam it passed into the hands of the Duke of York, who in turn sold it (1682) to William Penn to give him an outlet to the sea. Thereafter it was known as the " Three Lower Counties," or " Territories " of Pennsylvania, and was governed as a sort of province of that colony. It had no separate governor, but secured a legislature of its own in 1702.

In New Jersey the Dutch built two forts, Fort Nassau and one on the Hudson; but the history of the colony really begins with its cession to Lord Berkeley and Sir George Carteret by the Duke of York in 1664. It was named New Jersey for the island of Jersey, which Carteret had governed and held for Charles II. during the Commonwealth. Colonization began the next year with the settlement of Elizabethtown. A few Dutch, Swedes, and New Englanders were already on the ground. More came from New England and settled Middletown and Newark. In 1668 the first assembly met at Elizabethtown. The severity of its code of laws

[30] Bancroft, "History of the United States," vol. ii. p. 297.

— the death penalty was attached to thirteen crimes — testifies to the predominance of the Puritan spirit. A period of turbulence began with the disputes over quit-rents in 1670, and Berkeley finally sold out his interest in disgust to a party of Quakers. They in turn soon sold out to William Penn.

The Dutch recaptured New Jersey in 1673, but gave it back on the conclusion of peace the following year. In 1676 a new charter was issued, giving the eastern part, or East Jersey, to Carteret, and the western, or West Jersey, to the Quakers. The two provinces were then governed separately. In West Jersey the proprietor " put the power in the people," giving them religious freedom and a representative assembly. This liberal government attracted settlers, and four hundred Quakers came over in 1677. Their first settlement was at Burlington. In 1682 the heirs of Carteret sold East Jersey to a company of twenty-four, including William Penn. This province then received a government very much like that of West Jersey, and all went smoothly for a time.

The disturbance came when James II. revoked the Jersey charters on writs of *quo warranto* (1686) and added them to New York with Andros as governor. A period of turbulence then followed, for the people of New Jersey were no less democratic in spirit than their neighbors. They resisted the effort of Andros to levy taxes without a representative assembly, and disputed with the proprietors about the quit-rents. At last the proprietors, weary of their profitless task, surrendered their claims to the Crown, and New Jersey became a royal province (1702). Although it was a separate province, it did not have a governor of its own. The governor of New York and a deputy performed the executive functions. This was a constant source of complaint on the part of the people of New Jersey, and finally in 1738 they were given a governor of their own.

During Revolutionary times New Jersey made at least one important contribution to constitutional government. This consisted in the decision of a court that an act of the Assembly was void because it violated the frame of government.[31] The case is that of Holmes vs. Walton, and it was a suit involving the validity of a law providing for a jury of six to condemn goods seized while being carried to the camp of the enemy. The courts held that the

[31] Whitehead, "The English in East and West Jersey," in Winsor, "Nar. and Crit. Hist.," vol. iii. ch. xi.

constitution provided for a jury of twelve and that a smaller jury was illegal.[32]

VIII

PENNSYLVANIA

William Penn, the founder of Pennsylvania, was born in 1644. His father was an admiral in the English navy, and William himself was popular at court until he became a convert to the Quaker faith, nothing of which could have been more at variance with the tastes of Charles II. The Quakers were guided by an " inner light," which led them to disregard all social distinctions, to refuse to engage in wars or pay taxes to carry them on, and to practice the utmost simplicity in their manner of living. Persecution drove them into many extravagant practices which members of the sect to-day would not defend; but on the whole they were fighting the battle which Socrates fought centuries before for religious and intellectual freedom. When William Penn became a convert to their faith he turned to the New World to see if there was not some spot where his people could be free from the pitiless laws of England and Massachusetts.[33]

Upon the death of his father, William Penn became heir to a claim of £16,000 against the English king. Penn petitioned the king for an extensive grant of land north of Maryland, not as payment for his debt, but in order that he might restore his fortunes. He evidently believed that by careful management of the plantation he would be able to meet an indebtedness caused by certain Irish losses and by the repudiation of the debt owed him by the king. This grant, in spite of Penn's protest, was named Pennsylvania in honor of Admiral Penn.[34] The grant also contained the seeds of the customary boundary dispute. It began between Penn and Baltimore, passed on to their heirs, and lasted nearly a hundred years. Finally the famous Mason and Dixon's Line was run between Pennsylvania and Maryland (1767) and the dispute was at an end. Nearly a century later another dis-

[32] " American Historical Review," vol. iv. p. 456.
[33] Fiske, " Dutch and Quaker Colonies," vol. ii. p. 99; Bancroft, " History of the United States," vol. ii. ch. xvi.
[34] Andrews, " Colonial Self Government," p. 169.

pute between the people on either side of this line was settled by an appeal to arms.

The charter clothed Penn with ample powers of government, but it differed from previous charters in at least two important respects. It did not guarantee to the settlers the rights of Englishmen and it reserved to the English Parliament the right to tax the colonists. Penn at once prepared a pamphlet advertising his scheme of colonization. This set forth the advantages of the colony, the kind of government that was to be established, and the manner in which land would be granted. One hundred acres of land could be had for two pounds, and the settlers were to have a share in framing the laws. This pamphlet was widely distributed in England, Ireland, Holland, and Germany.[35] In this effort Penn proved himself one of the most successful advertisers of " cheap western land."

The liberal terms attracted many settlers, and three shiploads came over in 1681, under the leadership of William Markham, who became the first governor. A few Swedes were already on the ground and they were asked to remain. Penn himself came over the following year and took up the work of supervising the colony. According to the constitution drawn up by him, the governor was to be appointed by the proprietor, but all other executive officers and both the council and the assembly were to be elected by the freemen. At first laws could be originated only by the governor and council, but the assembly protested against this and finally won. All Christians, except servants and convicts, enjoyed political rights. The first legislature met at Chester in 1682, and the second at Philadelphia in 1683. Among the laws adopted were some providing for the humane treatment of the Indians, the teaching of a trade to each child, the useful employment and reformation of criminals, and religious toleration.

After some time had been spent in allotting lands, Penn passed up the Delaware and laid out Philadelphia, determined to make it unlike the crowded cities of the Old World. In this he succeeded, for Philadelphia, with its broad streets running at right angles to each other, has become the model followed by most American cities. Soon after this he met the chiefs of the Delaware Indians to discuss with them the terms of purchase for their lands. It took the Indians some time to form a resolution, but

[35] Andrews, " Colonial Self Government," p. 178.

they finally came to terms and Penn met them in council to ratify the agreement. Benjamin West's celebrated painting gives an idea of the simplicity and mutual confidence which characterized the meeting. The promise to " live in love with William Penn and his children as long as the sun and moon give light " was kept long after those who made it had passed away.[36]

Penn desired to make his home in the colony, but was forced to return to England in 1684 by the boundary dispute with Lord Baltimore. In 1685 he succeeded in getting a report in his favor from the Lords of Trade. He was also of great help to his Quaker friends, who were being severely persecuted as dissenters. Owing to his intimate relations with the Stuarts, and his success in receiving the royal pardon on so many occasions, he was suspected of siding with them at the time of the revolution (1688), and was deprived of his colony (1692). It was restored to him two years later. When he returned to America in 1699 he found that this little colony had grown to one of twenty thousand inhabitants and that the child in its maturer growth had forgotten some of its filial regard. Delaware clamored for a separate legislature, and Penn granted it. The assembly of Pennsylvania complained of the council, and its influence was still further reduced. " If," said the greatest of all the colony planters, " the people want of me anything that would make them happier, I shall readily grant it." Still dissensions went on. In 1701 he again left the scene of his philanthropic labors, never to return. He died in 1718, and so passed one who was indeed the greatest and best of our colonial founders. Yet he had his limitations. He appears to have been sincere in his attempts to found a government based on the equality of human rights, yet saw no inconsistency in enslaving the black man, though his will did provide for the emancipation of the slaves. Not quite a century later a celebrated statepaper drawn up in Philadelphia declared that all men were created equal, yet nobody dreamed that the black man was a part of " all men." Upon Penn's death the colony passed to his heirs and remained to them a source of perhaps more annoyance than profit until the Revolution.

The growth of Pennsylvania was rapid and substantial. By the time of the Revolution she hardly yielded to Virginia and

36 Fiske, "Dutch and Quaker Colonies," vol. ii. p. 159.

Massachusetts in importance. The Germans, the Dutch, the
Scotch, and the Scotch-Irish came to swell her numbers, and their
influence exists there to this day.[37]

[37] For a comprehensive constitutional history of Pennsylvania during the
Colonial period, see W. R. Shepherd, "History of Proprietary Government in
Pennsylvania."

Chapter V

COLONIAL GOVERNMENTS
1606-1776

BLACKSTONE, in his commentaries,[1] classified the English colonial governments in America as charter, royal or provincial, and proprietary, and this classification continued until very recently to be accepted by historical writers as the most convenient and logical arrangement which could be devised.

The charter colony was described as one whose governmental organization was set forth in a charter granted by the Crown, which charter served as a limitation on the power of the king. It was a sort of civil corporation empowered to make by-laws not repugnant to the laws of England. The royal colony was under the direct and immediate authority of the Crown, subject to his pleasure and without limitation upon his power. The royal commissions to the governors and the instructions accompanying them constituted the basis of the government of the colony. The proprietary colony was one in which supreme authority was vested in a proprietor or proprietaries, who received a grant of land from the king in the nature of a feudatory principality.[2]

A more scientific and logical classification is that suggested by Professor Osgood, one of the leading authorities on American colonial history. He classifies the thirteen colonial governments under two heads, namely, the corporation and the province. The former included those colonial establishments which were in the nature of a corporation possessing certain privileges of government, which were set forth in a charter. At the beginning of the Revolution there were three such colonies, namely, Massachusetts, Rhode Island, and Connecticut. The provincial group included the three so-called proprietary colonies of Pennsylvania, Delaware,

---

[1] Blackstone, " Commentaries on the Laws of England," vol. i. sec. 3.
[2] Story, " Commentaries on the Constitution," sec. 10.

and Maryland, and the royal colonies of Virginia, the Carolinas, New Hampshire, New York, New Jersey, and Georgia.[3]

The form of government in the several colonies varied from time to time, and, as a matter of fact, but two of them, namely, Connecticut and Rhode Island, continued under the same form from their establishment until the Revolution. The corporate and proprietary forms were the most general at first, and until 1685, in fact, there were no royal governments in America except in Virginia and New Hampshire. From the standpoint of the Crown, however, there were serious objections to the corporate and proprietary governments, and they gradually fell into disfavor. This was due mainly to the fact that the former possessed rather too much local autonomy to admit of effective royal control, while the latter had certain inherent defects in the nature of their form of organization that led to prolonged controversies and embarrassments to the royal interests.[4]

During the last years of the Stuart period, therefore, a policy looking toward the establishment of a more effective royal control over the colonies was adopted. In pursuance of the new policy one colony after another was deprived of its charter, often on mere technical grounds, by means of the writ of *quo warranto* instituted by the Attorney-General. The result was that by 1729 all of the colonies except four (Pennsylvania, Maryland, Connecticut, and Rhode Island) had been brought directly under royal control, and the colony of Georgia, founded after this date, suffered the same fate in 1752. It is but fair to say, however, that in making this change the Crown was not always animated by a spirit of hostility to the liberties of the colonists, but its action was adopted partly in the interests of stricter enforcement of the laws and the establishment of a more efficient government. In the place of the liberal charter originally granted Massachusetts, and under which it had existed for nearly three-quarters of a century as a

[3] See his article in the " Political Science Quarterly," vol. ii.; also his " American Colonies in the Seventeenth Century," vol. i. pp. 28–29. Professor Osgood shows that the term " charter " cannot be used to describe a form of government, that it signifies nothing as to internal organization, and that such a term relates only to the method of origin. Moreover, the proprietary colonies also had charters, and the royal colonies were, so far as internal organization was concerned, essentially the same as the proprietary colonies.

[4] E. B. Greene, " The Provincial Governor," pp. 11–15; see also the author's later and more comprehensive work. " Provincial America," chs. iii. and iv.

practically self-governing commonwealth, a less liberal instrument was substituted in 1691, which virtually reduced the colony to the position of a royal province. Connecticut successfully warded off all attacks upon its charter and continued alone with Rhode Island to enjoy virtual self-government throughout the entire colonial period, the liberal charters of both being retained, in fact, as constitutions long after the two colonies had become commonwealths of the American Union. As colonies they occupied a class by themselves and rarely had cause of complaint against the colonial policy of the mother country.

On the whole, there was a striking similarity in the forms of political organization prevailing in the several colonies. In each there was a governor, who was the chief executive of the colony, a legislature consisting of a council and a popular assembly and a judiciary. The governor was chosen in the self-governing commonwealths of Connecticut and Rhode Island by popular vote; in the so-called royal colonies he was appointed by the Crown, usually upon the recommendation of the Board of Trade; and in the so-called proprietary provinces by the proprietor with the approval of the Crown. The methods by which appointments to colonial governorships were secured were often corrupt and dishonorable, and not infrequently non-residents of poor character, persons broken in fortune, or individuals who had become political outcasts at home were sent over to govern in America and incidentally to recover their lost prestige and fortune.[5]

The tenure of the governor was usually stated in his commission to be at the king's pleasure; the average term in Massachusetts, after the new charter of 1691, being about eight years. Life commissions such as that granted to Lord Delaware were rare. The territorial jurisdiction of the governor sometimes included several colonies, as was the case with Sir Edmund Andros, who in 1688 was made governor of New England, New Jersey, and New York, and of the Earl of Bellomont, who in 1697 became governor of Massachusetts, New York, and New Hampshire.

The governor's salary was larger in proportion than at the present time, to enable him to maintain a semi-regal dignity, as the representative of the Crown. In addition to a stipulated salary he received fees and perquisites of various kinds and sometimes a

---

[5] Greene, " The Provincial Governor," p. 47.

share of fines and forfeitures, or a percentage of the property of persons dying intestate.

The legal position of the governor in the royal colonies was of a two-fold character: he was the chief executive of the colony and the resident agent of the home government. As the representative of the Crown he recommended to the colonial assembly legislation which the Crown desired to have enacted, kept the home government informed of the condition of the province and of its needs, transmitted statutes, records of legislative proceedings and other documents, and exerted himself to prevent the passage of laws injurious to the interests of the Crown and the mother country. The organ through which the governor communicated with the home government was the "Board of Trade," or the "Lords of Trade and Plantations," as it was called. This board was created by an Order in Council in 1696 for "promoting the trade of the Kingdom and for inspecting and improving his majesty's plantations in America and elsewhere." It examined the royal instructions intended to be sent to the governors and recommended alterations where changes seemed desirable; to it colonial governors made regular reports; it recommended to the Crown suitable persons for appointment as governors or councilors; made an annual report of the condition of the colonies; and exercised general supervision over colonial administration.

The powers of the royal governors were embodied in their commissions and the instructions which were issued to them from time to time, or were drawn by implication from the vice-regal character of the governor's position. Besides the powers expressly conferred by the commission or letter of instructions, they inherited various traditions of the royal prerogative, such for example, as the custom of approving the choice of the speaker by the assembly, which was not always a mere formality as in England, administering oaths of allegiance, and other similar functions. As the military representative of the king the governor commanded the local militia, conducted campaigns against the Indians, constructed fortifications, declared martial law, and, as vice-admiral, had the right to grant letters of marque and reprisal and erect admiralty courts.

The power of the Crown in matters of executive clemency naturally passed to his representative in the colonies, and so we find that as a general rule the governor could grant pardons to offenders, except in cases of treason or impeachment and sometimes of murder.   Included under this head also was the power to remit fines and forfeitures.   In the relations of the colony with the Indian tribes, as well as the relation of one colony to another, the governor was the representative of the Crown.   In the domain of internal administration a source of great power was the right to create offices and appoint their incumbents.   In Massachusetts, however, the higher administrative officers were appointed by the General Court, as the legislature was called, while in some of the other colonies they were appointed directly by the Crown. But in all the colonies the governor appointed the local judicial, administrative and military officers.

The financial powers of the governor were large at first, but steadily decreased with the growth of the popular assembly, which took away from him important powers and reserved them for itself.   Among the powers of the governor under the head of legislation were those of summoning, proroguing, adjourning and dissolving the legislature, the right to recommend measures for enactment into law, and sometimes the right to initiate them in the assembly.   In case of revenue bills, however, the governor gradually lost the right of initiation on account of the objection raised by the popular assemblies.   The home government usually required that all acts passed by the provincial assemblies, and approved by the governor, should be sent to England within three months after their passage for approval or disallowance by the Crown, although in Pennsylvania the period was five years.   If not expressly disallowed, they were to be enforced as valid laws.   The governor was forbidden to approve certain measures, which unduly favored the interests of the colony against those of the Crown.   The requirement that laws enacted by the colonial legislature should be sent home for examination was so often evaded that the royal restrictions upon the power of the governor to give his assent to bills were not strictly enforced.   Among the miscellaneous powers of the governor were the right to establish ports, markets, and fairs, grant lands, issue charters of incorporation, make appointments to certain ecclesiastical benefices, grant marriage licenses, take care of the great seal, exercise a censorship over the press and oversee the Established Church.[6]   In most of the colonies there

[6] For a scholarly discussion of the powers of the Colonial Governor, see Greene; "The Provincial Governor," pp. 91-165.

was a lieutenant governor, who discharged the duties of the governor during his absence from the colony.

In every colony there was a council which acted as an advisory body to the governor, sometimes shared the executive power with him, usually served as the upper house of the legislature and frequently acted as the highest court of appeal in the colony. There was a long list of executive acts which could not be performed without the advice and consent of the council, such as calling the legislature, the erection of courts, the declaration of martial law, and the making of appointments. The number of councilors varied from three in Maryland to twenty-eight in Massachusetts, the usual number being twelve. In the royal colonies the council was appointed by the governor, sometimes by the Crown. It was appointed by the proprietor on the nomination of the governor in the proprietary colonies, and in Massachusetts by the General Court. Where the executive power was vested in the governor and council jointly, which was not infrequently the case, there were often bickerings and clashes of authority between the two. The governor often showed a disposition to treat the council merely as an advisory restraining body rather than a coördinate and equal authority, a procedure which the council strongly resented. During the early colonial period the governor claimed and exercised the right to sit with the council when it was serving as the upper house of the legislature, and to make motions and vote as other members, but the assembly objected and the right was gradually lost either by act of the Crown or by act of the legislature, as in South Carolina, where the presence of the governor during the debates was declared to be of an " unparliamentary nature," in consequence of which the house refused to proceed with its business until he withdrew.

The lower house of the legislature, variously called the Assembly, the House of Delegates, the House of Commons, and the General Court, was chosen by the people, but the franchise was so narrow as to be hardly entitled to be called popular suffrage. Besides higher property qualifications, church membership or other religious tests were frequently required. In structure the legislature was bicameral in every colony except Pennsylvania and Georgia, where the single chambered body was preferred, but soon after the adoption of the Federal Constitution these two colonies **changed** to the bicameral form. The first representative assembly in America was called in Virginia in 1619 and was known as the House of Burgesses. The principle of representation was soon adopted in other colonies, as possessing distinct advantages over that of the pure democracy. It was introduced in Massachusetts in 1634, in Maryland in 1647, and in Georgia in 1752.

Between the governor, who represented the royal interests, and the legislative assembly, which represented the interests of the people, there were frequent conflicts of authority which led to important constitutional results in the relations between the executive and the legislature. The governor, as the agent of the king, was anxious to see that the interests of the Crown were advanced, that the dependence of the colonies upon the king was perpetuated, and that, in short, whatever was the king's due should be forthcoming regardless of popular interests. But it was utterly impossible for the governor to protect the imperial powers and maintain the royal prerogative intact without encroaching upon the popular interests, as they came to be understood by the colonists themselves, and the defense of these latter interests against royal encroachment virtually fell to the popularly elected legislative assemblies. In the contest which ensued they had the main advantage as a result of their power to grant or withhold supplies. But over against this was the power of the governor to prorogue or dissolve a refractory assembly—a power which was frequently resorted to, but seldom with permanent effect. The governor's dependence upon the assembly for his salary placed him, of course, virtually at the mercy of that body.

Very early in the history of the American colonies the Crown adopted the policy of throwing the burden of supporting the royal government upon the colonies, and the legislatures had very generally persisted in making the supply grants for the civil list annual instead of permanent, as the Crown urged and ordered, for they realized that if the governors ceased to be dependent upon the legislature for their salaries they would be beyond legislative control. This gave the assembly an effective weapon and it was used with success. Sometimes the legislature would refuse to consider appropriation bills for the payment of the governor's salary until he had signed certain acts which had been passed and which the assembly wished approved by that executive. The system became practically one of bargain and sale, the people buying from the governor for cash such laws as they needed. The custom grew

WILLIAM PENN'S SECOND VISIT TO HIS COLONY, 1699

Drawing by Howard Pyle

—page 112

up in some colonies of presenting the governor with a purse of a thousand dollars or more at the close of each session, providing he agreed with the assembly; otherwise it was withheld.[7]

The assembly soon found other means of limiting the power of the executive. Thus, in making appropriations of money, it directed the purposes for which the money should be spent. In military matters this enabled the assembly to direct in a large measure the course of military operations, leaving the governor little more to do than carry out its orders. The next step was for the assembly to claim the right to appoint the officers who were charged with the collection, custody, and disbursement of the public funds. The right of the assembly in this matter was soon established, and thus again the executive prerogative was reduced. In the course of time the appointment and control of other offices was transferred from the governor to the legislature, so that by the time of the Revolution the governor retained but a shadow of his former great appointing power. As already stated, the governor frequently exercised his power of dissolution to prevent refractory assemblies from encroaching upon his prerogative, but it was usually in vain, because he could not administer the government without the coöperation of the legislature, and a new one was not likely to be more subservient than the one dissolved. The result, therefore, of the long struggle between the legislature and the governor for power was the triumph of the former, just as the somewhat similar struggle between king and Parliament in England had resulted in the victory of the Parliament.

The colonial judiciary began with the justice of the peace, who was usually appointed by the governor for short terms and whose jurisdiction included the trial of petty civil cases. Next above the justice court was the county court, which tried more important civil cases and minor criminal cases, and which frequently performed various administrative duties relating to highways, case of the poor, and like things. The crown of the judicial system was a supreme court to hear cases of appeal and exercise original jurisdiction in certain cases; but appeals were allowed to be taken to the Privy Council of England. The erection of courts of justice was usually one of the prerogatives of the governor, as was also the appointment of the judges. In many of the colonies the terms of the judges were fixed at good behavior; but the Crown

[7] "Franklin's Works," Bigelow edition, vol. iii. pp. 311 *et seq.*

came to discourage this practice and ultimately to forbid it for the reason that life terms made the judges too independent of the Crown. The king, therefore, gave instructions to the governors that judicial commissions be granted " during pleasure " only, and in 1761 notified them that a violation of this instruction would be a cause for removal. Likewise the assemblies insisted on paying the judges' salaries by annual grants as a future means of controlling them. If the Crown both appointed the judges and allowed them permanent salaries, the subserviency of the judiciary to the Crown would be complete and the decisions would all be Crown decisions.

The colonies were of course unrepresented in the imperial Parliament, and it was this fact that subsequently led them to protest when the mother country undertook to impose taxes upon them. They bore, however, the expense of local administration, and sometimes upon the request of the Crown made voluntary grants for imperial purposes. In matters of interest to the empire, Parliament legislated directly for the colonies; but unless expressly mentioned in the act no parliamentary statute applied to them. Nevertheless, the colonies were supposed to enjoy all the rights of natural-born Englishmen. Being without representation in Parliament, the colonies adopted the practice of maintaining resident agents in England to look after their political and commercial interests. Just before the Revolution, when the controversy between the colonies and the mother country was ripening, the duties of these agents became very important and they gradually acquired a *quasi* diplomatic character. They were sometimes called upon to give testimony before Parliamentary committees and frequently appeared before the Board of Trade in the interests of the colonies. Not infrequently several colonies employed the same agent to represent them at London. Thus Benjamin Franklin acted in this capacity for Massachusetts, Pennsylvania, New Jersey, and several other colonies at the same time.

The system of local government in the colonies possessed less uniformity than did the central governments. They were, in fact, three general types of local government, namely, that which prevailed in New England, that of the middle colonies and that of the southern colonies. In New England the town with its unpretentious church and schoolhouse was the unit of local government, and was represented in the legislature. Instead of electing representatives to lay their taxes, enact local regulations and attend to various other matters relating to religion, care of highways, the poor, and the like, the people themselves assembled in town-meeting and enacted their own local laws and voted the taxes. The local government of New England was in other words a pure democracy. Originally all male inhabitants of legal age were allowed to participate in its deliberations. The town-meeting, summoned by the constable under authority of the selectmen's warrant, was usually held in the church or "meeting-house," and non-attendance was punished by a fine. The frequency with which meetings were held must have involved a serious encroachment upon the ordinary business of the community.[8] The meeting, once assembled, was organized by the election of a moderator or presiding officer, the town clerk always as *ex-officio* secretary. No one could speak without the permission of the moderator, and fines were imposed for disorderly conduct. The principal officers elected at the meeting were the selectmen, the number varying from three to nine, who looked after the enforcement of local regulations and the general supervision of the poor of the town. Other officers were the town clerk, assessors, treasurer, constables, school-committees, overseers of the poor, fence-viewers, pound-keepers, field-drivers, sealers of weights and measures, and surveyors. In addition to this rather imposing list of officials there were various other functionaries in some of the New England towns, such as inspectors of hides, fish and brick, measurers of various articles, preservers of deer, deer-reeves, wood-corders, rebukers of boys, swine-yokers, and ringers, overseers of chimneys, persons to keep dogs out of church, branders of cattle, and even town fishers, town grubbers, and town doctors. Boston, in 1690–1691, had ten constables, seven surveyors of highways, four clerks of the market, four sealers of leather, six hog reeves, three criers, sixteen wood-corders, eight overseers of wood-corders, four overseers of chimneys, and thirty-six tithingmen.[9] The county in New England as a political unit played an insignificant role, and that is true to-day, local government being carried on mainly through the agency of town-meeting, while the county survives rather as a judicial and elective district[10]

[8] See Howard, "Local Constitutional History of the United States," p. 62; also McKinley, "The Suffrage Franchise in the English Colonies," p. 361.
[9] Howard, "Local Constitutional History of the United States," p. 99.
[10] Goodnow, "Comparative Administrative Law," vol. ii. ch. ii.

The southern colonies differed from those of New England quite as much in their local polity as in their social and economic life. Here the pure democracy of New England never gained a foothold; it was in fact impracticable, if not impossible. Instead of populous, compact towns, as in New England, there were large plantations scattered throughout the colony and cultivated mainly by slave labor. This, with other causes, both economic and social, interfered with the natural growth of towns and villages, and consequently made necessary a more representative type of local government than that which prevailed in New England. Instead of the town, therefore, the parish became the unit of local government. The governing body of the parish was the vestry, composed of twelve men, at first popularly elected, but eventually becoming a close corporation with power to fill its own vacancies.[11] It appointed the local administrative officers, the principal of which were the two churchwardens, and levied the taxes, but was not, as in New England, the unit of representation in the legislature, that unit being the county. About the middle of the seventeenth century most of the secular duties of the vestry in Virginia were taken over by the county court, leaving the vestry merely ecclesiastical functions. At the head of the county was a lieutenant who corresponded in a rough way to the Lord Lieutenant in England, was a sort of deputy to the governor and bore the honorary title of " Colonel." He was the commander of the county militia, and as a member of the governor's council exercised other important non-military duties. The chief civil officer of the county was the sheriff, who was appointed by the governor upon the nomination of the county justices. He was collector of the taxes, acted as treasurer, executed the judgments of the courts, and performed many other important duties. Other local officers were the justices of the peace, usually eight in number, for each county, who, like the English justices, were probably the most important of all the local officials. They were not only judicial magistrates, but administrators as well. In the former capacity they held courts usually four times a year, after the manner of the English quarter sessions, while in the latter capacity they levied the county taxes, passed local regulations and acted as the general administrative authority of the county in the management of a great variety of interests, such as the care of highways, the repairing of bridges,

[11] Howard, "Local Constitutional History of the United States," p. 119.

and the appointment of officers. The justices were appointed by the governor and held office during his pleasure. The Virginia system of local government was of course wholly undemocratic, quite as much so as the Virginia social order. In the other southern colonies there were variations from the Virginia type, but the broad outlines were the same.

In the middle colonies the system of local government was in the nature of a compromise between the New England town meeting and the southern county commission. Here the county was neither the supreme local unit, as in the south, nor a mere survival as in New England. In New York the county was divided into townships, each of which elected a supervisor to represent it on the county board of supervisors, which authority was charged with the general management of the affairs of the county.

The townships, however, did not lose their individuality as local units of government. For a time purely township affairs were even regulated by a town meeting, but rather rudimentary in form, as compared with that of New England. In Pennsylvania the form of local government was very similar to that of New York; that is, it was administered by a county board of commissioners. Here, however, the commissioners were chosen from the county at large and did not therefore represent a particular township. But each township had its own local government and cared for such matters as local police, the assessment and collection of taxes, the maintenance and repair of highways, and the like. The system of local government in the middle colonies was more democratic than that of the south, yet it did not go to the other extreme of the New England pure democracy. It was well adapted to secure efficiency and local autonomy and has come to be adopted in the great majority of the States of the Union.

Chapter VI

COLONIAL LIFE AND INSTITUTIONS
1606-1776

I

POPULATION, RACES AND CLASSES

AT the beginning of the eighteenth century the total population of the thirteen colonies was estimated by Bancroft at
262,000. At the outbreak of the Revolution it was between 2,000,000 and 2,500,000 inhabitants, of whom not less than
400,000 were African slaves.[1] It ranged from about 8,000 in
Georgia to over 300,000 in Virginia; Massachusetts and Pennsylvania being next to Virginia the most populous States.
The English were everywhere the dominant race, although
there was a large Dutch element in New York. There was
a sprinkling of Dutch, Swedes and Germans in New Jersey and Delaware, many Germans and some Welsh, Dutch
and Irish in Pennsylvania, as well as a large element of
Scotch-Irish. Pennsylvania became the distributing center for
Germans and Scotch-Irish. From her borders streams of emigrants flowed south and southwest down the valleys of the Alleghanies into western Maryland, Virginia and the Carolinas, and
over the mountains into the country afterwards erected into the
States of Kentucky and Tennessee. At the outbreak of the Revolution the Germans constituted about one-third of the population
of Pennsylvania, or a total of about 100,000. Indeed, the German
immigrants were so numerous that the English authorities felt

---

[1] Bancroft's " History of the United States," vol. vi. p. 390. The estimate
of the Board of Trade was somewhat larger than that of Bancroft. An estimate of the white population made in 1783 for the purpose of assessment placed
the number at 2,389,300. No census was taken until 1790, at which time the
population was found to be 3,900,000. The least populous State, according to
the census of 1790, was Delaware, with 59,094 inhabitants, and the most populous was Virginia, with 747,600.

alarmed for the safety of the colony. As a whole they were an honest, industrious, religious people, so conservative and tenacious of their customs and language that whole communities of their descendants to-day speak a dialect commonly known as Pennsylvania Dutch.

The Scotch-Irish element, as it is popularly called, consisted of Presbyterians from Ulster, Ireland. Here their ancestors had made their home for generations, but driven by English oppression and religious persecutions, they began to flock to America about the opening of the eighteenth century. It is estimated that before the Revolution half the Presbyterian population of Ulster had emigrated to America. Some went to New England, some to Virginia; but by far the greater part settled in Pennsylvania, and from there spread southward into the Carolinas, Georgia, Kentucky and Tennessee. By the time of the Revolution they practically constituted about one-sixth of the total population, and their descendants have played an important part in the history of the country. There were many French Huguenots in New York, the Carolinas and Georgia, and some of them in almost every colony. They were an industrious, thrifty people, who came over in large numbers after the revocation of the Edict of Nantes in 1685, and a number of their descendants occupied prominent stations during the Revolution. Except for some Scotch-Irish in New Hampshire and some Huguenots in Massachusetts and Rhode Island, New England was purely English.[2] There were some small groups of Jews, Finns, Salzburgers and Moravians in various parts of the country, but they were so inconsiderable in number as to be without effect upon the general character of the population.

The population at this time was mainly rural, and in the south wholly so. The largest city probably in America was Philadelphia, which in 1760 had a population of 25,000. Boston had about the same number and New York some 15,000 to 18,000. Boston and Philadelphia were then among the largest towns outside of London in the king's dominions, ranking with Bristol and Liverpool. In 1790 only about three persons in a hundred lived in cities[3] having a population exceeding 5,000; now the proportion is about thirty-five out of one hundred; from half a dozen cities with

[2] Read Greene, "Immigration and Expansion," in "Provincial America," ch. xiv.

[3] Webber, "Growth of Cities," p. 23.

populations exceeding 8,000 each we have grown to be a country having not less than 545 such cities.[4]

In addition to the white inhabitants every colony had a more or less considerable negro population, practically all of which at this time was held in slavery. By far the greater number of blacks, however, were in the southern colonies, where they were well adapted to the warm climate, and where slave labor was profitable, if not indispensable, to the cultivation of the great tobacco, rice and indigo plantations. Here the institution of slavery throve and grew until by the invention of Eli Whitney it became an important factor in the southern economic system.

In the colonies of the north the number of slaves was comparatively small and they were held mainly as house servants. Neither the climate nor the industries of this region was favorable to negro slavery, and so, after 1750, the number rather declined than increased. Some of the colonies had very early foreseen the evils of a large slave population and had undertaken to restrict the importation of negroes from Africa; but these attempts were vetoed by the Crown on the ground that it interfered with a lucrative trade in which the Crown was pecuniarily interested as a stockholder of the Royal African Company, which had a monopoly of supplying the American colonies with slaves. Colonial governors were charged with furthering the interests of the company, and by 1695 the traffic in negroes was considered the best and most profitable branch of British commerce.[5] It is stated upon the authority of a careful investigator that in the twenty years from 1713 to 1733 not less than 15,000 slaves were annually imported into America by the English, of whom from one-third to one-half went to North American colonies. From 1680 to 1688 the African Company sent 249 ships to Africa and carried away to America 46,396 slaves after losing over 14,000 in the middle passage.[6]

It was not until after the achievement of independence that the colonies were free to adopt restrictive measures against this abominable traffic. In New England, where general conditions were unfavorable to the growth of slavery, the number of slaves was inconsiderable, and being employed mainly as domestic servants they were not as a rule harshly treated and were generally

[4] See "Census Bulletin," 1900, No. 4.
[5] Weeden, "Social and Economic History of New England," vol. ii. p. 451.
[6] DuBois, "Suppression of the African Slave Trade," p. 5.

instructed in the art of reading. After the slave population became relatively large as compared with the white population, the colonial assemblies began to pass drastic police regulations intended to secure the obedience and good behavior of the blacks and to prevent servile insurrection. The fear of slave outbreaks was never absent from the mind of the white man, and, indeed, the fear was not without foundation, for as early as 1687 an uprising of rebellious blacks occurred in northern Virginia, creating great terror and alarm among the whites. The slave code in consequence was made especially severe in Virginia and South Carolina, where the black population was large; but such laws, severe as they may seem to us now, were not condemned by the public sentiment of the day.

At law the slave was a mere chattel like any other personal property, and could be sold, hired or otherwise disposed of at the pleasure of his master. He could not leave the plantation without a permit, under penalty of a certain number of lashes, nor was he allowed to carry arms, keep dogs or own property of consequence. Except in rare instances he was never taught to read or write; indeed the teaching of slaves was generally forbidden by law. It was the undoubted right of the owner to punish his slave for disobedience, and in case of resistance he might take his life, for ordinarily there could be no " malice aforethought " in destroying one's own property. However, the willful killing of a slave was treated as murder, in the criminal codes, but it was not always easy to convict in such a case, because a white jury was loath to return a verdict of guilty against a white offender. Slave testimony was of course not admissible in the courts, if either party was a white man.

Despite the severity of the slave code, the unfortunate blacks were fed and clothed, and their health and comfort cared for; everywhere they were allowed to own gardens and poultry, and probably, except on some of the large plantations, they were not overworked. Their condition was much better than in Africa, and we have reason to believe that they were happy and contented. While there was a strong sentiment against the slave trade, our forefathers could see little wrong in holding the ignorant African in slavery. It rather seemed to them to be a blessing to the slave that he should be cared for and supported by the white man, and given the advantages of a Christian civilization. Shiftless and improvident, his own welfare required the stimulus and the incentive of the superior race. Contrary to this view, however, was the sentiment entertained by the Pennsylvania Quakers, or Friends, as they preferred to be called, who, before the close of the seventeenth century, had started an agitation against slavery on moral grounds.[7] Two of their foremost anti-slavery agitators were Woolman and Benezet, who by their speeches and writings aroused among the Friends a strong sentiment against slavery and led many of them to set their negroes free.[8] After the Revolution the Quaker hostility to slavery became more general and they were the first people to petition Congress for the enactment of legislation to restrict the spread of the institution. In Massachusetts an anti-slavery sentiment slowly grew up, the first anti-slavery advocate of that colony being the able and well-known Judge Samuel Sewall, who as early as the year 1700 published a pamphlet attacking the institution of slavery as inconsistent with the teachings of the Bible, as well as contrary to the principles of economic expediency.[9]

Next above the slave in the ascending social scale was the class of indented white servants, so called from a written instrument called an indenture which defined their obligations to their masters. Superior to the slaves in race, they were nevertheless an inferior class, consisting often of convicted criminals transported to America by the mother country and dumped upon the colonists, or of voluntary emigrants representing the idle and worthless from the larger English cities.[10] Others were of shiftless, impoverished characters who sold themselves into servitude for a term of years, sometimes as a means of paying the cost of their passage across the Atlantic. Still others consisted of children kidnaped from the streets of London or sold by inhuman parents. Their legal and social status was but little better than that of the slaves. Strict laws were enacted by the colonial assemblies to hold them in servitude, and they were subjected to the same degrading punishments. They were frequently illiterate, degraded,

---

[7] See Hart, "Contemporaries," vol. ii. p. 291.
[8] Bancroft, "History of the United States," vol. ii. p. 398.
[9] Weeden, "Economic and Social History of New England," vol. i. p. 429.
[10] "American Historical Review," vol. ii. p. 12. Some writers have estimated the number of convicted criminals sent to the colonies by the British Government at from ten thousand to twenty-five thousand, most of them being sent to Maryland and the middle colonies. See Scharf, "History of Maryland," vol. i. p. 371.

worthless, often despised even by the negroes. They were especially numerous in Pennsylvania and Virginia, and in the latter colony exerted a deteriorating influence. They were, it is said, the source of that class of Southern society known later as " poor white trash."

Next in the ascending social scale were the merchants, traders, shopkeepers and small farmers, who constituted, especially in the New England colonies, the substantial element of the population. They were of good English stock, were socially respected, and from their ranks a great leader occasionally rose by dint of genius and character. In some of the southern colonies, notably Virginia and South Carolina, this middle class hardly existed as a distinct group. Here there were only two well-defined classes, namely, large plantation owners and slaves.

Finally, at the top of the social pyramid was the aristocratic class, which in all the colonies was well differentiated from the lower classes. In New England this class consisted of the clergy, the magistrates, the professional men and those who were " wellborn." Here the aristocracy was more largely official than elsewhere, and was based on education and birth rather than on wealth. Although politically New England was the home of democracy, socially class distinctions were very sharp, and matters of social precedence were much more important than now. Until late in the eighteenth century the people were carefully seated in the churches according to social standing, while the names of Harvard students were arranged in the catalogue according to a similar method.[11] While substantially all the offices were open to the middle classes, the more important ones were reserved for the aristocrats of education. good birth and distinguished ancestry.

In the southern colonies the upper class consisted of the wealthy planters and large land holders. They occupied much the same position as the landed gentry in England; indeed, the Virginia planter had much in common, as regards his dress, manners and habits, with the English landlord. Surrounded by their slaves they lived like lords, on great plantations which sometimes extended for miles along the river banks. Not infrequently Virginia planters had their own wharfs, at which vessels from the Old World arrived and departed at irregular intervals. They were of the

[11] Weeden, "Economic and Social History of New England," vol. i. pp. 280, 289, 417.

best English stock and possessed the virtues as well as the faults common to landed aristocracies. With a high sense of honor, chivalrous, hospitable and proud, they held the chief offices of state, and in the struggle for independence furnished a large number of able leaders to the patriotic cause. It was from this aristocracy that the new Republic drew four of its first five Presidents, and a good many of its other leading statesmen and diplomats.

In the middle colonies, as in New England and the southern colonies, the differentiation of society into classes was clearly marked. In New York the existence of the patroon system gave society something of a feudal cast. The patroons owned vast estates along the Hudson and lived after the manner of feudal barons in spacious mansions built of imported brick or stone, and handsomely decorated and furnished. Notable families of this class were the Van Rensselaers, the Van Cortlandts, the Livingstons and the Schuylers, all prominent leaders in the political and social affairs of the colony. Their estates were cultivated by tenants, who looked to the patroon for protection and justice and who paid him rent at stated periods, patronized his grist mill and wine press and performed various semi-feudal services. The proprietor regularly held manorial courts and at stated intervals gave his tenants a great feast at the mansion. The most famous of these estates was that of Stephen Van Rensselaer, who owned 600,000 acres of land in the neighborhood of Albany.[12]

Below the aristocratic class in New York were the small land owners and tradesmen, a thrifty and well-to-do element of both Dutch and English stock. Then there were some 20,000 slaves, largely a remnant of Dutch occupation, and comprising about one-sixth of the population. Their status was substantially the same as the slaves in the southern colonies. A threatened slave insurrection in New York City in 1711 led to a massacre by the whites of nineteen negroes, and again, in 1741, in consequence of what was known as the "Negro Plot" formed to burn the city, a number of the blacks were seized and twenty-one of them were put to death after trial, some by hanging, others by burning, and still others by breaking on the wheel.[13]

In Pennsylvania, New Jersey and Delaware class distinctions were less sharply drawn than in either New York, New England

12 Fiske, "Dutch and Quaker Colonies," vol. i. pp. 265–269.
13 Lodge, "Short History of the English Colonies," p. 322.

or in the southern colonies. So far as there was an aristocratic class in Pennsylvania and Delaware it was made up of the descendants of Penn's principal followers and of the landed gentry; but it was not homogeneous and compact, nor was it separated from the middle class by the same impassible barriers which existed elsewhere.[14]

The distinctive feature of Pennsylvania society was the presence of the Quaker element, with their quaint habits of dress and peculiar customs. Racially and religiously there was unusual diversity. Besides English, there were Germans and Irish in large numbers, Scotch-Irish, Welsh and Swedes, while Lutherans, Presbyterians, Dunkards, Dutch Calvinists, Moravians, Baptists and Roman Catholics were some of the religious sects which played an important part in the life of the colony.[15] Naturally there was friction and some strife where so much racial and religious diversity existed. The Germans and Scotch-Irish could not live harmoniously together in the same community, nor were the Quakers and Scotch-Irish ever on good terms in political matters. Slaves there were in Pennsylvania, New Jersey and Delaware, but their number was not large, probably not exceeding one-fourth of the entire population,[16] and the practice of slave-holding was discountenanced by the unwavering hostility of the Quakers. Much more numerous was the class of indented servants, which consisted mainly of Irish and German redemptioners who sold themselves to pay their passage, or of transported convicts.

II

INDUSTRIES, OCCUPATIONS AND PROFESSIONS

The occupations and professions of the colonists were much more lacking in variety than at the present day. The most general of the occupations was agriculture. At first the chief industry in the New England colonies, it gradually declined in relative importance on account of the inadaptability of the soil and climate. Here the soil was rugged and barren, while the seasons were too short to grow the great staples that were raised with

[14] Lodge, "Short History of the English Colonies," p. 240.
[15] Read Fiske, "Dutch and Quaker Colonies," vol. ii. ch. xvii.
[16] Bancroft, "History of the United States," vol. ii. p. 391.

profit in the more southerly latitudes. Nevertheless, grain was raised in considerable quantities for export, mainly to Europe and the West Indies. Stock-raising was also an important industry and large quantities of cattle were likewise exported to the West Indies. Of scarcely less value was the trade in furs and peltries with the Indians. As the unsuitability of the country for agriculture became more and more apparent, the people turned their attention to manufacturing and maritime industries. At first manufacturing was conducted on a small scale, the articles produced being chiefly textile fabrics, iron, nails, shoes, and similar articles intended for domestic use. The setting up of slitting mills being forbidden by act of Parliament, the iron industry was greatly handicapped.

It was not until after the Revolution that the present supremacy of New England as a manufacturing section began. Lumber and grist mills were common, linens and coarse woolens were made, particularly by the Scotch-Irish of New Hampshire and Massachusetts, while hats and paper in small quantities were manufactured in various places. Fishing, shipbuilding and commerce became the most important of New England industries.[17] The fishery industry in particular afforded an occupation for thousands of bold and hardy men who braved the rough weather and perilous seas to make voyages to Newfoundland, Labrador and other places in pursuit of cod, whale and mackerel. As early as 1750 there were employed in the mackerel fishery and other small catch for the West Indian market 200 vessels; in cod fishing, 400 vessels, and in the pursuit of whales on the North American coast, 100 vessels.[18]

In 1764 New England employed 45,880 tons of shipping and 6,000 men in the cod fishing industry, and at the outbreak of the Revolution Nantucket alone had 150 vessels of 15,000 tons employed in the various fisheries. The output of the whale fishery was 45,000 barrels of sperm, 8,500 barrels of oil and 7,500 pounds of bone.[19] It was the fishery industry which laid the foundation of the greatness of Massachusetts, and it has continued to this day to be one of the sources of the industrial strength of this progressive commonwealth.

[17] Weeden, " Social and Economic History of New England," vol. i. p. 115.
[18] Ibid., vol. i. pp. 359–360.
[19] Ibid., vol. ii. p. 748.

Very soon after the planting of the New England colonies shipbuilding on a small scale was begun, the coasting trade was presently monopolized by New England vessels, and at the time of the outbreak of the Revolution an extensive and profitable commerce with the West Indies and with Europe was being carried on mainly by ships built in New England yards. Dried fish, beef, pork, oil, lumber, staves, hay, grain and cattle and horses were carried to the West Indies, and exchanged for sugar, molasses, coffee, cotton, salt and other tropical products.

By the British Sugar Act, passed in 1733, the American colonies were practically forbidden to trade with any of the West Indies not under British control, but the act was systematically evaded by the colonists. Thus, in 1763, of the 15,000 hogsheads of molasses which were imported into Massachusetts from the West Indies, only 500 came from the British Islands.[20] Rhode Island brought in 14,000 hogsheads in one year, only 2,500 of which were imported in conformity to the law.[21] The molasses thus imported was not infrequently taken to New England, converted into rum, which in turn was shipped to Newfoundland, along with tar and provisions, and exchanged for fish. The latter article was carried to southern Europe to supply the large Catholic demand, and exchanged for goods needed in America. A common practice also was to ship cargoes of rum to the west coast of Africa, where it was easily exchanged for slaves, and these were brought to America and sold to the Southern planters or carried to the West Indies and exchanged for more rum. In 1750 Massachusetts could boast of sixty-three distilleries, while Rhode Island had thirty. Of all the articles of colonial traffic rum was the most important. Negroes, fish, lumber, vessels, all felt the impulse of its power. It was merchandise on the coast of Guinea, as well as on the banks of Newfoundland, and furnished cargoes for about 900 vessels. Newport, Rhode Island, became the chief center of the rum-distilling, negro-importing business. It was the port of clearance for hundreds of vessels bound for the West Indies or for the Gold Coast. From a port of the third-class it rapidly grew to rival Boston. Governor Stephen Hopkins, one of the signers of the Declaration of Independence, stated that for more than thirty years prior to 1764 Rhode Island sent to Africa every year eighteen

[20] Weeden, "Social and Economic History of New England," vol. ii. p. 754.
[21] *Ibid.*, vol. ii. p. 756.

vessels carrying 1,800 hogsheads of rum, which was exchanged for slaves. This article by reason of its cheapness completely displaced French brandies in the Gold Coast traffic, and gave the Americans, the advantage in the slave trade. Among those who engaged in the African traffic was Peter Faneuil, the builder of Faneuil Hall, Boston.

In the middle colonies agriculture was the chief industry, except in New York and Pennsylvania, where the traffic in furs and peltries was of considerable importance. The soil was better adapted for farming in these colonies, and consequently agriculture was carried on with more success and profit than in New England. The principal staple was wheat, while cattle and other live-stock were raised in considerable quantities for export to England and the West Indies. In New York the most profitable industry was the traffic with the Indians in furs and peltries. Shrewd and adventurous traders, supplied with trinkets, novelties, firearms and rum, met the Indians at Albany and exchanged their cheap wares for valuable furs, which were in turn sold in Manhattan at a large profit.

The town of New York soon became an important center of trade and commerce, although it was not until the nineteenth century that it passed Philadelphia and Boston in population and importance. Before the outbreak of the Revolution the iron industry, which was subsequently to become a source of enormous wealth to Pennsylvania, had already made a beginning, although it was greatly hampered by the restrictive trade acts of the mother country. The first iron furnace was set up in 1720 and by 1750 the annual export of pig iron amounted to 3,000 tons.[22]

In the southern colonies agriculture was almost the only occupation of the inhabitants, and the great staples were tobacco, rice and indigo. Cotton was raised in small quantities, but the growing of this plant did not become an important industry until after the invention of the cotton gin. The economic wealth of Virginia lay in the tobacco industry. The colony was dotted with great plantations devoted almost exclusively to the cultivation of this one crop. On account of its importance in the economic life of the colony it was for a time used as currency for the payment of salaries and taxes and the purchase of supplies, while its cultivation was carefully supervised and regulated by the government. No

[22] Lodge, " Short History of the English Colonies," p. 230.

community was probably ever so completely absorbed in the production of any one article. It was the chief subject of export, and in many cases the vessels which carried it to Europe came directly to the wharf of the planter where the cargo was taken aboard. The profits were large and the desire to extend the acreage created a demand for more slaves. By the time of the Revolution not less than 100,000 hogsheads, valued at a million pounds sterling, and requiring about 300 vessels for their transport, were being annually exported from this colony.[23]

Its importance at the time was illustrated by an incident that occurred on the occasion of the visit of a delegation of Virginians to London in 1692 for the purpose of soliciting aid for William and Mary College. Addressing the attorney-general, the spokesman of the delegation called attention to the influence a college for the higher education of the people might exert in the saving of souls. To this allusion the attorney-general bluntly replied, "Souls! damn your souls, raise tobacco!" In South Carolina the cultivation of rice was at first the chief industry of the people. This grain was introduced near the close of the seventeenth century, and by the middle of the following century it occupied almost the same place in the economic and industrial life of the colony as did tobacco in Virginia. In 1770 the lieutenant-governor reported to the English Board of Trade that about 3,000 wagons came to Charleston in one year from the back country loaded with this product. A calculation made in 1768 placed the total value of rice produced in the colony at £500,000.[24] At first exceedingly profitable, it gradually became less so, and was superseded in a large measure by the cultivation of indigo. The cultivation of this latter plant was the chief industry of South Carolina at the time of the Revolution, although the cultivation of cotton was rapidly becoming a close rival. In North Carolina lumber and naval stores, such as tar, pitch and turpentine, were produced largely for export to New England and to Europe, while in all the southern colonies live stock and cereals were raised in large quantities, also for the foreign trade.

Manufactures did not flourish in the southern colonies, for the people found it more profitable to raise the great staples and purchase their necessary articles of manufacture from New Eng-

[23] Lodge, "Short History of the English Colonies," p. 65.
[24] McCrady, "South Carolina under the Royal Government," pp. 388–391.

land or the mother country.   Furthermore, it soon became evident that an industrial system founded on slave labor was ill adapted to the growth of manufacturing, and so the South continued throughout the colonial period, and indeed until very recently, an almost exclusively agricultural section.

The learned professions were comparatively few in all the colonies and played a subordinate part in the intellectual and economic life of the times.   The practice of law as a learned profession hardly existed, and lawyers were generally looked upon with suspicion.[25]   Litigation was rather small in amount, retainers were not large, and the opportunities for distinction few.   Consequently the bar did not attract the best classes of young men. Barristers there were in abundance, but they were frequently sharpers, pettifoggers or adventurers from London, and were largely lacking in that sense of professional honor which is the pride of the American bar to-day.   The qualifications for admission to the bar were few; in fact laymen were frequently allowed to act as attorneys, and the opportunities and facilities for the study of law were meager.   At the beginning of the eighteenth century lawyers were so few that even the most important judicial positions were often filled by men without specific legal training, and this was true in the southern and middle colonies as well as in New England.[26]   Before the outbreak of the Revolution, however, there had come a great improvement in the character of the bar.   Men of high position and talents, college graduates and ambitious young men generally, turned to the legal profession as affording the best opportunity for careers of honorable distinction. Especially in Philadelphia did the bar attain a position of respectability and influence, and the saying, " Smart as a Philadelphia lawyer," was a popular aphorism that has come down to the present day.   It was a Philadelphian, Andrew Hamilton, who rose to the leadership of the colonial bar, his reputation as a barrister even extending to Europe.   In Virginia, Patrick Henry, Thomas Jefferson, George Wythe and John Marshall were already laying the foundations of those remarkable careers which were to add dignity and prestige to the legal profession.

[25] Osgood, " The American Colonies in the Seventeenth Century," vol. ii. p. 434; Lodge, " Short History of English Colonies," p. 53; see also McCrady, " South Carolina Under the Royal Government," p. 459.
[26] Greene, " Provincial America," p. 317.

The medical profession was in but little better repute at this time than that of the law. The practice of medicine was in the crudest state. Quacks and impostors were numerous, and nostrums were a common reliance. Medical knowledge was scant, surgical skill almost unknown and medicinal drugs few. Preparations made from bark and herbs sufficed for ordinary ills, while generous bleeding was supposed to be the first remedy for the worst cases.

The methods of treatment were often barbarous; besides cupping and leeching, the patient was subjected to other torments believed to be efficacious. Water was denied the victim tormented with fever, and in its stead small quantities of clam-juice were given. Inoculation was practically unknown until well on in the seventeenth century, and on account of the prevalent superstition it was not frequently resorted to until much later. Hardly one of the many remedies now in general use for assuaging pain and destroying diseases were then known.[27]

In New England the most influential and respectable profession was that of the ministry. The clergy were usually men of high education; almost without exception they were university graduates, and many of them could read the Bible in Hebrew or Greek and expound it in Latin. They exercised a predominant influence in political affairs, directed public policy to a large extent, secured the passage of such laws as they desired, and were frequently consulted by the magistrates, by whom their advice was usually followed. They were held in great affection and esteem by all classes, and were looked upon as oracles of wisdom. The most powerful New England preacher of the eighteenth century was Jonathan Edwards, whose work, entitled "Freedom of the Will," is regarded as one of the greatest productions of colonial literature. Other notable divines were Thomas Hooker, Increase Mather, Cotton Mather, John Cotton, Samuel Willard and Mather Byles.

III

EDUCATION, LITERATURE AND PRINTING

In all the colonies education facilities were poor. In New England apparently the need of education was most highly appre-

27 McMaster, "History of the People of the United States," vol. i. p. 30.

ciated, and the means of instruction first supplied in 1635. Four
years after the founding of Boston the town meeting voted to establish a school with Philemen Parmount as teacher,[28] and in the
following year Harvard College was founded. It received its
name from the Rev. John Harvard, who bequeathed one-half his
property and his entire library of 400 volumes to the institution.[29]
Antedating Harvard College by two years was the famous Boston
Latin School, largely due to the Rev. John Cotton. In 1647 the
General Court of Massachusetts directed that a common school be
established in every township containing fifty families, and a grammar school in the larger towns. This was the beginning of the
excellent system of public schools which has ever been the pride
of the people of this noble commonwealth. Connecticut and New
Hampshire were hardly behind Massachusetts in educational
growth, although in Rhode Island progress was poor in spite of
legislation.[30] In all these colonies private schools were early established, public school systems soon followed, and compulsory attendance was ultimately adopted in all, if poorly enforced in practice.

In 1701 Yale College, the second institution of the kind in
New England, was founded at New Haven, taking its name from
Elihu Yale, a man of Boston birth who lived most of his life in
England, and who made various bequests of small amount to the
young institution. Brown University in Rhode Island was founded
in 1764, and Dartmouth in New Hampshire in 1770. In the Middle States the interest in education was fair, though the public school
facilities did not compare in excellence with those of New England. In 1633 a school was opened by the Dutch Reformed Church
at New Amsterdam, which was apparently the first school opened
in the colonies, and its lineal descendant is still in existence. Many
other schools were established by the burghers for their children,
and we have reason to believe that a high rate of intelligence prevailed among these sturdy settlers. Under English occupation
even more progress was made. In 1754 King's College was established in New York, with Dr. Samuel Johnson as president and
sole teacher. After the Revolution it was rechristened Columbia
College, and numbered among its early graduates Alexander Hamilton, John Jay and Gouverneur Morris. Before the Revolution,

[28] Howard, "Local Constitutional History," p. 67.
[29] Dexter, "History of Education in the United States," p. 226.
[30] Channing, "History of the United States," vol. i. p. 433.

New Jersey, although a small colony, could boast of two colleges, Princeton, founded in 1746, and Rutgers, founded about twenty years later.

A noteworthy educational institution in Pennsylvania was the Academy of Pennsylvania, founded mainly through the efforts of Benjamin Franklin, in 1749, and which subsequently grew into the University of Pennsylvania. In 1765 the University established a medical school, the first institution of the kind in the colonies. In the southern colonies, for various reasons, public education did not make much headway. Here the plantation system prevailed, towns and villages were few, and the democratic spirit which lies at the basis of the public school system was largely lacking, although in Virginia the vestry was charged with seeing that all poor children were taught to read and write, and in practice every minister maintained a school.[31] Situated far apart as the planters were, schools of any kind were maintained with difficulty. Most of the wealthier families employed private tutors to instruct their sons, as was the case with the Washington family, while some of them sent their sons to London to study at the Temple, or to Oxford, Edinburgh or Cambridge. Colleges and universities were few in the southern colonies, yet it is a noteworthy fact that the second college to be established in America was in Virginia. This was the College of William and Mary, founded in 1692, largely through the efforts of the Rev. James Blair, who was sent to London to solicit aid, and who succeeded in securing a charter from William and Mary, together with a grant of £2,000 " out of the rents " for the erection of buildings.[32]

The college had a president and six poorly-paid professors and a library of 3,000 volumes, which was considered a large one for that day. This college alone of the higher colonial educational institutions has been unable to hold its own with its contemporaries, so far as number of students is concerned. During the eighteenth century it declined, and by the time of the Revolution it was little more than a grammar school. Nevertheless its contribution of distinguished men to the cause of American independence was probably unequaled by that of any other college. Five of the signers of the Declaration of Independence, and sixteen members of

[31] L. G. Tyler, " England in America," p. 116.
[32] Dexter, " History of Education," p. 324; Greene, " Provincial America," ch. xviii.

the Continental Congress were among its alumni. Of these may be mentioned Peyton Randolph, Thomas Jefferson, James Monroe and John Marshall.

In all the colleges of the time the courses of study were narrow, being limited chiefly to Greek, Latin, metaphysics, logic, and theology; the facilities of instruction, such as are afforded by the modern library, laboratory, and museum, were almost wholly lacking, and the attendance was distressingly small. From all, women were excluded, while the conditions of life were such that few aside from the sons of the well-to-do were able to enjoy the meager opportunities thus offered. It is a curious fact that some of these colleges were either founded or supported by lotteries, and that the chief purpose of most of them was to train young men for the ministry. So far as the standard of their curricula was concerned, hardly any of them were more than academies.

In literature and arts, as in education, New England took the lead among the colonies, although there even here was little to excite pride. Before the Revolution the literature of New England belonged to two classes, namely, chronicles and theological writings. The former were marked by a spirit of partisanship and want of critical style, while the latter consisted mostly of sermons, controversial treatises and polemical essays, usually ponderous with metaphysical abstractions and dogmas. In New England nearly all the writers of note were theologians. Of these, Jonathan Edwards was the most powerful. His writings were characterized by a force of style and a profundity of thought which placed him among the greatest thinkers of this time. Other American writers of note were Hugh Peters, afterwards chaplain to Oliver Cromwell; Roger Williams, whose most important work, " Bloody Tenent of Persecution " appeared in 1644; John Cotton, who wrote in reply to Williams's treatise, " The Bloody Tenent washed and made white in the Blood of the Lamb "; William Bradford, author of a " History of Plymouth "; John Winthrop, author of a " History of New England "; Cotton, Mather, author of the " Magnalia," an ecclesiastical history of New England from 1620 to 1698; and Benjamin Franklin, whose autobiography and " Poor Richard's Almanack," are works of a high order, which, with his scientific achievements, won him the distinction abroad of being the best known American. Franklin's autobiography was the most widely current book in our colonial literature, while " Poor Richard's Almanack," first begun in 1732, continued for twenty-five years, and had an annual circulation of ten thousand copies.[33]   It was replete with proverbial sayings told in prose and verse and inculcated the virtues of industry, honesty, and frugality.   A writer who exercised a powerful influence during the Revolutionary period was Thomas Paine, who published, anonymously, at Philadelphia, in January, 1776, a pamphlet entitled " Common Sense," which was a series of essays advocating the independence of the colonies and the establishment of a republic.[34]   It was followed in December by the " Crisis," which began with the famous saying: " These are the times that try men's souls."   Full of crudities of thought and superficiality, " Common Sense " was withal a masterly pamphlet, and it was eagerly read and rapidly went through many editions.   It convinced multitudes of wavering patriots that the true interest of the colonies required their immediate separation from Great Britain.[35]

Outside of New England and Pennsylvania, however, there was little written which is worthy of the name of literature if we except some attempts at historical writing in Virginia by a clergyman named William Stith, and by Robert Beverly, and the really amusing diary of Colonel William Byrd.   Stith and Beverly wrote histories of the Virginia colony, while Colonel Byrd left his memoirs, including an account of his experiences as a commissioner for running the boundary line between North Carolina and Virginia.   The latter is replete with wit and humor, shows power of keen observation, and is by no means lacking in literary merit.[36]

The first printing press in the colonies was set up at Cambriage in 1639, and in the following year the first book ever printed in America was issued from it.   This was the " Bay Psalm Book," a collection of psalms made by various ministers, one of whom, John Eliot, translated the Bible into the Algonquin tongue for the benefit of the Indians.   There were no printing presses in Virginia until 1729, and Governor Berkeley thanked God in 1671 for it, as " printing presses," he said, " bring heresies in the world and libel

[33] Beers, " Studies in American Letters," p. 39.
[34] Conway, " Writings of Paine," pp. 67–169.
[35] M. C. Tyler, " Literary History of the American Revolution," vol. i. p. 474
[36] See Bassett, " Writings of William Byrd."

the best government that the world ever saw." [37]   The early printing press was, of course, a crude and cumbersome affair, was
worked by hand and had a capacity of hardly more than a hundred
tiny sheets per hour.   Few of our early inventions afford greater
objects of curiosity to-day than the printing press of Benjamin
Franklin's time.

Newspapers were few and of the very poorest kind.   Ordinarily they were but a few times larger than a man's hand in size,
were printed on coarse paper, and seldom circulated more than
fifty miles beyond the place where they were printed.   Their small
columns were often filled with essays on politics, morals, religion
or metaphysics, by writers who signed themselves Cincinnatus,
Cicero, or some other classical name.   There were no editorials,
and the little news from abroad was forgotten in the Old World
ere it crossed the Atlantic.   Their small columns were often filled
with quaint advertisements of runaway slaves or servants, or with
extracts from some standard history.   For lack of news a Boston
paper published Robertson's " History of America " as a serial,
while another reprinted Cook's " Voyages." [38]   Not infrequently
" broadsides," or extra sheets, were printed on eventful occasions
and sold on the streets.   The first newspaper published in the
colonies was the *Boston News Letter,* founded in 1704, and which
fifteen years later was flourishing with a circulation of 300 copies.[39]
The first newspaper founded in the south was the *Virginia Gazette,*
started in 1736, and at the outbreak of the Revolution there were
thirty-seven newspapers in circulation in the thirteen colonies.   Of
these fourteen were in New England, four in New York, and nine
in Pennsylvania; Virginia and North Carolina had two each,
Georgia one, South Carolina three.   The contents of the whole
thirty-seven would scarcely fill a dozen pages in a single one of
our modern dailies, and their combined circulation did not exceed
a few thousand copies.   Not one of them was a daily, and, as for
magazines and other periodicals, they were not even thought of.

As with newspapers, so it was with books: there were few
and they were of poor quality.   Most of those read in America
were, of course, imported from the mother country; but there were
few who, like Lewis Morris of Morrisania, could instruct their

[37] Hart, " Contemporaries," vol. i. p. 241.
[38] McMaster, " History of the People of the United States," vol. i. p. 37.
[39] Weeden, " Social and Economic History," vol. ii. p. 546.

London bookseller to send a long list " lettered and gilt as usual."
They consisted chiefly of theological treatises, essays on logic and
metaphysics, biographies and treatises on the law of nations.
Among the books most widely read in the colonies were Fox's
" Lives of the Martyrs," Vattel's " Law of Nations," Bunyan's
" Pilgrim's Progress," Rollins's " Ancient History," Plutarch's
" Lives," Watt's " Improvement of the Mind," and various Latin
and Greek authors.

IV

RELIGION AND RELIGIOUS WORSHIP

Religious worship played an important part in the life of the
colonies, and the church was an institution of vast power and
influence in social and political affairs. The basic idea of all the
colonial foundations assumed the necessity of a vital relation between church and state.[40] In every New England town there was
a Congregational church, which was in a sense the center of the
town life, and it was not merely the creature of the state, but was
the state itself.[41] The moral support which the clergy, the most
influential element in the New England colonies, gave to the government was very powerful, and in times of crises they were leaders
at the forefront. They were held in great respect by all classes,
and their advice was frequently sought by the magistrates, and
nearly always followed. They acted as referees on many questions
of policy; their expositions of the laws were the most authoritative
that we have; they frequently prepared the first draft of the laws
of the colony, and together with the magistrates they acted as
censors of the press; they were, in short, political as well as moral
leaders.[42] Attendance upon the church was usually required by
law and was strictly enforced by the magistrates. Apparently the
people did not consider it a great hardship to be compelled to sit
shivering for hours on wooden benches and to listen to harangues
on the torture of a lost soul, the awful wrath of God, the salvation
of the elect, or some other doctrinal question.

The Sabbath day was observed with characteristic Puritan

[40] Cobb, " Rise of Religious Liberty in America," p. 1.
[41] Trevelyan, " The American Revolution," part ii. p. 281.
[42] Osgood, " The American Colonies in the Seventeenth Century," vol. i. p
218.

strictness. It began at 6 P. M. on Saturday and lasted until sundown on Sunday, and during this period amusements of every kind were absolutely prohibited. Traveling and lounging on the streets, as well as the entertainment of strangers, were likewise regarded as sinful and forbidden by law. The people of the town were summoned to church by the beating of a drum or the blowing of a horn, for bells had not yet come into use. In the early days, when Indian outbreaks were common, the parishioners went armed and the minister frequently delivered his discourse with a musket by his side and a sentinel at the door. That such precautions were not ill-timed, the Indian tragedy on that fateful Sunday morning at Hadley bears witness. The worldly individual who absented himself from the house of God on the Sabbath day was waited upon by the tithing-man and punished either by fine or imprisonment. The thoughtless maiden who smiled during the service was in danger of banishment, while those who slumbered received admonitions from the tithing-man of such a nature as not to be soon forgotten. If the offender belonged to the male sex he received a rap over the head from a pole in the hands of the tithing-man; if a female, she was awakened by the gentle brush of a rabbit's foot.[43]

The church services strongly reflected the Puritan character. There was no music except the singing of hymns, the prayers compared in length with that of the sermon, and sacraments were a regular part of every service. The men were seated on one side of the aisle and the women on the other, with the pulpit steps and the rear seats occupied by the children and negroes. With regard to distance from the pulpit the worshipers were carefully seated according to age, social rank, estate, office, or amount contributed toward the erection of the church. In one Long Island town those who contributed forty shillings to the minister's salary, together with the justices of the peace, were given seats at the table, the trustees of the church were given the front seat, while the remaining ones were assigned on the basis of church contributions. One Massachusetts town had a standing committee of five to seat the church members and another committee of two to seat the committee with their wives.[44]

Religious worship in New England was characterized by a

[43] Lodge, " Short History of the English Colonies,' p. 480 et seq.
[44] Weeden, " Social and Economic History," vol. i. pp. 280, 417, 418.

superstition and intoleration which to one of our day seems almost incredible. Having fled from the intolerance of England, we of this generation might expect to see the New England church founded on the rock of toleration, if not of religious liberty; but such was not the case, for it soon transpired that they did not want religious liberty for any others than themselves. To the early religious leaders of Massachusetts especially, toleration of dissent from the "established order" of religious worship was as sedition in the state and sin against God, John Cotton going so far as to say that "it was toleration that had made the world anti-Christian." [45] Outside of Rhode Island, Catholics, Jews, Baptists, Quakers, and Episcopalians were at times subjected to various forms of persecution — flogging, imprisonment, exile, and even death. The New England hatred for those who adhered to the Church of England was especially bitter. No attempt was ever made by the home government to force this church upon the inhabitants of the New England colonies, but only to secure for it a foothold. But in this the government was unsuccessful and the church never made any headway outside of Connecticut and Boston. The seventeenth century was an age of fierce and narrow bigotry, but as time passed there was a tendency toward a wider toleration of religious liberty and gradually the spirit of persecution died away.

Rhode Island was, of course, an exception to what has been said concerning religious intolerance in New England. This colony was a haven for despised sects of every class, and in consequence of the complete religious liberty which it allowed in an intolerant age, it became a community of fanatical sects, and, to some extent, of turbulence, disorder, and laxity of morals. There never was, said Cotton Mather, such a variety of religions on so small a spot of ground. [46] For a long time church membership in some of the New England States was a qualification for the exercise of the suffrage, while moral and religious tests for office were not uncommon. Plymouth denied the privileges of a freeman to those who were not of a "sober, peaceful conversation," to those who were "grossly scandalouse or notoriously vitious," and to those who spoke "contemptuously" of the laws enacted by the General Court. By a latter statute Plymouth required freemen to be

[45] Cobb, "The Rise of Religious Liberty in America," p. 68.
[46] Richman, "Rhode Island, Its Making and Its Meaning," vol. i. p. 106.

" orthodox in the fundamentals of religion." Massachusetts (until 1691) and New Haven required church membership, and after 1664 Massachusetts required a certificate from the minister that the applicant was not " vitious " in his life. Connecticut at first denied the privilege to those whose conduct was known to be " scandalous," while Rhode Island required a profession of Christianity, though Roman Catholics were debarred. Virginia denied the franchise to transported convicts even though freeholders. South Carolina, by a statute of 1716, required voters to profess the Christian religion. Roman Catholics were expressly disfranchised by the statutes of New York, Maryland, Virginia, and Rhode Island, and were in practice not allowed to vote in most of the other colonies. Quakers were debarred from becoming freemen in Massachusetts and Plymouth, and there is evidence that Jews were excluded in New York and South Carolina.[47] In Massachusetts, Connecticut and New Hampshire the Congregational Church was established by law and was supported by public taxation, and in the first mentioned State it was not completely disestablished until 1835.

In New York under Dutch rule the Dutch Reformed Church was established by law, and other sects, notably Lutherans, Catholics, Jews, and Quakers, were not tolerated, but were arrested, imprisoned and even driven from the colony.[48] After the colony passed under English rule the Dutch Reformed Church was disestablished and an act was passed to maintain the Anglican Church, and later (1686) it was forced upon English and Dutch alike, all being taxed for its support. But this policy of coercion injured the growth of the church, and at the time of the Revolution the dissenters in New York probably outnumbered the Anglicans twelve to one. Catholics were bitterly persecuted by the English authorities, and by the Act of 1700 were threatened with imprisonment for life should they persist in their " heretical " teachings. In 1744 an act was passed against Moravian preaching and severe penalties were attached.

In New Jersey, Congregationalists and Scotch Presbyterians were the predominant sects, and the Church of England never gained a foothold there, although certain of the governors gave it support and precedence. Pennsylvania was distinctly the land of

[47] Bishop, " History of Elections in the American Colonies," pp. 53-64.
[48] Cobb, " Rise of Religious Liberty in America," pp. 314-320.

Quakers and Lutherans, and to a less extent was her little neighbor, Delaware. Here there was an unusual degree of religious tolerance; as a consequence of which a number of sects, such as Dunkards, Pietists, Mennonites, Baptists, and Dutch Calvinists, sprang into existence. The Anglican Church, though set up in Pennsylvania, never flourished. The only anti-religious legislation was that directed against Catholics, who were charged with inciting the people to join the French during the Seven Years' War, and the motive of this legislation was not religious oppression. There were no instances of religious persecution in Pennsylvania or of personal hardships for religion's sake, unless exclusion from office can be so termed.[49]

In Maryland, Virginia, the Carolinas and Georgia the Church of England was established by law and supported by taxation. In all of these, however, dissenters were numerous, almost equal in fact in numbers and influence to the Episcopalians. The Episcopal clergy in the southern colonies did not always come up to the standard of intelligence and piety of the Congregational ministers of New England and played a far less important role in the social and political life of their communities. In the south intolerance was quite as strong as in New England. In the seventeenth century Catholics, Baptists, Presbyterians, Puritans, and Quakers in Virginia were persecuted, thrown into prison, banished and harassed by vexatious laws, while at the outbreak of the French and Indian War an act was passed disarming all Catholics, as in Pennsylvania, on account of a popular belief that they were in sympathy with the French. Non-conformists' meetings were broken up and their adherents expelled from the colony. But no amount of persecution could break up the dissenters; only a handful at first, they largely outnumbered the Episcopalians at the time of the Revolution.

It is a singular fact that the British Government never established an episcopate in America, and never appointed a bishop for the colonies. Repeated efforts were made to induce the government of England to send over a bishop and otherwise aid the Virginia churches, but to no avail.[50] They remained until the Revolution attached to the diocese of London, and were often supplied with discarded English clergymen who were not wanted at home. As a consequence the Episcopal clergy, in addition to

[49] Cobb, "Rise of Religious Liberty in America," p. 450.
[50] Campbell, "History of Virginia," p. 251.

their intellectual inferiority, were often dissolute and worthless, and there was no bishop nearer than London to encourage, admonish or discipline them. The Bishop of London had, it is true, " commissaries " in America, but they had no power to restrain or punish their erring brethren, and could only report what came under their observation. The good Bishop Meade, in his memoirs, constantly complains of the worldliness and incompetency of the clergy. They were altogether too fond, he says, of horse-racing, gambling, card-playing, hunting, drinking, and were, besides, profane swearers, brawlers, and licentious. " One of them," says Bishop Meade, " was for years president of a jockey club; another fought a duel in sight of the very church in which he had performed the solemn offices of religion; another quarreled with his vestry violently, and on the next Sunday preached from the words of Nehemiah: ' And I contended with them, and cursed them, and smote certain of them, and plucked out their hair.' "[51] So low, in fact, did the clergy sink that by acts of the legislature of Virginia, passed in 1669 and 1705, the customary exemption of clergymen from the operation of the laws against infidelity, blasphemy, swearing, Sabbath-breaking, and adultery was withdrawn and they were made subject to the penalties of the law for such offenses.[52] Not a few of the clergy, however, remained steadfast, were worthy, pious leaders, and enjoyed the respect and admiration of the people; but they were exceptions to the general character of the clergy. On account of the failure of the Crown to appoint a bishop for the colonies, no native-born American could be ordained as a minister without incurring the long delays and indescribable discomforts of a journey across the Atlantic. In other respects candidates for ordination were compelled to face difficulties which were enough to have discouraged the most zealous of churchmen.[53]

The Episcopal clergy were generally remunerated in kind, usually a stipulated quantity of tobacco, often supplemented by fees. In 1748 the amount was fixed by the Virginia legislature at 16,000 pounds, including a glebe and a parsonage. The cash equivalent, of course, varied with the quality of the tobacco and the state of the market, but at the time it was estimated to be £400

[51] " Old Churches and Families of Virginia," pp. 14–18.
[52] Hening, " Statutes of Virginia," vol. iii. pp. 171, 358.
[53] Trevelyan, " The American Revolution," part ii. p. 288.

at sixpence per pound. In consequence of bad crops and heavy taxes on account of the French and Indian War the legislature in 1758 enacted the so-called "Two-Penny Act," providing that all debts payable in tobacco might, at the option of the debtor, be discharged in money at the rate of £18 and 8*d*. per one hundred pounds of tobacco, thus in effect reducing the salary of the clergy by two-thirds. In view of the early rise of the price of tobacco the act was clearly unjust to the clergy, as well as to others whose salaries were payable in tobacco, and they lost no time in seeking relief in the courts. In due course the "Two-Penny Law" was held to be invalid and it was generally believed that the jury would award damages to the plaintiffs. But at this juncture Patrick Henry, a young, obscure country lawyer, whose past life had been a virtual failure, appeared for the defendants and delivered a speech which at once raised him to the front rank of American orators. After he had concluded, the jury rendered a verdict assessing the damages at one penny. The clergy attempted no further suits, but waited for relief from a wiser legislature. The persistence of the clergy in attacking the act of the legislature had the effect of still further arousing public sentiment against them, for it was now asserted that they had no sympathy with the people in their poverty and burdens, but were only concerned with their own enrichment.

V

MEANS OF TRAVEL, SOCIAL CUSTOMS AND CRIME

Compared with conditions of to-day, life in the colonies was extremely narrow and monotonous. There was an isolation and stagnation about it which would be intolerable to the twentieth century. Each community was a life unto itself; it was to a large degree self-sufficing as a matter of necessity, for means of intercourse were crude and imperfect. There were no railroads in existence and travel by sailboat was not always convenient or possible, and besides it was too uncertain to rely upon. Travel by horseback or stage-coach was, therefore, the chief alternative. Besides indescribable discomforts and hardships, there was the element of time involved. In 1756 the first regular stage between New York and Philadelphia was established. It required three days to make the trip, and four days more to extend the journey to

Boston.[54] Something of a sensation was caused in 1765 by the announcement that a coach, described as "a good wagon with seats on springs," would thereafter make the journey between Philadelphia and New York in two days, and at the low cost of twenty shillings for the through trip. This record seemed so marvelous that the vehicle was popularly dubbed a "flying machine." Ordinarily the conveyances were shackling old vehicles drawn by jaded and ill-fed horses. In dry weather and on the best roads they made from thirty to forty miles per day, at other times rarely more than twenty-five, and only by frequent relays could this rate of speed be kept up. The tired passengers, after a restless night in a tavern, were called up at four in the morning by the sound of the driver's horn. At steep hillsides and mud-holes the passengers were required to alight and help the heavy vehicle over. The hardships and dangers of crossing large rivers in unsafe ferryboats often deterred many from traveling and were a source of anxiety to the friends of those who did. Greater still were the difficulties of ocean travel. It required months to cross the Atlantic, and news of events in the old country was ancient history when it reached the remote settlements of America. Nothing but the most urgent business in Europe could induce an American to undertake such a journey.

At first there were no postal facilities except such as were supplied by private enterprise. Letters from abroad were delivered at the wharf to those who called for them or sent to a nearby store or coffee-house for delivery whenever requested. The colony of Massachusetts apparently was the first to take steps looking to the establishment of a postal system under government control. In 1639 the General Court enacted the following law: "It is ordered that notice be given that Richard Fairbanks his house in Boston is the place appointed for all letters which are brought from beyond the seas, or are to be sent thither to be left with him; and he is to take care that they are to be delivered, or sent according to directions; and he shall be allowed for every letter a penny, and he must answer all miscarriages through his own neglect in this kind, provided that no man shall be compelled to bring his letters thither except he please."

Toward the close of the seventeenth century the colonial government of New York established a monthly mail between the towns

[54] McMaster, "History of the People of the United States," vol. i. p. 44.

of New York and Boston.   In 1692 the Virginia legislature passed an act reciting that one Thomas Neale had been empowered by letters patent from William and Mary to take charge of the postal business of the colonies.   Neale's patent authorized him " to erect, settle and establish offices in America for the receiving and dispatching away letters and packquettes," and to appoint such assistants as were necessary to aid him.   This patent created the first intercolonial postal service.   The charges for carrying a letter ranged from 4*d* to 15*d,* according to the distance.   Benjamin Franklin was in a sense the father of the American postal system. In 1753 he received, with William Hunter, a royal commission as deputy postmaster-general for the colonies, and he at once proceeded to organize the service and made a tour of personal inspection, visiting every post office in the colonies except that at Charleston.   Franklin established a regular system of offices and carriers, with a schedule of postage averaging a penny for about thirty miles.   He adopted the practice of requiring subscribers to pay for having newspapers carried, and " advertised " uncalled for letters and established three mails per week during the summer season between New York and Philadelphia.[55]

The post office department was soon placed on a paying basis, and by 1774 it was yielding a clear annual revenue of three thousand pounds to the British treasury.   In the latter year Franklin was removed by the home government on account of his activity in the Revolutionary movement, but in the following year was unanimously appointed postmaster-general by the Continental Congress and authorized to establish a line of posts from Falmouth, Maine, to Savannah, Georgia, and as many cross posts as might seem necessary.   As compared with those of the present day, the postal facilities of the colonial period were of the crudest kind. The rates of postage were very high, the mails were slow and irregular on account of the difficulties of travel, and postriders and postmasters frequently were untrustworthy.   Letters were not infrequently opened and read by the postmaster, to guard against which important communications were often written in cipher. Newspapers at first were not allowed to be sent through the mail, but were carried by private arrangement between the sender and the postrider.

During the colonial period few luxuries of the present day

[55] Sparks, " Expansion of the American People," vol. i. p. 64.

were to be had, and the same was true of many articles now considered as necessaries of life. Everywhere, however, there was an abundance to eat and drink, and the evidences of satisfaction and contentment were seldom wanting. In New England social life had a Puritanic cast which found its fullest expression in religious services. The gathering at the "meeting house" on Sunday was the chief social event of the week, as the sermon was the principal intellectual event. The regulation by statute of the dress, daily habits and social usages of the people was a distinctive feature of Puritan polity. The wearing of gaudy or costly apparel did not, in the eye of the Puritan, comport with good moral conduct, and it was therefore forbidden in many New England communities. Thus by a statute of 1634 the General Court of Massachusetts forbade the purchase of any cloth with lace on it or the making of a dress with more than one slash on the sleeve or adorned with embroidery or silver buckles. There were apparently a good many prosecutions under the act.[56] By a statute of 1677 the wearing of gold or silver lace or buttons or silk ribbons or other superfluous trimmings was forbidden, but magistrates, their families and miltary officers were exempted from the law. Connecticut forbade the wearing of silk, but Rhode Island enacted no sumptuary legislation.

Many were the statutes for the regulation of the morals of the people. In Connecticut these regulations were marked by such extreme severity that they have come down to us under the name of the "Blue Laws." To mention a few of them: no one was allowed to give lodging to a Quaker or other heretic, to walk about town on the Sabbath day except reverently to and from meeting, no one could travel, or cook victuals, make beds, sweep house, cut hair or shave on the Lord's day, nor bring cards into the colony, nor dance, nor play on any instrument of music except the drum, the trumpet and the jewsharp.[57] Many innocent amusements were suppressed. Drinking and smoking were placed under strict regulations. The harboring of strangers and even relatives was regulated and sometimes forbidden, and outsiders were not allowed to enter the colony without the permission of the magistrates. In spite, however, of the austerity and soberness of Puritanism,

[56] Weeden, "Social and Economic History of New England," vol. i. p. 289, 226.
[57] Ibid., vol. i. pp. 225, 272.

human nature occasionally asserted itself and the monotony of New England life was enlivened by corn husking and quilting parties, spinning bees, house raisings, sleigh rides, Thanksgiving feasts, militia musters and athletic sports of various kinds, often followed by the drinking of rum. As time passed the old restraints upon amusement were relaxed and there were picnics, tea parties, and even dances, horse races, and bull baitings.

The New England farmhouse, with its scanty furniture and unattractive exterior, had a redeeming feature in the great fire-place, around which the family gathered during the long winter evenings to read books, tell stories or perform various domestic duties, such as wool-carding, spinning and corn-husking. In the large towns of New England there were, of course, more of the comforts and luxuries of life. The houses were frequently built of brick or stone and richly furnished with carpets, silver and glassware, tapestries and mahogany furniture imported from England. There, as in New York, was to be found a gay and fashionable society. The people dressed handsomely and lived luxuriously. In New England towns and villages were numerous and situated near together, mainly for the purpose of defense and convenience of worship.

In the southern colonies, especially in Virginia, social life was affected by the existence of a landed aristocracy of Cavalier instincts, among whom extreme Puritanic ideas scarcely prevailed. Plantations were large and towns few and insignificant, in spite of the attempt of the legislature to create them by artificial process, as it did in 1680 by the Cohabitation Act, which ordered towns to be built at certain specified places for the benefit of trade.[58] The wealthy planters stood at the apex of the social pyramid. They occupied spacious mansions built sometimes of imported brick or stone, paneled and wainscoted in hard woods, with great fireplaces and rich mantels and furnished with an elegance befitting the manor houses of old England. They had carriages, servants, blooded horses, packs of hounds in abundance and enjoyed to the fullest the few luxuries which the times afforded. The wealthy planters were fond of hunting, horse racing, dancing, gaming and other amusements, as well as of politics, in which field they were the leaders. They were fond of drink, and in this respect were not far ahead of their fellow countrymen of New England. In fact drinking was

[58] Lodge, "Short History of the English Colonies," p. 51.

common in all the colonies. Every tavern or ordinary inn kept liquor for sale, while every well-to-do householder usually had it on his sideboard.

The liquors most commonly drunk were rum, beer and cider. A peculiar custom was the practice of drinking at funerals, on which occasions large quantities of liquor were consumed by the mourners.[59] Besides being occasions of pomp and excesses, funerals were expensive affairs on account of the custom of giving presents, and the practice led to the enactment of laws in some colonies to limit the expense of burials. The wife of the great patroon Stephen Van Rensselaer, is said to have been interred at an expense of $20,000. Two thousand scarfs were given away as presents and all the tenants on the manor were entertained for three or four days at the expense of their landlord. The custom of heavy drinking at funerals, as well as the practice of giving presents, was general throughout the colonies, but it was carried to more extreme lengths in New York during the Dutch supremacy than elsewhere.[60]

While drunkenness was probably regarded with less disfavor than now, there was in other respects a much stricter code of morality. Laws against crime were severe and many offenses were capitally punished that to-day carry a penalty of small consequence. Thus blasphemy in Massachusetts was made a capital offense in 1646. Playing in the streets, " uncivilly " walking in the streets or fields, traveling from town to town, going on shipboard, frequenting taverns and other places to drink were forbidden under severe penalties.[61] Furthermore, the manner of punishment often tended to degrade and needlessly humiliate the offender. It was the custom to give as much publicity as possible to punishments in the belief that it would serve as a deterrent to other evil-doers. Criminals were branded, labeled with conspicuous letters indicative of their offense, and flogged through the streets, while the whipping-post, the ducking-stool, the pillory and the stocks were familiar objects in the public square of many towns.

[59] It is related that at the funeral of Mrs. Cornelia Van Cortlandt, mother of General Philip Schuyler, 140 gallons of wine and two barrels of ale were thus consumed. Trevelyan, "The American Revolution," part ii. vol. i. p. 280.
[60] Lodge, "Short History of the English Colonies," p. 338.
[61] Osgood, "The American Colonies in the Seventeenth Century," vol. i. p. 215.

Chapter VII

INTER-COLONIAL WARS. 1689-1748

I

KING WILLIAM'S WAR. 1689-1697

THE rivalry between Great Britain and France in America had been steadily increasing for many years when the English Revolution of 1688 gave to that rivalry a new turn. The bigoted and despotic James II. had been forced by his subjects to abandon the English throne, and the crown had been conferred jointly upon William and Mary. James, upon abdicating, fled to France, where he was cordially received by Louis XIV., who at once espoused his cause and undertook to restore the exiled monarch to his lost throne. War accordingly broke out between the two countries in 1689, and soon spread to their colonies in America, although none of them had any direct interest in the issues involved. In Europe the contest was known as the War of the Palatinate; in America it was called King William's War.

As compared with the English possessions the French colonies in America were so inferior in resources and population that they did not undertake to conduct a regular campaign against the English, but resorted to savage raids and expeditions for the purpose of harrying their settlements and massacring their unoffending inhabitants. The French population in America probably did not exceed 12,000 as against 100,000 English settlers in New England and New York. But the French had an invaluable resource in their Indian allies, who were well fitted by nature for the purposes for which they were employed by the hardly less barbarous white commanders.

The governor of Canada was the aged Count Frontenac, the most distinguished of the French officials in America and a man who did not scruple to employ whatever methods were available to destroy the English colonists to the south of him.[1] One of the

[1] Parkman, "The Struggle for a Continent," edited by Edgar, p. 233; Greene, "Provincial America," p. 121.

expeditions which he sent against the English settlements, consisting of one hundred and ten men, a considerable number of whom were Iroquois Indians, reached Schenectady in February, 1690, after traveling over the snows for nearly a month, and while the quiet little village lay wrapped in slumber they stealthily entered its unguarded gates, gave the war whoop and began their work of slaughter. Sixty of the inhabitants were massacred, of whom seventeen were children, many were taken captive and carried off to Canada, while a few escaped and fled half-clad through the snows to Albany.[2] Another party of fifty-two French and Indians, commanded by Hertel de Rouville, fell upon the village of Salmon Falls, New Hampshire, burned many of its houses, massacred a goodly number of the inhabitants and carried off fifty-four prisoners, mainly women and children. The towns of Dover, Casco and Pemaquid were subjected to similar cruelties and barbarities.

In consequence of the general alarm to which these events gave rise a colonial congress was called, mainly through the initiation of the Massachusetts General Court. It met at New York in May, 1690, commissioners being present from the colonies of Massachusetts, Plymouth, Connecticut and New York. The congress took into consideration the state of affairs occasioned by the French and Indian massacres and decided to make an attempt to conquer Canada by sending an army overland to attack Montreal and a fleet by sea to capture Quebec. Sir William Phipps took command of the fleet, consisting of thirty-four vessels, furnished by Massachusetts and manned by two thousand of her citizens.[3] Within less than a month from the adjournment of the congress Phipps had taken Port Royal (now Annapolis), but in the following year it was retaken by the French.

On October 16 the fleet reached Quebec, and Phipps made a pompous demand upon Governor Frontenac for its surrender and gave him an hour for an answer, saying, " If you refuse forthwith to do, I am come, provided, and am resolved, by the help of God, to revenge all wrongs and injuries offered and bring you under subjection to the Crown of England, and, when too late, make you wish you had accepted of the favor tendered." Frontenac immediately informed the messenger who delivered the demand

[2] Bancroft, "History of the United States," vol. ii. p. 180.
[3] Ibid., vol. ii. p. 181.

that he did not recognize King William; that he knew no king of England except King James, and that he would answer Phipps's demand only by the mouth of his cannon.[4]   Phipps was not able to carry out his threat.   Quebec was strongly fortified and well garrisoned, while Phipps's vessels were small wooden craft and manned by inexperienced gunners, as subsequent events showed.   A plan of attack, however, was arranged and the fort was bombarded, but without effect.   Thereupon the fleet weighed anchor, sailed away and returned to Boston in November, after having been badly scattered by storm and many of the men lost.   All was now dismay and gloom in Boston.   The colony was already impoverished and burdened with debt, and now it was compelled for the first time in its history to issue a quantity of paper currency with which to pay clamorous soldiers and sailors whose services had resulted only in failure and disaster.   The land force sent against Montreal met with no better success, and after being repelled by Frontenac, it returned to New York.

All attempts at offensive war were now given up, and the disappointed, impoverished colonists contented themselves with defending their frontiers as best they could against the barbarous incursions of the enemy.   For several years longer the war dragged on.   In January, 1692, a band of French and Indians came down on snowshoes from Canada and fell upon the town of York, Maine, sacked the place and offered the inhabitants the choice between captivity or death.   In the following year a village in New Hampshire was destroyed and ninety-four of its inhabitants killed or carried away.   Various other New England villages suffered similar and even worse fates.   A familiar story of the barbarity of the enemy, one which illustrates the heroism of the English settlers, is that of Hannah Dustin, the wife of a farmer near Haverhill, Massachusetts, who, having seen her house burned and her children murdered by savages in the French service, and having been herself carried off into captivity, killed and scalped ten of her captors while they lay asleep, and finally made her escape and returned home.[5]

At last, in 1697, this unrighteous war, which had brought such great disaster, sorrow and desolation to the English settlements in America, was ended by the Treaty of Ryswick.   The

[4] Parkman, "Count Frontenac and New France under Louis XIV.," ch. xiii.
[5] Bancroft, "History of the United States," vol. ii. p. 182.

only provision affecting America was that which called for the restoration of Acadia to France.

II

QUEEN ANNE'S WAR. 1702–1714

The Peace of Ryswick proved to be only a truce. Within four years after the conclusion of the treaty England and France were again at war, and the conflict of necessity extended to their colonial settlements in America. In Europe the contest was known as the War of the Spanish Succession from the fact that it grew out of the attempt of Louis XIV. to place his grandson, Philip of Anjou, on the Spanish throne. Great Britain was unwilling to see such an enormous extension of her old enemy's influence in European affairs, and so went to war with her to prevent it. Although her colonies in America were only remotely interested, if at all, in the question, they were dragged into the conflict and became the chief sufferers. In method and results it was King William's War over again. Instead of regular campaigns and hard fought battles, there was the usual harrying by savage red men and Frenchmen of the English settlements on the coast, and the massacring of the inhabitants, irrespective of age or sex.

Early in 1704, in the dead of winter, a party consisting of about fifty Canadians and two hundred Indians, according to French accounts, commanded by the same Hertel de Rouville who had burned the village of Salmon Falls during William's War, after journeying nearly three hundred miles on snowshoes through the vast wilderness lying between Canada and the Massachusetts frontier, fell upon the peaceful village of Deerfield with a terrible war whoop and massacred not less than fifty of its three hundred unsuspecting inhabitants. One hundred and eleven persons were carried away into captivity, only one-half of whom ever succeeded in returning, while the remaining one hundred and thirty-seven escaped with their lives only to have their homes destroyed by their barbarous enemy. Among those carried off as captives were the village minister, Mr. Williams, his wife and five children. Mrs. Williams was soon put to death with a tomahawk, but the others, with the exception of a seven-year-old girl, were subsequently rescued. This girl grew to womanhood among her savage captors, and afterwards married one of them and reared a family of children. Subsequently visiting Deerfield, she was entreated by old friends to forsake her Indian husband and children and resume her residence among the associates of her childhood; but this she refused to do, and returned to the fires of her wigwam and to the love of her Indian children.[6] During the ensuing years of the war other towns in Massachusetts suffered a fate similar to that of Deerfield. One of these was Haverhill, a village of thirty cottages and log cabins surrounded on three sides by a great primeval forest. On the night of August 29, 1708, a party of French and Indians commanded by De Rouville rushed into the peaceful hamlet and began the work of massacring the inhabitants. Some were shot, others tomahawked, while still others, especially children, had their brains dashed out against stones and trees.[7]

Meantime the home government was making an effort to capture Port Royal, which, as has been said, was taken by the English in the previous war, but was recaptured by the French. In 1704 and again in 1707 a fleet from Boston made ineffectual attempts to take the place. Finally, in 1710, a fleet under command of Colonel Nicholson was sent over from England, and being re-enforced by New England vessels, it sailed from Boston in September, and in the following month succeeded in taking Port Royal, which was thenceforth called Annapolis, in honor of the Queen, while Acadia was renamed Nova Scotia.[8] Encouraged by this victory, Colonel Nicholson urged the home government to undertake a conquest of Canada. His recommendations were approved and a fleet of fifteen warships and forty transports, together with seven veteran regiments from Marlborough's army, altogether about 12,000 men, were sent over under the command of Sir Hovenden Walker.[9]

It was the most formidable naval display ever seen in American waters, and caused quite a commotion in Boston. In July, 1711, it sailed from Boston for Canada, while at the same time a land force consisting of militia from New York, Connecticut and New

[6] Parkman, "Half Century of Conflict," vol. i. ch. iv.; Bancroft, "History of the United States," vol. ii. p. 196; Greene, "Provincial America," p. 145.

[7] Bancroft, "History of the United States," vol. ii. p. 197.

[8] Parkman, "Half Century of Conflict," vol. i. p. 148.

[9] Bancroft, "History of the United States," vol. ii. p. 200. Parkman says the fleet consisted of nine ships of war and about sixty transports and other vessels. "Half Century of Conflict," p. 163.

Jersey, together with almost six hundred friendly Iroquois Indians, set out from Albany for the purpose of taking Montreal. Not since the outbreak of the war nine years before had the hopes of the English colonists been so high as now. But they were soon to end in disappointment. After considerable delay Walker's fleet entered the St. Lawrence, but instead of taking Quebec, as his government had a right to expect, the apparently timid and incompetent admiral was seized with fears lest the freezing of the river would bring his ships to ruin, and he accordingly refused to procede. Becoming involved in a dense fog near the mouth of the river, a number of ships and about 800 lives were lost through his blundering. Thus the expedition ended in failure and disgrace, although Walker was able to find consolation in the reflection that the wreck " was a blessing in disguise and a merciful intervention of Providence " to save the expedition from the freezing, starvation and cannibalism which his imagination had conjured up.[10]

Few episodes in American colonial history are more humiliating than this expedition against Quebec, and many in New England loudly attributed it to cowardice, if not to treachery.[11] Nicholson, learning of the failure of the naval expedition against Quebec while in camp near Lake Champlain, burned the forts he had built, marched back to Albany and disbanded his army of 2,300 men. Thus far only defeat and disaster had crowned English operations in America. In Europe English successes had been brilliant and numerous, and now that both nations were tired of fighting peace was concluded by the Treaty of Utrecht, April, 1713. By this treaty the " five nations," known as the Iroquois, who had been allies of the English, were recognized as subjects of Great Britain; while Hudson Bay, Newfoundland and Acadia, with its " ancient limits," were ceded by France to England, the latter territory being yielded only with the greatest reluctance on the part of the aged French monarch who made strenuous efforts to retain this favorite province. The net result of the war was a real advance in the prestige of Great Britain in North America, and a serious though not decisive defeat for France.[12]

[10] Parkman, "Half Century of Conflict," p. 170.
[11] Greene, "Provincial America," p. 160.
[12] *Ibid.*, p. 165.

III

KING GEORGE'S WAR. 1744-1748

The Treaty of Utrecht, like that of Ryswick, brought but a temporary peace to Europe and America. Its great defect was that it did not settle definitely several important questions, the settlement of which was absolutely necessary to the future peace of the two contending nations. The limits of Acadia, as well as the boundary between New France and the English colonies both in the north and the west, were left undetermined, and therefore made a future conflict inevitable. The next thirty years were, therefore, years of nominal peace, but of actual smothered war in disguise.[13]

While France was forced to give up Acadia she was allowed to retain Cape Breton Island, which commands the entrance to the gulf and river of St. Lawrence. The French now determined to fortify and garrison the place as a means of guarding the approaches of Canada and of furnishing a base for attacking the English colonies in the event of another war. Accordingly on the southeastern part of the island, at a place well chosen for its strategic importance, a mighty fortress was erected, to which was given the name of Louisburg, in honor of the king. It cost not less than six million dollars, and was twenty-five years in course of construction. It was flanked by solid walls of masonry, from the tops of which scores of cannon frowned, and was altogether the strongest fortress in America, with the possible exception of Quebec, which owed its chief strength to nature and not to art, and was believed to be impregnable against attack.

Scarcely was this great defensive stronghold completed when France and England were again at war, and the conflict, as formerly, was soon extended to their colonies in the New World. The contest which now broke out was known in Europe as the War of the Austrian Succession. In 1740 the Austrian Emperor, Charles VI., the last of the male line of the house of Hapsburg, died; whereupon a number of the European powers straightway laid claims to certain of his dominions, although they had solemnly united in an agreement to respect the integrity of his empire and recognize his daughter, Maria Theresa, who had succeeded to

[13] Parkman, "Half Century of Conflict," vol. i. p. 177.

the crown. As a result of this policy of spoliation nearly all the powers of Europe became involved in war either on the side of Maria Theresa or on the side of Frederick of Prussia, the chief claimant to Austrian territories. As might have been expected, England and France were ranged on opposite sides. It is to be noted that the cause of the war between these two nations did not grow out of the questions left unsettled by the Treaty of Utrecht. The quarrel over these questions had not yet reached a climax. The present dispute was a European dynastic question, and although the American colonies had not the slightest interest in the issues involved, it was a foregone conclusion that their settlements would again be subject to the desolating and murderous ravages of bands of Indian savages. There were, however, fewer of these forays than in the preceding wars, but there were enough to keep the frontier settlements in constant terror.

Aside from these incursions the great event of the war was the capture of Louisburg. This remarkable military feat was conceived and planned by Governor Shirley of Massachusetts. When the doughty governor proposed the scheme to the Massachusetts General Court it was rejected as utterly impracticable, and the legislature refused to provide the necessary funds or ships. The scheme seemed audacious, especially as an undertaking for a single colony. But the indefatigable governor induced the legislature to reconsider its action, and upon reconsideration it decided by a majority of one vote to authorize the undertaking, a rumor in the meantime having got abroad that the garrison was mutinous and living on half rations. Shirley invited the coöperation of other colonies as far south as Pennsylvania; but favorable responses were received only from Connecticut, New Hampshire and Rhode Island. The governor of New Hampshire agreed to furnish 500 men provided Massachusetts would pay and feed 150 of them, while the governor of Connecticut promised as many more upon the condition that a Connecticut man should have the place of second rank in the expedition. Rhode Island, always on bad terms with her more powerful neighbor, grudgingly and rather tardily furnished 500 men. Massachusetts herself furnished 3,300 men, making altogether about 4,500 men, mostly farmers, fishermen and mechanics.

To command the expedition Governor Shirley chose William Pepperell, a well-to-do merchant of Kittery, and the selection proved to be most wise. A little fleet of twenty or thirty vessels, carrying not more than 150 guns, was collected and placed under the command of Captain Tyng, and before it reached its destination a considerable number of fishing vessels were added, and to these four British men-of-war from the West Indies, commanded by Commodore Warren, were soon joined. Early in May this motley fleet appeared under the great walls of Louisburg. Detachments of the men landed, dragged their batteries into position with great difficulty and laid siege to the mighty fortress. On May 7 a summons to surrender was sent to the commander, who replied that he would answer with his cannon. On the 23d of the month 189 of the American force were killed or captured while making a desperate attempt to take a battery which commanded the entrance to the harbor. But this disaster did not discourage the English. More cannon and mortars were dragged into position and planted under the orders of Colonel Gridley, who thirty years afterwards directed the fire of the batteries at Bunker Hill. Under his direction a deadly cannonade was now opened upon the island battery with telling effect. Gradually the place became untenable, and just as Warren and Pepperell were preparing to make a combined attack the fortress surrendered on June 17, 1745, six weeks after the beginning of the siege. On the same day the fleet sailed into the harbor, while Pepperell with a part of his army entered the town.

The news of the fall of Louisburg reached Boston a little after one o'clock in the morning of July 3, and soon the slumbering town was astir with shouting crowds who were induced with difficulty to believe the truth of the report. Great demonstrations of rejoicing were made in New York and Philadelphia and a general thanksgiving day was appointed for the purpose of giving expression to the popular gratitude for what had seemed to be an interposition of Providence. In England the glad news was received with equal joy, and Pepperell was made a baronet and Warren an admiral. But the news caused astonishment in France, where it had been said that Louisburg was so strongly fortified that a dozen women could successfully defend it, and the French king refused to believe the report so long as there was a shadow of a doubt. That a handful of New England farmers and fishermen could take such a place seemed incredible. But they had nevertheless done it. It was more than the French could bear, and so they determined to make a supreme effort to recapture the lost fortress. A fleet of sixty-five vessels was accordingly fitted out under the command of Duc d'Anville, and in June, 1746, it sailed for America to undertake the work of recovering Louisburg.[14] But from the first the fleet encountered unforeseen difficulties, and soon after its arrival in American waters in September Duc d'Anville died, his successor, D'Estournel, committed suicide, and the enterprise resulted in failure.

Undaunted, however, by this failure, the French Government fitted out another fleet under La Jonquiere for the conquest of Acadia and Louisburg, and in May, 1747, it sailed for America, but it was totally defeated by an English fleet before reaching its destination. Six of the ships of war were captured, and a large number of its men taken prisoners, among them Jonquiere himself. Finally both nations tired of the weary and barren conflict, with its enormous financial burdens, came to terms of agreement, and in October, 1748, signed a treaty of peace at Aix-la-Chapelle. It was agreed that there should be a mutual restitution of all conquests made during the war, and this meant that Louisburg would be given back to the French. George II. is said to have doubted whether it was his to give, considering the circumstances of its capture by New Englanders, but whatever may have been the facts as to this point, the great fortress was quietly restored to the French without the consent of the American colonies, and of course to their great indignation. This act increased the already growing dissatisfaction of the colonists with the course of the mother country, and was doubtless one of the causes that eventually led to the desire for separation. Nevertheless it brought about temporary peace and gave the colonists a short breathing space until the coming of that great struggle which was to settle conclusively the question of British supremacy in America.

[14] Parkman. "Half Century of Conflict," vol. ii. p. 175.

Chapter VIII

THE FRENCH AND INDIAN WAR. 1754-1763

I

THE DISPUTE

THE Treaty of Aix-la-Chapelle, like those which preceded it, proved to be a mere truce in the long struggle between France and England for the mastery of North America, and only postponed the greater and decisive conflict. The vague language employed in the Treaty of Utrecht with regard to the limits of Acadia had given rise to a boundary dispute between the two rival powers, and this had not been definitely settled by the Treaty of Aix-la-Chapelle. The English claimed that Acadia comprehended not only what is now Nova Scotia, but the immense tract of land extending westward to the St. Lawrence River — about twenty times as much as that conceded by French interpretation.[1] In pursuance of a provision in the latter treaty, a commission was appointed for adjusting the rival claims of the two powers in America, but after sitting at Paris for three years it broke up without reaching an agreement and only leaving four quarto volumes of allegations, argument and documental proofs as the result of its labors.

Meantime the dispute assumed larger dimensions by the claim which each nation now put forward for the possession of the valley of the Ohio, and the conflict was precipitated by the action of France in attempting to occupy the territory in dispute. France based her claim to the Ohio Valley on the ground of discovery and occupation. French explorers had sailed up and down the St. Lawrence and Mississippi Rivers, and had made their way along the shores of the Great Lakes from Ontario to Superior. The principles of international law as interpreted by the French gave them a right to the adjacent country drained by the rivers flowing

[1] Parkman, "Montcalm and Wolfe," vol. i. p. 123.

167

into these bodies of water; that is to say, the Mississippi valley extending eastward to the crest of the Alleghany Mountains. Had this claim been allowed they would have received half of New York and a goodly share of Pennsylvania, leaving the English nothing but a narrow strip along the coast. The inchoate title thus gained by discovery and exploration was made definitive by the establishment of a line of forts and trading posts which extended like a great bow from Biloxi in Louisiana around by way of the Great Lakes to the mouth of the St. Lawrence, and including New Orleans, Fort Rosalie (Natchez), Chickasaw Bluffs (Memphis), Cahokia, Kaskaskia, Chartres, Vincennes, Detroit, Montreal, Kingston, Quebec and eventually about fifty others of less importance. Another line of posts, more recently erected, and intended to exclude English fur traders from the headwaters of the Ohio and the region about Lake Erie, extended southward from Lake Ontario to the forks of the Allegheny and Monongahela Rivers. Most of these posts were garrisoned by French troops, and were relieved at regular intervals of six years.

The British claim to the territory in dispute was based, first, on the Treaties of Utrecht and Aix-la-Chapelle, the provisions of which were too vague and uncertain to throw much light on the merits of the controversy; second, on the old " sea to sea " grants by which the western boundaries of the English colonies were made to extend to the South Sea, or Pacific Ocean, these charters being granted prior to the French settlements in the Mississippi Valley; and third, on Indian cessions. By the Treaty of Utrecht in 1713 the Iroquois Indians of New York had been declared British subjects and, at various times during the forty years following, bands of these savages had made raids into what is now Ohio, Indiana, and Illinois, and in some cases had driven off the native Indians and killed and scalped many of them. Great Britain claimed the right to the lands thus " conquered " by her dusky subjects, and in 1744 entered into a treaty with them at Lancaster, Pennsylvania, by which they formally ceded to the British Government an indefinite extent of these lands situated west of the mountains. Again in 1752 another treaty was concluded at Logtown by which Virginia was given the right to erect a fort at the " forks of the Ohio." [2]

The British claims were quite as extravagant and unfounded

[2] Winsor, " Narrative and Critical History," vol. v. pp. 487, 490.

as those of the French, and had they been conceded the French power in America would have been restricted to a comparatively small territory north of the St. Lawrence River. By the middle of the century the rivalry of the two nations for the possession of the valleys of the Ohio was becoming acute. Both French and English colonial governors made urgent recommendations to their respective governments to take steps to occupy and fortify the territory in dispute. The French Government acted first. English fur traders from New York, Pennsylvania and Virginia were penetrating the territory claimed by France and participating in a profitable trade, which the French insisted should be reserved exclusively to them.[3]

Worse still, English land speculators were at work and English emissaries were "tampering" with the Indian allies of France. To expel these intruders the governor of Canada in 1749 sent Chevalier Celeron de Bienville with a detachment of Canadian soldiers and Indians to the junction of the Allegheny and Monongahela Rivers, where they took formal possession of the region in dispute by nailing the arms of France to certain trees and by burying leaden plates with appropriate inscriptions at the mouths of various streams flowing into the Ohio. This performance was enacted at the mouth of the Muskingum River, the Great Kanawha and other streams, and late in the nineteenth century some of the plates were washed up and discovered by the local residents.[4]

Celeron, having thus warned all intruders, returned to Montreal, from which place he summed up his opinion of the situation in the following words: "All I can say is, that the nations of those countries are very ill-disposed towards the French and devoted entirely to the English."

[3] "The traffic of the French in peltries," says Parkman, "was far more important than all the rest together; one which absorbed the enterprise of the colony, drained the life sap from other branches of commerce and, even more than a vicious system of government, kept them in a state of chronic debility— the hardy, adventurous, lawless fur trade. In the eighteenth century Canada exported a moderate quantity of timber, wheat, the herb called ginseng, and a few other commodities; but from first to last she lived chiefly on beaver skins." —"The Old Régime," p. 302.

[4] Parkman, "Montcalm and Wolfe," vol. i. p. 48. Much earlier in the century Gov. Spottswood, of Virginia, had taken possession of this part of the country in the name of George I., by burying bottles containing proclamations setting forth the facts of English occupation. Winsor, "Narrative and Critical History," vol. v. p. 483.

Meanwhile the English were trying the scheme of colonization as a more effective method of frustrating French encroachments. In the previous year (1748) the Ohio Company had been formed for colonizing the lands on the Ohio in what is now West Virginia, and the crown had been induced to grant the company a tract of 500,000 acres, " which," said Governor Dinwiddie, " are his majesty's undoubted right by the treaties of Lancaster and Logtown," in consideration that a hundred families be settled thereon within seven years, and a fort built and garrisoned. Among the members of the company were young George Washington and two of his brothers. Other companies were formed and other grants made, so that by 1757 more than 3,000,000 acres of Virginia lands had thus been granted away. The outbreak of the war soon thereafter put an end to the activities of these land companies, so that they never had an opportunity of accomplishing the purpose for which they were organized.

Soon after Celeron's expedition the French erected and garrisoned several new forts in the disputed territory with a view to checking the English advance. These forts were Presque Isle, on the site of the present city of Erie, Pennsylvania; Fort le Bœuf, about twenty miles to the south of Presque Isle; and Fort Venango, still farther south, near the headwaters of the Allegheny River, or about midway between Lake Erie and the " forks of the Ohio." A third fort was planned at the junction of French Creek and the Allegheny, but was never erected.

II

PRELIMINARY OPERATIONS

The continued activity of the French alarmed Governor Dinwiddie of Virginia, and he decided to send a message to the commandant of the fort at the junction of the Allegheny and Monongahela, protesting against further encroachments. As the bearer of this message the governor selected Major George Washington, at the time adjutant-general of the Virginia militia, who as a surveyor for Lord Fairfax, had seen something of western Virginia and of life on the frontier. Early in November, 1753, with Christopher Gist and an Indian chief called Half King as guides, together with French and Indian interpreters and the necessary

number of servants, Washington set out upon his long journey of
nearly a thousand miles for the "forks of the Ohio."[5]   After a
month or more of perilous journeying through an unbroken wilderness, over the mountains, across swollen rivers and encountering
heavy snows and drenching rains, Washington reached Fort le
Bœuf on December 11.

To the commandant, Saint Pierre, the governor's letter was
delivered and an answer requested.   The letter expressed "astonishment" that the French should have presumed to build forts on
lands belonging to the Crown of Great Britain, demanded to know
by whose authority Celeron's expedition had been undertaken, and
requested the withdrawal of the French troops from the newly
erected forts.   Washington was courteously received by Saint
Pierre, who promised to send the letter to the governor of Canada,
saying that until an answer could be received he would remain
at his post.   Having accomplished his mission Washington set out
on his return journey, which was full of incident and peril.   On one
occasion he narrowly escaped death at the hands of an Indian who
fired at him through accident, as his assailant pretended, and at
another time he was nearly drowned in the swollen Allegheny River
while crossing on a raft.   Finally, after enduring hardships almost
incredible, Washington reached Williamsburg in the middle of
January, 1754, after an absence of nearly eighty days.

Meantime Dinwiddie had sent a report of the French encroachments to the British Government, and had received orders to demand the withdrawal of any persons presuming to erect forts
within the limits of Virginia, and, if the demand should not be
complied with, to "drive them off by force of arms."   The Virginia legislature, refusing aid at first, finally voted ten thousand
pounds under special conditions to enable the governor to carry out
the orders of the king.   Two hundred militiamen were called out
and placed under the command of Joshua Fry, an Englishman, and
a graduate of Oxford, as colonel, with George Washington as second in command.[6]   Before beginning the march a party of Virginians had been sent forward to build a fort at the forks, and while
engaged in this work were driven off, in April, by a French
force which demolished the unfinished fort and began on its site

[5] Parkman, "Montcalm and Wolfe," vol. i. p. 133; Winsor, "Narrative and
Critical History," vol. v. p. 492.
[6] Winsor, "Narrative and Critical History," vol. v. p. 493.

a much more powerful one, which was called Du Quesne, in honor of the governor of Canada, the Marquis Du Quesne. Meantime the militia was on the march. Roads through the wilderness had to be cut for wagons and artillery. Streams were forded with difficulty, and the mountainous character of the country made rapid advance impossible.

In May the army reached the neighborhood of Ohio, and at a place called Great Meadows a detachment of the militia fired on a body of Frenchmen who were lurking in the woods near by; a fight ensued and the French commander, Jumonville, and nine of his men were killed and the rest of his force captured.[7] The war now began in earnest. "A cannon shot fired in the woods of America," said Voltaire, "was the signal that set Europe in a blaze." Such were the complications of European interests that not France and England alone were involved, but the greater part of the Old World.

After the skirmish at Great Meadows, Washington threw up intrenchments at a place which he called Fort Necessity and awaited the coming of reënforcements from Colonel Fry. Before they arrived, however, Fry had died and Washington was made commander of the regiment, which consisted of about 300 men. After the death of Jumonville, his brother, Villiers, took command of the French forces, which greatly outnumbered those of the English.

On July 4 the enemy, consisting of some 900 French and Indians, rushed out of the woods yelling and firing their guns, and at once began the attack upon the English. For nine hours, during most of which time the rain fell in torrents, the fire on both sides was kept up without ceasing, but with the approach of darkness the French proposed a parley. The English were in a bad plight; they had little ammunition, their muskets were in foul condition, and they themselves, were half starved, and drenched

---

[7] The precipitancy of the attack led to the French charge that Jumonville's death was the result of assassination rather than an act of war, and through the treachery of a Dutch interpreter Washington was made to admit this in the articles of capitulation, which were drawn up in French. The French claimed that the party attacked was simply an armed escort with a summons from the commander of Fort Du Quesne seeking an interview with Washington. But the fact is the French had been lurking several days within a few miles of Washington's camp and had made no effort to deliver the summons. Winsor, "Narrative and Critical History," vol. v. p. 493; Parkman, "Montcalm and Wolfe," vol. i. pp. 148–149.

to the skin with rain. In this situation Washington accepted the offer of the French; two officers were sent to confer with Villiers, and presently they returned with terms of capitulation, which Washington signed about midnight. The terms allowed the English to march out with drums beating and with the honors of war, and permitted them to retain all their property. The loss of the Virginians was twelve killed and forty-three wounded; that of the enemy being somewhat smaller. The morning after the surrender Washington's force abandoned the fort and marched back to Will's Creek, fifty-two miles distant, while the French, exultant over their victory, returned to Fort Du Quesne. Not an English flag now waved west of the Alleghanies.

III

RESOURCES OF THE CONTENDING BELLIGERENTS.

Before proceeding further with the narration of the military operations of the war, it is well to turn aside for a moment to consider the strength and resources of the two belligerent powers in America. The territorial possessions actually occupied by the two contestants were not very unequal in extent. Great Britain controlled the Atlantic Coast from Maine to Florida and westward to the watershed of the Alleghany Mountains. France held Louisiana, the Mississippi Valley and Canada. The French population in America in 1754, including that in Louisiana and Acadia, did not exceed 80,000 persons, of which about 55,000 were in Canada. The population of the English colonies in America was not less than 1,100,000. This disparity of population alone was an immense disadvantage to the French, but it was to some extent offset by other circumstances. In the first place, the French power in America was centralized and united. There were, to be sure, territorial subdivisions of provinces, but they were without local autonomy. When it came to raising troops and supplies the governor of Canada was not dependent upon the will of a dozen local legislatures, each free to vote the necessary funds or withhold them as it pleased. The king had but to command and the French colonies acted as a unit, a condition of the highest value in the prosecution of war. The English power in America, on the other hand, was a "mosaic of little republics," each with a large degree of local autonomy, free to grant or withhold supplies for the prose-cution of the war as its sense of right and justice dictated.   United action was difficult to secure, as the appeals of Governor Dinwiddie to the neighboring colonies clearly showed.

The need of closer union among the colonies for purposes of mutual defense, as well as domestic tranquility, was strongly felt by the colonial leaders, and in 1754, the very year the war broke out, a plan of union proposed by Benjamin Franklin was laid before a congress which assembled at Albany for the purpose of renewing the treaty with the Six Nations.   The plan proposed a grand council of forty-eight members to represent the various col-onies on the basis of their respective contributions, no colony to have more than seven nor less than two members.   The members of the grand council were to be elected by the colonial legislatures for a term of three years.   The council was to be empowered to provide for the defense of the colonies, the apportionment of quotas of men and money, the control of the colonial armies, and the care of the general welfare.   There was to be a president general ap-pointed by the Crown, with the power of appointing military offi-cers, supervising military affairs and vetoing ordinances.[8]   This scheme was adopted by all the delegates present except those from Connecticut; but it seemed to the colonial assemblies to give the Crown too much power, and was therefore rejected.   For the opposite reason it found just as little favor with the home govern-ment.   It was the first notable attempt to bring about a union of the English colonies, and of it the historian Bancroft well says: " America had never seen an assembly so venerable for the States that were represented, or for the great and able men who com-posed it."

In addition to the advantage which the French derived from the character of their political organization, the powerful influence which they exerted over the Indians was a source of incalculable strength to them.   The French fur trader in America had been followed by the Jesuit priest, and while the one bargained with the savage for his furs and peltries, the other sought to convert him to the Roman Catholic faith.   The French explorers, traders, soldiers and missionaries placed themselves on an equality with the red men, lived with them in their huts, adopted their customs and sometimes married Indian squaws and reared families, apparently

[8] Frothingham, " Rise of the Republic," p. 143.

without any sense of degradation. The Indian fondness for display, as well as his weakness for spirits, were not neglected.[9] Their festivities were participated in by Frenchmen, and it is said that no less a personage than Governor Frontenac himself donned their uncouth but picturesque costume and engaged in their dances.[10] By these means the French gained a remarkable ascendency over the Indians and were thus enabled to enlist them as allies in the war with the British.

The Englishman showed an unwillingness to treat the Indian on a footing of equality, and, moreover, he lacked the resources of artifice and flattery which the French turned to so great advantage. Besides, the Indian realized that the Englishman wanted his lands, while the Frenchman did not, and consequently cherished a suspicion of the former. It was not unnatural, therefore, that the Indians should have taken sides with the French in the war that now ensued. To this, however, there was a notable exception in the case of the Iroquois, or Six Nations of New York, who withstood French influence and cast their lot with the British.[11] This was due to two causes. In the first place the Iroquois had a traditional dislike of the French, which dated back to the year 1609, when Champlain made a raid into Iroquois territory and killed some of their chiefs. Secondly there was a bitter hostility between the Algonquin and Iroquois nations, and the fact that the Algonquins were on intimate terms with the French led the Iroquois to reject the diplomatic advances of the latter, and to become allies of the former.[12]

With all their hatred for the French it is extremely probable, however, that the Iroquois would have yielded to French seductions had it not been for the powerful influence exercised over them by Sir William Johnson. Johnson was a native of Ireland who came to America in 1738 and settled near Schenectady. Engaging in trade with the Indians, he soon won their confidence to a remarkable degree. He adopted the French method of social intercourse

[9] While Washington was at Fort le Bœuf on his mission in 1753 he says he found it almost impossible to prevent the French from seducing Half King by means of gifts and brandy and winning him over to their side.

[10] Sloane, "The French War and the Revolution," p. 33.

[11] "Iroquois" was the French name for the confederacy of Cayugas, Senecas, Oneidas, Onondagas and Mohawks. In 1713 they were joined by the Tuscaroras of North Carolina. By the English, they were known as the "Six Nations" after 1713. They called themselves Hodenosaunee.

[12] Sloane, "The French War and the Revolution," pp. 34-35.

with the Indians, became a master of their language, married an Indian squaw, and was elevated to the rank of Sachem, an honor rarely accorded by an Indian tribe to a white man. In 1744 he was appointed by Governor Clinton as colonel of the Six Nations, and when the war broke out he was made a major general of British forces. He used his influence with the Iroquois to turn them against the French, and to him, more than to any other man, the alliance with the British was due.

IV

BRADDOCK'S EXPEDITION

The English authorities, both in America and at home, were sorely disappointed at the result of the affair at Fort Necessity, and at once began to devise plans for retrieving the disaster and driving out the French. The Cabinet, at the head of which stood the Duke of Newcastle, proposed to take rigorous measures to insure British control of Acadia and to organize three expeditions to proceed against Fort Du Quesne, Niagara and Crown Point respectively.[13] Early in 1755 a fleet was dispatched to Virginia with two regiments of soldiers under the command of Major General Braddock who was to have chief command of His Majesty's forces in America. Braddock had seen forty years of service in the British army, had gained distinction for gallantry, and meritorious conduct, but he possessed personal qualities which, to a large degree, unfitted him for military service such as he was to see in the mountains and woods of North America. Soon after the departure of Braddock with his feeble force, a French fleet, under the command of Vaudreuil, the new governor of Canada, with 4,000 soldiers, sailed for the Gulf of St. Lawrence.

Braddock arrived in Virginia early in February, 1755, called a conference of colonial governors at Alexandria in April, and discussed with them the question of raising men and money, and plans for expelling the French. This done, he assumed command of the expedition and entered upon the long march through the wilderness to a point on Will's Creek named Fort Cumberland in honor of the general's patron, the Duke of Cumberland. The

[13] Sloane, "The French War and the Revolution," p. 40; Winsor, "Narrative and Critical History," vol. v. p. 495.

force consisted of a detachment of British regulars, together with several regiments of provincial troops, whom Braddock contemptuously referred to as "raw recruits." He further showed his contempt of the provincials by issuing an order which withheld from the higher American officers all rank when regulars of the same rank were in the field, and made matters worse by declaring that whatever incapacity the American "recruits" might exhibit in the presence of savage warriors His Majesty's regulars would be more than a match for them. Nevertheless, he suffered Washington to attend him as aide-de-camp. After a weary march of nearly a month Braddock reached Fort Cumberland in May, where a large body of militia was already waiting. Through the efforts of Benjamin Franklin, who had preceded Braddock to Will's Creek, the neighboring farmers had been induced to lend their wagons and teams in large numbers for the transportation of supplies. After a rest of several days, during which the militia was put through a rigorous course of training and discipline, the army set out for Fort Du Quesne, one hundred and thirty miles distant. Great were the difficulties of that march, for there were no roads except Indian paths, and the country was an unbroken wilderness covered with steep hills and traversed by rough ridges. A force of five hundred axemen had to be sent forward to clear a wagon road and construct bridges. In the narrow twelve-foot road thus constructed the army slowly made its way over the mountains, sometimes drawn out four miles in length and giving the appearance of a gigantic parti-colored snake trailing through the forest.[14]

By June 18 it was within thirty miles of Fort Du Quesne, but was advancing scarcely more than three miles per day. Growing impatient, Washington induced Braddock to leave the heavy baggage behind under Colonel Dunbar and send forward 1,200 picked men as an advance corps. By July 7 this body of troops had reached the mouth of Turtle Creek, about eight miles from Fort Du Quesne. Early on the morning of the 9th, when the army was within five miles of the fort, a force, consisting of some two hundred Frenchmen and six hundred Indians dressed in their customary war paint, was sent out from the fort to meet the English. Concealing themselves in the high grass and underbrush which flanked the narrow roadway near the ford of the Monongahela, they waited until the advance guard under Lieutenant Colonel Gage

---

[14] Parkman, "Half Century of Conflict," vol. i. p. 205.

had reached a convenient point, and then at a signal from a French officer they rose with a terrible war whoop and began to pour a merciless fire right and left upon the terrified and demoralized English and Americans.[15]

It seemed to the astonished English that the woods were swarming with savages. From behind trees, stumps, bushes, bunches of grass and crags the unseen enemy poured volley after volley into the British ranks. As soon as Gage recovered his equanimity he wheeled his men into line and made several discharges with remarkable steadiness. But for the most part they took effect only against trees and stones. When Braddock heard the firing he pushed rapidly forward to the aid of Colonel Gage, but his forces were soon thrown into the utmost confusion, with the exception of the Virginians, who fired upon the enemy from behind stumps and trees, according to their own method of warfare. Braddock was unaccustomed to the Indian manner of fighting, and what was worse, he refused to adopt it upon the advice of Washington, and expressed disgust at such unmilitary conduct. Dashing to and fro, apparently oblivious to every thought of danger, he endeavored in vain to form the regulars in line and to prevent them from breaking ranks and taking advantage of the trees and stumps. Under this pressure the regulars stood their ground for a brief interval, firing aimlessly at foes whom they could place only by puffs of smoke; but finally they broke in confusion and fled, their scarlet uniforms offering excellent targets for the enemy. The militia, more accustomed to the war whoop of the savage, were less easily terrified, and contested their ground for about two hours, during which time the regulars were mowed down like grain before a reaper. The panic was indescribable.

In reply to Braddock's entreaties some of them replied, " We would fight if we could see anybody to fight with." The ground was covered with dead and wounded soldiers, maddened horses rushed neighing about the field, while the roar of cannon and the clatter of musketry added further to the terror caused by the hideous yells of Indian savages. Braddock's courage never deserted him. He was always in the thickest of the fight. Four horses were shot under him, and while dashing forward on the

[15] The ambush theory is questioned by some authorities. Thwaites in his " France in America," pp. 177–178, says " what occurred was a regulation forest fight in which the French and their allies flanked the British on either side."

fifth he was mortally wounded by a bullet which entered his lung. Carried to the rear he died a few days later and was buried in the middle of the road. Washington, too, barely escaped, for two horses were shot under him, and four bullets tore his clothes to pieces. Out of 86 officers, 63 were killed or disabled, while of 1,373 men, but few more than 400 escaped unhurt. The losses of the enemy were insignificant, being about 30 killed and as many wounded. Among the killed on the English side were Sir Peter Halket and young Shirley, secretary of General Braddock and son of Governor Shirley of Massachusetts. Among the wounded were Horatio Gates and Thomas Gage, well known names in the history of the Revolution.

After the fall of Braddock the army retreated in utter rout. The arrival of the fugitives at Dunbar's Camp with the tidings of defeat threw the camp into commotion, and orders were at once given that the wagons, stores and ammunition should be destroyed, to prevent their falling into the hands of the enemy. The order was carried out and hundreds of wagons were burned, scores of cannon disabled, many barrels of gunpowder thrown into the river, and large quantities of provisions scattered through the woods and swamps. This done, the depleted, disorganized and disheartened army took up its return march for Fort Cumberland, sixty miles distant. Thus ended the first attempt to expel the French from the Ohio Valley.

V

EXPULSION OF THE ACADIANS

A tragic feature of the war was the expulsion by the British authorities of the Acadians from Nova Scotia. This province, as we have seen, was settled by the French in 1604, three years before the first English settlement in America, and through all the changes of a century and a half it had remained largely French in race, religion, manners and customs. By the Treaty of Utrecht of 1713, Acadia, with indefinite boundaries, was ceded to England; but the treaty contained a stipulation which relieved the French inhabitants from taking up arms against France in any war between Great Britain and that country. During the forty years they had lived under British rule they had increased in numbers and had become prosperous and contented. They were a simple-minded, peasant people, thrifty, frugal and industrious, lived in rustic plenty, and were deeply attached to their homes. But notwithstanding their quiet, peaceful habits, they were a thorn in the side of the British, for they were British subjects only nominally, and their neutrality proved to be ostensible rather than real. They remained devoted to the Catholic religion and were completely subject to the influence of their priests, for the most part Canadians, who encouraged them to retain their native language and to refuse the oath of allegiance to the British Crown.

Toward the middle of the eighteenth century the British Government, fearing that France might attempt to reassert her sovereignty over Acadia, sent out several thousand settlers and founded the town of Halifax as a means of strengthening its power in the peninsula. In the spring of 1755 a British fleet, commanded by Colonel Robert Monckton, arrived in the Bay of Fundy, captured a number of French vessels and expelled the French from this region and took Forts Beau Sejour and Gaspereau, the only places of strategic importance on the isthmus still held by the French. To the surprise of the British they found Acadians with arms at Beau Sejour, fighting on the side of the French, in violation of their neutral obligations. They had thus forfeited their right to be treated as neutrals, and so something had to be done to curb their French propensities. To order them to leave the country would be merely to drive them to Canada or Cape Breton and thus to strengthen the enemy. To place garrisons in their midst to enforce their neutrality would require more men than the government could spare, besides the entailment of a large expense.

It was therefore decided to remove the whole population, root and branch, from the province, if they refused to take oaths of allegiance, and transplant it to various parts of the country, in such a way as to destroy all possibility of its ever giving the English further trouble. It was a harsh decision, but the English believed it to be justified on the grounds of military necessity, and they proceeded to carry it out with a severity and relentlessness rarely equalled in the sad history of warfare. A plan for kidnaping the unsuspecting peasants was carefully worked out and kept a profound secret from them. In September they were assembled under false representations at their various parish churches, by order of Colonel Winslow, when the king's proclamation ordering their expulsion was read to them, after which they were surrounded by the soldiers, made prisoners and hurried on ships that lay in a nearby harbor. Families were not infrequently broken up by the separation of the husband from the wife, and both from the children, although the English commanders endeavored to keep families together. The heartrending scenes that occurred at Grand Pré have been well portrayed by Longfellow in his poem "Evangeline," and the whole affair has been charmingly described by Francis Parkman in his "Half Century of Conflict." Lands, crops, cattle, houses, everything except their little money and household goods, were forfeited to the Crown, and to insure the starvation of those who fled to the woods the growing crops were destroyed and the barns and houses burned. Their beautiful country, smiling in the autumn with well cultivated gardens and fields of waving grain, was left not only a solitude, but a desert. Once on board the English vessels they were carried away to distant provinces of the British colonial empire. More than a thousand were sent to Massachusetts, where they long remained a burden on the public. Their wretched condition of course excited commiseration, but the New England intolerance for Catholicism was too great to make the exiles welcome guests, and they were regarded with suspicion. The governors of several States refused to receive them, and the ships bearing them were forcibly turned back. Some were sent to Pennsylvania, some to far-away Georgia, and others to the West Indies —altogether about 7,000 being carried off.[16] Many resigned themselves to their fate, while others yearned for their former homes and endeavored to return to Acadia or to Canada. In some cases the colonial assemblies, only too anxious to be rid of Papists, defrayed the expenses of their transportation. Several hundred who were sent to Georgia built rude boats and tried to reach the Bay of Fundy. Some were sent to England and France, while some made their way to the French province of Louisiana, where their descendants are still found, constituting a numerous and distinct population. Of those who were deported only an insignificant portion ever lived to see Acadia again, while many died broken-hearted.

It is difficult for the impartial historian to find justification for so severe and harsh a policy. As a military measure it was without precedent in modern times, and must always remain a dark

[16] As late as 1762 the General Court of Massachusetts turned back five transports loaded with these unfortunate persons. Winsor, "Narrative and Critical History," vol. v. p. 417.

spot in the history of Great Britain.   It is often claimed, however, that the provocation of the English was not inconsiderable, and that they did not take this extreme step until every resource of patience and persuasion had been tried in vain to induce the Acadians to take an oath of allegiance and preserve a neutral attitude. As long as they remained in Nova Scotia they were deemed a source of perpetual danger to the English colonists, and kept the English constantly filled with a feeling of insecurity.[17]

VI

ENGLISH DISASTERS AND FAILURES

The disaster at Fort Du Quesne was a sore disappointment to the Newcastle ministry and caused general dismay throughout the English settlements in America, for it left the people of the middle colonies exposed to the savage raids of the Indians and their French allies.   They were quickly aroused to this danger, and the legislatures of Pennsylvania and Virginia at once appropriated large sums for defense, while the neighboring colonies offered to furnish men and supplies to the extent of their ability.

Braddock's defeat also spoiled another well-laid scheme of the British authorities — the expedition against Fort Niagara.   This place was the center of the fur trade in the lake region and constituted an important link in the chain of posts from the St. Lawrence to the Ohio.   Governor William Shirley, of Massachusetts, with some good regulars, militiamen and Indians, had already undertaken to capture the fort, expecting to be joined by Braddock's army after the latter had taken Fort Du Quesne.   He had set out from Albany early in the summer, and after a long and toilsome march through the wilderness of western New York, reached Oswego, on Lake Ontario, with the expectation of embarking for

[17] Parkman, "Half Century of Conflict," ch. viii.; Sloane, "The French War and the Revolution," pp. 46–48; Winsor, "Narrative and Critical History," vol. v. pp. 415–417. This melancholy subject is of too great extent to be adequately examined in the limits of a few pages. The most scholarly as well as the most patient investigation of this intricate question is comprised in the two volumes by Edouard Richard, a great grandson of one of the transported Acadians. This author's conclusions are not in perfect harmony with our text or with the opinions of many previous writers. See "Acadia, Missing Links of a Lost Chapter in American History."

Niagara. Here he fitted out a number of vessels and made great preparation for the advance on Niagara, but at this juncture came the discouraging news of Braddock's defeat, in addition to innumerable delays occasioned by heavy rains and other obstacles. On account of the lateness of the season, therefore, it was decided to abandon the expedition, and this was accordingly done after building a fort and leaving a garrison of seven hundred men to defend it.

It now began to look as if the first year of the war would end in total failure so far as the English were concerned, but fortunately they were saved from this by a victory over the French in northern New York. As has been said, the fort, Crown Point, on the west shore of Lake Champlain, or, as the French called it, Lake Sacrament, was, with Du Quesne and Niagara, one of the objective points in the British programme. It stood as a gateway on the road to Canada, and was a place of some strategic importance. William Johnson, the great friend of the Iroquois, was selected to lead the expedition against the fort, with General Phineas Lyman of Connecticut as second in command. Among the officers were Israel Putnam and John Stark, afterwards famous generals in the Revolution, and Colonel Ephraim Williams, the founder of Williams College. Johnson succeeded in raising nearly 4,000 men, mainly New England militiamen, and marched up to the shores of Lake George, while the opposing French army, consisting of some 3,000 men, including 700 Indians, and commanded by Baron Dieskau, pushed down from Montreal and made ready to attack him.

The advance guards of the two armies met on September 8, at a place some distance south of Crown Point, a battle ensued, and Dieskau was defeated and mortally wounded. His troops thereupon fled in terror back to Crown Point, while Dieskau himself was taken prisoner. The loss of the French was about 1,000 men; that of the English about 300. Johnson was knighted by the Crown and given £5,000 by Parliament as a reward for his services; but General Lyman of Connecticut claimed the chief honor, on the ground that while Johnson lay wounded in his tent he forced the rout of the French; however, Johnson did not even mention Lyman's name in his report.[18]

[18] Winsor, "Narrative and Critical History," vol. v. p. 504; Parkman, "Montcalm and Wolfe," vol. i. p. 316.

Although receiving reënforcements, Johnson made no attempt to follow up his victory by an advance on Crown Point, but against the advice of Lyman, timidly suffered the French to erect Fort Ticonderoga near by, while he withdrew his army to the south. He was accused by many in New England of incapacity, and apparently the charges were not without foundation. Thus the year 1755 ended with the outlook for the English anything but encouraging. They had sustained one overwhelming defeat, had met with utter failure in the Niagara expedition, and had, after a decisive victory on Lake George, neglected to follow it up and reap the fruits which it offered.

The next year (1756) saw formal declarations of war by both belligerents — after war had been in actual existence for two years — and renewed preparations for the prosecution of hostilities in America. The Earl of Loudon was made commander-in-chief of the British forces in America, with General Abercrombie as second in command. General Montcalm was made commander of the French forces, to succeed the dying Dieskau, and, while the English were pursuing a policy of masterly inactivity, he marched upon the fort which Shirley had built and garrisoned at Oswego, and in August captured it, together with about 1,600 prisoners. Some of these unfortunates were tomahawked by drunken savages, and about 100 pieces of artillery and considerable ammunition were taken.

It was the most important victory that the French arms had yet achieved in America, but the French success was partially offset by the erection of a British fort on the Tennessee to guard Georgia and the Carolinas against incursions of the French from their posts east of the Mississippi. The destruction also of Kittanning, an Indian village some fifty miles north of Fort Du Quesne on the Allegheny River, served further to offset in a small way the French victory at Oswego. From Kittanning Indian raids had been made upon the frontier settlements of Pennsylvania, and many of the inhabitants massacred or carried away into captivity. It was finally taken by a militiaman, Captain John Armstrong, who, with a party of 300 frontiersmen, pushed his way through the wilderness in September and fell upon the town in the early morning, taking the Indians unawares just as they were closing a night of festivities. After a hot and stubborn fight the Indians were badly routed and their town utterly destroyed, together with a quantity of ammunition which they declared was sufficient for a ten years' war with the English.

Throughout the winter which followed hostilities were suspended with the exception of a few raids upon the enemy undertaken by partisan bands from New England or from the forts in New York. An unsuccessful attempt was also made by a French party to strike a blow against the fort at the head of Lake George,

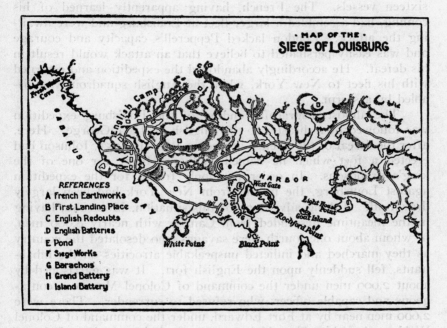

• MAP OF THE •
SIEGE OF LOUISBURG

REFERENCES
A French Earthworks
B First Landing Place
C English Redoubts
D English Batteries
E Pond
F Siege Works
G Barachois
H Grand Battery
I Island Battery

but the garrison proved too strong, and their assailants were compelled to retreat without inflicting any greater injury than the burning of neighboring houses and the desolation of the adjacent country.

The military operations of 1757 were even less successful from the English standpoint than those of the preceding year. It was indeed a year of humiliation and disaster.[19] One of the principal objects of the war was the capture of Louisburg, the impregnable fortress on Cape Breton Island, which, as we have seen, had been taken by Pepperwell and his New England militiamen in 1745 and

[19] Thwaites, "France in America," p. 215.

restored to France by the Treaty of Aix-la-Chapelle, to the great chagrin of the New Englanders. Loudon planned to lead an attack upon the stronghold, but his preparations were characterized by extraordinary tardiness and inactivity. Finally, he embarked from New York with a large fleet, and reached Halifax in June, where he was joined by a squadron from England, his effective strength consisting altogether of ten or twelve thousand men and sixteen vessels. The French, having apparently learned of his coming, had assembled a larger fleet at Louisburg and were awaiting the attack. Loudon lacked Pepperell's capacity and courage and was easily persuaded to believe that an attack would result in his defeat. He accordingly abandoned the expedition and returned with his fleet to New York, while the English squadron was disabled by a storm.

The almost disgraceful ending of the Louisburg expedition was followed by a disaster to the English on Lake George. Here, after the defeat of the French at Crown Point in 1755, Johnson had erected a fort which he named William Henry for one of the king's grandsons. In order to supply troops for the expedition against Louisburg, the militia from New York had been largely drawn off. Taking advantage of this situation, Montcalm, having in the meantime descended from Canada with nearly 8,000 men, of whom about one-fourth were savages who desolated the country as they marched and inflicted unspeakable atrocities on the inhabitants, fell suddenly upon the English fort. It was garrisoned by about 2,000 men under the command of Colonel Munro, a courageous and capable officer, who refused to surrender. There were 2,600 men near by at Fort Edward, under the command of Colonel Webb, and to this officer Munro sent appeals in vain for reënforcements. For four or five days the brave garrison held out, but was finally forced to surrender, being accorded generous terms and allowed to march out with the honors of war.

Montcalm found it impossible to compel the Indians to observe the terms of the treaty, although he had exacted from the chiefs a promise of obedience. Disappointed at not finding plunder in the fort, they turned upon the sick and wounded left there, murdered them in cold blood, and horribly mutilated their bodies. Proceeding early next morning to the camp, partly intoxicated with rum, they began the work of butchering the soldiers who were waiting to be marched out. In vain did Montcalm appeal to his bloodthirsty allies to spare the English who were under his protection; he even begged them to kill him instead. But neither threats nor entreaties, nor the promise of presents, could restrain them, and so they kept on with their bloody work until seventy or eighty persons, including a number of women and children, had been massacred. Two hundred prisoners and a quantity of plunder were carried away, the fort was razed to the ground and the ruins, with the dead bodies of the slain, were heaped in a vast pile and burned to ashes.[20]

Thus the year 1757 ended as the preceding one, in gloom for the British, and the great mass of the people were in despondency.[21] The war had now been going on for more than two years, and they had scarcely won a single substantial victory. The record was mainly a succession of disasters and failures, both on land and sea. To this, however, there was a notable exception. In far-away India the British had won the Battle of Plassey, by which they had destroyed the French power in that part of the globe and laid the foundation for a great empire in the East. But in America the French still controlled three-fourths of the continent, including the great waterways that led to the heart of the continent, the Mississippi and the St. Lawrence, and the several portages which connected them. Not a foot of the disputed territory in the valley of the Ohio or on the Great Lakes was held by Great Britain, and the only fort she had established there had been taken by the enemy. The British commanders in America had shown themselves inefficient and incapable. Popular sentiment attributed this state of affairs to the imbecility and incapacity of the Newcastle ministry, which had held the reins of power since the outbreak of the war.

VII

THE VICTORIES OF PITT

It was now felt that what England needed more than anything else was an able leader at the head of the government, a man who was capable of directing and managing a great war. Public sentiment had already found such a statesman in the person of William Pitt, the Great Commoner, as he was called, but the

[20] Parkman, "Montcalm and Wolfe," vol. i. p. 513.
[21] Thwaites, "France in America," p. 215.

king and the ruling Whig families looked upon him with jealousy and caused his dismissal in April, 1757. But the popular enthusiasm for Pitt was irresistible, and in June of the same year he was called to the head of the government. Almost instantly the situation began to improve under his magic touch. He had worked out well-conceived plans for prosecuting the war and now proceeded to carry them out with masterly success. "England has long been in labor," said Frederick the Great, "and has at last brought forth a man." Pitt proposed to take Louisburg, Ticonderoga, Du Quesne, and finally Quebec, and under his direction the organization of the army was speedily reformed and new and able leaders like Howe, Forbes, Amherst and Wolfe were selected to carry out his program.

In the early part of 1758 England became an ally of Frederick the Great, who had been struggling single-handed against a coalition of Russia, France and Austria; the combined forces of the allies soon began to win startling victories over the enemy, in spite of the great odds against them. The moral effect of these brilliant European victories upon the spirits of the disheartened Americans was soon perceptible. Early in 1758 Pitt sent a fleet to America under the command of Admiral Boscawen to capture Louisburg. It consisted of more than forty vessels and had on board over eleven thousand troops, nearly all regulars, including two able commanders, Generals Jeffrey Amherst and James Wolfe. On May 28, after a long and tempestuous voyage, the fleet arrived at Halifax, and early in June began the attack upon the powerful French fortress, the "Dunkirk of America." The gallant Wolfe, in the face of a deadly fire, captured the outposts and drove in the enemy's lines, killing and capturing 120 men. A regular siege was then begun against the fortress. Day after day Boscawen's guns bombarded the fort, until by the latter part of July the French cannon were silenced and a breach made in the crumbling walls. Part of the fort was also on fire and the condition of the garrison was truly pitiable. In one day no less than 1,200 bombs were thrown, and there was scarcely a house in the town that had not been injured by the artillery fire. In this situation it seemed useless for the garrison to attempt to hold out further, and it surrendered upon receiving promise of honorable terms. Altogether about 5,700 men were made prisoners, while 240 cannon and a large quantity of ammunition and stores were captured. This splendid success, really the first of the war, aroused genuine enthusiasm throughout the American colonies and raised Pitt to the first place in the hearts of the English people. Addresses of congratulation poured in upon the king from every quarter, thanksgiving sermons were preached in New England, and displays of fireworks and illuminations were made in all the large towns of the colonies. It proved to be the beginning of a series of successes which were to result ultimately in the downfall of the French.

It was also a part of Pitt's programme to capture Ticonderoga, an important stronghold held by the French at the north end of Lake George, and which, besides controlling the highway to Canada, was a thorn in the side of New York. While the siege of Louisburg was in progress a large army was assembling in New York under the leadership of Abercrombie and Lord Howe, brother of the two Howes of Revolutionary fame, for the purpose of marching against Ticonderoga. The army consisted of 15,000 men, of whom 6,300 were British regulars and 9,000 were provincials, mainly from New England and the middle colonies, among them being Israel Putnam and John Stark. It is believed to have been the largest army of white soldiers ever assembled in America up to that time.[22] Besides. there were about 900 bateaux, 135 whale boats and a large number of heavy flatboats for transporting the men and artillery on the lake.

Early in July the flotilla, bearing the army and presenting a magnificent spectacle, sailed down the lake and prepared to attack the fort which was occupied by Montcalm with about 4,000 men.[23] A skirmishing party had been thrown out by Montcalm and this was attacked by an advance guard of the English force, with the result that Lord Howe, the real, though not nominal, commander of the army, was killed in the sharp fight which followed. The death of this brave leader threw the army into confusion and produced a languor and consternation from which the timid, incapable Abercrombie was never able to completely rescue it. On July 8 the English troops undertook to carry the breastworks of the fort, but were mowed down in frightful numbers, while Abercrombie himself remained at a sawmill a mile and a half away, secure from all danger. By his direction six frantic assaults were made against the intrenchments, but each time the

22 Sloane, "French War and the Revolution," p. 69.
23 Parkman, "Montcalm and Wolfe," vol. ii. p. 93.

soldiers were driven back, leaving in the end about 2,000 of their dead and wounded on the ground. In this situation Abercrombie decided to abandon the attack and retreat with his shattered army to the south. This he did, leaving Ticonderoga in the hands of the enemy. His military career, like that of Loudon, having ended in failure, he returned to England, reëntered politics, was elected to Parliament, and we hear of him no more.

While the English were sorrowing over their awful disaster at Lake George, there occurred an event which served to cheer, in a slight degree at least, their drooping spirits. This was the capture and destruction of Fort Frontenac, on the western shore of Lake Ontario. This daring exploit was accomplished by John Bradstreet, who with some 3,000 militiamen marched to Oswego, which he easily recaptured, after which he crossed the lake in such boats as could be procured, and in the latter part of August captured the coveted fort with its garrison of more than a hundred men and nine armed vessels — the whole of the French naval force on Lake Ontario — besides a large quantity of valuable spoils, including 60 cannon, and some ammunition and stores intended for Fort Du Quesne. Next to the loss of Louisburg, this was the heaviest blow that the French had yet received. Their command of Lake Ontario was now gone and New France was cut in twain.[24]

The last military campaign of the year was that against Fort Du Quesne. This expedition was entrusted to the command of General Forbes, a Scotch veteran, with the able assistance of Colonel George Washington, who marched at the head of 1,400 Virginia troops. To these were added 2,700 men from Pennsylvania under John Armstrong, about 2,000 men from the Carolinas, and a corps of Royal Americans, commanded by a Swiss officer, Colonel Bouquet, making altogether an army of about 6,000 men, nearly all of whom were Americans. After some discussion it was decided not to follow the road constructed by Braddock in 1754, but to cut a new path through the forest from the headwaters of the Juniata across the ridges to a tributary of the Allegheny. It was a shorter route, but was more broken and required a vast amount of time and labor to construct the road. The proposition was opposed by Washington, who, not insensible to the interests of his colony, which had western lands to develop, insisted on following Braddock's road. The Pennsylvanians, on the other hand,

---

[24] Parkman, "Montcalm and Wolfe." vol. ii. p. 129.

wished to have a new road cut from Carlisle direct to Fort Du Quesne.

The expedition was delayed in getting started, and when at last, in June, it began to move, General Forbes was seized with a mortal illness and had to be carried on a litter before his troops. On account of the additional delay thus occasioned, it was not until September that the expedition reached the neighborhood of the forks. Major Grant with 800 skirmishers was sent forward to reconnoiter, and if possible decoy a portion of the garrison from the fort and capture them; but he was surprised by overwhelming numbers and badly beaten in a fight which cost him nearly 300 men. At this juncture it was decided not to proceed farther until spring, but on November 12 news was brought to the camp by friendly Indians that the garrison of Fort Du Quesne had been diminished by withdrawals and was badly weakened for lack of supplies. Thereupon it was resolved to resume the march, and Washington and Armstrong, with 3,500 men, pushed forward through the forests, only to find upon reaching the forks of the Ohio a heap of smoldering ruins on the site of the fort.

The French garrison, reduced to five hundred men, seeing that they were greatly outnumbered and on the verge of starvation, had burned the barracks and storehouses, blown up the fortifications, and departed in various directions, leaving the heads of their slaughtered captives stuck on poles for the delectation of their living comrades. Upon the arrival of Washington the English flag was hoisted on the spot and a thanksgiving service followed the next day. Few campaigns have ever been conducted so successfully from a litter of pain.[25] The name of the place was changed to Pittsburg, in honor of the Great Commoner, who had made the English triumph possible. The name was retained after the colonies became independent States, in recognition of Pitt's unselfish stand for the liberties of the Americans at the outbreak of the Revolution, and on the site of the ruined fort has grown up a mighty city which stands the most enduring monument ever erected to an Englishman on this continent. General Forbes was carried back to Philadelphia on a litter, and after lingering in great pain, died in March and was buried with military honors in Christ Church, that city.

The year 1758 opened under more auspicious circumstances

[25] Winsor, "Narrative and Critical History," vol. v. p. 530.

for the English than any preceding year since the outbreak of the war.   Since the accession of Pitt, the military situation had undergone a marvelous transformation.   A succession of victories had followed where hitherto only disaster and failure had characterized English operations.   The important strongholds of Louisburg, Du Quesne, and Frontenac, constituting the left, right and center, respectively, of the French lines, had been taken, and barring the repulse of Abercrombie at Ticonderoga, the English forces in America had not suffered a defeat since Pitt assumed the reins of government.   The great West was now open to English enterprise, the frontier settlements were relieved from the scourge of Indian warfare and the French had lost half their savage allies.[26]   Encouraged at the prospect, Pitt mapped out an elaborate and well-conceived plan of campaign for the new year.   The region of territory between the lakes and the forks of the Ohio was to be taken and held secure by General Stanwix; an expedition under the direction of General Prideaux and Sir William Johnson was to be sent against Niagara and Montreal; while General Amherst, who had been made commander-in-chief, was to be sent against Ticonderoga, after which his forces were to join the army of the St. Lawrence under Wolfe and advance upon Quebec.[27]

The campaign opened with the advance on Fort Niagara, Prideaux leading a division of English regulars and American provincials, with Johnson at the head of a band of Iroquois braves. Leaving strong garrisons at Fort Stanwix and Oswego, they embarked at the latter place early in July and in due course arrived at Niagara and laid siege to the fort.   Shortly after beginning the bombardment, Prideaux was killed by a shell and was succeeded in the command by Johnson.   The siege continued for several weeks, and, although the French received large reënforcements, they were compelled to surrender.   It is a relief to be able to record that the surrender was not followed by an Indian massacre, such as had occurred at Fort William Henry when the English surrendered to the French and their savage allies, although Johnson, remembering the atrocities perpetrated upon his countrymen on the latter occasion, did not object to the Indians pillaging the fort and enjoying the spoils.   The result of the fall of Fort Niagara was to make possible the speedy establishment of English control

[26] Parkman, "Montcalm and Wolfe," vol. ii. p. 162.
[27] Sloane, "French War and the Revolution," p. 78.

over the intervening country between the lakes and the Ohio, and it was immediately followed by the abandonment of the neighboring forts between Niagara and Pittsburg. In a few weeks not a fighting Frenchman was to be found in all this part of New France.

Ticonderoga, at the head of Lake George, was now the only remaining French stronghold within American territory claimed by the Crown of Great Britain. Preparations for the advance against this place were rapidly pushed, and in June an army of over ten thousand men, about equally divided between regulars and provincials, was assembled at Lake George under the command of General Amherst. On July 21 the army sailed down the lake for Ticonderoga, but as it neared the walls of the fort the garrison, numbering about 3,500 men, abandoned it and withdrew to Crown Point. Subsequently the latter place was also abandoned and the French army retreated to Isle-aux-Noix in the Richelieu River. Instead of following the retreating enemy, as he should have done, Amherst settled down with his superior army to building a fortress and constructing vessels, until the season for conducting hostilities was past.

VIII

THE FALL OF QUEBEC

The year 1759 was to see the crowning event of the war in the capture of Quebec, the capital of New France. This city stands on a high promontory overlooking the St. Lawrence River and occupies an angle formed by the confluence of the St. Charles and the St. Lawrence Rivers. In the rear of the city is a plateau stretching back some eight miles toward the west and known as the Plains of Abraham. The defense of Quebec had been entrusted to Montcalm, who, in spite of a bitter controversy with the jealous governor of Canada — a quarrel which was carried to the court of the king for settlement — had been retained in the American service, although his requests for additional men and supplies had been refused. His total available strength was about 17,000 men, including a considerable number of Indians.[28] Defended by such a force and possessing such natural advantages of position, the city was believed to be impossible of capture. Nevertheless, Gen-

[28] Parkman, "Montcalm and Wolfe," vol. ii. p. 202.

eral Wolfe resolved to make the effort.   Though still a young man, just lately turned his thirty-second year, he had been in the military service sixteen years, had taken part in the battles of Culloden, Sterling and Perth, and had given evidence of bravery, fertility of resource and even genius.   He had at his command a fleet bearing 9,000 men, which in June had sailed up the St. Lawrence and anchored a short distance below the city.   Among the officers of his army were some whom we shall meet again during the Revolution, notably Guy Carleton, William Howe and Isaac Barré.

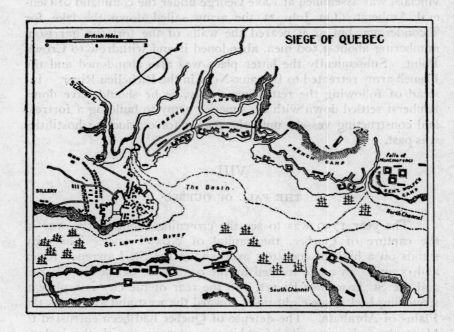

Wolfe's army was disembarked and a camp established on the north bank of the St. Lawrence, near the mouth of the Montmorency River, about seven miles below Quebec and within sound of the Montmorency Falls.   The north bank of the St. Lawrence from Montmorency to Quebec frowned with French batteries, while the opposite shore was lined with English cannon and redoubts. The English batteries were able to destroy the lower part of Quebec (that part near the mouth of the St. Charles River) with hot shot, but the citadel, of course, could not be reached.   For weeks after Wolfe's army had gotten into position nothing was done but wait and watch for an opportunity to strike. Montcalm acted strictly on the defensive, and, much to Wolfe's chagrin, avoided a general engagement. To be sure, there were desultory operations, occasional skirmishes and artillery bombardments, but in effect they amounted to little. From time to time the French attempted to destroy the English fleet by sending down floating rafts of fire-ships against it. On July 27 a raft of seventy vessels loaded with old cannon, bombs, mortars, swivels, and the like, charged with powder and ball and the whole smeared with tar and pitch, was fired and set adrift on the river. The effect was terrific. The heavens were made lurid with darting tongues of flame, while the earth trembled with explosions of infernal machines, as the whole slowly floated down the stream. The vigilant English, however, were able to steer them aside or run them ashore, so that no harm was done.

Wolfe, eager for a fight with the French, crossed the Montmorency below the falls on July 31, and with a detachment charged the French redoubts on the opposite bank. But the attacking party was driven back and forced to retreat, suffering a loss of 440 men, many of whom were scalped by the Indians.[29] This repulse, together with Wolfe's impatience and his disappointment at the failure of Amherst to come to his aid, threw him into a dangerous fever from which he barely recovered. Plan after plan had been worked out, but had been found impossible of execution; nearly a thousand men had been sacrificed; the season was rapidly passing, and yet the position of the French was as secure as ever. The thought of abandoning the campaign frightened him. He now proposed what seemed to everyone except himself an audacious, if not impossible, task — namely, the scaling of the Heights of Abraham.

Revived by the prospect of activity, he arose from his sick bed and began preparations for the execution of his daring scheme. Abandoning the camp at the mouth of the Montmorency, he moved his fleet noiselessly up the river under the cover of darkness, past the batteries of the enemy, and landed at a quiet eddy just north of the city, ever since known as Wolfe's Cove. A narrow zigzag path led from the cove to the top of the heights, and up this the

[29] Sloane, "The French War and the Revolution," p. 87; Parkman, "Montcalm and Wolfe," vol. ii. p. 233; Winsor, "Narrative and Critical History," vol. v. p. 545.

men silently clambered, single file, through the darkness, and when morning dawned Montcalm was amazed to find not less than five thousand of the enemy drawn up along the crest of the height within a mile of the city ready for battle.   The indefatigable, vigilant Montcalm had been completely outwitted.   He had either to fight Wolfe in the open or abandon the capital of New France. His army outnumbered that of Wolfe's, but was inferior in fighting qualities, being composed largely of raw Canadian militia and Indian savages.[30]   The brave Frenchman determined to contest the ground with Wolfe, and, if possible, drive him over the heights into the river.   Accordingly he made a fierce onslaught upon the British lines.   The latter cooly withheld their fire until the enemy was within a few yards, when they poured a deadly volley into their ranks and sent them flying for their lives.   The route of the French was complete, and altogether the affair was one of the most heroic and far-reaching achievements ever wrought by Englishmen in any land or age.[31]   But the victory of the English had cost them the life of their general, to whom, more than anyone else, the victory was due.

Twice during the charge Wolfe had been wounded; nevertheless he continued to ride up and down the lines encouraging his men to do their duty.   Finally he received a third wound, which was destined to prove fatal.   Being carried to the rear he refused medical aid, saying it was of no use, as his end was near.

Being informed that the French were retreating, he roused himself, gave an order for dispatching a regiment to cut off their retreat at the Charles River bridge, turned upon his side and murmured, " Now, God be praised, I shall die in peace."   In a few moments he was dead.[32]   Only a few months before he had parted in England from his affianced bride, to whom he hoped soon to return.   He had, however, a strong presentiment that death would overtake him before Quebec was captured.   In the evening before the landing at the cove he deliverd to a friend a picture of his betrothed, together with a farewell message for her.   He was also heard to quote from Gray's " Elegy " those solemn lines of which he said he would rather have been the author than to be the hero of Quebec:

[30] Sloane, " The French War and the Revolution," p. 93.
[31] Thwaites, " France in America," p. 254.
[32] Parkman, " Montcalm and Wolfe," vol. ii. p. 297.

"The boasts of heraldry, the pomp of power,
     And all that beauty, all that wealth e'er gave,
     Await alike the inevitable hour,
     The paths of glory lead but to the grave."

By a strange fate Montcalm was also wounded at the moment
at which his men began to retreat. Carried to the rear, he was
told that he had but few hours to live, whereupon he is said to
have replied. "I am happy that I shall not live to see the surrender of Quebec." He died on September 14, and was buried the
same day beneath the floor of the Ursuline convent in the city
which he had given his life to defend. His wish not to see the
surrender of Quebec was realized, for it was not until four days
after his interment that the city was formally occupied by an English garrison.

The fall of Quebec practically ended the war, although it continued after a desultory fashion some time longer. The French
power in America was broken. One by one the most powerful
French strongholds had fallen before the skillful operations of
the British, until France no longer held any place of importance in
America.

Throughout the winter skirmishing operations were kept up
by the French, and in the spring of 1760 a determined effort was
made to recapture Quebec. A hard-fought battle took place on
the Plains of Abraham, on the identical spot where Wolfe and
Montcalm had struggled the previous year, and the English were
driven back with great loss, while French war vessels poured a
deadly fire into the city. Quebec would doubtless have been retaken
had it not been for the timely arrival in the latter part of May of an
English fleet, which immediately engaged and destroyed the besieging French squadron. In September Montreal surrendered to
Amherst, and with the surrender ended the French and Indian
War in America. Still Pitt insisted on continuing the war in
Europe, in spite of the enormous burdens which it was entailing
upon the people of England; but in October, 1761, he was forced
to resign and a Tory ministry in favor of peace was brought into
power. The deplorable condition of France finally made her anxious for peace, and in February, 1763, the famous Treaty of Paris
was signed—an instrument remembered chiefly for the magnitude
and number of the territorial changes which it brought about. The
great question to be settled was, what disposition should be made

of the English conquests in America and elsewhere. England held Canada, the Ohio Valley, which was the original subject of dispute, the French West Indies, Cuba and the Philippine Islands, which had been taken from Spain, who had become an ally of France in 1762, and various conquests in India.

The terms finally agreed upon provided that practically all the French possessions in America, including Canada, Nova Scotia, Cape Breton and the Ohio Valley, and that part of Louisiana situated east of the Mississippi River and north of the River Iberville (now Manshac), and Lake Ponchartrain, should be ceded to Great Britain. After considerable wavering as to whether Canada should be restored to France, and Guadaloupe, with its profitable sugar industry, retained instead, the British Cabinet decided to retain the former and restore the latter. France was allowed to retain only the two small islands of St. Pierre and Miquelon, in the Gulf of St. Lawrence, together with a share in the St. Lawrence and Newfoundland fisheries. In the West Indias, Great Britain restored the French possessions of Guadaloupe, Martinique and St. Lucia, but in East India France was required to relinquish all her claims, and in Africa she lost Senegal. In exchange for the cession of Florida, Great Britain restored to Spain, Cuba and the Philippines, which had been captured by British squadrons during the preceding year. To compensate Spain for her loss of Florida, the King of France, out of gratitude to his Most Catholic cousin, ceded to him, through a secret agreement, what was left of Louisiana, namely, that portion which stretched westward with indefinite boundaries from the Mississippi River, and that part east of the Mississippi and south of the Iberville, including the town of New Orleans.[33]

The result of all these cessions and gifts was the virtual extinction of French dominion and the annihilation of French power in America — a fact which was destined to have important results upon the future relations of Great Britain and her American colonies. America was now divided between two powers: England held the eastern part from the Gulf to the Arctic; Spain all west of the Mississippi, including both sides of the mouth of that great river. The loss of her American empire was a severe blow to the pride of the French, but France was utterly exhausted and could do nothing but accept the hard terms imposed by her victorious

[33] See Thwaites, "France in America," ch. xvii.

adversary, now recognized as the leading colonial and maritime empire of the world.[34]

The "Old French" War, as it was called in America, had important political bearings on the subsequent history of the colonies. It meant that the civilization of North America was to be dominated by English-speaking people, and that meant liberal political institutions and rapid economic and political development for the New World. The war was also the means of furnishing the colonists with valuable military experience, which in a later time was to be of great service to them, and it taught them, above all things, the value of united action in matters of common interest. But they had been compelled to make enormous sacrifices for whatever gains they had derived. They had lost large numbers of men, while their frontier communities had been ravaged and desolated by inhuman savages in the French service. They had also imposed heavy taxes upon tnemselves and incurred large debts for the prosecution of the war. Especially was this true of the New England and middle colonies, the expenditures of Massachusetts alone aggregating $2,500,000, while New York emerged from the struggle with a debt of $1,000,000. Part of the expenditures incurred by the colonists for the equipment of their troops were, it is true, reimbursed from the imperial treasury after the accession of Pitt; but these constituted but a small portion of the entire outlay.

But if the financial burdens of the colonies were large, those of the mother country were much greater. England, in 1763, staggered under the weight of the national debt which the long struggle had necessitated, and the government was compelled to look around for new sources of revenue. It turned to the American colonies, in whose behalf the war had, to a large extent, been waged, and who were alleged to have been the chief beneficiaries from the expulsion of the French and the subjugation of the Indians. They were asked, for the first time, to contribute a small tax to be levied by the home government. The manner of their response will be the subject of another chapter.

One result of the extinction of French power in America was to stir up a great Indian uprising against the English settlements in the Northwest. The Alqonquin tribes, who throughout the war had been active allies of the French, now found themselves without

[34] Mahan, "Influence of Sea Power," p. 291.

friendly protection in America, and, entertaining a strong hatred for their new masters, the English, who instead of treating the Indians with flattery and cordiality, regarded them as old enemies, they secretly entered into a great conspiracy for the purpose of driving the English inhabitants off the frontier and recovering the country for themselves. "The English shall never come here so long as a red man lives," was the message sent by them to the French settlers of Illinois, who were not unwilling to encourage the uprising, provided the Indians would do the fighting.[35] The leader of the conspiracy was Pontiac, an Ottawa chief, who Parkman thinks was the greatest Indian warrior in America, and who had in 1755 led his braves against Braddock. Like Tecumseh in a later war, he visited various tribes in the Northwest and by his eloquence and diplomacy induced them to join the conspiracy. Others were won over by his emissaries, until finally nearly every Algonquin tribe, and even one of the Iroquois nations, had entered the conspiracy. By concerted agreement an attack was made simultaneously (May, 1763) on most of the English posts of the Northwest from Oswego to Mackinaw, fourteen in number. All but four of these—Niagara, Pitt, Ligonier and Detroit—were captured, the entire garrison of Mackinaw being massacred. Throughout the summer of 1763 a veritable reign of terror existed along the western frontier, hundreds of families were murdered and scalped, whole towns were destroyed by fire, travelers were waylaid and shot, in fact the very existence of the English settlements in the West was threatened. The plot to capture Detroit was betrayed by an Indian girl, a fact which gave the commanding officer time to prepare for defense. Pontiac himself laid siege to the fort, but after several months of desultory fighting he was compelled to withdraw, mainly as a result of desertion from his own ranks and the failure of expected reënforcements.

The war dragged on for several years, until August, 1765, when Pontiac entered into a treaty of peace with Sir William Johnson. A few years later he suffered the fate of King Philip, being killed at Cahokia, Illinois, by one of his own race. He was buried on the site of the city of St. Louis, where, says Parkman, "the race whom he hated with such burning rancor trample with unceasing footsteps over his forgotten grave."[36]

35 Thwaites, "France in America," p. 278; Moses, "Illinois," vol. i. p. 124.
36 "Conspiracy of Pontiac," vol. ii. p. 313.

Chapter IX

THE RUPTURE WITH THE MOTHER COUNTRY
1763–1775

I

CAUSES OF THE DISPUTE

PETER KALM, a Swedish trader who visited America in 1748, predicted that the extinction of the French power in Canada would soon be followed by the revolt of the English colonies against the mother country.[1] So long as France held Canada the English colonies needed the protection of the imperial government against this old enemy which hung upon their borders and sent down bands of Indian savages to desolate their settlements. They felt a sense of fright at the thought of becoming colonies of a Roman Catholic power, and consequently held in abatement their passion for extreme local autonomy. The expulsion of the French from America as a result of the war removed this danger, and consequently lessened the dependence of the colonies upon the mother country. No longer under the necessity of shaping their policies to secure imperial protection, they became more self-assertive, showed an increasing disposition to oppose such acts of Parliament as seemed to them injurious to colonial interests, and soon came to entertain ideas of separation. France thus occupied the peculiar position of encouraging our independent spirit and at the same time checking its extreme development.[2]

Occasions for the exhibition of the spirit of independence were soon afforded by the new colonial policy of the British Government. It must not be understood, however, that the causes of the rupture had their origin entirely in the period subsequent to the French and Indian War. Some of the grievances of the colonists against the mother country were of long standing — in fact, dated back to the middle of the preceding century. The principal of these

[1] "Travels in North America," vol. i. p. 265.
[2] Fisher, "True History of the Revolution." p. 32.

grew out of the commercial policy of Great Britain toward her colonial possessions. According to the views of European statesmen in the seventeenth century, colonies were planted by nations solely for their own benefit, were, in fact, expected to serve as feeders for home industries, and consequently there was neither injustice nor inexpediency in exploiting their resources in monopolizing their trade.[3] These were the underlying principals of the colonial system which prevailed in England from the time of Charles II. Nowhere was this view more strongly held than in England, until Adam Smith, on the eve of the Revolution, published his " Wealth of Nations," showing the impolicy of the old theory which was soon to cost Great Britain her most valuable and prosperous possessions.[4] The adoption of this narrow commercial policy really begins with an act of Parliament passed in October, 1651, by which it was provided that no goods of the growth of Asia, Africa or America should be imported into England or the English colonies except in English ships, and that no goods of the growth or manufacture of Europe should be imported into England or the dominions thereof except in English ships or ships belonging to the country where the goods were produced or manufactured. The obvious purpose of the act was to strike a blow at the vast carrying trade of the Dutch, and the ill feeling it engendered ultimately led to a naval war, in which the two great admirals Blake and Van Tromp contended for the mastery.[5]

The particular effect of the act was to exclude the Dutch as carriers between England and the colonies, to give the English carrier the monopoly of this trade, and, by thus diminishing the advantages of competition, to greatly injure the colonies, as they maintained. The products of Europe, however, might still be brought to the English colonies in non-English ships if transported in vessels owned in the country where the goods were produced or manufactured. Thus a French cargo might be brought to America in a French vessel, but not in a Dutch vessel. By the famous act of 1660, for " The Encouraging and Increasing of Shipping and Navigation," this latter advantage was taken away by providing

---

[3] Seeley, " The Expansion of England " ch. i.; see also Thorold Rogers, " Economic Interpretation of History," p. 323; Andrews, " Colonial Self-Government," ch. v., and Howard, " Preliminaries of the Revolution," ch. iii.

[4] Adam Smith, " Wealth of Nations," book iv. ch. vii.

[5] Beer, " Commercial Policy of England toward the American Colonies," p. 32.

that no goods should be imported into the colonies or exported therefrom except in English or colonial built and owned vessels. This excluded every continental European vessel from the ports of the colonies, and left them at the mercy of the English carrier, in so far as the colonies themselves were unable to carry their own imports and exports.

These provisions were primarily for the benefit of the maritime interests of Great Britain, but the clamors of the mercantile class were too loud to be ignored, and so a provision was inserted in the same act prohibiting the colonies from exporting certain of their important articles of produce and manufacture except to England and to the other colonies. These articles were sugar, tobacco, cotton, wool, indigo, ginger, fustic and other dyeing woods, mainly the products of the southern colonies and the West Indies. Other commodities were added to the list later. The actual effect of this provision was to make England the sole market for the chief staples of the southern colonies, thus compelling them, as they asserted, to sell their surplus in overstocked markets. On the other hand, the northern colonies could export their grain, fish, live stock and naval stores whithersoever they pleased, provided only they were sent in English or colonial ships.[6]

In 1673 another act was passed prohibiting the exportation from one colony to another of various articles of produce unless they were shipped first to England, or, if shipped direct to a colony, upon payment of an export duty equivalent to the English import duty. Thus a cargo of Virginia tobacco intended for Boston had either to be shipped to England and reshipped to Boston, or pay the English import duty for the privilege of shipping direct for Boston.[7] Finally in 1733 Parliament passed the so-called Sugar Act, imposing a heavy duty on sugar and molasses imported into the American colonies from any other than English sugar-producing possessions. The purpose of this legislation was of course to prevent the English colonies from importing sugar from the French West India islands, and to compel them to import only from the British islands. As they exported large quantities of merchandise and produce to the French islands and received in exchange sugar and molasses, which were brought to the colonies and converted

[6] Chamberlain, "The Revolution Impending," in Winsor, "Narrative and Critical History," vol. vi. p. 7.

[7] Howard, "Preliminaries of the Revolution," p. 57.

into rum or otherwise consumed, the act was a real hardship, and had it not been systematically evaded it would have seriously crippled a large and profitable trade between America and the West Indies.

Other laws were passed to protect the mercantile classes against the competition of colonial made goods. Thus the colonists were forbidden to set up steel furnaces and slitting mills, although the iron industry in Pennsylvania was already full of promise; to export colonial made hats, or send them from one colony to another; to export woolen goods, while a variety of other legislation was enacted for the purpose of discouraging the growth of colonial industries.[8]

In extenuation of this legislation it should be said that it was not enacted in pursuance of any spirit of hostility toward the colonists, but was rather the result of the narrow and false economic theories of the age. Moreover, its effect on the industrial progress of America was not so unfavorable as it might seem, for while the colonies were compelled to find a market for certain of their produce in England, they had a monopoly of the supply for that market. Thus the English consumer of tobacco was not allowed to grow a pound for his own use or import it from other countries, but was compelled to draw his supply from the colonies, while the cultivation of indigo, rice, and the exportation of tar, hemp, flax, ship timber, and allied products to England were encouraged by liberal bounties.[9] From 1714 to 1744 it is alleged that over one and a half million pounds sterling were paid in premiums on colonial goods carried to British ports.[10] As for the Navigation Acts, some of them encouraged colonial shipping, and whether they did or not, they were not very different from those to-day which confine the carrying trade between the United States and its insular dependencies exclusively to American vessels. As to the restriction on the sale of domestic made hats, it was maintained by the British that such articles could be imported from England for less than they could be made in the colonies. Finally, it must be said that the Navigation Laws were never strictly enforced, and the revenue acts brought little or nothing into the

[8] For a summary of these restrictive laws see Beer, " Commercial Policy," pp. 66–90.

[9] Lecky, " The American Revolution," p. 45 (Woodburn's Edition); see also Beer, ch. v.

[10] Howard, " Preliminaries of the Revolution," p. 60.

imperial treasury; in fact, it not infrequently cost seven or eight thousand pounds a year to collect two thousand pounds of revenue. The total remittance from the colonies on an average for thirty years did not exceed nineteen hundred pounds a year, the expense of collection being not less than three times this amount.[11]

The evasion of the Navigation Laws by smuggling became notorious, and the British customs officials made little effort to put a stop to it, if they did not actually wink at it. Everywhere public sentiment favored it, and juries returned verdicts of not guilty in the face of the most undoubted facts. It is stated by an impartial authority that not less than nine-tenths of the tea, wine, sugar and molasses imported into New England for many years before the Revolution were smuggled in violation of the acts of trade.[12] Persons of the highest social standing and influence in New England, like John Hancock, of Boston, were guilty of such conduct, and it was not regarded as reprehensible. Even during the French and Indian War, when the mother country was straining every nerve to defeat the French, it was found that their fleets and garrisons were systematically supplied with provisions from New England, the highest officials conniving at it on the ground that it was good policy to make money out of the enemy.

After the close of the French and Indian War, however, the British Government felt called upon to adopt a new policy with regard to the administration of the Navigation Laws and Acts of Trade. George Grenville, who now became prime minister, was resolved to enforce the laws strictly, and if possible derive a revenue therefrom for the benefit of the overburdened imperial treasury. The agencies which he purposed to employ were revenue cutters, admiralty courts, without juries, commissioners of customs, writs of assistance and naval forces. Accordingly, old customs officials who had grown rich by bribery were dismissed and new ones sent out to the colonies with strict orders to enforce the laws and break up smuggling. But the smugglers had been so long unmolested that it was found to be an extremely difficult task to discipline them. When, therefore, the sloop *Liberty* was seized for violating the customs laws, a Boston mob rescued the cargo, demolished the windows of the collector's house, dragged his boat through the town,

---

[11] Bancroft, "History of the United States," vol. iii. p. 31; Beer, "Commercial Policy," ch. vii.

[12] Lecky, "The American Revolution," p. 47.

publicly burned it on the Common, and compelled the customs officials to take refuge for their lives on the British man-of-war *Romney,* which lay in the harbor.   Before the outbreak of the Revolution mobs and tar-and-feather parties had become so active in Boston that the customs officials were necessarily compelled to abandon all further attempts to discharge their duties.   To enable them to carry out effectively orders, they had been instructed to apply to the courts for writs of assistance, or general search warrants, empowering them to search anywhere for smuggled goods. This was an extraordinary procedure, for it had always been recognized as a part of the common law that the premises of an individual could be searched only in pursuance of a special search warrant, particularly describing the place to be searched and the things to be seized.   The writ of assistance neither contained the name of the person suspected nor described the premises to be searched; it was good for an indefinite time, was not returnable to the court, and authorized seizure at all hours.[13]

When Paxton, the chief customs official at Boston, applied to the chief justice of the Province, Thomas Hutchinson, for one of these writs, James Otis, who had recently resigned his position as royal advocate for the colony, appeared for the Boston merchants and resisted the granting of the writ as unconstitutional. Otis's speech was a powerful one, and had a profound influence on the popular mind, not only in New England, but everywhere in the English colonies of America.   He described the hardships of the colonies on account of the Acts of Navigation and Trade, denounced the granting of writs of assistance as a species of tyranny such as had " cost one king of England his head and another his throne," and declared that taxation without representation is tyranny.[14]   The speech stirred the people of the country to resistance as no other utterance had done, and made the speaker one of the leaders of the revolutionary movement, which had now set in.   John Adams, then a Harvard student, heard the oration, took notes of it, and long afterwards, in speaking of it, declared that " then and there the child Independence was born."[15]   Although Otis lost this case and the writs were issued, yet on account

[13] General search warrants are forbidden by the fourth amendment to the Federal Constitution.

[14] See Hart, " American History Told by Contemporaries," vol. ii. no. 131.

[15] Hosmer, " Life of Samuel Adams," p. 44.

of the strong popular opposition which he had done most to create, they were seldom used thereafter.

A year or two later a note of resistance was sounded by a southern orator, Patrick Henry, who stirred the people to even greater depths than Otis had done. Henry was a young lawyer whose early life had given little promise of success, and at the time of his speech he had only a local reputation. Being employed by the local authorities to defend the people in the celebrated Parsons' Cause, to which allusion has already been made, Henry took occasion to denounce the action of the Crown in vetoing the Virginia law relating to the salaries of the clergy, and launched forth into a general discussion of the relations between the mother country and the colonies. The action of the king, he declared, was arbitrary and unwarranted; that instead of being a father to his people he had " degenerated into a tyrant and had forfeited all right to the obedience of his subjects." This was indeed bold language for a subject of George III. to utter, but the cries of treason with which he was greeted by some of his hearers did not deter him from proceeding with his oration.[16] Henry's fame as an orator spread rapidly throughout the colonies, and the courage with which he had publicly denounced British tyranny made him, with Otis, one of the leading pioneers of the Revolution.

Next to the enforcement of the Navigation Laws the chief feature of the Grenville policy was the proposition to maintain a standing army in America and levy a tax on the colonists to defray a part of the expense for its support. Although the danger to the colonists from the French had been removed, in the opinion of the home government a small standing army was required in America for the maintenance of a " stable government " among the French colonists who had been subjected to British rule, while protection against the western Indians was now needed, as the recent conspiracy of Pontiac seemed to show.[17]

The number of troops necessary for this purpose was estimated at not less than 20,000, besides a proportionate number of officers. The estimated expense for the military and civil establishment was 300,000 pounds sterling, one-third of which it was proposed to collect from the colonists in the form of import duties and a stamp tax. It was said in justification of the proposition

[16] Tyler, "Life of Patrick Henry," p. 48.
[17] Winsor, "Narrative and Critical History," vol. vi. p. 688 *et seq.*

to tax the colonies that the French and Indian War, so glorious to the empire and to the colonists in America, had added 140,000,-000 pounds sterling to the British national debt, and that the people of the United Kingdom, already staggering under the weight of the load, objected to the imposition of additional burdens, while the colonists in whose interest the war had been largely waged went free. Moreover, it was said that as the primary purpose of sending the troops to America was to protect the colonists, they ought not to object to bearing a share of the expense. It was readily admitted that so far as the expense of conducting the war was concerned, they had borne their share, but that was no reason, Grenville insisted, why they should seek to escape the burdens which the results of the war had entailed upon the empire.

Every source of revenue at home had been drained, and the ministry now as a sort of last resort turned to their prosperous colonies of America, on which the empire had during the last fifty years expended over 30,000,000 pounds sterling for their maintenance. England and Ireland each maintained, it was said, its own army, and the American colonies should do the same. They were not to be asked to contribute a penny for the support of the navy which protected their coasts, or to the payment of interest on the national debt, a large part of which had been incurred in their own behalf. To make the proposition as palatable as possible, Grenville proposed that none of the revenue collected in America should pass to the imperial exchequer, and thus drain the colonies of their specie, but that every farthing of it should be expended in America for their defense, protection and security. [18]

In explanation of the reason why a stamp tax had been decided upon, Grenville stated that it seemed to him to be the most equitable and easy of collections, and as it had been variously recommended by Americans years before, he did not think it would meet with opposition. He stated, furthermore, that if it was objectionable to the colonists and they preferred to raise the money in some other way, it would be agreeable to him. He seemed anxious to know the sentiments of the leaders of public opinion in America on his proposed scheme, and called in Benjamin Franklin, who was then acting as the agent of several of the colonies at London, and requested his views. Franklin told him frankly that the stamp tax would meet with strong opposition in America, not be-

[18] Lecky, "American Revolution," ch. xi.

cause it was objectionable in itself, but because the colonies denied
the right of Parliament to tax them in any shape or form except
such as might be incidental in the regulation of their foreign commerce. [19] He pointed out that they drew a distinction between
" internal " and " external " taxes, the former having reference
to such as were intended to raise revenue, the latter to such as had to
do with the regulation of trade, and that while they admitted the
right of Parliament to impose the latter, they denied its right to levy
the former. But this distinction, which, it must be admitted, was
wholly illogical as a matter of constitutional law, was not recognized by all colonial statesmen, and in fact both James Otis and
Governor Hutchinson of Massachusetts publicly declared that there
was no foundation for it. [20]

As to the legal competence of Parliament to tax the colonies,
the highest authorities still differ. Probably the weight of opinion
is in favor of the right as claimed, although it is worth remarking
that of all the charters granted to the colonies, only that of
Pennsylvania expressly reserved the right of taxation to Parliament. Aside from the question of constitutional competence, the
colonists opposed the Grenville scheme, first, on the ground that
they had not asked for the troops, that they did not want them, and
that they were able to protect themselves against the imaginary
dangers which the British statesmen had conjured up in their minds.
Moreover, the French and Indian War had been waged not primarily in their interests, but in the interests of the realm of which
they were not a part. By monopolizing their trade and commerce
the British government had received, in the form of profits and
other benefits, more than the colonial share of the expense necessary
to provide for their protection. This was their contribution to the
imperial treasury, and it was enough, as they believed. Taxation
by a Parliament 3,000 miles away, in which they had no representation, would mean a destruction of their liberties, and the reduction
of the people " from the character of free subjects to the miserable
state of tributary slavery." [21] But it was said in answer to this
objection that under the rotten borough system then existing in

[19] For a fair and reasonable statement of the British view, see Lecky,
" History of England in the Eighteenth Century," vol. iii.; reprinted also in his
" American Revolution " (edited by Woodburn), ch. xi.

[20] Also compare Bancroft, " History of the United States," vol. iii. pp.
79, 82, 85.

[21] Otis, " Rights of the British Colonies Asserted," p. 100 *et seq.*

England nine-tenths of the people of the United Kingdom were virtually unrepresented in Parliament, and that in this respect Boston and Philadelphia were no worse off than Manchester, Sheffield, and other English cities.

What the colonists really objected to was taxation without their consent; they did not object to making voluntary contributions through their legislative assemblies to the imperial treasury when called upon to do so. "The imposition of our own taxes," declared the Assembly of North Carolina, "is our inherent right and exclusive privilege." [22]   In the course of Franklin's interview with Grenville, he entered into a defense of the old method of requisitions, whereupon Grenville inquired if the thirteen colonial legislatures could agree upon the proportion each colony should raise, adding that it had been shown to be impossible to induce them to do so during the late war. Franklin was, of course, obliged to return a negative answer. Reliance upon voluntary contributions was wholly insufficient, and the government was determined to levy and collect the tax directly without the intervention of the local legislatures.

In March, 1765, the Stamp Act, without attracting unusual attention, and without exciting serious opposition, passed both Houses of Parliament and received the assent of the king. It provided that bills, bonds, leases, insurance policies, newspapers, broadsides and legal documents used in America should be written on stamped paper, and that the proceeds therefrom should be applied exclusively to the protection of the colonies. The act was to go into effect on the first of November following. To soften the opposition, the distribution of the stamps was to be left to the colonists, and their agents at London were requested to recommend suitable persons for appointment as stamp distributors — a request with which they readily complied. An objectionable feature of the act was the provision that offenses arising under the law were not to be tried by juries, the popular belief in England being that no jury could be found in the colonies which would convict a violator of such an unpopular law. This feature, however, was of little consequence; it was the principle of the act to which the colonists objected, and their opposition proved to be out of all proportion to what the government had expected.[23]   Indeed, the

    [22] "Colonial Records of North Carolina," vol. vi. p. 1261.
    [23] Frothingham, "Rise of the Republic," p. 177 et seq.

calm judgment of the present day must be that the law was not necessarily an evil or tyrannical measure. It had years before been recommended by the governors of several colonies, and at the time little objection was raised.[24]   To-day the government of the United States imposes taxes on its colonial subjects beyond the seas, although they are not only unrepresented in Congress, but have very few rights of local self-government, and whether the policy be right or wrong it is the same in principle as that to which our forefathers objected at the time of the Revolution.

When the news of the enactment of the law reached America a wave of indignation swept over the colonies, and here and there impassioned speakers urged the people to resist the execution of the law. The Virginia House of Burgesses, aroused by the fiery eloquence of Patrick Henry, who asserted in the course of a notable speech that George III. might suffer the fate of Cæsar and Charles I. if he did not " profit by their example," passed a series of resolutions declaring that the people of the colonies were entitled to all the privileges of natural born subjects of England; that the colonial assemblies had the exclusive right to levy taxes upon the inhabitants of America; and that every attempt of Parliament or of any other authority outside the colonies to exercise such power was unconstitutional, unjust and destructive of the liberties of the colonists.[25]

The announcement of the arrival of the stamps in August was at once followed by riots and disorders in various parts of America. Stamp distributers were hanged in effigy and forced to resign their positions, the supply of stamps was seized and destroyed, and in some cases the records of the courts were burned. In Boston especially were the disorders serious. The house of Lieutenant Governor Hutchinson, the finest in the town, was sacked, his large library, containing rare and valuable books, burned, and his plate, furniture and public records destroyed. The houses of other prominent supporters of the government were similarly plundered, and some of the leading sympathizers with the government were compelled to flee from the colony.

In New York the effigy of the governor was paraded with that of the devil around the town and publicly burned. Non-importation agreements were entered into by the citizens; bells

[24] Howard, " Preliminaries of the Revolution," p. 121.
[25] Tyler, " Patrick Henry," p. 62.

were tolled and flags placed at half-mast, and organizations known as " Sons of Liberty " were formed everywhere. Not a box of stamps could be found in the colonies, not a legal document was properly stamped, and the newspapers appeared with a death's-head in the place of the stamp required. It was found absolutely impossible to enforce the law, and the governors were compelled to authorize non-compliance with it.[26]

Meantime, at the instance of James Otis, the Massachusetts General Court had issued a call for a general congress to take into consideration the state of affairs caused by the British Government. In response to this call delegates from nine colonies, practically all whose legislatures were in session during the summer, met at New York on October 7, and drew up a Declaration of Rights and addressed petitions to the king and to both Houses of Parliament.[27] The Declaration of Rights asserted that while the colonists owed allegiance to the Crown they were entitled to the same liberties as natural born subjects, that for geographical reasons they could not be represented in the British Parliament, and that no authority beyond their local legislatures could levy taxes upon them.

It was now clear that they were determined to resist the execution of the law, and the proceedings described above soon showed that they were quite able to do so with marked success. English merchants were suffering from the loss of American trade caused by the non-importation agreements. Besides, the requirement that the new duties should be paid in specie and the cutting off of the supply from the West Indies by the strict enforcement of the Acts of Trade made it impossible to import manufactured articles from England, and compelled the colonies to depend upon home industries. Thus American trade with the mother country was reduced to a minimum. Thousands of artisans were thrown out of employment, and petitions from all over the United Kingdom poured in upon Parliament praying for the repeal of the Stamp Act.[28] At this juncture the unpopular Grenville ministry fell, and was succeeded by a new one formed by the Marquis of Rockingham.

[26] Lecky, " The American Revolution," p. 84.
[27] Frothingham, " Rise of the Republic," p. 188; Fiske, " The American Revolution," vol. i. pp. 22–23.
[28] Helen Hodges, " Repeal of the Stamp Act," in *The Political Science Quarterly*, June, 1904.

Under the leadership of the new ministry Parliament, in January, 1766, took up the question of the repeal of the Stamp Act, and in order to ascertain as nearly as possible the sentiments of the colonists, Benjamin Franklin, then residing at London as colonial agent, was summoned before the bar of the House of Commons and interrogated on the situation in America. He told the Commons that the people of America felt a genuine pride in being a part of the great British Empire, and that they had a real attachment for those of the old world with whom they were so closely connected by ties of blood and interest, but that they denied the right of the imperial government to tax them without their consent, since the colonies were unrepresented in Parliament, and since they were not a part of the realm — not a part of the dominions of England, but of the king's dominions. They were, he insisted, subordinate only to the king, both in matters of legislation and taxation; that he alone was the bond of union between them and England. In the course of his examination Franklin dispelled many popular illusions concerning the colonies, and produced convincing proof of their determination to resist to the bitter end the attempt of Parliament to tax them.

Next to Franklin's examination the principal features of the session were the great speeches of Burke and Pitt in behalf of the rights of the colonists and the profound constitutional discussions of Lords Mansfield and Camden. Pitt was the foremost champion of the rights of the colonists. Rising from a bed of sickness, he dragged himself into the House of Commons and entered an eloquent protest against what he regarded as the wicked and short-sighted policy of the Government. "The kingdom," he declared, "has no right to lay a tax on the colonies because they are unrepresented in Parliament. The Commons of America, represented in their assemblies, have ever been in possession of this their constitutional right of giving and granting money. They would have been slaves without it. I rejoice that America has resisted. Three millions of people so dead to all the feelings of liberty as voluntarily to submit to be slaves would have been fit instruments to make slaves of the rest." The profits of Great Britain from the colonies, he said, were not less than 2,000,000 pounds a year, and this was price enough for them to pay for their protection.[29]

[29] See Pitt's speech in Hart, "American History Told by Contemporaries," vol. ii. no. 142.

Lord Camden, in the House of Lords, spoke in a similar strain. "Taxation and representation," he declared, "are inseparable." Both Pitt and Camden, however, admitted the right of Parliament to regulate colonial trade, and insisted that there was "a plain distinction between taxes levied for the purpose of raising revenue and duties imposed for the regulation of trade," although the latter might incidentally yield revenue. Conway, Burke, Rockingham and others argued in favor of repeal on the ground of expediency without reference to the legal right of Parliament to tax the colonies.

Lord Mansfield, on the other hand, speaking for the opposition, upheld the right of Parliament to impose the tax, pronounced the distinction between external and internal taxes fallacious, and declared that the colonies were as much represented in Parliament as were the non-voters of England. " The notion," he said, " that every subject must be represented by deputy, if he does not vote in Parliament himself, is merely ideal," and asserted that the imperial legislature had "authority to bind every part of and every subject without the least distinction, whether such subjects have a right to vote or not, or whether the law binds places within the realm or without." The outcome of all this remarkable debate was the repeal of the Stamp Act, but to lighten the fall of the ministry as much as possible, the repealing act was accompanied by a "Declaratory Act" affirming the right of Parliament to legislate for the colonies in all cases whatsoever, and the subordination of the Americans to the Crown and Parliament of Great Britain.[30]

Benjamin Franklin doubtless expressed the general opinion of the colonists when he stated that the "Declaratory Act" would cause little concern if no attempt was ever made to put it into effect.[31] The announcement of the repeal was followed by general rejoicing in America. The colonial assemblies voted thanks to the king, Pitt, Camden and others; the Quakers of Pennsylvania showed their loyalty on the king's birthday by donning suits of English cloth, giving their homespun garments to the poor, and in many towns statues were erected in honor of the king and the Great Commoner. Speaking a few years later of these evidences of loyalty Pitt declared that "the Americans had almost forgot in the excess of their gratitude for the repeal of the Stamp Act any

[30] Winsor, "Narrative and Critical History," vol. vi. p. 32.
[31] "Parliamentary History," vol. xvi. p. 145.

interest except for the mother country; that there seemed an emulation among the different provinces as to who should be the most dutiful and forward in their expressions of loyalty."

The Rockingham ministry fell shortly after the repeal of the Stamp Act, and Pitt, who had just recently been made a peer with the title of Earl of Chatham, became the head of a coalition ministry consisting of various elements, including even Tories.[32] On account of ill health, however, he was compelled to relinquish the active management of the government to the Chancellor of the Exchequer, Charles Townshend, an able and brilliant statesman, but sadly lacking in Pitt's foresight and conciliatory disposition. Townshend assumed the reins of government with the full determination of enforcing the Declaratory Act, and of showing the colonists that England was still their master. Accordingly, he passed (1767) a series of bills commonly known as the Townshend Acts. One of these, evidently drawn with due deference to the colonial distinction between " external " and " internal " taxes, provided for the levying of a customs tax on tea, wine, oil, glass, paper, lead and painters' colors imported into the colonies; another provided that the salaries of the colonial judges and governors should be paid out of the royal treasury instead of out of the colonial treasuries, as a means of rendering these officials independent of the local assemblies; and another act legalized writs of assistance and gave the admiralty courts jurisdiction of offenses against the revenue laws without the benefit of a jury. To provide for the more efficient administration of the revenue laws a board of customs commissioners, with large powers of supervision, was created. Finally, because the legislature of New York had refused to provide quarters and supplies for the British troops stationed in the city of New York, as required by a previous act, Parliament suspended its functions.[33] These several acts constituted severe infringements upon the right of trial by jury, the right of local self-government, and the independence of the judiciary of the colonies, aroused them to a high pitch of indignation and drove them still further to resist the measures of the home government. Everywhere non-importation agreements were proposed for the purpose of boycotting English products, while men like Samuel Adams in

[32] Fiske, " The American Revolution," vol. i. p. 28.
[33] Fiske, " American Revolution," vol. i. p. 30; Frothingham, " Rise of the Republic," p. 205; Winsor, " Narrative and Critical History," vol. vi. p. 35.

Massachusetts, John Dickinson in Pennsylvania, and Patrick Henry in Virginia stirred the masses to the verge of rebellion by their impassioned eloquence.

In the year following the enactment of these laws, Townshend was succeeded as Chancellor of the Exchequer by Lord North, but no change of policy toward the colonists was made. In February, 1768, the Massachusetts legislature passed certain resolutions setting forth the rights of the colonists, and sent a circular letter to the assemblies of the other colonies inviting them to take similar action. The British authorities took great offense at these proceedings, and instructed the governor to demand the recall of the circular. This the assembly refused to do, whereupon the governor dissolved it, and at the same time the other assemblies were warned not to follow the example of Massachusetts. Some of them did not heed the royal admonition, however, and were promptly punished by dissolution.

The Virginia Assembly in particular showed unusual boldness and determination. In May, 1769, it passed a series of resolutions emphatically denying the right of England to tax the colonies, affirming their right to act in concert to secure a redress of grievances, and denouncing in strong language the Parliamentary suggestion that the king should transport to England for trial all persons in America charged with treason.[34] Being dissolved by the governor, the legislature repaired to a near-by tavern, where the members entered into a solemn agreement not to use any goods imported from England which were taxed under the Townshend law. Similar agreements were entered into in the other colonies, and by this means English merchants were soon forced by loss of trade to exert all the pressure they could command to secure the repeal of the Townshend duties.

The importation of the taxed commodities became so inconsiderable and the expense of collection so great on account of the elaborate administrative machinery necessary to prevent smuggling, that the revenue obtained was scarcely worth the trouble; indeed, it is stated that the total net amount derived from the Townshend law was but 295 pounds above the cost of collection, while the increased expenditures made necessary by the local opposition exceeded 170,000 pounds. As a revenue producer, therefore, the Townshend law was a failure, and was repealed in April, 1770, ex-

[34] Frothingham, "Rise of the Republic," p. 234.

THE RUPTURE

cept that the duty on tea, glass and painters' colors was retained more to serve as a precedent in case of future taxation than anything else. The partial repeal of the act, however, did not allay the opposition, because the principle involved had not been abandoned by the British Government. The attempt to enforce the unpopular law had been attended by riots and disorders, and at times Boston, in particular, was well-nigh at the mercy of mob rule. Informers were tarred and feathered and led through the streets, and English goods belonging to merchants were destroyed.

In March, 1770, occurred one of these conflicts, which has come down to us as the "Boston Massacre." To preserve order and aid the revenue officials in the discharge of their duties, several regiments of troops had recently been sent to Boston, and their presence in the town had from the first served to excite popular indignation. On March 5 a party of soldiers, provoked by the action of a crowd of men and boys who taunted them with such epithets as "lobsters" and "bloody backs," and dared them to shoot, fired into the crowd and killed several of their number. Immediately the town was in an uproar. The cry was raised that the "bloody and brutal myrmidons of England had shot down the inoffensive citizens of Boston." The church bells were rung, drums called the people to arms, and an immense meeting of the citizens resolved that the soldiers must go.

Lieutenant Governor Hutchinson was waited on by a committee and informed of the action of the meeting. He hesitated, and endeavored to make excuses, but the meeting remained in session and demanded a positive answer before nightfall. Under these circumstances Hutchinson yielded, and removed the troops to Fort William, in the harbor, three miles from the city.[35] The soldiers accused of the murder of the citizens were placed on trial and were defended by two of the leading patriots of the colony, John Adams and Josiah Quincy. They were all acquitted by a local jury except two, who were convicted of manslaughter and given slight punishments.

Already in the year 1771 the battle of Alamance, sometimes called the first of the Revolution, had occurred in North Carolina between the troops of the royalist Governor Tryon and a band of "regulators," who, being goaded by extortion and unlawful im-

[35] Lecky, "American Revolution," pp. 128-129.

prisonment, had risen in rebellion [36] against the royal authorities. In the course of a severe fight they were defeated, two hundred of their number being killed while several were captured and hanged for treason.   An incident in 1772 which attracted wide attention, and which had important consequences, was the *Gaspee* affair. The *Gaspee* was an armed British schooner which was engaged in patrolling the coasts of Narragansett Bay to prevent violation of the revenue laws.   The conduct of the commander in trying to perform his duty greatly offended the inhabitants living along the coast, and they made complaints, without result.   Finally, one day in June, while chasing an American vessel, the *Gaspee* ran aground, and on the following evening she was boarded by a party of respectable citizens, who burned the vessel to the water's edge.   The British authorities were furious at this outrage and ordered the arrest of the offenders and their delivery up for transportation to England for treason, but no evidence could be obtained against them, although probably every person in the community knew who the guilty parties were.

Moreover, the chief justice, Stephen Hopkins, afterwards one of the signers of the Declaration of Independence, openly declared that he would not take cognizance of any case arising out of the affair, and that no one of the accused should be removed from the colony for trial in England or elsewhere.   Arising from the event was the appointment by the Virginia House of Burgesses of a " committee of correspondence " to ascertain the facts concerning the burning of the *Gaspee* and " to maintain a correspondence with our sister colonies." [37]   Half a dozen other colonies soon followed the example of Virginia, and thus was created a system of revolutionary machinery that in time was adopted generally in America and proved of inestimable value in bringing about concert of action among the colonies.[38]

All these evidences of a mistaken policy had no effect on George III., who was not only dull, but vindictive.   He was resolved to try the issue with the Americans regardless of consequences.   To force them to pay the duty on tea he hit upon an ingenious scheme.   At this time the financial affairs of the English East India Company were in a bad way, mainly because Americans

[36] Fiske, "American Revolution," vol. i. p. 75.
[37] Channing, "History of the United States," p. 181.
[38] Frothingham, "Rise of the Republic," pp. 280–283.

were no longer buying tea from England, but were smuggling it from Holland. Being anxious to help the English East India Company out of its straits, and at the same time induce the Americans to buy English tea, it was decided to make the English article cheaper than the Dutch tea, which had to be smuggled. Accordingly, the English East India Company was allowed a drawback on the tea which it imported into England from the Orient and re-exported to America. The remission of the customary duty enabled the English company to undersell the Dutch East India Company, and of course it was believed that the Americans would buy the cheaper article (it was only threepence per pound), and thus admit the principle involved in the duty collected in America.[39] But this assumption proved wholly unwarranted. The scheme thus ingeniously devised to inveigle them into paying the duty was too thinly veiled to cover its real purpose, and they determined not to be ensnared by it.

In the autumn of 1773 several cargoes of tea were sent to America consigned to agents at Boston, New York, Philadelphia and Charleston. In several of these cities indignation meetings were held and the consignees forced to resign their commissions. In Charleston the tea was offered for sale by the customs officials to pay the duty, but nobody would buy, and it was stored in damp cellars, only to rot. In Philadelphia a town meeting was held and a resolution passed requesting the captain of a tea ship, recently arrived, to take his cargo out of the harbor, and he promptly obeyed, returning with his ship to England. The tea was similarly disposed of in New York. In Boston no amount of pressure could force the consignees to resign; town meetings were held to consider what action should be taken upon the arrival of the tea, and the committees of correspondence throughout the colony took up the question and discussed it as though the fate of the nation was at stake.

On Sunday, November 28, one of the expected tea ships arrived in the harbor. An immense town meeting was held at the Old South Meeting House, and it was unanimously voted that the tea should not be allowed to land. Other meetings followed in the course of the week, and the excitement of the populace reached a high pitch. Finally, on the night of December 16, a mob of fifty persons, disguised as Indians and armed with hatchets,

[39] Hutchinson, "History of Massachusetts," vol. iii. pp. 331-332.

proceeded to the wharf and threw the cargoes of three ships — three hundred and forty chests in all — into the sea.[40]　The excited crowd looked on with approval for three hours, and not a man was arrested for the deed.　As to the moral aspect of this conduct historians have differed, and will probably continue to differ, according as their sympathies are with the Americans or British.　The eminently candid and fair English historian, Lecky, describes it as nothing more than an " outrage,"[41] while John Fiske speaks of it as a " heroic act," full of grandeur and deserving of greater praise than it has received from the hands of historians.[42]　Be this as it may, the news of the affair caused intense indignation among the government authorities in England, and led them to resolve upon stringent measures for the punishment of the turbulent and rebellious inhabitants of Boston in particular, and of Massachusetts in general.

" If we take a determined stand now," said the great jurist, Lord Mansfield, " Boston will submit and all will end in victory without carnage."　To the same effect was the boast of General Gage that " they will be lions while we are lambs; but if we take the resolute part they will prove very meek, I promise you."　With the object, therefore, of bringing the colonists to submission, Parliament passed five laws, which, from their stringent and repressive character, were popularly known as the five " intolerable " acts. The first of these was the so-called Boston Port Bill, which closed the port of Boston to commerce until the city should indemnify the owners of the £15,000 worth of tea thrown overboard and the customs officials for the damage done by mobs in 1773 and 1774. The act, furthermore, made Marblehead the port of entry and Salem the seat of government in the place of Boston.

The second measure, known as the Regulating Act, annulled the liberal charter of Massachusetts and virtually took away the large measure of self-government which the colony had always enjoyed.　It provided that the executive council should be appointed by the Crown instead of by the Assembly, empowered the governor to appoint and remove at pleasure all judges and administrative officers, made the judges' salaries a charge upon the Crown instead of upon the legislature, prohibited town meetings except with the

[40] Hosmer, "Life of Samuel Adams," p. 242.
[41] Lecky, "American Revolution," p. 153.
[42] Fiske, "American Revolution," vol. i. pp. 90-91.

approval of the governor, and vested the selection of juries in the hands of sheriffs instead of in the people. The third measure, often called the Transportation Act, provided for the removal to England for trial of any royal official, including soldiers who might be accused of murder in suppressing riots, the purpose being, of course, to secure a fair trial of such persons as the soldiers who were responsible for the " Boston Massacre," but the result of which, the Americans insisted, was to encourage the British soldiery to shoot inoffensive citizens.

The fourth law, known as the Quartering Act, made it obligatory upon Massachusetts towns to furnish quarters to British troops, while the fifth, passed about the same time, and usually known as the Quebec Act, extended the boundaries of Canada to the Ohio River, in spite of the territorial claims of the Eastern colonies. Furthermore, the act involved the introduction of the Catholic religion into the Northwest, and a centralized system of administration, the effect of which the English colonists claimed would be to shut them out from immigration to this region. The purpose of the act was probably misunderstood by the colonists, for there is no reason to believe that it was passed out of hostility to them,[43] but in the then excited state of mind they interpreted it as one of the additional blows by which the British Government was riveting the chains of slavery upon them.[44] General Gage was now sent over with several regiments to close the port of Boston, and, if possible, starve or awe the turbulent inhabitants into submission. He was given a sort of *carte blanche* in dealing with those who resisted the execution of the law, and was ordered to arrest and send to England for trial on the charge of treason the leading " agitators " who, in the opinion of the king, were chiefly responsible for the recent disorders. It soon became evident, however, that all the colonies would make common cause with Massachusetts, and that the attempt of the king to punish one of them would be resisted by all.

When the news of the Boston Port Bill reached Massachusetts a town meeting was called and a circular was prepared and sent to the other colonies, asking their aid and sympathy. The responses were prompt and generous. When the first of June had

[43] Coffin, " The Quebec Act " in the " Annual Report of the American Historical Association " for 1894; also, Hinsdale, " The Old Northwest," p. 141.

[44] Fiske, " American Revolution," pp. 93-97; Channing, " History of the United States," p. 184.

arrived, the day on which the Port Bill was to go into effect, droves
of cattle, loads of grain, vegetables, fruit, fish, etc., were pouring
into Boston from the neighboring colonies, even from communities
as far away as South Carolina. Everywhere the first of June was
observed as a fast day; bells were tolled and flags on the ships in
the harbors placed at half-mast.[45]   The town refused to indemnify
the tea merchants or the customs officials, in fact claimed that it
had no legal right to do so, and neglected to punish any of the
offenders, although their identity was known to everyone.   There
could be no doubt of the state of public opinion in America, and
had George III. possessed the average amount of common sense he
would have readily seen how untenable his position was.

II

THE FIRST CONTINENTAL CONGRESS

Matters had now reached a point where the cause of the colonists required a more efficient agency for securing concert of action
and unity of purpose than that afforded by the inter-colonial committees of correspondence.   The New York Sons of Liberty had
earlier in the year 1774 proposed a Continental Congress as contra-
distinguished from the provincial or State congresses, which should
contain representatives from all the colonies, and which should take
into consideration the present state of affairs and adopt measures
for the future conduct of the people.   The legislature of Virginia,
after the dissolution referred to above, assembled unofficially at the
Raleigh tavern, approved the suggestion and invited Massachusetts
to fix the date and place of meeting.   The legislature of the latter
colony, assembled at Salem, acted promptly and favorably on the
Virginia invitation.   The leading patriot in Massachusetts at the
time, or, as the English preferred to say, the leading " agitator,"
was Samuel Adams, and it was through his shrewd and bold action
that the legislature outwitted the governor and adopted resolutions
appointing delegates and fixing Philadelphia as the place, and
September 1 as the time, of the proposed meeting.[46]

Knowing full well that the governor would dissolve the legis-

---

[45] Fiske, " American Revolution," vol. i. p. 103.
[46] For an unfavorable opinion of Adams, see Lecky, " American Revolution," p. 121.

lature should it attempt to consider such a proposition, Adams coolly locked the door of the assembly hall and kept the members in their seats, Tories and all, and denied admission to the governor's secretary, when presently he arrived with a writ dissolving the Assembly. Thus undisturbed, the House quietly passed its measures and adjourned. The invitation to take part in the proposed Congress was generally accepted, and all the colonies except Georgia chose delegates, some of them in an irregular way, before the end of the summer.

The Congress met at Carpenters' Hall, Philadelphia, September 5, 1774. Forty-four members were present, and the number was subsequently increased to fifty-two. Some of the prominent delegates in attendance were Peyton Randolph of Virginia, who was chosen president; Samuel and John Adams of Massachusetts; Roger Sherman and Silas Deane of Connecticut; John Jay of New York; Stephen Hopkins of Rhode Island; George Washington, Patrick Henry, Benjamin Harrison, Richard Henry Lee, and Edmund Pendleton of Virginia; John Dickinson and Joseph Galloway, the latter a famous loyalist, of Pennsylvania; McKean, Rodney and Read of Delaware; the two Rutledges, John and Edward, of South Carolina, and others of less prominence in the future history of our country. It was the ablest, as it was the first, general assembly of the English colonists of America.[47] It was, of course, not a legislative body, but a revolutionary assembly, and did not, therefore, attempt to do much more than adopt recommendations for the guidance of the colonists in the approaching conflict with the mother country. After a month of deliberation marked by an exhibition of remarkable moderation and conservatism, the Congress put forth a declaration of the rights of the colonists, including their grievances; adopted addresses to the king, the people of Great Britain and the inhabitants of Canada; and entered into an association of non-intercourse with Great Britain. Some idea of the spirit which permeated these addresses may be gathered from the following extract from the address to the people of Great Britain:

"We believe there is yet much virtue in the English nation. To that justice we now appeal. You have been told that we are

[47] Of this Congress, William Pitt, lately become Earl of Chatham, said: "For myself I must declare and avow that in all my reading and observation, for solidity of reasoning, force of sagacity and wisdom of conclusion, no nation or body of men can stand in preference to the Congress of Philadelphia."

seditious, impatient of government and desirous of independency. Be assured that these are not facts, but calumnies. Permit us to be as free as yourself, and we shall ever esteem a union with you to be our greatest glory and our greatest happiness; we shall ever be ready to contribute all in our power to the welfare of the Empire; we shall consider your enemies as our enemies and your interests as our interests. But if you are determined that your ministers shall wantonly sport with the rights of mankind — if neither the voice of justice, the dictates of law, the principles of the Constitution nor the suggestions of humanity can restrain your hands from shedding human blood in such an impious cause, we must tell you that we will never submit to be hewers of wood or drawers of water for any ministry or nation in the world." [48]

The non-intercourse resolution pledged the colonists not to import after December 1 following any goods, wares or merchandise from Great Britain, or any tea, molasses or coffee from the British colonies, and after September 10, 1775, if the obnoxious acts of Parliament were not repealed, they would export no merchandise or produce to Great Britain. The delegates further pledged themselves to do all in their power to make the colonies economically independent of the mother country. They agreed to improve the breed of their sheep; not to eat or export any mutton; to encourage economy, frugality, and industry; to promote agriculture, arts, and manufactures, especially that of wool; to discountenance every species of extravagance and dissipation, particularly horse-racing and all kinds of gaming, cock-fighting, shows, plays, and other diversions and entertainments; and that upon the death of any friend or relative they would wear the plainest of mourning dress and discontinue the practice of giving gloves and scarfs at funerals. It was further agreed than any person who should take advantage of the scarcity caused thereby to raise prices should be boycotted by the people, that a vigilance committee should be appointed in every community to " observe the conduct of persons touching the agreement," and that all persons so violating it should be " published in the *Gazette* and universally contemned as the enemies of American liberty." Finally the Congress adjourned in October, after adopting a resolution providing for the assembling of a new Congress in

[48] Journal First Continental Congress. For the legal status of the Congress, see Friedenwald in the " Annual Report of the American Historical Association " for 1894.

May, 1775, if in the meantime the grievances of the colonists were not redressed.

III

LEXINGTON AND CONCORD

The day on which the Congress assembled at Philadelphia General Gage set to work fortifying Boston Neck for the purpose of defending the only approach to the city. On September 17 a meeting representing all the towns of Suffolk County was called, and it adopted a series of " resolves " arraigning the British Government for its acts, expressed astonishment at the military activities of General Gage, and appointed Dr. Joseph Warren to wait on the governor and inform him that " the country are alarmed at the fortifications beginning on Boston Neck." The convention also adopted an address to the governor, assuring him that the people of America, " by divine assistance," were resolved never to submit to the late acts of Parliament. The Suffolk resolves were laid before the Continental Congress and its advice requested. The Congress promptly indorsed the resolutions, pledged the aid of the other colonies in case armed resistance became necessary, and recommended to their brethren in Massachusetts "a perseverance in the firm and temperate conduct " as expressed in their resolutions.

Thereupon the people of Massachusetts proceeded to organize a provisional government of their own with the intention of repudiating the sovereignty of Great Britain. The legislature, which had been dissolved by the governor, assembled at Salem upon its own authority and organized itself into a Provincial Congress under the presidency of John Hancock, a wealthy merchant of Boston, a graduate of Harvard, and one of the three leading patriots of the colony. The Congress chose a committee of safety and placed at its head Dr. Joseph Warren, one of the most active and resourceful of the early Revolutionary leaders. Early in 1775 another Provincial Congress was assembled, and it entered actively upon the task of putting the colony on a war footing. The militia was strengthened, officers appointed, bodies of " minutemen " ready to act at a moment's warning were organized, and soon every village square was the scene of active military drill.

Everywhere there was evidence of rebellion against British

authority; in every heart there was the feeling that death itself was preferable to submission. The British had found it impossible to enforce the Regulating Act in Massachusetts; royal officers were forced to resign, juries were awed and intimidated into rendering verdicts against the Crown wherever the rights of the people were at issue; the courts were broken up and Gage found himself powerless, for no one would work for him or sell him supplies. He attributed most of his troubles to the "seditious" utterances and activities of Samuel Adams and John Hancock, the two chief arch-conspirators, and after vainly endeavoring to win over Adams by bribery, he undertook to arrest both in pursuance of instructions from the king, that they should be sent to England for trial. But both were among friends who shielded them from the king's officers, and while they deemed it the better part of valor to elude the royal officers, they did not cease their opposition to the late acts of Parliament.

On April 15, having learned that both Adams and Hancock were staying at a house in Lexington, a village nine miles northwest of Boston, Gage secretly dispatched an expedition of some eight hundred troops with instructions to arrest the two patriot leaders, after which they were to proceed to Concord, ten miles farther on, and capture a quantity of military supplies that had been collected there by the "rebels." Gage, however, was unable to conceal the movement of the troops from the vigilance of the patriots, and one of their number, Paul Revere, volunteered to ride to Lexington and inform the citizens of the approach of the regulars. Booted and spurred, he waited for a given signal from a lantern hung in the tower of the Old North Church, which indicated the direction the troops had taken, after which he galloped away through the darkness shouting the news at every farmhouse as he passed along. Reaching Lexington about midnight, he roused the sleeping citizens and informed Adams and Hancock of the coming of the troops in time for them to escape.

In the gray dawn of April 19, Major Pitcairn, who had been sent forward with several companies of infantry, entered the quiet village only to find himself confronted by a well-drilled company of minutemen under the command of Captain Parker, a veteran of the French and Indian War. Riding up, Pitcairn commanded them with an oath to disperse, but not a man budged. Thereupon he gave the command to fire, and after some hesitation his troops obeyed, killing seven of the Americans and wounding ten others. The minutemen bravely returned the fire, but being greatly outnumbered, prudently retired and waited for reënforcements.

The British troops marched on to Concord unopposed, only to find that the bulk of the arms and ammunition had been removed from the town and concealed by the inhabitants. The only damage the invaders did was to cut down the " liberty pole," disable a few cannon and destroy a small quantity of supplies. While this was going on a force of some 400 minutemen fell upon a detachment of 200 regulars which had been left to guard the bridge north of the town, and chased them back to the village. The British, realizing their perilous situation, now determined to return to Boston. By this time the adjacent country was well aroused and troops were swarming to the scene from every quarter, and as the regulars marched back toward Lexington they were harassed and shot by the farmers, who concealed themselves behind hedges, trees, rocks and other natural objects. The British retreat soon degenerated into an utter route. All was disorder and confusion; the day was dry and hot, and the soldiers were well-nigh exhausted from their long march. At Lexington they were saved by the arrival of Lord Percy, who with 1,200 men had been sent to their rescue. Thus reënforced, the British held the Americans at bay and gained time for rest and refreshment, after which they resumed their march to Boston. But the roadside along which they now traveled was fairly alive with American troops. They flew at the retreating British from every direction and gave them one continual battle from Lexington to Boston. Finally, at sundown, the retreating soldiers, weary and with depleted ranks, reached Charlestown, where they found a welcome cover afforded by the gunboats. Altogether they had lost 273 men, while the Americans had lost less than 100.

The battles of Lexington and Concord were the first of the Revolution, and so far as moral results were concerned were a distinct victory for the Americans. The British forces had barely escaped capture and the fighting qualities of the Americans had been abundantly shown. If further evidence was needed that they could not be frightened into abject submission by the presence of a British regiment, it was furnished by the retreat from Concord. The news of the affair spread rapidly, and from all parts of the colony troops began to pour into the vicinity of Boston. Leaders like Israel Putnam, who, according to the story, left his plow in the field, John Stark, Benedict Arnold, and others, came at the head of well-drilled companies, and within three days it was estimated that not less than 16,000 American volunteers had gathered in the neighborhood of Boston and were ready to begin a siege of the town. Everywhere the people rose in revolt against the royal authorities, and in a short time British rule in America had utterly collapsed. The royal governors were compelled to abandon their governments; some of them resigned, others returned to England, while still others took refuge on near-by war vessels and went through the hollow form of attempting to govern their provinces from a distance. Nowhere was there a thought of submission or reconciliation. On May 11, three weeks after the battle of Lexington, Ethan Allen, a "Green Mountain" patriot, with a handful of backwoodsmen, captured the fortress of Ticonderoga in eastern New York, and a little later Crown Point, on Lake Champlain, also fell into the hands of the Americans, with a large number of cannon and a quantity of ammunition. Such were the beginnings of a revolution which was destined to result in the independence of the American colonies, and which was to have political consequences of tremendous import to the future of mankind.

Chapter X

REVOLUTION AND INDEPENDENCE
1775-1776

I

THE SECOND CONTINENTAL CONGRESS

ON May 10, 1775, the very day on which Ticonderoga fell into the hands of the Americans, the second Continental Congress came together at Philadelphia, in pursuance of a resolution of the preceding Congress. The address to the king drawn up by the last Congress had been unanswered, and instead of redressing the grievances set forth therein, the king had resolved upon the subjugation of his rebellious American subjects. Important events had taken place since the adjournment of the Congress in October; an armed conflict had occurred between the royal forces and the American militia, and blood had been shed on American soil. As a result the country was rising in arms, and already the British forces were besieged in the town of Boston, and the king was preparing to send to their aid large reënforcements from England.

Among the delegates chosen to the second Continental Congress were the two Adamses, the Livingstons, Edward and Robert, John Jay, Patrick Henry, Richard Henry Lee, and George Washington, all of whom had been members of the first Congress. In addition to these were two new members who were destined to win great fame in American history, namely, Thomas Jefferson, who had just turned his thirty-second year, and Benjamin Franklin, already the most widely known man in America. Another new member was John Hancock, who, after eluding the British at Lexington, had hastened to Philadelphia to be present at the opening of Congress. Hated and proscribed by the British, he was very popular among the patriots of America, and the Congress made him its president, partly " to show Great Britain how much they valued her proscriptions." Like the preceding Congress, this one was a revolutionary body, a sort of advisory organ, assembled without legal authority, and consequently without constitutional power to enact legislation binding on the colonies. Nevertheless, during the course of the long war that now ensued it assumed both legislative and administrative functions, as a matter of necessity, always relying, of course, upon the acquiescence of the people as the measure of its powers. It was the only general legislative body for the colonies during a period when some such authority was absolutely necessary, and the fact that the colonies acquiesced in its acts, unsupported by legal authority as they were, must always stand as high evidence of their unity of purpose and patriotism. The great and almost only task of the Congress was to raise, organize and support the army. One of its first duties, and at the same time probably the wisest and most far-reaching of its acts, was the selection of George Washington as commander-in-chief of the army.

The Continental Army at this time consisted mainly of raw, untrained New England militia, and the selection of a Virginia planter, upon the nomination of a New Englander, John Adams, to organize and command them, was striking evidence of the determination to sink local prejudices and present a united front to the enemy. All the more was this true in view of the fact that several prominent New England men, chief of whom was Hancock, desired the position of commander-in-chief. At the time, Washington was colonel of the Virginia militia, and his experience in the French and Indian War, his fondness for military service, and his natural genius as a commander made him eminently qualified, as subsequent events showed, for the high office to which he was now called; in fact, there was no one who could for a moment be compared with him in fitness. In the debates of the Congress Washington had taken no part, so far as the record shows, but " for solid information and sound judgment," said Patrick Henry, " he was unquestionably the greatest man on the floor of Congress." [1] With becoming modesty he now rose in his seat and in trembling voice said, " But I beg it may be remembered by every gentleman in this room that I this day declare with utmost sincerity I do not think myself equal to the command I am honored with." Nevertheless, he agreed to " enter upon the momentous duty," and announced that he would accept no pay for his services,

[1] Lodge, " Life of Washington," vol. i. p. 127.

but would keep an account of his personal expenses, which Congress might reimburse if it wished at the close of the war.

In addition to selecting Washington as commander-in-chief, Congress appointed four major-generals, Ward, Lee, Schuyler and Putnam, and eight brigadiers; it also authorized the issue of two million dollars of paper currency, set apart a day of prayer and fasting, and recommended the States to adopt constitutions and organize local governments in place of the defunct British authority — a recommendation which they all followed in the course of the next two years.

II

BUNKER HILL AND BOSTON

While the Congress at Philadelphia was providing for the organization and equipment of the " Continental Army," affairs were reaching a crisis at Boston. Fifteen or twenty thousand American volunteers were encamped in the neighborhood of the town, while the arrival of Clinton, Howe and Burgoyne with re-enforcements from England had increased Gage's strength to over ten thousand men. The American army, under the command of General Artemas Ward, was arranged in the form of a great semicircle about sixteen miles in length, stretching from Cambridge to Charlestown Neck, while the British forces occupied Boston. At this juncture Gage, feeling confident of victory, issued a proclamation offering amnesty to all "rebels" who would lay down their arms and return peaceably to their homes. Excepted from the benefits of the proposed amnesty, however, were Adams and Hancock, the chief conspirators, in Gage's opinion, and who, if captured, were to be summarily hanged. The proclamation had no more effect than if it had been issued against the moon — hardly a man returned to his allegiance. Gage, now feeling certain that he would have to fight in order to hold Boston, and fearing that the rebels would seize some of the surrounding hills and make his position untenable, decided to occupy the two most important of these defenses, namely, Bunker Hill and Dorchester Heights, to the north and south of the town, respectively.

Learning of Gage's intention in this respect, the Americans resolved to forestall him, and on the night of June 16, 1775,

General Ward dispatched 1,200 men under Colonel Prescott to take possession of Bunker Hill. Disregarding orders, they passed over that hill and occupied Breed's Hill, a lower elevation between Bunker Hill and the Charles River. On the morrow the British were astonished to find that they had been forestalled by the vigilant Americans, who were now strongly posted behind intrenchments on the eminence which they had expected to occupy themselves. Instead of sending a detachment to cut the Americans off at Charlestown Neck, as he might have done with success,

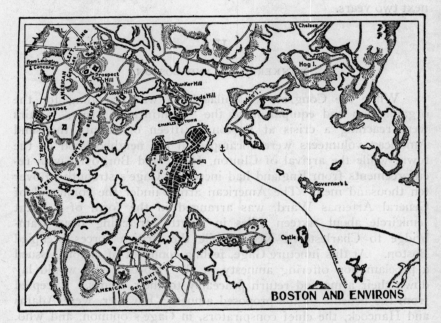

BOSTON AND ENVIRONS

Gage decided to attack them from the front and drive them back over the hill. Accordingly, 3,000 troops under General Howe were sent across the river, and in the afternoon of June 17 they started up the ascent prepared to storm the breastworks of the enemy. The Americans calmly withheld their fire until the British troops were within convenient range, when suddenly they poured a terrible volley into the ranks of the enemy and sent them down the hillside in utter rout and confusion. Recovering their equanimity after a brief pause the British advanced to a second charge, only to be driven back again with frightful losses. Toward five

BENJAMIN FRANKLIN
(Born, 1706. Died, 1790)
Painting by Joseph Silfrede Duplessis, Art Museum, Boston

o'clock in the afternoon, to the amazement of everybody but the British themselves, a third assault was made with remarkable courage and desperation.[2]

In the meantime the American supply of powder having run short and their muskets being without bayonets, Prescott's men were reduced to the necessity of repelling the attack of the enemy with their gunstocks, which were used as clubs. Under these circumstances the Americans were driven back, and the British were left in possession of the hill. The British loss in killed and wounded was something over 1,000 men, that of the Americans being less than half that number. The loss of officers among the British was especially heavy, among the killed being Major Pitcairn. The Americans suffered an irreparable loss in the death of Dr. Joseph Warren, who was shot while imprudently lingering on the field after the close of the battle. With the Adamses, Hancock and Otis, he was one of the leading patriots of New England, and had played a conspicuous part in the events by which the Revolution was inaugurated. From the standpoint of purely military results the battle of Bunker Hill (or more properly, Breed's Hill) was an English victory and enabled Gage to hold Boston nine months longer. But the moral advantages were largely with the Americans, for until disabled by the exhaustion of their ammunition they had shown themselves more than a match for the enemy. Instead of discouragement at the result there was general elation, while praises for the fighting qualities of the New England militiamen were widely expressed, both in America and in Europe.[3]

Two weeks after the battle of Bunker Hill, Washington, after a tiresome journey of eleven days by stage from Philadelphia, arrived at Cambridge, and on July 3 took command of the " Continental Army," of some sixteen thousand men.[4] All were New England militiamen, and all, except about five thousand, were inhabitants of Massachusetts. Shortly afterward they were reënforced by some three thousand troops from Pennsylvania, Maryland and Virginia. Washington's journey to Boston had been in the nature of an ovation, and his assumption of the chief com-

[2] See Lodge, " Story of the Revolution," ch. v.
[3] Fiske, " The American Revolution," vol. i. pp. 137-146. Winsor, " Narrative and Critical History," vol. vi. pp. 130-140.
[4] Lodge, " Life of Washington," vol. i. p. 134.

mand was attended by every circumstance of popular rejoicing. Among his subordinate commanders who were destined to achieve fame in the near future were Nathanael Greene, who, next to Washington, was the greatest soldier the war produced; John Stark of New Hampshire, who had already in the battle of Bunker Hill given evidence of his brave and rugged character; Daniel Morgan, the gallant leader of a company of Virginia sharp-shooters; Benedict Arnold of Connecticut, a brilliant soldier, whose promising career was to have a sad ending; and Henry Knox, a Boston book-dealer, who was destined to become one of the first Cabinet officers under the Constitution, and one of the most trusted advisers of Washington.

Never was the task of a military commander greater than that which faced Washington when he took charge of the Continental troops under the shades of the great Cambridge elm. Without uniforms, armed with every variety of weapon, having no commissariat worth the name, untrained, undisciplined, and hardly yet having learned the lesson of military subordination, this motley crowd of farmers, fishermen, and shopkeepers presented a spectacle which was enough to discourage the most experienced of commanders. Nevertheless, it afforded a body of excellent raw material, and out of this Washington proceeded to organize an army. Many of the men had volunteered for short periods, and as their terms of enlistment expired they insisted on going home, and many of them went. The work of reënlisting proceeded apace; in fact, the army was practically disbanded and reënlisted within cannon-shot of the enemy.

For months Washington toiled away drilling the men, re-enlisting those whose terms had expired, securing arms and ammunition and creating a commissariat.[5] During this period of preparation and organization no active military operations were undertaken except an invasion of Canada in the autumn, largely in the hope of freeing the Canadians from British rule and attaching them to the American cause. In the latter part of August, General Richard Montgomery, with some 2,000 men, set out from Fort Ticonderoga and in November captured Montreal. To aid Montgomery in what promised to be a highly successful campaign, Washington, in September, sent Colonel Benedict Arnold with

[5] For an interesting account of this phase of the Revolution, see Hatch, 'The Administration of the Revolutionary Army."

1,200 men to join Montgomery's forces in the attack on Quebec. After a march of more than a month through the dense wilderness of Maine, during which the men suffered indescribable hardships from cold and hunger, their flesh torn and lacerated by thorns and briers, exhausted by fatigue and tormented by disease, the expedition reached the neighborhood of Quebec early in December. On the last day of the year 1775, while a blinding snowstorm was raging, the two armies made a combined attack on the city. Although the Americans fought with a courage amounting to desperation, they were driven back with frightful losses, the gallant Montgomery being among the killed. Such was the disastrous ending of one of the most daring and heroically conducted campaigns of the Revolution.[6]

After about eight months of organizing and drilling Washington was at last ready to begin the attack upon Boston. A great quantity of cannon had been collected, some of them dragged on sledges all the way from Ticonderoga, where they had been captured by Ethan Allen the year before, and thus equipped the operations were begun in earnest against the British. Washington's first move was to seize and occupy, on the night of March 4, 1776, Dorchester Heights, which commanded the town from the south, as Bunker Hill did from the north. All night long the Americans labored with pick and shovel, and when the British awoke on the morning of March 5 they were astonished to find two thousand men strongly intrenched behind earth-works, and ready to begin the bombardment of the British vessels in the harbor. Howe was greatly puzzled to know what to do. His first thought was to storm the American works, but it soon became evident that only disaster could result from such an attempt, and it was accordingly abandoned. Nothing seemed left but to evacuate the city, and on March 17, his whole army of 8,000 troops, together with a considerable number of loyalists, who were resolved to sacrifice their all for the mother country, sailed away to Halifax, leaving to the enemy two hundred cannon, a quantity of small arms and a large amount of ammunition. Thus by one brilliant stroke, and almost without the loss of a man, New England was freed from the rule of the British.[7]

[6] Read Codman, "Arnold's March to Quebec."
[7] Fiske, "The American Revolution," vol. ii. p. 172; Winsor, "Narrative and Critical History," vol. vi. p. 158.

While Washington was besieging Boston several noteworthy events were happening in the southern colonies. The first of these was the burning of Norfolk, the principal town of Virginia, by Lord Dunmore, the royalist governor, who, having stirred up the wrath of the Virginians, had been compelled to take refuge on a war vessel in the harbor. On January 1, 1776, Dunmore set fire to the town to prevent its falling into the hands of a body of patriot troops, and laid it completely in ashes. In the same month General Clinton with 2,000 troops was sent from Boston to take possession of the southern colonies and hold them for the Crown, being subsequently joined by Sir Peter Parker with a fleet of ten ships and seven regiments from England. Meantime, a body of 1,000 troops under Colonel Richard Caswell had defeated and utterly routed 2,000 Scotch Highlander Tories under the leadership of Donald MacDonald, on Moore's Creek, North Carolina, in February, 1776. Immediately following this brilliant victory, the North Carolina patriots flew to arms in such numbers that Clinton was afraid to land. After cruising up and down the North Carolina coast for some time, he decided to capture Charleston with the aid of Parker's fleet, which had now arrived, and thus provide a refuge for the large number of loyalists which he was made to believe were settled in South Carolina. On June 28 the combined fleets attacked Fort Moultrie, which the Americans had hastily constructed, mostly out of palmetto logs, but the British fire was unavailing. The British fleet was badly injured and more than 200 of their men were lost; the American fort was little damaged and their loss was inconsiderable. After ten hours of fruitless bombardment the British fleet sailed away and later returned to New York, leaving the southern colonies unmolested for nearly three years longer, after which they became the chief seat of military operations and continued as such until the close of the war.[8]

III

THE DECLARATION OF INDEPENDENCE

In the meantime a strong sentiment was growing up among the colonies in favor of formally renouncing all allegiance to the king and declaring themselves independent of the mother country.

[8] Lodge, "Story of the Revolution," ch. vi.

During the first stages of the war hardly any American of prominence, possibly with the exception of Samuel Adams, entertained any idea of separation. Benjamin Franklin declared that whatever else the Americans might desire, they did not want independence, and Washington asserted that at the time he took command of the army (July, 1775) he abhorred the idea of separation.

There can be little doubt that the opinions of these two leaders expressed the general sentiment of their countrymen in the summer of 1775. They all hoped and prayed for a reconciliation with the mother country, for there were few who did not feel a certain sense of pride in being a part of the great British Empire. It was therefore with genuine regret that they were forced to abandon all hope of reconciliation.

But by the time of the evacuation of Boston a great revulsion of sentiment against the continuance of the union with Great Britain had taken place. This was due to a combination of circumstances. In the first place, the Continental Congress had, in July, 1775, addressed a respectful petition to the king, praying for a repeal of those statutes of Parliament which had borne with so much oppression upon the Americans. This " olive-branch " petition the king contemptuously refused to receive, and in the place of an answer issued a proclamation denouncing the Americans as a dangerous, ill-designing and rebellious people. This, in itself, contributed much to the alienation of his American subjects and to the development of a strong sentiment in favor of separation.

In addition to this insulting treatment of his subjects the king further aroused their indignation by hiring an army of foreign soldiers with which to complete their subjugation. These were the so-called " Hessians," about 20,000 in all, who were hired from the Landgrave of Hesse-Cassel and other German princes, after an effort had been made to secure troops from Catherine of Russia.[9] They were not mercenaries, as is often asserted, for they did not voluntarily engage to fight the Americans for personal profit, but were hired to the British by their sovereigns without their consent, the king agreeing to pay a fixed sum for each one who was killed outright, while three wounded men were to be

[9] Fiske, "American Revolution," vol. i. p. 161; Winsor, "Narrative and Critical History," vol. vi. pp. 18–24.

counted as one dead.[10]   Having no interest in the war, many of
them were easily induced to desert the British upon promise of
grants of land by Congress.

The employment of foreign troops against the Americans was
bitterly condemned by some of the leading members of Parliament
as impolitic and incompatible with the rules of legitimate warfare.
In America it created intense indignation and cost the king the
most of the friends he had left on this side of the Atlantic.   Thousands who had been lukewarm on the subject of independence now
became enthusiastic supporters of a declaration severing all connection with Great Britain.   Congress adopted a bolder policy and
prepared for a long struggle, feeling certain that all hope of reconciliation was gone.   In November, 1775, it appointed a " Secret
Committee of Correspondence" to communicate with friends of
America in Europe, and sent out Silas Deane to France to procure
arms and other supplies for the use of the American army.   Deane
was shortly afterwards followed by other agents, and soon they
were bestirring themselves at various Continental capitals in the
endeavor to secure aid for the struggling colonists.   In the same
month also Congress recommended to the good people of New
Hampshire, as it had already recommended to those of Massachusetts in the preceding June, to adopt a constitution of government
in conformity with the views of the inhabitants, to last during the
continuance of the struggle.   Finally, on May 15, 1776, Congress
recommended all the colonies to establish permanent governments
without regard to the possibility of reconciliation.   The royal
authority having practically collapsed everywhere in America, and
the colonies being without settled forms of government, most of
them acted promptly upon the advice of Congress, and before the
Revolution had advanced very far they had all adopted constitutions, except Rhode Island and Connecticut, both of which continued under their liberal charters for many years longer.

Judged by the present-day standards these early instruments
of government were a little crude in content and arrangement; some
of them were framed by Revolutionary legislatures or Provincial
Congresses, as they were called, and all but one of them were
put into effect without popular ratification.   The most noted of
them were the constitution of Virginia, adopted in 1776, and that of
Massachusetts of 1780.   The former was accompanied by an elab-

[10] Trevelyan, "The American Revolution," part ii. vol. ii. p. 123.

orate bill of rights drawn up by George Mason and containing the most admirable statement of the principles of American civil liberty then in existence. The Massachusetts constitution, drawn mainly by John Adams, likewise contained a lengthy bill of rights, and as a whole the constitution was so satisfactory that it has been retained in all essential particulars by the people of Massachusetts until this day.[11]

Public sentiment in favor of separation from Great Britain was further crystallized by the arguments of Thomas Paine in a pamphlet entitled " Common Sense," published in January, 1776, and soon spread broadcast over the country. Containing a good deal of scurrilous abuse of the English people, it was, nevertheless, replete with sensible argument in favor of the advantages to be derived from a declaration of independence. The pamphlet found thousands of readers; in fact, the primitive presses of the time could not supply the demand, and many who were lukewarm were thoroughly convinced by Paine's logic of the expediency of independence.

As a result of these several causes the people of the colonies, in the spring of 1776, had arrived at the conclusion that Congress should proclaim a formal separation from the mother country. The first colony to take official action was North Carolina, whose provincial Congress, on April 12, instructed its delegates in the Continental Congress " to concur with the delegates of the other colonies in declaring independency." Other colonies soon followed the example of North Carolina. Finally Virginia took an advanced step on May 6 by instructing her delegates to propose to the members from the other colonies a declaration of independence. In pursuance of these instructions Richard Henry Lee, chairman of the Virginia delegation, on June 7, offered a resolution, " that these United Colonies are, and of right ought to be, free and independent States, that they are absolved from all allegiance to the British Crown, and that all political connection between them and the State of Great Britain is, and ought to be, totally dissolved." After a brief debate on this resolution it became evident that the delegates were not ready to vote, most probably because they

[11] For a learned discussion of the legal aspects of Revolutionary constitution-making, see Jameson, " The Constitutional Convention," sects. 125–169. See also Morey, " Revolutionary State Constitutions " in " Annals of the American Academy of Political and Social Science," vol. iv.

preferred to get instructions from their constituents before taking action on so vital a question. Upon motion, therefore, further discussion was postponed until July 1, by which time the States could be heard from.

Meantime a committee consisting of Thomas Jefferson, Benjamin Franklin, John Adams, Roger Sherman, and Robert R. Livingston was appointed to make a draft of a declaration to be used in case Lee's motion should prevail. Prompt action was taken by the States, and by the time July 1 arrived all except New York had empowered their delegates to vote for independence. Lee's resolution was now taken from the table for debate, and a lively and protracted discussion ensued. The great majority of the delegates were in favor of the declaration, but the minority was able and respectable and was led by John Dickinson, famous as the author of the " Letters of a Pennsylvania Farmer." His principal arguments were that the proposed action was rash, that it would cause the Americans to lose their last friend in England and that the declaration ought to be delayed until independence had been achieved as an actual fact. In spite of all opposition Lee's motion was adopted on July 2, all the States, except New York, voting in the affirmative. On July 4 the Declaration of Independence was formally adopted by the unanimous vote of twelve colonies, and a little later the New York delegates, having received instructions, gave their adhesion. The Declaration was not signed on the 4th, as is popularly believed, but received the signatures of the members present on August 2.[12]

The draft of the Declaration, probably the most famous of American state papers, was prepared by Thomas Jefferson, a young Virginian, then but thirty-three years of age, and the youngest member of the committee. It began with a recital of certain " self-evident " truths, such as the equality of man; the inherent right of life, liberty, property, and the pursuit of happiness; the doctrine of the consent of the governed as the basis of government, and the right of revolution when governments become destructive of the ends for which they are created. Then followed a long indictment against the British king (Parliament being completely ignored), charging him with many crimes against the rights and liberties of the colonies, one or two of which, however,

[12] Winsor, " The Narrative and Critical History," vol. vi. p. 268; also Friedenwald, " The Declaration of Independence."

were stricken out by Congress on the ground that they were not well founded.[13] Finally there was the declaration also of absolution from all allegiance to the British Crown and of independence of Great Britain, for the maintenance of which the signers pledged their " lives, their fortunes, and their sacred honor."

The news of the adoption of the " Declaration of Independence " was carried to all the colonies as rapidly as the crude means of communication then existing would permit, and was received by extraordinary demonstrations of popular rejoicing. It was read at the head of the army, from the pulpit and the public platform, and was welcomed everywhere with firing of cannon, ringing of bells, and pyrotechnic displays. Thus after years of protest against British tyranny, after the advances of the colonies in the direction of reconciliation had been rejected, and armies sent over to coerce them into submission, the Americans had formally renounced all allegiance to the mother country. The die was cast, " a new empire had suddenly risen in the world, styled the United States of America." [14]

[13] Schouler, "Life of Thomas Jefferson," p. 80.
[14] See Lodge, "Story of the Revolution," ch. vii.

Chapter XI

THE WAR IN THE MIDDLE COLONIES. 1776–1778

I

LOSS OF THE LOWER HUDSON

DRIVEN out of New England, and foiled in their attempt to gain a foothold in the south, the British now conceived the plan of capturing New York and holding the line of the Hudson, thereby cutting the American confederacy in twain. By isolating the New England States from those of the south concert of action among them would be hindered, and thus they might be forced to return to their allegiance. According to the plan worked out by the ministry, General Howe was to bring his army from Halifax to New York, where he was to be joined by the army of Clinton and Cornwallis from the south, and by a fleet under the command of his brother, Admiral Howe, from England. This combined force was to capture New York City and occupy the valley of the Hudson, while General Guy Carleton, with another army, reënforced by many of the Tories who inhabited New York, was to descend from Canada and form a junction with Howe's army on the upper Hudson. The execution of this well-conceived scheme was at once entered upon.

Howe reached New York in August, 1776, but before beginning operations he decided to offer the rebels an opportunity to return to their allegiance. Accordingly a letter offering a full and free pardon to all who would lay down their arms and aid in restoring order was sent to the American headquarters under a flag of truce, addressed to " George Washington, Esq." This " olive-branch " communication " General Washington " refused to receive, because not properly addressed, and so hostilities were renewed. Howe's combined army aggregated about 20,000 well-equipped and disciplined troops, opposed to which were about 18,000 Americans under the command of Washington, who, divining Howe's purpose, had moved his army from Boston to New York earlier in the year. General Greene had been sent to occupy and fortify Brooklyn Heights on Long Island, an eminence which commanded New York much as Bunker Hill and Dorchester Heights did Boston, and there, on August 27, one-half of the American army, commanded by General Putnam, was attacked by the British. The Americans were greatly outnumbered, and as a consequence were defeated. About 400 men were killed and wounded on each side, and over 1,000 Americans were taken prisoners, among them the brave General Sterling. The Americans now retired within their works, and, being reënforced by troops from New York, made ready to resist the beseiging operations of General Howe. Upon sober second thought, however, Washington decided to abandon this place and withdraw his army from Long Island. Accordingly, on the night of August 29, having collected every sloop, yacht, fishing-smack, rowboat and other craft to be had on East River, Washington quietly transported his army across the river to New York, without leaving behind a man or valuable article of any kind. Next morning Howe was astonished and bewildered to find that the enemy had escaped and his opportunity of capturing the American army had been lost through his own lack of vigilance and energy. This successful retreat of Washington, involving as it did the saving of his army from capture, was one of the most brilliant military exploits in the history of the Revolution, and was the beginning of a series of events which were to bring out in striking relief his remarkable qualities as a resourceful and vigilant strategist.

Howe, however, soon followed in pursuit, and Washington, being unable with his relatively small army to hold New York, abandoned it to the enemy (September 15) and withdrew to Harlem Heights north of the city. On September 16 the British attacked the Americans at Harlem Heights, near the present site of Columbia University, but were repulsed with considerable loss. The task to which Howe now bent his energies was to cut off Washington's retreat by sending troops up the Hudson and East Rivers to gain his rear. But on the northern extremity of Manhattan Island British ascent by way of the Hudson was obstructed by two strongholds on opposite banks of the river. Fort Washington on the east, and Fort Lee on the west. The East River was unobstructed, however, and Howe accordingly sent the greater part of his army up this stream to Throg's Neck, with the purpose of gaining Washington's rear. But the vigilant American commander was not to be thus outwitted, and accordingly changed his base to White Plains, some miles above Fort Washington, where his whole army was presently concentrated. Here, on October 28, the American army was attacked by the British, but the attack was repulsed, the enemy losing about 230 men, the Americans about 150. Thus baffled, Howe withdrew to a point on the Hudson in the neighborhood of Fort Washington with the evident intention of attacking the fort or crossing the river into New Jersey.

II

THE RETREAT ACROSS NEW JERSEY

Washington having become convinced that it would be impossible to hold the forts on the Hudson, neither of which had been effective in preventing ships from passing up the river, decided to evacuate both and fortify West Point, a more important place up the Hudson. Colonel Magaw was accordingly instructed to evacuate Fort Washington in certain events, but before he had done so an order from Congress was received directing that the fort be held. Magaw therefore disregarded Washington's orders and made an effort to hold the fort, but he found it an impossible task. On November 16 Howe stormed the fort, carried the works, and captured the entire garrison, consisting of 3,000 of Washington's best-drilled troops, together with a large quantity of artillery and small arms — all of which the Americans could ill afford to spare. The captured Americans were subjected to some rather rough, insolent treatment, but the charge often made, that the surrender was followed by a wholesale butchery of the captives, seems to be without good foundation.[1] The loss of Fort Washington with the garrison and supplies was the greatest disaster that the American cause had suffered since the outbreak of the war, and greatly depressed the spirits of the patriots. If the truth must be told, it was mainly due to the meddlesomeness of Congress. Worse still, it was the beginning of a series of disasters which threatened to end in the utter overthrow of the American cause.

Washington's army was now divided by the Hudson River.

[1] See Trevelyan, "The American Revolution," part ii. vol. ii. p. 10.

In this situation he ordered General Charles Lee, who was at North Castle, on the east side of the Hudson, to cross the river and join him in the defense of Fort Lee. Instead of moving promptly, Lee made excuses, and being only too anxious to cause the downfall of Washington, in the hope of superseding him in the chief command, he neglected to go to the latter's relief. In the meantime

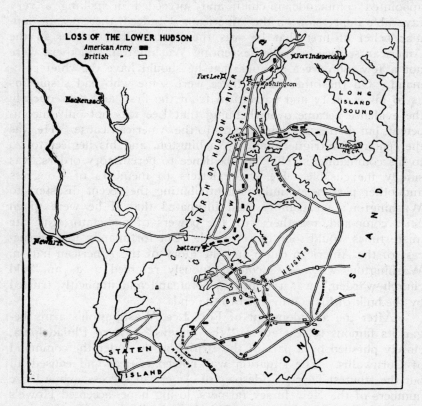

a detachment from Howe's army had scaled the palisades and were before Fort Lee, and General Greene, finding it impossible to hold the fort, abandoned it and narrowly escaped with his army, on November 19. Lee's men were saved, but all his artillery, camp equipage and provisions were left behind for the use of the enemy. To the outrageous conduct of General Lee, more than any other circumstance, was this disaster due. Lee was an English soldier of fortune, who had served in various European wars without achieving any special distinction. Deserting the English army, he came to America and offered his services to the Continental Congress for a major general's commission and thirty thousand dollars, the estimated value of his English estates.

He was chosen a major general at the time Washington was appointed commander-in-chief, and succeeded in making a very favorable impression on the Americans. Indeed, there was a popular belief at first that he was the most skillful soldier in the American service, not even excepting Washington, and there were not a few who were anxious that he should have the chief command. On the other hand, there were some who had suspicions as to his capacity and patriotism from the first, and subsequently the evidence became overwhelming that Lee was not only incompetent, but distressingly lukewarm to the American cause. He was the center of intrigue against Washington, and his neglect to go to his commander's relief, in obedience to peremptory orders, was simply inexcusable. He wrote letters to members of Congress and other persons of influence, attributing the recent disasters to Washington's incapability, and intimated that if he were given chief command, together with the powers of a dictator, the late misfortunes would soon be retrieved. But fortunately for the success of the American cause and the glory of the American nation, Washington, whom Lee contemptuously referred to as an "old church warden," was retained in command and implicitly trusted by the bulk of his countrymen to the end.

After the abandonment of Fort Lee, Washington's army began its famous retreat across "the Jerseys" toward Philadelphia, closely pursued by a part of the British army under the command of Cornwallis. The situation was indeed critical and caused all but the stoutest hearts to despair of American success, while large numbers of the New Jersey farmers, losing hope, accepted Howe's amnesty offer and returned to their British allegiance. "The conduct of the Jerseys," wrote Washington, "has been most infamous. Instead of turning out to defend their country and offering aid to our army, they are making submissions as fast as they can." The seriousness of the situation was further complicated by the embarrassments occasioned from the expiration of the terms of enlistment of large numbers of the soldiers, many of whom it proved difficult to induce to reënlist.

The nominal strength of the American army soon fell to less than six thousand men and the real strength did not exceed four thousand. Five thousand Americans had been taken prisoners during the last three months and the contagion of desertion was spreading like a plague. Winter was setting in, the supply of tents and blankets was inadequate, the army had few arms except muskets, and the soldiers were homesick and discouraged. The best of them were clothed in threadbare garments, with worse stockings and shoes. Many of them were overrun with vermin, and altogether the army was in a truly pitiable condition. Added to these difficulties were the discomforts occasioned by inclement weather, incessant marching, and exposure and hunger. At this season of the year the country through which they marched was bare of grain, fruit, and vegetable, so that they were unable to live " off the stalk," as did Sherman's army in the Civil War. " They starved all the way," says one writer, " from Hackensack to Newark, and from Newark to Brunswick; and by the time they came in sight of the Delaware, those mothers and sisters who had spun and dyed their garments would with difficulty have recognized their pinched faces and discolored rags." Finally Washington's depleted army reached Princeton, and on December 8 it crossed the Delaware, after which he seized every boat within sight to prevent the enemy from following in pursuit. Meantime, Lee, taking his own time, had crossed the Hudson and was proceeding leisurely across New Jersey to Morristown. Fortunately for the American cause, he was captured by a party of British dragoons on December 13, just after he had finished a letter to Gates, describing Washington as " damnably deficient." This capture of Lee was regarded by the Americans as a terrible misfortune, but could they have known what historical investigation has since revealed, they would have reckoned his riddance as one of the happy incidents of the campaign.

In this situation, when the gloom of despondency hung like a pall over the land, and when all but the bravest hearts had lost hope, Washington, his little army reënforced to 6,000 men, resolved to strike a desperate blow, in the hope of reviving the drooping spirits of his countrymen.* His project was to recross the Dela-

---

* After the capture of Lee, General Sullivan with the remnant of the army advanced rapidly across northern New Jersey. Crossing the Delaware at Easton he marched quickly toward the southward and joined Washington in Bucks

ware and fall upon the enemy unawares. Accordingly, on Christmas night, 1776, with an army of 2,500 men, he braved the difficulties of the icefloes borne swiftly along by the powerful current. Not a man or gun was lost; but the cold was intense, the wind high, and the poor soldiers left blood-stained tracks as they marched. For nine hours the Marblehead fishermen contended with ice and flood, but at four o'clock in the morning the last boatload of soldiers was safely landed on the Jersey side. Before sunrise the army was on the march for Trenton, nine miles distant, and toward evening came upon the enemy just settling down to thoughts of the Old World. After a sharp battle the British were defeated, and over 1,000 Hessians were taken prisoners, and a hundred killed in the fight. The American loss was four men, two frozen to death and two killed. A thousand fine muskets, forty hogsheads of rum, and a quantity of other supplies also fell into the hands of the Americans, much to their delight.[2] This brilliant victory, coming at a time when the patriot cause was at its lowest ebb, caused great rejoicing among the people, who had been stirred to intense indignation against the conduct of the German soldiers in the employ of the king, and greatly raised the spirits of the little band that had never lost hope in the ultimate success of the American cause. " It may be doubted," says the English historian, Trevelyan, " whether so small a number of men ever employed so short a space of time with greater and more lasting results upon the history of the world."[3]

Cornwallis, receiving news of the American victory at Trenton when on the eve of sailing from New York to England, abandoned his proposed trip and hastily returned to Princeton, from which place he proceeded with 8,000 men to march upon Trenton. Washington in the meantime, being convinced of the impossibility of holding Trenton, had retired to a position on the banks of the Assunpink, some miles to the southward. Here Cornwallis decided to attack him and capture his army, or drive it into the Delaware. Reaching Trenton late in the afternoon, the British commander retired to his bed full of hope, saying that at last he had run the

County, Pennsylvania. However unfortunate at Long Island, Sullivan rendered splendid services in the timely victory at Trenton.—Trevelyan, " The American Revolution," vol. ii. part ii.

[2] Winsor, " Narrative and Critical History," vol. vi. p. 264; Trevelyan, " The American Revolution," part ii. vol. ii. p. 112.

[3] " The American Revolution," part ii. vol. ii. p. 113.

old fox down and would "bag him in the morning." But the fox was not so easily bagged as the hunter had calculated. One of Washington's sources of strength was his remarkable ability to extricate himself from dangerous positions. This had been the resource that had saved his army more than once since he assumed the command in July, 1775; he was now to employ it with greater success than ever.

Keeping his camp fires burning all night to deceive the British, who lay in front of him, he marched his army quietly out of camp, passed around Cornwallis's left wing, and by sunrise was well on the road to Princeton, the seat of a college which was the pride of the central colonies. By this means he escaped with his entire army as effectively as he had done at Brooklyn Heights the year before.

When Cornwallis awoke in the morning, to his utter amazement the American camp was empty and no enemy was to be seen. Presently he heard the boom of cannon in the direction of Princeton. It was the noise of an encounter between the Americans, under General Mercer, and a detachment of British on their way to join Cornwallis. The British were as much astonished, said General Knox, to find themselves confronted by the Americans, as if an army had dropped perpendicularly upon them from the clouds. But they were not confounded, and at once made ready for battle. Being largely outnumbered they were easily defeated by the Americans, losing four hundred of their men—one hundred killed and three hundred wounded. General Mercer, the American officer, was mortally wounded. The result of the engagement was a complete victory for the Americans. Realizing from the roar of the distant cannon that the Americans had escaped and were engaged with British troops, Cornwallis hastened off to New Brunswick, where a large quantity of British stores were collected, in order to save them from falling into the hands of the enemy.

The victory of the Americans over the British at Princeton was all the more welcome because of the outrageous conduct of Howe's army in pillaging the college buildings. Apparently unrestrained by their commander, they gutted the library, museum and lecture rooms; carried off or destroyed every volume on the shelves, broke up the philosophical and mathematical instruments, and destroyed various other objects of value, among them the celebrated "orrery" of Rittenhouse, said to have been the finest in the world.   The dwelling house of the president of the college, Dr. Witherspoon, as well as most other private buildings in the town and vicinity, were pillaged by Howe's brutal soldiery.   Hundreds of families were reduced to poverty and ruin and left in the middle of winter to wander through the woods without clothing.[4]

The most flagrant offenders in this particular were the Hessians, who regarded plunder as the right of war, and indiscriminately robbed all civilians with whom they came in contact.   Unlike the English depredators who, it is said, were usually content with pilfering chickens and pigs, the Hessians entered dwelling houses, broke open wardrobes, ransacked drawers and carried off every object of value which fell into their hands.   After the battle of Princeton Washington retired northward to the heights of Morristown, where he went into winter quarters for the rest of the season.   Thus during a brief campaign of less than a month he had retrieved the disasters of the last six months and raised the hopes of his despondent countrymen to a high pitch.   " The most important results of Trenton and Princeton," says Sir George Otto Trevelyan, "were not of a temporary or local character.   The permanent and paramount consequence of those masterly operations was the establishment of Washington's military reputation and the increased weight of his political and administrative authority throughout every State of the Confederacy."[5]   Henceforth Washington's military capacity was generally recognized, not only throughout America, but in Europe as well.   " He had," said Horace Walpole, " shown himself both a Fabius and a Camillus "; and his march through the British lines was conceded to be a prodigy of leadership.   Even from far-away Prussia came the praise of Frederick the Great, who is said to have pronounced the recent campaign the most brilliant in the annals of warfare.   After the close of the war, at a dinner given at the American headquarters, Cornwallis, responding to a toast proposed by Washington, said: " When the illustrious part that your excellency has borne in this long and arduous contest becomes a matter of history, fame will gather your brightest laurels rather from the banks of the Delaware than from those of the Chesapeake."   It is a pleasure to be able to record that Washington's soldiers, who had longed for an opportunity to get at the throats of the conscienceless Hessians who had

---

[4] Trevelyan, " The American Revolution," part ii. vol. ii. pp. 31–32.
[5] *Ibid.*, part ii. vol. ii. p. 142.

devastated New Jersey and maltreated the Americans at Fort Washington, did not retaliate at the battle of Trenton, but treated the Hessians with magnanimity and even hospitality. Washington set the example and gave orders that their knapsacks and port-manteaus should be turned over to them unopened and that they should be treated with consideration and respect. After giving their paroles they were taken to Philadelphia where, strange to say, they received no little attention from the inhabitants.

III

BURGOYNE'S INVASION AND THE STRUGGLE FOR THE UPPER HUDSON

The capture of New York City, together with Fort Washington and Fort Lee, and the driving of Washington out of the State, gave the British the control of the lower Hudson. Following the defeat on Long Island, General Putnam had been sent to Philadelphia, but in May, 1777, was assigned to the command of the Continental army in the highlands of New York. With the strongholds in the north still in the hands of the Americans, the British had only made a beginning toward the execution of their project for the separation of the middle and eastern colonies along the line of the Hudson. A renewal of efforts for the control of the upper Hudson was now entered upon. According to the plan worked out by Lord George Germain, an army under the command of General Burgoyne was to proceed from Canada to Albany, New York, recapturing Ticonderoga in the course of the advance; another but smaller army, under the command of Colonel St. Leger, was to go by water to Oswego, thence across New York State, following the line of the Mohawk Valley and capturing Fort Stanwix, after which he was to join Burgoyne at Albany; and finally Lord Howe was to move at the same time up the river from New York and effect a junction with the other two armies. This project of an invasion of New York along converging lines was well worked out and received the approval of the ministry as one easy of execution, and at the same time, one which would give the British control of upper New York. But there was an inherent danger in the plan which was destined to spoil it, namely, the possibility that the junction of the converging armies might be prevented by some unforeseen circumstance.[6] Through an over-sight of Lord George Germain, who at the time was hurrying off for his summer vacation, the dispatch to Howe, ordering him to move up the river, was not sent, and so Burgoyne was deprived of the coöperation of the army upon which his success mainly depended.[7] Ignorant of Howe's movements, Burgoyne with some 8,000 troops, about one-half of whom were British regulars, set out from Canada in June, 1777, and a month later appeared before the walls of Fort Ticonderoga, in New York. Since its capture by Ethan Allen in the early days of the war the fort had been greatly strengthened, and was now held by a garrison of 3,000 men, under the command of General Arthur St. Clair. It was deemed impregnable and probably could have been easily held had it not been for the blunder of St. Clair in allowing the British to seize and occupy an eminence which commanded the fort from the south.

The Americans had not supposed it possible for the enemy to scale this elevation with artillery; great, therefore, was their amazement when on the morning of July 5 they awoke to find Fort Defiance, as the British called the eminence, covered with red coats and dotted with cannon. They were evidently trapped, and so there was nothing to do but surrender the fort and, if possible, make their escape. Accordingly, under the cover of night, St. Clair transported his garrison across the lake and set out for the Green Mountains. Early in the morning the British, being awakened by a burning building, discovered the retreating Americans and soon set out in hot pursuit. Their rear guard was overtaken at the village of Hubbardton, and after a sharp fight was badly beaten, losing about one-third of their number, killed and wounded. A few days later the remainder of the garrison reached Fort Edward, where it joined the main army under General Schuyler.

The loss of Fort Ticonderoga was a sore disappointment to the Americans, and greatly depressed their spirits. St. Clair was court-martialed for allowing the British to occupy Fort Defiance, but was acquitted. Schuyler was also greatly censured, and John Adams asserted that a general should have been shot for the effect it would have. In Great Britain, on the other hand, the news caused great rejoicing, and the king declared that the Americans were already beaten. Meantime Burgoyne had reached

---

[6] Fiske, "American Revolution," vol. i. p. 263.
[7] Lodge, "Story of the Revolution," p. 230.

the head of Lake Champlain, at a point about twenty miles from Fort Edward, where Schuyler's army was encamped. To impede his progress Schuyler now set to work obstructing the roads with the trunks of fallen trees, destroying the bridges and filling up the fords with huge stones and logs. In the face of these obstacles Burgoyne was able to push along at the rate of only a mile a day, reaching Fort Edward the last of July, 1777. Believing his position to be untenable, Schuyler abandoned the place and escaped with his army unmolested.

Burgoyne's next move was to send a detachment of six hundred men, one hundred of whom were Indians, to the village of Bennington, near the border line between New York and Vermont, for the purpose of capturing a large quantity of stores and ammunition which the Americans had gathered there. The detachment was commanded by Colonel Baum, who proceeded on his mission with the expectation of being joined by large numbers of loyalists who, he had been told, inhabited the Green Mountain region, and who would flock to his standard as soon as he appeared. His expectations, however, were not realized; the loyalists proved to be a myth, and hardly a man came to his aid.

John Stark, who was in command of the Americans, was one of the ablest generals on the American side, and although Congress had recently passed him over in making out its list of promotions, a fact which had caused his temporary retirement, he now came forth from his retreat, quickly raised a force of less than one thousand men, and hastened to meet the enemy.

On August 16, 1777, Stark's force, which he divided into two equal parts, attacked the British front and rear, and after a fierce fight which lasted two hours, completely routed them. Both sides receiving reënforcements at this juncture, renewed the fight and continued it until dark — but the Americans won the day, and when the results were footed up it was found that they had killed and wounded over 200 of the enemy and taken about 700 prisoners, leaving less than one hundred to escape. Besides, they had captured a large quantity of small arms, both muskets and swords, several valuable pieces of artillery, and had themselves lost only fourteen men killed and forty-two wounded. This brilliant victory, in which a body of untrained mountaineers had annihilated a detachment of British regulars, greatly raised the hopes of the patriots and led to an inpouring of volunteers. Stark, to whom the victory was mainly due, was now restored to the army and promoted to the rank of brigadier general.

Two weeks before the battle of Bennington, St. Leger, who had landed at Oswego about the middle of July, according to the ministerial plan, and had slowly made his way across western New York, arrived at the headwaters of the Mohawk, a few miles from Fort Stanwix. He had, all told, about 1,700 men, many of whom were Tories, and a band of Iroquois Indians under the leadership of their chief, Thayendanegea, better known as Joseph Brant. Fort Stanwix, then on the New York frontier, was, as we have seen, erected during the French and Indian War, and at the time of the approach of St. Leger's motley army it was garrisoned by about 600 Americans, a force hardly adequate to repel an enemy of the character which now threatened it. Nicholas Herkimer, an aged German resident of the neighborhood, raised 800 men and went to the relief of the garrison.

At Oriskany, about eight miles from the fort, Herkimer's army was caught in an ambuscade prepared by Brant, and a terrible battle ensued, which presently degenerated into a hand-to-hand contest made hideous by the terrific yells of the Indians and the roar of a heavy rain and thunder storm. Wounded by a musket ball, Herkimer seated himself at the root of a tree, lighted his pipe and coolly continued to direct his men. Finally, after more than 500 men had been killed or wounded, the Tories and Indians fled, leaving Herkimer's little band in possession of the field. About one-third of the number engaged on each side was lost in this obstinate and sanguinary contest. St. Leger might still have taken the fort had it not been for the arrival a few days later of Benedict Arnold, who, with 1,200 men had been sent to the relief of the garrison. Sending a half-witted Tory into St. Leger's camp to spread the story that the American forces were as numerous as the leaves of the forest, Arnold succeeded in causing a panic among the enemy. Apparently frightened out of their wits at the prospect of capture, they fled, leaving behind their artillery and supplies for the use of the Americans, and scarcely pausing for breath until Oswego was reached.

The outlook for the American cause now began to grow brighter. Unfortunately at this juncture, however, Congress, with its habit of meddling, removed General Schuyler from the command of the army in New York and appointed Gates in his stead.

For some time Gates had been intriguing against Schuyler, and had persuaded Congress to believe that the latter officer was inefficient. But the truth is, Schuyler was an able, patriotic and true-hearted man, while Gates was an unscrupulous, boastful, intriguing self-seeker, whose military ability, as subsequent events showed, were far over-rated by Congress. Burgoyne's position had now become critical. St. Leger's army, which was expected to coöperate with him, had been turned back by the Americans, and Howe's army, on which he mainly relied, was now in Pennsylvania marching in the opposite direction, wholly ignorant of the dispatch which Lord Germain had intended for it.

To retreat was impossible; Burgoyne therefore resolved to risk a battle with the Americans, whose aggregate strength now amounted to 15,000 men, strongly posted on an eminence called Bemis Heights, on the west side of the Hudson. Toward the middle of September Burgoyne crossed to this side of the river, and on the nineteenth was attacked at Freeman's Farm by 3,000 Americans under the command of Benedict Arnold. Being hard pressed Arnold sent imploringly to Gates for reënforcements, and although that officer had over 10,000 men in reserve, none were sent. Nevertheless, Arnold kept up the fight until dark, the results being substantially in his favor. The jealous Gates, who had refused to send reënforcements, at once claimed all the credit for what little had been accomplished, and in his report to Congress never so much as mentioned the name of Arnold. In the course of the quarrel that ensued Gates informed Arnold that he had no further need of his services, and that he might return to Washington's camp, if he liked. Upon the advice and entreaties of his friends, however, Arnold decided to remain and take part in the decisive battle which was expected to occur at an early date.

For nearly three weeks after the fight at Freeman's Farm the two armies lay watching each other and waiting for an opportunity to make a decisive blow. On October 7 Burgoyne moved out of his camp with 1,500 picked men, with the intent of flanking the American left. They were at once attacked by Morgan's sharpshooters, aided by the New England "regulars," and completely routed. Arnold, nominally without a command, sat watching the fight from the heights until he could no longer restrain himself. Springing upon his horse, he rode quickly to the scene of action, where he was greeted with deafening cheers by the men of his old

command.   Putting himself at their head, he charged the enemy
and drove their line from the field.   Burgoyne now planned to retreat, but presently discovered that he was practically surrounded,
that his supplies were cut off, and that escape was impossible.   In
this situation he asked for terms.   At first an unconditional surrender was demanded, but the terms were rejected by Burgoyne,

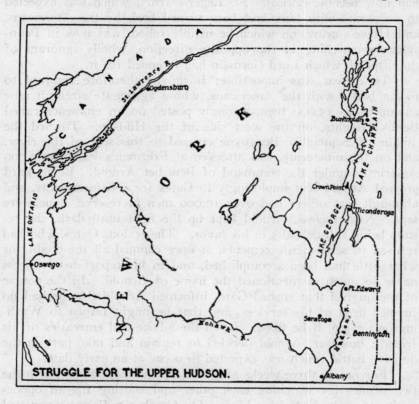

STRUGGLE FOR THE UPPER HUDSON.

and better ones were finally granted.   The British army was allowed to march out with the honors of war and stack their arms at
a designated place, after which they were to be permitted to return
to England upon promise not to take up arms against the United
States again during the existing war.   Altogether nearly 6,000
men were surrendered, besides a large quantity of arms, ammunition and stores.   The terms of the surrender, be it said to the

discredit of Congress, were never carried out. When it occurred to that body that the return of Burgoyne's army to England would be followed by the sending over of others to take their places, Congress began to find pretexts for the evasion of its duty. It insisted on payment for the subsistence of the troops since the surrender, and yet refused to accept its own notes in extinguishment of the claim. It then demanded other conditions with which Burgoyne could not with self-respect comply. Finally, all intention of sending them home was abandoned, and they were accordingly removed to the neighborhood of Charlottesville, Virginia, where they remained until the end of the war. Some of them returned to England upon the conclusion of peace, but the greater number, especially of the Germans, preferred to remain in America, and became citizens of the United States.

The battle of Saratoga, or Bemis Heights, as it is sometimes called, is usually regarded as the turning point of the Revolution. Up to that time the success of the American cause had been in doubt. Now, however, the hope of independence seemed assured, and the result which the American victory accomplished soon set in motion a procession of events that was destined to lead to the ultimate triumph of the American cause.

IV

BRANDYWINE, GERMANTOWN, AND VALLEY FORGE

It is now necessary to return to Morristown, New Jersey, where we left Washington after the battle of Princeton in January, 1777, and to follow his operations during the following year. Having, by his recent successes, gained the unqualified confidence of his countrymen, he was now given by Congress a virtual dictatorship for the conduct of the war. He was vested with " full, ample, and complete powers " to raise sixteen additional battalions of infantry, three thousand light-horse, three regiments of artillery, and a corps of engineers; to call upon the States for militia; to dismiss and appoint all officers below the rank of brigadier general; to impress, at a fair price, all provisions and other supplies necessary for the use of the army; and to arrest and send to the courts for trial any persons charged with disaffection to the American cause. " Such an expression of confidence, unstintedly and unanimously accorded, during the closing hours of the very darkest season in American history, will remain on record through all ages as a tribute to the man, and not to his fortune."[8]

Feeling certain that Howe would remain in New York throughout the winter, and leaving him unmolested, Washington

THE ADVANCE ON PHILADELPHIA, 1777

quietly settled down for the winter in Morristown, and set himself to reorganizing and reënforcing the Continental army, and the force which he here brought together followed him obediently and devotedly to the end. With the approach of spring, military operations were renewed. Instead of marching up the line of the Hudson to coöperate with Burgoyne, as the ministry had intended,

[8] Trevelyan, "The American Revolution," part ii. vol. ii. p. 141.

Howe decided to march across New Jersey and capture Philadelphia, the rebel capital. Divining his purpose, Washington, with
his army now numbering 8,000 men, threw himself across Howe's
line of march, and, by a campaign of remarkable strategy, in which
he harassed and outwitted the enemy, compelled him to change his
plan and return to New York. Nevertheless, the British general
did not abandon his attempt to capture Philadelphia, as he thought
that its possession would greatly affect the final result. He therefore resolved to send his army by sea and approach the city by
way of the Delaware. Accordingly, in July, he embarked at New
York and sailed for the mouth of the Delaware; but finding obstructions in the river, he sailed around the peninsula and up
Chesapeake Bay, landing at Elkton, Maryland, in the latter part of
August, with the intention of marching his army overland to
Philadelphia, some fifty miles distant. Upon receiving news of
Howe's landing, Washington resolved to meet him, and, if possible,
turn him back, as he had done in New Jersey earlier in the spring.
Planting himself at Chad's Ford on Brandywine Creek, about midway between Elkton and Philadelphia, he prepared to oppose the advance of the British. The chances were all against Washington,
as his entire force did not exceed 11,000 men, as against 18,000
British troops. His position, however, was well chosen, and he
was aided by able subordinate commanders, among them Generals
Greene and Anthony Wayne. Howe's right and left wings were
commanded by Knyphausen, an able Hessian soldier, and Cornwallis, respectively. On September 11, just a week before the fight
at Bemis Heights, the two armies met, and the battle which ensued
resulted in the defeat of the Americans, their loss exceeding 1,000
men, or nearly one-tenth of the number engaged.

The way to Philadelphia was now open, although Washington
was able to harass and detain Howe's army with a view to preventing him from sending aid to Burgoyne. Establishing his
headquarters at Germantown, near by, Howe sent Cornwallis to
take possession of the rebel capital, which he did with colors flying
and bands playing, the Congress fleeing first to Lancaster, and
later to York, where its sessions were resumed without molestation.
The importance of the capture of Philadelphia was greatly overestimated by the British. The town possessed no strategic value,
it was not a military post, and its importance as an administrative
center was inconsiderable. It was, indeed, the meeting-place of the

Continental Congress, but the Congress could easily retire and hold its sessions as well at some other place. The loss of the town, therefore, had no perceptible effect upon the course of military operations.

After the battle of the Brandywine, Washington followed the British army to Germantown, a village several miles to the northwest of Philadelphia, and there, on October 4, five days before the final engagement at Saratoga, gave them battle. His plan was to advance along converging lines from the north and attack the enemy at daybreak, but unfortunately this well-conceived scheme was spoiled by a dense fog which enveloped the village just at the time the attack was to begin. In the confusion which followed the beginning of the battle, a division of Wayne's men, mistaken for the enemy, were fired upon by a brigade of American troops commanded by General Stephen. This led to a panic among the Americans, and caused them to retreat, leaving the enemy in possession of the field. The result, therefore, was a victory for the British, although their losses in killed and wounded were almost as large as those of the Americans. Freed from further danger, Howe now gave his attention to the opening of the Delaware, and after a month of effort succeeded in reducing Forts Mercer and Mifflin, which commanded the lower part of the river. This done, he settled down to spend the winter of 1777-1778 in the American metropolis.

After the defeat at Germantown, Washington withdrew to Valley Forge on the Schuylkill, some twenty miles to the northwest of Philadelphia, where he went into winter quarters. The sufferings of his men during that terrible winter have excited not only the pity, but the admiration, of all students of American history. For days the American troops were without bread or meat, and at one time Washington reported that nearly 3,000 were " barefoot and otherwise naked." When, in December, they took up their march for winter quarters, the line of march could be traced on the snow by the blood that oozed from their bare frostbitten feet. As is so often the case in war, much of the suffering was due to the mismanagement of the commissary and quartermaster departments. At the time the men were marching barefoot and naked to their quarters, we are told by a contemporary historian of the Revolution that hogsheads of shoes, stockings and clothing were lying at different places on the roads and in the woods, rotting for want of teams or of money with which to pay the cost of transportation. As a result, not infrequently the poor fellows had to sit up all night by the fire to keep from freezing. Soon, also, the rudely constructed huts were filled to overflowing with the sick; many died, and at one time barely 2,000 were able to take the field had the exigencies of the campaign required it. Much of the responsibility for this terrible suffering lay at the door of Congress. Since the first meeting in 1774 it had steadily declined in character, and by 1778 it was far from being the able body which it once was. Great leaders like Washington, Franklin, Jefferson, Patrick Henry, and Jay were no longer members, and in their places sat men of third-rate ability and character. Instead of giving its attention to the welfare of the soldiers in the field, Congress too often occupied its time with needless meddling and intriguing.

It was just at this time that the " Conway Cabal " undertook to secure the removal of Washington from the command of the army and the appointment of Gates in his place. Almost from the beginning of the war there were a few unscrupulous, self-seeking individuals like Lee and Gates, who secretly labored in and out of season to bring about Washington's downfall, and who never lost an opportunity to criticise and even malign him for not doing what obviously he was unable to do with the poor resources at his command. Their complaints were carried to Congress, and, unfortunately, there were some members of that body who were ready to lend willing ears to all the absurd stories about Washington's incompetency. The head of the present plot was Thomas Conway, an Irish officer who had served in the American army in the battles of Brandywine and Germantown, and had taken offense at Washington's opposition to his promotion. Allied with him were Thomas Mifflin, quartermaster-general; Dr. Benjamin Rush, a prominent citizen of Philadelphia, and James Lovell, a member of Congress. This coterie of defamers set to work by an anonymous correspondence and other reprehensible methods to convince Congress and the country of Washington's incapability, compared his failures with the success of Gates at Saratoga, and asserted that the appointment of the latter hero to the chief command would be followed by a series of magnificent military successes. Just as the plot reached its height some of Gates's secret correspondence fell into the hands of Washington, and was published. The revelations of these underhand attempts to bring about his overthrow caused a feeling of public indignation against the plotters, and the cabal soon collapsed without having accomplished its nefarious purpose. Henceforward the powerful influence of Washington steadily increased, and he came to occupy a higher place in the hearts of his countrymen than ever before — a place from which no amount of defamation and censure could dethrone him.

V

CHARLES LEE AND THE BATTLE OF MONMOUTH

While Washington's hungry, half-clad troops were induring the sufferings of Valley Forge, and incidentally being thoroughly drilled by the Baron von Steuben, a skilled Prussian soldier in the American service, Howe's army was enjoying a comfortable winter at Philadelphia. There was an abundance to eat and drink in this, the largest of American cities; many loyalist friends were ready to minister to their wants, and a round of balls, theaters and parties furnished all the amusements and diversions that could be desired. Nevertheless, Howe had derived no military advantage from the possession of the place; further occupation was not only useless, but dangerous, for the city had no natural defenses, and a French fleet was then approaching America, possibly bound for the mouth of the Delaware.

Under these circumstances the British Government recalled Howe and appointed Clinton, with instructions to evacuate the city and transfer his army to New York. Accordingly, on June 18, the British forces marched out, carrying with them 3,000 loyalists, and the Americans shortly afterwards took possession. The Congress which had during the British occupation held its sessions first at Lancaster and then at York, now returned to its old place of meeting and resumed its sittings. After the evacuation the British army took up its march across New Jersey for New York, but it was not to be an unmolested retreat. Taking courage from the favorable outlook now presented by the prospect of French aid, Washington resolved to pursue the retreating enemy, and, if possible, annihilate it before it could reach New York. Accordingly, with 15,000 well-drilled troops — thanks to Von Steuben — he set out in hot pursuit on a parallel line of march, and on June 27 came up with Clinton near Monmouth Court House. Detaching a force of 6,000 men under Charles Lee, who had recently been exchanged for the British General Prescott, and restored to his old rank as senior major general, Washington sent him with peremptory orders to turn the British left wing of 8,000 men under General Cornwallis, while he was to follow up the attack with the main army and complete the discomfiture of the enemy. On June 28, a torrid Sunday morning, Lee advanced to the attack with every prospect of success, but soon after the fight began, to the astonishment of the British and the bewilderment of his own men, Lee ordered a retreat. The young Marquis de Lafayette, to whom Washington had first entrusted the command, and later bestowed it upon Lee, was filled with suspicion at this behavior, and sent a dispatch to Washington requesting his immediate presence. When the commander-in-chief appeared on the scene all was disorder and confusion. Trembling in his saddle and white with anger he inquired of Lee: "What is the meaning of all this?" Severely rebuking him for disobeying explicit orders, Washington wheeled about and undertook to stop the disorderly rout and retrieve the disaster which Lee's conduct had occasioned. This proved a difficult task, but in spite of an obstinate resistance, the British were forced back along the ground over which Lee had retreated, until night put an end to the struggle. During the night Clinton withdrew, leaving the Americans in possession of the field, the British loss being somewhat over 400; that of the Americans somewhat smaller. Shortly afterward the British loss was further increased by the desertion of 2,000 Hessians, who joined the American cause.

So far as military results were concerned, the battle of Monmouth—the last of the Revolution to be fought in the north—was indecisive; but the moral advantages, however, were on the side of the Americans. Had it not been for the extraordinary behavior of Lee, there can be little doubt that the Americans would have won a decisive victory. During the course of the battle Washington ordered him to the rear, after which Lee addressed an impudent letter to the commander-in-chief demanding an apology. Washington's reply called out another letter so full of impertinence from a subordinate officer, that he ordered the arrest of Lee and his trial by court-martial.

After a lengthy trial Lee was found guilty of disobedience of orders, of misbehavior on the field, and of gross disrespect to the commander-in-chief, but was let off with the light punishment of suspension from his command for the term of one year.[9]   There were many who felt that the offense warranted a far more serious punishment; certainly many European soldiers have been shot for acts less serious in character.   The discovery many years later of certain of his private correspondence seems to establish what was not generally believed in 1778, namely, that Lee was grossly indifferent if not actually a traitor to the American cause.   Before the close of the war he got into a quarrel with Congress and was expelled from the army.   Thereupon he retired to a plantation in the Shenandoah valley, where he lived surrounded by his dogs, apart from the world, until 1782, when he died on the occasion of a visit to Philadelphia.   His last injunction that his body should not be buried within a mile of any church was disregarded, and his bones to-day repose in the cemetery of Christ Church, Philadelphia, with those of some of America's greatest heroes.   Lee was unfitted by temperament and character for the position to which he had early been appointed by Congress.   His head was soon turned by early successes, and at the time of his insubordination, says an English historian of the American Revolution, was kept in a state of effervescence by a great deal of extraordinary, and, in some cases, of rather interested flattery.   Of inordinate vanity, he possessed an insufferable disdain of American soldiers, sneered at his comrades of rank, lectured them constantly about the arts of strategy and fortification, and inundated America with his imperious advice and his unsparing and most offensive criticism.[10] Unlike the career of Benedict Arnold, says Fiske, a career into which there enters the element of avarice and pity, the whole story of Charles Lee, from first to last, is little more than a vulgar melodrama.

Shortly after the battle of Monmouth the two opposing armies resumed their march for New York, Washington going to White Plains, Clinton to the city of New York, and here they remained for the next three years facing each other, while the operations of the war were being conducted in the south.

[9] Fiske, "American Revolution," vol. ii. p. 67.
[10] Trevelyan, "The American Revolution," part ii. vol. ii. p. 53.

VI

THE FRENCH ALLIANCE

Meantime the American cause had been strengthened by a notable diplomatic achievement. As early as November, 1775, the Continental Congress had appointed a " Secret Committee of Correspondence," of which Benjamin Franklin and John Jay were members, to correspond with the friends of the colonies in Europe, and as has already been said, Silas Deane was sent to France in the spring of 1776 with instructions to appear in the character of a secret agent, to seek an audience with Vergennes, the French minister of foreign affairs, and ascertain whether, if the colonies should declare their independence of Great Britain, France would acknowledge that independnce and enter into a treaty of alliance with them. In 1777 the name of this committee was changed to the " Committee on Foreign Affairs." [11]

Deane was also instructed to solicit aid for the Americans in the shape of arms, ammunition, clothing and other supplies. He reached Paris in June, 1776, and was received in audience by Vergennes, who, while declining to commit himself on the question of independence, promised to furnish a quantity of supplies, and early in 1777 several vessels laden with stores, cannon and small arms were actually sent to America for the use of the army. Deane succeeded in enlisting in the American cause a rather romantic character of humble origin, named Beaumarchais, then at the height of his fame as a dramatist, and remembered chiefly as the author of those charming plays, " Figaro " and " The Barber of Seville." Beaumarchais became the head of a fictitious mercantile firm, through which the French Government secretly aided the Americans, for it was necessary to conceal every movement from the British ambassador, who kept a sharp lookout to see that French neutrality was not violated. What France had to give the Americans, therefore, was placed in the hands of " Hortalez & Company," and through it transmitted to America. It is, of course, a breach of neutrality for a neutral government to give aid to either belligerent in war, but it is a legitimate transaction for private individuals to sell supplies to whoever will buy in the regular course of trade.

[11] For its history see " The Department of State, Its History and Functions " (Government Printing Office, 1893).

Through this roundabout method the French Government was able to offer substantial aid to the Americans, and at the same time conceal the fact that it was violating its neutral duties. Considerable sums of money were also transmitted to the colonies through this channel, Deane agreeing to repay with cargoes of tobacco and other products sent over by Congress. Unfortunately, when the Congress came to settle accounts with Beaumarchais, a dispute arose as to how much of the amount was a gift from the king and how much a loan from Beaumarchais. Beaumarchais claimed that the the amount advanced through him was a loan and not a gratuity; but this was denied by Congress, and he was unable to get a settlement and died in 1779 with the claims still pending. His heirs, supported by the French Government, pressed their claim against the United States for sixty years, until 1831, when a small appropriation was made by Congress in final settlement of the long-standing account.[12]

After the Declaration of Independence Congress adopted a more systematic policy of foreign intercourse, and in September, 1776, drew up a " plan " of treaties to be proposed to foreign powers, and Franklin, Deane, and Arthur Lee were commissioned as ministers to France to lay it before Louis XVI.,[13] Franklin reached Paris in December, where he was joined by Deane and Lee, and on the 23d they addressed a note to Count Vergennes, proposing a commercial treaty.[14] Franklin was at the time the best-known American abroad, and his popularity in France, where he had temporarily resided before the Revolution, was especially great. His philosophic and scientific writings, his republican simplicity, his quaint dress and good humor, made him the idol of the people of the gay and learned French capital, and the testimonials of esteem which he received from their hands were scarcely ever equalled in the history of diplomacy. Before he left Paris in 1774 he had an interview with Vergennes, who had pointedly reminded him that France had contributed to the independence of the Netherlands, and that she might aid the American colonies in a similar manner. Franklin now called upon him for the fulfillment

[12] James B. Angell, "Diplomacy of the Revolution," in Winsor, "Nar. and Crit. Hist.," vol. vii. chap vii.; see also Foster, "American Diplomacy," p. 16.

[13] See Snow, "Topics in American Diplomacy," pp. 12–24.

[14] John Bassett Moore, "The Beginnings of American Diplomacy," *Harpers Magazine*, vol. cviii. p. 500.

of his promise. But the winter of 1776–1777 was an inauspicious time to secure diplomatic concessions. The American cause was at a low ebb, the authority of Congress was disregarded, the American forces were depleted, and a series of disasters had crowned the operations of the Continental army. The proposition of the American commissioners was, therefore, rejected, and they were compelled to wait for victories in the field to move the French Government to action. For a year, therefore, nothing was accomplished.

Early in December, 1777, news of the American victory at Saratoga reached Paris and at once gave a new turn to the negotiations. The Americans assumed a bolder front and proposed a treaty of alliance. Almost immediately they were informed that the king had decided to recognize their independence, and to enter into a treaty with them, his decision being evidently hastened by the report that the British authorities were negotiating with them with a view to the termination of the war. The motive of the French king was, of course, not so much the result of personal solicitude for the welfare of the colonists, as a desire to humiliate the old enemy of France, who had despoiled her of her American empire. Nevertheless, the aid was gladly accepted, and the commissioners did not trouble themselves to inquire into the nature of the motive back of the deed. The negotiations rapidly proceeded, and on February 6, 1778, a treaty of alliance and one of commerce were signed at Versailles by Conrad A. Gerard on the part of the king, and by Franklin, Deane and Lee on the part of the United States.

By the treaty of alliance France recognized the independence of the colonies and declared the object of the alliance to be the maintenance of that independence; she stipulated that if Great Britain should declare war against France, which she soon did, the two contracting parties should make common cause and aid each other with their good offices, their counsels and their forces; that they would not lay down their arms until the independence of the United States should be acknowledged, and that neither would conclude peace without the formal consent of the other. Moreover, the treaty stipulated for a division of probable conquests in America, and contained a guarantee upon the part of the United States of the existing French possessions in America and a similar guarantee upon the part of France of any dominion which the United States might obtain by conquest from Great Britain in America.[15]   The formation of the alliance with France was by all odds the most important diplomatic triumph of the Revolution.   It secured the aid of a powerful European government at a time when the outlook for American success was anything but bright, and insured the ultimate independence of the American nation.   It is probable, however, that the colonies would have succeeded without French aid, and the time eventually came when the alliance was repudiated by act of Congress.   It was the only alliance ever entered into between the United States and a foreign government, and the embarrassment to which it subsequently gave rise was the foundation of the American policy laid down by Washington, that the United States should enter into no entangling alliances.[16]

No other treaties were concluded with European nations before the surrender of Cornwallis at Yorktown, although commissioners were sent to various European capitals to negotiate for concessions similar to those secured from France.   Henry Laurens of South Carolina was appointed minister to the Netherlands in 1779, but was captured off the coasts of Newfoundland by the British, and imprisoned in the Tower of London, while his papers, containing the plan of a treaty with the Netherlands, which he had vainly tried to sink in the Atlantic, were confiscated.   Arthur Lee was sent to Berlin to negotiate with Frederick the Great, who refused to enter into a treaty with the United States, but showed his friendliness to the Americans by prohibiting several regiments of Hessians from passing through his territories with a view to joining the British army in America.   An incident of Lee's residence at Berlin which illustrates the unscrupulous methods of diplomacy then practiced, was the stealing of his papers by the British minister, whose suspicions had been aroused by Lee's activity at the Prussian capital.[17]   William Lee, Francis Dana, and Ralph Izard were sent to Austria, Russia and Tuscany, respectively, but were not received.   John Jay and William Carmichael were dispatched to Madrid to secure the aid of Spain, but they had no success, although the King of France proposed that his Catholic brother should join him in the alliance with America, and although Spain

---

[15] Snow, "Topics in American Diplomacy," pp. 32–35.
[16] Foster, "A Century of Diplomacy," p. 31.
[17] Moore, "Beginnings of American Diplomacy," *Harper's Magazine*, vol. cviii. pp. 503–505.

ultimately went to war with Great Britain as the ally of France. In the early part of the war the Spanish Government secretly advanced a million livres to the American cause through the fictitious house of Hortalez & Company, but further than that it contributed little to American independence.[18]

The news of the French alliance caused general rejoicing in America, and greatly raised the hopes of the struggling patriots. A powerful French fleet was soon on its way to America, and presently a number of French engineers and higher officers arrived to contribute their services to the prosecution of the war. The most distinguished of all the foreigners who came was the young Marquis de Lafayette, who fitted out a vessel at his own expense, offered his services to Congress, and was made a major general in the Continental army. His services to America were inestimable, and no man in the army came to enjoy the confidence of Washington to the same extent that he did. Others who came were the Baron de Kalb, an able officer, who rose to the rank of major general and gave his life for the American cause; Kosciusko, a Polish patriot, whose services as an engineer were of great value to Washington; Count Pulaski, also a Pole, who was fated to fall at Savannah; and Baron von Steuben, a German, whose services in the army as a drillmaster have already been referred to. While rendering valuable service to the American cause, the importunities of many of the foreigners for office was a source of constant embarrassment to Washington. Irritated on one occasion at the conduct of Steuben, he declared: " Though I think the Baron an excellent officer, I do most devoutly wish that we had not a single foreigner among us except the Marquis de Lafayette, who acts upon very different principles from those which govern the rest."

The conclusion of the French treaty was soon known in England in spite of all efforts to keep it a secret, and the government at once declared war on France for what in international law was an act of unwarranted intervention in British affairs. Feeling certain that if the war continued the colonies would be lost, the ministry, in a last effort to conciliate them, repealed the Townshend Act and sent three commissioners to America to propose terms of

[18] By a lax enforcement of their neutral obligations the Spanish authorities at New Orleans permitted both men and supplies to pass up the Mississippi, and the brilliant campaign of Galvez on the Gulf contributed to weaken the common enemy.

reconciliation. But it was too late, and Congress refused upon their arrival to appoint commissioners to confer with them. The Rockingham Whigs now proposed to end the war and abandon the colonies without a further struggle. At this juncture the dying Chatham appeared for the last time in the House of Lords to protest against the voluntary surrender of the English possessions in America. Swathed in flannels and leaning on the arm of that younger son who was destined in a few years to rival his fame, with sunken eyes and ghastly face, he hobbled into the chamber and entered his last plea in a voice barely audible in the almost breathless silence of the House, saying: " My lords, I rejoice that the grave has not closed over me; that I am still alive to lift up my voice against the dismemberment of this ancient and noble monarchy." [19] While trying to speak a second time, he fell into a swoon and died four days later, being spared the cruel humiliation of witnessing the disruption of the empire with whose greatness his name of all men was most inseparably associated. But his wish that the colonies should not be voluntarily surrendered was respected, and so the war continued for four years longer.

[19] Lecky, "The American Revolution," p. 354.

Chapter XII

THE WAR IN THE SOUTHERN COLONIES
1778–1782

I

THE GEORGIA CAMPAIGN

AFTER the disastrous failure of the attempt to gain a foothold in the Carolinas in the spring of 1776, the British desisted in that quarter, and for three years turned their attention entirely to the conquest of the eastern and middle colonies. After four years of war the British forces had overrun a large part of New York, New Jersey and Pennsylvania, had destroyed a vast amount of property at an enormous sacrifice of their own resources, but outside of the city of New York still held no place of importance.[1]

In despair the ministry again determined to strike at the weaker and less populous section of the country. In the Carolinas and Georgia, the character of the country and the sparseness of population would make organized resistance more difficult; the resources of these colonies were inferior to those of the north and east, and, besides, it was believed there were large numbers of loyalists ready to join the British armies as soon as they should make their appearance in the south.

In the late autumn of 1778 a force of 3,500 British regulars from New York landed near Savannah, quickly overcame the feeble resistance which the Americans were able to offer, and in December took the town, together with 500 prisoners and a quantity of artillery and stores. Most of the inhabitants submitted, others fled

---

[1] British power in the Illinois country was effectually broken by a frontiersman, George Rogers Clark, who, with a commission from Governor Patrick Henry of Virginia, captured Kaskaskia in 1778 and Vincennes in 1779, thus laying the basis of the future claim of Virginia to the Northwest Territory.

to South Carolina or to the hill country of the interior. A few days later another British force under Colonel Campbell captured Augusta, and shortly afterwards various other places of less importance in Georgia suffered the same fate. Thus by a short, quick blow Georgia had been completely reduced to subjection to the Crown.

Meantime, General Robert Howe, commander of the American forces in this quarter, was superseded by General Benjamin Lincoln, who had served in the New York campaign, and who, though a brave man, was slow and without military capacity. Lincoln assumed command in December, and sent a detachment of 1,500 men to recapture Augusta, which it easily did; but the army was afterwards defeated (March, 1779) and routed by the British with great loss at Briar Creek, all of the Americans being captured except some 450, who succeeded in swimming the river.

The British General Prevost then crossed the Savannah River into South Carolina, and with 3,000 troops, together with a band of Indian allies, devastated the adjacent country somewhat as General Sherman did eighty-five years later in the great Civil War. Continuing his campaign of devastation until Charleston was reached, he demanded the surrender of the town; but at this juncture he was confronted by Lincoln, who drove him back into Georgia. Early in September the French fleet under the command of D'Estaing arrived from the West Indies, where it had been cruising, and in the latter part of the month laid siege to Savannah in the hope of recapturing it from the British. Aided by Lincoln's artillery from the land side, he bombarded the town at intervals for three weeks, but being unable to force a surrender decided to make an attempt to take it by storm. Accordingly, on October 9, a desperate assault was made by the combined French and American forces, but the assailants were driven back with a loss of some eight hundred men. Among the killed was the gallant Pulaski, whose memory is worthily perpetuated by a handsome monument in the picturesque old town for the defense of which he gave his life. After the defeat D'Estaing sailed away and never again came to the aid of the Americans with his fleet, and Lincoln withdrew disheartened to Charleston.

The outlook was now very gloomy for the unaided Americans. Without men and money South Carolina seemed helpless. The French had gone and thousands of the inhabitants, seeing themselves exposed to war, came forward and declared their allegiance to the Crown. Following D'Estaing's withdrawal from southern waters, a British fleet from New York, bearing 8,000 men under the command of Sir Henry Clinton and Lord Cornwallis, the same who had failed to effect a landing in the south in 1776, arrived at Savannah, and having received reënforcements of three thousand men proceeded overland to Charleston, which was their main objective point. This was the largest town in the south, and the third largest in America. For its defense General Lincoln had gathered a small force which, in view of the additional reënforcements which the British received from New York, proved wholly insufficient for an effective defense. Slowly Clinton invested the city on the land side while the British fleet menaced it from the sea. Thus surrounded it seemed useless to offer further resistance, and on May 12, 1780, Lincoln surrendered the place, together with his whole army and a vast quantity of supplies. The fall of Charleston was a severe blow to the American cause.[2] Besides the loss of an entire army the way was opened to British control of South Carolina.

After the surrender of Charleston, Clinton with the larger part of his army returned to New York, leaving Cornwallis with 5,000 men to continue the task of subjugation in the South. The British forces soon overran the State, and like Georgia, it now lay at the feet of the king. Three weeks after the fall of Charleston Sir Henry Clinton wrote to the ministry, "I may venture to assert that there are few men in South Carolina who are not either our prisoners or in arms with us." At this time the Americans were able to offer but little organized resistance, although irregular bands of patriot volunteers greatly harassed and annoyed the British, and on several occasions inflicted heavy losses on their advancing columns. Suddenly descending from the mountains or emerging from the swamps, they swooped down upon the enemy, threw their ranks into confusion, captured their wagon trains, released their prisoners and frequently engaged them in hand-to-hand contests and then disappeared from sight as suddenly as they had appeared. Some of these partisan bands were commanded by daring and resourceful leaders whose services were such as to entitle them to high rank as leaders of the Revolution. The most prominent of them were Francis Marion, Thomas Sumter and Andrew Pickens. Marion,

[2] Sloane, "The French War and the Revolution," p. 316.

called by the British half in fear, half in hatred, the " Swamp Fox," was a dashing but kind-hearted man of Huguenot descent, whose exploits read like a mediæval romance. He had served in the Old French war and had lately been wounded at Savannah. Hardly second to Marion as a daring commander was Sumter, likewise a soldier in the Old French war, who, too, had recently been turned out of doors by the British and his house burned. After the formation of the Constitution he became a United States Senator, and lived to the great age of ninety-eight years, dying in 1832. During the summer of 1780 this method of warfare was kept up in South Carolina, and British detachments were routed at several points, notably at " Ninety-Six " and Hanging Rock.

In the meantime some 2,000 troops under De Kalb had been dispatched by Washington to South Carolina, and they arrived in the early summer. General Gates, who ever since the battle of Saratoga had been held up as a military hero hardly second to Washington, was appointed to the chief command of the American forces in the south, and preparations for an energetic campaign were entered upon. He arrived in July and proceeded at once to march upon Camden in the hope of taking it before Cornwallis could go to its relief.

Through injudicious choice of a route and lack of promptness in movement, Gates allowed Cornwallis to effect a junction with Rawdon's force at Camden, and thus lost the golden opportunity of capturing the latter. While endeavoring to take each other by surprise, the two armies suddenly found themselves face to face before daybreak on the morning of August 16, and soon after dawn the fight began. After holding their ground stubbornly and successfully, the untrained, undisciplined militia, outnumbered and outflanked, gallantly rallying twice in the midst of their enemies, finally threw away their arms and fled, panic-stricken and pursued by the British, who cut down eight hundred of them on the field. Gates was caught in the struggling mob and borne from the field. Making no effort to rally his men, he continued his flight for three and a half days until he had reached Hillsborough, North Carolina, some two hundred miles distant. Here the North Carolina legislature was in session, and Gates doubtless felt relieved, for he always seemed to be more at home with Congress and legislatures than with armies.

His northern laurels had indeed, as a critical observer remarked, been changed to southern willows. Never had an American army suffered such a disastrous defeat; it was utterly broken and dispersed. Not less than one thousand of Gates's men were killed, the loss of some of the regiments being severe, while another thousand were taken prisoners, and a large quantity of artillery and small arms were captured. De Kalb, after having been wounded eleven times, died a prisoner in the hands of the British. The British loss was about four hundred men — a severe loss to an army no larger than Cornwallis's. The battle of Camden virtually ended Gates's career; his failure was not due to cowardice or lack of patriotism, but rather to hesitation at the critical moment and the weakening of his army on the eve of battle by the detachment of four hundred of his ablest troops for service under Sumter;[3] in short, he failed on account of bad generalship.[4]

II

TREASON OF BENEDICT ARNOLD

To the gloom of despondency caused by the ignominious rout of the American army at Camden was now to be added the treason of one of the most gallant of the American commanders, General Benedict Arnold. Arnold's expedition to Quebec in the early part of the war, and the sufferings which he endured for the American cause, had greatly endeared him to General Washington, although we know now that he possessed neither moral courage nor conviction. While suffering from wounds, he was placed in command of Philadelphia — after its evacuation by the British in 1778, and while occupying this post he became engaged to an attractive and prominent lady of Tory family Miss Margaret Shippen, and it was said that he moved altogether too much in Tory social circles for the good of the American cause. Falling into habits of extravagance, he soon began to gamble and to engage in reckless speculations to keep up his style of living. It was not long, therefore, until charges were preferred against him for fraudulent transactions, abuse of official power, and other acts of misconduct.

Stung by the accusations, the high-spirited Arnold demanded an investigation, and a committee was appointed by Congress to

[3] Fiske, "The American Revolution," vol. ii. p. 194.
[4] Sloane, "The French War and the Revolution," p. 318.

examine into the truth of the charges.   After diligent inquiry the
committee virtually acquitted him.   Instead of accepting the report,
however, Congress referred the case to a court-martial in April,
1779, new testimony having in the meantime been adduced.   In
January, 1780, the court-martial completed its trial and acquitted
Arnold of all the serious charges preferred against him, but directed
Washington to reprimand him for imprudence in using army
wagons for private purposes and for improperly granting a pass.
This disagreeable task General Washington performed as gently as
his sense of duty and dignity would permit.   Added to this grievance, Arnold was irritated by the action of Congress in passing him
over in the matter of promotions, five junior major generals being
appointed above him.   There is no doubt that in this particular
Arnold was wrongfully treated by Congress, and no satisfactory
reason has ever been given for its extraordinary action.   His services had been marked by courage and gallantry, as well as a spirit
of self-sacrifice and devotion to the American cause.   Nevertheless,
he was ignored by Congress in the distribution of rewards, and unable to control his sensitive, high-strung nature, and burning with
indignation, he resolved to wreak vengeance upon Congress by
betraying the American cause to the enemy.   Accordingly, under
the guise of commercial correspondence, he opened communications
with General Clinton, and in the meantime requested from Washington, and easily secured, the command of the important post of
West Point, which had recently been elaborately and strongly fortified, and which controlled the Hudson.

On the night of September 21, 1780, in pursuance of a previous arrangement, he held an interview in a dense thicket near the
bank of the Hudson with Major John André, an attractive young
Anglo-Frenchman of fine accomplishments and an adjutant general
in the British service.   André had been taken up the river by the
British sloop of war *Vulture,* and was carried ashore in a boat
rowed by three men who were entirely ignorant of what was going
on.   At this midnight interview it was arranged that Arnold should
deliver up to the British, West Point with its three thousand men
in consideration of the payment to him of six thousand pounds
sterling, and the promise of a command in the British army.
André not having returned at the approach of dawn, the *Vulture*
was compelled to drop down the river to escape the fire of the batteries on land.   In this situation André decided to attempt to make

his way back to New York by land, and accordingly set out on foot in the prosecution of his long and perilous journey.

All went well until, as he passed a lonely spot just north of Tarrytown on September 23, he was suddenly stopped by three Americans named Paulding, Williams and Van Wert, who suddenly appeared from the bushes and inquired his name and business. Mistaking them for friends, André revealed his identity, only to be informed to his amazement that he had fallen into the hands of enemies. The men insisted on searching him, and found in his stocking several papers and drawings relating to the works at West Point in Arnold's own handwriting. No promise of money, entreaties or threats could induce his captors to release their prisoner, and accordingly they took him to headquarters and delivered him up to Colonel Jameson. On the morning of September 25, while at breakfast, Arnold was handed a note by a courier, informing him of the arrest of André with compromising documents in his possession. Quietly reading the missive with but slight appearance of emotion, he rose from the table, excused himself, bade his wife farewell, and hurried away. Mounting a large barge anchored in the Hudson near by, he rowed eighteen miles down the river to where the *Vulture* was still waiting for André, was taken aboard and in due course reached New York in safety, thus escaping the ignominious death that he would have received as a traitor had he been captured. When Washington received the news he remarked to Lafayette and Knox with tears in his eyes: "Arnold is a traitor, and has fled to the British! Whom can we trust now?" for the thought that the conspiracy might be widespread was apparently the first to flash into his mind.

Arnold had escaped, but not so André. A military commission was promptly organized and André was put on trial charged with being a spy. With equal promptness he was found guilty and sentenced to be hanged, and on October 2, nine days after his capture, the sentence was carried into execution. Every means was exhausted by the British authorities to save him from the gallows, but nothing except the surrender of Arnold for punishment in his stead could have sufficed, and this the British authorities declined to do. While there was a feeling of general sympathy for the cruel fate of this gallant young officer, whose handsome figure and charm of manner captivated the crowds who saw him die, especially in view of the fact that the traitorous wretch who most deserved punishment had escaped, yet he was a spy and the laws of war allowed no other alternative. Moreover, it was identical with the case of Nathan Hale, a young American, who had been captured and hanged as a spy by the British during the Long Island campaign of 1776. Major André's remains were interred at Tappan on the banks of the Hudson near by; but in 1821 were removed to England and given a place in Westminster Abbey alongside of those of England's greatest heroes. The inscription on his tomb recites the simple truth that " he fell a sacrifice to his zeal for his king and country," and that he " was universally beloved and esteemed by the army in which he served, and lamented by his foes."

Soon after this act of treason Arnold was sent by Sir Henry Clinton on a marauding expedition into Virginia, where he inflicted all the injury that lay within his power on the inhabitants whose cause he had betrayed. After the war he moved to England, where he spent the remainder of his days, leaving descendants, who at a later time rose to distinction. Tradition relates that while on his deathbed in June, 1801, his mind dwelling on the triumphs of his better days, he called for his old American uniform — a present from Washington in recognition of his gallantry at Saratoga, and put it on, asking that he might be permitted to die with it around him, and praying forgiveness for having ever worn another.

III

RECOVERY OF THE CAROLINAS

The gloom and despair caused by the rout of Gates and the treason of Arnold was but the darkness before the dawn. The tide now turned, and henceforth until the close of the war the military operations of the Americans were crowned by an almost unbroken series of victories. In September, 1780, an expedition of British and Tories was completely routed near Camden by the Americans, and a little later the gallant Marion fell upon a British force on the Santee, captured a considerable portion of it and released a hundred and fifty American prisoners.

After the battle of Camden Cornwallis set out for an invasion of North Carolina. With the approach of his army to the North Carolina frontier the hardy backwoodsmen from beyond the mountains rose almost to a man and swarmed in from every direction under their leaders, James Williams, William Campbell, Isaac Shelby, John Sevier and others. By the last of September 3,000 of these picturesque mountaineers, dressed in buckskin hunting shirts and fringed leggins, armed with long knives and rifles, had assembled at a point near the northwest boundary, between North and South Carolina, prepared to dispute Cornwallis's advance. On October 7 a detachment of them, over one thousand strong, fell upon a British force of about 1,000 men under General Ferguson at King's Mountain, near the border line.

Ferguson was bitterly hated by the Carolina patriots on account of his brutality and for his remarkable success in winning over loyalists and enlisting them under his standard. He had not, however, like Tarleton, permitted his troops to massacre prisoners and outrage women, and was a brave and formidable fighter. The British were posted on a mountainous ridge, from which they boasted that all the rebels in America could not dislodge them. But the backwoodsmen knew how to scale mountains; they crept up the sides of the ridge in the face of the British fire, and, although driven back again and again, finally drove the enemy from the crest. The British lost one-third of their entire force, over four hundred men, including Ferguson, who was killed by a North Carolina rifleman, while six hundred of their men were taken prisoners. The American loss did not exceed thirty men killed, but among them was one of their leaders, James Williams. The remnant of Ferguson's army was surrendered to the Americans, who, after the battle, retired with the spoils to their homes beyond the mountains as suddenly as they had come forth, and took no further part in the contest.[5]

King's Mountain was one of the most picturesque battles of the war as it was one of the most decisive. The outlook now began to grow brighter, and the hopes of the patriots were further raised at this juncture by the arrival in December of Daniel Morgan, the famous commander of the Virginia riflemen, and of General Nathanael Greene, who came as the successor of Gates, and who was soon to earn a military reputation second only to Washington's. Greene had already won the full confidence of the commander-in-chief, yet, like Arnold, he had been slighted by Congress and driven into retirement. Washington, however, was quick to appreciate

[5] Lodge, " Story of the Revolution," p. 390; Sloane, " The French War and the Revolution," p. 320.

his military talent, and when requested by Congress to select a commander to succeed Gates he promptly chose Greene. Greene called upon Congress for men, money, arms, stores and ample authority, and sent requests for similar aid to various State executives.

SOUTHERN CAMPAIGNS

The remnant of Gates's army added to some two thousand militia raised in Virginia gave him a force of about five thousand men, though rather poorly equipped and badly disciplined.

Dividing his army into two parts, he sent Morgan with some nine hundred men to the western part of the State to coöperate with the mountaineers and annoy the British who occupied several important posts in that region. Cornwallis likewise divided his army and sent Colonel Tarleton, also a noted cavalry leader, with over one thousand men to capture Morgan. On January 17, 1781, the two armies met at a place known as the Cowpens, in the northwestern part of the State, a few miles from King's Mountain. The British began the attack about sunrise, and for a time the advantage was on their side, but eventually they began to waver under the charges of the militia, and finally threw down their arms and fled in complete rout. Their loss reached nearly two hundred men in killed and wounded, besides two cannon and one thousand stand of small arms.[6] The greater part of the remainder of Tarleton's men were taken prisoners, while he and a handful of his followers escaped to the mountains. The battle of Cowpens, a fit supplement to that of King's Mountain, was one of the most brilliant victories which the Americans had won, although the numbers engaged were small and the results relatively unimportant. It was now no longer a question of how much territory the British would overrun; but of how long they could hold the ground which they already occupied.

Flushed with victory, Greene turned his attention to Cornwallis, whose effective strength had been greatly weakened by the destruction of Tarleton's army. In the hope of drawing Cornwallis away from his base of operations and attacking him, Greene set out on a long retreat to the northward. Cornwallis fell into the trap and followed in hot pursuit. Across the State of North Carolina the two armies raced, covering altogether a distance of two hundred miles. On February 9, 1781, Greene reached Guilford Court House, thirty miles from the Virginia border, and being joined by Morgan's forces, faced about, and after several weeks of maneuvering offered the enemy battle, March 15. Greene had the advantage in numbers, his army outnumbering his opponents two to one, although his men were largely raw recruits, and consequently greatly inferior in discipline to the trained veterans of his adversary, and besides were destitute and worn out.[7]

In the beginning of the battle the American militia were driven back by the heavy charges of Cornwallis's veterans, but a rout was prevented by the resistance offered by Colonel William Washington's cavalry. After several hours of stubborn and desperate fight-

[6] McCrady, "History of South Carolina in the Revolution, 1780–1783," p. 95.
[7] Sloane, "The French War and the Revolution," p. 332.

ing, the British retired to an elevation, from which it proved impossible to dislodge them. Thereupon, Greene withdrew, leaving the enemy in possession of the field, but too badly weakened to renew the attack. Cornwallis lost over four hundred men killed, wounded and missing, while Greene's loss reached about two hundred, not including several hundred militia " who went home," as Greene said, " to kiss their sweethearts and wives." Cornwallis claimed the victory, but Charles Fox, on learning the true facts, is alleged to have declared that " such another victory would destroy the British army."

Instead of pursuing the enemy Cornwallis resumed his march and proceeded into Virginia, leaving his own wounded as well as the American on the field. Greene soon started after him; but in a few days changed his plan and returned to South Carolina with the intention of clearing the State of the British who still held Camden, Ninety-Six and Augusta. Sustaining a defeat at the hands of Lord Rawdon, a bold and energetic officer, at Hobkirk's Hill, on April 25, he nevertheless forced his adversary to abandon the place in the following month, thus gaining easily the great prize for which Gates had vainly contended more than a year before. Other victories now followed in quick succession. Augusta fell early in June, opening the way to the heart of Georgia, and before the end of the month Ninety-Six, the last stronghold of the enemy in upper South Carolina, and altogether the strongest post in the south, was taken after a siege lasting nearly a month.

Thus within a period of ninety days after Greene's return to South Carolina he had recovered the greater part of the State, and had dispossessed the enemy of all its strongholds except Charleston.[8] Finally Greene completed his remarkable campaign — the last of the Revolution but one — by attacking the British at Eutaw Springs, near the Santee, September 8, and, so far as strategic results were concerned, winning a decisive victory. After nearly three years of effort to subjugate the south, having lost large numbers of men and made enormous sacrifices, the British had been driven out of South Carolina with the single exception of Charleston, which they continued to hold until the middle of December, 1782.[9]

[8] For a criticism of Greene as a military strategist, see McCrady, "History of South Carolina in the Revolution, 1780–1783," pp. 3–10.

[9] McCrady gives a list of 137 "battles, actions and engagements" which

IV

YORKTOWN

Cornwallis, after the battle of Guilford Court House, instead of following Greene back to South Carolina, continued his march toward the northeast, and in May reached the neighborhood of Petersburg, Virginia, with some 5,000 veterans, bent on the conquest of the Old Dominion, a rich and populous State, which was quite undefended, and which untouched had been a strong resource and support to the general cause of the Revolution.[10] Here he was confronted by the young Lafayette, then in his twenty-third year, who, with 3,000 raw militiamen, had been sent to Virginia by Washington to check the raids of Benedict Arnold. With this inferior force the young Frenchman outwitted his antagonist, harassed him on every side, all the time skillfully avoiding a battle, and by a campaign of adroit maneuvering held Cornwallis in check, thus proving himself a strategist of high order.

During the summer Lafayette's army was reënforced from various sources until it numbered more than 4,000 men. It was now evident to Cornwallis that he would be unable to " catch the boy," as he had boasted, and so he abandoned upper Virginia and retreated to the coast, taking up his position at Yorktown near the mouth of the York River. This afforded a safe base of operations, and insured ample supplies and reënforcements through connection with England. Lafayette followed and took up a position at Malvern Hill, directly in front of him, and waited for developments.

Ever since the battle of Monmouth in 1778 Washington's army had been keeping guard of the Hudson and had taken no part in the campaigns of the south. During all this time he had looked anxiously toward the city of New York, then held by Clinton, and had longed to recover it from the enemy. Early in 1781 he began to devise schemes for an attack upon this, almost the last stronghold of the British in America, being encouraged thereto by the arrival of 6,000 French troops from Rhode Island under Count Rochambeau. In August the situation was changed by the arrival of news

took place in South Carolina during the Revolution, 103 of which were fought by South Carolinians alone. See his " South Carolina in the Revolution, 1780-1783," pp. 734-736, and also appendix B.

[10] Lodge, " Story of the Revolution," p. 497.

that a powerful French fleet under Admiral de Grasse was on its way from the West Indies to Chesapeake Bay and that Cornwallis had taken up his position at Yorktown.   Washington now changed his plan, and decided to transfer the combined French-American army to Virginia, and with the aid of De Grasse's fleet overwhelm and capture Cornwallis's army.   Leaving General Heath with 4,000 men to hold West Point, he crossed the Hudson on August 19, and with 2,000 Americans and 4,000 Frenchmen set out on his march

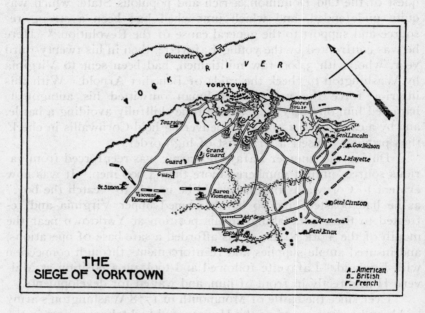

THE SIEGE OF YORKTOWN

A — American
B — British
F — French

for Virginia.   The destination cf the army was kept a profound secret from everyone except Rochambeau, for it was necessary to keep Clinton in the dark as to Washington's movements.   So skillfully was this done that it was not until the army had reached Philadelphia that Washington's purposes were definitely known to the British.   The march through Philadelphia was the occasion of a great popular demonstration, for the joy of the inhabitants at the prospect of the early capture of Cornwallis knew no bounds. Finally, toward September 18, the army had reached the neighborhood of Yorktown after a month of tiresome marching in the heat and dust of summer. There were now not less than 12,000 American troops on the ground ready to attack Cornwallis.

Meantime, De Grasse's fleet had arrived at the mouth of the York River, and 4,000 French troops had been sent ashore to reënforce the American army. An English fleet under Admiral Hood had followed De Grasse from the West Indies, but had sailed past him, and seeing no trace of the fleet in the Chesapeake proceeded on to New York to get instructions from Admiral Graves, who commanded the naval force in the north.[11] Learning the true situation, Admiral Graves put back for the Chesapeake, where, on September 5, he found the French fleet at the mouth of the bay and proceeded to attack it. After a sharp fight of several hours the British fleet withdrew and sailed away, leaving De Grasse in control of the bay. This insured the capture of Cornwallis, for he was now surrounded on all sides and escape was impossible. Slowly the toils were drawn about him; all efforts to cut his way out were thwarted by the vigilant Americans. Likewise the attempt of Clinton to divert Washington by sending Arnold to devastate and plunder the coast of Connecticut was unavailing. Day after day the works of the British crumbled under the artillery fire of the Americans, and, the last hope of escape being gone, Cornwallis hoisted the white flag October 17, 1781. Two days later he formally surrendered, and his entire army of 8,000 men became prisoners of war. Cornwallis, feigning illness, sent his sword by General O'Hara, and the army marched out with colors furled, while the band played "The World's Turned Upside Down," — a tune which probably expressed very accurately the feelings of the men engaged in the unhappy business of laying down their arms that October afternoon.

The surrender of Cornwallis virtually ended the war, and no further campaigns were undertaken, although a state of hostilities legally existed until the signing of the definitive treaty of peace on September 3, 1783, nearly two years later. It was five days before the joyful news of the surrender reached Philadelphia, and immediately the city was astir with evidences of popular rejoicing. Congress marched in a body to the Lutheran church, where a thanksgiving service was held in gratitude to Almighty God for the result. Everywhere the event was celebrated by blazing bonfires, the singing of triumphal hymns and the holding of thanksgiving services.

[11] Fiske, "The American Revolution," vol. ii. p. 279.

A month later the news reached England, and when it was laid before Lord North, Prime Minister, it is said he threw up his hands and exclaimed: "Oh, God! it is all over!" His ministry was now doomed, and on March 20, 1782, it resigned — an event which was full of good omen for the English race the world over.[12]

The way was now open for peace. In March, 1782, Franklin, at Paris, addressed a letter to Lord Shelburne, with whom he was personally acquainted, and who as secretary of state for colonial and home affairs, was charged with the conduct of all matters relating to the colonies, expressing the hope that a "general peace" might soon be restored. Shelburne replied by sending over to Paris a Scotchman, named Richard Oswald, who by marriage and purchase had acquired large estates in America, to talk with Franklin, to ascertain the conditions upon which a treaty could be concluded, and to acquaint him with the views of the British Government. Franklin at first placed his terms rather high, demanding among other things the cession of Canada to the United States, whether seriously or not, it is difficult to say. Returning to London, Oswald laid before Shelburne Franklin's views, and, after a brief absence, was sent back to Paris to say that Canada could not be ceded, and that, moreover, the Americans would be expected to indemnify the loyalists for the losses which they had suffered at the hands of American legislatures, and possibly to make some compensation for the surrender of New York, Charleston and Savannah, then held by British troops. In July the short-lived Rockingham ministry fell, and, after some difficulty, a new one was formed with Shelburne as Prime Minister. This change of government together with the defeat at this time of the French and the Spaniards by the British in several notable engagements, simplified the task of making a treaty. In the meantime, also, Congress had appointed John Adams, John Jay, then in Spain, and Henry Laurens, now out of the Tower on parole, to join Franklin in the conduct of the negotiations. France had hoped that her ally, Spain, would be able to recover Gibraltar from the British, but being disappointed in this hope, she now undertook to repay Spain for her losses by inducing the British Government to cede to the latter power a large tract of land in America between the Alleghany Mountains and the Mississippi River. In other words, France proposed to pay Spain for her services out of the territory which the Americans had con-

[12] Fiske, "Critical Period," p. 1.

quered from England in 1779, and the cession of which they expected to insist upon in the treaty of peace.

When they discovered, therefore, as they believed, that the French Minister of Foreign Affairs, Count Vergennes, was attempting to steal a march on them, the American ministers (Adams and Jay had recently arrived to aid in the negotiations) decided to begin a separate negotiation with England. This action of the American commissioners was contrary to the letter of the Treaty of Alliance of 1778 with France, which prohibited either party to the alliance from concluding peace with Great Britain without the knowledge and consent of the other, and was also contrary to the instructions of the American commissioners, but they justified their action on the ground that the attempt of France to enrich her ally at the expense of the United States required independent negotiations — a proceeding founded on the law of self-preservation. Franklin did not share the suspicions of Adams and Jay as to the conduct of Vergennes, but he nevertheless acted with them in negotiating independently with Great Britain.[13]

Of the various questions to be settled in the negotiations, that of independence was the most important. The American demand for an unqualified recognition of the independence of the United States was conceded without hesitation. The question of boundaries was likewise easily disposed of, Franklin's demand for the cession of Canada being abandoned as too extravagant. The St. Croix River was to be the boundary on the northeast, the crest of the highlands between the St. Lawrence River and the Atlantic Ocean, the forty-fifth parallel and the Great Lakes to the source of the Mississippi west of the Lake of the Woods was to be the boundary on the north. The Mississippi River on the west and the thirty-first parallel on the south completed the boundaries.[14]

With regard to the Newfoundland fisheries which the colonists had enjoyed without restriction, and which were a source of enormous profit to the New England inhabitants, as well as a nursery of American seamen, the treaty provided that the right of the Americans to take fish on the Grand Banks should be conceded by Great Britain, and that they should be accorded the liberty to fish in the Gulf of St. Lawrence and in the bays and on the coasts of New-

[13] See Moore, "American Diplomacy," p. 30.
[14] For the settlement of various controversies over the boundary stipulations see J. B. Moore, "International Arbitrations," vol. i. chs. i.–vi.

foundland, but not to dry their catch on the shores of the island. With regard to private debts due from Americans to British creditors, aggregating some three millions sterling, mostly contracted before the Revolution, it was provided that the debts should be paid in full sterling money, that no unlawful impediments or obstacles should be placed in the way of the collection of such debts, and that British creditors should be free to resort to American courts to prosecute their claims.

A question which proved difficult of settlement was the demand of the British negotiators that the Americans should provide an indemnification for the loyalists. To this demand Franklin and his colleagues returned an emphatic *non possumus*. These people, said Franklin, were largely responsible for their own unfortunate condition, inasmuch as they had by their misrepresentations aided in bringing on the war; moreover, they had forfeited all right to an indemnity by the ruthless and cruel manner in which they had, in league with savages, plundered and desolated the frontier settlements of New York and Pennsylvania; and, lastly, the people of America were too impoverished by the long war to provide pensions for their own patriots, much less compensate those who had, by word and deed, aided their enemies. No amount of pressure could move the American commissioners from this position, and the only concession that could be secured was a stipulation to the effect that Congress would recommend to the several States to desist from further proceedings against the loyalists, to reconsider their harsh laws, and afford legal redress to such persons as desired to have recourse to the courts for the recovery of their estates. Congress, indeed, duly made the recommendation, but it was not generally followed, and thus the treaty stipulation proved worthless.

With these important questions settled the minor points were quickly agreed upon, and the preliminary treaty was signed November 30, 1782, although it was nearly a year later before the definitive treaty received the signatures of the commissioners. In nearly every particular the Americans had secured an acknowledgment of their demands, and had themselves granted few concessions. It was truly a great diplomatic triumph, and will ever stand as a monument to the diplomatic skill and shrewdness of the American negotiators.[15] But in violating their instructions, as well as the stipulations of the treaty of 1778 with regard to joint negotiations

[15] Lecky, "History of England in the Eighteenth Century," vol. iv. p. 263.

with the French, the American commissioners had brought down upon their heads the denunciation of the King of France, who charged them with duplicity and bad faith. Franklin undertook to defend their conduct in a letter to Vergennes, in which he admitted that they had " been guilty of neglecting a point of *bienséance*, but that it was not from want of respect for the king, whom," he said, " all Americans loved and honored," and he hoped that it would be overlooked and that the " great work which has hitherto been so happily conducted, and is so glorious to his reign, will not be ruined by any indiscretion of ours." [16] The terms of the treaty were unanimously approved in America, but the feeling of the majority of Congress was that the commissioners were not warranted in departing from their instructions, and in signing without first making known the terms of the treaty of the French Government.[17] The Americans had hoped to be able to conclude a commercial treaty with Great Britain, but in this they were disappointed, and many years were to pass before Great Britain would consent to treat on the subject.[18]

V

GENERAL OBSERVATIONS

It would be insufficient to dismiss the Revolution without a brief reference to several important aspects of the struggle which could not be well described above without interfering with the thread of the narrative. One of these was the naval achievements of the war. At the beginning of the Revolution the colonies, of course, had no navy, although they possessed a considerable merchant marine, which became the basis of an effective privateering service. Letters of marque and reprisal were freely issued, both by Congress and the States, to privateers, and at one time it was estimated that not less than 70,000 persons were engaged in preying on the commerce of Great Britain.[19] A comparison between the military and naval forces shows that the navy, in its various forms,

[16] John Bassett Moore, "Beginnings of American Diplomacy," in *Harper's Magazine,* vol. cviii. p. 507.
[17] Foster, "Century of American Diplomacy," p. 69.
[18] See Jay, "The Peace Negotiations," in Winsor, "Nar. and Crit. History," vol. vii. ch. ii.
[19] Sloane, "French War and the Revolution," p. 373.

embodied almost as many men as the army, and sometimes, indeed, more.[20]　From first to last, over fifteen hundred armed vessels were fitted out as privateers in the United States, Massachusetts heading the list with over five hundred.　Congress, devoting its main energies to the support of the army, gave little attention to the question of organizing a navy.　Nevertheless, it made a beginning in 1775 by ordering the construction of thirteen cruisers, which were in the course of time completed, but less than half of them ever succeeded in getting to sea.　Later, some forty vessels of various types were put into the service of the Continental Congress, but more than half of them were captured by the enemy.　Yet notwithstanding the feeble character of the navy, it accomplished much.

Before the French alliance more than six hundred British vessels had been taken by daring American seamen who hovered about the coasts of England and Scotland.　The three men whose names are most closely associated with these naval triumphs were Lambert Wickes, who in the early years of the war captured many prizes in the eastern Atlantic; Gustavus Conyngham, whose operations in the English Channel sent marine insurance rates up 25 per cent.; and John Paul Jones, a Scotch sailor, who shortly before the Revolution had taken up his residence in Virginia, and who was destined to become the greatest naval hero of the war.[21]　Appointed captain in the American navy, Jones sailed for the English Channel, and, with a single vessel, captured several British prizes, and caused general consternation in maritime circles.　In the summer of 1779 he took command of a squadron of three vessels, of which the *Bonhomme Richard* (40 guns) was the chief, and in September arrived off the east coast of Scotland, where he proceeded to destroy or capture English vessels as they came along.　While at this business, near Flamborough Head, he descried a merchant fleet bound for the Baltic and convoyed by the *Serapis* and the *Countess of Scarborough,* both together carrying sixty-four guns.　Jones gave chase in the *Bonhomme Richard,* and after dark on the evening of September 23, 1779, attacked the *Serapis,* and a duel between the two ships ensued, which was one of the most obstinate and sanguinary in the history of naval warfare.　At intervals for several hours each vessel poured a terrific broadside into its antagonist, the lurid flashes of

[20] Winsor, " Nar. and Crit. History," vol. vi. p. 588.
[21] For an account of the exploits of these daring seamen see Hale, " Naval History of the Revolution," in Winsor's " Nar. and Crit. Hist.," vol. vi. ch. vii.

the cannon lighting up the inky darkness which prevailed. Finally Jones succeeded, by the use of grappling irons, in lashing the *Bonhomme Richard* to the *Serapis,* after which the fight became more of the nature of a hand to hand contest. While the American vessel was being raked by British cannon, parties of her crew climbed into the *Serapis,* and with hand-grenades and other implements of warfare played terrible havoc with their opponents. Both vessels were now in a sore plight; each was badly damaged and afire in places, while their decks were strewn with the dead and dying. In this situation the *Serapis* surrendered, but her adversary kept afloat with difficulty during the night and sank next morning. While the fight between the *Serapis* and the *Bonhomme Richard* was proceeding, the *Pallas* captured the *Countess of Scarborough,* thus completing the greatest naval victory of the Revolution. Though the military results of the fight were insignificant, the moral results were of great consequence. The fighting qualities of American seamen were clearly established, and Europe soon rang with praises for the daring captain who had bearded the lion in his den, and inflicted upon him a crushing defeat. From various countries of Europe decorations, honors, and pensions were showered upon Jones, and he was held up as the greatest naval hero of the time, although the English government insisted that he was, in legal status, only a pirate.[22]

Though not so picturesque as the famous victory of Jones, the capture by Captain John Barry of the *Mermaid* and the *Kitty* demonstrated in quite as high a degree the qualities of enterprise and courage. This, however, was only one of Barry's exploits. His captures were numerous and his services scarcely surpassed, and in 1777 he was publicly thanked by General Washington. Shortly after his appointment to command by Congress, in 1776, he succeeded in taking the British tender *Edward,* after a sharp action, and this was the first capture of a vessel by a commissioned officer of the United States navy.

Another phase of the Revolution which also deserves a brief mention was the financial aspect of the struggle — the provision of ways and means for the support of the army. The Continental Congress, having no constitutional power of taxation, and afraid to assume an authority so likely to excite popular opposition, was compelled from the first to devise other schemes than taxation for filling its treasury. The most prolific of these was the issuance of

[22] Fiske, "The American Revolution," vol. ii. p. 129.

treasury notes—always a favorite resource of governments in time of war. During the first year of the war $6,000,000 of paper was thus put into circulation; in 1776, $19,000,000 more was added; in 1777, $13,000,000; in 1778, $63,500,000; in 1779, $140,000,000; making a total issue of $241,500,000. To this volume of paper currency were added also the notes issued by the several States. During the first year of the war "continental currency" was willingly received by the people at par, but as the issues increased beyond the requirements of trade, an inevitable increase of prices followed, and with it a depreciation of the value of paper money. At the beginning of 1709 a dollar in paper currency was worth but twelve cents in specie, a year later it was worth but three cents, and before the end of the war it was practically worthless, and all specie had disappeared from circulation. As prices of labor and commodities soared to fabulous heights, the States began to pass laws to fix the price of both, and for the punishment of those who violated such enactments or who refused to receive paper money at its par value. Likewise, Congress enacted a law authorizing Washington to seize whatever supplies he needed for the army, to pay what he deemed reasonable prices, and to punish those who should refuse to receive continental money in payment thereof. It went even further, and adopted a resolution declaring that every person who should refuse to accept continental bills should be published, and treated as a public enemy, and be precluded from all trade or intercourse with the inhabitants of the colonies.

Notwithstanding Congress had solemnly pledged the faith of the nation to redeem this flood of paper, it ultimately repudiated the pledge and passed a resolution providing for the redemption of all bills of credit at one-fortieth of their face value. The first issues were apportioned among the States according to the population, with the recommendation that each should make provision for redeeming its quota by special taxes for the purpose. This recommendation was followed in 1775, but unfortunately was disregarded in the case of the succeeding issues, notwithstanding the urgent appeals of Congress. The loss inflicted on the people by the depreciation of the continental currency can never be estimated.[23]

But without resort to this resource it is difficult to see how the war could have been carried on, in view of the opposition of the

[23] For an account of the burdens of the war see Sumner, "The Financier and the Finances of the Revolution," vol. i. ch. xxiv.

people to taxation. Had Congress possessed the power to lay and collect taxes which it now has, the evils of depreciated currency could have been largely diminished. But it possessed no such power, and had it attempted to exercise it its authority would have been destroyed and the war stopped. In this situation Congress resorted to various expedients for obtaining specie, the most important of which was by requisitions on the States. Again and again the States were asked to contribute their quotas to the support of the war, but their responses were tardy and ungenerous, they, like Congress, preferring to issue notes rather than to tax themselves.[24]

In 1781 Robert Morris was put at the head of the continental treasury with the title of Superintendent of Finance, and he was able to bring about a great improvement in the national finances, among other things the placing of continental affairs on a specie basis. He established the Bank of North America at Philadelphia, with a capital of $400,000, and the institution rendered great service to Congress by aiding it to place its loans. Altogether Morris's services were hardly second to those of Washington or Greene. In the dark days of the Revolution, when the army was on the verge of starvation and naked for lack of clothes, Morris was able to raise small amounts and send them to Washington for the support of his suffering troops.[25]

Franklin urged Congress to cease issuing bills of credit, and borrow what it needed. But it proved harder to borrow than to issue paper money. Nevertheless the suggestion was tried and some specie acquired in this way, both at home and abroad. Nearly $8,000,000 was borrowed in Europe. Of this $6,352,000 was secured from France; $1,304,000 from Holland, and $174,000 from Spain, and the domestic loans aggregated nearly $12,000,000. The debts incurred by the several States amounted to more than $18,000,000. Taxes to the amount of nearly $6,000,000 were levied and collected by the States, and nearly $3,000,000 raised from miscellaneous sources, such as gifts from France and Spain, lotteries, confiscation of loyalist estates, sales of public land, and prizes taken at sea. Altogether the war cost, according to a competent authority, about one hundred million dollars.[26]

[24] See Oberholtzer, "Robert Morris, Patriot and Financier," ch. iv.
[25] *Ibid.*, ch. v.
[26] C. J. Bullock, "Finances of the Revolution."

A word remains to be said concerning the fortunes of that large class of Americans who were opposed to the Revolution, and who either refused to take up arms in defense of the American cause, or openly joined the ranks of the British forces. These persons were known indiscriminately as Tories or Loyalists. It is impossible to estimate their numbers, but it is certain that they were a very large body, and in some communities outnumbered the patriots. John Adams declared, after the close of the war, his belief that they numbered nearly one-third of the people of the colonies,[27] while Joseph Galloway, himself a Loyalist, thought the proportion was four-fifths or nine-tenths.[28] Altogether not less than 50,000 American Loyalists served in the British army, either as regulars or militia.[29] The English historian, Lecky, a fair and impartial authority, expressed the opinion that at least one-half of the more honorable and respected Americans were either openly or secretly hostile to the Revolution. It is certainly true that the Loyalists were among the principal men of substance in their communities, leaders in political, industrial and social circles, and generally persons of the highest type of character. Prominent examples were Governor Hutchinson of Massachusetts, the DeLanceys of New York, Joseph Galloway of Pennsylvania, and William Temple Franklin, son of Benjamin Franklin, of New Jersey. The Tory element was made up mainly of royal officials and their friends; the Anglican clergy, whose attachment to the Crown was stronger than their desire for independence; conservative persons of all classes, who disapproved revolution for any purpose, or who believed that Parliament had a moral and legal right to tax the colonies; and finally those who, after the outbreak of the war, became disgusted with the financial policy of Congress, the Declaration of Independence, and the French alliance, and were induced to return to their old allegiance.[30]

Among the New England States, Connecticut, by reason of its proximity to New York and Canada, had the greatest number of Loyalists. Of the larger and more popular colonies, Massachusetts had the fewest, although 1,100 embarked with Howe for Nova Scotia upon the evacuation of Boston, in March, 1776.[31]

[27] Works of John Adams, vol. x. p. 193.
[28] Fisher, "True History of the American Revolution," p. 229.
[29] Van Tyne, "Loyalists of the American Revolution," p. 183.
[30] Ibid., pp. 25–26.
[31] Ibid., p. 59.

New York, of all the American colonies, was the principal Tory stronghold. By reason of its nearness to Canada, and the large commercial interests of the colony, the number of its inhabitants who were opposed to the Revolution was very considerable. Besides, the city of New York, including the valley of the lower Hudson, after the spring of 1776, was held by the British, thus affording a convenient refuge for those of British sympathies. New York furnished altogether 23,000 Loyalists to the British army. When Washington was driven from Long Island in 1776 almost the entire population went over to the side of the British.[32] Two-thirds of the property of the State was believed to have been in Tory hands. Next to New York, Pennsylvania and New Jersey had the largest number of Loyalists of any of the colonies. When Howe evacuated Philadelphia in 1778 he took with him over three thousand of these persons. In Virginia practically all of the upper class were patriots; in North Carolina the two parties were pretty equally divided; in South Carolina the Loyalists were in the majority. When South Carolina and Georgia were abandoned by the British in 1782, over 13,000, including nearly 9,000 negroes, accompanied the British troops.

The trials and hardships of the Loyalist class were especially severe, and their fate in many cases peculiarly sad. By means of "sounding committees" appointed by Sons of Liberty organizations, the timid and vacillating were forced to declare their sentiments. If adverse to the American cause the offender was given a coat of tar and feathers, which seems to have been the usual antidote for Toryism. Sometimes they were ducked in pools, ridden on rails, whipped, branded, boycotted, plundered, drummed out of the community and warned not to return, or otherwise maltreated by patriot mobs. Everywhere they were disfranchised and proscribed. The courts of law were closed to them and means of legal redress denied them. An unrelenting social ostracism made their life a perpetual misery, and most of them were forced into exile or to seek refuge within the British lines. In November, 1777, Congress adopted a resolution recommending the States to confiscate and sell the property of all persons "who had forfeited their right to protection," and turn the proceeds into State treasuries.[33] The confiscation of Loyalist property, begun in some

[32] Lecky, "American Revolution," p. 256.
[33] Van Tyne, "The Loyalists in the American Revolution," p. 277. The

States before this resolution, now proceeded by wholesale in all of them. In some States they were given an opportunity to return to their allegiance and save their estates from confiscation; in others no such opportunity was allowed, and many were attainted without hearing, without jury trial, and often in their absence. By a single act of the New York Legislature fifty-nine persons, including three women, were thus attainted of treason, their property confiscated, the death penalty imposed on any who should be found in the State, and a special tax levied on every parent who had a Loyalist son.[34] In this State alone over $3,600,000 worth of property owned by such persons was acquired by the State. By a similar act of the Massachusetts Legislature, passed in 1778, the death penalty was affixed to 310 self-exiled Loyalists, provided they should ever return to the colony, and in Pennsylvania 490 persons were likewise attainted by a similar process. Thousands of the exiles went to England, the West Indies, the Bermudas, the Bahamas, Nova Scotia, and New Brunswick, and in most cases their lot was a hard one. Attainted of treason and debarred from returning to their homes, they were compelled to start life anew.[35]

While the fate of these unhappy people must excite the sympathy of the historian, it must be admitted that to their own conduct is to be largely attributed the severity of the policy adopted by the State legislatures toward them. Their opposition to the American cause was not merely passive. They not only took up arms against their patriot brethren, but what was worse still, they joined the Indians in devastating the New York and Pennsylvania frontiers and became actual participants in several massacres of their fellow-inhabitants. The most atrocious of these massacres occurred on July 4, 1778, in the beautiful Wyoming Valley, where Colonel John Butler, with some 800 Tories and Indians, suddenly fell upon a peaceful village, easily defeated the small force gathered for its defense, and put to death over 200 of its inhabitants. The survivors fled to the mountains, leaving the valley practically deserted. The Tories attributed the slaughter of the inhabitants to

popular hatred of Tories is shown by the following definition which appeared in the public prints of the time: "A Tory is a thing whose head is in England, whose body is in America, and whose neck ought to be stretched."

[34] Sabine, "Loyalists of the Revolution," pp. 78–81.

[35] For a good account of the experience of a prominent Loyalist in exile see Hosmer. "Life of Thomas Hutchinson," ch. xiv.

SIGNING THE PRELIMINARY TREATY AT PARIS, NOVEMBER 30, 1782

Painting by C. Seller

—page 288

the Indians, but the colonists held them no less responsible for employing savages in civilized warfare.   In the following year a somewhat similar occurrence took place at Cherry Valley, Otsego County, New York, in the course of which over thirty persons, most of them women and children, were massacred by a band of Tories under the command of Walter Butler, son of John Butler, and the noted Mohawk chieftain, Joseph Brant.

The British Government felt under an obligation to provide for those who had sacrificed so much for the sake of the king, but as has been said, it was practically forced to abandon them in the treaty of peace.   After the war, however, many of them were given lands in Canada, and several million dollars were expended in establishing settlements for their benefit.   Some were given offices and a few were granted pensions.   In 1782 a Parliamentary committee was appointed to investigate their claims for losses sustained by reason of their adherence to the British cause.   After an investigation lasting through five years, the committee recommended the payment of $19,000,000 in settlement of all claims. This amount was appropriated, which, with the sums expended for estalishing the Loyalists in Nova Scotia and Canada, raised the total amount expended by the British Government on account of the Loyalists to not less than thirty million dollars.[36]

[36] Van Tyne, " The Loyalists in the American Revolution," p. 303; see also Ellis, " The Loyalists and Their Fortunes," in Winsor's " Nar. and Crit. Hist.," vol. vii. pp. 211–212.

Chapter XIII

TRANSITION FROM COLONIES TO STATES. 1781–1789

I

THE ARTICLES OF CONFEDERATION

BY united exertions and common sacrifices the thirteen colonies had at last achieved their independence of Great Britain, and had concluded with her an honorable treaty of peace, embodying a recognition of substantially all the principles for which they had fought and suffered. The war had, indeed, been a glorious one to American arms, and had brought out in bold relief the true character of that branch of the English race which was soon to build a new nation and carry it forward upon a career unexampled in the history of the world. The future of this new nation, if the great opportunity which opened before it were wisely used, was now abundantly assured. It was, however, destined to pass through a period of severe trial, in the course of which many of the wisest and strongest men, the leaders of the Revolution, together with those destined to leadership in the great work of reconstruction, were led to doubt whether, after all, their condition had been bettered by separation from the mother country. The peril which threatened the very existence of the United States at the outset was the lack of a suitably endowed, efficient central government to take the place of the British sovereignty which had been superseded. So long as British supremacy remained intact there was a common authority to which each colony owed allegiance — an authority which made it impossible for one colony, actuated by motives of selfishness or of particularism, to encroach upon the rights of another, or upon their common welfare as determined by the general consciousness and by the policy and opinions of the mother country.

The Declaration of Independence, although the result of concerted action upon their part, left the thirteen colonies without a common and acknowledged superior. So far as any constitutional limitations were concerned, each State was virtually an independent nation, free to follow any course or pursue any policy it might choose.   But inasmuch as their independence of Great Britain at the time of the Declaration was not an established fact, the prosecution of the war for the actual realization of what as yet existed only in theory made necessary common action and deference, if not actual submission to, a common authority.   Without the action of some central organ armies could never have been raised, equipped or commanded, and the aid of foreign nations could never have been secured.   In short, the improvization of a central government acting for all the colonies, temporary and ill adapted though it might be, seemed indispensable as a result of the situation created by the necessities of the war and the Declaration of Independence. To meet this situation the Continental Congress was called into existence and, until peace was nearly reached, it was the guiding authority for the management of the common concerns of the colonies, which at this stage included few matters of importance except such as related to the prosecution of the war.   The Congress thus created was a revolutionary body summoned to meet a temporary emergency, but the force of events soon compelled it to assume, so far as it could, sovereign powers of government, and to undertake the general management of the war.   Its members were chosen by the legislatures in some of the colonies, in others they were chosen by popular conventions, and in still others they were selected by committees of correspondence or other extra-legal bodies.   Each colony was free to send as many delegates to the Congress as it saw fit, to authorize them to serve for such period of time as it wished, and to pay them for their services or not, as it seemed best.   The delegates represented colonies or States, and voted as States, and not as individuals.   There being no written constitution or agreement among the States, the powers of this extraordinary assembly were of course wholly undefined, and its acts were without sanction or means of enforcement.[1]   The Congress accordingly exercised such authority as was deemed necessary to the successful conduct of the war, and which it was believed would meet the approval of the people of the colonies.   The only measure of its powers, therefore, was to be found in the voluntary assent of the several States and general popular acquiescence, limitations which the Congress kept steadily in mind in all its delibera-

[1] Curtis, "Constitutional History of the United States," vol. i. ch. iv.

tions. A body whose powers were thus undefined by any written instrument, whose composition was lacking in uniformity, whose decrees had no binding force, which dealt only with States and touched no individual citizen, and whose organization was unicameral in character, was obviously unfitted, not only for the general purposes of government, but even for legislation itself. No attempt was made to apply the modern principle of the separation of governmental powers by providing distinct organs for the exercise of executive and judicial functions, but reliance was placed upon boards and committees for administrative purposes and upon the State courts for the judicial enforcement of its commands.

Notwithstanding the general unfitness of the Continental Congress as an organ of government, its services in bringing about the independence of the colonies were, as already stated, indispensable. It raised, organized and supported the army, it adopted a declaration of independence, it established a committee of correspondence and maintained diplomatic relations with foreign countries, it assumed control of Indian affairs, it established a postal system, it undertook the settlement of boundary disputes among the colonies, it issued a national paper currency and negotiated loans, and performed many other duties of government which properly belonged only to a central authority.[2] But the objections to a scheme of government whose powers were wholly undefined and unsupported by any sanction or means of enforcing its decrees, which in short rested only on a revolutionary basis and was as inefficient as it was revolutionary, were too obvious to be ignored, and the war had barely entered upon the second year of its progress when the necessity for a change had become apparent to all. On June 11, 1776, the same day on which Congress chose a committee to draft a declaration of independence, a committee was also appointed to prepare a constitution of government. It was clearly foreseen that the creation of an efficient general government ought to follow the Declaration of Independence; otherwise the purposes for which the separation from Great Britain was desired would be difficult, if not impossible, of realization. In short, independence without government and union would be worthless. In the second week of July the committee finished its labors and made a report, John Dickinson being the supposed author. The report

[2] See an article on the Continental Congress by Herbert Friedenwald in the Annual Report of the American Historical Association for 1894, p. 227.

embodied a plan of government entitled " Articles of Confederation and Perpetual Union," but unlike the Declaration of Independence, it was destined to be the subject of debate for a year and a half, and was not to be put into operation until the expiration of nearly five years. In the meantime the Continental Congress continued to direct the common affairs of the country, and to exercise such powers as the acquiescence of the States permitted. As the plan recommended by the committee proposed to limit in some measure the powers of the individual States, it provoked strong opposition in Congress. At this time most of the States, acting upon the advice of the second Continental Congress in 1775, had adopted constitutions and set up governments of their own, and were therefore loath to surrender their sovereign rights to an outside authority. There were also very grave difficulties of detail, such as whether each State should be allowed one vote in Congress, according to the existing plan, or whether it should have a number of votes, proportioned according to its population; difficulties also as to the matter of assessing and raising revenue, the apportionment of powers between the general government and the States, the settlement of disputes among the States, and many others. Finally, on November 15, 1777, the proposed Articles were adopted by Congress, and were then sent to the States for ratification by their respective legislatures.[3]

Accompanying the Articles was a circular letter prepared by Congress, recommending the acceptance of the scheme as the only plan likely of adoption. In little more than a year the Articles were ratified by all the States except Maryland, which refused to give its adhesion until the States laying claim to lands northwest of the Ohio should promise to surrender their claims for the benefit of the nation. Maryland had no claim to western land, while her nearest neighbor, Virginia, laid claim to an immense region in the west, which would make her by far the most powerful State of the Confederation, and many times greater in area than her less powerful neighbor. A Confederation of such grossly unequal States, argued the Marylanders, was out of the question. The proceeds from the sale of Virginia's western lands would in time be sufficient to defray the expenses of her government, and her citizens thus relieved of the burdens of taxation. Besides, the wealth and influence of Virginia would give her the balance of

[3] Van Tyne, "The American Revolution," ch. xi.

power in the Confederation, and make it possible for her to tyrannize over her neighbors. Finally, it was said that the western lands had been acquired by conquest from Great Britain in a common war waged by all the colonies united, and should, therefore, be reserved for the common benefit of all. The States claiming western lands came to appreciate the justice of these arguments, and made ready to yield to the demands of their less favored sisters. New York and Virginia agreed to cede their claims to the United States, and on the strength of this promise Maryland came forward and ratified the Articles in March, 1781.[4]

Tested by the principles of sound political science, the scheme of government provided in the Articles of Confederation, and so tardily accepted, was one of the most inefficient in the whole range of history, and after a few bitter years, during which the country gradually drifted toward anarchy, escape from its evils was effected only by what were practically revolutionary methods. According to the language of the Articles the thirteen States entered into a perpetual league of friendship with each other for common defense and general welfare, and it was expressly declared that each State retained its sovereignty, freedom and independence, and every power not expressly delegated to the United States in Congress assembled. The Union thus created was not a federal State, *Bundesstaat,* as the Germans say, with sovereignty in the nation, but a confederation or *Staatenbund,* the sovereignty remaining in the individual States. Experience has taught that this latter form of government is one of the most inefficient of all forms, and it has been abandoned by nearly every civilized nation that has tried it. But a hundred years ago, when the sentiment of particularism was much stronger than now, it was cherished as the safest and also as being the most consonant with the liberties of the people. By the Articles of Confederation a sort of general citizenship was created, it being provided that the free inhabitants of each State should be entitled to all the privileges and immunities of free citizens in the different States. It was moreover required that full faith and credit should be given in each State to the judicial records and proceedings of every other State, and that fugitives from justice, as well as runaway slaves escaping from one State to another, should, upon demand, be returned to the State from which they had escaped.

[4] Curtis, "Constitutional History of the United States," vol. i. pp. 90–94.

But it was in the organization of government that the most glaring defects of the Articles appeared. The legislative power of the Confederation was vested in a Congress composed of at least two and not more than seven delegates appointed annually by each State. No delegates could serve more than three years in six, they were paid by the States which they represented, were subject to instructions, and could be recalled at the will of the States. Ignoring all differences between the States, the Articles provided that each should have one vote in Congress, regardless of its population or wealth, the vote to be cast by a majority of the State's delegates.[5]

Disregarding also the advantages to be derived from the employment of the check and balance principle in legislative procedure, the Articles provided for a single chamber, which was better adapted perhaps for administrative purposes than for legislation, and was very bad and ineffective in both directions. In the apportionment of power between the United States on the one hand and the States on the other, the Articles exhibited the prevailing fear of the central government. To the Congress was given the sole and exclusive power to declare war and to make peace, to send and receive ambassadors, to make treaties, to settle disputes between the States, to establish rules for the disposition of captures and prizes in war, to establish courts of appeal in cases of capture, to regulate the value of all coin struck by the United States or by any State, to regulate trade with the Indian tribes, to establish post offices, to appoint all officers of the army above the rank of colonel, to appoint all naval officers, to make rules for the government of land and naval forces, to fix the standard of weight and measures, and to borrow money.

No State, without the consent of Congress, could send or receive ambassadors, make treaties, lay duties or imposts which would interfere with any treaty between the United States and foreign powers, or keep troops or vessels of war in time of peace, or engage in war. An almost fatal defect in the Articles was the provision which required an extraordinary majority for the enactment of all important measures of legislation. Thus the consent of nine States was required to pass any measure for engaging in war, to granting letters of marque and reprisal, to make treaties, to coin money or regulate the value thereof, to emit bills of credit, to borrow or appropriate money, to establish a navy, to raise land forces, or to

[5] McMaster, "History of the People of the United States," vol. i. pp. 130–132.

appoint a commander-in-chief. As the total number of States was but thirteen, it followed that the most important measures of government could be defeated by any five States. On account of the frequent non-attendance of members from some of the States, and the jealousy of others, it often happened that sorely needed measures were defeated by an insignificant minority.[6]

As for the executive department, there was none. True, there was a President of Congress, who enjoyed a certain precedence over other officials, and represented in a way the dignity of the United States; but he was in reality only a moderator or speaker, not an executive officer charged with the enforcement of the laws, and in fact had no more executive power than any other member of Congress. Congress was thus both executive and legislative. If the mails were robbed or the currency counterfeited, the United States must depend upon the States for the punishment of the offenders. With the exception of a short-lived tribunal of appeal for hearing and determining prize cases, there was no national judiciary and consequently the United States was dependent upon the State courts for the interpretation and enforcement of its statutes.

If the State courts were friendly the national authority was upheld and respected; otherwise it was disregarded, as only too frequently happened. The lack of a national executive and judiciary machinery contributed immensely to the inefficiency of the government, and was one of the causes of its ultimate downfall.[7]

But perhaps the most serious defect in the scheme of government embodied in the Articles of Confederation was the lack of the two essential powers of laying and collecting taxes, and of regulating trade among the States and with foreign nations. Not a word was said in the Articles with regard to the power of Congress to lay and collect taxes. In the controversy with Great Britain the colonies had contended that the right of taxation belonged exclusively to their legislative assemblies, and when they came to form a national government, after the Revolution, they still exhibited the same jealousy of surrendering any part of that power. The collection of taxes remained, therefore, with the States, Congress having only the right to determine upon the sums needed and then to apportion the amount among the States for

---

[6] Winsor, " Narrative and Critical History of America," vol. vii. p. 217.
[7] Curtis, " Constitutional History of the United States," vol. i. pp. 99-101.

collection on the basis of the value of real estate in each. If any State refused to collect and pay into the national treasury the quota assigned to it, Congress was powerless. It had neither constitutional nor physical power to coerce a delinquent or recalcitrant State into fulfilling its obligations to the Union; nor had it the necessary legal means to collect the tax itself. In fact, the whole theory underlying the Articles of Confederation was that the power of the national government should be limited to dealing with the States and not with individuals, which of itself was fatal to the entire scheme. In practice such a system is impossible, since refractory States cannot be dealt with in the same manner as refractory individuals. Such an individual can be arrested and imprisoned and thus forced to fulfill his public obligations, but the coercion of a State is a far more serious undertaking. If it had been tried in 1781, it is almost certain that a rebellion would have been stirred up, and the feeble Union would have been speedily dissolved. The only resource was moral suasion and appeals to the pride of the States — an alternative which generally proved ineffective, leaving the government paralyzed for lack of revenues to pay current expenses of administration and to meet its obligations to creditors. It is doubtful if there is another instance in history of a government so poorly endowed with the means of support and whose struggles to replenish its treasury in a time of peace were marked by so much of imbecility, if not of actual pathos.

Likewise, the power of the government over its means of defense depended upon the will of the individual States. Congress, to be sure, was empowered to fix the quotas of men which each State should furnish, but it had no power to compel obedience, and the States complied with the request of Congress for recruits if they sympathized with the purposes for which the army was wanted, or refused to comply if they happened to disapprove. The refusal to vest Congress with the regulation of foreign and interstate commerce, as we shall see, led to incessant quarrels and commercial retaliations among the States, and made it impossible to present a united front to foreign countries in respect to commerce. They levied duties upon imports and exports, each according to its own selfish views of its local interests, without any regard to the general welfare. Moreover, they shared with Congress the right of coining money, of emitting bills of credit, and of making their notes a legal tender in payment of debts.[8]

[8] McLaughlin, "The Confederation and the Constitution," pp. 48–52.

II

FAILURE OF THE CONFEDERATION

Such was the nature of the Confederation and the constitution of government under which the new nation entered upon its career of independence, and under which it was soon drifting toward dissolution. As has been well said, the Confederation was merely a league of friendship, while the government was so organized as to produce a minimum of result with a maximum of effort. But what was worse than all, the Articles could not be altered without the consent of every State — a fact which made its displacement possible only through revolutionary methods.[9] The new government had barely gone into operation before its inherent weaknesses were discovered. The first trouble came with the army, on account of the failure of Congress to fulfill its obligations to the poorly clad, half-starved soldiers. As early as 1778, yielding to the strong appeals of General Washington, Congress had voted half pay for life to the officers, and provision had been made for bounty lands for the men. During the ensuing years the measure for the payment of the officers was repealed, and as a result the army began to show signs of impatience and discontent. In January, 1781, before the Articles of Confederation had yet gone into effect, there had occurred an ugly mutiny of New Jersey and Pennsylvania troops, which for a time it was feared would prove serious.

Again, early in 1782, many of the officers became discouraged at the meager prospect of receiving their pay, and disgusted with the imbecility of Congress, began to entertain the idea, whether seriously or not it is difficult to ascertain, of making Washington king. One of the officers, Colonel Nicola, addressed a letter to the commander-in-chief, setting forth the almost anarchical condition of the country resulting from the weakness of Congress, and inviting him, in the name of the army, to come forward, assume dictatorship, and put an end to the troubles. But Washington repelled the suggestion as totally abhorrent to his sense of patriotism, and

[9] For an illuminating discussion of the Articles of Confederation and their inefficiency as a constitution of government, see George Ticknor Curtis, "Constitutional History," vol. i. chs. iv-vi., and Joseph Story, "Commentaries on the Constitution," vol. i. book iii. ch. iv. For a more popular account, see John Fiske, "The Critical Period," chs. iii.-iv.

one which he could not for an instant entertain.[10] The incident, although without result, was clearly symptomatic of the general discontent and confusion. A year later the dissatisfaction in the army came near resulting in a serious outbreak, which was only averted by the tact and firmness of Washington. An inflammatory address to the army having been issued by a disaffected officer at Newburgh, calling a meeting for the discussion of grievances and the formulation of a plan of action by which their rights could be secured — a plan which seems to have contemplated the intimidation or overthrow of Congress and the coercion of the delinquent States into the payment of their quotas, — Washington seized the initiative, attended the meeting and made an eloquent and sympathetic appeal to the soldiers to abstain from further action, and to continue their faith in Congress. His appeal was successful, the threatened outbreak was prevented, and a resolution of confidence in Congress was adopted by the officers. Washington thereupon appealed to Congress to make provision for the just payment of the officers, his advice was promptly followed, and an act was passed commuting half pay for life into a lump sum equal to five years' full pay to be paid at once in six per cent. certificates of indebtedness.

This tardy recognition and settlement of a long-standing claim did not, however, entirely end the troubles with the army. In June, 1783, two months after the virtual disbandment of the army, a band of mutinous soldiers, some of whom were drunk, while all were riotous and excited on account of the failure of Congress to treat them justly, marched to Philadelphia, surrounded the meeting place of Congress, taunted and insulted the members and threatened to seize them or make a raid upon the federal treasury if their demands were not answered favorably. Nothing showed more clearly the impotence of the government so far as its power to maintain peace and order was concerned than this disgraceful incident. Congress was powerless to disperse the disorderly mob or to arrest those who composed it, and accordingly an appeal was made to the State government of Pennsylvania for protection; but the governor of the State feared to call out the local militia lest they might take sides with the mutinous soldiers. In this situation Congress yielded to the intimidation of the rioters, fled from the city and took up its official residence at Princeton, safe from the jeers and insults of the drunken mutineers. To all thoughtful men the affair ap-

[10] Lodge, " George Washington," vol. i. pp. 337-338.

peared far more serious than ludicrous, for it revealed too plainly the weakness of the government and the disordered condition into which the country was drifting. Such a government neither merited nor could command respect at home or abroad.[11]

The government was likewise unable to fulfill its treaty obligations with foreign countries on account of the large autonomy left with the States. By the Treaty of 1783 with Great Britain, the United States had solemnly agreed to recommend to the State governments that they repeal all laws which had been enacted from time to time for the persecution of the Tories and the confiscation of their estates, and it was further stipulated that all debts due from Americans to British creditors should be discharged at their full value in sterling money, without the interposition of any lawful impediment upon the part of any State. In pursuance of the treaty Congress appealed to the States to desist from further persecution of the Tories, but the recommendation went unheeded. The hard lot of these unfortunate people has already been recounted in a previous chapter. It is sufficient to say here that many were banished from the country, others fled of their own accord, while still others remained and endured as best they could the hardships to which they were subjected. Besides disfranchisement, imprisonment and social ostracism, their estates were confiscated, and they were denied all means of recovering them. Upon the conclusion of peace, instead of milder treatment, the severity of the legislation against the Tories seemed to increase. Between 1783 and 1785 it was estimated that more than one hundred thousand left the United States, those in the northern States going mostly to Canada, while those from the south went to Florida and the British West Indies. Those who remained soon became the object of social persecution and victims of the most unfriendly legislation.[12]

One of the most noteworthy of these laws was the New York Trespass Act, by which all persons who had abandoned their homes on account of the presence of the British troops were empowered to recover damages in an action of trespass against such persons as took possession of the abandoned estates, and no military order could be pleaded in justification of the occupation. Nearly every

[11] McMaster, "History of the People of the United States," vol. i. pp. 181-185.

[12] See Fiske, "Critical Period of American History," chs. iii.-iv.; also Hart, "Formation of the Union," ch. v.; and McMaster, "History of the People of the United States," vol. i. ch. ii.

Whig owner whose house had been occupied by a Tory, however short the time, instituted an action of trespass for damages. As most of the estates on Manhattan Island had at one time or another during the Revolution been thus occupied, it may readily be seen what a state of confusion would have resulted from such a policy. Accordingly a test case was made up — the famous case of Rutgers v. Waddington, in which the constitutionality of the Trespass Act was tried.

In this case Elizabeth Rutgers sued Joshua Waddington, a Tory merchant, for trespassing upon her premises during the war, and although public sympathy was largely with the act, the court held that it contravened the provisions of the treaty with Great Britain, as well as the law of nations, and was therefore void. The case is further interesting from the fact that Alexander Hamilton, but a few years before a waif from the West Indies, but now a distinguished soldier, a rising statesman, and a powerful advocate, although only twenty-seven years of age, appeared as counsel for the Tory defendant. It was an unpopular act to defend a Tory, and Hamilton was roundly abused for his course, but he firmly believed that he was in the right, and he had the courage to follow his convictions.[13]

Gradually such evidences of bitter hatred of the Tories wore away; social ostracism became less general, and confiscating acts in most States were repealed. So far as the Tories were concerned Congress had complied with the letter of the treaty when it recommended to the States to cease their persecution; but with regard to the debts due British merchants, its obligations were not merely advisory. If unlawful impediments were placed in the way of the collection of the debts the United States could not rightfully plead that its power was only recommendatory, and yet, as a matter of fact, five of the thirteen States passed acts for the total or partial confiscation of the debts, the action of two of them taking place after the ratification of the treaty. Although the United States had stipulated that this should not be done, it was found impossible to prevent it, since Congress lacked the requisite power to enforce its treaty stipulations.

This failure of the United States to carry out its treaty stipulations left Great Britain to retaliate by refusing to fulfill her own

[13] McMaster, "History of the People of the United States," vol. i. pp. 125-127.

obligations, and for this reason she declined to withdraw the troops from certain posts on the northern and western frontiers which had been surrendered to the United States by the Treaty of 1783. In spite of this stipulation British garrisons continued to occupy the posts until 1796. Moreover, she refused to make compensation for the large number of slaves which had been carried away by the British fleet at the time of the evacuation. In justification of this conduct the British alleged that the negroes in question came into their lines and were presumed to be freemen and could not therefore be remanded to slavery.

Besides declining to carry out the provisions of the treaty, Great Britain took advantage of the weakness of the Union and the impotency of the government to refuse us much needed commercial privileges, and at the same time to interfere materially with American trade. By an order in council American built vessels were excluded from the West India trade — an act which seriously crippled a large and lucrative commence upon which thousands of American citizens depended for a livelihood. Great indignation was aroused in America, and loud threats of retaliation were made; but the British Government knew well that thirteen States could never be made to agree upon a common line of policy, as regards commercial regulations, while separate retaliation was out of the question. Great Britain, therefore, refused to modify her policy and declined to enter into a commercial treaty with the United States. In 1785 John Adams was sent over to England as our first minister to that country, and he labored in and out of season to negotiate a treaty, but without avail.[14]

Our participation in the Newfoundland fisheries was restricted, while American markets were flooded with British manufactured goods upon which the government had no power to levy import duties. Great Britain, of course, was not anxious to conclude a commercial treaty, since she enjoyed all the privileges which she desired without a treaty, and moreover taunted our government with being powerless to enforce its treaties, saying: " You are one nation to-day and thirteen to-morrow, according as one or the other best subserves your selfish interests." Unfortunately there was a large measure of truth in the taunt. Meantime Great Britain refused to send a minister to the United States, and treated the new nation as unworthy of having a diplomatic representative ac-

[14] Fiske, " Critical Period of American History," pp. 138-141.

credited to its government.[15]   Eventually some of the States were
induced to pass discriminating navigation acts against British commerce, imposing duties on imports brought in English ships, and
prohibiting English vessels from carrying goods out of their ports.
Other States, taking advantage of the opportunity to gain profit
thereby, threw their ports open to British ships and invited commercial intercourse, thus making it impossible for the country as a
whole to present a united front to Great Britain in respect to commercial retaliation.

What was needed to bring England to terms was, above all
things, a uniform navigation act; but this Congress had no power
to pass; nor would the States consent to invest it with such power.
In 1785 ten States yielded to the demand created by the deplorable
condition of affairs and granted to Congress the power to regulate
commerce with foreign nations for a period of thirteen years; but
Georgia, South Carolina and Delaware, fearing that if competition
were destroyed the New England States would obtain a monopoly
of the carrying trade and oppress the non-commercial States by
charging exorbitant transportation rates, refused to surrender their
power of regulating commerce.   As it required the unanimous consent of all the thirteen States to amend the Articles of Confederation, the scheme necessarily fell through, and the almost intolerable
condition of affairs continued unchanged until the adoption of the
Federal Constitution in 1789.   Trade and commerce were further
deranged by the petty wars of retaliation among the States themselves.   Imposts and tonnage duties were levied upon the ships
and produce of neighboring States as though they were foreign
nations, each trying to build up its own trade at the expense of its
neighbor; Pennsylvania levied a tax on produce from Delaware,
while New Jersey discriminated against by both New York and
Pennsylvania was compared by Madison to a cask tapped at both
ends.   Not content with levying a tariff on the produce of the Jersey
kitchen gardens, New York went to the length of taxing firewood
brought over from Connecticut.   Her central position gave her an
advantage in this respect over her less favored neighbors, and under
the influence and teachings of her States rights governor, George
Clinton, she pursued a narrow and selfish policy, scarcely equaled in

[15] See McLaughlin, "The Confederation and the Constitution," chs. v.-vi.;
Curtis, "Constitutional History of the United States," vol. i. ch. xi.; McMaster,
"History of the People of the United States," vol. i. ch. iii.

any of the other States.   But New Jersey, better favored than Connecticut in this respect, retaliated upon her more powerful neighbor by imposing an annual tax of $1,800 on the lighthouse which New York had recently erected at Sandy Hook within the jurisdiction of New Jersey.[16]

In such manner the States quarreled and disputed.   Pennsylvania and Connecticut wrangled over the title to the Wyoming Valley, and after the dispute was settled in 1782 by a special tribunal constituted in accordance with the Articles of Confederation the Connecticut settlers were so maltreated by the Pennsylvanians that for a time war between the two States seemed imminent.[17]   Likewise New Hampshire and New York nearly came to blows over the disputed territory of Vermont and long after a sort of *modus vivendi* had been patched up between the disputants the debatable territory was the scene of disorders at times approaching border warfare.   These incidents, although not the most disgraceful events of the time, afforded evidence, if such were needed, of the progress toward anarchy under the existing régime.

III

ON THE VERGE OF ANARCHY

Of far greater consequence were the financial and economic disorders of the time.   The national debt was over $50,000,000 and Congress could not raise the money to pay either principal or interest; indeed, it was impossible to raise enough to meet the current expenses of administration.   Each State had its own war debt, besides the burden of maintaining its own government.   The nation had not recovered from the desolating effects of the war, business was deranged and the people were poor.   The States, therefore, found it difficult to raise more than was needed for local purposes and Congress had to be content with what it could get.   Strong appeals were sent to the States from time to time, but the responses were few and the small amounts granted were grudgingly given.   Of the $5,000,000 quota assigned to the States for the year 1781, but little more than $400,000 had been paid into the Confederate

[16] Fiske, "Critical Period of American History," p. 147.
[17] McMaster, "History of the People of the United States," vol. i, pp. 210-216.

treasury at the end of the year, none of which came from Georgia, the Carolinas or Delaware. Of the amount assessed for 1783 scarcely any had been paid in by the end of the year. From 1781 to 1788 the total requisitions made upon the States amounted to about $16,000,000. Of this amount not more than $6,000,000 was paid into the treasury of the Confederation and but little more than half of this was specie. Some of the States flatly refused to contribute anything, and there was no way of compelling them to pay a dollar of their quotas.[18]

Ere the Articles of Confederation had gone into effect Congress had proposed an amendment empowering the national government to levy an import duty of five per cent. on goods entering the United States, the proceeds to be applied to the discharge of the principal and interest of the public debt. In the course of a year twelve States with more or less reluctance agreed to this reasonable amendment, but Rhode Island stood out in opposition and the plan failed. Again in 1783 the States were asked to allow Congress to levy certain specific duties on imports for a period of twenty-five years, and to obviate objections raised against the five per cent. scheme of 1781 the duties were to be collected by officers appointed by the States. The result was as before: twelve States agreed to the amendment, but one stood out and defeated it. Every attempt to amend and improve the Articles of Confederation resulted in failure, and the country drifted helplessly on toward chaos.[19]

As a consequence of the inability of Congress to raise money the public credit of the government was so low that a loan could not be effected. Few things are more pathetic in our history than the efforts of John Adams, minister to England, to raise money with which to meet the drafts upon him by the Superintendent of Finance. He first applied to the Dutch Government at Amsterdam, but being refused he appealed to some private money lenders, from whom, after a long delay, he succeeded in obtaining a small loan at a high rate of interest. It is no surprise that money lenders hesitated to trust a government which was neither respected at home nor abroad, and had no control over the sources from which its treasury was replenished. In these struggles to raise money and establish public credit, one man stands out above all others, and is entitled to the lasting gratitude of his countrymen. This was Robert Morris,

[18] See Story, "Commentaries on the Constitution," ch. v.
[19] Hart, "Formation of the Union," pp. 109-111.

a wealthy merchant and unselfish patriot of Philadelphia, who had come over from England when a boy, and who, as already stated, became Superintendent of Finance under the Confederation, and shortly thereafter established the Bank of North America as an agency for the negotiation of loans. For three years this patriotic man struggled hard to weather the storm, but in 1784 resigned his office to a board of finance, and be it said to the discredit of his ungrateful countrymen, he was many years afterwards, when he had failed in business, allowed to languish in a debtor's prison.[20]

The condition of finances and of business generally was largely affected by the economic vagaries of the time. It often happens in times of business depression that people are seized by a craze for cheap paper money, which they think is a panacea for all their troubles. This feeling prevailed during the period from 1783 to 1786, and it led to increased disorders and distress. In all the States, except Connecticut and Delaware, the paper money craze seized the popular mind, and in seven States believers in cheap money controlled the legislatures. In these States large quantities of paper currency were issued and all sorts of expedients were resorted to to get it into circulation at its face value, and to keep it on a par with specie. In spite of all efforts, however, it declined in value and the people refused to take it except at a discount. In some States ostracism and intimidation were resorted to in order to compel its acceptance, and in others laws were passed for the punishment of those who discriminated against it. But it was soon discovered that no amount of intimidation and no form of legislation could force people to accept notes at more than their real value.[21]

Hand in hand with its depreciation business declined and the distress of the people increased. As always happens in such times, speculators arose to take advantage of the situation. Loss of confidence followed, trade declined, debts increased and general business demoralization prevailed. Of all the States that were affected by the paper currency Rhode Island and Massachusetts suffered most. Here, indeed, it wrought havoc, and in Massachusetts led to a dangerous insurrection. In Rhode Island the advocates of paper money secured control of the legislature, and an act was passed requiring everyone to accept paper at par with gold under

[20] Oberholtzer, "Robert Morris, Patriot and Financier," pp. 348–454.
[21] McMaster, "History of the People of the United States," vol. i. pp. 281–304; Fiske, "Critical Period," pp. 168–180.

penalty of a fine of five hundred dollars and disfranchisement.
The merchants thereupon closed their shops, and by 1786 business was paralyzed. The farmers, indignant at the action of the
merchants, undertook to starve them into submission, and either
sent their produce to New York and Connecticut or destroyed it.
Indignation meetings were held throughout the State, and riots
occurred in a number of places. Finally, like the Trespass Act
in New York, the act to enforce the acceptance of the unlimited
issuance of paper money was resisted in the courts and declared unconstitutional. This was the decision of the Supreme
Court of Rhode Island in the noted case of Trevett v. Weeden, in
which a butcher refused to accept paper money in payment for
meat except at a large discount and was sued for violation of the
act. The trial was attended by great excitement, and after the
verdict was announced a special session of the legislature was
called and four of the judges who had opposed the law failed of
reëlection to the bench. This case deserves to be remembered
further as one of the very first instances in which the courts
enunciated that peculiar doctrine of American jurisprudence that
the judges are not bound by statutes which conflict with the constitution. Presently the Force Act was repealed, but not until
after a great deal of harm had been done and the State had won
the unenviable distinction of being a land of vagaries and the
nickname of " Rogue's Island." [22]

In Massachusetts the paper currency advocates did not succeed
in getting control of the legislature, but the business depression
and distress were so great that an insurrection broke out which it
taxed the resources of the State to suppress. Private debts in
the State increased enormously, farms were mortgaged, taxes were
high, and thousands were thrown out of employment. The distress was especially great among the farmers, who were led to at-
tribute the source of their troubles to the merchants and lawyers.
A sentiment in favor of wiping out all debts was developed, and
a movement set on foot for the issue of a paper currency. The
legislature refused to enact a law for this purpose and then an
outburst of popular wrath followed, under the leadership of one
Daniel Shays, an old captain in the Continental army. The malcontents undertook to prevent the courts from sitting, and went

[22] McMaster, "History of the People of the United States," vol. i. pp.
330-338.

on to destroy public and private property and to plunder houses. Governor Bowdoin acted promptly and energetically, called out the militia, placed it under the command of General Lincoln, and after several skirmishes, in which a few lives were lost, the re-

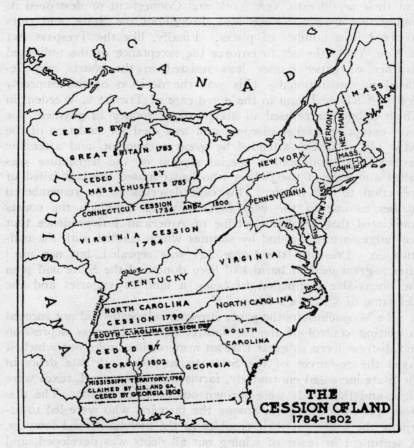

THE CESSION OF LAND 1784-1802

bellion was put down. Fourteen of the leaders were convicted of treason and sentenced to death, but were subsequently pardoned by Governor Hancock. It is to be noted that in all these disturbances, which extended to Vermont and New Hampshire as well, the government of the Confederation was too weak to interfere. At one time a requisition was made for troops to check the anticipated spread of the disorders, but Congress was too timid to disclose the real purpose for which the call was made, declaring that the troops were wanted for an expedition against the western Indians.[23]

Almost the last, and by far the most important, piece of legislation enacted by Congress under the Confederation, was the ordinance of 1787 for the government of the territory northwest of the Ohio River. This territory had been claimed by the States lying directly to the east, and, as we have seen, had been ceded to the United States to overcome the objections urged by Maryland to the adoption of the Articles of Confederation. The territory ceded by Massachusetts constituted a considerable portion of what is now Wisconsin and the lower part of Michigan. That ceded by Connecticut consisted of a long, narrow strip extending across Northern Ohio, Indiana and Illinois to the Mississippi River. The claims of both these States rested on grants of their old charters. New York claimed a vast undefined area in the west on the ground of cession from the Iroquois Indians, who had asserted jurisdiction over it, and who had placed themselves under the protection of New York. The largest cession was that of Virginia, whose title was based on an early charter and also on the conquest of George Rogers Clark, a citizen of the State, who, acting on its behalf, conquered the territory from the British during the Revolution.

The surrender by the State of this magnificent domain for the common benefit of the nation — a domain to which Virginia had a clear title, has been pronounced by a great American historian as an act of splendid magnanimity. It certainly was an act of large patriotism and far-seeing wisdom, deserving of the highest praise. Maryland's persistence in forcing the cession of these western lands is deserving of scarcely less commendation. A measure of approbation should also be accorded New York, which set the ball in motion by offering, early in 1780, to cede her lands. Congress hastened the movement by pledging itself that the proceeds from the sale of the land should be applied to national purposes, and that as soon as practicable the territory should be formed into distinct republican States to be admitted to the Union on an equality with the original States. Then Connecticut agreed

[23] See an article by J. P. Warren, *American Historical Review*, vol. xi. p. 42.

to cede; Virginia followed in January, 1781, and finally Massachusetts surrendered her claim in April, 1784. In ceding their claims both Connecticut and Virginia reserved certain lands for the use of their own citizens; Connecticut retaining some 3,000,000 acres for school purposes in the northern part of what is now Ohio, and still known as the "Western Reserve." Virginia retained a tract in the southern portion of the State, as bounty lands for her Revolutionary veterans.[24] It is not easy to over-estimate the influence of these cessions on the future development of the United States. They made possible the completion of the Union under the Articles of Confederation, and led eventually to the creation of five powerful States — Ohio, Indiana, Illinois, Michigan and Wisconsin.

Shortly after the completion of the cession Congress took up the matter of providing a government for the Northwest Territory. Thomas Jefferson, a member from Virginia, who was to be largely instrumental at a later period in the territorial expansion of the United States, submitted a plan for the government of the entire Territory, which was adopted, but which never went into effect. Jefferson proposed to divide the Territory into ten States bearing the names Sylvania, Michigania, Chersonesus, Assenisipia, Metropotamia, Illinoia, Saratoga, Washingtonia, Polypotamia and Pelesipia. In each State the inhabitants were to be permitted to establish local governments under the direction of Congress, and when the population of any State should equal any one of the original States, it should be admitted to the Union with the consent of nine States. Jefferson also proposed that slavery should be forever prohibited there, after the year 1800, but this suggestion was not adopted.

Meanwhile, by the efforts of General Rufus Putnam, the Ohio Company had been organized, and under its auspices Marietta, a flourishing settlement, was growing up on the Ohio River. The movement of population in that direction made it highly necessary that provision be made for the government of the Territory, and this was brought about by the celebrated ordinance of 1787, pronounced by Daniel Webster to have been one of the most notable pieces of legislation in its effects in ancient or modern times. The authorship of the ordinance is disputed, but it was probably the work of Rufus Putnam and Manasseh Cutler, supported in Con-

[24] See Hinsdale, "The Old Northwest," chs. xii., xiii.

gress by Nathan Dane of Massachusetts, and also contained some
of the ideas embodied in Jefferson's proposed ordinance of 1784,
but happily abandoned his names.[25]

It provided a constitution of government and a bill of rights
for the inhabitants. Not less than three nor more than five States
were to be formed from the Territory, and when any one of
these should have a population of 60,000 inhabitants it was to be
admitted to the Union on an equality with the original States.
Until then the Territory was to be governed by officials appointed
by Congress. These were to be a governor, a secretary, and
three judges; the governor and judges being empowered to adopt
such laws in force in the old States as were suitable for the government of the Territory. As soon as the population should
reach 5,000 a representative legislature, chosen by a limited suffrage was to be introduced. Freedom of religious worship
was to be allowed and no religious qualification for office was
to be required. The right of trial by jury and the privilege of the
writ of *habeas corpus* were to be a part of the jurisprudence of the
Territory. The future policy of the Northwest was well summed
up in the phrase that "religion, morality and knowledge being
necessary to good government and the happiness of mankind,
schools and the means of education shall be forever encouraged."
But the most important provision of the ordinance was that which
declared that neither slavery nor involuntary servitude, except as
a punishment for crime, should be permitted.[26] This dedicated the
great Northwest unreservedly to freedom and thus affected immeasurably the future history of the nation. It is worthy of note
that this clause was unanimously adopted by Congress, nine States
being represented, the southern members favoring it quite as
much as those from the northern States. The scheme of government was put in operation by the appointment of a Revolutionary
veteran, General Arthur St. Clair, as the first governor. The land
was surveyed and offered for sale at a nominal price; immigrants
flocked to the Territory, and within a decade and a half a new
State, Ohio, the first of the five, was carved from the Northwest
Territory and admitted to the Union.

In the meantime, under the Articles of Confederation, the country was showing increased signs of disintegration. As a consti-

[25] Hinsdale, "Old Northwest," ch. xv.
[26] Preston, "Documents Illustrative of American History," p. 240.

tution of government the Articles had proved well-nigh a failure, notwithstanding the fact that under their authority Congress had performed some conspicuous services for the nation. It had concluded a treaty of peace with Great Britain; it had negotiated treaties with the Netherlands, Sweden, Prussia and Morocco; it had established our system of decimal currency; it had acquired the Northwest Territory for the nation, and had provided a constitution of government and a bill of rights therefor; it had in a most imperfect way supplied the need of a general government during the formative period of the Republic. Whatever we may say of its defects, its weaknesses and its failures, it was better than no government at all, for it maintained some sort of relation between the States and so kept alive the idea of union and of common action. But this was all. The course of events had now reached a point where a more perfect union with a more efficient government must be devised, put in operation, and made to work, unless the Revolution was to prove a failure and the country was to sink into anarchy and the disorders of jarring States, only to become the prey of some European power.

Chapter XIV

ESTABLISHMENT OF THE REPUBLIC. 1785-1789

I

ORIGIN OF THE PHILADELPHIA CONVENTION

THE events of the year 1786-1787 settled conclusively the fate of the Confederation. All the disorders and troubles described in the preceding chapter, and others besides, seem to have culminated at this time. Shay's rebellion, the rejection of the proposed amendment to the Articles of Confederation, the paper money craze, the disorders in Vermont and New Hampshire, the dispute with Spain concerning the navigation of the Mississippi River, and the trouble with the Barbary powers, all occurred during this period and afforded abundant proof, if proof were necessary, that the nation was in danger of utter disintegration for lack of a more perfect union and a more efficient government. The three attempts to amend the existing constitution had all resulted in failures, and many began to despair of escape from its evils except by armed revolution.

The train of events which led up to the calling of a national convention and the adoption of a new constitution had its origin in the disorders occasioned by the lack of uniform commercial arrangements, resulting from the power of the individual States to regulate commerce among themselves and with foreign nations. It began with a conference of commissioners representing the States of Maryland and Virginia, which was called to meet at Mount Vernon in 1785 for the purpose of discussing a common commercial policy with regard to the navigation of the Potomac. In the course of the deliberations it was suggested that other States, particularly Pennsylvania, were interested in the navigation of the Potomac, and should, therefore, be invited to participate in any discussion looking to the framing of regulations for that purpose. Acting upon this suggestion James Madison induced the legislature of Virginia to invite commissioners from all the States to meet at

Annapolis, Maryland, on the first Monday in September, 1786, to discuss a uniform system of legislation with regard to interstate commerce. The convention was duly called, and met September 11, but the attendance of delegates was so small that it was decided not to enter upon a discussion of the purposes for which the meeting had been called. No delegates appeared from any State east of New York, or from any State south of Virginia. Massachusetts, New Hampshire, Rhode Island and North Carolina appointed delegates, but they did not attend; while no action was taken by Maryland, Georgia, South Carolina and Connecticut.[1]

But the opportunity which the convention afforded, small as it was, could not be allowed to go unimproved; and, accordingly, before adjourning, an address prepared by Alexander Hamilton, one of the delegates from New York, was adopted after a lengthy discussion, and sent to the people. The address urged the appointment by all the States of delegates to a convention to be held at Philadelphia on the second Monday in May, 1787, empowered " to devise such further provisions as shall appear to them necessary to render the Constitution of the federal government adequate to the exigencies of the Union, and to report to Congress such an act as when agreed to by them and confirmed by the legislature of every State would effectually provide for the same." This was striking at the root of the difficulty. No mere trade convention was to be called, but a constituent assembly, authorized to remodel the Articles of Confederation, and to endow Congress with more effective powers; and yet the requirement that the approval of every State should be necessary for the change presented the same old obstacle which had already defeated amendment on three previous occasions.

At first Congress refused to approve of the proposed convention; but the rejection of the impost amendment by New York, together with other events occurring at this time, showing the inadequacy of the existing system, caused a change of sentiment which led that body to give its endorsement to the movement and to issue the call in February, 1787. The decision of Congress was doubtless hastened by the action of the States, which from the first took a lively interest in the proposed convention. Before Congress had given its approval, in fact, Virginia, New Jersey, Pennsylvania, North Carolina and Delaware had chosen their dele-

[1] Gay, "James Madison," pp. 52–60.

gates, among them many of the most distinguished men of the country. This gave prestige to the project, and immediately following the recommendation of Congress, Massachusetts, New York, Georgia, South Carolina, Connecticut, Maryland and New Hampshire fell in line and chose their delegates. Of the thirteen States Rhode Island alone refused to appoint delegates or to take any part in the convention. Ever since the Revolution that State had pursued a narrow and selfish policy, and it was, therefore, no surprise when it was announced that she would take no part in the movement which had for its purpose the revision of the Articles of Confederation. Under the existing arrangement Rhode Island was free to profit by her favored geographical position by collecting duties on trade coming into her ports, whether from abroad or from the neighboring States, and she naturally, therefore, preferred not to surrender such advantages even for the common good of all the States.[2]

The convention met May 25, 1787, in the old State House at Philadelphia, a building already famous as the place where the Continental Congress had many times assembled, and where the Declaration of Independence had been adopted and published to the world. It was by far the most distinguished assembly which America had ever seen, and with a few exceptions included all the great characters of the country who enjoyed anything like national reputations. Seven of them had signed the Declaration of Independence and four had signed the Articles of Confederation. Nearly all had had legislative experience, either in Congress or in the State legislatures, while some had distinguished themselves on the bench or in the army.

Altogether there were fifty-five delegates present, while eighteen others who had been chosen did not attend. More than half of them were graduates of universities, including Harvard, Yale, Columbia, Princeton, William and Mary, Oxford, Glasgow and Edinburgh. The most illustrious delegates, neither man of university training, were Washington and Franklin, the latter being then in his eighty-first year, and the oldest member of the convention. Other delegates, whose names are both famous and familiar, were Elbridge Gerry and Rufus King of Massachusetts, the one a future Vice President, the other a leading senator; Roger

[2] McMaster, "History of the People of the United States," vol. i. pp. 390–399.

Sherman and Oliver Ellsworth of Connecticut, the latter a future
chief justice of the Supreme Court; Alexander Hamilton of New
York, one of the youngest members, destined to a brilliant though
short career; James Wilson, Gouverneur Morris and Robert Morris of Pennsylvania, the first mentioned a learned jurist and future
justice of the Supreme Court, the two latter, future senators in
Congress; James Madison of Virginia, the "father of the Constitution," a future President, destined to outlive all his confrères
of the convention; and John Rutledge and Charles C. Pinckney of
South Carolina.

Of the distinguished Americans who were not members of the
convention, John Adams and Thomas Jefferson were both ministers
abroad, while Samuel Adams, John Hancock, Patrick Henry and
Richard Henry Lee opposed the convention and refused to serve
as delegates. John Jay, another able and distinguished man, was
left at home because his State, New York, not being in sympathy
with the purposes of the convention, preferred a commonplace delegation and accordingly chose two narrow States' rights men to
offset the influence of Hamilton. This fact, together with Hamilton's well-known leanings towards the British form of government, prevented him from exerting the full influence which his
brilliant talents would otherwise have made possible. The convention organized by electing George Washington as president;
the doors were then closed to outsiders, and the work of making
a new Constitution began. It was foreseen that the deliberations
of the convention would be marked by dissension and strife, and
it was believed that the ratification of their work would be most
likely assured if it were presented to the people as the unanimous
product of the convention. The delegates were, therefore, put under a pledge of secrecy, and had it not been for the industry and
foresight of Madison, who kept a journal of the daily happenings,
which was published some fifty years later, we should know very
little of the proceedings of that famous assembly.[3]

II

FRAMING THE CONSTITUTION

Upon the completion of the organization several "plans" were
brought in by individuals or State delegations, and these served

[3] Curtis, "Constitutional History of the United States," vol. i. ch. xvi.;
Fiske, "Critical Period," ch. vi.

to furnish a basis for discussion and at the same time led to the grouping of the delegates into several indistinct parties. The first of these projects was that known as the "Virginia plan," introduced by Governor Randolph as the spokesman of the Virginia delegation. One of the resolutions declared "that a national government ought to be established, consisting of a supreme legislature, executive and judiciary." One of the main defects of the government under the Articles of Confederation was that it was not national; it rested upon the States rather than upon individuals. Furthermore, there was no supreme executive or judiciary. The Virginia plan proposed to go further than a mere revision of the Articles; it contemplated an entirely new scheme of government involving a substantial limitation upon the autonomy of the States and a corresponding enlargement of the powers of the national government. It proposed to create a Congress of two houses, modeled after the organization of the State legislatures (except in Georgia and Pennsylvania, where single chambered legislative bodies existed) and in both the votes were to be by individuals and not by States, as under the Articles of Confederation. The States were to be represented in the Congress in proportion to their population, so that the large State of Virginia would have sixteen representatives, whereas Georgia would have but one. The executive authority, whether vested in one or several persons, was to be chosen by the Congress, and the judiciary was to be given power to determine questions arising under the Constitution and laws of the United States, and to settle disputes between the States.[4]

This radical scheme created strong opposition among the delegates from the small States, who saw in it the destruction of the Congressional equality which they had hitherto enjoyed with the large States, and the curtailment of some of their powers of sovereignty, for the benefit of the Union. They denied that the convention had any power to go further than a mere revision of the Articles of Confederation. It was well known, they said, that Congress in issuing the call for the convention had declared that it was for the "sole and express purpose of revising the Articles of Confederation," while the credentials of the delegations of most of the States restricted their action in the same way. The

[4] McMaster, "History of the People of the United States," vol. i. pp. 439-444.

Articles of Confederation, they maintained, did not need to be rejected *in toto;* in principle they were good enough and only needed revision along certain lines where experience had shown them to be defective. The views of this party were formulated in the "New Jersey plan," submitted by William Patterson, one of the delegates from that State. This plan proposed to amend the Articles so as to provide for a national judiciary and executive, while retaining the unicameral Congress, but increasing its powers, notably with regard to taxation and commerce. But the old theory of the relation between the States and the central government was to be retained; the national government was to continue to act upon the States rather than upon the people, and worst of all, the old principle of equality of representation in Congress was to be retained. The most that can be said for the New Jersey plan was that it was but a halfway measure. In general it was favored by the delegates from Connecticut, New York, Delaware and Maryland, and opposed by those from Massachusetts, Pennsylvania, Virginia, North Carolina, South Carolina and Georgia. A long and at times heated debate between the advocates of the two plans followed, and occasionally it appeared as if the convention would be compelled to break up without having attained any result. Some of the delegates from the small States indulged in threats of disunion, Bedford, of Delaware, declaring that if their rights could not be secured there were foreign powers ready to take them by the hand.[5] On one occasion, when the situation was at its worst and further progress seemed impossible, the venerable Franklin rose in his seat and suggested that the temper of the convention might be improved by opening the morning sessions with prayer; but his motion did not meet with favor, for the reason that it might arouse the suspicions of the public as to what was happening behind the doors.

The rock upon which the convention came near splitting was the question of representation. The group of delegates representing the larger States won its first victory when it was decided that the Congress should consist of two houses instead of one. This party then insisted that the States should be represented in both houses in proportion to population, while the smaller States contended with the same insistence for equal representation in both. "There is no more reason," said a delegate from one of the smaller

[5] Fiske, "Critical Period," p. 250.

States, " why a large State should have more votes in the legislature than that a large man should have more votes than a small one." Without equality of representation, the smaller States would be tyrannized over by the larger ones; it was their only weapon of defense. On the other hand, Madison, Wilson, King and others pointed out with convincing logic the injustice of allowing one State with a population sixteen times as large as that of its neighbor no more representatives in the national legislature. For a long time both parties held out, but finally the convention came to the scheme proposed by Sherman and Ellsworth, by which the representation was to be popular in the lower branch and by States in the upper. Known as the Connecticut Compromise, this famous arrangement saved the convention from dissolution and made the Constitution a possibility and a success. Thus it was agreed that each State should have two senators in the upper branch and one representative in the lower house for every 30,000 of its population. As an illustration of the practical operation of the rule of apportionment today it may not be out of place to note that while the States of New York and Nevada, with populations of 7,000,000 and 42,000 respectively, have equal representation in the Senate, New York's representation in the lower house is thirty-seven times as great as that of Nevada.[6]

This, the greatest of the compromises of the Constitution, was adopted on July 16 by the close vote of five to four. Although it disposed of the greatest obstacle to the further progress of the convention, it by no means insured smooth sailing to the end. As soon as it was determined that representation in the lower house should be apportioned according to the basis of population, it became necessary to determine who constituted the population. Unfortunately this led to a differentation of parties along sectional lines, and gave rise to the discussion of slavery. It was no longer a contest between large and small States, but between slave States and free States. On this question the delegates from the southern States insisted that both the slave and free population should be counted in determining the basis of apportionment. They said, what was perfectly true, that the slaves were a part of the population, and contributed largely to the economic development of the country. To this the northern delegates replied that the slaves were, in the eye of the law, mere chattels, and as they were denied

[6] Curtis, " Constitutional History of the United States," vol. i. chs. xii.–xiii.

the right of suffrage it would vastly increase the weight of the south in the councils of the nation in proportion to the voting population if it were allowed representation for the slaves. If, said, a northern delegate, negroes are not represented in the States to which they belong, why should they be represented in the general government. On this point Gouverneur Morris declared, " I would sooner submit myself to a tax for paying for all the negroes in the United States than saddle posterity with such a Constitution." But the good sense of the delegates prevailed, and a way of settling the dispute by compromise was found, as in the case of the controversy between the large and the small States over the basis of representation.

The question had come up in 1783 when Congress was endeavoring to find an equitable basis for the apportionment of the revenue quotas among the States. The southern States then objected to the counting of the slaves in determining the basis of apportionment, since it would increase their quotas. On the other hand, the north favored counting the slaves. As a compromise, Madison had suggested that for the purpose of apportioning taxes five slaves should be counted as three free men, and the suggestion met with favor. It was now proposed to employ the same illogical method for settling the dispute with regard to representation, and it was adopted. According to this provision, in determining the population for the apportionment of direct federal taxes and representation in the lower house of Congress, but three-fifths of the slaves were to be counted. By counting part of the slave population the south got a corresponding increase of representatives but suffered the disadvantage of an increase of direct taxes. But as the imposition of direct taxes has been rarely resorted to, while the south continued to enjoy the increased representation as long as slavery existed, the advantage was greater than the disadvantage. The operation of this rule afterwards became the subject of complaint in the north, since it resulted in almost doubling the representation of some of the southern States in Congress, in proportion to their voting population. But it is clear that without it the Constitution could not have been adopted; it was the best solution attainable under the then existing circumstances.

The third great compromise was also of a sectional character and related to the foreign slave trade. The States of South Carolina and Georgia refused to consent to a prohibition of the importation of slaves, although the other southern States were in favor of stopping further importation. The northern States were also anxious to confer upon Congress power to regulate foreign and interstate commerce, the sad experience under the Articles of Confederation admonishing them that such power could not be left safely with the States. But here again the southern States were at issue with those of the north. None of them favored vesting Congress with control over commerce, for fear the New England States might, by a simple majority of Congress, secure a monopoly of the carrying trade and then oppress the south by charging high transportation rates. Here, again, were the materials for a compromise, and a bargain was accordingly struck by which it was agreed that Congress should have no power to prohibit the importation of slaves prior to the year 1808, during which time the southern planters would have an opportunity to stock their plantations with an adequate supply of negroes. In return for this concession the southern States consented to invest Congress with the power to regulate foreign and interstate commerce.[7] It is worthy of note that this compromise was carried through against the strong opposition of Virginia, one of whose delegates, Mason, denounced the slave trade as an " infernal traffic," while the State as a whole opposed the investment of Congress with the absolute power over commerce. This compromise has been criticised as an undue concession to slavery but it secured the adhesion of South Carolina and Georgia, without which the adoption of the Constitution would have been doubtful, if not impossible. It is certain that the settlement by compromise, however open to criticism and objection, of these three great questions which divided the northern and southern States and the large and small States, insured the adoption of the Constitution.[8]

The most difficult work of the convention was thus accomplished and what remained was comparatively easy of settlement. But it must not be overlooked that there were many other minor antagonisms, and consequently many other compromises of less note than the three mentioned above. In fact, the Constitution is an instrument of compromises, like all the great legislative work of the English-speaking people; is perhaps the most notable instance in history of what a judicious spirit of compromise can effect. Moreover, just as the Constitution is an instrument of compromises,

[7] Fiske, " Critical Period," p. 262.
[8] Curtis, " Constitutional History of the United States," vol. i. ch. xxvi.

so is it an admirable example of judicious selection and adaptation of materials already at hand. The mistake is frequently made of eulogizing the Constitution as if it were solely or primarily an original creation; one of its admirers, William E. Gladstone, going so far as to say that it was the greatest piece of work ever struck off at one time by the brain and purpose of man. But the fact is, there is little absolutely new matter in the Constitution, and on the other hand there is much that is as old as Magna Charta.

Political institutions are not the result of invention, but of growth, adaptation and combination. The framers of our Constitution realized this and did not, therefore, commit the French error of attempting to break with the past, but followed the teachings of British and colonial experience wherever practicable. Many of the delegates had helped to frame the State constitutions under which they lived; and all were familiar with the practical working of these, as well as of the British Constitution. Many, if not most, of the institutions of government under which we live, therefore, have their prototype in the colonial and British constitutions, and experience shows that in the few instances where the framers of the Federal Constitution broke away from the past and attempted to create new institutions which did not have the sanction of long usage, the Constitution has proved least successful in practice. This is well shown in the working of the electoral machinery created for the choice of the President — a device which has totally failed to meet the expectations of the framers.[9] Other sources of the Constitution were the English common law and the writings of Blackstone, Montesquieu and Locke, while the "Social Contract" of Rousseau was not without its influence upon American thought then turned almost exclusively to questions of government. Blackstone was the most noted expounder of the English Constitution, and his commentaries were widely read and studied in America, while Montesquieu was the ablest political writer of the time, and his theory of the separation of legislative, executive and judicial powers unquestionably had a large influence in determining the broad outlines of the national government.[10] The influence of Dutch institutions probably amounted to something, but it was not considerable.

[9] Bryce, "The American Commonwealth," abridged edition, ch. ii.
[10] See Merriam, "American Political Theories," ch. ii.; also Stevens, "The Sources of the Constitution."

The most purely original part of the convention's work was naturally the formulation and apportionment of the powers of government between the national authority on one hand and the States on the other. Profiting by the experience of the Confederation, the majority of the convention were in favor of investing the national government with more adequate powers. It was therefore given the sole and exclusive right to coin money, fix the standard of weights and measures, establish post offices and post roads, grant patents and copyrights, raise and support armies, maintain a navy, declare war, grant letters of marque and reprisal, suppress insurrection, repel invasion, regulate foreign and interstate commerce, maintain diplomatic relations with foreign nations, control naturalization and bankruptcy, borrow money on the credit of the United States, etc. Certainly these were powers which experience had taught could not be safely left with the States, while subsequent history has abundantly justified the wisdom of vesting them in the national government. Realizing the impossibility of expressly enumerating all the powers of Congress, the convention finally inserted a sort of sweeping clause which empowers Congress to make all laws which shall be necessary and proper for carrying into execution the enumerated powers. Under this clause has been built up the doctrine of implied powers which has developed such an important branch of our constitutional law.

On the other hand Congress was expressly prohibited from suspending the privilege of the writ of *habeas corpus* except in time of rebellion or invasion, from passing bills of attainder and *ex post facto* laws, from laying duties on articles exported from any State, from discriminating in favor of any port in respect to commercial regulations, from granting titles of nobility, etc. It was also deemed wise to place certain limitations upon the power of the States in the interest of the general welfare. They were accordingly forbidden to enter into treaties or alliances, grant letters of marque and reprisal, coin money, emit bills of credit, make anything but gold or silver a legal tender in payment of debts, a provision suggested by the paper money craze in the States, pass bills of attainder, *ex post facto* laws, or laws impairing the obligation of contracts, or grant titles of nobility. They were also forbidden to exercise certain other powers, notably the levying of duties on imports or exports and the keeping of troops or ships of war in time of peace, except with the consent of Congress. The theory underlying the relations between the national government and the States was that the powers of the former should be enumerated, while all others except those prohibited should be left to the States. That is to say, the States have reserved or residuary powers, while the national government is one of enumerated powers. But it is a mistake to assume, as is sometimes done, that the United States was made supreme over the States. The truth is, the Constitution marked out a sphere for each, and each is supreme within that sphere. Thus each individual is subject to two jurisdictions and two sets of authorities, and even has two allegiances, and while the Federal Constitution and laws are declared to be the supreme law of the land, it must not be understood that the supremacy of national law affects the action of the States in the sphere reserved to them. They are subordinate only in the extent of their jurisdiction. Their powers seem insignificant as compared with those of the United States merely because the latter are enumerated. They include, as a matter of fact, the whole domain of civil and religious liberty, education, suffrage, marriage, divorce, domestic relations, contracts, business, property, trade, and, for the most part, the administration of the criminal law. Their powers are impossible of enumeration; to detail them would be to catalogue all social and business relationships, to examine all the foundations of law and order.[11]

As already noted, the Congress was made to consist of two houses — a Senate and a House of Representatives, the Senate to consist of two senators from each State, chosen by the legislatures thereof for a term of six years, the House of Representatives to be composed of members chosen by popular vote for a term of two years. Congress was required to assemble at least once in every year, and each chamber was to be the judge of the elections and qualifications of its own members. The executive power was vested in a President to be chosen for a term of four years by electors from each State. Each State was to choose as many electors as it had senators and representatives in Congress; these were to meet at the State capital, cast their ballots and transmit the same to the president of the Senate, Congress to serve as a canvassing board. Eligibility to the office was restricted to natural-born citizens, and provision was made for a Vice President, to be chosen in the same

[11] Wilson, "The State," p. 487.

manner and at the same time, to succeed the President in case of death, resignation, removal or inability to discharge the duties of the office.[12] Among the duties of the President were the command of the army and navy, the granting of reprieves and pardons for offenses against the United States, except in cases of impeachment, the negotiation of treaties with the advice and consent of two-thirds of the Senate, the appointment of officers of the United States, the furnishing of Congress with information regarding the state of the Union, the recommendation of legislative measures, the calling of Congress in extraordinary session, the reception of ambassadors and ministers from foreign countries, and the execution of the laws.

The judicial power was to be vested in a Supreme Court, and such inferior courts as Congress might establish. It was made to include all cases arising under the Constitution and laws of the United States and all treaties made in pursuance thereof; all cases affecting diplomatic agents; all cases of admiralty and maritime jurisdiction; all cases in which the United States or a State is a party, and a few others. The objection to allowing State courts jurisdiction in such cases is obvious, and the lack of a national judiciary to take cognizance of such matters under the Confederation was one of the defects of the old scheme of government. Hardly any feature of the Constitution has given so great satisfaction as the national judiciary, and the Supreme Court in particular has been the admiration of students of political science throughout the civilized world. Such is a brief outline of the constitution of government on which the convention labored long and assiduously throughout the summer of 1787. From May 25 to September 17 its great work slowly assumed shape, and on the latter date the result was ready for submission to the people.[13]

During the course of the long summer many members of the convention had despaired of ever reaching on agreement, but there were enough, like Randolph, who were ready, as he said, to bury their bones in Philadelphia before breaking up without performing the task for which they had been called together. Their determination and faith were at last rewarded. The great document was

[12] Citizens of the United States at the time of the adoption of the new Constitution were also declared eligible to the office of President.

[13] McMaster, "History of the People of the United States," vol. i. pp. 440–452.

finished and placed in the hands of Gouverneur Morris, an adept in the use of grammar and rhetoric, for final draft. In his skillful hand it was freed from redundant phrases and ambiguous expressions, and in this form was signed by the delegates. Of the fifty-five members, thirty-nine attached their signatures. Four members, Luther Martin of Maryland, George Mason and Edmund Randolph of Virginia, and Elbridge Gerry of Massachusetts, were dissatisfied and refused to sign. The other delegates whose signatures are not attached were not present at the time of the signing. Before adjournment it was agreed to send the Constitution to the Congress of the Confederation, inasmuch as the resolution of February 1, 1787, which summoned the convention, had declared that it should report to Congress. It was further agreed that the Congress should transmit the document unchanged to the State legislatures; that these in turn were to submit it to conventions in their respective States for ratification; and when nine States should have given their approval it should go into operation between the States so ratifying. It should be noted that this latter provision was in conflict with the amending clause of the Articles of Confederation, which declared that no amendment to that instrument should be made without the unanimous consent of the thirteen States. This provision was now disregarded, the Articles totally set aside, and the approval of but nine States was required. This stamps the Constitution of the United States as revolutionary, for it was ratified by a process unknown to the existing fundamental law. But if ever revolutionary procedure was justified, it was now; experience had shown that it was impossible to amend the Articles according to the methods therein prescribed; continued progress and tranquillity under them were out of the question.

III

THE CONSTITUTION RATIFIED

The day after the adjournment of the convention the new Constitution was laid before the legislature of Pennsylvania, but it was thought improper by that body to take action until Congress should give its approval. A few days later it was laid before Congress and at once the opposition began, under the leadership of Richard Henry Lee of Virginia, Nathan Dane of Massachusetts, and the members from New York. Every objection which the mind of man could conceive was raised against the new instrument, but the sound arguments of Madison and others prevailed, and, after more than a week's discussion, it was agreed to submit the document to the States for ratification or rejection.[14] A great issue was now before the people, and the division into parties followed. Those who favored ratification came to be known as " Federalists "; those opposed as " Anti-Federalists." A war of pamphlets and essays in the newspapers ensued, the most notable of which became famous as the " Federalist," a collection of papers written by Hamilton, Madison and Jay, and originally published in the *Independent Gazeteer,* over the signature of " Publius." There were eighty-five numbers, of which Hamilton probably wrote fifty-five, Madison fourteen, Jay five, Hamilton and Madison three jointly, leaving ten which were written either by Hamilton or Madison, with the probabilities in favor of the former's authorship. These essays were devoted to explaining the different parts of the Constitution, and to setting forth the arguments in favor of ratification. It is the most valuable contemporary commentary on the Constitution which we have, and indeed one of the greatest political treatises in the history of the world. It was widely circulated and largely read, and perhaps accomplished more than any other single agency toward insuring the popular ratification of the Constitution.[15]

In the meantime the contest in Pennsylvania was raging; every conceivable objection was raised, and all sorts of obstructive tactics were employed by the opposition to bring about the rejection of the Constitution. In the course of the struggle two Anti-Federalist obstructionists were forcibly seized, carried to the State House and held in their seats so as to make a quorum. But the eloquence and logic of James Wilson overcame all opposition, and on December 12 the Constitution was ratified by a vote of forty-six to twenty-three. Already on December 6 the little State of Delaware, whose delegates had so vigorously opposed the Constitution in the convention, gave her adherence, thus acquiring the honor of being the first State to come under the " New Roof." On December 18 New Jersey, another one of the small States which at first opposed the overthrow of the Articles of Confederation, ratified by a large majority. Two other small States, Georgia

[14] Thorpe, " The Const. Hist. of the United States," vol. ii.
[15] Lodge, " Alexander Hamilton," pp. 65–69.

and Connecticut, ratified January 2 and January 9, respectively, the former by a unanimous vote, the latter by a vote of 128 to 40. All eyes were now turned toward Massachusetts, where it was known that the opposition was very strong, and whose action would doubt-less influence the decision of the conventions in other States. Elbridge Gerry and Samuel Adams were at heart hostile to ratifica-tion, while the sympathy of Hancock was of the feeblest sort; but Adams and Hancock were both brought round to at least a nominal support, and an actual vote, so that the sound and able arguments of King, Gorham, Strong, Cabot and Bowdoin carried the day. After a prolonged discussion, the convention ratified the Constitu-tion by a narrow majority of 187 to 168 votes on February 6, 1788, making the sixth State to ratify. But this ratification was accom-panied by a number of proposed amendments. Shortly afterwards Maryland ratified by a large majority, despite the strong opposition of the extreme Anti-Federalist, Luther Martin, a leading citizen of the State, who, after serving as a delegate to the Philadelphia convention, did not remain to sign the Constitution.[16]

In South Carolina there was considerable opposition, but the Constitution had able and influential supporters in the two Pinck-neys, the Rutledges and others, who, after a contest of eleven days, overcame all obstruction and secured the ratification by a vote of 149 to 73. The New Hampshire convention, which had early as-sembled, but later adjourned to await the action of other States, now reassembled, and with the good news from South Carolina ringing in their ears, ratified, after a short session, by a vote of 57 to 46. The ratification of but one more State was now necessary. Before New Hampshire had ratified, the Virginia convention had assembled, but was making poor progress, on account of the strong opposition. In no other State did the Anti-Federalists have so many able leaders. Chief among them were Patrick Henry, one of the most popular orators in America, Richard Henry Lee, George Mason and James Monroe. But the Constitution had powerful champions in James Madison, Governor Randolph, who, having refused to sign, now threw his great influence in favor of adoption, "Light Horse" Harry Lee, and John Marshall, the latter destined to become the foremost jurist of the country. The sound logic and calm reasoning of these men was too

[16] Thorpe, "The Const. Hist. of the United States," vol. ii. pp. 25-55.

much for even the eloquence of Patrick Henry and his associates, and after three weeks of debate the convention ratified the Constitution by a vote of 88 to 79. The ratification of Virginia, the greatest of the States, and then regarded as the leader in the Union, was followed by great rejoicing, for the general acceptance of the Constitution now seemed assured.[17] New York, North Carolina and Rhode Island, however, had not yet ratified, and the adhesion of New York, on account of its geographical position, was highly necessary to insure the completion of the Union. Her attitude, therefore, was watched with the greatest interest by all friends of the Union. The convention which assembled at Poughkeepsie on June 17, 1788, contained an overwhelming majority of avowed Anti-Federalists, the chief of whom was George Clinton, a States' right champion of distinguished ability and of influence by virtue of his long service as governor of the State.

In no one of the conventions yet assembled had the opposition been so active and determined. But the few Federalists were equally determined and equally resolute. Their leader was Hamilton, whose services as a member of the Federal Convention had been, owing to his adverse colleagues, confined to one great speech setting forth his system of government, and to exertions with the delegates from other States. Handicapped as he had been at Philadelphia, he was now free to labor with all his might for ratification. As chief author of the "Federalist" and leader of the friends of the Constitution in the State of New York, his services in bringing about the acceptance of the scheme of government under which we live are second to none of the "fathers." No higher tribute can be paid to his ability and influence than to say that in spite of an opposition that seemed insurmountable, he secured the adoption of the Constitution by a vote of 30 to 27. Great was the rejoicing over the news that New York had at last decided to cast her lot with the Union, for this insured the geographical unity of the Republic.[18]

The North Carolina convention, after a stormy session, adjourned without coming to any decision, while Rhode Island did not show sufficient friendliness to call a convention for the purpose of even considering the Constitution. In view of her course

[17] Hunt, "Life of James Madison," ch. xvi.
[18] Lodge, "Alexander Hamilton," pp. 69-79; Thorpe, "The Constitutional History of the United States," vol. ii. ch. iv.

since the Revolution it was hardly expected that she would exhibit any great enthusiasm for it. But it was not necessary now to wait for the ratification of these two States. The eleven ratifying States were able to put the new government into operation at once, and trust to the course of events to bring the recalcitrants into the Union sooner or later. In the course of time this happened. In November, 1789, North Carolina gave her adhesion, and in May of the following year Rhode Island joined the Union, the action of both being hastened, perhaps, by the threat of compulsion from the national government as regards the payment of their share of the national debt incurred in the conduct of the War of Independence.

The great struggle was now over, but it had abundantly demonstrated the truth of John Adams's statement that the Constitution was extorted as a grinding necessity from a reluctant people. For the first time in the history of the world a written Constitution applied to the federal form of government had been established, and although framed for thirteen agricultural communities with a population of less than four million inhabitants, it has proved equally adapted to forty-six powerful commonwealths with a total population of about eighty millions. Many objections were raised against the Constitution in the State conventions, but hardly any of them have proved as serious as predicted. One of the most general of these was the lack of a bill of rights securing to the individual a sphere of liberty upon which the national government should be forbidden to encroach. Accordingly, several of the States accompanied their ratifications by proposed amendments embodying a number of important prohibitions upon the power of Congress, as a means of safeguarding civil liberty. Within the course of a year after the adoption of the Constitution twelve of these were proposed to the States by Congress, and ten of them were promptly ratified. They prohibit the national government from abridging the freedom of conscience, of speech or of the press; from interfering with the right of petition or of assembly or with the right of the citizen to bear arms; from quartering soldiers on the inhabitants, or from depriving an individual of life, liberty or property without due process of law. They furthermore guarantee the right of trial by a jury of the vicinage, of due process of law in Federal judicial procedure, together with a number of other safeguards for the benefit of persons accused of crime. With two comparatively unimportant exceptions no further amendments were made until after the Civil War in spite of numerous attempts to bring about needed changes.[19]

[19] Ames, " Proposed Amendments to the Constitution of the United States."

Chapter XV

THE FIRST EIGHT YEARS OF THE CONSTITUTION
1789–1796

I

GEORGE WASHINGTON ELECTED PRESIDENT

ON September 13, 1788, the old Congress of the Confederation made formal announcement that the Constitution had been ratified by the required number of States, and on the 23d of the same month it held its final session, the representatives of but two States being present. One of its last acts was to provide for putting the new government into operation. It was enacted that the Presidential electors should be chosen on the first Wednesday in January, 1789; that they should meet and cast their votes for President and Vice President on the first Wednesday in February, and that the new Congress should assemble on the first Wednesday in March. The latter date happened to fall on March 4, and that day was subsequently fixed by act of Congress as the beginning of each new Congress and of each Presidential term. Representatives and senators were duly chosen in the various States, the former by general ticket in some States, by district ticket in others, and at the same time Presidential electors were appointed in all those that had joined the Union, except New York, where they was a delay. The choice was made by the legislatures in some cases and by popular election in others. When the electors met at their various State capitals in February, Washington was the only man who was thought of for the Presidency. It was well understood that he preferred to spend his remaining days on his fine estate at Mount Vernon, but the electors, knowing that with him personal considerations were never allowed to outweigh public obligations, unanimously chose him President, and he promptly accepted.[1] Under the Constitution, as it then stood, John Adams,

[1] McMaster, "History of the People of the United States," vol. i. pp. 525–532.

who received the next highest vote to Washington in the electoral college, thirty-four out of sixty-nine, was elected Vice President.

The fourth of March came and found but a handful of senators and representatives in New York, where the new government was to make its beginning. The old and evil habits of the Confederation still clung to the representatives and senators under the new system, and the two houses did not have a quorum until April 6. Some of the members had long distances to come; the means of transportation were crude; the season was unfavorable for travel, and, besides, the results of the elections in some States were not yet definitely known. Formal announcement was then made to Washington of his election, and of the organization of the houses, by Charles Thomson, the old secretary of the Continental Congress, who had proceeded to Mount Vernon for that purpose. As soon as he had received his notifications Washington left his home and journeyed by easy stages to New York, receiving a continual ovation from the people in every town through which he passed, although he traveled as a plain citizen in his private carriage.

Through Philadelphia he rode a white charger accompanied by an escort of troops, and at Trenton he passed under a triumphal arch supported by thirteen pillars and bearing the inscription " The Defender of the Mothers will be the Protector of the Daughters." He arrived at his destination on April 23, and was escorted to the house which Congress had provided for his residence by Governor Clinton and his staff, a committee of Congress and a body of militia, while the air rang with the plaudits of the throng and the boom of artillery. On the 30th, one week later, he took the oath of office, and was duly inaugurated on the balcony of Federal Hall, at the corner of Nassau and Wall Streets. The ceremony was simple but impressive. The President was dressed in a dark brown suit, wore white silk stockings, shoes with silver buckles, and carried a dress sword at his side, while his hair, according to the prevailing fashion, was powdered and gathered in a bag behind his uncovered head. Chancellor Livingston administered the oath, and then lifting his hand cried out, " Long live George Washington, President of the United States," and the people responded with acclamation, while the artillery thundered the first of the Presidential salutes.[2]

[2] For a contemporary account of the inauguration of Washington see Griswold, " Republican Court."

In the Congress, which Washington found waiting him, were many distinguished men, most of whom were cordial supporters of the great experiment which was now to be undertaken. Among them were some who had been chosen because they were friends to the Constitution in preference to those already distinguished, but were believed to be opposed to or lukewarm toward the experiment thus set on foot. For this reason Fisher Ames, an eloquent speaker and able lawyer, had defeated Samuel Adams in Boston, for the House, and Elbridge Gerry, another signer of the Declaration, was elected only on a pledge of support to the Constitution. The high character of these two men was well maintained by the members of the House sent by the other States. From Connecticut came Roger Sherman, one of the most eminent men of the older generation, and Jonathan Trumbull, former governor of Connecticut and a powerful supporter of Washington during the Revolution; Benson and Lawrence represented well the mercantile interests of New York; New Jersey sent Elias Boudinot, a noted philanthropist; Pennsylvania, George Clymer, the two Muhlenbergs, both Lutheran ministers, one of whom, Frederick, was chosen Speaker, and Thomas Fitzsimons, a wealthy merchant; South Carolina, Thomas Sumter, a famous Revolutionary soldier, who was destined to live nearly one hundred years, and Adamson Smith, soon to prove himself one of the ablest debaters in the House; and Georgia, Abraham Baldwin, of New England antecedents, already well known by his services in the Philadelphia convention, and James Jackson, an eccentric man who had served as secretary of the convention. The delegation from Virginia was not a very strong one, but it included Madison, one of the great champions of the Constitution, who, defeated for the Senate, had been elected to the lower branch, in which he became at once the most conspicuous figure.

In the Senate also we find but few of the Revolutionary leaders, although Richard Henry Lee and Robert Morris were both there. Their colleagues, as in the House, were chiefly younger members of the convention or noted supporters of the Constitution. Among them were many men of marked ability, and some who were destined to great distinction in the future. Such were John Langdon of New Hampshire, a wealthy man, and a future president of the Senate, who in after years put aside the proffered Vice Presidency of the United States; Caleb Strong of Massachusetts, who was to be for many years one of the leading Federalists and several times governor of the State; General Schuyler and Rufus King of New York, the latter recently removed from Massachusetts, and destined to become the most famous member of the Senate; Ellsworth, the future Chief Justice from Connecticut; Daniel Carroll from Maryland, a wealthy man of Roman Catholic faith, a kinsman of the more celebrated signer of the Declaration; Pierce Butler of South Carolina, and William Few of Georgia. On the whole the Congress was composed of able and earnest men, greatly in advance of the decrepit Assembly under the Confederation. Politically it was strongly Federalist, the only senators chosen avowedly as opponents of the Constitution being Lee and his colleague, William Grayson, from Virginia.

Among the distinguished names which we do not find on the rolls of either house in the first Congress under the Constitution are those of Hamilton, Jay, Wilson, George Clinton, Samuel Adams, Luther Martin, Patrick Henry and the South Carolina Pinckneys. Some of these being Anti-Federalists, like Adams, had been defeated by Federalist candidates; others, like Clinton, preferred to hold State offices. Some, like Luther Martin, had retired from politics; while still others, like Henry, had lost their political influence and were kept at home. After taking the oath of office Washington pronounced a brief inaugural address, in which he alluded feelingly and sincerely, no doubt, to the hope which he had entertained of being allowed to spend his declining years in retirement, suggested the amendment of the Constitution in accordance with the proper demand as revealed in the recent State conventions, and with becoming modesty announced that he desired no compensation for his services further than the defrayal of actual expenses incurred in the discharge of his official duties. According to the British parliamentary custom, both houses of Congress drew up formal replies to the Presidential address and waited upon him in turn, the President of the Senate presenting the address of the Senate, the Speaker of the House that of the latter body, and to both the President made a brief reply.

II

ORGANIZATION OF THE NEW GOVERNMENT

As soon as the ceremonies of the inauguration were over Congress set to work in earnest upon the great task before it, nothing less than converting the bare clauses of a written document into a living organism, a real and effective government. For this it had to provide at the start the very framework of administration by which alone all other laws could be enforced and executed.

In organizing the administrative departments Congress decided that the employment of boards and commissions, as had been the practice under the Articles of Confederation, should no longer be resorted to, but that departments, each with a single head, should be created instead. It was provided that there should be three of these, to have charge respectively of foreign affairs, war and finance, each under the direction of an officer called a secretary.[3] As head of the Department of Foreign Affairs, the name of which was changed before the end of the session to the Department of State, the President chose Thomas Jefferson, author of the Declaration of Independence, and at the moment minister to France, from where he soon returned. In addition to the conduct of foreign affairs the Department of State was entrusted with certain purely domestic duties, such as the custody of the great seal, the publication and promulgation of the laws, and the management of business relating to public lands and patents. When he came to select a Secretary of the Treasury, Washington turned naturally first to Robert Morris, the "financier of the Revolution," but Morris declined to serve, and recommended Alexander Hamilton, who was appointed. The law organizing the Treasury Department was very elaborate, and contained various provisions designed to insure the safe keeping of the public funds, and to fix the responsibility of the Secretary. For this purpose it required, among other things, the Secretary to make annual reports to Congress, while the other heads of departments were left to report to the President. General Knox of Massachuetts, a gallant Revolutionary soldier, and for some time head of the Board of War under the Confederation, was appointed Secretary of War, and was also given charge of naval affairs. Edmund Randolph, late Governor of Virginia, was

[3] Schouler, "History of the United States," vol. i. p. 104.

WASHINGTON TAKES THE OATH OF OFFICE AS FIRST PRESIDENT OF THE
UNITED STATES, ON THE BALCONY OF THE OLD CITY HALL, NEW YORK

Drawing by J. R. Wiles   —page **343**

made Attorney-General, with a seat in the Cabinet, although no regular Department of Justice was as yet organized, and for a good many years the duties of the Attorney General were inconsiderable. The post office continued under the management of a Postmaster General, who, however, did not become a Cabinet officer until many years later.   During the debate on the organization of the executive departments the question arose whether the President alone could remove an officer whose appointment required the advice and consent of the Senate, the Constitution being silent on that point.   The Senate insisted that its advice and consent was as necessary to remove as to appoint, while the House contended for the independence of the President in such cases.   The question was finally settled by the casting vote of the Vice President in favor of the right of the executive to remove without restraint, and this continued to be the rule until changed by Congress as a result of its unfortunate breach with President Johnson in 1867.[4]   The heads of the executive departments, which have now increased to nine, came in a short time to be known collectively as the Cabinet, a body quite unknown to the Constitution or to the laws, but now well established in practice and importance, although without any such share in legislation as the European and British ministries possess.   The members do not have seats in either house of Congress, have no right to participate in the Congressional debates, nor is their tenure affected in the slightest by any adverse vote, or by the resolutions of either house.   At first Washington consulted with the heads of departments as single individuals, and usually by writing; but toward the end of his first term the situation caused by the outbreak of war between England and France led him to convene the members for the purpose of general consultation.   This established the precedent of collective consultation which has since been followed by all his successors.

Another question which arose in connection with the organization of the executive departments, and which caused prolonged and animated discussion in both houses, related to the title by which the President was to be addressed.   Again the two houses differed, the Senate preferring the pompous title of " His High Mightiness, the President of the United States and Protector of their Liberties," — which it was understood the President desired — while the House contended for a less ostentatious one.   The result was that

---

[4] Curtis, "Constitutional History of the United States," vol. ii. pp. 142-145.

no form whatever was agreed upon, and the title of the chief magistrate is simply " The President of the United States," and he can properly be addressed in no other way.   Notwithstanding Washington's declaration that he desired no fixed salary, Congress enacted that the compensation attached to the office should be twenty-five thousand dollars per year, and the style in which our first President lived was such that his expenses did not fall below that sum.[5] The salary of the Vice President was fixed at five thousand dollars per year, that of Senators and Representatives at six dollars per day, with double pay for the Speaker, and the yearly salary of the Chief Justice at four thousand dollars.

The third branch of the government to be organized and put into operation was the judiciary.   The Constitution had provided that there should be a Supreme Court, but had left the details of organization to Congress, as well as the creation and organization of the inferior courts.   By the act of September 24, 1789, drafted by Senator Oliver Ellsworth, who had been a member of the Constitutional Convention, and was destined later to become Chief Justice of the Supreme Court, the Federal courts were organized on substantially the same basis as at present.   Under this law, one of the most remarkable of many acts in this period of great constructive legislation, the Supreme Court was to consist of six judges, and John Jay of New York, recently head of the old Department of Foreign Affairs, was chosen by Washington to be the first Chief Justice, and of him it has been well said that when the ermine fell upon his shoulders it touched a man as pure and spotless as itself.

Two grades of inferior courts were also created, namely, the district and circuit courts.   The territorial jurisdiction of the district courts, each of which was held by a single district judge, was as a rule coterminous with one of the States.   The circuit courts were to be held by a supreme justice and a district judge sitting together, no circuit judges having been provided for.   Prosecuting attorneys and marshals were to be appointed, and brief rules regulating the procedure of the courts were enacted.   To secure uniformity in the interpretation of federal law, and to insure its supremacy throughout the Union, as the Constitution required, appeals were to be allowed to the United States Supreme Court from the supreme courts of the States, where a decision had been ren-

[5] Schouler, "History of the United States," vol. i. p. 116.

dered denying the validity of a Federal statute, or where some right or privilege claimed under the Federal Constitution or laws had been denied. During the early years of its existence the business of the court was small, and few important decisions were rendered. There was little then to warrant the belief that the Supreme Court of the United States, perhaps the most remarkable of all the creations of the makers of the Constitution, would soon become the most powerful judicial tribunal in the world. It is an evidence of the slight regard in which a seat on the Supreme bench was held at the beginning, that in 1795 John Jay resigned the chief justiceship to become governor of New York.

While the discussion of the necessary measures for the organization of the government was proceeding, Congress was considering means for raising revenue, for creating a national currency, and for placing the public debt on a sound basis. For the first mentioned purpose Congress passed a tariff act imposing a duty on certain articles imported from abroad. Strangely enough, it was entitled " An Act for the Encouragement and Protection of Manufactures," although the average rate of duty hardly exceeded five per cent., while the highest did not exceed twelve and a half per cent. Distilled spirits, certain manufactures of iron, paper, and leather, cotton and wool cards and coal were the principal articles upon which an *ad valorem* duty was imposed, while certain others, notably hemp and cotton, were subjected to a specific duty. An attempt to lay a head tax of ten dollars on each slave imported into the country failed on account of the opposition of the Southern members.[6] The tariff of 1789 proved insufficient to provide the government with the necessary revenues, and a year later the duties were slightly increased. Another revenue measure was a tonnage act which, based upon the principles of protection and reciprocity, imposed a tax of six cents a ton on all vessels built and owned in the United States and a tax of thirty cents a ton on those built but not owned in the United States, as well as those owned by inhabitants of countries having commercial treaties with the United States, which countries at that time were France, Prussia, Sweden and Holland. Upon the ships of countries like England, which had not yet concluded commercial treaties with us, a tonnage duty of fifty cents per ton was imposed. Still later a third revenue

[6] McMaster, "History of the People of the United States," vol. i. pp. 552–555.

measure — a part of Hamilton's general scheme — was an excise tax on whisky, for the assumption of the State debts described hereafter, made necessary the discovery of new sources of income. Hamilton argued that besides producing needful revenue the excise tax would discourage the extensive consumption of an article which many believed to be a source of great moral and physical evil to the country. The proposed measure was bitterly opposed as an unwarranted exercise of the Federal taxing power, but it passed Congress by a small majority in March, 1791. Although the rate was low — it did not exceed twenty-five cents per gallon in any case — it excited strong opposition, especially in Pennsylvania and the South, and led to open resistance in some communities. The tax was repealed during Jefferson's administration by a Republican Congress.

All this financial legislation was due to Alexander Hamilton, who not only organized the Treasury Department and all machinery for the collection and disbursement of revenue, but devised and set forth in a series of great State papers the policies which established our credit and financial system upon the rock of good faith, and which stamped him as the great organizing and constructive mind of the epoch.[7] Upon the request of Congress, Hamilton prepared an elaborate report on the state of the public debt, which he submitted to the House of Representatives at the autumn session of 1790. This report showed that the debt was of three kinds: the foreign debt, the domestic debt and the debts of the individual States. The first with the accrued interest amounted to at least $12,000,000, most of which was due to France, some to Holland and a little to Spain. The domestic debt with accrued interest amounted to about $42,000,000. The State debts incurred in the common cause of the Revolution aggregated about $25,000,-000.[8] Hamilton proposed to fund the foreign and domestic debt into United States bonds running for a definite period and bearing lower rates of interest than the government was paying on the old certificates of indebtedness, and he recommended that both debts should be paid in full, dollar for dollar. So far as the foreign debt was concerned there was no objection to paying off according to contract; but as to the domestic debt it was said that justice did not require payment in full because the old evidences of indebted-

[7] Lodge, "Alexander Hamilton," ch. v.
[8] Schouler, "History of the United States," vol. i. p. 145.

ness had long since passed from the hands of the original holders into the hands of speculators at varying rates of discount. Indeed, while his report was being read, agents for Eastern capitalists were hurrying to remote parts of the country to buy up certificates whose value a day later had increased fifty per cent. Hence payment at par would only reward those who were least deserving. If the certificates could be scaled down the speculators would still reap a handsome profit, while there would be an enormous saving to the government. Madison proposed that an effort be made to ascertain what the present holders had paid for the certificates, that this amount be paid to them, and that the face value should be paid only to the original holders. To all arguments against payment in full Hamilton replied that it was bad faith for the government to pay less than it had solemnly promised to pay, and that if in the future the credit of the nation was to be strong, the record of the government for keeping faith with its creditors must be unimpeachable. Hamilton's view was accepted by Congress after a spirited contest and much debate, and the funding scheme with the faith of the nation inviolably preserved was carried through. The example which the new nation thus set under the direction of its first great finance minister, of keeping full faith with its creditors has been of incalculable aid to the Republic in times of great crises, when the government was compelled to borrow large sums, besides teaching a most valuable lesson of political ethics.

But Hamilton's policy did not end here. He proposed to the astonishment of Congress and the country, that the national government should assume the payment of the outstanding State debts. The secretary argued that these debts had for the most part been incurred in a common cause, and as the States had surrendered the power of laying duties on imports, one of the chief sources of their revenue at the time the debts were incurred, the national government should now assume the payment of them. This final proposition, which not only was wise financially, as it was intended to be, but was also a powerful instrument of consolidating the government and developing the national sentiment, excited a most bitter opposition, far more than had been aroused by any of the preceding measures, and the bill was at first defeated in the House by a majority of two votes. Some of the States like Virginia, which had already arranged for the liquidation of their war debts, naturally opposed assumption; others like New Hampshire and Maryland, which had small debts, opposed it for a similar reason; while those like Massachusetts, Connecticut and South Carolina, which had large debts, enthusiastically favored the assumption scheme. Still others were divided in their opinions.

While the great financial policy was being carried out, the question of selecting a permanent site for the National Capital had been hotly discussed and had awakened great feeling and many jealousies. The Northern members wished to have the capital somewhere in the North, preferably at New York or Philadelphia, while the Southern members were eager to carry it southwards. But as the supporters of a Northern capital were slightly in the majority it was evident that the Southern members would be outvoted unless a deal of some kind could be made. Hamilton, to whom the assumption project, far-reaching and essential to the new government, was infinitely dearer than the situation of the capital, proposed to Jefferson a means of settling both questions. Jefferson was to induce a sufficient number of his Southern friends to vote for the assumption measure in return for which Hamilton was to secure Northern votes for a Southern capital. The bargain was struck; the bill for the assumption of State debts amounting to $21,500,000 passed both houses, and it was agreed that for the next ten years the seat of government should be at Philadelphia, after which it should be placed permanently on the Potomac River.[9] Shortly thereafter a body of commissioners, at the head of which was President Washington, selected the site, the land was acquired by purchase, and Major l'Enfant, a French engineer, who had been employed for the purpose, laid out the plan of a great " Federal city " with magnificent avenues, parks, public fountains, and stately edifices.

Having carried through his schemes for raising revenue and for reorganizing the national finances, Hamilton next proposed the establishment of a national bank. He urged the measure upon Congress in one of his famous reports as a means of aiding the government in negotiating loans, effecting exchanges and otherwise carrying on its financial business, besides supplying the country with a stable and useful paper currency. The capital stock of the proposed bank was to be $10,000,000, of which the government was

[9] McMaster, "History of the People of the United States," vol. i. pp. 574–581.

to own one-fifth; one-fifth of the directors were to be appointed by the government, and they were required to make periodical reports of all the operations of the bank. This proposal to establish a government bank aroused vehement opposition, both in and out of Congress, among those who feared the association of the government with banking. Moreover there were many who denied the necessity of such an institution to furnish a circulating medium because of the many State banks in existence, while there were not a few who doubted the constitutionality of such a measure. The latter insisted that as the Constitution nowhere empowered Congress to embark in such an enterprise, it had no right to do so.

To the Constitutional arguments Hamilton replied that Congress was empowered to do anything which was "necessary and proper" to carry into effect any power expressly delegated by the Constitution to Congress. Among the powers expressly delegated were the collection and disbursement of the revenues, the borrowing of money and the payment of the debts of the United States. A bank, he argued, was a proper agency for these purposes, as well as for conducting other fiscal operations of the government, although, he admitted, it was not absolutely indispensable. Here was involved for the first time the doctrine of "implied powers"; that is, powers drawn by implication from those expressly conferred by the Constitution on Congress. According to this rule of interpretation the Constitution is not to be construed strictly as a legal document, but in the light of the general purposes for which the government was created, due emphasis being given to those powers which, while not expressly conferred by the Constitution, yet exist by reasonable implication. The advocates of this theory were popularly called "loose constructionists."[10]

Those who opposed the establishment of the bank contended that if the powers conferred upon the national government by the Constitution were not strictly construed, the whole theory of the relation between the national government and the State governments would be destroyed, since the powers of the former might be magnified and extended almost without limit at the expense of the latter. It was a view which, if put into practice, would lead to danger, they said, because it opened the way for Federal usurpation with its accompanying possibilities of revolution. The only safe method of interpretation was to follow literally the plain lan-

[10] Lodge, "Alexander Hamilton," pp. 98–105.

guage of the Constitution, and if no express authority could be found for the exercise by the national government of the power claimed, it should be presumed to have been left with the States in accordance with the constitutional principle that all powers not delegated to the national government nor prohibited to the States are reserved to the States. The advocates of this school of interpretation came to be popularly known as " strict constructionists." Its founder and ablest exponent was Thomas Jefferson. So it came to pass that when Hamilton in an argument, still unsurpassed in power of statement, set forth the doctrine of " implied powers," he not only laid the foundation for party divisions, but for two schools of constitutional and political thought. The conflict between these schools and their parties has made the political and constitutional history of the United States, and once brought the Union to the verge of destruction by civil war. The national school, which Hamilton founded, has triumphed and the national principle is now supreme. But it must not be forgotten that the States embodying the great principle of local self-government are essential to our national existence.

In the case of the national bank the liberal constructionists won the day. The bill passed both houses by a small majority, and it is not without significance as showing the geographical distribution of the two schools of constitutional interpretation that the Northern members almost unanimously favored the bank, while the Southern members almost solidly opposed it.[11] When the bill was presented to the President for approval he was apparently impressed with the importance of the constitutional questions at issue, and requested the opinions in writing of his Cabinet. Hamilton, of course, defended the measure with all the power which he could command, and his argument remains, as has been said, one of the ablest expositions in existence of the doctrine of implied powers. Jefferson, on the other hand, urged the President to veto the bill, as neither a " necessary " nor " proper " measure, and his argument against the constitutionality of the bank is one of the best expositions of the theory of strict construction. But Hamilton's argument prevailed with the President, and the bill was signed.[12]

The period for which the bank was chartered was twenty years. It was established at Philadelphia with branches in all the

[11] McMaster, "History of the People of the United States," vol. ii. p. 32.
[12] Schouler, "History of the United States," vol. i. p. 177.

principal cities of the Union. The four-fifths of the stock allowed to the public was quickly subscribed. Besides doing a general banking business, the bank served as a sort of fiscal agent for the United States, and on numerous occasions was of great service to the government in placing its loans and aiding it to meet its obligations. The banknotes supplied a sound national currency; they were receivable for all debts, taxes and duties; and were accepted on a par with gold everywhere throughout the world. Probably no institution ever created by our government better fulfilled the purposes of its founders; but those who believed that it was a monopoly unwarranted by the Constitution and represented an encroachment upon the rights of the States increased in numbers, until presently the bank had more enemies than friends. In this connection it ought to be repeated that aside from financial considerations Hamilton had ulterior motives in wishing the national government to engage in the banking business and to assume the State debts. He saw clearly that both would strengthen the national government by rallying to its support the moneyed interests of the country and by getting the people generally accustomed to federal laws and federal institutions, and also interested in government securities as an investment. These motives, however, were strictly honorable and stand as a silent tribute to his political sagacity and wise statesmanship.

A fifth and final project in the great financial policy of the Secretary of the Treasury was the establishment of a national mint and the creation of a uniform metallic currency. During the period of the Confederation, Gouverneur Morris had prepared a plan for a decimal system of currency, but it was never adopted. At the time the Constitution went into operation, therefore, no uniform national currency existed, a fact which caused great inconvenience to business and hampered trade very considerably. The metallic money in common use consisted of a variety of English, French and Spanish coins—shillings, crowns, dollars, moidores, joes, half-joes, pistareens, and picayunes, while the paper currency of the country consisted of thirteen kinds of notes issued by as many different States. Now that there was a national government expressly empowered by the Constitution to coin money and regulate the value thereof, the want of a uniform Federal currency could easily be supplied. The plan sketched by Gouverneur Morris and which had been improved upon as to certain details by

Jefferson was now made the basis of Hamilton's report to Congress and was adopted as law. A national mint was established at Philadelphia, and later, as the demand for an increase in the volume of coin grew, mints were established elsewhere.

The system of coinage adopted provided for a gold and silver standard with the dollar as the unit, together with various denominations arranged according to the decimal scale — the ratio between the two metals being fixed at fifteen to one. That is, the weight of the silver coins was made fifteen times that of the corresponding gold coins of the same denomination, the market price of an ounce of gold at the time being fifteen times that of an ounce of silver. In other words, the mint ratio was made to correspond to the market ratio. But the difficulty of maintaining this ratio was soon discovered, since it involved the fixing by statute of the price of a commodity. As a result of the law of supply and demand, the price of gold soon began to increase so that it was really worth sixteen times as much as the same quantity of silver. The market ratio no longer corresponded to the mint ratio, and the decree of the government could not make it so without increasing the weight of the silver coin or decreasing the weight of gold. Gold was undervalued, and it soon disappeared from circulation, its place being taken by the cheaper metal, silver. It thus happened that gold was more valuable as bullion than as coin; consequently it was exported or used in the arts, so that for a good many years, instead of a double standard, we really had a single silver standard.[13] But the advantages of having a uniform metallic currency easy of computation far outweighed the inconveniences flowing from the difficulties of adjusting the ratio.

The establishment of a mint and the creation of a system of coinage completed Hamilton's financial program. But he also made a report on manufactures in which he set forth an elaborate scheme for the protection and encouragement of manufacturing industries by means of tariffs and bounties, and although nothing was done at the time to carry his proposals into effect this famous discussion of " Free Trade, Protection and the Diversification of Industry " became later the foundation of the " American System," and made protective duties the national policy. Hamilton's services to the United States in reorganizing its finances and establishing the public credit were of the first order. No nation ever

[13] Laughlin, " Political Economy," p. 307.

started upon its career with a greater constructive genius as one of its founders and guides. It was due to him more than to any other man that the foundations of our government in all financial matters were firmly laid in honesty and integrity. As an organizer he was by far the most conspicuous leader in the government during its first years, and his dominant influence was apparent in every policy adopted by Washington's administration, whether at home or abroad.

With financial confidence thus established, with public and private credit restored and a stable government in operation, uncertainty and distrust disappeared. Trade among the States was now unhampered; the volume of exports increased rapidly, business expanded and signs of a healthy prosperity were everywhere visible. The Federal census of 1790 showed a population of nearly four million inhabitants, and settlers were flocking to the Northwest in large numbers. The revenues of the government were adequate, its obligations were met with punctuality, domestic tranquillity existed throughout the Union; from every point of view, in fact, the government under the Constitution had proved to be an undoubted success and the prospects for the future career of the nation were of the most favorable kind.

But the financial measures which Hamilton had proposed and carried through had given rise to divisions which soon culminated in the organization of two hostile political parties.[14] The debates on the funding scheme, and especially those on the bank bill, the bill for the assumption of the State debts and the excise scheme had developed a wide difference of opinion concerning the method of interpreting the Constitution so far as the power and scope of the national government were concerned. The two leaders of the parties thus produced, Hamilton and Jefferson, were, to use the latter's own expression, soon " pitted against each other like two fighting cocks." Jefferson, fresh from the ultra-democratic society of revolutionary Paris, his head filled with Jacobin ideas, looked with aversion upon the centralizing schemes of Hamilton and the aristocratic ways of the Federalists, as the followers of Washington and Hamilton were now called. He was by nature suspicious, and soon came to believe that the Federalists, under the leadership of Hamilton, **were** plotting to overthrow the Republic and set up a monarchy.

---

[14] Lodge, " Life of Alexander Hamilton," pp. 136–152.

Seizing upon bits of conversation and current gossip, he magnified them into full-fledged conspiracies against the Union.

The Federalists wished the government to be conducted with more or less ceremony and dignity, somewhat after the British fashion, while Jefferson and his followers, who at first could find no better name than Anti-Federalists, but who later called themselves Republicans, preferred an administration of extreme democratic simplicity. Hamilton was obliged to carry out his programme against the opposition of his ministerial colleague, whom he denounced in due time as a demagogue and a hypocrite — " a man of profound ambition and violent passions, seeking the Presidency." Secret at first, Jefferson's hostility very soon came to the surface; he denounced Hamilton unsparingly and vehemently; the division in the Cabinet became public, and each side began to organize as a party. The *Gazette of the United States* became the organ of the Federalists, while Jefferson aided in the maintenance of an opposition journal, the *National Gazette,* by the appointment of its editor, Philip Freneau, to a clerkship in the Department of State. This newspaper was devoted mainly to scurrilous abuse of the Federalist chiefs, including the President, who once spoke of its editor as " that rascal Freneau, who sent me three copies of his paper every day, as though he thought I would become a distributor of them." Between the two hostile secretaries stood the calm figure of Washington, always a peacemaker, striving to maintain harmony in the Cabinet and to keep down party spirit, which he regarded as one of the chief dangers to the Republic. But his efforts were fruitless, and the close of his first term was marked by so much bitterness and rancor that he desired to retire to private life. The attacks upon his ministers he regarded as assaults upon himself, and once in the heat of passion declared that he would rather go to his farm and earn his bread by the use of a spade than remain where he was.

III

REËLECTION OF WASHINGTON; TROUBLES WITH FRANCE AND ENGLAND; THE WHISKY REBELLION

The country, however, was not yet ready to dispense with Washington's services. All of his Cabinet united in urging him to serve a second term, and the general sentiment of the people was probably correctly expressed by Jefferson, who wrote to him, saying, "The confidence of the whole Union is centered in you; North and South will hang together if they have you to hang on." With unfeigned reluctance, he consented to stand for reëlection, and in 1792 was unanimously chosen to succeed himself, being supported by both Federalists and Republicans with equal spontaneity and enthusiasm. He received 132 electoral votes, the number having been increased by the admission of Vermont to the Union in 1791 and Kentucky in 1792. For Vice President there was no such unanimity: John Adams (Federalist) received 77 electoral votes; George Clinton (Republican), 50; Thomas Jefferson, (Republican), 4; Aaron Burr (Republican), 1. The electors were chosen by the State legislatures in Connecticut, New Jersey, Pennsylvania, Delaware, South Carolina and Georgia; elsewhere they were elected by popular vote. The old Cabinet was retained without change, although it suffered a break the following year by the retirement of Jefferson and a year later by the resignation of Hamilton. Washington then abandoned the attempt to carry on the government with the leaders of both parties as his ministers and made up his Cabinet wholly of Federalists.

Washington's second administration, unlike the first, was stormy and warlike, with party dissensions at home and perils and difficulties brought on by the French Revolution abroad. The troubles abroad grew immediately out of the war between Great Britain and France in 1793. Ordinarily this would have been a matter of little or no concern to the United States, but the sympathies of the American people were naturally with the French Republic, which seemed to be superficially akin to our own, and the result of American example. The progress of the French Revolution was watched, therefore, with the deepest solicitude by the people of the United States. There were, aside from considerations of a sentimental character, other reasons which led Americans to sympathize with France. During the dark days of our own struggle for independence France alone among European nations had made a treaty of alliance and commerce with us and had contributed both men and money to the success of the American cause. In return for this, the United States had agreed to allow her certain privileges in our ports, such as shelter to French privateers and prizes, which were not allowed to other nations, and to guarantee the integrity of her colonial possessions in the West Indies in case of defensive war. It was now certain that an attempt would be made by England to seize the possessions of France in the West Indies, and consequently the fulfillment of the American promises was certain to be demanded by our former ally.

We were, in short, bound to France by an alliance, by gratitude, and by the sympathy which one republic must needs have for another in an age when republics were still new and very unpopular among the monarchies of the Old World. American sympathy with France was still further elicited by the treatment which we received from the hands of her old enemy, Great Britain. She was still our enemy, although she might easily have made us her friend. Ten years had passed since the formal recognition of our independence had been extorted from her, yet she had refused to enter into commercial arrangements with us; she had persisted in holding the military posts in the Northwest which she had agreed by the Treaty of 1783 to surrender, and had only very recently condescended to accredit a minister to our government. It is true that our failure to comply with our treaty obligations as to debts gave England justification of her attitude, yet that did not alter our feelings.

But there were, nevertheless, most serious objections to our joining France in a war against Great Britain. War would have meant the loss of a large and rapidly increasing commerce, besides entailing other sacrifices which the new Republic could ill afford to make at this stage of its career. Certainly it would seem that nothing could have been more unfortunate for our growing prosperity than a second war so soon after the achievement of independence. On the other hand, our obligations to France were not so certain or so binding, either morally or legally, as they seemed at first sight to enthusiastic and irresponsible minds. In the first place, we had made the treaty with Louis Capet, the head of the French monarchy, and there was no longer a French monarchy, the French king having been put to death and a republic established, which was struggling for existence both at home and abroad. In the second place, France had aided us during the Revolution not through any special desire to see American independence achieved, but rather to injure England. Finally, and this was the decisive legal point, it can be said very justly that France was not engaged in a war of defense, but had undertaken to wage war against all Europe for the purpose of extending the ideas engendered by the French Revolution. For these reasons Hamilton and the Federalists generally were in favor of strict neutrality, while Jefferson and his followers regarded the treaty obligations with France as binding and were somewhat inclined to favor war with Great Britain.

In April, 1793, when the news of the outbreak of war between Great Britain and France reached Philadelphia, Washington was at Mount Vernon, whither he had gone shortly after the inauguration to enjoy a brief and well-earned repose from his public duties. Hastening at once to the capital, he summoned, for the first time, the members of the Cabinet to meet him in council for the purpose of collective consultation with regard to our treaty obligations with France and as to the proper course to be pursued by the United States in the approaching struggle. The Cabinet united in advising a policy of neutrality, and accordingly on April 22 the President issued a proclamation announcing that the United States would take no part in the war, and warning all citizens from giving aid to either belligerent upon pain of prosecution in the courts. In this famous document Washington laid down the principles of neutrality which our government has always followed with regard to European affairs and which undoubtedly was the only wise policy at the time.[15] Shortly before the issue of the proclamation the French minister, Genêt, an over-zealous, excitable democrat, arrived at Charleston well supplied with blank letters of marque and reprisal, which he proceeded to issue to such American citizens as were willing to become privateers against British commerce. A number of privateering vessels manned by American seamen were actually fitted out in American ports as though the United States were an ally of France, and several British vessels were captured and brought in for condemnation as good prizes. Proceeding leisurely overland to Philadelphia, Genêt was the recipient throughout his entire journey of a continual ovation. Democratic associations, in imitation of the French Jacobin clubs, were organized everywhere and at their banquets the " rights of man " were enthusiastically proclaimed. Liberty-poles were erected, Americans dressed like Frenchmen, dropped the old titles of " Sir " and " Mr." and called each other " Citizen." [16] French revolutionary songs were sung, the tri-color was displayed with the Stars and Stripes, and various other manifestations of sympathy with France were to be seen on every hand. Genêt was feasted at Philadelphia and the enthusiasm

[15] Lodge, " Life of Washington," vol. ii. p. 115.
[16] McMaster, " History of the United States," vol. ii. p. 93.

for the cause he represented was unparalleled in the history of the city. Meantime, Hammond, the newly arrived British minister, had filed a formal complaint against the fitting out of French privateers in American ports, and the President had informed Genêt that no more letters of marque and reprisal must be issued and that the territorial jurisdiction of the United States must be respected. But the popular manifestations of sympathy for this fervent champion of the " rights of man " were so loud that Genêt allowed himself to believe that Washington did not represent the feeling of the nation, and he therefore threatened to make an appeal to the people to override the President. Thereupon the popular enthusiasm at once subsided, and upon the demand of our government he was recalled in disgrace. The French Government demanded his delivery up for punishment, but this the United States refused to do " for reasons of law and magnanimity "; Genêt, therefore, remained in the United States and so escaped the guillotine. He later married the daughter of Governor Clinton of New York and lived to a ripe old age. It is but just to say that he has been the subject of much unmerited obloquy; the truth is he did not violate his instructions, which in reality contemplated the fitting out of hostile enterprises in the United States.[17] After this episode sympathy for France declined and the administration regained its strength with all the most important and conservative elements among the people.

But the effort of the administration to pursue a policy of neutrality did not prevent the United States from becoming involved in disputes with both belligerents, due mainly to the French and English interpretation of several usages of international law regarding neutral commerce. One of the effects of the war between England and France had been to drive their own commerce from the seas. Thereupon the American neutral carriers acquired almost a monopoly of the European and American commerce, and it presently came about that nearly three-fourths of the world's carrying trade was in the hands of Americans, whereas they had formerly carried only about one-fourth. When French merchantmen were driven from the seas and France could no longer get the sorely needed products of her colonial possessions, she opened her colonial trade to neutrals, and soon American vessels were plying between the French West Indies and the continent of Europe, supplying France with products which she could not obtain elsewhere. Great

[17] See John Bassett Moore, "American Diplomacy," p. 48.

Britain denied the right of France to throw her colonial trade open to neutrals, since by the so-called " Rule of 1756 " a nation which forbade neutral trade with its colonies in time of peace could not allow it in time of war. Great Britain, therefore, claimed and exercised the right to seize American merchant vessels trading between France and her West India colonies. England also took the extraordinary ground that provisions and food stuffs were contraband of war, and accordingly American vessels laden with such cargoes bound for continental ports were seized and paid for at such prices as the British chose to give. The French Government followed the same course with regard to cargoes destined to British ports. Moreover, the British Government insisted that after notice of a blockade had been given, vessels bound to blockaded ports might be seized anywhere on the high seas, whether a blockading squadron was stationed at the entrance to the interdicted port or not. Finally, Great Britain denied the American doctrine that " free ships make free goods "; that is, that neutral vessels are not liable to capture when carrying enemy's property unless such property is contraband of war. In disregard of this view American vessels carrying French goods were stopped on the high seas by British cruisers and their cargoes confiscated as good prize.

As a result of these several interpretations of international law, the carrying trade of the United States was seriously crippled by the cruisers of both England and France; but as the maritime power of the former was much greater than that of the latter, the feeling in the United States was proportionately more bitter against England. The resentment against England was still further heightened by her practice of impressing seamen from American merchant vessels on the ground that they were still British subjects, notwithstanding naturalization by the courts of the United States. In many instances native-born Americans were mistaken intentionally or unintentionally for British seamen and were seized under peculiarly irritating circumstances.

Spurred on by the popular excitement aroused by these aggressions, Congress in the spring of 1794 laid an embargo for sixty days on American shipping, prohibiting all vessels from departing from American ports. A measure for absolutely interdicting intercourse with England was proposed, and was defeated only by the casting vote of the Vice President in the Senate. For a time war with England seemed inevitable, but the President, knowing well the enormous danger of war to our new government, determined to make a last effort to come to a friendly understanding with England. Accordingly, in April, 1794, he appointed the Chief Justice, John Jay, as special envoy to England to act in conjunction with the resident minister at London in the negotiation of a treaty for the settlement of the questions at issue. Jay reached England in June, was received with the utmost cordiality, and in November concluded a treaty with the British Government, but it was not received by the President until after the adjournment of Congress in March, 1795.

The announcement of its provisions, which were given out by a member of the Senate to whom it had been communicated in confidence, caused an outburst of popular wrath. The treaty contained no agreement on the part of the British to give up the right of search, no mention was made of impressment nor of blockade, nor of recompense for the actions of British commanders in carrying away negro slaves in 1783 in violation of the treaty; in fact, there was no assurance whatever in regard to the rights of neutrals, the violation of which had been our chief grievance.[18] The treaty provided that the Western posts still held by Great Britain, and which included Detroit, Mackinaw, Fort Erie, Niagara, Oswego and several others, should be evacuated in June, 1796; that mixed commissions should be appointed for the adjustment of the northeast boundary dispute arising from the difficulty of determining what was the St. Croix River mentioned in the Treaty of 1783, and for the settlement of the claims arising out of the action of the States in obstructing the payment of debts due British creditors in violation of the Treaty of 1783, which stipulated that creditors on either side should meet with no lawful impediment to the recovery of the full value in sterling money of all *bonâ fide* debts contracted before the peace. Finally, a mixed commission was provided for adjusting all claims arising from the action of British cruisers in unlawfully capturing American vessels in 1793. The most objectionable provision of all was that which restricted American trade with the British West Indies to vessels of seventy tons burden, but which allowed all British vessels without regard to tonnage to compete in our West India trade unrestrained. In return for this poor concession for twelve years the United States was not to export molasses, sugar, coffee, cocoa, or cotton to any part of the world, and

[18] McMaster, "History of the United States," vol. ii. pp. 246-247.

agreed to throw open all her ports to Great Britain and permit reciprocal trade on the footing of the most friendly nation.[19] In June the Senate was called together in extraordinary session to ratify the treaty, and it was with the greatest difficulty that the necessary two-thirds majority was obtained. The article relating to trade with the West Indies and the prohibition upon exports was promptly rejected, after which the Senate ratified the treaty by a narrow majority. The House of Representatives, being called upon at the ensuing session to appropriate the necessary funds for the payment of the expenses of the several commissions provided for in the treaty, indulged in a fierce debate, in which the treaty was bitterly attacked, and a resolution was passed calling on the President for the papers relating to the negotiations. Washington refused to comply with the request, on the ground that the House had no share in the treaty-making power, and that the executive must be the sole judge as to the publication of such papers. Finally the House gave way, and by a vote of forty-eight to forty-one passed the necessary appropriation bills.

The treaty was now a part of the supreme law of the land, but the popular indignation which it excited throughout the country was very great. Jay was hanged and burned in effigy from Maine to Georgia. Hamilton was stoned while defending the treaty at a public meeting in New York.[20] State legislatures, conventions and massmeetings condemned it as a surrender to Great Britain, and an offense to our old ally, France. Even Washington was savagely reviled in language which he said " could scarcely be applied to a Nero, to a notorious defaulter, or even to a common pickpocket." But after all the treaty was probably the best that could have been obtained from Great Britain at the time. The commissions settled in a satisfactory way the disputed questions of boundaries and claims referred to them, and altogether over $11,000,000 were awarded to the United States in the form of indemnities in consequence of this much abused treaty, as against $2,664,000 awarded Great Britain on account of judicial obstructions to the payment of British debts.[21] More important still, the treaty postponed for a term of years the war with Great Britain and gave the new nation time to grow in strength and to prepare for the

---

[19] Schouler, "History of the United States," vol. i. p. 307.
[20] Lodge, "Life of Washington," vol. ii. p. 183.
[21] See John Bassett Moore, "International Arbitrations," vol. i. pp. 298, 344.

struggle which came seventeen years later, besides otherwise proving of immense benefit to the country.[22]

While the excitement over the Jay treaty was at its height, another agreement of special importance to the West was also being negotiated. This was the treaty with Spain concluded by Thomas Pinckney in October, 1795, and which secured to the citizens of the United States the valuable privileges of freely navigating the Mississippi River to its mouth and of " deposit " at New Orleans for a period of three years, for as the territory at the mouth of the river was owned by Spain, the right of navigation was worthless without a " place of deposit," where goods could be stored for trans-shipment. It settled, besides, a boundary dispute by fixing the thirty-first parallel of latitude as the boundary between the United States and Spanish West Florida. The principle that " free ships make free goods " was also recognized, and Spain agreed to indemnify the United States for losses sustained on account of unlawful captures of American merchant vessels in the late war between France and Spain. The treaty was very popular in the West, since it secured an outlet for the trade of the western inhabitants and threw open to them a section of disputed territory, although on account of the tardiness with which Spain evacuated the posts therein it was some years before the United States reaped the full benefit. In the same year a treaty was concluded with Algiers by which the crews of various American vessels that had been captured and held for ransom by Algerine corsairs were released in consideration of the payment by the United States of a large sum aggregating not less than a million dollars, and the promise of an annuity to the Dey of sixty thousand dollars.[23]

The domestic tranquillity of the United States was disturbed during Washington's administration by Indian outbreaks in the West, and by the resistance to the enforcement of the excise law in Pennsylvania. In 1788 the first white settlement west of the mountains was made at Marietta on the Ohio River, in the southeastern part of what is now the State of Ohio. The settlers were made up chiefly of immigrants from New England, many of them being veterans of the Revolutionary War. During the years immediately following, a stream of pioneers poured over the mountains to the neighborhood of Pittsburg, whence they embarked on flatboats for

[22] Foster, " Century of American Diplomacy," p. 165.
[23] Haswell, " Treaties and Conventions," p. 776.

points upon the Ohio, where settlements were quickly made. As has already been said, Congress in 1787 provided a scheme of government for the rapidly growing West, and this was shortly afterwards put into operation by the appointment of General Arthur St. Clair as governor. At these encroachments of the whites the Indians looked on with jealousy, and kept the frontier in constant dread by their hostile demonstrations. The faraway posts of Detroit and Mackinaw were still occupied by the British forces, in disregard of the Treaty of 1783, and it was popularly believed that the English incited the Indians to attack the white settlers. Be this as it may, it is certain that the presence of the British, old-time allies of the Indians, lent courage, if nothing more material, to their unfriendly attitude. The demonstrations of the Indians at last became so hostile that in 1790 the President sent General Harmar with a force of 1500 men to attack them; but he was badly defeated near the present site of Fort Wayne, many of his men being slaughtered and their bodies thrown into the river. Harmar was court-martialed and acquitted, but the verdict did not change the popular opinion that he was incompetent, if not guilty of cowardice, and shortly afterwards he resigned his commission. In the following year the governor, General St. Clair, was dispatched against them with a new and more formidable force in spite of Washington's caution to beware of an ambuscade, he allowed himself to be surprised by the Indians, and his little army was cut to pieces, November 4, 1791. After a fight of several hours St. Clair, severely wounded and with his clothes cut to shreds by eight bullets, gave the order for retreat. Many of his men were left behind only to be scalped, tortured and plundered by the infuriated savages. Altogether about six hundred men were killed or missing, and a large quantity of arms, ammunition and government stores was lost. Terrible, indeed, was Washington's wrath when the news reached him that St. Clair had been defeated, and in a tempest of passion he poured out awful imprecations upon his old Revolutionary comrade, who had allowed his army to be " hacked, butchered, and tomahawked by a surprise." [24]

But he did not delay to indulge his feelings of grief and resentment. In order to retrieve the disaster, he appointed Anthony Wayne, one of the bravest and most daring of the Revolutionary soldiers, to succeed St. Clair as major general, and although the

[24] Lodge, "Life of Washington," p. 96.

appointment was criticised, events soon justified Washington's judgment. In the summer of 1794 Wayne completely broke the power of the Indians in a battle on the Maumee, not far from the present site of Toledo, and in the following summer (1795) concluded with their chiefs the Treaty of Greenville, by which the pacification of the Northwestern Indians was completed and the greater part of northern Ohio was ceded to the United States and thrown open to prosperous settlement.

While Wayne's campaign against the Indians was in progress, the power of the new government to enforce the laws and maintain domestic tranquillity was for the first time being put to the test in western Pennsylvania. In this remote region, far from the markets of the East, the farmers, finding it unprofitable to transport their grain across the mountains, had adopted the practice of turning it into whisky, and in this more portable form it was sent over the mountains to the tide-water region and there sold for about a shilling a gallon, while in the mountainous country it served the purpose of a currency. The excise tax of seven to eighteen cents a gallon, according to proof, bore hard, therefore, on these trans-Alleghany distillers, who were not accustomed to paying high taxes, and accordingly they resisted the efforts of the officers to collect the revenue, all the more so because of the insistence of the government upon specie.

The principal seat of the opposition was in the four western counties. The collectors in several instances were tarred and feathered, and when the United States marshals appeared with process for service on the delinquent distillers, the officers received the same treatment. Public meetings were held at which the iniquitous excise was denounced and resistance to its enforcement urged. The law was amended and softened; a commissioner was sent to the scene of the disaffection for the purpose of conciliating the malcontents, but the resistance increased rather than diminished, and Federal officers were fired upon by armed mobs, driven out of the community, and their houses burned.[25]

The ordinary machinery of courts and marshals being thus powerless to enforce the law, Congress passed an act, which is still in force, empowering the President to call out the militia when, in his judgment, combinations too powerful to be dealt with by ordinary methods exist against the enforcement of the laws. The

[25] McMaster, "History of the United States," vol. ii. p. 189.

President was not at all sure, in view of the strong States rights feeling then prevailing, and the opposition which such a display of Federal authority would excite, that the States would respond to the call for militia to execute an unpopular Federal law. As this was the first test of the new government's ability to maintain the supremacy of its laws, it was necessary that no risks should be taken, for if it proved unable to collect its revenues on account of the opposition of a community of backwoodsmen, respect for its authority would be gone. Accordingly Washington called upon the governors of Pennsylvania, New Jersey, Maryland and Virginia for fifteen thousand militia to put down the rebellion. Happily the governors responded promptly, and leading their forces in person they marched toilsomely over the mountains to the scene of the disorder, making a great display of Federal authority as they proceeded. Before this ample and well-timed exhibition of power the insurrection speedily collapsed, the ringleaders fled, the authority of the United States was vindicated and the national government immeasurably strengthened in the respect of the people. Some of the ringleaders were arrested and tried for treason, but none were convicted. Several were tried for other offenses and convicted, but later were pardoned by the President, who felt that being frontiersmen, unaccustomed to that respect for the majesty of the law which usually prevails in older communities, they did not understand the gravity of the offense of rebellion. The affair, which is usually dignified by the name of the Whisky Rebellion, cost the government over a million dollars, but the lesson was not without its moral value to the new republic.[26]

As the end of Washington's second term approached the country began to concern itself with the task of finding a successor for the great office which many had felt that only Washington could fill. His last term had been stormy and full of dissensions, but at the same time strong and victorious. The difficulties with England and France, the unpopularity of the Jay Treaty, the Whisky Insurrection, the bitter party rivalry, the discord in the Cabinet, and its ultimate disruption as well as the scurrilous abuse heaped upon the President, had made his position far from enviable, although he had triumphed over every obstacle. It was well known that he had with reluctance consented to serve a second term, and now he meant, with a determination nothing could shake, to retire to his long-

[26] Lodge, "Life of Washington," vol. ii. p. 126.

sought, well-earned repose at Mount Vernon. He accordingly issued a farewell address announcing his determination not to be a
candidate for a third term, although there can be no doubt that he
could have been easily elected again had he been willing to stand.
The abuse which he received was by no means a reflection of the
popular feeling, but we have abundant evidence that it greatly annoyed him and increased his distaste for public life. As the first
President of the new republic he had to face difficulties such as
none of his successors ever had to meet. He had no precedents by
which to be guided in the administration of an office which at the
time was unlike any other in the world. It therefore devolved upon
him to set an example, involving a greater responsibility in that he
well knew it would probably be followed in all essential particulars
by his successors. Forunately for the country he made no mistakes
in his conduct of affairs, or in the usages which he established. As
the chief civil magistrate of the country he displayed the same wisdom and tact, the same calm, judicious attitude on all public questions, the same dignity of behavior and magnanimity of soul, which
he had shown as the commander of the armies of the Revolution.
It is impossible to estimate the effect of his personal character upon
the office which the Philadelphia Convention seemed to create especially for him, and of which he was destined to be the first and
most illustrious incumbent. The petty discords and troubles of his
administration are forgotten when we repeat the story of the great
constructive work which marks the inauguration and the first years
of the new government. Every storm and difficulty had been
weathered; the wisdom of the builders of the nation had been
abundantly proved. The Constitution was no longer a mere experiment; its permanence was assured, so far as eight years of brilliantly
successful administration could assure it. Everywhere was evidence
of prosperity, of renewed hope and of love of country.

In taking final leave of public office, the great President who
had served the public for forty-five years, took occasion to give his
countrymen a few words of advice, and to warn them against what
he considered to be the chief dangers to the country. In a farewell
address which he put forth in September, 1796, and which he had
carefully prepared with the aid of others, he pleaded earnestly for
a full appreciation of the " immense value of union and unrestrained
intercourse between all parts of the republic "; admonished the people to beware of the baneful effects of party spirit, for he had but

recently felt its embittering influences; urged them to cherish public credit and good faith, and advised them to deal justly with all nations, but to avoid entangling alliances with anyone. His words upon this subject have served as a creed for all parties, and have been the basis of our foreign policy for over a hundred years. "The great rule of conduct for us," said he, "in regard to foreign nations is, in extending our commercial relations, to have with them as little political connection as possible; if we remain one people under an efficient government, the period is not far off when we may defy material injury from external annoyance, when we may take such an attitude as will cause the neutrality we may at any time resolve upon to be scrupulously respected; it is our true policy to steer clear of permanent alliances with any portion of the foreign world." This declaration was completed by the next generation, when Adams and Monroe added the famous doctrine which was the corollary of that announced by Washington. The President's valedictory was cordially approved by the people of all sections of the Union, and many public and private bodies testified through formal addresses to their respect and affection for him, who, by the common consent of posterity, has earned the title, "Father of his Country." "The well-chosen words," says Schouler, "in which America's venerated captain bade farewell to public station hushed faction into silence; and, the last rapids past, his bark went fitly down to a rich sunset through smooth waters, applauding multitudes crowding the banks, and parties emulating in respect as though to borrow glory from his departing radiance." [27]

[27] Schouler, "History of the United States," vol. i. p. 346.

Chapter XVI

THE FEDERALIST SUPREMACY. 1796-1801

I

JOHN ADAMS ELECTED PRESIDENT

THE third Presidential election was the first to be characterized by anything like a strict party contest. Both in 1789 and 1792 Washington had been the unanimous choice of the electors; but the development of political parties during his second term made inevitable a party struggle for the choice of his successor. Jefferson, who had retired from the Department of State in 1793, was the natural leader of the Republicans, while John Adams, who was then completing his second term as Vice President, was the most available Federalist candidate. As no party machinery for nominating Presidential candidates had yet been devised, Jefferson and Adams were put forward by the general consent of their respective followers. Aaron Burr, a New York politician of prominence and ability, and Thomas Pinckney, now honored as the negotiator of the Spanish treaty, were the Republican and Federalist candidates respectively for Vice President.

Adams received the electoral vote of all the Northern States except Pennsylvania, and also those of Delaware and a part of Maryland, making a total of seventy-one, while Jefferson received nearly all the Southern votes, and also the vote of Pennsylvania, a total of sixty-eight.[1] The Constitution then provided that each elector should vote for two persons, and that the one receiving the highest number of votes, if a majority of the whole number, should be President, and that the person receiving the next highest number should be Vice President. It thus happened that the Republican candidate for President was elected Vice President, and the country was presented with the anomalous spectacle of an administration with a Federalist head and with a Republican occupying the second

[1] McMaster, "History of the United States," vol. ii. p. 307.

place. In ten States the electors were chosen by popular vote, in the other six by the legislatures.

On March 4, 1797, Adams was formally inaugurated in the Hall of Representatives at Philadelphia, in the presence of a large concourse of spectators, among whom was Washington. After delivering a brief address replete with common sense and dignity of expression, he took the oath of office, which was administered by the Chief Justice of the Supreme Court, Oliver Ellsworth. The first and only President elected as a Federalist was a graduate of Harvard College, and a statesman of long experience and training, being then in his sixty-second year. He had been a member of the Continental Congress, and was one of the signers of the Declaration of Independence; he had served as minister to England, and with Franklin and Jay had negotiated the Treaty of 1783; while as Vice President, for eight years, he had influenced largely the course of legislation by his casting vote in the Senate. Although an able and distinguished patriot, with only the highest interests of the Republic at heart, he occasionally showed a lack of discretion and forbearance as President which involved him in difficulties. He was somewhat headstrong, irritable and inclined to vanity, but withal a most conscientious and able President.

Although it is customary to call Adams the first Federalist President, it is well to remember that the conduct of Washington's administration was entirely in keeping with the Federalist ways of thinking, and the policies which it pursued were purely Federalist and not at all Republican. In his social relations President Washington conducted himself in accordance with the views of those whom Jefferson and his followers were wont to call Federalist aristocrats and monarchists. His demeanor was anything but democratic, judged by the standard of Paris, which then set the fashion of what was termed democracy. His manner was reserved and stately; he had few intimate friends and no familiars, never forgetting that he was the chief magistrate of the Republic. His receptions were exceedingly formal, and were thought by his political opponents to be characterized by a certain frigidity. It was reported that he preferred a title of some kind in keeping with the dignity of his position, and we know that he did not object to his wife's being called " Lady Washington." Having no precedents to guide him with regard to the manner in which he should conduct himself while in office, he very sensibly addressed

a number of written questions to his Cabinet asking whether he
should associate with all or see none; what would be said if he
were sometimes seen at quiet tea parties; what he should do in
the way of receptions; whether he should make tours through the
country, and similar questions.   The rules which he laid down
in regard to all these matters of ceremony, as well as the principles
which guided him in the determination of his policies of state were
in the main followed by Adams.   Even Washington's Cabinet was
retained by his successor, and this proved to be one of the first
errors of the new administration, for several of these gentlemen
gave their first allegiance to Hamilton, who was the real leader
of the Federalists, rather than to the President, who was their
nominal chief.[2]

II

THE FRENCH IMBROGLIO

Thus it was with divided counsels that the new administration
entered upon its career confronted by a grave situation in regard
to the foreign relations of the country.   France had felt angered
at what she regarded as the ingratitude of the United States in
refusing to join her in the war against England in 1793, and this
was increased to rage when it became known in 1795 that the
United States had concluded a treaty with England, instead of
declaring war against her.   Up to that time France had confidently
hoped that the United States would be forced by the increasing
aggressions of the British to make common cause with her.   Great
was the surprise and indignation, therefore, of the French Government when news of the Jay Treaty reached Paris, and with it the
destruction of this last hope.   This treaty, the French Government
held, virtually made the Americans the allies of the British and
released France from the obligations of 1778.

Soon after the announcement of the conclusion of the Jay
Treaty the French Directory issued a decree announcing that the
cruisers of France would in the future treat neutral vessels in the
same manner as such governments suffered England to treat them.
Thereupon, French cruisers began to plunder American commerce
more ruthlessly than ever.   James Monroe, whom Washington had

[2] Morse, "Life of John Adams," p. 275.

sent to France to secure redress for outrages on American commerce, was recalled in 1796 for failure to press the American claims, and Charles Cotesworth Pinckney, an elder brother of the late Federalist candidate for Vice President, was appointed as his successor. Monroe had not only shown indiscretion, but disobeyed his instructions. "The truth is," said President Washington in severely criticising him, "Mr. Monroe was cajoled, flattered and made to believe strange things. In return he did, or was disposed to do, whatever was pleasant to that nation, reluctantly urging the rights of his own." [3] Upon his return to the United States Monroe, contrary to all displomatic usage, published a four hundred page vindication of his conduct, bitterly attacking the administration, and disclosing diplomatic information of a confidential nature.

Shortly after Adams's inauguration news came that the Directory had refused to received Pinckney upon his arrival at Paris in December, 1796; that he had been treated with discourtesy, by not being permitted to reside in France even as a private alien, although Monroe by reason of his French predilections was the object of constant flattery; and that the Directory had declared that no minister would be received from the United States until the French grievances had been redressed, as though the United States, instead of France, were the real aggressor. Burning with indignation the President called Congress together in special session, advised that "the action of France ought to be repelled with a decision which shall convince her and the world that we are not a degraded people, humiliated under a colonial spirit of fear and sense of inferiority," and recommended the adoption of measures of defense, especially the augmentation of the naval force. This language highly offended the French Government, and served further to increase the tension between the two countries.

The President, however, was extremely desirous of reaching a friendly understanding with the French Government in spite of his dislike for French manners and institutions, and he determined to send a special commission to Paris and make in this way another effort to bring about, if possible, an amicable settlement of the dispute. For this purpose he appointed John Marshall, a moderate Federalist, and Elbridge Gerry, a Republican, though not of the radical type, to join Pinckney at Paris. In October, 1797, they reached Paris, and instead of being allowed an official interview with

[3] "Washington's Writings," vol. xiii. p. 484.

Talleyrand, the Minister of Foreign Affairs, they were approached by the agents of the Directory, who informed them in a vague and roundabout way that if they wished to conclude a treaty with France, the United States must make a loan of some $6,000,000 to the French Government, pay each of the five directors $50,000 as private *douceurs,* and apologize for the President's language at the opening of Congress. The demands for *douceurs* were indignantly refused by the astonished envoys with the reply, " No, no, not a sixpence," although they offered to consult their government with regard to the loan, provided the Directory would suspend its measures against American commerce. This it refused to do.[4] Thereupon the negotiations were broken off and Marshall and Pinckney returned to the United States, leaving behind Gerry, who, by reason of his Republican sympathies, was better liked by the French diplomatists. In April, 1798, the President laid before Congress their dispatches, the name of Talleyrand's go-betweens being designated by the initials X, Y and Z. As soon as these communications were made public they were popularly described as the " X, Y, Z Dispatches," and the popular indignation was summed up in the universal cry, " Millions for defense, but not one cent for tribute," a famous phrase erroneously attributed to Pinckney. The President recommended the adoption of vigorous measures of defense, and announced that he would " never send another minister to France without assurances that he would be received, respected and honored as the representative of a great, free, powerful and independent nation.[5] The war fever swept over the country from Maine to Georgia, the Federalists and Republicans now standing on common ground as regarded their attitude toward France. The Republicans donned the cockade, the Federalist emblem, while tricolors and liberty poles which had been fervently displayed by the Republicans at the time of the outbursts of enthusiasm for France in 1793 were thrown aside with contempt. Hopkinson's popular song " Hail, Columbia," was composed at this time and set to the " President's March." [6]

There was no longer any external difference between Federalists and Republicans concerning the attitude toward France, and the treaties with France were deliberately suspended by act

[4] J. B. Moore, " American Diplomacy," p. 59.
[5] Morse, " Life of John Adams," p. 287.
[6] McMaster, " History of the People of the United States," vol. ii. p. 380.

of Congress. Preparations for war were actively begun; volunteer companies were formed in the towns, and popular subscriptions for building and fitting out ships were taken, $125,000 being raised in Boston alone. In the seacoast towns forts were built and earthworks erected. No formal declaration of war was ever made, but Congress authorized the issue of letters of marque and reprisal, and soon the ocean was swarming with privateers seeking French merchant vessels. A Navy Department was created, with George Cabot, a rich Boston merchant, as the first secretary, and a number of naval vessels were authorized to be built.

As early as 1794 Congress had authorized the construction of six frigates, and of these the *Constitution,* the *Constellation,* and the *United States,* famous names in our naval annals, were now ready for use, and with lesser vessels made a navy of some three dozen sail. The little squadron, commanded by such men as Decatur, Bainbridge, Hull and Rodgers, was then sent to the West Indies to search for French ships and protect American commerce. In February, 1799, the *Constellation,* carrying thirty-eight guns, in command of Captain Truxton, captured the French frigate *L'Insurgente,* carrying forty guns, in the Caribbean Sea, and a little later the *Vengeance,* carrying fifty-four guns. A number of captures were likewise made by the privateers. Steps were also taken to reorganize and increase the strength of the army, and Washington was appointed commander-in-chief with the rank of lieutenant general with the understanding that the chief command, except in case of actual war, should be exercised by Hamilton, who was made second in rank. Knox and Charles C. Pinckney were also appointed major generals, and a number of brigadiers were authorized.

In the meantime, Talleyrand having become convinced that the United States would resist to the last the aggressions of France, and that nothing but an honorable treaty would be acceptable to the Americans, notified the American minister at the Hague in a round-about way, that " if a minister from the United States were sent he should be received with the respect due to the representative of a free and independent nation." The grace with which he did it was not the finest, and would be resented today; but then the Republic was in its swaddling clothes, and it was thought best to avoid war, if possible, even if it involved the sacrifice of a little dignity. Accordingly, the President appointed the Chief

Justice, Oliver Ellsworth, Governor Davie of North Carolina, and William Vans Murray, then minister to Holland, and an able member of the bar, as special envoys to negotiate a treaty. When they reached Paris they found that the Directory had been overthrown by Napoleon Bonaparte, who as First Consul was at the head of the government. Bonaparte was disposed to be friendly with the United States, and in September concluded with the envoys a treaty of peace, commerce, navigation and fisheries, which released the United States from the obligations of the treaty of 1778, and exempted France from all responsibility for damages inflicted upon American commerce by French cruisers.[7] This ended the so-called quasi war between the two nations, and reëstablished friendly relations.

III

FEDERALIST MEASURES

The French hostilities made Adams popular, discredited the Republicans, who cherished a traditional sympathy for the French, and brought the Federalists to the front with a majority in both houses of Congress. In this situation the party proceeded to enact four laws which destroyed its popularity and led to its ultimate downfall as a political organization. These were a naturalization act, two alien acts, and the sedition act. The general purpose of all these measures was to crush out foreign influence and repress domestic opposition, but the attempt proved ruinous to the Federalists. It was believed that the chief strength of Republican opposition was the foreign element. Many Republican newspapers were edited by foreigners, chiefly Frenchmen and Irishmen, who indulged in scurrilous abuse of Federalist leaders and Federalist measures. Adams's administration was reviled in a manner which greatly annoyed him, and he felt that a limit ought to be set to the right of editors and pamphleteers to criticise the government, and inasmuch as many of these were naturalized citizens it might be well to place greater restrictions upon the right of aliens to acquire American citizenship. Accordingly a new Naturalization Act was passed, which increased the term of residence required

[7] Foster, "A Century of American Diplomacy," p. 179.

for citizenship from five to fourteen years; established a more stringent procedure, and required a registration for purposes of surveillance of all white aliens thereafter arriving in the United States. An Alien Act was then passed authorizing the President, for a period of two years, to expel from the country any alien whom he might deem dangerous to the peace and safety of the United States, or who was suspected of being concerned in any treasonable or secret machinations against the government, and another empowering him in time of war to order the removal of all subjects or citizens of a hostile government. In case an alien warned to depart was afterwards found in the United States, he could be fined and imprisoned for three years, at the President's discretion; and if any alien having been banished should return to the United States without permission, he might be imprisoned at the discretion of the President for an indefinite term.

The Sedition Act, to prevent and restrain " seditious practices," was a measure of greater severity, and excited more opposition. It ordered the punishment of any person who should conspire to oppose the execution of any act of Congress, or who should write or publish any false, scandalous or malicious matter against the government, either house of Congress, or the President, or seek to bring them into contempt or disrepute. Any person convicted of an offense against the first mentioned provision was to be punished by a fine of $5,000 and five years' imprisonment; while the punishment for the second was a fine not exceeding two thousand dollars and imprisonment for two years.[8] The Alien Acts were criticised as depriving accused persons of the right of trial by jury, and as vesting the President with arbitrary powers, since any suspected alien was liable to summary banishment at the pleasure of the President without the slightest regard for due process of law. No occasion, however, seems to have arisen for the employment of the powers thus conferred upon the President, and the act expired without ever having been enforced. But not so with the Sedition Act. It was immediately taken advantage of by the Federalists, and a number of Republican editors were prosecuted for libeling the government, one of whom was Callender, a Scotch pamphleteer and friend of Jefferson. He was convicted of saying, among other things, that Adams had completed a scene of ignominy which Washington had begun.

[8] Schouler, "History of the United States," vol. i. p. 432.

Mathew Lyon, of Irish birth, a member of Congress from Vermont, was fined $1,000 and sentenced to prison for a term of four months for criticising in the course of a political canvass the government for its "ridiculous pomp, foolish adulation, and selfish avarice," and being virtually offered a pardon by the President, he refused to accept it, and was reëlected to Congress while in prison.[9] Other convictions for similar utterances followed. The trials under this act aroused intense indignation among the Republicans, who affirmed, and not without some truth, that the Federalist journals were allowed to publish what they pleased without molestation. The least that can be said of the Alien and Sedition Acts is that they were short-sighted party measures, intended to crush out political opponents rather than win them, wholly repugnant to the spirit and genius of American institutions, and instead of accomplishing the purpose for which they were passed did the Federalist party irreparable injury. This was the first and only attempt by the national government to suppress free speech, shackle the press and outlaw those who had sought our shores as an asylum from oppression.

Among those who opposed these measures as destructive of the liberties of the people, no one was more active than the Vice President, Thomas Jefferson, who proposed to organize public opinion against them by an appeal through the legislatures. In pursuance of this plan he wrote a series of resolutions, which the legislature of Kentucky adopted in 1798, with certain modifications, while another set, prepared at his suggestion by Madison, was adopted by the legislature of Virginia in the same year. The "Kentucky and Virginia Resolutions," as they have come to be known, contain the first clear enunciation of the compact theory of the Union — a theory which was destined to have an immense influence on the constitutional development of the country. The Kentucky resolutions, which were the first to be adopted, declared that the Constitution is a compact under which are united equal sovereign States, that the general government is one of delegated powers, and when it assumes undelegated powers its acts are unauthoritative, void and of no force, and in such case the States (which are the parties to the compact) have the right to judge for themselves of the infractions and of the mode of redress.[10]

[9] McMaster, "History of the People of the United States," vol. ii. p. 399.
[10] See Warfield, "The Kentucky Resolutions of 1798."

Incidentally, the Alien and Sedition Acts were declared to be null and void, on account of their repugnance to the Constitution. In the following year the Kentucky legislature passed another set of resolutions in which the right of the States to judge of infractions of the Constitution was reasserted, and the additional view advanced that nullification by the States of unauthorized Federal acts was the rightful remedy. The Virginia resolutions, written by Madison, were milder in tone, although they presented the "compact" theory of the Union, and called upon the other States to join Virginia in declaring the obnoxious Alien and Sedition Acts unconstitutional. The resolutions were sent to all the State legislatures for an expression of opinion, but the nullificationists received little encouragement or sympathy. All the Northern State legislatures formally condemned as pernicious the doctrine that the supreme law of the land might at the discretion of a single State legislature be set aside, while the action of the Southern legislatures did not indicate any very great sympathy with the doctrines thus set forth.

The most important effect of the Kentucky and Virginia Resolutions was to arouse public opinion against the recent acts of Congress, and to create a reaction in favor of the rights of the States. Some have fixed the stigma of responsibility for the theory of nullification, which was to play such an important part in our history, upon Jefferson and Madison.[11] Years afterwards, when the country was greatly aroused over the attempt of South Carolina to nullify the tariff act, the venerable Madison indignantly repelled the imputation that either he or Jefferson ever contemplated the nullification of an act of Congress by a single State.[12] The probability is that all that was intended was to arouse public opinion by a formal denunciation of the recent arbitrary measures of the government, and thereby prevent similar legislation in the future.[13]

While the excitement over the trouble with France was at its height, and the Alien and Sedition Acts were under discussion, the President announced the ratification of the eleventh amendment to the Constitution. This amendment grew out of a decision of the Supreme Court in 1794 (Chisholm v. Georgia), which held that

[11] Morse, "Life of Jefferson," p. 194; also Von Holst, "Constitutional History of the United States," vol. i. p. 149.
[12] Houston, "A Study of Nullification in South Carolina," p. 24.
[13] See Schouler, "Life of Thomas Jefferson," p. 193.

the jurisdiction of the Federal Courts extended to suits brought by private citizens against a State, provided the plaintiff were a resident of another State.

At that time, when the idea of State sovereignty was strong, it was regarded as little less than an outrage upon the dignity of a State to make it the defendant in a suit at the instance of a private individual, and the decision in question came near provoking the State of Georgia, against which it was directed, to resistance. To prevent the State from carrying out its threats, and to avoid similar difficulties in the future, Congress proposed, and the States ratified, an amendment providing that the judicial power of the United States shall not be construed to extend to any suit commenced or prosecuted against one of the United States by citizens of another State or of a foreign state. The amendment accomplished its purpose, but it has proved to be an evil, in that it has enabled States to repudiate their debts, leaving their non-resident creditors without judicial remedy except in the State courts.

As the eighteenth century drew to a close the country was thrown into mourning by the death of its most illustrious citizen, George Washington, who since the expiration of his presidential term had been living in retirement at Mount Vernon. Born in 1732, he had been a witness of and a participant in the chief events of the century. His death was announced in Congress by John Marshall, his young friend and neighbor. By Richard Henry Lee he was pronounced to have been " First in war, first in peace, and first in the hearts of his countrymen." To no other man was the Republic so indebted. He had been the leader in the war for independence; he had helped to make the Constitution, and as the first chief magistrate he had started the nation upon its great career, and had successfully guided it clear of the early perils.

At the close of Adams's administration the seat of government was removed from the gay city of Philadelphia to Washington, then a dreary village of two or three hundred inhabitants. It had been laid out in the woods a few years previous, its houses were mostly huts of the rudest sort, while its streets were deep, muddy roads flanked by rows of scrub oaks and pines. There was no business, no industry, no society. For those who wished to live comfortably, says McMaster, " the only resource was to go to Georgetown, three miles away." [14]   Most of the government build-

[14] McMaster, " History of the People of the United States," vol. ii. p. 489.

ings were but half finished, the Capitol was hardly ready for the meeting of Congress, and the noise of hammer and saw in the partly finished Presidential mansion disturbed the quiet of the village. Such was the rude beginning of one of the finest capitals of the world.

Meantime the Presidential election was claiming the attention of the country. The Federalist members of Congress had met in caucus and renominated Adams and Pinckney; the Republican members had in the same way nominated Jefferson for President and Aaron Burr for Vice President. The Alien and Sedition Acts, and the bitter quarrel which had broken out between Hamilton and Adams, had destroyed the chances of the Federalists, so that when the electoral votes were counted it was found that Jefferson and Burr had each received seventy-three, Adams sixty-five, and Pinckney sixty-four votes. According to the Constitution the election now devolved upon the House of Representatives, voting by States, there being a tie between the two leading candidates. Under the system by which each elector voted for two persons, it was natural that as soon as strict party organization was introduced the two candidates of each party would tie, since every elector who voted for one would probably vote for the other. This happened at the first election after the rise of political parties, and it doubtless would have continued to happen had not the Constitution been amended. The framers had evidently not foreseen the time when the President and Vice-President would be chosen by a strict party vote. Another difficulty was that in voting the electors did not indicate which of the two candidates was being voted for as President and which for Vice President. In the present case there was nothing on the face of the returns to show whether the electors wished Jefferson for President, or Burr, although, as a matter of fact, it was well known to be Jefferson. If the House had been Republican, Jefferson would have been promptly chosen, in obedience to the well-known wishes of the party. But the situation was complicated by the fact that the Federalists were in a majority in the House, and as the Constitution provided that in such cases the choice should be made from the two highest candidates, they were forced to choose between two evils, as they regarded it. Therefore they were inclined to choose that one of the candidates who would most likely do them the least harm as President, and that one in their opinion was Burr.

They also discussed the plan of balloting fruitlessly for a President until the expiration of Adams's term, March 4, when both the offices of President and Vice President would become vacant, and a new election could be held. Intrigues were then entered into with a view to securing terms with the candidates. Jefferson declared unequivocally that he would not " receive the government on capitulation," that he would not " go into it with hands tied." Hamilton, Jefferson's most bitter enemy, now came forward with true high mindedness and political sagacity, and advised the Federalists to choose Jefferson as a less dangerous man than Burr, whom he pronounced as " true a Cataline as ever met in midnight conclave." " If there be a man in the world I ought to hate," said Hamilton, " it is Jefferson; but the public good must be paramount to every private consideration.[15]   After a long struggle, lasting through more than a week, during which threats and ugly rumors of various kinds were afloat, Jefferson was chosen on the thirty-sixth ballot, receiving the vote of ten States, as against four for Burr, two States casting blank votes.[16]   In a letter to Governor McKean Jefferson declared that if the election had resulted in the choice of Burr no one would have submitted more cheerfully than himself; but in the event of a usurpation he was decidedly with those who were determined not to permit it. Burr is said to have secretly schemed for the office and held out promises to the Federalists, although he well knew that the electors never intended to choose him for the Presidency. Threats of war had been made by the Republicans in case the Federalists should choose Burr, and in order to avoid similar dangers in the future a movement was at once set on foot for the amendment of the Constitution with regard to the manner of electing the President, and before another Presidential election occurred the amendment had become a part of the Constitution.

[15] Stanwood, " History of the Presidency," p. 70.
[16] McMaster, " History of the People of the United States," vol. ii. p. 524.

Chapter XVII

JEFFERSONIAN REPUBLICANISM. 1801-1809

I

CHARACTER OF JEFFERSON

WITH the accession of Jefferson to the Presidency on March 4, 1801, a new political party came into power, holding principles widely different from those upon which the government had been administered during the preceding twelve years. He was the first President to be inaugurated at the new capital city of Washington, and the first Chief Magistrate whose political tastes were ostensibly democratic. Although democratic in politics, he belonged to the Virginia aristocracy, from whose ranks so many of our early Presidents were destined to be drawn. After graduating from William and Mary College he studied law under Chancellor Wythe, a distinguished Virginia barrister, and was admitted to the bar in 1767. As a member of the Continental Congress he wrote the Declaration of Independence, while still in his thirty-third year. As a member of the legislature of Virginia he was the author of notable legal reforms, particularly the abolition of the law of primogeniture and entail as regards land inheritance, and the establishment of religious freedom. He was also the author of a general system of education, and was the founder of the University of Virginia.[1] As a member of the State legislature, governor of Virginia, minister to France, Secretary of State, and Vice President, he had acquired large experience as a statesman, and had shown himself to be a most successful politician.

In person he was tall, loosely built, freckled faced, somewhat awkward in movement, inclined to carelessness of dress, retiring in disposition, extremely democratic in his habits, and hostile to ceremony and parade. Senator Maclay of Pennsylvania described him

[1] Schouler, "Life of Thomas Jefferson," ch. vi.

in 1790 as a man whose figure had a "loose, shackling air," his countenance a "rambling vacant look," and as one who talked brilliantly almost without ceasing. To the British Secretary of Legation at Washington in 1804 he appeared "very much like a tall, large-boned farmer," dressed in a blue coat, thick gray-colored hairy waistcoat, with a red underwaist lapped over it, green velvet breeches with pearl buttons, yarn stockings and slippers down at the heels.[2] He was benevolent of disposition, hospitable almost to self-impoverishment, and the most indulgent of slavemasters. He had a quick and inquiring mind, and touched on many subjects; but his acquirements were, in the opinion of some, various and superficial rather than solid or profound. He read easily several languages, studied with enthusiasm botany, music, mathematics, architecture and other sciences; kept a record of meteorological phenomena, made experiments in astronomy, practiced scientific agriculture, took great interest in the proposed application of steam to machinery, discussed with familiarity zoölogy and archæology, and is said to have invented an improved plow. He kept up with the literature of the day, and maintained a constant correspondence with leading men, both at home and abroad, as his twenty thousand letters show.[3] As an architect he drew the plan for his home at Monticello. He was an expert violinist and a bold horseman. But the one subject he thoroughly understood was politics, and it was as a manager of men that he stands unrivaled.

Although Jefferson charmed his friends by his delightful correspondence, and excited their admiration by his versatility as a thinker, yet as an orator he was ineffective and consequently rarely resorted to speech-making on public occasions. His religious views were those of a free thinker and materialist, with preferences for Unitarianism. But he was no scoffer at divine truths, no enemy of the moralities and decencies of life, but one whose private life was singularly pure.[4] The New England Federalists, especially the clergy, charged him with being an atheist; but we have his testimony that he believed in God, although, like Benjamin Frank-

[2] See Henry Adams, "History of the United States," vol. i. p. 186.

[3] Concerning Jefferson's many-sidedness someone said: "He could calculate an eclipse, survey an estate, tie an artery, plan an edifice, try a cause, break a horse, dance a minuet, and play the violin." Buffon, the naturalist, in a letter to him, expressed regret at not having consulted him before publishing his natural history.

[4] Schouler, "Life of Thomas Jefferson," p. 229.

lin, he did not accept the teachings of orthodox Christianity, so far as they related to the divinity of Christ and Scriptural interpretations. His social peculiarities were quite as striking as his mental characteristics. His theory was that all were equal, and titles and distinctions were exceedingly distasteful to him. Aristocracies founded on birth were to him worthless shams; no race of kings, he said, ever presented above one man of common sense in twenty generations, and as for existing sovereigns, he did not believe there was one in Europe whose talents or merits would entitle him to be elected a vestryman by the people of any parish in America.[5] He objected to the stamping of his likeness on the coinage, and to the celebration of his birthday by his friends; he did not scrupulously observe the customary ceremonial in the reception of foreign ambassadors, ignored the formal system of precedence at social functions, and established the "rule of *pêle-mêle*," by which each guest selected his own seat at the dinner-table, the ladies being escorted by those nearest them when dinner was announced.[6]

The first Republican President was duly inaugurated at the new Capitol March 4, 1801, the oath being administered by the new Chief Justice, John Marshall. He did not, as an English traveler wrote two years later, ride horseback to the Capital unattended, and after hitching his horse to the palings, go in to take the oath; but he walked from his lodgings escorted by a body of troops and a number of political friends, including several members of the Cabinet. In a somewhat inaudible voice he delivered an inaugural address, which for a long time, says Henry Adams, was almost as well known as the Declaration of Independence. Besides a certain charm of style, it was in a way the first platform of a new political party, and it has continued until this day to embody the political philosophy of one of the two great parties into which the people of the United States are divided. After a few remarks, intended to soothe his political opponents, such as "We are all Republicans, we are all Federalists," "brethren of the same principle called by different names," and a few others in praise of the American system of government, which he pronounced "the strongest on earth — the only one where every man, at the call of the laws, would fly to the standard of the law," he proceeded with an epitome of his political principles, those which were to guide him

[5] "Jefferson's Works," vol. iv. p. 426; also vol. v. p. 8.
[6] "Jefferson's Works," vol. viii. p. 277.

in the conduct of his administration. Compressed in the narrowest compass, they included, he said:

"Equal and exact justice to all men, of whatever state or persuasion, religious or political; peace, commerce, and honest friendship, with all nations —entangling alliances with none; the support of the State governments in all their rights, as the most competent administrations for our domestic concerns and the surest bulwarks against anti-republican tendencies; the preservation of the general government in its whole constitutional vigor, as the sheet anchor of our peace at home and safety abroad; a jealous care of the right of election by the people—a mild and safe corrective of abuses which are lopped by the sword of revolution where peaceable remedies are unprovided; absolute acquiescence in the decisions of the majority—the vital principle of republics, from which there is no appeal but to force, the vital principle and immediate parent of despotism; a well-disciplined militia—our best reliance in peace and for the first moments of war, till regulars may relieve them; the supremacy of the civil over the military authority; economy in the public expense, that labor may be lightly burdened; the honest payment of our debts and sacred preservation of the public faith; encouragement of agriculture, and of commerce as its handmaid; the diffusion of information and the arraignment of all abuses at the bar of public reason; freedom of religion; freedom of the press; freedom of person under the protection of the *habeas corpus;* and trial by juries impartially selected—these principles form the bright constellation which has gone before us, and guided our steps through an age of revolution and reformation. The wisdom of our sages and the blood of our heroes have been devoted to their attainment. They should be the creed of our political faith—the text of civil instruction—the touchstone by which to try the services of those we trust; and should we wander from them in moments of error or alarm, let us hasten to retrace our steps and to regain the road which alone leads to peace, liberty, and safety." [7]

The rather aristocratic but certainly dignified manner in which the Federalists had conducted the government was especially distasteful to him, and he accordingly abandoned several of their practices and established others, which have since been followed without deviation. One of the Federalist customs was to have the President meet Congress at the opening of each session, and read to it a formal address, after which the two houses separated, prepared appropriate replies, and then marched to the Executive Mansion and presented their reply to the executive. This was the British practice, and if for no other reason was obnoxious to Jefferson. He accordingly communicated with Congress by written message, and dispensed altogether with the reply of Congress.

[7] Richardson, "Messages and Papers of the Presidents," vol. i. p. 323.

The Federalists asserted, probably with some truth, that the innovation was due to Jefferson's incapacity as a speaker quite as much as to his fidelity to democracy. However this may be, the practice has been followed by all his successors, and levees, as they had been maintained by Washington and Adams, were also done away with.

Jefferson was inclined to interpret the election of 1800 as a revolution against what he called the monarchial tendencies and usurpations of the Federalists — a revolution as real in the principles of the government as that of 1776 was in its form, he maintained; and he therefore determined to put the ship of state on the Republican tack, as he expressed it, in order that she might show the beauty of her motion and the skill of her builders.[8] His political philosophy was summed up in the ideas that government rests on the consent of the governed, and that the government which governs least is the best, and is more in harmony with the true theory of individual liberty. So far as the general government was concerned, this course was not only wise, but obligatory under the Constitution. For, according to his interpretation of that instrument, the function of the general government was limited chiefly to foreign concerns, the great sphere of internal government being left chiefly to the States. The general government, he contended, should be a " very simple organization and a very inexpensive one; a few plain duties to be performed by a few servants." He thought the country, under the Federalist rule, had been too much governed, that unnecessary legislation had been enacted, that the number of officers had been needlessly multiplied, that the taxing power had been unnecessarily employed, and that the public expenditures, notably for the maintenance of the army, the navy, and the diplomatic establishment, were greater than the public welfare demanded.[9] This general line of policy Jefferson believed to be in accordance with the theory of strict construction of which he was the most distinguished advocate, and which had been wholly disregarded by the Federalists during their supremacy. Thus he came into power on a platform of principles wholly at variance with those which had been in force, and fully persuaded

---

[8] "Jefferson's Works," vol. iv. p. 365; vol. vii. p. 133.
[9] "Jefferson's Works," vol. iv. p. 330. For a discussion of Jefferson's political philosophy see Merriam, " American Political Theories," ch. iv.

that the Federalists had abused their powers he was resolved to bring about reform.

II

REPUBLICAN " REFORMS "

Among his constitutional advisers, Jefferson selected Madison to be Secretary of State, and Gallatin to be Secretary of the Treasury. The other members were men whose names were hardly known beyond their States. In both houses of Congress the Republicans had a majority, completely under Jefferson's influence, but the Supreme Court, the authority charged with interpreting the Constitution, was still composed of Federalist judges, while the great majority of the administrative offices of the government were likewise held by Federalist incumbents, for while Washington and Adams had never failed to appoint men of high character, they uniformly gave the preference to those of their political faith. This was a source of anxiety to the new President, who thought that there ought to be a more equitable division of the offices among both parties. He lamented that " nearly the whole of the offices of the United States were monopolized by a particular sect," and declared that it would have been a circumstance of great relief had he found a " moderate participation of office in the hands of the majority." It was intolerable, he said, that this monopoly should continue after the recent verdict of the people, and as few incumbents died and none resigned, the only means of making places for Republicans was by removal. It was a painful duty, he professed, but he was ready to meet it as such.[10]

The Federalists, foreseeing their early downfall, had during the last months of Adams's administration created a number of new offices, which had been promptly filled by the appointment of men of their own party. Among the offices thus created were sixteen Federal circuit judgeships and twenty-four minor judicial positions in the District of Columbia, which were filled during the last hours of Adams's term by the appointment of staunch Federalists. " Thus," said Jefferson, " they have retired into the judiciary as a stronghold; there the remains of Federalism are to be

10 " Jefferson's Works," vol. iv. p. 402.

preserved and fed from the treasury; and from that battery all the work of Republicanism are to be beaten down and destroyed." [11]

The story is, that as midnight of the last day of Adams's term approached, the office of the Secretary of State, John Marshall, was all astir with the work of preparing commissions for the recent appointees, when General Dearborn, representing Jefferson, walked in to take charge. Such commissions as had not been delivered were withheld by Madison, the new Secretary of State, on the ground that Adams had no authority to make appointments during the last hours of his term, when a new administration was coming into power. One of these "midnight" appointees, Mr. Marbury, whom the President had appointed justice of the peace for the District of Columbia, brought suit in the Supreme Court for a writ of mandamus to compel the Secretary of State to deliver his commission. The court refused to issue the writ, on the ground that it had no authority under the Constitution to do so, and that the provision of the Judiciary Act of 1789, which undertook to give the court that power, was not warranted by the Constitution. The court, therefore, laid down the new and far-reaching doctrine that an act of Congress, which in the opinion of the judiciary is in conflict with the Constitution, is null and void, and everyone is thus relieved from all obligation to be bound thereby. Although there were some loud protests among the Republicans against the assumption of such authority upon the part of the court, the decision was acquiesced in, and thus was established the peculiar American doctrine of the right of the courts to override the statutes of the legislature. The author of this great opinion of the court in the case of Marbury vs. Madison was John Marshall, recently Secretary of State, who had been appointed Chief Justice of the Supreme Court to succeed Oliver Ellsworth, about a month before the expiration of Adams's term. Marshall was destined to become the foremost American jurist, and one of the greatest judges of modern times. For thirty-four years as Chief Justice he dominated the Supreme Court, and during all this period, while the other two departments of the government were in the hands of the Republicans, the Federalists continued to possess this "stronghold" and to interpret and apply the Constitution and laws according to Federalist theories of constitutional law. The appointment of Mar-

[11] "Jefferson's Works," vol. iv. p. 424.

shall was the most far-reaching act in its effect of President Adams's administration. Marshall not only elevated the Supreme Court to a place of great dignity and respect, but his decisions on the many difficult questions of constitutional law arising during the early years of the government built up the national sentiment and increased the strength of the central government. He was, with Hamilton and Washington, one of the three great founders of the Republic.

The effort of the Federalists, already condemned by the popular verdict, to intrench themselves in the government by methods which, to the Republicans, seemed disreputable, Jefferson was determined to defeat. Shortly after his inauguration he wrote to Dr. Benjamin Rush of Philadelphia: "I will expunge the effects of Mr. A.'s indecent conduct in crowding nominations after he knew they were not for himself. Some removals must be made for misconduct — of the thousands of officers in the United States a very few individuals only, probably not twenty, will be removed; and these only for doing what they ought not to have done." [12] "That done," he again wrote, "I shall return with joy to that state of things when the only questions concerning a candidate shall be, is he capable, is he honest, is he faithful to the Constitution?" [13] Jefferson accordingly removed a number of Adams's so-called midnight appointees; then followed a few who had made themselves offensive as partisans, or were guilty of official misconduct; and finally a group consisting mainly of attorneys and marshals, against whom no charge was made, but who were removed, as Jefferson said, "to make room for some participation for the Republicans." The courts were so "decidedly Federal," he said, that the removal of attorneys and marshals, "they being the doors of entry into the courts," was indispensably necessary as a "shield to the Republican part of our fellow citizens." [14] In order to retain their places undisturbed many of the Federalist incumbents joined the Republican party and became outspoken maligners of those with whom they had formerly affiliated. Few removals had been made by Jefferson's predecessors. Washington, during his two terms, had removed but 9, and Adams had displaced but 19, most of them in the

[12] "Jefferson's Works," vol. iv. p. 382.
[13] Letter in reply to the "Remonstrance of New Haven Citizens," July 12, 1801; "Jefferson's Works," vol. iv. p. 402.
[14] Letter to Giles, March 23, 1801; "Jefferson's Works," vol. iv. p. 381.

interest of the public service, a few for political reasons.[15] During the eight years of Jefferson's administration he removed 109 officials out of a total of 433 belonging to the Presidential class. This, however, does not include the number of subordinates who lost their positions as a consequence of the displacement of their superiors.[16] Technically, perhaps, Jefferson must bear the odium of introducing the spoils system into the national service, for with him party allegiance was made the basis of appointment, and party dissent a cause for removal. But it was not the sole cause, and certainly the civil service was not corrupted and enfeebled by the adoption of a policy of wholesale proscription. The adoption of this innovation belongs to one of his successors.[17]

There was one class of officers, however, which was believed to be beyond Jefferson's reach, namely, the Federal judges, whose tenure is fixed by the Constitution at good behavior. In spite of this provision, Congress, at the suggestion of the President, repealed the law passed during Adams's administration for the creation of the sixteen circuit judgeships, and thus the incumbents were legislated out of office, much to the chagrin of the Federalists. A clause of the repealing act provided for a suspension of the sessions of the Supreme Court for a period of fourteen months, for the purpose, says Henry Adams, of preventing Marshall from declaring the judiciary act unconstitutional.[18]

To reach the other judges nothing remained but to try impeachment. Some of them had gone out of the way to express from the bench their opinions of Jeffersonian democracy. In February, 1803, John Pickering, district judge in New Hampshire, was impeached for drunkenness and violence, and was removed from office. The weapon of impeachment was then turned against one of the Supreme Justices, Samuel Chase, who had on several occasions shown strong political bias on the bench, and who, in the course of a charge to a grand jury, had taken occasion to express his condemnation of Jefferson's election, and his belief that the government under Republican rule would soon sink into "mobocracy." Although Chase's display of partisanship on the

---

[15] Fish, "The Civil Service and the Patronage," p. 21.

[16] *Ibid.*, p. 42

[17] For the character of his appointments see Henry Adams, "History of the United States," vol. i. p. 227 *et seq.*

[18] Henry Adams, "History of the United States," vol. i. p. 298.

bench was fully established, the requisite two-thirds of the senators could not be secured for conviction, and he was accordingly acquitted, greatly to the chagrin of Jefferson. Articles of impeachment were also prepared against Peters, one of the district judges, for arbitrary conduct, but no action was taken by the House. Thus this desperate effort to seize the courts and make them the creature of the administration, for the time being, failed; henceforth the judiciary was unmolested by the Republicans, and Jefferson was compelled to accept its inexorable decrees, although he believed it to be dangerous to the rights of the people, saying, of the Supreme Court, that it " was a body like gravity, ever acting with noiseless feet, gaining ground step by step, and engulfing insidiously the State governments." There can be little doubt that his hostility to the Supreme Court was partly the result of personal dislike for Marshall, whom he wished to have impeached.

After repealing the Judiciary Act, the Naturalization Act and other obnoxious Federalist measures, Congress took up Jefferson's recommendations with regard to retrenchment, reorganization of the finances and the reduction of the civil, military and naval establishments. The Secretary of the Treasury, Albert Gallatin, was an able financier, second only to Hamilton, and, like Hamilton, a citizen of foreign birth. Gallatin, upon request of the President, drew up, after long and laborious study, an elaborate scheme of finance for the payment of the public debt and the reduction of the government expenditures. Under the Federalists, so the Republicans complained, the taxes had increased threefold, while the expenditures had increased in even greater proportion; yet the highest point which the expenditures had ever reached was only $11,500,000, attained in the year 1800, when increased expenses were made necessary on account of the quasi war with France. Of this amount more than one-third was on account of the national debt. The average annual expenditures had been about $9,000,000, a smaller sum than was expended in any one year of Jefferson's administration.[19] One of the sources of revenue, namely, the internal tax on whisky, refined sugar, stamped paper, etc., amounting all told to about $650,000 annually, was especially obnoxious to the Republicans, and was accordingly abolished, and at the same time provision was made for setting aside $7,300,000 annually for the

[19] Henry Adams, " History of the United States," vol. i. p. 253.

THOMAS JEFFERSON
(Born, 1743.   Died, 1826)
After an engraving by Baron Desnoyers, Paris

payment of the public debt, which nominally amounted to about $80,000,000. Then, upon Jefferson's recommendation, the army was given a "chaste reformation." Its strength was reduced from 4,000 to 2,500 men, the peace establishment of 1795 leaving only one regiment of artillery, two of infantry, and a corps of engineers. Likewise, the new President favored a large reduction of the navy, and suggested that the remaining vessels might be hauled up into the eastern branch of the Potomac, where they would be under the immediate eye of the department, and where " it would require but one set of plunderers to look after them." [20] The numbers of vessels in commission was therefore reduced from about twenty-five to seven, work on fortifications was stopped, and the construction of ships on the stocks was abandoned. The number of naval officers was reduced about three-fifths, and the President was authorized to sell the gallant little squadron which the Federalists had constructed, excepting thirteen frigates, of which only seven were to be retained in commission.[21] An effort was also made to abolish the navy department and place the management of naval affairs under control of the Secretary of War, as had been the case before the advent of the Federalists to power, but the bill failed. Jefferson had the satisfaction of seeing the fruition of his policy of economy, and before he retired from the Presidency the public debt, under the wise management of Gallatin, was reduced over forty millions, or about one-half, the taxes had been reduced by a million and a half, while there had been a large increase of the revenues from customs duties.

III

FOREIGN RELATIONS; WAR WITH TRIPOLI; PURCHASE OF LOUISIANA

At the very time when the reduction of the army and the dismantling of the navy were going on, the country was called upon to prepare for war with Tripoli, one of the Barbary States in North Africa. Ever since the middle ages these countries had followed piracy as one of their chief pursuits, and the European nations apparently without any sense of common interest had sub-

[20] Letter to S. Smith, April 17, 1801.
[21] Schouler, "History of the United States," vol. ii. p. 24.

mitted to the demands of petty Mohammedan despots for black-
mail, and from time to time sent them large sums of money or an
equivalent in presents, in order to secure immunity for their merchant vessels on the Mediterranean.   When the United States became independent it adopted the European custom of paying for a
similar immunity, and from time to time sent cargoes of presents,
including barrels of money, to the rulers of Algiers, Morocco,
Tripoli and Tunis for the privilege of navigating the high seas,
the common property of all nations.   During the last ten years not
less than two million dollars had been thus expended in the form
of ransoms, gifts and tributes; but in spite of this generous tribute
our consuls were insulted, our vessels seized and our sailors were
frequently captured and reduced to slavery, and to secure their
ransom additional sums were occasionally sent over.   In 1801 the
Pasha of Tripoli, who had received presents and $83,000 in cash
under the treaty of 1796, complained that the United States was
not treating him with the same liberality that it was the ruler of
Algiers, as evidenced by the recent treaty with that potentate, but
instead was putting him off with empty professions of flattery.   He
therefore demanded an increase of the tribute; but receiving no
satisfaction he declared war.   Instead, however, of sending over
a handsome bribe, Jefferson, who years before, as a member of
of the Continental Congress, had advocated war instead of tribute
as the proper method of dealing with the Barbary pirates, dispatched to the Mediterranean a squadron under Commodore Dale
— consisting of some of the same vessels which he was preparing
to lay up in the east branch of the Potomac to furnish food for
Maryland worms — to teach the petty despot that the United
States would no longer submit to his insults and demands for black-
mail.   Reaching the Mediterranean in July, 1801, Dale captured
a Tripolitan cruiser, blockaded Tripoli, and made such a display
of his vessels as to overawe not only Tripoli but the other Barbary
powers, and to cause them to respect the American flag and to be
contented with the presents to which they were entitled under the
treaty.[22]   This was a new method of dealing with these pirates,
and the honor of its adoption belongs to the United States.   Jefferson's conduct in this respect was applauded at home by men
of all parties, and the whole affair must have gone far toward

[22] Henry Adams, "History of the United States," vol. i. p. 245.

convincing him of the fallacy of his theory with regard to the uselessness of a navy.

While the war with Tripoli was in progress Jefferson's administration had scored a great diplomatic triumph, as a result of which the territorial area of the United States was more than doubled. This was the conclusion of a treaty with France for the purchase of Louisiana. From the time of the Revolution the question of the navigation of the Mississippi River had been one of continual agitation, since this great waterway afforded the only practicable outlet to the sea for the inhabitants of the West. It was essential to their prosperity, and, as Jefferson said, whoever controlled New Orleans and the mouth of the Mississippi was the natural enemy of the United States.[23] Spain had owned the mouth of the river, a fact which was a source of continual annoyance to the inhabitants of the United States, and in 1795 had granted to the citizens of the United States a right of deposit at New Orleans for a period of three years. Since 1763 she had also owned all the territory west of the river, but the government had no fear of her, in spite of the vexatious restrictions which she might impose upon the right of navigation. Indeed, Jefferson in a letter to Governor Claiborne of the Mississippi Territory in July, 1801, went so far as to say that the people of the United States considered the Spanish possession of Louisiana as " most favorable to our interests," and that we should " see with extreme pain any other nation substituted for her." [24] But already rumors were reaching the United States that Spain contemplated retroceding Louisiana to France, and the reports caused intense anxiety. " Nothing," said Jefferson, speaking of this report, " has produced more uneasy sensations through the body of the nation since the Revolution." [25] Finally, in May, 1802, the suspicions of Jefferson were confirmed by the receipt of news that Spain had already by the secret treaty of San Ildefonso, concluded in October, 1800, nearly two years previous, ceded Louisiana to France. Jefferson, upon receiving the news, declared that " the day France takes possession of New Orleans fixes the sentence which is to restrain her forever within her lowwater mark. It seals the union of two nations, who, in conjunction, can maintain exclusive possession of the ocean. From

[23] Read Ogg, " The Opening of the Mississippi," ch. ix.
[24] Henry Adams, " History of the United States," vol. i. p. 404.
[25] Foster, " Century of American Diplomacy," p. 189.

that moment we must marry ourselves to the British fleet and nation." [26]   About the same time matters were further complicated by the act of the Spanish intendant at New Orleans in withdrawing from the Americans the right of deposit under which the inhabitants of the West had been permitted to send their goods down the Mississippi River to the sea without the payment of duties at New Orleans.[27]   In this situation it was decided that an effort should be made to purchase New Orleans and West Florida from France, which would insure to the United States the control of the mouth of the Mississippi, and this was all that was wanted. For this purpose the President appointed James Monroe, acting with the resident minister, Mr. Livingston, to conduct the negotiations — " negotiations upon the outcome of which," said Jefferson, in giving them their instructions, " the future destinies of our country hang."   After the brief Peace of Amiens, England and France were on the point of renewing the war, and Napoleon quickly came to the conclusion that his American possessions would doubtless be an element of weakness instead of strength.   According to Marbois, the negotiator upon the part of France, and the historian of the Louisiana Purchase diplomacy, the First Consul submitted to his counselors the American proposition with the following remarks: " They only ask of me one town in Louisiana; but I already consider the colony as entirely lost, and it appears to me that in the hands of this growing power it will be more useful to the policy and even to the commerce of France than if I attempt to retain it.   Irresolution and deliberation are no longer in season. I renounce Louisiana.   It is not only New Orleans that I will cede, it is the whole colony without any reservation. . . . I direct you to negotiate this affair with the envoys of the United States. Do not even await the arrival of Mr. Monroe.   Have an interview this very day with Mr. Livingston." [28]

The offer of Napoleon to sell his whole domain in America came as a great surprise to Monroe and Livingston, and at first they were quite as much puzzled as delighted, since they had no instructions to buy more than the territory necessary to secure control of the mouth of the river.   It was impossible to have recourse to the government for more ample instructions, for on account of the

[26] " Jefferson's Works," vol. viii. p. 144.
[27] Henry Adams, " History of the United States," vol. i. p. 421.
[28] Marbois, " History of Louisiana," pp. 264, 274.

crude means of communication then existing a delay of not less than six months would have been required — a delay which in the present case would doubtless have proved fatal to the negotiations. In this situation the envoys proceeded with the negotiations, and with remarkable speed, considering the traditional slowness of diplomacy a hundred years ago, concluded a treaty with Napoleon, not only for the cession of New Orleans and West Florida, but for the whole of the Louisiana territory, stretching far away, north and west, to the Canadian frontier. The price finally agreed upon was sixty million francs for the territory and twenty millions in satisfaction of American claims against France for unlawful captures — a total of about $15,000,000. The terms of the treaty provided that the inhabitants of the ceded territory should be admitted to the rights, privileges and immunities of citizens of the United States, and incorporated into the Union as soon as consistent with the principles of the Federal Constitution. The seventh article granted to the inhabitants of France and Spain special privileges in the ports of Louisiana for twelve years.

On account of English naval supremacy Napoleon knew that he would probably not be able to hold Louisiana, and accordingly offered it to the Americans for a small sum, remarking after the conclusion of the treaty that he had just given England a maritime rival that would sooner or later humble her pride.[29] Moreover, the failure of the expedition to San Domingo had dampened his colonial enthusiasm and turned his thoughts toward a European empire. The territory acquired by the treaty was over eight hundred thousand square miles, thus costing less than four cents an acre. When the treaty was sent to the President he was half-delighted, half-perplexed. He was the founder and leader of the party whose one overshadowing principle was strict interpretation of the Constitution so far as the powers of the general government were concerned. Now he was called upon to do an act for which no authority could be found in the Constitution. To purchase Louisiana would be the most flagrant instance of loose construction in the history of the government. " The Constitution," he said, in a letter to John Breckenridge, " has made no provision for our holding foreign territory, still less for incorporating foreign nations into our Union. . . . The executive, seizing the fugitive occurrence which so much advances the good of our country,

[29] Ogg, " The Opening of the Mississippi," p. 582.

have done an act beyond the Constitution." [30] And again: "Our peculiar security is in possession of a written Constitution; let us not make it a blank paper by construction." His first thought was to propose an amendment to the Constitution, an "act of indemnity," as he called it, empowering the government to acquire foreign territory, and he actually prepared a draft for this purpose, but after a brief reflection he readily saw that under the clumsy method of amending the Constitution speedy ratification would be impossible, and that delay might lead to the failure of the treaty. For once Jefferson threw aside his theory of a strict construction, decided to send the treaty to the Senate for ratification, and suggested that the less said about the necessity of amendment the better.[31] The treaty was duly ratified by a vote of 24 to 7, the strict constructionists thus presenting to the country the spectacle of a party scattering its own cherished theories to the winds and supporting with unanimity those which it had always regarded as dangerous and unconstitutional, and relying for its justification upon the wisdom and necessity of the act and hearty wish of the people for its consummation.[32]

Curiously enough, the only opposition to the acquisition of Louisiana came from the party of liberal construction — the Federalists — some of whom for once became strict constructionists, and insisted that the government had no power to acquire foreign territory, at least no power to incorporate it in the Union as an integral part of the Republic. It thus happened that Federalists and Republicans each drew their arguments from the other's arsenal. But the Federalists advanced the further argument that the Union was a partnership, and that new members could not be admitted except by unanimous consent,— Griswold of Connecticut, the House leader, going so far as to predict that the accession of so vast a territory would at no distant day lead to the subversion of the Union. This was mainly the result of New England's traditional jealousy of the West, which was first prominently brought out in the Philadelphia convention of 1787. It was but natural that the people of this section should look with apprehension upon the extension of the western boundaries, since in the course of

[30] "Jefferson's Works," vol. viii. p. 244.

[31] "Jefferson's Works," vol. viii. p. 245. For a rather severe criticism of Jefferson for "violating the Constitution," see Von Holst, "Constitutional History of the United States," vol. i. pp. 190–192.

[32] Foster, "Century of American Diplomacy," p. 201.

time it would mean the destruction of New England's balance of power and the diminution of her influence in the Union. Others objected that the boundaries of Louisiana were in dispute and might, therefore, lead to war; while still others insisted that the price paid was too high — that it would equal over four hundred tons of silver, would require over eight hundred wagons to contain it, would provide every man, woman and child in the country with three dollars, and the like.[33] The Federalist opposition, however, was futile in the face of the general belief that the country had made a splendid bargain. The treaty was ratified, as stated, and possession of the Territory was formally entered upon in December, 1803, by the new governor, William C. C. Claiborne, late governor of the Mississippi Territory. The American flag was hoisted over the Cabildo a few days before Christmas, " amidst the acclamations of the inhabitants." Thus Louisiana passed forever from the control of France. Few diplomatic events have had a more important influence on the history of the United States than the conclusion of the treaty for the purchase of Louisiana. Besides adding 900,000 square miles to the national domain, it removed an old source of disaffection in the West, increased immensely the strategic power of the nation, made necessary the acquisition of Florida, brought about the annexation of Texas and the Mexican War, increased the thirst for slavery, and thus indirectly contributed to the chain of causes which led ultimately to the Civil War.[34] Fortunate it was that Jefferson had enlarged views of the future of the country, and was able to put aside his narrow and preconceived opinions as to the interpretation of the Constitution, and welcome an opportunity of such vast import to the Republic. In March of the following year Congress passed an act providing a government for the Territory. The northern portion, embracing Missouri, the only inhabited part north of New Orleans, was made the District of Louisiana, and for purposes of government was attached to the Territory of Indiana, greatly to the disgust of the inhabitants of this region, who in time held a convention and formally protested against this quasi-foreign bondage.[35] The southern portion, embracing roughly what is now the State of Louisiana, was called the Territory of Orleans, and placed tem-

---

[33] McMaster, "History of the People of the United States," vol. ii. p. 630.
[34] Foster, "Century of American Diplomacy," p. 204.
[35] Thomas, "Military Government of Newly Acquired Territory," p. 44.

porarily under the administration of the President of the United
States, who was authorized to exercise all the military, civil and
judicial powers at the time exercised by the officers of the existing
government.   Thus Louisiana started on its career as an American
territory, under the absolute authority of Thomas Jefferson.[36]

Louisiana had been lightly acquired, but with it came a perplexing boundary dispute.   The treaty of cession gave us the
Territory, " with the same extent that it now has in the hands
of Spain, and that it had when France possessed it, and such as it
should be after the treaties subsequently entered into between Spain
and other states."   Neither phrase explained the other, but they
were on the contrary contradictory.   The United States at once
claimed West Florida on the ground that Louisiana in the hands
of France extended to the Perdido River, while Louisiana, in
the hands of Spain, extended only to the Iberville River.   Both
Monroe and Livingston firmly believed that it was actually included
in the purchase, and Marbois seems to have been of the same opinion.[37]   A territory with uncertain boundaries had, therefore, been
annexed, and the outcome of the long dispute will only appear
at a much later time.   Little was known of the great region thus
acquired.   Except along the Mississippi from St. Louis to New
Orleans the country was uninhabited save by Indians.   The inhabitants of the lower Territory consisted principally of French,
with a few Spanish Creoles, English, Germans and negroes, the
aggregate being less than 50,000, of whom 16,000 were slaves and
1,300 free persons of color.   The upper portion of the Territory
contained about 6,000 inhabitants, mostly about St. Louis.   In
a special message to Congress concerning the cession, Jefferson referred to an immense glittering white salt mountain somewhere in
Louisiana, said to be one hundred and eighty miles long and forty-
five in width, and also mentioned other marvelous natural curiosi-
ties supposed to exist in the new domain.[38]

Even before the acquisition of Louisiana Jefferson had shown
a lively interest in the exploration of the West, and now that it
belonged to the United States he sent Meriwether Lewis and William Clark to make an official exploration, having in the meantime

[36] For a good account of the legal nature of this Government, see Thomas,
"Military Government of Newly Acquired Territory," pp. 24-44.
[37] Schouler, "History of the United States," vol. ii. p. 56.
[38] McMaster, "History of the People of the United States," vol. ii. p. 631.

induced Congress to appropriate the necessary funds to cover the expenses of the party.   The expedition, consisting of some thirty of forty individuals, started from St. Louis in May, 1804, ascended the Missouri River, crossed the great divide, and floated down the Columbia River, reaching the Pacific Ocean in November, 1806.   The explorers then returned to St. Louis in September, 1807, having traveled 9,000 miles, and made a report, furnishing the first definite information of the geographical condition of the new Territory.

In the year of their return Zebulon Pike was sent to explore the region about the headwaters of the Mississippi, and after finishing the task he penetrated the mountainous region of Colorado and New Mexico, discovering the great peak in Colorado which still bears his name.   These western expeditions were but another phase of the interest in the country's progress and the eagerness for scientific knowledge.   Following closely upon them in 1807 came the first successful operation of the steamboat by Robert Fulton on the Hudson.   Before a crowd of excited spectators the little boat which he had named the *Clermont* started on its trial trip August 17, and proved to be a success.   Four years later the first steamboat passed down the Mississippi from Pittsburg to New Orleans.   These events are important landmarks in the material progress of the country, and are quite as worthy of note as political or constitutional changes, for they were to make the Union possible over an extent of territory undreamed of by the founders.

As the time for the Presidential election of 1804 drew near, it was clear that the Republicans would win by a large majority. The country had been prosperous during Jefferson's first term, the government had been conducted with economy; the national debt had been largely reduced; the national honor had been defended against the Barbary pirates, and above all the national domain had been doubled in extent.   Jefferson's popularity was now at its zenith, and he was unanimously renominated in February, 1804, by a caucus of the Republican senators and representatives, with George Clinton, many times governor of New York, as his associate for Vice President.   The Federalists, now most unpopular, numbered but a handful, and their strength was confined almost entirely to New England.   Some of them had vigorously opposed the purchase of Louisiana, while others, like Timothy Pickering, had proposed the withdrawal of the Eastern States from the Union, and the formation of an Eastern confederacy.[39]

The disaffected elements now made a desperate effort to secure control of New York State with the aid of Aaron Burr, then Vice President, who had been repudiated by the Jefferson wing of the Republican party.[40] The former contingent proposed to support Burr as an independent candidate for Governor, to succeed Clinton, the Republican nominee for Vice President, but Hamilton threw his influence against the scheme as a disgraceful plot, and Burr was defeated. Brooding over his downfall, and blaming Hamilton for his defeat, Burr challenged him to a duel and killed him on the field of Weehawken, July 11, 1804, on the same ground where Hamilton's eldest son had fallen the victim of a duel three years before.[41] Thus was the country deprived by a duelist's bullet of one of the founders of the Republic—a statesman of precocious intellect, of prodigious energy, of remarkable executive ability. The firm friend of Washington, the idol of the Federalists, of whom he was the real though not the nominal leader, yet he loved his country better than he did his party. At the time of his death at the early age of forty-seven he had had the most brilliant career of any American then living. What might he not have accomplished had he been spared to devote his maturer years to the good of his countrymen? The awful tragedy shocked the entire country, and it was felt that the act was little short of murder. Burr was indicted and fled the State, despised and execrated by his countrymen, not only as a political outcast, but as a murderer. His career henceforth is in dark contrast to that of his earlier days. One result of the affair was to arouse the public sentiment of the North against the barbarous practice of dueling and to bring about its early abandonment. Unfortunately, the practice continued much longer in some sections and was frequently resorted to as an honorable method of settling disputes among gentlemen.

When the results of the Presidential election were known, nobody was surprised at the result. Jefferson was reëlected President, and with him, George Clinton, as Vice President, the ticket receiving one hundred and sixty-two electoral votes, as against

[39] See Henry Adams, "History of the United States," vol. ii. pp. 160–191.
[40] Schouler, "History of the United States," vol. ii. p. 70.
[41] Lodge, "Life of Alexander Hamilton," p. 250.

seventy-three at the last election. The Federalist candidates, Charles C. Pinckney of South Carolina and Rufus King of New York, received only fourteen electorial votes, as against sixty-five at the last election. Only Connecticut, Delaware, and a part of Maryland, remained true to what was once the great party of Washington and Hamilton.[42] The party seemed now on the verge of disintegration, although it was to regain strength and continue in existence for a few years longer. Just before the presidential election a new amendment to the Constitution — the twelfth — had secured the ratification of the requisite number of States, and had become a part of the law of the land. The purpose of the amendment was to remove the difficulties which arose in the Presidential election of 1800. By requiring each elector to designate as such the person voted for as President and the person voted for as Vice President, the possibility of the two candidates coming before the House of Representatives in case of a tie was removed, and with it the possibility of electing the leading candidate of one party as President and the leader of the other as Vice President.[43]

IV

THE BURR CONSPIRACY; TROUBLES WITH GREAT BRITAIN AND FRANCE

Jefferson's first term had been a period of domestic tranquillity, while, with the exception of the little war with Tripoli, peace had marked our relations with foreign powers. But the same good fortune did not attend his second term. Besides foreign complications there were troubles enough at home. The first of these to claim attention is the so-called Burr conspiracy. After the killing of Hamilton, Burr, now bankrupt in fortune and politically ruined, but brilliant and still ambitious, entered upon a desperate undertaking in the West. Just what he purposed to do is hard to ascertain. He unfolded vague schemes of colonization and conquest to several persons of prominence in the West, notably General Wilkinson of the United States Army, who villainously entered into Burr's scheme and then betrayed him, and Andrew Jackson, then a lawyer of Tennessee.

[42] Stanwood, "History of the Presidency," p. 84.
[43] See House, "The Twelfth Amendment."

Finally, in December, 1806, he collected a small party of adventurers, not exceeding one hundred in number, and mustered them at Blennerhassett's Island, in the Ohio River. Enlisting the aid of Blennerhassett, the wealthy owner of the island, Burr, with his adventurers, floated down the river on flatboats for a destination and purpose unknown to the public. Meantime wild rumors were afloat that he had designs upon Mexico, and even contemplated the detachment of the Southwest from the Union. Acting upon such reports as he could gather, Jefferson issued a proclamation offering a reward for his capture. Early in 1807 Burr was arrested near Natchez by the authorities of the Mississippi Territory, and while awaiting trial forfeited his recognizance and fled for parts unknown. Shortly afterwards he was captured near Fort Stoddert, Alabama, and taken to Richmond, Virginia, where he was arraigned on the charge of treason against the United States. After a trial before Chief Justice Marshall, sitting as circuit judge at Richmond, he was acquitted, August, 1807, on the ground of insufficient evidence, since it could not be proved that his offense consisted in levying war against the United States or in giving its enemies aid and comfort, as required by the Constitution. " The overt act," said the Chief Justice, " must be proved according to the mandates of the Constitution and of the act of Congress, by two witnesses. It is not proved by a single witness." [44] After his acquittal Burr disappeared from public notice. Abandoning the country which had called him to its highest honor but one, he wandered abroad several years, living incognito upon scanty remittances from personal friends, but returned to New York in 1812, confirmed in sensual and impecunious habits, and there resided until his death in September, 1836. Being asked shortly before his death whether he had meditated designs against the Union, he answered, " No; I would as soon thought of taking possession of the moon, and informing my friends that I intended to divide it among them." [45] His correspondence with the British and Spanish ministers, Merry and Yrujo, contains appeals for financial aid from England and Spain, ostensibly to enable him to effect the secession of the West. Many of the inhabitants of the West were not without feelings of disaffection toward the Union on account of the jealousy and neglect of their interests by the

[44] McCaleb, " The Burr Conspiracy," p. 350.
[45] Parton, " Life of Aaron Burr," vol. iii. p. 327.

East, and Burr proposed to encourage the spirit of disaffection and to make himself the leader in the movement to bring about a separation of that section from the Union. Knowing that England and Spain would rejoice at the disruption of the United States, he solicited their aid in carrying out his treasonable scheme, but it was never given. Recent investigation, however, seems to show that Burr only sought to hoodwink the British and Spanish ministers, and really intended to use whatever aid might be given for an expedition against the Spanish Territories in the southwest.[46] An incident of the trial at Richmond was a collision of authority between the executive and the judiciary, arising from the action of Marshall in issuing a *subpœna duces tecum* against Jefferson, ordering him to produce a certain paper regarding Burr's transactions. This Jefferson refused to obey, and the court was powerless to enforce its commands. Jefferson's action may have been possibly due to his dislike of Marshall. He was greatly disgusted at Burr's acquittal and declared that " the scenes which have been enacted at Richmond are sufficient to fill us with alarm; now it appears that we have no law but the will of the judges." [47]

By far the most perplexing difficulty, however, of Jefferson's administration, arose from the aggressions of England and France upon American commerce. It will be remembered that war between these two powers had broken out in 1793, and had raged without interruption until 1802, when by the Peace of Amiens a brief suspension of hostilities followed. In 1803 the war was renewed; nation after nation was dragged into the contest, and the struggle raged with increasing fury until Napoleon went down to defeat at Waterloo, ten years later. England was mistress of the seas, while Napoleon was invincible on land. The ships of France, Spain and Holland were driven from the ocean; consequently these countries found it impossible to obtain the much-needed products of their colonies in the West Indies, South America and elsewhere.

In this situation, as we have seen, nothing remained to France but to throw her colonial trade open to neutrals, and American vessels very soon acquired a monopoly of this trade, and became, in fact, the principal carriers of the world. But by the so-called " Rule

[46] McCaleb, "The Burr Conspiracy," p. 8.
[47] McCaleb, "The Burr Conspiracy," p. 358; Henry Adams, "History of the United States," vol. iii. p. 451.

of 1756 " a belligerent was not permitted to open to neutrals in time of war its colonial carrying trade which was not open to them in time of peace, and England therefore claimed the right to seize any neutral vessel carrying a cargo directly between a belligerent port and a colony of that belligerent. This harsh rule was soon evaded in a legitimate way by the ingenuity of enterprising American sailors. The rule of 1756 did not apply to trade between a neutral port and that of a belligerent, and, hence, all that was necessary to make the voyage between a belligerent and its colony lawful was to break the voyage by landing at a neutral port and re-shipping the cargo. Thus an American vessel sailing from a French or Spanish port in the West Indies, touching at New York or Charleston, entering the cargo at the custom house, reloading on the same ship and proceeding to France or Spain was pursuing a lawful voyage.

Such was the decision of the British admiralty court in April, 1800. Under this ruling American shipping swarmed upon every sea. Hundreds of vessels sailed to the colonial possessions of France, Spain, Holland and Italy, loaded with the products needed by belligerents, proceeded to the United States, broke the voyage, and sailed for Europe. In one year the customs revenue increased from thirteen to twenty million dollars. England discovered that under this practice her naval supremacy would avail nothing. If her continental enemies were to be supplied with all the products needed, in spite of her maritime power, she could never cope successfully with them. Accordingly, in 1805, the British admiralty court reversed its previous decision, and held that breaking the voyage at a neutral port was an obvious evasion of the rule of 1756; that the intent of the voyage must be taken into consideration, and hence a voyage as above described was unlawful. Captures of American vessels at once began, and a prosperous carrying trade was soon well-nigh destroyed. The number of captured vessels increased the first year after Lord Stowell's decision from 39 to 116, and within three years 350 American vessels were thus captured by the British.[48]

Such were the British aggressions upon American commerce. Those of France were scarcely less. Napoleon, having suffered a great defeat at Trafalgar at the hands of Lord Nelson, resolved to

[48] McMaster, "History of the People of the United States," vol. iii. pp. 220–227.

destroy English trade with the continent regardless of the rights of neutrals, by means of the " Continental System "; that is, by the exclusion of English goods from the ports of that part of Europe which was under his control, or in alliance with him. This meant the virtual cutting off of commercial intercourse between Great Britain and the continent. The announcement of this resolution was followed in May, 1806, by a retaliatory British Order in Council, which declared the whole coast of Europe, from the Brest to the Elbe River, a distance of some eight hundred miles, to be under a blockade, and, of course, closed to neutral trade. No blockading squadron was stationed outside the interdicted ports to give notice of the blockade and to warn approaching vessels; and, what was worse, American ships bound for Europe were presumed to be destined for a blockaded port, and, therefore, liable to capture by British cruisers. In November of the same year Napoleon retaliated with the Berlin Decree — so called from the place of proclamation — declaring all the British Islands to be in a state of blockade, interdicting all trade therewith, and forbidding all vessels touching at British ports from entering French ports. This order was directed against neutral trade, and as the Americans were practically the only neutral carriers left, they were the chief sufferers. Notwithstanding the stipulations of the treaty of 1800, Great Britain again retaliated by an Order in Council in January, 1807, which forbade all neutral trade with France and her allies and dependencies, and by an order of November, the same year, neutral vessels bound for blockaded ports were authorized to be seized unless they had touched at a British port and paid duties. These orders were followed by a counter decree of Napoleon in December, 1807, — the Milan Decree, — which directed the seizure and forfeiture of every neutral vessel which allowed itself to be searched by a British vessel, which should touch at a British port and pay duty, or which should be found on the high seas or elsewhere bound to or from any British port.[49] These orders and decrees virtually put all Europe under a paper blockade, and whether the American vessels sailed from or to a British port or a continental port, it was liable to capture. In 1807, 194 American vessels were captured by the British authorities, and a considerable number by the French.

But the aggressions upon neutral commerce were not the only

[49] J. B. Moore, " American Diplomacy," p. 60.

grievances of the Americans against the European belligerents. There was the old question of the impressment of American seamen by British cruisers. Almost from the foundation of the government Great Britain had claimed and had exercised the right of stopping American merchant vessels on the high seas and reclaiming any British subject found thereon. The matter had been aggravated by the great increase in the number of English subjects who had lately enlisted in the American merchant service, mainly as a result of the enormous expansion of American commerce, and the consequent increase in the demand for trained seamen. With the expansion of commerce came also an increase in the wages of seamen, the amount being some three times that allowed by British merchantmen, as a consequence of which British seamen deserted in great numbers and entered the American merchant marine. Whole crews would sometimes go ashore in an American port and join the American service. Many of these seamen took out naturalization papers and became American citizens; but Great Britain stood by the doctrine of indefeasible allegiance, and insisted that no British subject could divest himself of his citizenship without her consent. Consequently American naturalization papers were of no avail against British searching officers, and their disposition to disregard naturalization certificates was heightened by the knowledge that they were readily transferable from one sailor to another, and easily forged.

Moreover, the task of distinguishing British sailors from American sailors was not always easy. At first the British naval officers seem to have made an honest effort to impress only those of British birth; but when the demand for seamen grew pressing on account of the Napoleonic wars, the officers were inclined to give themselves the benefit of every doubt, and sometimes able-bodied seamen were presumed to be of English birth unless they could prove the contrary, which was usually a difficult, if not an impossible task. As the aggressions on American rights continued, the feeling in favor of war, especially against England, increased. But to Jefferson war did not appear necessary, and, besides, as a result of his own policy, we were not prepared for war. The army and navy had been reduced to insignificant proportions, and the fortifications had been neglected. To build new war vessels and fortify the coast and harbors would interfere with his cherished policy of retrenchment. He, therefore, resorted to schemes which served only to excite the ridicule of the Federalists and of some Republicans as well. One of these was the " gunboat system," by which the defense of the country was entrusted to a fleet of gunboats which were built according to Jefferson's orders. They were unpretentious looking little craft, each carrying a small gun at the stern, and were to be used against the enemy in time of war, but in time of peace were to be hauled up under sheds and protected from the weather. They were utterly useless when war came, and rendered no service except to afford amusement for the Federalist wits.

Meantime, Jefferson was trying to reach an understanding with Great Britain, and for this purpose he sent James Monroe and William Pinkney to London as special envoys. In December, 1806, they concluded a treaty which contained no prohibition against impressment, no definition of a lawful blockade, made no provision for indemnification of American owners for unlawful captures, no recognition of the right of the United States to participate in the British West India trade, and no acknowledgment of the American doctrine that " free ships make free goods." It was so unacceptable to Jefferson that he did not even communicate it to the Senate.[50] In the next place Jefferson recommended a non-importation act as applied to English manufactured goods and the goods of English colonies, and the act was passed in April, 1806, but it was suspended after a duration of about one month and a half. All these measures, as well as diplomatic remonstrances, were without avail. Finally, in June, 1807, the last straw was added by a British outrage near Norfolk. As the American frigate *Chesapeake* was proceeding down the Potomac for a cruise to the Mediterranean, the British frigate *Leopard* overhauled her, after exposing the vessel to a raking fire and killing a number of the crew, sent on board a searching party against the will of her commander and carried away four sailors, of whom three were Americans. The commander of the *Chesapeake* was unable to resist the attack of the *Leopard,* his guns not being ready for action, his crew untrained, and the vessel altogether unfit for immediate action. The news of this last outrage set the nation aflame with indignation, and in many towns and cities public meetings were held and resolutions passed denouncing the outrage and demanding reparation or war.

[50] Schouler, "History of the United States," vol. ii. p. 159; Henry Adams, vol. iii. p. 419.

Jefferson declared that "the country had never been in such a state of excitement since the battle of Lexington"; yet he was still opposed to war, and the extent of his action was to issue a proclamation ordering all British armed vessels out of American waters. He then summoned Congress in extra session, October, 1807, and recommended an embargo on American shipping. This was a part of his policy of "peaceable coercion," by which he believed that the European nations could be forced to respect our rights by withholding from them American commerce. But, as events showed, Jefferson had overestimated the value of that commerce to England; it did not prove to be absolutely essential to her existence and its paralysis was ruinous to us. Jefferson's influence with Congress, however, was omnipotent, his recommendation was enacted into law, and no American merchant vessel could any longer leave American water for any foreign port, and coasting vessels were required to give bonds to land only at American ports.

The French and English aggressions had seriously crippled American commerce, but Jefferson's embargo completely destroyed it. "It was," said John Randolph of Roanoke, "like cutting off the toes to cure the corns." Ships, with their cargoes, rotted in port, and thousands of seamen were thrown out of employment. No foreign market was available for disposing of surplus products, industry was at a standstill, and general business stagnation prevailed throughout the country. Exports dropped in one year from $110,000,000 to $22,000,000; in 1809 import duties fell from $16,000,000 to $7,000,000. The price of wheat declined three-fifths. The distress was especially great among the shipping interests of New England, and among the tobacco growers of Virginia. As the ruinous effects of the Embargo Act increased, the difficulty of enforcing it increased also, and smuggling and evasion became a fine art.[51] The coasting trade, as said, was permitted, and vessels bound for New Orleans often found it convenient to run into West India ports, exchange their cargoes for tropical products, and with false manifests proceed to New Orleans. Systematic smuggling across the Canadian and Florida borders was also carried on, in some cases through most ingenious methods. The stringency of the embargo law was increased by several supplementary acts requiring heavier bonds of those engaged in

[51] See McMaster, "History of the People of the United States," vol. iii. pp. 300–306.

the coasting trade, and imposing other restrictions, including a force provision. Had the embargo brought England to terms there might have been some compensation for the suffering which it occasioned; but Lord Castlereagh was able to boast that it was " operating more forcibly in our favor than any measure of hostility we could call forth without war actually declared." Its operation as against France was equally ineffective, the French minister declaring that it was applauded by the emperor. In April, 1808, Napoleon issued the Bayonne Decree, directing that all American vessels entering Continental ports should be captured, since, under the American embargo, they had no right to be out of American ports. In other words the emperor, in the kindness of his heart, proposed to help the United States enforce its policy of non-intercourse.

Meantime the dissatisfaction with the embargo at home continued to increase. In New England the discontent ripened almost to rebellion, and caused the great majority of the people to desert the ranks of Republicanism and go over to the Federalists. Jefferson was compelled to admit that his policy of peaceable coercion was not a success, and, finally, in February, 1809, one week before the expiration of his term, the Embargo Act was repealed, after being in force about fourteen months. The principle of peaceful coercion was not entirely abandoned, however, and in place of the embargo a Non-Intercourse Act was substituted. This forbade intercourse with Great Britain and France so long as they should persist in their hostility to American trade. Jefferson signed the act to repeal the embargo, thus condemning the principle which underlay his whole theory with respect to neutral trade. This was the last important act of his administration. He retired from the Presidency with less popularity than when he entered upon it; yet in spite of the effects of the embargo, loving and respectful tributes poured in upon him from every section of the Union except New England. His first term was a successful one, but its brilliancy was eclipsed by the troubles of the second. The one overshadowing event of his administration was the purchase of Louisiana, and this is generally remembered, while too often the failures of his general policies are largely overlooked and forgotten; but when all is said, it must be admitted that his political career was unparalleled in the history of the Republic. Probably no President has so fully impressed his personality upon the country; no one has exerted so powerful an influence upon his political followers. In his last annual address to Congress he pronounced a brief valedictory to his countrymen, saying: "Looking forward with anxiety to their future destinies, I trust that, in their steady character unshaken by difficulties, in their love of liberty, obedience to law, and support of the public authorities, I see a sure guarantee of the permanence of our republic; and, retiring from the charge of their affairs, I carry with me the consolation of a firm persuasion that Heaven has in store for our beloved country long ages to come of prosperity and happiness." [52]

[52] Richardson, "Messages and Papers of the Presidents," vol. i. p. 456.

Chapter XVIII

THE SECOND WAR WITH GREAT BRITAIN
1809–1815

I

PRELIMINARY INCIDENTS

AS Jefferson's second term drew to a close he announced that he would not be a candidate for a third term, thus following the example of Washington. "If," he said, "some period be not fixed either by the Constitution or by practice, the office will, though nominally elective, become for life and then hereditary." Besides, he had now reached his sixty-fifth year and longed to retire from public life to the quiet of his beloved Monticello. Nevertheless he was invited, through affectionate addresses, by many legislatures to stand for reëlection, and there can be little doubt that had he consented to do so he could easily have triumphed over any other candidate. He lived almost a generation longer after his retirement from the Presidency, and devoted his later years to the work of higher education in Virginia, particularly the university which he had himself founded many years before and which was "the darling child of his old age." While refusing the Presidency for himself, however, he practically named his successor, so great still was his influence with his party. The Republican members of Congress met in caucus January, 1808, and nominated Jefferson's choice, James Madison, for the last eight years Secretary of State, for President, and George Clinton for Vice President.[1] Clinton had been Vice President during the last term, and as his office had been regarded as the stepping-stone to the Presidency, he was a candidate for first place on the ticket. Monroe, supported by some of his Virginia friends, who disliked Madison, was also a candidate to succeed Jefferson. Pinckney and

---

[1] Hunt, "Life of James Madison."

413

King were renominated by the Federalists, but Madison was easily elected, receiving 122 electoral votes.[2]   The Federalist candidates, who received only fourteen electoral votes in 1804, now received forty-seven, the increase being due chiefly to the unpopular measures of Jefferson's second term and the wide-spread discontent occasioned by the embargo.   The dissatisfaction in New England was shown by the fact that the Federalists carried all that group of States except Vermont.   They also carried Delaware, two districts in Maryland, and three in North Carolina.   The electors were chosen by the legislatures in six States and by popular vote in the others.

The new President, like his predecessor, belonged to the Virginia "dynasty," and was inclined to follow in the footsteps of his former chief.   He was a statesman of wide experience, having served in the Continental Congress and in the Federal Convention of 1787.   His great services in the Convention had been so important as to win for him the enviable title of "Father of the Constitution."   He had also served in the legislature of Virginia, had been a member of the first Congress under the Constitution, and during the eight years of Jefferson's administration had been Secretary of State.   He was, therefore, thoroughly familiar with the duties of the office to which he was now called; and, as Schouler properly observes, was entitled to the office by every consideration of merit, seniority, public experience and patriotic as well as party service.[3]

The chief problem confronting the new administration at the outset was the settlement of the troubles with England and France — a heritage bequeathed by Jefferson.   Commercial retaliation having failed to bring these nations to a sense of justice, diplomacy and war remained as the only alternatives.   Like Jefferson, Madison was opposed to war, preferring to try peaceful measures so long as they promised success.   By some he was charged with being timid and irresolute, and certainly for the first two years of his administration he seemed to be without a definite policy.   The Non-Intercourse Act which took the place of the embargo was enforced throughout the year 1809 without accomplishing the purpose for which it was intended.   It was then superseded by an act passed in May, 1810, which provided that if either England or France

[2] Stanwood, "History of the Presidency," p. 95.
[3] Schouler, "History of the United States," vol. ii. p. 187.

would withdraw its offensive decrees against American commerce, and the other would not, non-intercourse would be continued against the one and suspended as to the other. This measure was known as the " Macon Bill No. 2." Napoleon thereupon promised to revoke the Berlin and Milan Decrees on the first of November, provided England would withdraw her Orders in Council, saying that he loved the Americans and wished to help them whenever opportunity afforded. Madison, believing that Napoleon was acting in good faith, issued a proclamation on November 1, reciting that the French decrees had been revoked, and establishing non-intercourse with England. Already, before the passage of the Macon Bill, Napoleon had issued (March, 1810) the famous Rambouillet Decree, ordering the capture and confiscation of all American vessels that had entered the ports of France, her colonies, or her allies since the adoption of the non-intercourse policy in March, 1809. As a result of this decree large numbers of valuable American cargoes were confiscated, and the proceeds turned into his treasury. These captures were continued after the lying promise which Madison had jumped at had practically been made, and, finally, on December 25, 1810, a general order was given for the capture of all American vessels in French ports. Under this order some ten million dollars' worth of property was seized and confiscated. Certainly nothing could have been more shameful and treacherous than Napoleon's conduct toward us at this time.

Meantime England was showing her true colors. In April, 1809, Mr. Erskine, the British minister at Washington, informed the government that he was authorized to make reparation for the damage inflicted upon American commerce by Great Britain. Thereupon, Madison, with great elation at what seemed to be an amicable settlement of the difficulty, issued a proclamation reciting these facts, and announcing a resumption of commercial intercourse with Great Britain. But again he was doomed to disappointment, for the British Government promptly disavowed the agreement made by Mr. Erskine, and so the President was forced to undergo the humiliation of issuing another proclamation reviving non-intercourse with Great Britain. Erskine was promptly recalled for his conduct and another minister, James Jackson, appointed as his successor. The new minister began his diplomatic career in America by accusing the administration of cajoling his predecessor into signing an agreement which the government knew he was not authorized to do, and made other insinuations of bad faith unusual in diplomatic correspondence, and of such a character as no self-respecting government could tolerate. He was, therefore, informed by the President that no further communication would be received from him, and he left Washington, and shortly thereafter (February, 1811) our minister at London, Mr. Pinkney, demanded his passports and left England. At the request of the United States Government Jackson was recalled; another minister, Mr. Foster, was sent over, and a tardy reparation was made in November, 1811, for the *Chesapeake* affair, but it was no settlement of the difficulty as a whole. Already a month earlier, the two countries had come to blows through the action of the English frigate *Little Belt* in firing upon the American frigate, *The President,* and the capture of the British vessel by *The President.*

During the excitement over the threatened hostilities with England and France, the attention of the country was momentarily diverted by a war with the Indians in the Northwest. For several years they had shown a restless spirit, which assumed dangerous proportions when an effort was made by the Shawnee chief, Tecumseh, and his brother, the Prophet, to organize them into a vast confederacy for the purpose of driving out the white settlers of this region. Tecumseh, together with some of his chosen braves, also visited the distant tribes of the South, the Choctaws, Chickasaws and Creeks, for the purpose of inducing them to join his alliance, but without success. These two leaders succeeded in inciting the Indians to attack the whites, and it was charged that they were encouraged in their attitude by the British, who probably hoped to secure their aid in the event of war with the United States. In the autumn of 1811 war broke out between the Americans and the Indians, and a great battle was fought at Tippecanoe in western Indiana, in the course of which the Indians were defeated by General William Henry Harrison, Governor of the Indiana Territory, and a future President of the United States. Tecumseh then joined the English in Canada, and fought in the war with Great Britain until killed at the battle of the Thames in 1814. The result of this victory was to relieve the Northwestern settlers from the menace of Indian depredations and to establish a high military reputation for General Harrison.[4]

---

[4] See Lossing, "History of the War of 1812," pp. 141-209.

WAR OF 1812

Three days before the battle of Tippecanoe a new Congress met at Washington to consider relations with Great Britain and France. It contained an overwhelming majority of Republican members, among whom were a number of new men filled with the vigor and fire of youth and with determination not to submit further to the insults of England on the one hand or of France on the other. Among them were Henry Clay of Kentucky, John C. Calhoun, Langdon Cheves and William Lowndes of South Carolina, Peter B. Porter of New York, and Felix Grundy of Tennessee.[5] The House gave earnest of its spirit by electing as speaker one of the young members from the West — Henry Clay — who had just entered the House of Representatives for the first time, but who had previously served a brief term in the Senate. He represented a section of the country which favored war, and was himself strongly in sympathy with his constituency on this point. He organized the committees of the House with a view to securing a declaration of war, giving Calhoun the chief place on the Foreign Relations Committee. The Eastern members had shown timidity in their attitude toward England and France because it was believed that in the event of war the Eastern States would be the heaviest sufferers. But the Western and Southern members had no such fear, and entered upon a warlike policy with eagerness, determined to avenge all insults upon American rights regardless of consequences.

There were several grounds of opposition. In the first place it was said, with entire correctness, that the country was unprepared for war as a result of the condition of the army and navy. Again it was urged with equal truth that our grievances against France were almost as numerous as those against England, and yet it was proposed to declare war against England alone. The Federalists, who had always been inclined to sympathize with England, made much of this point. Finally it was said that no more reason for war existed then than had existed five years before. All forms of opposition, however, were overcome, and Congress entered at once upon active preparations for war. An act for raising 20,000 troops was passed, and the President was empowered to call for 50,000 volunteers. The President was also authorized to require the State executives to organize and hold in readiness

[5] Schouler, "History of the United States," vol. ii. p. 372.

100,000 militia; the army was reorganized; appropriations were made for the purchase of ship timber and other materials, and orders were given for the repair and equipment of the frigates.[6]   Following these preliminary acts an embargo for ninety days was laid, and, finally, on June 1, 1812, Madison yielded to the pressure brought upon him by the young Republicans, who told him frankly that unless he abandoned his dilatory policy his renomination and election could not be assured, and sent a message to Congress recounting the long series of aggressions upon American commerce by Great Britain, and recommending a declaration of war.

The reasons assigned for the recommendation were the impressment of American seamen, depredations by British cruisers on American shipping along the Atlantic coast, capture of American cargoes in violation of the rules of international law governing blockades, and the Orders in Council.[7]   The vote on the declaration of war was seventy-nine to forty-nine in the House, and nineteen to thirteen in the Senate.   The members from every State east of Pennsylvania voted against the declaration, while those from Pennsylvania and from the South and West voted in favor of war.[8]   Of the ninety-eight members who voted for the declaration of war, seventy-six came from south of the Delaware River.   Thus the war was brought on by the South and the West against the opposition of the East, whose chief industry had been so nearly destroyed by British aggressions, and the section which it was expected would be the greatest beneficiary of a successful war.   The probable explanation of the New England attitude was the fear that war with Great Britain would result in a total destruction of its commerce, and so its merchants preferred to take its chances of escaping capture under existing conditions.   On June 23, five days after the declaration of war, and before it was possible for news of the declaration of war to have reached England, the Orders in Council were formally withdrawn.   This news reached the United States before active hostilities had actually begun, but too late for any practical result.   Past insults had to be avenged, and, besides, there were other grievances than the Orders in Council for which no

[6] "Statesman's Manual," vol. i. p. 353.
[7] See his message, Richardson, "Messages and Papers of the Presidents," vol. i. p. 505.
[8] Von Holst, "Constitutional History of the United States," vol. ii. p. 232; also " Statesman's Manual," vol. i. p. 354.

redress was promised.   The news of the revocation of the Orders, therefore, had no effect upon the course of events in America.

Now that the United States had at last decided upon war, it may be worth while to consider her resources, as well as those of her adversary, with a view of gaining some idea of their comparative strength for the contest which was soon to begin.   At the outbreak of war the United States had a population of about eight millions; that of England was about twenty millions.   The total annual revenue of the United States was less than ten million dollars; that of England was some three hundred and fifty millions. The war cost the United States about thirty million dollars a year, and sums aggregating nearly one hundred millions were borrowed during its continuance.   The financial system had been thrown into confusion by the expiration of the charter of the national bank in 1811, and the refusal of the Republicans to recharter it on account of their old-time prejudice to a government bank.   Thus, at the very time when the government most needed an efficient fiscal agency to aid in conducting its vast financial concerns, it was deprived of this great element of strength.   In point of national spirit and unity the United States was also at a disadvantage.   The war was opposed by the Federalists, who contemptuously referred to it as " Mr. Madison's war," and who gave the government hardly a lukewarm support.[9]   Indeed, their conduct at times was not far from treasonable, and we know that England profited greatly by our failure to present a united front against her.

As to the military strength of the United States, the weaknesses were most glaring.   The regular army was composed of less than seven thousand available men, the organization was markedly inefficient and the service most unpopular.   The chief officers were Revolutionary veterans who had outgrown their usefulness, and their incompetency led to several disasters in the early stages of the war.   As to the naval strength of the two combatants comparison was almost impossible.   The United States navy consisted of sixteen seagoing vessels, of which the *United States,* the *Constitution* and the *President,* all forty-four gun frigates, were the largest.[10]   The number of enlisted men was less than 6,000, of

[9] For a discussion of Federalist opposition to the war, see Von Holst, " Constitutional History of the United States," vol. ii. p. 244 *et seq.*
[10] Henry Adams, "History of the United States," vol. vi. p. 362.

whom 1,500 were marines.   The British navy consisted of 830 ships, manned by 150,000 seamen, who were well equipped by training and experience in the long war in which England had been engaged.   From almost every point of view, then, England was not only better equipped for the contest, but was incomparably more powerful.   It should be remembered, however, that at this time England was engaged in a life and death struggle with Napoleon and his allies, and consequently was unable to devote her whole strength to the task of overcoming her American enemy.   The United States had the single advantage of fighting for the most part on the defensive.

II

MILITARY AND NAVAL OPERATIONS

According to the original plan of operations, the war was to be initiated by an attack upon Canada from two points, Buffalo on the eastern border, and Detroit on the western.   From the latter point the veteran, General William Hull, crossed the border and attacked the Canadians with a pompous proclamation in which he threatened them with extermination.   Laying siege to Malden, he soon found his communication threatened, retired to Detroit, then a town of 800 inhabitants, and on August 16, 1812, surrendered the place to General Brock with 2,500 men and thirty-three guns, without firing a shot, and in spite of the eagerness of his men to fight, and notwithstanding also his superior force.   His explanation was that he feared a massacre of the women and children at the hands of the Indians, of whom there were some 600 in the British army.   But the surrender caused universal indignation, the old general was court-martialed for cowardice and was sentenced to be shot, but was pardoned by the President on account of his gallant services in the Revolutionary War.[11]

Shortly after the disgraceful affair at Detroit, Fort Dearborn, occupying the present site of Chicago, was destroyed by the Indians and the garrison massacred to a man.   Mackinaw had already fallen.   The invasion of Canada had proved a failure, Michigan was in the hands of the enemy and the whole Northwest exposed to the danger of Indian raids.   On the Niagara frontier the operations of

[11] Schouler, "History of the United States," vol. ii. p. 398.

1812 were equally unsuccessful. A body of New York militia under the command of General Van Rensselaer was defeated at Queenston, chiefly on account of the refusal of 3,000 militiamen, for constitutional reasons, to cross the American border to aid their comrades, notwithstanding repeated and almost pathetic appeals of General Van Rensselaer, who, crippled and wounded, crossed the river and personally implored the militiamen to come to his aid. Nine hundred American prisoners were captured, among them

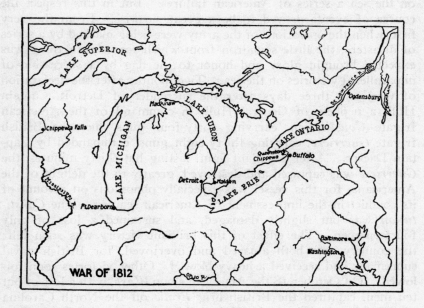

WAR OF 1812

Colonels Winfield Scott and John E. Wool; but the British suffered an irreparable loss in the death of the young and gallant Brock, who was killed in battle.[12] Van Rensselaer resigned in disgust, and was succeeded by General Alexander Smythe, who, after a few feeble movements, marked mainly by the issue of several belligerent proclamations, gave up the attack on Canada and was cashiered for his failure. In the region of Lake Champlain several campaigns were undertaken, but like the others they were failures. The only American success was the defeat of a British force at Ogdensburg,

[12] Lossing, "War of 1812," ch. xix.; McMaster, "History of the United States," vol. iv. p. 12.

New York, by a body of militia under the command of Jacob Brown.

It was the navy, the arm of the service from which least was expected, that proved to be the salvation of the Americans. At the beginning of the contest they calculated that their chief resource, compared with which Great Britain's strength was insignificant, was in their power to raise land forces. It was believed, therefore, that the war on land would be a succession of American victories, and on the sea a series of American failures. But in this respect the course of events proved to be a great surprise. From the very first, when the operations of the army were being marked by a series of disasters, the little squadron from which scarcely anything was expected brought glory and honor to the flag by a succession of unparalleled victories on the sea. Two months after the declaration of war, and three days after the surrender of Detroit, Captain Hull, a nephew of General Hull, in command of the American frigate *Constitution,* carrying forty-four guns, met the British frigate *Guerriere,* carrying thirty-eight guns, commanded by Captain Dacres. After a gallant fight, lasting but thirty minutes, the *Guerriere* was captured and destroyed, greatly to the delight of the Americans, for this vessel was especially obnoxious on account of its conduct in the impressment of American seamen. The *Constitution* was but slightly damaged, and sustained a loss of only fourteen men. The effect of this brilliant victory was soon felt; the country was both amazed and overjoyed, for British naval supremacy had received a heavy blow.[13] Other victories soon followed. On October 18 the American sloop *Wasp,* with a loss of but ten men, captured the British brig *Frolic* off the North Carolina coast, and a week later the *United States,* commanded by Stephen Decatur, took the *Macedonian* after a hard fight of more than an hour and with only thirteen casualties.[14] Toward the last of December the *Constitution,* now commanded by Captain Bainbridge, again distinguished itself by destroying the *Java* off the coast of Brazil and killing one-third of her crew, including the captain.

During the six months since the war had begun the American navy had captured three British frigates, besides several smaller vessels; had captured privateers by scores, and had ravaged severely British commerce on the high seas. The powerful British navy on

[13] Henry Adams, "History of the United States," vol. vi. p. 375.
[14] Lossing, "History of the War of 1812," p. 434.

the other hand had succeeded in capturing only three small American vessels.[15] In the following year, 1813, other notable American naval victories were added to the list, the most important being that of the battle of Lake Erie. It was highly important to the American cause that this body of water should be under American control in order to facilitate land operations against Canada. To bring this to pass Commodore Perry had hastily built a rude fleet of nine vessels, carrying fifty-five guns, from such materials as were at hand, and went forth to dispute with the British the control of the lake.[16] On September 10 he came up with the British fleet of six vessels under command of Commodore Barclay, carrying all told sixty-five guns. A fierce and well contested action followed, in the course of which Perry was exposed directly to the fire of the enemy while passing from the sinking *Lawrence* to the *Niagara,* but escaped unhurt and finally won the battle, thus securing to the Americans the undisputed control of the lake and making possible the recovery of Michigan. The tale was briefly told in the following dispatch which Perry sent to General Harrison: " We have met the enemy and they are ours; two ships, two brigs, one schooner, and one sloop." In the following year, September 11, 1814, the Americans crowned their naval exploits by a victory on Lake Champlain. won by Commodore McDonough, one of the ablest of all American naval commanders. The whole British fleet on the lake, with the exception of a few gunboats, was surrendered to the American commander, making one of the most vital victories in its results that the Americans gained during the war. As a whole, the record of the navy was one of which the nation had reason to be proud, for never were the expectations of a people so greatly surpassed. The Americans were fighting the most renowned naval power in the world, but the fighting ability of the ships and the superior skill of the American gunners carried the day. By the end of 1813 the Americans had captured twenty-six British war vessels carrying 600 guns.

There were, however, several engagements in which the Americans were defeated, the most notable being the fight between the thirty-eight gun American frigate *Chesapeake* and the British ship *Shannon,* off Boston, in June, 1813. The *Chesapeake* was com-

[15] Henry Adams, "History of the United States," vol. vi. p. 386.
[16] For an interesting account of the building of Perry's fleet see McMaster, "History of the United States," vol. iv. pp. 31-34.

manded by Captain Lawrence, who eagerly sought the encounter, but who was killed in the course of the short and bloody fight which followed. His dying words, " Don't give up the ship," became the watchword of the Americans and it was an inspiration on the march and in the camp. The capture of the *Argus* by the British vessel *Pelican,* in the English Channel in August, 1813, and the destruction of the *Essex* off the west coast of South America in December, 1814, were other American naval disasters of note.

The achievements of the navy were supplemented by the exploits of the privateers. Responding to the call for a privateering force, many persons fitted out small but fast sailing vessels, and with commissions of marque and reprisal scoured the seas in pursuit of English merchant vessels. From October, 1812, to May, 1813, they made prizes of 500 British merchantmen, one alone, the *Trueblooded Yankee,* capturing twenty-seven vessels in little over a month. Another captured twenty prizes in thirty days. In two years and a half American privateers took over fourteen hundred prizes, valued at many million dollars, thus inflicting incalculable damage upon English commerce, and increasing enormously the rates of marine insurance. But American foreign trade was practically destroyed, while the coast traffic was seriously interrupted by the blockade maintained by British cruisers.[17]

In the land operations of 1813 there was some improvement over those of 1812; and the army came to be better organized, younger and abler officers being put in command. Among these younger commanders were William Henry Harrison, Winfield Scott and Jacob Brown. The year, however, opened in discouragement. In January an American detachment of about 1,000 Kentucky troops, commanded by General James Winchester, was defeated at Frenchtown on the River Raisin, in Michigan, by an equal number of British and Indians. About 400 Americans were killed or wounded, while the rest became prisoners of war. A disgraceful feature of the affair was the conduct of the British general, Proctor, in allowing the Indians to inflict horrible atrocities upon their wounded captives, some thirty being massacred after having surrendered to their captors, and in spite of Proctor's solemn promise that they should be protected. After plundering the village the half-drunken savages set fire to the dwellings, and burned a number

[17] For the achievements of the navy and the exploits of the privateers see McMaster, "History of the United States," vol. iv. ch. xxv.

of wounded soldiers occupying them. Others who attempted to escape were thrown back into the flames or were tomahawked or scalped by their fiendish captors.[18] Thenceforth, " Remember the River Raisin," became one of the rallying cries of the American soldiers.

In spite of this check upon the effort to recover Michigan, success soon came. In May, General Harrison, who now commanded in the West, defeated the British under Proctor at the battle of Fort Meigs in northern Ohio, and his further advance into Canada was now made possible by Perry's victory on Lake Erie in September. Accordingly, in October, Harrison recaptured Detroit, drove the British out of Michigan, pursued their retreating army into Canada, defeated it at the battle of the Thames, and recaptured eight guns which Hull had surrendered at Detroit, and the greater part of the men. Besides shattering the British army, the Americans had the satisfaction of ending the career of Tecumseh, the Indian chief who had been the leading instigator of the Indians to hostilities against the inhabitants of the Northwest. He was said to have been killed by Colonel Richard Mentor Johnson, of Kentucky, a future Vice President of the United States. This victory broke the alliance between the British and the Indians, completed the recovery of Michigan, and freed the Northwest from the further presence of the enemy.[19]

On the eastern line of the frontier American operations were distinguished by the advance of the Americans upon York (now Toronto) in April, 1813, and the burning of part of the town wantonly, as the British historians have charged. This incident was followed shortly afterward by the capture of Fort George on the Niagara River by General Boyd. The next year, 1814, was generally marked by defeat and disaster to the American arms. With the abdication of Napoleon in April, English resources were released, and twelve thousand veterans were dispatched to America to prosecute the war with renewed vigor.

The campaign on the Niagara frontier was renewed under the direction of General Jacob Brown, an able commander of the New York militia. Under his direction Colonel Winfield Scott, with some 1,300 men, was sent to engage a somewhat larger detachment of British at Chippewa, a short distance from Niagara Falls,

[18] Schouler, "History of the United States," vol. ii. p. 424.
[19] Lossing, "History of the War of 1812," pp. 545-562.

on the Canadian side. After a sharp battle, July 5, the British were repulsed with a loss twice as great as that of the Americans. On the twenty-fifth of the same month the most hotly contested battle of the war was fought between the two armies at Lundy's Lane, within sound of the mighty Falls. The American army, commanded by Colonel Brown and Colonel Scott, consisted of about 2,600 men; that of the British of about 3,000 regulars. For five hours during the darkness of night a fierce battle raged, each side struggling for possession of a small hill, which was held first by the British and later by the Americans. Finally toward midnight the firing on both sides ceased, and the Americans retired, leaving their heavy artillery in possession of the enemy. The total American loss was over eight hundred men. Brown and Scott being among the wounded. The British loss was about the same, both of their commanders, Drummond and Riall, likewise being wounded. Both sides claimed the victory. The American army next proceeded to Fort Erie, where it was attacked on August 15, but the British were repulsed with heavy losses and were compelled to withdraw.

Meantime an attempt to invade the United States from the East was in progress. The coast of Maine was occupied in the summer of 1814, and later other parts of the sea coast were harried somewhat according to the methods frequently employed by Generals Sherman and Sheridan in the Civil War. The inhabitants were even compelled to take oaths of allegiance to Great Britain. The attempt to invade New York by way of Lake Champlain was defeated by McDonough's victory at Plattsburg, to which reference has already been made. In August some 4,500 British troops under command of General Ross disembarked in Chesapeake Bay, and after routing the Americans at Bladensburg, a few miles northeast of Washington, advanced upon the capital and easily took it, owing to the feeble preparations which had been made for its defense, and the lamentable confusion and disorder which reigned in the War Department. It was a shame and a disgrace that the capital of the Republic should have been captured as easily as the most insignificant village in the land. The character of the defense made is shown by an order said to have been given by General Winder to the artillery just before the advance of the British: "When you retreat," he said, "do so by the Georgetown road," and they did.[20]

[20] Henry Adams, "History of the United States," vol. xiii., ch. v.; McMaster, "History of the United States," vol. iv. pp. 143–144.

The approach of the British caused great excitement in the capital; the President and Cabinet fled, leaving the public buildings at the mercy of the invaders.[21] A number of these including the capitol, which contained the library of Congress, the presidential mansion, the Treasury, the navy yard, besides numerous private buildings — a total of $2,000,000 worth of property — were wantonly destroyed by the British in retaliation, it was said, for the burning by the Americans of the Parliament House at York. The Americans, however, asserted that the destruction of the public buildings at York was done by private soldiers acting without authority, while the destruction of Washington was the act of the British commanders themselves.[22] This piece of vandalism has been condemned by American historians without exception, and has not been defended by any reputable British writer. After plundering Alexandria and raiding the adjacent country, the British made an attack on Baltimore; but a more effective resistance was offered there, and the invaders were beaten back. General Ross, who was mainly responsible for the burning of Washington, and three hundred other British soldiers were killed and a number wounded during the attack. After an unsuccessful bombardment of Fort McHenry on an arm of the Chesapeake, an incident of which was the writing of " The Star Spangled Banner," by Francis S. Key, while pacing the deck of a vessel, the British fleet sailed away and gave the Americans no further trouble.

Toward the close of the year 1814 the British prepared to attack New Orleans, the town of chief importance in the Southwest, and fifty vessels bearing sixteen thousand Peninsula veterans under the command of General Pakenham, brother-in-law of the hero of Waterloo, were sent over to conduct the operations, and in December the fleet made the attack. Andrew Jackson of Tennessee (recently the leader of an expedition against the Creek Indians of Alabama, who, in August, 1813, had risen against the white settlers, destroyed Fort Mims on the Alabama River, and massacred 400 persons, including many women and children) was selected to take charge of the defense of New Orleans. He had in the meantime been promoted to the rank of major general to succeed Harrison, who

[21] At the approach of the British, Mrs. Madison carefully cut from the walls of the White House Stuart's famous portrait of Washington and carried it away to a place of safety.

[22] Lossing, " War of 1812," p. 935.

had resigned. In his own vigorous way Jackson, after raising a
force of several thousand Southern militiamen, proceeded first to
Spanish West Florida, treating it as though it was British territory,
and threatening to punish the Spanish authorities for allowing their
ports to be used as bases of operations by the British. After expelling the British from Pensacola, he marched to New Orleans in
December, erected defenses below the city with cotton bales and
other such articles as could be procured, and behind these awaited
the attack.

The British approached within a few miles of the city, and
after two unimportant preliminary battles the two armies met on
January 8 for the final contest. Jackson's army numbered about
5,500 men; that of Pakenham about 10,000. The battle began
about daybreak and continued furiously for two hours; volley after
volley was poured into the ranks of the British from the American
artillery and musketry. The fire of the Kentucky and Tennessee
riflemen proved most deadly, the enemy being mowed down by the
hundred. Over 700 British soldiers were left dead on the battle-
field, among the number being General Pakenham, who, after having two horses shot from under him and being twice wounded,
was finally killed by a Kentucky rifleman. The number of British
wounded was about 1,900 men; the American loss was but eight
killed and thirteen wounded. The American troops consisted
chiefly of Kentucky and Tennessee militia, with a few soldiers
from other States, but rough and untrained as they were, well led
and fighting behind entrenchments, they defeated with heavy slaughter the veterans of the Peninsula campaigns.[23] This was the last
and greatest battle of the war, but it was entirely unnecessary, for
a treaty of peace had already been concluded two weeks before, and was then on its way to America. Had there been an
Atlantic cable to bring the news this last effusion of blood might
have been spared; but it had its value in showing how Americans
could fight when properly led, and in redressing the miserable
humiliations we had endured at Washington and on the Canadian
frontier.

Shortly after the outbreak of hostilities the Emperor of Russia
tendered his good offices to both powers to bring about peace, and
Madison had taken advantage of the offer to send James A. Bayard
and Albert Gallatin to St. Petersburg to negotiate a treaty of

[23] Lossing, "War of 1812," pp. 1034-1050.

peace. Great Britain, however, refused to accept the proffered mediation of Russia, and the peace movement came to an end.[24] Later on in the war the British Government expressed a willingness to negotiate directly, and the President appointed John Quincy Adams, Henry Clay and Jonathan Russell to serve with Bayard and Gallatin as a peace commission. In August, 1814, the commissioners, with those of Great Britain, met at Ghent, in Belgium, and after a long and weary negotiation concluded a treaty on December 24. Curiously enough, the treaty contained no provisions relative to neutral rights, blockades or the impressment of American seamen — the chief questions which led to the war. The British encroachments of this character had been abandoned, and the British commissioners virtually admitted that they would not be resumed, by failure to insist on articles recognizing the old principles for which they had previously contended. The American doctrines were now tacitly admitted.[25] With regard to the territory captured it was agreed that there should be a mutual restitution as before the war. Over the question of the fisheries the commissioners themselves disagreed somewhat. The British contended that the fishery privileges granted by the Treaty of 1783 had been abrogated by the war, and they did not now propose to renew the privileges gratuitously. Clay insisted that the British right of navigating the Mississippi River had also been forfeited. To him, as a Western man, the navigation of the Mississippi seemed of far more importance than the Eastern fisheries. With Adams, an Eastern man, the opposite view prevailed, and he insisted to the last that the fishery clauses of the Treaty of 1783 were in the nature of a recognition of preëxisting rights rather than a grant or concession, and therefore belonged to that class of agreements which remain unaffected by war.[26] But the British negotiators refused to yield, and, consequently, no mention was made of either question in the treaty, the settlement of the matter being left to future negotiation. There was one other question which proved to be vexatious. That was the proposition of the British negotiators to create a large buffer State through Ohio, Kentucky and Tennessee for the Indians who had served as allies of the British during the war; but to this the Americans presented a determined opposition and the question

[24] McMaster, "History of the United States," vol. iv. p. 250.
[25] Foster, "Century of American Diplomacy," p. 246.
[26] J. B. Moore, "International Arbitrations," vol. i. pp. 705–707.

was abandoned. Provision was made for the appointment of a joint commission for the determination of a dispute which had arisen concerning the northeastern boundary of the United States, and the two powers agreed to use their best efforts for the suppression of the African slave trade.

III

OBSERVATIONS ON THE WAR

On the whole, the peace was an honorable and satisfactory one to the United States, considering that it was concluded before the British disaster at New Orleans, but it had cost the country enormous sacrifices. Besides the expenditure of over a hundred million dollars, 30,000 valuable lives had been sacrificed, and the country had suffered great loss of property and seen its commerce practically destroyed. The export trade had fallen to about one-twentieth of its former volume; some 1,400 American vessels, with over 20,000 seamen had been captured by British cruisers, while the unpopularity of the war had created disaffection among a portion of the inhabitants. With a few exceptions the military achievements were not highly creditable to the nation nor to the government whose management of the war was marked by a series of blunders. Moreover, the naval victories, although highly creditable to the little squadron that achieved them, had no real strategic value. The capture of 2,416 British vessels, including 56 warships, was overbalanced by the destruction of American trade and commerce.[27]

Throughout the war great reliance was placed on the militia, and it may be truly said that this branch of the service bore the brunt of the contest, and contributed far more to the success of the war than did the regular army. From the beginning of the struggle, however, the New England States, on account of their opposition to the war, had refused to furnish militia at the call of the President. The governor of Connecticut refused to permit the militia of his State to serve beyond its borders, and the legislature supported him in his rebellious attitude. The Massachusetts legislature characterized the war as a "wanton sacrifice of our best

[27] "Statesman's Manual," vol. i. p. 377. The victories of Perry and Mc-Donough are to be regarded as exceptions to this statement.

interests," and the governor declined to furnish militia, assigning as a reason for his action that there was no invasion, and that consequently no constitutional obligation rested upon him to call out troops. The executives of New Hampshire, Rhode Island and Vermont made similar responses, the governor of the latter State declaring that the military forces of the State must be reserved for its own exclusive defense and protection.

All this did not interfere with the volunteer service, and Massachusetts even furnished its quota, and bore its proportion of the expense. Being the chief seat of Federalism, the people were inclined to sympathize with England as against France, and would have preferred war with the latter power instead of with the former. The English took advantage of this feeling to encourage the disaffection of the people, and probably cherished a faint hope of inducing them to withdraw from the Union. Thus during the early stages of the war English cruisers were instructed not to blockade the coasts of New England or to capture vessels owned in New England. At one time it was reported that English emissaries were at work in this section seeking to encourage disaffection among the inhabitants, and events soon justified the report. At a Massachusetts public meeting one of the leading Federalist extremists, Josiah Quincy, offered a resolution declaring that " in a war like the present, waged without justifiable cause, and prosecuted in a manner which indicates that conquest and ambition are its real motives, it is not becoming a moral and religious people to express any approbation of military or naval exploits which are not immediately connected with the defense of our sea coast and soil." There were many others of his way of thinking.

The legislature of Massachusetts took the initiative on October 16, 1814, in voting to raise a million dollars with which to maintain a State army, and at the same time issued a call to the other New England States to appoint delegates to meet in convention for the purpose of considering such action as the situation seemed to demand. On December 15 the convention met at Hartford, and began its deliberations behind closed doors, with George Cabot as president, and Theodore Dwight as secretary. It was made up of twenty-six delegates from Massachusetts, Connecticut, Rhode Island, New Hampshire and Vermont, the representatives from the two latter States being chosen by unofficial bodies.[28] The general

[28] Von Holst, " Constitutional History of the United States," vol. ii. p. 263.

belief was that the secession of the New England States would be recommended, and the subject may have been discussed by some of the more extreme delegates, but it apparently did not meet with the favor of the majority. The President sent Colonel Jessup, an officer of the army, to watch the proceedings of the convention, as well as an outsider could, and make daily reports to him; but there seems to have been nothing to report, and the convention attracted little attention, not even enough, declared Jefferson, to make a subject of conversation either public or private.[29] An official report of the proceedings was published as a means of vindicating the convention from the charge of plotting to break up the Union, and from this it appears that only moderate measures were discussed, although there is evidence of great want of patriotism among the members. The conduct of the war was severely criticised, the Federal authorities were accused of violating the Constitution, and in language similar to that of the Kentucky and Virginia Resolutions, the convention declared that " in cases of deliberate, dangerous and palpable infractions of the Constitution affecting the sovereignty of a State and liberties of the people, it is not only the right, but the duty, of such a State to interpose its authority for their protection," and that " States which have no common umpire must be their own judges and execute their own decisions." The President could, of course, take no exception to this interpretation of the Constitution, since it was almost identical with that laid down by him in the Virginia resolutions of 1798. The New England Federalists in 1814 were standing on the identical ground occupied by the Republicans in 1798–1799, and in each case the right of the States was asserted as against those of the general government, and for similar reasons. Before adjourning the convention drew up a list of proposed amendments to the Constitution, the general purpose of which was to protect the individual States from the power of the majority of States, and which requested that the commonwealths which they represented should be allowed to retain the customs duties collected within their ports. The resolutions contained an implied threat of secession should this request not be complied with, but just as the convention broke up the news of peace arrived, and their demands were no longer insisted upon.[30] The legislatures of but two States,

29 " Jefferson's Works," vol. vii. p. 425.
30 For a good account of the Hartford Convention see Von Holst, " Consti-

Connecticut and Massachusetts, formally approved the resolutions
of the convention, although there is reason to believe that the other
New England States would have followed the action of these two
had the war continued.

The Hartford Convention was the deathblow to what remained of the Federalist party. This party had opposed the war
from the first, and at a time when the government was straining
every nerve to repel the invasion of the enemy it was meeting in
secret conclave to consider the expediency of seceding from the
Union. Their factious opposition had undoubtedly embarrassed
the government in the prosecution of the war, perhaps had delayed
its termination, and now that an honorable peace had been concluded they were justly held up to execration. After 1816 the
Federalists as a party never cast another vote. Its great service
to the nation had been the organization of the government upon
broad and liberal principles, after which its record was chiefly
a series of blunders until its final dissolution. Although disappear-
ing as a party, the principles for which it stood, namely, adequate
powers for the general government and the maintenance of the
national dignity, were adopted and put into practice by the Republicans. During both Jefferson's and Madison's administrations this
theory of constitutional interpretation was acted upon time and
again, and after the war the Federalists gradually came into the
Republican ranks, so that when Jefferson, in 1801, said "we are
all Republicans, we are all Federalists," he expressed what had
come to be the truth in 1816. Bringing this to pass was one of the
chief political results of the war of 1812.

What may be termed one of the military results of the war
was the development of a school of young soldiers, who were
afterwards to render the country valuable service in the war with
Mexico. Among those who rose to leadership were Winfield Scott,
who eventually came to be the highest officer in the army; William
Henry Harrison, the hero of Tippecanoe, who, in 1840, became
President of the United States; and Andrew Jackson, who rose to
the Presidency in 1828. Among the leading naval heroes of the
war were Decatur, Perry, Hull, McDonough, Bainbridge, Stewart
and Blakely.

tutional History of the United States," pp. 250–269; see also Lodge, "Life of
George Cabot," and Dwight, "History of the Hartford Convention."

Chapter XIX

THE ERA OF GOOD FEELING AND INDUSTRIAL DEVELOPMENT. 1816–1824

I

THE TARIFF OF 1816 AND THE SECOND UNITED STATES BANK

IN 1812 Madison had been reëlected President, receiving 128 electoral votes, and Elbridge Gerry, Vice President, receiving 131. The Federalist candidates were DeWitt Clinton of New York, and Jared Ingersoll of Pennsylvania. Clinton received 89 electoral votes, which was the largest ever cast by the Federalist party in its history. Following the example set by Washington and Jefferson, Madison declined, in 1816, to be a candidate for a third term, and in accordance with what had now come to be a well-established precedent, his Secretary of State, James Monroe, received the Republican nomination for President, with ex-Governor Daniel D. Tompkins of New York for Vice President. Rufus King was put forward as the candidate of the Federalists, both parties nominating their candidates through the congressional caucus. Monroe was elected, receiving 183 electoral votes, King obtaining only 34 votes. This represented the expiring effort of the Federalist party; before the next election it had dissolved, and consequently never nominated another candidate. The Republicans, soon to divide into Democrats and National Republicans, or Whigs, who absorbed the Federalists, had an overwhelming majority in both houses of Congress, and with brief intervals the more extreme wing, or the Democratic element, were to control the government until the Civil War. But the Supreme Court for a good many years longer, under the domination of Marshall, continued, to the great disgust of the old Republicans and new Democrats, to interpret the Constitution according to the purest Federalist theories of construction.

The new chief magistrate was the last of the Revolutionary statesmen to reach the Presidency, and the last of the " Virginia dynasty," which, with the exception of the brief period from 1797 to 1801, had furnished the Republic its chief magistrates since the adoption of the Constitution.   Monroe had served in the Revolution, rising to the rank of lieutenant colonel, was a member of Congress under the Confederation, a United States senator under the Constitution, minister to France, governor of Virginia, one of the commissioners who purchased Louisiana, and Secretary of State under Madison.   He lacked the brilliancy of Jefferson and Madison, but was industrious, amiable, generous and had had long experience in civil affairs.   The appointment as Secretary of State of John Quincy Adams, who had in 1807 gone over to the Republicans, was virtually the selection of his successor to the Presidency.

With the accession of Monroe to the Presidency an era of peace and prosperity set in.   The long series of English and French outrages upon American commerce were at an end, and the country was no longer divided in its sympathies between England and France.   Politics had ceased to be colonial and had become American.   There was only one party and that was an American party.   Old issues had disappeared; new ones had arisen to take their place, and new leaders were at hand to champion them. The War of 1812 is sometimes called the Second War of Independence.   As the Revolutionary War freed us from political dependence upon England, the War of 1812 started us upon the road to economic and industrial independence, and freed our politics from the colonial habit of basing our opinions upon what happened in Europe.   Until the latter date our economic development was impeded by European restrictions which held us in a semi-colonial dependence.   The country was now free to devote its energies to internal development, and the chief questions which came to occupy the attention of Congress related to tariff protection, the construction of public improvements, and the establishment of a stable currency.

Of all the results of the War of 1812 none were more important than the improvement of the distressing economic and industrial conditions which it had brought into existence.   During the period of the embargo and the war capital and labor were compelled to find new fields of employment.   Ship-building and commerce were practically at a standstill, consequently those who were engaged in these industries at the outbreak of the war now found it more profitable, in fact were compelled, to turn their attention to the manufacturing industries. As soon as the policy of commercial restriction began in earnest, the American supply of manufactured articles from abroad was cut off. Hardware, crockery, pottery, cutlery, tools, clothing and many other articles of necessity, for the supply of which we had depended upon Great Britain, could no longer be had from this source. Home production now became a necessity, and manufacturing enterprises, mills, factories, foundries, rope walks, and many other industries sprang up in various parts of the country. Premiums were offered for the encouragement of home industries of various kinds, and in many large cities associations were formed the members of which were pledged to wear only garments of domestic manufacture. In various ways the State legislatures encouraged the movement, and the census of 1810 showed that already nearly $200,000,000 worth of goods were being manufactured annually in the United States. The extraordinary increase of cotton manufactures is shown by the fact that from 1808 to 1811 the number of spindles increased ten-fold, and during the next four years, ending in 1815, they increased over six-fold. Within a radius of thirty miles of Providence there were one hundred and forty factories spinning each year 29,000 bales of cotton, which would make not less than 28,000,000 yards of cloth worth $6,000,000.[1] The iron and woolen industries also made immense gains. So long as the war lasted and British manufactured articles were excluded, the home manufactures had a monopoly, and consequently their business was prosperous. Both with the close of the war and the resumption of friendly relations with Great Britain, our ports were thrown open to the commerce of the world, and a flood of British goods poured in upon the American markets, which had once been the chief outlet of British trade. From 1814 to 1816 the imports of the United States rose from $12,000,000 to $147,000,000.[2] Great Britain's manufacturing industries were old and well established; British skilled labor was cheap and plentiful, and consequently the British manufacturer could supply the American market with goods at lower prices than was possible for the American manufacturer. It was evident, therefore, that the American manufacturing industries which had sprung up under the stimulus which the war had afforded could

[1] McMaster, "History of the People of the United States," vol. iv. p. 328.
[2] Stanwood, "Tariff Controversies in the Nineteenth Century," vol. i. p. 131.

not successfully encounter British competition, and must sooner or later succumb, unless aided by a protective tariff.   As fleet after fleet laden with British goods began to arrive in our ports, the manufacturers turned to Congress and appealed to that body to come to their rescue, and by means of a protective tariff preserve their home markets from the effects of the British flood.   Millions of dollars had been invested in manufactures and this would be lost; besides the owners could not return to the shipping industry with advantage, since the general peace would subject their vessels to a competition which they could not meet.[3]

The demand for a protective tariff raised a new question of politics and economics, one which has ever since afforded an issue upon which politicians and economists have divided.   The preamble to the Tariff Act of 1789 declared that the purpose of the tariff was for the "encouragement and protection of manufactures," among other things, but as the average rate imposed by the law did not exceed five per cent. *ad valorem*, it afforded little or no stimulus to the establishment of new industries.   It was in fact a revenue tariff, pure and simple, but nevertheless each party to the controversy now claimed to find in it justification of its position.   This first Tariff Act, with amendments, continued in force until the outbreak of the War of 1812, when the rates were doubled to meet the increased demand for more revenue, and were to continue in force until a year after the close of the war; but the destruction of our foreign trade made the increase of little avail.   Congress now acted favorably upon the appeal of the manufacturers, and in 1816, under Southern leadership, passed a new Tariff Act which was really the first in which the principle of protection to home industries was a prominent feature.   It imposed a duty of twenty-five per cent. on cotton and woolen goods until 1819, when the rate was to be reduced to twenty per cent. A duty of thirty-five per cent., meant to be prohibitory, was imposed on articles of which a full supply could be made at home, a duty of twenty per cent. on those which could not be, and a tariff for revenue on a class of articles consumed in large quantities and almost entirely made abroad.   The average rate under this Tariff Act was twenty-five per cent. *ad valorem*.[4]   There was also

[3] Read McMaster, "History of the People of the United States," vol. iv. ch. xxxi.

[4] For the constitutional aspect of the tariff question see Stanwood, "Tariff Controversies in the Nineteenth Century," vol. i. ch. ix.

a schedule of over a hundred articles on which a separate and specific duty was imposed; there was in addition a free list, a discriminating duty on goods brought in vessels not owned in the United States, and a continuation of the bounty and drawbacks on pickled fish and sugar exported.[5]

In view of subsequent tariff history it is worthy of note that Webster, speaking for New England, opposed the tariff, believing that it would operate as a hardship upon the shipping industry of that section by increasing the price of ship-building material; Calhoun, speaking for the South, advocated the policy of protection as a legitimate means of encouraging domestic industries, evidently believing that the establishment of cotton factories would provide a home market for cotton, which was fast becoming the chief Southern staple. As a source of strategic strength in time of war Calhoun also wished to see the United States industrially independent of Europe, a position which he thought would be hastened by a protective tariff.[6] In the course of the next ten years we shall see New England and the South reversing their positions on this question. During that period New England became a manufacturing section, while the South discovered that a high duty on coarse goods was a heavy burden upon the slave-holders. The West, where flax and hemp were the chief staple articles which needed protection against foreign competition, also favored the tariff, Henry Clay, Speaker of the House, being the chief advocate from that section. But the rate of protection granted did not satisfy the manufacturers; agriculture and trade did not seem to return to their normal condition as before the war; the currency was deranged, and finally, as a result of these and other causes, a wide-spread financial panic, resulting in the failure of many banks and mercantile establishments, swept over the country in 1819.

Next to the Tariff Act the most important legislative measure immediately following the war was the recharter of the United States Bank. It will be remembered that the charter of the old bank had expired in 1811, and the bill introduced the same year to grant it a new lease of life was defeated by a narrow majority — one vote in the House and the casting vote of the Vice President

[5] McMaster, "History of the People of the United States," vol. iv. p. 339.
[6] Burgess, "The Middle Period," p. 11; Von Holst, "Constitutional History of the United States," vol. i. p. 309.

in the Senate. The excellent currency which it had supplied to the country was now withdrawn, and its place taken by a currency issued by State banks which quickly sprang into existence in large numbers. From 1811 to 1816 the number of State banking institutions increased from 88 to 246. The flood of paper which they issued could not be redeemed in specie; in fact there was no penalty attached to a refusal to redeem, nor any real check to prevent an issue of bills far beyond the legal limit. Under the stress of the embargo and non-intercourse policies, the currency soon began to depreciate in value, and during the war most of the banks were compelled to suspend specie payments, causing great derangement to business and general economic distress.

In this situation the Secretary of the Treasury, Alexander Dallas, proposed to establish a national bank, but Congress differed with him as to certain details, and it was not until April, 1816, that the bill was passed. It was rather curious that the Federalists, who had always stood for a national bank, opposed this one, chiefly on the ground of factional opposition; while the Republicans, traditional enemies of a federal bank, supported it with the same line of argument used by the Federalists in 1791.[7] Never did two political parties shift their ground more completely than did the Federalists and Republicans in 1816 on the bank issue. The only explanation which the Republicans ever gave as to why most of them opposed the bank in 1811, and favored it in 1816, was that the times had changed, and the conditions which confronted the country in 1816 were quite different from those prevailing in 1811. The new bank was planned on the same lines as the old one, except that its capital stock was to be $35,000,000, instead of $10,000,000, and the government was to hold $7,000,000 of the stock and appoint one-fifth of the twenty-five directors. As before, the main bank was to be established at Philadelphia, with branches in the different States. The funds of the government were to be deposited in the bank, in return for which it was to pay a bonus of $1,500,000, and to aid the government in the negotiation of loans and the transaction of other fiscal business. The stock was quickly subscribed; the bank at once went into operation, and for twenty years it provided a sound currency, which circulated at face value throughout the country, and was a source of strength to the govern-

[7] See McMaster, "History of the People of the United States," vol. iv. pp. 310–311.

ment. One of its first acts was to force the State banks to resume specie payments in February, 1817.[8]

Shortly after the establishment of this second Bank of the
United States the attempt of Maryland to impose a tax upon its
circulation led to one of the most notable of the early decisions of
the Supreme Court concerning the powers of the general government under the Constitution. This decision was rendered in the
case of McCulloch vs. Maryland, in 1819, the opinion being written by Chief Justice Marshall. In upholding the constitutionality
of the act of Congress, Marshall restated in clear and forcible language the doctrine of implied powers first laid down by Hamilton.
" A national bank," he said, " is an appropriate means for carrying
out certain of the expressed powers conferred on the national
government by the Constitution. Let the end be within the scope
of the Constitution, and all means which are plainly adapted to
that end, which are not prohibited but consistent with the letter
and spirit of the Constitution, are constitutional." Few decisions
of the Supreme Court have been more often quoted than this one.
It settled once for all the question of the existence of implied powers
under the Constitution, and immensely strengthened the authority
and influence of the general government.[9]

Other decisions were rendered about the same time, notably
those of Fletcher vs. Peck, and the Dartmouth College case,
which placed substantial limitations upon the power of the States.
In the former case the court held that the clause of the Constitution
which forbids the States from passing laws impairing the obligations of contracts covered land grants made by the legislature and
protected them from subsequent abrogation by the States. In the
latter case it was held that a charter granted to an educational
institution was likewise a contract, and could not be altered, much
less repealed, by subsequent act of the State. These decisions materially limited the autonomy of the States, and correspondingly
exalted the power of the general government, to the great disgust
of the States rights Republicans.

[8] For a comprehensive history of the bank, see Catterall, " The Second
United States Bank."
[9] See Dillon, " The Decisions of John Marshall," pp. 252–299.

II

INTERNAL IMPROVEMENTS; TERRITORIAL EXPANSION; THE MONROE DOCTRINE

Next to the protection of home industries and the creation of a national bank currency, the most important question of domestic interest related to the power of the general government to construct internal improvements or aid the States in constructing them. Up to 1816 the construction of roads, canals, harbors, and similar public works had been recognized as a matter of State enterprise, except that in 1806 the general government had undertaken to build the Cumberland Road, for the purpose of providing better transportation facilities between the East and the West. During Jefferson's second term Secretary Gallatin had made an elaborate report recommending the construction of a system of roads and canals throughout the country at an estimated cost of ten million dollars, but with the outbreak of the war and the disappearance of the surplus Gallatin's scheme was abandoned.

After the passage of the second bank bill in 1816, the question arose as to the disposal of the bonus of one and a half millions which the bank was to pay to the United States for its charter. It was now proposed to apply the fund to the construction of roads and canals, and to the improvement of river navigation. Calhoun, afterwards distinguished as an extreme advocate of strict construction, favored the proposition as entirely within the scope of the Constitution, and a bill embodying its substance passed both houses of Congress, but was vetoed by President Madison, just before he went out of office, on the ground that the power to engage in internal improvements was not conferred by the Constitution on the general government.[10] Madison's successor, Monroe, interpreted the Constitution along similar lines, and in 1822 vetoed a bill making appropriations for the repair of the Cumberland Road,[11] at the same time giving notice that if Congress proposed to embark in schemes of internal improvement the Constitution would have to be amended. But in the following year Congress began the practice of making appropriations for the improvement of harbors. This was followed by appropriations for preliminary surveys, and

[10] McMaster, "History of the People of the United States," vol. iv. p. 415.
[11] Von Holst, "Constitutional History of the United States," vol. i. p. 390.

in 1825 the government became a large stockholder in the Chesapeake and Delaware Canal. The precedent was thus established by which the United States undertook to aid in the construction of works deemed to be of national interest. This aid was sometimes in the form of direct appropriations and sometimes in the form of government subscriptions to stock, and to this principle the nation may be said to have become finally committed, not, however, without strong opposition on the part of the South.

One of the principal reasons for the growth of the sentiment in favor of internal improvement at this time was the extraordinary development of the West and Southwest. The immigration to this region from the Eastern States had been steadily and continuous since the adoption of the ordinance of 1787, and more especially since the defeat of the Northwestern Indians by General Wayne in 1794. Between 1810 and 1816 the population of Ohio had increased from 200,000 to about 400,000, and during the same time the population of Indiana increased three-fold. In fact it looked as if the population of the Eastern States would be drained off to people the West. Most of the immigrants were seeking new homes where land was cheap and opportunities plentiful. The Western rivers swarmed with steamboats, prosperous settlements sprang up on their banks, which soon grew into populous towns, while the country was presently covered with productive farms.[12]

In 1816 Indiana was admitted to the Union as a companion to Ohio, then a flourishing State rapidly filling with immigrants from New England. In the next year the importance of the Southwest was increased by the admission of Mississippi, to be followed two years later by Alabama. In 1818 Illinois was admitted, and Missouri, lying west of the Mississippi, was already making application for statehood. There were now eight States in the Mississippi Valley, and the center of population, which in 1789 was thirty miles east of Baltimore, had moved westward considerably over one hundred miles. The Republic was no longer a fringe of Atlantic States, but an empire stretching far to the west, big with possibilities and capable of commanding respect from the outside world.

Closely associated with the expansion of the Republic by the erection of new States was the acquisition of foreign territory, and the rectification of the national boundaries through the treaty-

[12] Read McMaster, "History of the People of the United States," vol. iv. ch. xxxiii.

making power. The joint commission provided by the Treaty of Ghent for the adjustment of the northeast boundary was unable to reach an agreement on several points, and so the settlement of the dispute was left to future negotiation.[13] Meantime a dispute had arisen between the two powers with regard to the northeastern fisheries and the northwest boundary. In the negotiations at Ghent the British commissioners gave notice that they did not propose to renew gratuitously the fishery privileges contained in the Treaty of 1783. The American commissioners expressed surprise at this announcement, for they regarded these provisions of the treaty in the light, not of a grant, but as the recognition of a preëxisting right which was not suspended or otherwise affected by the War of 1812. Failing to reach an agreement on this point the commissioners decided to omit the matter altogether from the treaty, and this was done. The British Government, however, was determined to enforce its views of the intent of the Treaty of 1783, and accordingly, soon after the close of the War of 1812, British cruisers began to seize American fishing vessels in the neighborhood of the Grand Banks. The government of the United States protested, and, in October, 1818, succeeded in concluding a convention with Great Britain by which the rights of American fishermen on the coasts of Labrador and Newfoundland were specifically set forth, and for a time the fishery dispute disappeared.[14] With regard to the boundary dispute the convention provided that the boundary between the United States and Canada should follow the forty-ninth parallel from the Lake of the Woods to the Rocky Mountains. Beyond the Rockies the dispute was more serious, and the only agreement that could be reached was that the disputed territory, commonly known as the Oregon Country, should remain open to the joint occupation of both powers for a period of ten years, with the privilege for either party to terminate the joint occupancy upon giving one year's notice.

With Spain there was also a boundary dispute which had a favorable termination. It will be remembered that Louisiana was acquired in 1803 with uncertain boundaries, the United States claiming that the cession included West Florida, a claim which Spain denied with equal steadfastness. The inhabitants of this district

---

[13] Moore, "International Arbitrations," vol. i. ch. xiii.

[14] Moore, "International Arbitrations," vol. i. ch. xiii.; Henderson, "American Diplomatic Questions," ch. v.

finally rose in rebellion against Spain and asked to be annexed to the United States, which was done by proclamation of the President in 1810. Spain refused to recognize the rightfulness of this action or to sell the disputed territory. She also refused to sell East Florida, which was eagerly desired by the United States to round out her southern boundary. Finding that the American Government was determined to hold the territory seized, and realizing that East Florida alone would be of little value, Spain finally consented to negotiate for the sale of the Floridas.

East Florida, by virtue of its geographical proximity to the United States, was a source of continual trouble to the government, since the territory afforded a convenient refuge for fugitive slaves and criminals, besides serving as a base for smuggling expeditions into the States. In 1816 an expedition was sent to Florida to break up a nest of desperadoes who had taken possession of an abandoned British fort and were terrorizing the adjacent country. Finally, Colonel Clinch threw a red-hot cannon ball into the fort and destroyed it, together with 270 persons. In 1818 its danger was further shown by the Seminole war. The United States had found it necessary to declare war upon the Seminole Indians who, together with some Spaniards and fugitive slaves, were committing depredations upon American settlements in Georgia, and when General Jackson undertook to punish them they retreated to the Everglades of Florida where they were aided by the Spanish settlers of St. Mark's and Pensacola. Jackson thereupon marched into Florida, without orders, seized these two towns, and arbitrarily executed two British subjects — Arbuthnot and Ambrister — whom he charged with aiding and encouraging the Indians in their rebellious attitude.[15]

Jackson's invasion of Spanish territory aroused indignation in Spain, and came near embroiling the two countries in war, while his summary execution of Arbuthnot and Ambrister stirred English feeling to a high pitch. His conduct was a subject of discussion in the Cabinet, and Calhoun, who was then Secretary of War, proposed that he be court-martialed, but nothing was done. This episode, however, convinced Spain of the expediency of disposing of Florida, and in the following year John Quincy Adams and the Spanish minister signed a treaty at Washington, concluded after

[15] Parton, "Life of Jackson," vol. ii. pp. 436-488; Sumner, "Andrew Jackson," pp. 56-61.

long and tedious negotiations, by which Florida was ceded to the United States for the sum of $5,000,000, the entire amount of which was to be applied to the payment of claims of American citizens against Spain for spoliations committed by Spanish cruisers upon American commerce. Spain abandoned all claim to lands north and east of a line beginning at the mouth of the Sabine River, extending up that stream to the 32d degree, thence north to the Red River, thence along that river to the 100th meridian, thence due north to the Arkansas River, and along the same to its source, thence to the 42d parallel and along that line to the Pacific Ocean. Following the provision of the Louisiana treaty it was stipulated that the inhabitants of the ceded territory should be admitted to all the rights and privileges of American citizens, and as soon as consistent with the principles of the Federal Constitution be incorporated into Union. By this treaty the United States gave up whatever claim it had to Texas, and at the same time acquired Spain's title to all the Oregon country. Some, like Henry Clay, believed the claim of the United States to Texas was well founded. The acquisition of Florida rounded out our southern boundary, gave us an unbroken line from the Sabine River to the Atlantic, and removed a source of danger to the peace and quiet of the Republic. On account of the action of the Spanish Government in making several large grants of land in Florida subsequent to the conclusion of the treaty, which action was presently discovered by the authorities of the United States, it was nearly two years before the treaty was finally ratified. General Jackson was appointed the first governor of the new territory, which he proceeded to rule after the manner of a military dictator.[16]

About the time that Spain was parting with Florida great events were happening in her South American possessions. One after another of her colonies, including Mexico, had risen in rebellion against the attempt of the restored Bourbons to reimpose upon them the colonial absolutism of the old régime. Between 1816 and 1822 a revolutionary government had been established in every Spanish-American colony, from the United States, on the north, to Cape Horn, on the south, and their independence of Spain had become an established fact. The people of the United States naturally felt a lively sympathy for the efforts of their struggling neighbors to throw off the despotic yoke of Spain, and as early

[16] Parton, "Life of Jackson," vol. ii. ch. xlv.

as 1820 the House of Representatives, under the leadership of its speaker, Henry Clay, had passed a resolution declaring that it was expedient to provide a suitable outfit and salary for such ministers as the President might see fit to appoint to those South American republics which had achieved their independence of Spain. But the Florida treaty being still unratified, the President did not deem it expedient to act. Clay, however, still continued his championship of the revolted colonies, and in 1822 his efforts were rewarded by the action of Congress in recognizing, so far as congressional action could recognize, their independence, and appropriating $100,000 to pay the expenses of sending ministers to their governments.

Recognition of their independence, however, by the United States did not insure the new republics against the danger of European interference. In September, 1815, after the reëstablishment of the old régime throughout Europe, a number of the great powers had entered into an agreement known as the " Holy Alliance," ostensibly for the purpose of " doing each other reciprocal service," but really to keep down the spirit of revolution within their respective dominions, and maintain unimpaired the régime of absolutism.[17] In Europe the Holy Alliance easily carried out its ends without hindrance, and whenever a revolutionary outbreak occurred some of the members of the league, as the agent of the allied powers, intervened to restore the old order. Thus in 1823 France interposed in Spain to restore the Bourbon sovereign, Ferdinand, whom the people had risen against in 1820, and driven out. In like fashion liberal uprisings in Naples and Piedmont were put down by Austria.[18]

Having restored absolutism everywhere on the continent, and having nothing further to fear in Europe for the present, the allies began to consider the possibility of restoring to Spain her revolted colonies in South America. France was willing to serve as the instrument of this unworthy undertaking, with the expectation, of course, of reimbursing herself with a generous slice of South American territory. England alone, of the European countries, was opposed to intervention, chiefly because a large and lucrative trade had sprung up between that country and South America since the overthrow of Spanish dominion in that region, and this

---

[17] See text of the treaty of the Holy Alliance in Snow, " Topics in American Diplomacy," pp. 243–245.
[18] Fyffe, "History of Modern Europe " (pop. ed.), p. 502.

was in danger of being destroyed should the revolted colonies be restored to Spain. The British Minister of Foreign Affairs, Canning, therefore turned to the United States minister, Richard Rush, and proposed that the two powers unite in a joint declaration against the threatened intervention of the Holy Alliance. Rush had no instructions, although he took the liberty of saying that the United States would regard intervention as "highly unjust and fruitful of disastrous consequences," and promised to join in the declaration if Great Britain would first recognize the independence of the revolted colonies, as the United States had done.[19] This Canning refused to do, and the declaration was never made.[20]

Meantime the position which the United States should assume with regard to the American continent was complicated by the attitude which Russia was taking in the Northwest. In 1821 the Czar had issued a *ukase* reserving exclusively to Russian subjects, all trade, commerce and fishing, and indeed all other industries on the northwest coast as far south as the fifty-first parallel of latitude, part of which region was claimed by the United States. Foreigners were forbidden to approach within one hundred miles of the interdicted coasts, and it was believed that Russia might attempt to extend her dominion much further down the coast. This seemed to the President to be an encroachment upon American rights, and a source of danger to the United States. The Secretary of State, John Quincy Adams, protested against this action, and told the Russian minister, Baron Tuyl, that the United States would contest the claim of Russia in this regard, and would assume the position that the American continents were no longer open to future colonization by European nations because of the independent position which they had assumed and maintained.[21] In this situation Monroe turned for advice to the two venerable ex-Presidents, Madison and Jefferson, and encouraged by them in the stand which he had already taken, announced in his annual message of December, 1823, the principles which have come to be known as the Monroe Doctrine.[22]

---

[19] Tucker, "The Monroe Doctrine," p. 10.
[20] Foster, "Century of American Diplomacy," p. 442.
[21] Morse, "Life of John Quincy Adams," p. 132.
[22] Jefferson in approving the proposed declaration said: "Our first and fundamental maxim should be never to entangle ourselves in the broils of Europe. Our second never to suffer Europe to intermeddle with cis-Atlantic affairs." Both he and Madison advised forcible resistance to the proposed inter-

The message contained a statement of three principles which collectively make up the so-called "doctrine." Concerning the proposed intervention of the allies in South America, the President said: "We owe it, therefore, to candor, and to the amicable relations existing between the United States and those powers, to declare that we should consider any attempt on their part to extend their system to any portion of this hemisphere as dangerous to our peace and safety. With the existing colonies or dependencies of any European power we have not interfered, and shall not interfere. But with the governments who have declared their independence and maintained it, and whose independence we have, on great consideration and just principles, acknowledged, we could not view any interposition for the purpose of oppressing them or in any other manner controlling their destiny, by any European power, in any other light than as the manifestation of an unfriendly disposition toward the United States." With regard to the attitude of the United States toward purely European affairs, the President said that it had always been our policy not to interfere in any of the internal concerns of those powers, but to cultivate friendly relations with them. 'It was impossible,' he said, 'that the Allied Powers should extend their political system to any portion of either continent without endangering our peace and happiness; nor could anyone believe that "our Southern brethren," if left to themselves, would adopt it of their own accord. It was equally impossible, therefore, that we should behold such interposition in any form with indifference.' Concerning the claims of Russia, it was declared that "occasion has been judged proper for asserting, as a principle in which the rights and interests of the United States are involved, that the American Continents, by the free and independent condition which they have assumed and maintained, are henceforth not to be considered as subjects for future colonization by any European power." [23]

The bold announcement of these principles accomplished the purpose for which it had been made. France was informed by Great Britain that intervention by the allies would lead the British Government to recognize the independence of the revolted Spanish American colonies. The proposed intervention of the allies was,

position in South America. See Jefferson's and Madison's Works, vols. x. and iii. respectively, pp. 277 and 339.

[23] Richardson, "Messages and Papers of the Presidents," vol. ii. pp. 210, 218.

therefore, abandoned, and shortly afterwards the dispute with Russia was settled by a treaty which fixed the parallel of fifty-four degrees, forty minutes, as the southern boundary of Russia, and recognized the right of the United States to the enjoyment of the fisheries in the North Pacific. As a matter of fact, however, the principles enunciated in Monroe's message did not originate with him or with Adams, who was the real author of the memorable sentences from which the above quotations have been taken, but may be traced directly to Washington's neutrality proclamation, of which the Monroe Doctrine is the necessary outcome and corollary.[24] The great credit, therefore, belonging to Monroe and Adams, and it is very great indeed, was the restatement in vigorous language of these original principles and their extension and application to new conditions, when the occasion was offered.

It should be remembered that the Monroe Doctrine, as it is called, is neither international nor statute law; it is simply a declaration by the President as to what had been the policy of the United States, and what should continue to be its policy concerning the particular question raised. But this policy so commended itself to the people as a wise and proper course, as so absolutely vital to the existence of the United States, that it has been cherished and enforced by all political parties and by all subsequent statesmen of the Republic. Many times in our history occasions have arisen for the assertion of the principles of the Monroe Doctrine, and in each instance our government has firmly adhered to this traditional policy, which commands the absolute devotion of the American people and which the world is now compelled to recognize. Daniel Webster, in a speech of April 11, 1826, in defense of the Doctrine, said: " I look upon the declaration as a part of its [the country's] reputation, and for one I intend to guard it; it is a bright page in our history. I will neither help to erase it nor tear it out; nor shall it be by any act of mine blurred or blotted. It did honor to the sagacity of the government, and I will not diminish that honor." [25]

[24] See Gilman, "Life of James Monroe," appendix ii.
[25] "Webster's Works," vol. iii. p. 205. For recent applications of Monroe's policy see Edgington, "The Monroe Doctrine"; see also Henderson, "American Diplomatic Questions," ch. iv.

III

THE MISSOURI COMPROMISE AND THE TARIFF OF 1824.

It was during Monroe's peaceful administration also that the anti-slavery agitation for the first time assumed threatening proportions — causing an alarm which rang out as suddenly as a firebell in the night, to use Jefferson's expression. During the thirty years which had elapsed since the adoption of the Constitution, the institution of slavery had been gradually extended by the admission of new States in the Southwest, while the number of slaves had largely increased. In all the Northern States slavery had been abolished, partly because the severity of the climate and the character of the industries rendered the employment of slave labor unprofitable; partly, no doubt, from the conviction that slavery was a moral wrong. In the South, however, where the warm, moist climate made the negro grow and thrive, where the character of the labor was such that the white man was at a disadvantage, slavery was profitable, although many of the ablest and most influential Southern men were convinced of the moral, and even of the economic evils of the " peculiar institution," and wished to see it abolished.

There is every reason to believe that slavery was in a fair way of ultimate extinction, when an event occurred which was destined to increase immensely the demand for slave labor, and consequently to perpetuate the existence of the system indefinitely. This was the invention of the cotton gin in 1793 by Eli Whitney, a native of Massachusetts, and a graduate of Yale College. By means of this invention a thousand pounds of cotton could be ginned in a day, whereas previously the output did not exceed a few pounds. Just at this time, also, the manufacture of cotton cloth in Europe was being greatly stimulated by the introduction of improved machinery, so that the demand for raw cotton was correspondingly increased. With the cotton gin the South was now able to supply the demand, and the export at once showed that the cultivation of the cotton plant had received a tremendous stimulus. In 1793 five hundred thousand pounds were exported, in 1800 over sixteen million pounds sent to Great Britain alone.[26] During the same period the price increased very largely, and the price of slaves increased proportionately with the increase in the price of cotton, and the

[26] Hammond, " The Cotton Industry," p. 31.

demand exceeded the supply. The result was an industrial revolution for the South and an enormous increase of the difficulties of emancipation.

Meantime the territory in which slavery was lawful was being extended. Already before Washington had retired from office Tennessee and Kentucky had been admitted to the Union as slave States. In 1803 came the acquisition of Louisiana, by which the

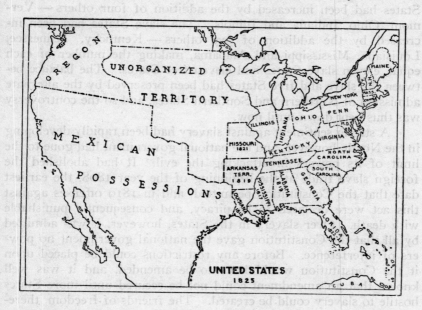

UNITED STATES
1825

Union was doubled in area, and in all this territory slavery existed by custom.[27] The rights of the slaveholders were guaranteed by a provision in the treaty which pledged the government of the United States to uphold the rights of property of the inhabitants of the ceded territory. But this obligation was to France rather than to the inhabitants of Louisiana, and the United States might have abolished slavery within the Territory without violating its obligation to any citizen of the United States.[28] No such action, however, was taken, and when Louisiana was admitted to the Union

[27] Phillips, "Economic Cost of Slaveholding," in *Political Science Quarterly*, vol. xx. p. 267.
[28] Burgess, "The Middle Period," ch. iii.

in 1812 it was admitted as a slave-holding State. The slave-holding commonwealths were further increased by the admission of Mississippi to the Union in 1817, and Alabama in 1819, and the acquisition of Florida in the latter year insured the addition of another slave State in the near future. As regards the slavery question, the situation was as follows: Of the thirteen original States seven had abolished slavery, while six still retained it. The free States had been increased by the addition of four others — Vermont, Ohio, Indiana and Illinois. The slave States had been increased by the addition of five others — Kentucky, Tennessee, Louisiana, Mississippi and Alabama, making the number of each equal, eleven slave States and eleven free States. The balance between the slave and free States had been preserved by the alternate admission of Northern and Southern States, and so the controversy was thus kept down until now.

A strong sentiment against slavery had been rapidly developing in the North, however, and the national government had gone to the limit of its powers in attacking the evil. It had abolished the foreign slave trade at the beginning of the year 1808, the earliest date that the Constitution permitted, and in 1819 offenses against this act were declared to be piracy, and consequently punishable with death. Over slavery in the States, however, it was admitted by all that the Constitution gave the national government no powers of interference. Before any restrictions could be placed upon it the Constitution would have to be amended, and it was well known that an amendment could not be secured until more States hostile to slavery could be created. The friends of freedom, therefore, bestirred themselves to secure the admission of free States.

At this time it was generally admitted by Southern statesmen, as well as Northern, that Congress had plenary powers in the Territories, and could, therefore, prohibit slavery in them. By this means these parts of the country might be settled by a free population, which would in time organize States from which slavery would be excluded, and when a sufficient number of these were created the Constitution could be amended so as to empower Congress to abolish slavery in the States where it already existed. On account of the extraordinary majority required to adopt an amendment, it was evident that this would be a slow and tedious process, all the more so if the South should continue to insist upon the maintenance of the equilibrium by the alternate admission of slave and free

States. Moreover, Congress had already lost an opportunity by admitting the southern portion of the vast domain acquired from France as a slave State, and it would, therefore, be difficult to prohibit slavery in the adjoining portions of the Territory.

The only other possible means which the Constitution seemed to afford was the power conferred upon Congress to admit new States to the Union from time to time. According to the language of the Constitution this power is both general and discretionary, and it was asserted by many that Congress might, in admitting a State, impose the condition upon it that it should have a constitution forbidding slavery. Congress had, in fact, imposed conditions, and the opportunity was now offered for testing its power in the case of slavery. The question was raised by the application in 1818 of the Territory of Missouri for admission to the Union as a State, but no action was taken upon the application at this session. In the same year a bill was brought in for the organization of a territorial government for Arkansas embracing the territory lying between Louisiana and the proposed State of Missouri. The question of slavery in the remaining territory of Louisiana was now seriously raised. A New York member moved that slavery be prohibited in the Territory of Arkansas, and the resolution was lost only by the casting vote of the speaker, Henry Clay. In the next year the Territory was organized with no mention of slavery.

In the meantime the discussion on the bill to admit Missouri was proceeding apace. On February 13, 1819, James W. Tallmadge of New York, proposed an amendment to the effect " that the further introduction of slavery or involuntary servitude be prohibited, and that all children of slaves born within the said State after the admission thereof into the Union shall be free at the age of twenty-five." The real question at issue was one of constitutional law rather than of practical expediency. It was whether Congress had the power under the Constitution to impose conditions upon the admission of new States which were not imposed by the Constitution on the original States. Those who defended the right of Congress in the premises relied chiefly upon the language of that clause of the Constitution which relates to the admission of New States to the Union. They pointed out that it did not *require* Congress to admit new States, but only *empowered* it to do so; Congress could, therefore, refuse to admit at its discretion; and that if it could admit or refuse to admit it could admit upon such conditions as it might choose to impose. The several precedents which Congress had created in this respect were pointed out to show that the question was not a new one, and that the restrictionists were occupying old ground.[29]

A strong argument was also made upon the lines of morals and public policy. To the first line of argument it was replied that if Congress could admit new States upon such conditions as it might choose to impose, it could create a Union of unequal States such as was never intended by the fathers of the Republic. Those who took this view insisted that Congress had no power to create new States — but only to admit those which had been created by the inhabitants of the Territory, and when admitted they were on an equality with the original States of the Union. Otherwise Congress could strike bargains with Territories seeking admission, and confer upon them the status of statehood in return for powers surrendered for the benefit of Congress. Such States would come into the Union lamed and crippled and shorn of the powers which properly belonged to them under the Constitution. With regard to the morals and policy of slavery extension, they argued that the withdrawal of a portion of the slaves from overstocked regions and their distribution upon new lands of the West would result in an improvement of the condition of the slaves. It was, in short, an argument in favor of the dilution of slavery.

A careful weighing of the arguments on both sides shows that while the advocates of slavery extension perhaps had an advantage from the standpoint of constitutional law, the restrictionists probably got the better of the argument as regards the policy and expediency of extending slavery. However this may be, the House passed the Tallmadge amendment by a vote of eighty-seven to seventy-six, and sent it to the Senate for concurrence. But the Senate refused to accept the amendment and passed the original bill, and the two Houses being unable to reach an agreement the session closed without definite action. The debate on the Missouri bill created great interest and excitement throughout the country; during the recess of Congress it was the all-absorbing question of discussion, and when the new Congress assembled in December, 1819, it was the leading measure for consideration.[30] In the mean-

[29] As to the practice of Congress in imposing conditions upon newly admitted states see Dunning, "Essays on Civil War and Reconstruction," pp. 304-352.

[30] Blaine, "Twenty Years of Congress," vol. i. p. 18.

time the Missouri controversy was complicated by the application for admission to the Union of the District of Maine, which had been a part of Massachusetts since 1691. Early in the session the House passed a bill to admit Maine, but when it came before the Senate for concurrence that body coupled with it the bill to admit Missouri without the Tallmadge amendment prohibiting slavery. The bill in this form passed the Senate, and was returned to the House, which refused its concurrence thereto. The deadlock was finally broken by a compromise proposed by Senator Thomas of Illinois, which provided that Missouri should be admitted without any restrictions upon slavery, but that in all the rest of the Louisiana Territory lying north of the parallel of thirty-six degrees and thirty minutes slavery should be forever prohibited. In this form the bill passed the Senate, was finally accepted by the House with the close vote of ninety to eighty-seven, and became law by the signature of the President, March 3, 1820. It admitted Maine with a constitution forbidding slavery, and authorized the people of Missouri to adopt a constitution legalizing or prohibiting slavery, as they might choose, and apply for admission to the Union.

At the next session of Congress the Missouri Constitution was laid before that body for approval, but unfortunately it contained a provision which gave rise to another difficulty and for a while longer delayed the admission of the State. This provision excluded free negroes from entering the State, a restriction believed to be a violation of the constitutional guarantee that the citizens of each State shall enjoy the privileges and immunities of citizens of the several States. The Northern members voted almost solidly against admitting Missouri with this provision in her constitution, but again the difficulty was settled by compromise, this time through the intervention of Henry Clay. The substance of Clay's compromise was that Missouri should be admitted upon the condition that its legislature should solemnly promise that no interpretation should ever be placed on the clause in question which should in any way impair the rights of citizens of the United States. With this understanding the State was admitted to the Union, thus ending the first great controversy over the slavery question — a controversy which for the excitement and sectional feeling it aroused had never been equaled since the adoption of the Constitution. The contention clearly revealed the increasing divergence of the North and the South, intensified sectional feeling, and merely postponed to a later day the settlement of the real issue involved. The compromise proved to be only a truce in the great struggle between slavery and freedom, of which this passage-at-arms may be said to have been the opening battle. The Missouri Compromise is sometimes called a Southern measure, but the ultimate advantage which the South derived from it was inconsiderable as compared with that of the North. The South gained as a result of it Missouri and Arkansas, while in the end the North gained the immense region now embracing the States of Kansas, Nebraska, Iowa, the Dakotas and Montana, and parts of Colorado, Wyoming and Minnesota. The Southerners were, moreover, made to understand that the welfare of slavery could be best secured by a strict interpretation of the Constitution with regard to the powers of Congress, while the North, on the other hand, was taught its power over slavery through a liberal interpretation.[31] Thus clearer ideas of constitutional law were formed, but the movement in the South in the direction of gradual emancipation was checked.

The last important measure of Monroe's administration was the Tariff Act of 1824. The tariff schedule of 1816 had proved a disappointment in many respects to its framers. It had been followed by a large falling off of imports, a contraction of the currency, a decline in prices, and a general derangement of business, which resulted in the financial crisis of 1819.[32] In 1820 an effort to revise the schedule in the interest of higher protection was defeated only by a single vote in the Senate. A great change of attitude was now taking place with regard to the position of the several sections on the question of protection. New England was fast becoming a manufacturing region, while the South was beginning to realize that its dependence upon the North or upon Europe for its supply of manufactured goods was likely to continue indefinitely, and a protective tariff would only increase the prices of these articles. The Middle States had always been in favor of protection, while the West, since 1816 at least, had clamored for it. The Western agriculturists hoped that the development of manufacturing industries in the East would afford more ready and convenient markets for their produce. President Monroe's annual

[31] For an excellent constitutional discussion of the struggle over the admission of Missouri to the Union, see Burgess, "The Middle Period," ch. iv.; see also Schouler, "History of the United States," vol. iii. ch. x, section ii.; and McMaster, "History of the People of the United States," vol. iv. ch. xxxix.

[32] Taussig, "Tariff History of the United States," p. 69.

HENRY CLAY
(Born, 1777.   Died, 1852)
After a daguerreotype

messages of 1821, 1822 and 1823 contained recommendations for the more adequate protection of manufactures as a necessary policy for the attainment of industrial independence, showing that down to that period at least the South had not yet abandoned the idea of protection.

In pursuance of these recommendations the House Committee on Manufactures entered upon the consideration of a new tariff project. Heretofore the consideration of this subject had devolved upon the Ways and Means Committee, indicating that up to that time the revenue feature of the tariff was of the first importance. Its reference now to the Committee on Manufactures is evidence of the change of sentiment which was taking place with regard to the purpose of tariff legislation. In January, 1823, Mr. Tod, chairman of the Committee on Manufactures, reported a bill largely increasing the duties on iron, coarse woolens and cotton goods. Being unable to secure action on the bill at this session, he brought in a more moderate measure at the next session (January, 1824). The time was now favorable for action, as a presidential election was approaching and none of the candidates felt like committing themselves against the principle of the bill. Henry Clay, Speaker of the House, came forward as the great champion of protection, the substance of his argument being that a protective tariff was necessary to secure industrial independence, and industrial independence was the necessary corollary of political independence. " The object of the bill," said Clay, " is thus to create a home market and to lay the foundation of a genuine American policy." Webster, speaking for Massachusetts, as he had done eight years before, opposed the bill; four years more were necessary to bring him over to the ranks of the protectionists. For the first time the South seems to have discovered that protection was inconsistent with the interests of slavery, and consequently voted almost solidly against the bill. But the votes of the Western, Middle and part of the Eastern States were sufficient to pass it in May, 1824.[33] As finally passed, it raised the duties on cotton and woolen goods from twenty-five per cent. to thirty-three per cent., while increased duties were also laid on iron, lead, wool, hemp and cotton bagging.[34] The general average was increased from twenty-five per cent. to

[33] For an analysis of the vote on the bill, see Stanwood, " Tariff Controversies in the Nineteenth Century," vol. i. p. 239.
[34] Taussig, " Tariff History," p. 75.

thirty-seven per cent. The tariff of 1824 was the first and most direct fruit of the early protective movement, but the protection afforded was modest; except on a few articles it was little more than a continuation of the tariff of 1816. The bill was, nevertheless, openly denounced in South Carolina as unconstitutional and oppressive, although elsewhere it was acquiesced in and was not regarded as sectional legislation. It was also the first of the so-called " political tariffs," its passage having been facilitated largely by the aid of the candidates for the Presidency in the approaching campaign.

Chapter XX

RISE OF THE DEMOCRATIC PARTY. 1824-1828

I

THE PRESIDENTIAL CONTEST OF 1824

A T the presidential election of 1820 James Monroe had been reëlected, and for the first time since 1796 there had been no organized opposition to the Republican candidate. Monroe received every electoral vote except that of the aged William Plumer of New Hampshire, a Federalist senator from that State, who cast his vote against Monroe because he was determined that Washington alone should have the honor of a unanimous choice to the Presidency.[1] The Federalist party, as an organization, had dissolved, and Federalists no longer existed except in the ranks of the Republican party or as a social reminiscence. The truth is, the Federalists had not so much disappeared as they had become absorbed by the Republicans, who had themselves adopted Federalist ways. It was this change which led Josiah Quincy to ask: "Why should we oppose the Republicans when they have become federalized?" Thus it was the Republican party — the party of strict construction — which had purchased Louisiana, established the second United States Bank, and indulged in other Federalist luxuries. On the other hand, we find Federalists — members of the party of liberal construction — for partisan reasons of opposition, abandoning their early principles, opposing the United States Bank and supporting Republican measures, as well as the old Republican theory of constitutional interpretation.[2] It was this dissolution of the old parties, or what would perhaps be more accurate, this disappearance of party spirit during Monroe's administration, which caused the period to be called the "Era of good feeling." Several events, notably the controversy over the admission of Missouri to the Union, had served to interrupt some-

---

[1] Sumner, "Life of Andrew Jackson," p. 73.
[2] See Macy, "American Political Parties."

what this peaceful era, but it cannot be said that a period marked by especial party violence set in until the administration of Monroe's successor.

After the enactment of the tariff law of 1824 the ground was clear for a new presidential election. The campaign which ensued was, as a result of party disintegration, mainly personal, and therefore both petty and bitter. Crawford claimed to be the congressional caucus candidate, but not one of the aspirants was any party's nominee. All the candidates were Republicans with varying shades of belief as to the relative importance of the general government on one hand and of the States on the other. Had the precedent of choosing the Secretary of State been observed as it had been followed for several terms, John Quincy Adams would have been the logical candidate; but there had grown up a dissatisfaction at this semi-hereditary practice, so that it is doubtful if Adams's position as Secretary of State was of advantage to him so far as his political ambitions were concerned. His chief distinction was that of being a diplomat and statesman of long experience and undoubted ability.

Two other members of Monroe's Cabinet were also candidates, namely, William H. Crawford, Secretary of the Treasury, and John C. Calhoun, Secretary of War. Crawford was a citizen of Georgia, a man of large wealth and imposing appearance, with the advantage of long experience as United States Senator, minister to France, Secretary of War and Secretary of the Treasury. He was a shrewd politician, and in 1820 had secured the enactment of a law limiting the tenure of many civil officers to four years, ostensibly to improve the civil service, but in reality, it has been generally asserted, to secure the appointment of Treasury officers known to be in sympathy with his presidential aspirations. He had also the advantage — a doubtful one, it must be said — of being the regular caucus nominee. It will be remembered that since 1800 presidential candidates had been put forward by a caucus of the members of Congress representing their respective parties. But there had grown up a widespread popular objection to this method of nominating candidates for the highest office in the land by a small clique of members of Congress, and consequently the caucus had fallen into such disfavor that at the meeting which nominated Crawford scarcely one-third of the members attended. He was therefore the last caucus nominee for the Presidency; other nominating machinery now had to be devised. Calhoun was the youngest candidate in point of years — he was but forty-two — but had already passed fourteen years in the public service as member of the State legislature, member of Congress and Secretary of War. He had won many friends by his liberal views of public policy, and was regarded as one of the most promising statesmen of the national school which the Republic had produced. Before the campaign was well advanced, however, he withdrew with the assurance of an undisputed election to the Vice Presidency.

The West furnished a candidate in the person of Henry Clay of Kentucky. Clay had long been Speaker of the National House of Representatives, was an orator of real eloquence, a political leader of engaging manners and great personal charm, and consequently had a large and enthusiastic following. He was the recognized champion of the protective tariff, of internal improvements, and of the cause of the South American republics. His hobby was Americanism, and he longed to see this country independent of the Old World in industrial as well as political matters. Like Calhoun, he belonged to the younger national school of American statesmen, and was then in his forty-seventh year. He was put forward as a candidate by the legislatures of five States, including his own State of Kentucky.[3]

Lastly, the West and South had a candidate in General Andrew Jackson of Tennessee, a rough and able Indian fighter, who had won distinction in the Creek War, and particularly by his victory over the British at New Orleans. Like Adams, he was in his fifty-seventh year, having been born before the Revolution. By profession he was a lawyer, had served a short time in both houses of Congress, was at one time a judge of the Tennessee Supreme Court, and was the first governor of the Florida Territory. In none of these positions had he won special distinction, but his service was marked by rugged honesty, patriotism and integrity. It was as a commander of militiamen that he had shown unusual talent, although in his rough way he was inclined to insubordination and was charged with arbitrary treatment of those who incurred his enmity. At the outbreak of the War of 1812 he was appointed major general of the Tennessee militia, and after inflicting a crushing defeat upon the Creek Indians at the Horse Shoe Bend in 1814, he was rewarded by an appointment as major general in the regular

[3] Schurz, "Life of Henry Clay," vol. i. p. 228.

army of the United States and put in command of the Southwest. In this capacity he defeated the British at New Orleans in an extremely well fought action, and one which in that day was very naturally regarded as a great victory.

In 1818, as already stated, he invaded Florida contrary to instructions, and Calhoun, as Secretary of War, had proposed that he be court-martialed for disobedience of orders; but he was ably defended by the Secretary of State, John Quincy Adams, whom Jackson had supposed was his chief enemy. Not until years afterwards did Jackson learn of this, and then without making amends to Adams used his powerful influence with success to destroy Calhoun's chances for the Presidency. Both in Florida and at New Orleans Jackson's conduct in several instances was arbitrary, if not lawless, and on one occasion he was fined $1,000 by a federal judge for contempt of court.[4] His actions had certainly given weight to the claim of his enemies that, like many other military chieftains in the past, he was a dangerous man for a civil magistracy. However this may be, from the standpoint of experience and training he was certainly the least qualified for the Presidency in 1824. But military heroes are always popular, and in a democracy, where political power is vested in the masses, they make formidable candidates for civil office, whether trained statesmen or not.

Jackson had the advantage, also, of being the representative of the rising democracy, and of all the candidates he alone came " pure, untrammeled and unpledged from the people," as the legislature of Pennsylvania expressed it. Our Republic had reached that stage in its progress when the masses were beginning to chafe and grow impatient at the restraints of government administered by statesmen of the old school. Up to this time the rulers of the country had been men qualified by long experience and training for public service. The masses had been content to let the few nominate the officers and were ready to submit to government by those who belonged to the upper ranks of society, respecting always the difference of capacity between man and man. But now this was all on the verge of change. In most of the States the elective franchise had been extended to the people, and thus they had become a factor with which the politician had to reckon. These new electors were coming to look with distrust upon rulers who were highly qualified by long experience and education; they were taught by demagogues

[4] Sumner, "Life of Jackson," p. 46.

to fear such men as too far removed from the people to be in sympathy with them; in short, high qualifications for office were coming to be regarded as disqualifications in the popular estimation. The masses were making ready to insist upon a full participation in political power, and regarded themselves as fully competent to govern.

Jackson was in thorough sympathy with this view, which cannot be said to have been true of any of the other candidates. He was brought forward by his old friend and neighbor, Major William B. Lewis, an astute political manager, the " father of wire pullers," says Sumner, and received the nomination of the Tennessee Legislature, and of two conventions in Pennsylvania.[5] " Hickory Clubs " were organized in many communities, and various public and private bodies passed resolutions endorsing Jackson, and at the same time denouncing the caucus and the " Secretary dynasty " as inconsistent with democratic traditions. During the autumn and winter of 1822 and 1823, says McMaster, it was not possible for a dozen men to be assembled for any purpose without somebody making a canvass of Jackson's strength.[6]

Jackson's remarkable letter to Monroe shortly after the latter's election to the Presidency, advising him to be the chief executive of the whole people, and to " exterminate that monster called party spirit " was now brought out and published for the first time. At this juncture also he wrote a letter intended for the latitude of Pennsylvania, which sought to convey the impression that he was a moderate protectionist in his political economy. The effect of these letters was to strengthen the chances of Jackson in quarters where his following was small, and to make him the leading candidate.

As was to be expected in a contest of this character, where there were so many candidates, no one received a majority of the electoral votes, although Calhoun was elected Vice President by a substantial majority. The result showed that Jackson led with ninety-nine votes; Adams came next with eighty-four, then Crawford with forty-one, Clay bringing up the rear with thirty-seven. Jackson had also received a plurality of the popular vote, which indicated that he was the choice of the people; but under the Constitution there was no election, and for the second time in our

[5] See Parton, "Life of Jackson," vol. iii. p. 21 *et seq.*
[6] "History of the People of the United States," vol. v. p. 58.

history decision devolved upon the House of Representatives voting by States.

As the Constitution provided that the choice in such cases should be made from the three highest candidates on the list, Clay had to be dropped from the contest. Had his name come before the House it is practically certain that he would have been promptly chosen, as his ascendency over that body was well-nigh complete; and had it not been for a bit of double dealing in New York, Clay, instead of Crawford, would have been third on the list. The friends of Adams and Clay in the New York legislature which appointed the electors (there were seven States in which presidential electors were chosen in this way) had agreed to divide the electors among their favorites, but the combination did not hold together, and it happened that four Crawford electors were chosen.[7] Likewise, in Louisiana, the Clay electors had been defeated by a trick and Adams electors chosen instead. This insured Clay's elimination from the contest before the House of Representatives, but he was left master of the situation with power to decide which one of his three rivals should be given the prize. It was well known that the representatives of those States which had cast their electoral vote for Clay, namely, Kentucky, Missouri and Ohio, would now vote with him in the House, and that many others would also follow his lead.[8] Henceforth the friends of the three candidates entered upon a campaign of forming " alliances " and " pulling wires " for Clay's support. Each candidate claimed that there were special reasons why Clay should cast his vote and influence for him. The friends of General Jackson asserted that as he was the leading candidate, both as regards the electoral vote and the popular vote, the House was under a moral obligation to choose him, otherwise the plain wishes of the people would be defeated.

But Clay was opposed to Jackson, whom he had repeatedly stigmatized as a dangerous military chieftain, saying that he did not regard the killing of two thousand British soldiers at New Orleans as a special qualification for the Presidency. He had frequently denounced Jackson's arbitrary conduct in the army, and it was therefore natural that he should oppose him for the Presidency. Besides, with an eye single to his own interest, he was quick to see that the election of a Western man at this time would

---

[7] McMaster, "History of the People of the United States," vol. v. p. 73.
[8] Schurz, "Life of Henry Clay," vol. i. p. 238.

endanger his own availability four years hence, as the country would not want two Western Presidents in succession. Crawford had practically been put out of the race by a stroke of paralysis which had so impaired his physical powers that it was not believed that he would live until the fourth of March next, although the efforts of his friends to counteract this impression were ceaseless and even ingenious. There remained only Adams, by experience and training perhaps the best qualified man in the country, and his views of public policy coincided more readily with those of Clay than did those of any other candidate. Clay announced that he had " interrogated his conscience as to what he ought to do, and that faithful guide had told him that he ought to vote for Adams." He similarly advised his friends to cast their votes; and Adams was chosen by thirteen States, as against seven for Jackson and four for Crawford.

In refusing to choose the highest candidate on the list the House did what was perfectly constitutional both in spirit and in letter. Had it been the view of the framers of the Constitution that the highest candidate in the popular count was entitled to be seated, provision for election by the House would never have been made, and a mere plurality of the electoral vote would have been declared sufficient. But the friends of Jackson asserted at once that the will of the people had been defeated and the spirit of the Constitution violated, and intimations were even made that Clay had acted from improper motives. This became an open assertion shortly afterward, when it was announced that Clay had been appointed Secretary of State. The cry of " corrupt bargain " was raised — a " coalition between Blifil and Black George," a combination unheard of until now, " of the Puritan and the blackleg " was John Randolph's pleasant way of expressing it. A member of Congress named Kremer, from Pennsylvania, asserted in the public prints that a " corrupt bargain " had been made between Adams and Clay, by which Clay was to be appointed Secretary of State in return for his support of Adams. As the Tennessee legislature expressed it, Adams wanted the office of President: he went into the combination without it and came out with it; Mr. Clay desired that of Secretary of State: he went into the combination without it and came back with it.[9] Clay at once demanded an investigation by the House, but Kremer sneaked out of it by re-

[9] Morse, " Life of J. Q. Adams," p. 183.

tracting.[10] There was probably no truth in the charge of corruption, but it was easy to persuade the new democracy to believe it, and the persistency with which it clung to Clay illustrates the tremendous vitality of a well-managed political lie. The whole affair, says Carl Schurtz, was " an infamous intrigue against the good name of two honorable men, designed to promote the political fortunes of a third." [11] The truth is, Clay's position was such that whatever course he might have elected to follow would have exposed him to censure.

II

THE PANAMA CONGRESS; THE CONTROVERSY WITH GEORGIA; THE TARIFF OF 1828

The election was hardly over before Adams's enemies entered upon a policy of determined opposition to the administration. The first evidence of this was the attempt of the Senate to reject his nomination of Clay to be Secretary of State, fifteen of the forty-one senators present voting against confirmation, and among the fifteen was Senator Andrew Jackson of Tennessee, who openly asserted the charge of " bargain and corruption." It was now evident that an organized opposition to the Adams-Clay administration was to be prosecuted by the followers of Calhoun, Jackson and Crawford, although there was no essential difference of principle between the views of Adams and those of his opponents.[12] Jackson, " the people's choice," had been cheated out of the Presidency, they asserted, by a dirty collusion, and everything possible must be done to make the new administration unpopular. Its policies must be opposed, and its recommendations must be ignored without regard to merit on the general principle that it was not the rightful administration, while the old hero must be constantly kept before the people as the victim of an unjust conspiracy, and be elected as the successor of Adams in 1828. This proved an effective weapon with which to destroy Adams's popularity and the success of his administration. " No President," says Thomas H. Benton, " could have commenced his administration under more unfavorable auspices or with less expectations of a popular career." Adams felt

[10] Schurz, " Life of Henry Clay," vol. i. p. 246.
[11] *Ibid.*, vol. i. p. 246.
[12] Morse, " Life of John Quincy Adams," p. 189.

keenly the charge that he was a "minority President," and he lamented in his diary that he had been elevated to the Presidency "not in a manner satisfactory to pride; not by the unequivocal suffrages of a majority of the people; but with perhaps two-thirds of the whole people adverse to the actual result." [13]

It cannot be denied, however, that in knowledge and experience, Adams was one of the best equipped men for the chief magistracy that the Republic had produced. At the early age of twenty-seven Washington had sent him as minister to Portugal, and later his father, upon the earnest advice of Washington, appointed him minister to Prussia. After serving a term in the United States Senate, and having quarreled with the Federalist party, to which he belonged, he reëntered the diplomatic service as minister to Russia. He was one of the commissioners that negotiated the Treaty of Ghent, and later served as minister to England. During the eight years of Monroe's administration he filled with conspicuous ability the office of Secretary of State. He was, in the full sense of the word, a statesman, was industrious, conscientious, and had a high conception of the dignity of the presidential office. He belonged to the national wing of the Republican party, and favored a liberal policy of internal improvements. In his first annual message his recommendations under this head were so advanced as to quite shock even some of his confidential advisers. He urged the construction of roads, bridges, canals, a national university, a national observatory, a naval school, the improvement of harbors, a strong navy, an efficient army, and the construction of suitable coast fortifications.[14] His recommendations, however, were ignored and the appropriations of Congress were confined chiefly to the construction and repair of roads and canals, and to subscription of stock in State enterprises. No actual advance was made upon the policy of Monroe's administration; in fact, there was retrogression, for the opposition professed to fear that the administration had a fixed purpose of encroaching upon the reserved rights of the States, and their leader, Martin Van Buren, went so far as to introduce a resolution in Congress denying the power of the general government to construct roads and canals within the States.

Another matter in which the administration took a special in-

---

[13] Morse, "J. Q. Adams," p. 177.
[14] Richardson, "Messages and Papers of the Presidents," vol. ii. p. 311.

terest was the proposed Congress of American Republics to be held at Panama. In 1824 General Simon Bolivar, the South American patriot, had issued an invitation to the several Spanish-American governments to send delegates to the proposed congress. These delegates were to be empowered to discuss various questions concerning American affairs, particularly those relating to liberal commercial intercourse and advanced principles of maritime neutrality in time of war. In the spring of 1825 the invitation was extended to the United States. The prospect of a grand confederation of American republics under the hegemony of the United States excited the imagination of the Secretary of State, who, in Congress, had been the brilliant defender of these republics against the despotism of Europe.[15] Nothing seemed to be more in harmony with his idea of an "American system," and after demanding and receiving definite information concerning the organization and procedure of the congress and the subjects to be discussed, he persuaded the President to accept the invitation, with the understanding that the delegates should not be empowered to take any action contrary to the traditional policy of the United States with regard to neutrality. Upon the meeting of Congress the President sent in a message saying that the invitation had been accepted, and that commissioners would soon be nominated to represent the United States at the proposed conference. Members of both Houses professed to feel that Congress had not been properly treated, and that instead of informing it that the invitation had been accepted, the President should have first consulted the Senate in regard to the expediency of the mission. Vehement attacks were made upon Adams by members of both Houses on the ground that he had exceeded his powers. When the President, therefore, sent in the nomination of Anderson and Sergeant as the delegates to the congress, the Senate referred the nomination to the Committee on Foreign Affairs and called for the correspondence relating to the subject. The committee reported against the nominations on the ground that participation in the congress would draw us into entangling relations with other countries. The Senate in secret session debated the report for about a month, and finally on March 14, 1826, confirmed the nominations by a vote of twenty-four to nineteen. The necessary funds ($40,000) were voted after a prolonged discussion in the House, but it was too late for the delegates to reach

[15] Schurz, "Life of Henry Clay," vol. i. p. 268.

Panama before the adjournment of the congress, and the whole scheme ended in failure.

It is commonly asserted that one of the reasons for the delay, and consequently the failure of the Panama mission, was the opposition of the Southern members on account of their objection to taking part in a congress of States which had abolished slavery, and in which there probably would be discussion of common measures for the suppression of the slave trade. It was claimed, furthermore, that the Southern slaveholders feared the effect of the action of the South American republics upon their slave population.[16] Benton of Missouri frankly declared that it was inadmissible that " our fixed policy should be discussed in a congress made up of five nations which have already put the black man upon an equality with the white, not only in their constitutions but in real life; five nations which at this moment have black generals in their armies and mulatto senators in their congresses." [17]

The chief domestic difficulty of Adams's administration arose over the controversy between the State of Georgia and the United States with regard to the Indians within her limits. As has been pointed out in another connection, the State of Georgia, in 1802, had ceded to the United States her claims to lands lying in what are now Alabama and Mississippi for $1,250,000. One of the conditions of this cession was that the United States should extinguish, as soon as it could be done in a peaceful way and on reasonable conditions, all Indian titles to land within the limits of Georgia. During the next twenty years the government made some progress in the direction of the fulfillment of its promise, but on account of the difficulties encountered the advance was not so rapid as the Georgians wished, or as the progress of the State demanded. Designing white men had joined the Indian tribes for the purpose, it was charged, of organizing an Indian State within the limits of Georgia, so that a rather serious problem was presented. The people grew impatient of the slow progress made by the United States in extinguishing the Indian claims, and in 1819 the legislature urged the President to hasten the fulfillment of the agreement of 1802. In 1824 the Indian chiefs in council decided to sell no

[16] Burgess, " The Middle Period," p. 153; see also, Snow, " Topics in American Diplomacy," pp. 295-312; Morse, " Life of John Quincy Adams," p. 192.

[17] Read Von Holst, " Constitutional History of the United States," vol. i. pp. 415-425.

more of their lands to the United States. In February, 1825, however, United States commissioners succeeded in concluding at Indian Springs a treaty with McIntosh, one of the Creek chiefs, by which all the lands occupied by the Creek Indians were to be surrendered to the United States. But when the State surveyors entered upon the task of examining the lands thus relinquished they were resisted by the Indians, who repudiated the treaty on the ground that it was obtained by fraud from chiefs who were unauthorized to make it. The indignation of the Indians was, in fact, so great that they put McIntosh to death and sent commissioners to Washington to protest against the enforcement of the fraudulent agreement. Thereupon the Secretary of War informed the governor of the State, Mr. Troup, that the surveys must be discontinued until the validity of the treaty could be inquired into.[18]

The governor took offense at what he regarded as an unwarranted interference of the United States in the affairs of Georgia, declared that he would not discontinue the surveys, and called upon the legislature to " stand to arms " and resist the " encroachments " of the general government upon the reserved rights of the State. At this juncture the President dispatched General Gaines to the territory in question with instructions to prevent the survey by force, if necessary, but if possible to obtain the assent of the Indians to the treaty. The governor protested at this order, entered into an angry correspondence with the Federal authorities, and threatened secession, but the President stood firm, and for a time matters were at a standstill. In January, 1826, another agreement was concluded with the Creek Indians by which the Treaty of Indian Springs was annulled and a smaller cession made to the United States, the Indians firmly refusing to yield all their claims. This time the governor repudiated the treaty, and directed the survey of the lands in accordance with the agreement of 1825, which gave Georgia a million acres more than did the later treaty. Again the Indians resisted, and again the President ordered the arrest of any person caught surveying Indian lands lying west of the line fixed by the treaty of 1826. A second time the governor defied the administration and ordered the release of the arrested surveyors and directed the militia to be held in readiness to resist the threatened invasion by the military power of the United States, and declared that any attempt to enforce the Indian claim should be

[18] Von Holst, " Constitutional History of the United States," vol. i. p. 437.

regarded as an attack upon the people and sovereignty of Georgia. Adams felt that he was bound to uphold the dignity of the national government, yet he hesitated to come to an open collision with the Georgia authorities for fear of provoking civil war. He therefore laid the whole matter before Congress, but the opposition, which controlled a majority of that body, was rather pleased at his humiliation and took no action upon the matter.[19] Thus Georgia had won in an open conflict with the United States. She had successfully nullified Federal authority, and she had gone far to establish her claim as a sovereign State.[20]

In one respect, and in one only, did the administration score a success. This was in the management of the foreign relations of the country. During Adams's term a considerable number of commercial treaties were negotiated; more in fact than had been concluded during the entire thirty-six years of national history preceding his inauguration; but unfortunately their good effect was largely impaired by the act of Great Britain in closing her West Indian ports to American commerce, thus destroying a lucrative trade, of which the Americans had enjoyed a monopoly for several years past. The British interdict upon American trade with the West Indies caused widespread discontent in the United States, and contributed much to the unpopularity of the administration, but it should be said in justice to Adams that he was not altogether responsible for Great Britain's action. Her discrimination against us was partly due to unwise legislation by Congress. Preferring to let the odium rest on Adams's shoulders, Congress refused to resent in a suitable manner Great Britain's conduct. In this situation the President did what he could to repair the wrong, and by authority of an old act of Congress he issued a proclamation reviving against Great Britain a number of trade restrictions.

The last year of his administration was marked by a renewal of the struggle over the tariff question — in the interest of higher protection. The tariff of 1824, which had been framed chiefly for the protection of the manufacturers of coarse woolens, had not given satisfaction. Much capital had been turned into the manufacture of woolen goods, which had the effect of glutting the home markets, and at the same time the output of woolen manufactures in Great Britain had largely increased on account of the admission

[19] Burgess, "The Middle Period," p. 215.
[20] Von Holst, "Constitutional History of the United States," vol. i. p. 447.

of free wool to British ports. This enabled the British manufacturer to compete with the American manufacturer in his own markets, and made it necessary, therefore, to increase the American duties or permit the ruin of the American manufacturer.[21] Moreover, it was alleged that the ruin of the home manufacturer was being accelerated by fraudulent undervaluation of imported goods.

In furtherance of the movement, a national convention of protectionists, made up mainly of manufacturers and wool growers from thirteen States, was held at Harrisburg, and it adopted resolutions recommending higher duties on wool and woolen goods, and also on the manufactures of cotton, hemp, flax, iron, and glass. Meetings of lesser importance were held at many other places throughout the country, all of which adopted memorials and petitions to Congress for an increase of the tariff duties. The petitions and memorials were referred to the Committee on Manufactures, and in January, 1827, the chairman, Mr. Mallery of Vermont, reported the famous woolens bill. It proposed to place a duty on coarse woolens so high as to amount practically to a prohibitory tariff. Massachusetts, which up to this time had opposed high tariffs, now came over to the ranks of the protectionists, while the South, including Kentucky, went over to the side of the opposition. the bill passed the House in February, 1827, but was lost in the Senate by the casting vote of the Vice President, Calhoun, who had in the meantime abandoned his original advocacy of the tariff, and had become a champion of free trade. The effect of the controversy in Congress was to arouse intense excitement and opposition in South Carolina, where at various public meetings in Columbia resolutions were adopted advocating the secession of the Southern States in case the proposed tariff bill were enacted into law.[22]

The main argument of these South Carolina protests was that the chief exports of the United States were Southern products, and therefore it was Southern industry which provided the means for the largest part of the merchandise imported from abroad; that the tariff, by adding to the cost of foreign merchandise, diminished the amount which could be purchased, and thus became a tax almost exclusively upon Southern industry; that the enforced diminution of imports placed a limitation upon the amount of cotton which

[21] Stanwood, "American Tariff Controversies," vol. i. p. 253.
[22] See "American State Papers," "Finance," vol. v., for a large collection of these resolutions.

foreign countries could purchase, and thus hampered the export trade; and that the taxes collected from the South were levied for the purpose of promoting Northern industry, the proceeds being expended mainly in making internal improvements in the North.[23]

At the beginning of the next session of Congress the Committee on Manufactures reported a new bill largely increasing the duties on iron, woolen goods, flax, hemp, and a number of other articles, thus introducing the new principle of high protection of raw materials used in the manufactures. It is sometimes asserted that the duties on raw materials were made purposely so high as to force the New England members into voting against it, and thus make them responsible for its defeat. And with this weapon Adams's defeat in the approaching election could be easily accomplished. But to the surprise of its authors the New England members voted for the bill with all its "abominable" features, preferring it to no bill at all. As finally passed, it increased very largely the duty on iron, wool, and hemp. The principle of minimum valuation was applied to the tariff on woolen goods, that is, all goods costing between forty cents and $2.50 were to be assessed as if they had cost $2.50.[24] The law was really in the interest of the hemp and wool growing section of the West. It is questionable whether the manufacturers derived any benefit from the measure; it is almost certain that the agricultural interests of the South did not, for it increased the price of woolen fabrics and did not extend the domestic market for raw cotton. The measure was stigmatized by its enemies as the "tariff of abominations," and John Randolph declared that it referred to manufactures of no kind except the manufacture of a President of the United States. Adams's approval of the bill was a fitting close to his unpopular administration.

The measure stirred up great excitement in the South, five legislatures formally protested against the act, and Calhoun, now the acknowledged Southern leader, drew up for the use of the South Carolina legislature an elaborate paper styled "The Exposition and Protest." In this paper he examined the nature of the Union, and argued with great force that the States were sovereign and possessed the constitutional power to nullify a law of the United States if deemed to be oppressive or unconstitutional.[25] He there-

[23] Stanwood, "American Tariff Controversies," vol. i. p. 262.
[24] Taussig, "Tariff History," p. 94.
[25] Von Holst, "Constitutional History," vol. i. p. 467.

fore suggested that a State convention be called to decide upon the proper manner of declaring the Tariff Act null and void in the State of South Carolina, but further action was postponed until the election of Jackson, whose sympathies, it was believed, were with the nullificationists.

The campaign for the election of Jackson in 1828 really began shortly after his defeat in 1824, and the four years of Adams's term were one long drawn-out contest upon the part of his opponents to discredit the administration and destroy his prospects for reëlection. As early as October, 1825, the Tennessee legislature had renominated Jackson by acclamation, received him with appropriate ceremonies at Nashville, and called upon the people to repudiate Adams, who had been foisted into the Presidency as the result of a corrupt bargain. In Congress a coherent organization of Jackson's friends was formed, and their activity in his behalf assumed a character calculated to create the impression that the administration was composed of rascals and that the government was reeking with corruption. Investigations into various departments of the government were undertaken, but little was discovered which reflected upon the honesty of the President, whom they were designed to discredit. Resolutions were passed intimating that the government was extravagant, and demanding retrenchment; others were introduced for no other purpose than that of bringing Adams into contempt; while still others, such as the resolution to appropriate $100,000 to paint a picture of the battle of New Orleans for the decoration of the Capitol, were intended to bring into prominence the merits of General Jackson.

Adams was criticised for his abuse of the appointing power, yet of all our Presidents he was perhaps the least deserving of criticism on this score. He absolutely refused to remove a single official for political reasons, although great pressure was brought upon him to do so, and it was probably true, as he said, that four-fifths of those in office were opposed to his election. Even when a New Orleans naval officer went out of his way to get up a demonstration for the purpose of insulting the administration, Adams could not be induced to remove him, for the reason that it could not be done upon "any fixed principle which would apply to others as well as to him."

Like his father, John Quincy Adams had many personal attributes which unfitted him for the career of a successful politician.

He was cold and austere toward his friends, would not stretch a point for his most ardent supporter, was needlessly disagreeable, preferred his books to discussing questions of patronage, never exchanged light compliments, and wholly lacked the gracious qualities that made General Jackson the idol of the masses. That he could have done much to stem the tide against him there can be little doubt; but he refused to attend political gatherings, would do nothing to placate antagonisms, to soothe disaffected State or conciliate those who differed with him on questions of public policy, declined to make political speeches under any consideration, and when asked by Edward Everett what he proposed to do to secure a reëlection, said, " Absolutely nothing." " If," said he, " the people wish me to be President I shall not refuse the office; but I ask nothing from any man or from any body of men." [26] It was well known that if reëlected he would not turn a hand toward those who had exerted themselves to secure his election.

With this conception of his duty in the premises it was impossible for Adams to organize a large and enthusiastic following ready to fight his cause in season and out of season. There were no well defined differences in the political and economic policies of the two candidates so far as could be ascertained. The people were simply called upon to choose between two personalities; one, a cold, highly trained statesman of distinguished family; the other, a gallant military hero, rough, genial, true to his friends, and apparently a strong, certainly a noisy believer in the virtue and capacity of the people, and an uncompromising foe to the " wicked aristocracy," which up to this time had filled the offices of the government to the exclusion of the common people. Under these circumstances there could be but one result. The new democracy of the South and West flocked solidly to Jackson, leaving, as Parton says, only the book-nourished, silver-forked aristocracy of the East to vote for Adams.[27] The result of the election showed that Jackson had carried every State west of the Alleghany Mountains, and every one south of Mason and Dixon's line except Delaware and Maryland. Through the aid of Martin Van Buren, a shrewd and influential politician of New York, Jackson also secured twenty of the thirty-six electoral votes of that State. He also received one electoral vote in Maine, five in Maryland, and stranger still, the

[26] Morse, "Life of J. Q. Adams," p. 167.
[27] Parton, "Life of Jackson," vol. iii. p. 150.

entire vote of Pennsylvania, a State noted for its strong protectionist tendencies, but which had been persuaded by Jackson's managers
to believe that he favored a high tariff. The total number of
electoral votes received by Jackson was one hundred and seventy-
eight, while Adams had but eighty-three.[28] Calhoun was reëlected
Vice President. The result of the election of 1828 was an overwhelming triumph of the new democracy. New political and social
forces in American life were now at work, and a race of new rulers
had risen up to guide and direct them. Adams was the last of the
great statesmen who belonged to the old school, and many years
were destined to elapse before another of his type was called to
occupy the White House and preside over the destinies of the
Republic.[29] "As President," says James Schouler, "the two
Adamses passed quickly out among the failures of the age, accomplishing little to be long remembered; but as fearless men on
the floor of an American Congress, stirring the blood, forcing conviction by example, and compelling willing or unwilling attention,
they stand on the canvas the most vivid figures of two remarkable
epochs of American history full sixty years apart. John Adams
stood among the immortals in youth as John Quincy Adams did in
old age."[30]

[28] Stanwood, "History of the Presidency," p. 148.
[29] Von Holst, "Constitutional History of the United States," vol. ii. p. 1.
[30] Schouler, "History of the United States," vol. iii. p. 400.

Chapter XXI

THE JACKSONIAN EPOCH. 1828-1841

I

ANDREW JACKSON

WITH the accession of Andrew Jackson to the Presidency in 1829 a new epoch in American history may be said to have begun. Socially and intellectually the distinguishing feature was the further development of the transition from colonialism to nationalism and democracy, which had begun after the close of the second war with England. Industrially, a change almost revolutionary in extent, stimulated by the policy of protection, was taking place as a result of the invention of labor-saving machinery and the application of steam to land transportation. Politically, a new party with a new policy had gained control of the government, and old traditions were soon to be swept away. A new and unique personality had been called to the chief magistracy. Born in 1767 in the backwoods of North Carolina of humble Scotch-Irish parents, Jackson passed his boyhood amid the wild scenes of that primitive region, his youth having been embittered by several incidents of the Revolutionary War from which he had suffered, and the scars of which he carried to his grave. He lacked the advantages of education and experience such as Adams and Jefferson had enjoyed, neither was he possessed of the unquenchable thirst for knowledge which marked the early life of Abraham Lincoln. The rude sports of the frontier, such as horse racing and cock fighting, had far more attraction for him than steady labor, either physical or intellectual. Picking up a smattering knowledge of the law from such books as were at hand, he crossed the mountains into that still more primitive part of North Carolina soon to become the State of Tennessee and entered upon the practice of his profession, first at Jonesboro and later at Nashville. Commending himself to his new neighbors, he was selected as the public prosecutor of the district, and acquired a local reputation full of terror

477

to evil doers.   When the district was ready to apply for statehood Jackson was chosen as a member of the convention which prepared its first constitution, and in the course of time was chosen the State's first representative in Congress.   He even became a justice of the State Supreme Court, and at two subsequent periods served short terms in the United States Senate, in each case resigning before the end of his term.   Apparently he cared little for public life at this time, and certainly the impression he made as a senator was anything but favorable.   Long afterward he was remembered by Albert Gallatin as a tall, awkward frontiersman with his hair arranged in a queue and tied behind his head in an eel skin.

Far different was his career as a military leader, however, for it was here that he exhibited those unusual qualities of mind and heart which were destined to make him the idol of the masses, and carry him into the Presidential office.   Until late in life he apparently did not think himself fitted for the Presidency, and when his name was first mentioned in 1821 he ridiculed the suggestion as preposterous, saying that he was fit only to command a body of men in a rough sort of way.   Few of our Presidents have so impressed their personality upon the history of their time as Jackson.   Some of his mental traits need to be mentioned in order to afford a proper background for the study of his administration.   Measured by the standard applied to his predecessors, Jackson was an ignorant man, hasty in judgment and tenacious of his opinions.   Having reached a conclusion, he could rarely ever be convinced of the possibility of error, certainly not by political opponents.   He always felt sure that he was right, and could never tolerate differences of opinion in anyone.   To differ with him meant to incur his enmity.   Those who were fortunate enough to win his friendship never lacked evidences of his favor; but with those who opposed him he had but one course, namely, eternal war.   Nor could he ever forget or forgive those who opposed him.   In action he was direct and aggressive, sometimes even lawless and violent.   Toward the accomplishment of a given object he moved along the shortest and straightest line, exhibiting no patience with circuitous methods, and destroying, if he could, whatever obstacle blocked his path.   His domestic life was pure, his integrity of character incorruptible, his patriotism of a high order, his energy unbounded, and his intentions generally good.   These were the qualities which seized the popular fancy, and gave him a hold upon the plain people such as none of his predecessors had ever enjoyed. By them he was loved and trusted, to them he spoke like an oracle, and whether the advice was good or bad their one response was "Hurrah for Jackson!"

At the time of Jackson's accession the population of the United States was about thirteen millions, or more than double that of twenty-five years previous. This increase represented a natural growth, but little being due at that time to foreign immigration. During the same period the area of the country had more than doubled while the Union had been increased by the admission of seven new States, all except one (Maine) being situated in the West or Southwest. The most populous States were New York and Pennsylvania, both of which had passed Virginia. The center of population was now near the western boundary of Maryland. The population at this time was chiefly rural, less than ten per cent. living in towns of over eight thousand inhabitants. The largest cities were New York, with a population of two hundred thousand; Philadelphia with one hundred and sixty-seven thousand; Baltimore with eighty thousand, and Boston with sixty thousand. In the South the largest cities were New Orleans, Charleston, Savannah and Richmond, none of which had a population of as many as fifty thousand. Cincinnati, the largest city of the West, was but an ordinary town, while Chicago did not yet have a legal existence. The foundations of Omaha, Denver, and other Western cities were not even laid. Differences of wealth had not yet become a menace to the nation; in fact there were only three millionaires in the country: Lawrence of Boston, Astor of New York, and Girard of Philadelphia. The increase of the slave population had kept pace with the growth of the white population, and now numbered over two millions.

Industrial conditions had been revolutionized by the improvements in transportation and by inventions of labor-saving machinery. Steamboats were plying on all the Western rivers and on the Great Lakes, and many improvements in steam navigation had been made. Considerable progress had also been achieved in artificial waterways, the most important of which was the Erie Canal, connecting Lake Erie with the Hudson River, a distance of 360 miles. This valuable watercourse was due to the energy and foresight of DeWitt Clinton, a nephew of George Clinton, at the time of completion the Governor of New York. Its effect upon the industrial developments of New York may be readily seen from the fact that the cost of transporting freight from New York to Buffalo dropped from one hundred dollars a ton to fourteen dollars, the year after its opening. New York City soon became the metropolis of the country, while a great impetus was given to the development of Ohio, Indiana and Illinois. The construction of the Erie Canal was followed speedily by others of less magnitude, and the Ohio Canal, connecting Lake Erie with the Ohio River, and the Chesapeake and Ohio Canal, connecting Pittsburg with Washington, were soon completed. It was estimated that at the time of the accession of Jackson some 1,300 miles of canal had been completed in the United States, while nearly 2,000 more were in course of construction. But the most important factor in the industrial and economic development of the country was the application of steam to land transportation. In 1828 the first spike was driven on the Baltimore and Ohio Railroad by the venerable Charles Carroll, of Maryland, the last surviving signer of the Declaration of Independence; and three years later a locomotive was hauling cars over a railroad in South Carolina. Within twelve years over two thousand miles of railroad were in operation. Intimately connected with the building of railroads was the development of the iron industry in Pennsylvania, which was greatly stimulated at this time by the application of anthracite to the process of smelting.

This period was also one of great social and intellectual transition. New and powerful forces were for the first time coming into play, and a general democratization of American life and institutions was rapidly taking place. Almost everywhere a wide extension of suffrage was made although free negroes were disfranchised about this time in two States, North Carolina (1835), and Pennsylvania (1837). Also, the old-time restrictions for eligibility to public office were removed, so that the humblest citizen was qualified for the highest station. At the same time many of the administrative offices which had formerly been filled either by appointment by the governor or by the legislature were now made elective by the people. This extreme democratic movement was soon to sweep into its grasp even the judiciary. In 1832 Mississippi adopted a new constitution, taking the selection of the judges out of the hands of the governor and placing it in the hands of the people. Mississippi's example was soon followed by other States, and before the outbreak of the Civil War less than half a dozen retained appointed judiciaries. Still another feature of the democratic movement was the introduction of the principle of the referendum in legislation, according to which the validity of certain important legislative acts was made to depend upon the approval of the electorate at the polls. By 1850 there was scarcely a State in which this principle of popular coöperation in law-making was not being resorted to in practice.

It was about this time, too, that the development of American literature proper had its beginning. William Cullen Bryant, Washington Irving, James Fenimore Cooper, Fitz-Greene Halleck, and Noah Webster were already at the height of their powers, while Emerson, Hawthorne, Longfellow, Lowell, Whittier, Poe, N. P. Willis, and George Bancroft were soon to be famous names. In law, Kent, Wheaton and Story, in science, Benjamin Silliman and others had already entered upon careers which were to make the world wiser by their productions. Andrew Jackson was a typical representative of the new democratic ideas, both political and social, of the time, and was eminently fitted by his character to give force and direction to them.

The character of his inauguration was in keeping with the Jacksonian idea that the government belonged to the people, and accordingly they descended upon the capital by thousands and tens of thousands from every part of the land. Judge Story, who was an eye-witness to the scene, declared that Washington City had never seen such a throng, and Daniel Webster wrote that men came from a distance of five hundred miles to see the " Old Hero," who, they seemed to think, had rescued the government from some great calamity.[1] It was generally believed that Jackson, upon coming into power, would reward his friends and punish his enemies, although, in a letter to Monroe shortly after the latter's election to the Presidency, he had advised him to avoid all appearance of party spirit, and to make no appointments except upon the basis of merit. But the office seekers, evidently believing that Jackson would make a clean sweep, appeared in large numbers; Adams asserted that the editor of every slanderous or scurrilous newspaper in the country attended the inauguration, and was easily distinguishable by his excessive enthusiasm for Jackson. Parton, who was an eye-witness, says that the descent upon Washington was like the inundation of Rome by the northern barbarians, save

[1] Curtis, "Life of Daniel Webster," vol. i. p. 340.

that the tumultuous tide came in from different points of the compass. On the night following the inauguration the visitors took possession of the White House, where barrels of orange punch had been provided for their refreshment, and in their eagerness to shake hands with the President, rough men stood with muddy boots upon the costly furniture of the White House and smashed the fine chandeliers which hung overhead. At one time during the reception the press was so great that Jackson was in danger of injury, and was rescued with difficulty from the onslaught of his friends.[2]

To none of these proceedings was Adams a witness. Disregarding the time-honored custom, according to which the outgoing and incoming President rode side by side to the Capitol on inauguration day, Adams refused to attend the ceremonies, and like his father at the time of the inauguration of Jefferson, he remained quietly at home. A few days later he returned to Quincy, Massachusetts, resolved "to go into the deepest retirement and withdraw from all connections with public affairs."[3] But in this expectation he was doomed to disappointment, for soon he was called again into the arena of politics as a member of Congress, and the seventeen years which he spent in the national legislature constitute perhaps the most brilliant period of his long public career.

II

THE SPOILS SYSTEM; CONTROVERSY WITH GEORGIA; NULLIFICATION IN SOUTH CAROLINA

Many who came to the inauguration with the expectation of being rewarded were not disappointed. Although the President-elect so carefully concealed his intentions that no one could tell what would be his policy, Webster, the day before the inauguration, predicted that "General Jackson would probably make some removals, but not a great many immediately."[4] In his inaugural Jackson gave an intimation of his intentions by an allusion to the "task of reform," which the "recent demonstration of public sentiment had inscribed on the list of executive duties," and gave assurances that "the causes which have disturbed the rightful course

[2] Parton, "Life of Jackson," vol. iii. p. 171.
[3] Morse, "Life of Adams," p. 216.
[4] Parton, "Life of Jackson," vol. iii. p. 168.

of appointments" would be "counteracted" and the abuses corrected. The work of reform was promptly begun. A wholesale removal of those in office followed, and the vacancies were filled with Jackson's supporters. Efficiency and skill acquired from long experience seemed to count for nothing; in fact long service was regarded as a good reason for removal.

Up to this time the civil service had been looked upon as a sort of life profession, and those who had secured appointments often arranged their private affairs with the expectation of spending their remaining years in the public service without the probability of disturbance by changes of administration. At the time of Jackson's accession there were not a few persons in office who had been appointed by President Washington. During the forty years intervening between the inauguration and that of Jackson no President had found cause to remove them.[5] The total number of removals during this long period had probably been less than one hundred, and nearly all of these had been for good cause, such as misbehavior or incompetency, and then only after investigation. It remained for Jackson to break the record by removing, in the first year of his term, nearly five hundred postmasters (Senator Benton says nearly seven hundred), and some two hundred and forty other officials, which necessarily affected a large number of subordinates, and thus involved in all probability two thousand changes. Of Jackson's predecessors since Jefferson, Madison had made five removals, Monroe nine, and John Quincy Adams but two.[6]

A reign of terror set in among the old office holders; several tragic occurrences followed in some of the departments, and many pathetic incidents happened in connection with the enforcement of the proscription.[7] No explanation was given when a resignation was demanded, unless it was that the offices were not hereditary, or that no one had a right to government support. Jackson's appointees were mainly those who had cheered lustily for him in the

[5] Concerning the appointment of a personal friend to office, Washington wrote: "He is welcome to my home and to my heart; but with all his good qualities he is not a man of business. His opponent, with all his politics hostile to me, is a man of business. My private feelings have nothing to do in the case. I am not George Washington, but President of the United States. As George Washington I would do this man any kindness in my power—as President of the United States I can do nothing."

[6] Parton, "Life of Jackson," vol. iii. p. 210; also Fish, "The Civil Service and the Patronage," pp. 126–127; Sumner, "Life of Jackson," p. 147.

[7] Read Parton, "Life of Jackson," vol. iii. pp. 212–220.

campaign or had otherwise actively shown their allegiance. Many of them had no other qualifications, and it turned out that some of them were thieves and rascals. John Quincy Adams expressed a common judgment when he declared that "very few reputable appointments have been made, and those confined to persons who were indispensably necessary to the office. The appointments are exclusively of violent partisans, and every editor of a scurrilous and slanderous newspaper is provided for." A few of the worst appointments were rejected by the Senate, but Jackson regarded this as an infringement of his prerogative and resisted it with his usual ultimate success. It is not at all probable that he desired the appointment of any but honest and capable persons to office under his administration, but it was impossible to avoid mistakes when the appointments were made for political reasons.

Perhaps a large share of the responsibility for introducing the spoils system should also rest upon his advisers, rather than upon himself. He was largely under the influence of the New York politicians, especially his Secretary of State, Van Buren, and is reported to have declared that he was no politician, but if he were, he would be one of the New York type. The view of a New York politician was well expressed by William L. Marcy, a United States Senator from that State, who in 1830, speaking of his party associates, said, "When they are contending for victory they avow the intention of enjoying the fruits of it. If they are defeated they expect to retire from office. If they are successful they claim, as a matter of right, the advantage of success. They see nothing wrong in the rule that to the victors belong the spoils of the enemy." Jackson accepted this view as a cardinal doctrine of his political ethics, without realizing the demoralizing effects of such a policy upon the character of the public service. Thus he became the instrument of what was for many years the most pernicious feature of our civil service — a policy which stimulated political strife, placed a premium upon corruption, enfeebled the public service, and debauched national politics, until the Civil Service Act of 1883 was passed, half a century later.

But it must be remembered that the spoils system had already been introduced into the politics of several States, notably New York and Pennsylvania, and doubtless would have appeared in national politics sooner or later whether Jackson had been elected or not. Popular opinion demanded its introduction into the national service and Jackson merely served as the agent of the public in adopting the policy as his own. But his conduct was strangely inconsistent with the good advice he had volunteered to Monroe just after the latter's election, and also inconsistent with his former opposition to the appointment of members of Congress, for in one year he appointed more than did any one of his predecessors in a whole term.[8]

Jackson chose for his official advisers a body of men none of whom, with a single exception, had gained national reputations for conspicuous public service. The exception was Martin Van Buren of New York, who had lately been elected governor of that State, and who now became Secretary of State in the new Cabinet. For Secretary of War Jackson selected John H. Eaton, an old Tennessee friend and neighbor, who had served in the United States Senate. The others are scarcely remembered by the general student of American history. Jackson, however, did not rely upon his Cabinet for advice, and in fact seldom had Cabinet meetings. He either formed his own opinions or sought the advice of a small coterie of personal friends who gathered about the White House at his call, or lived with him upon terms of great familiarity. This little group was popularly known as the "Kitchen Cabinet." [9] Its most conspicuous member was Major William B. Lewis, another old friend and neighbor, who, for four years had been his political manager and was now a member of the presidential household, and an unofficial adviser to the President. Another member was Amos Kendall, a graduate of Dartmouth College, and a newspaper editor of some literary ability, who rendered great service to Jackson in the preparation of his state papers. Still another was young Henry Lee, who likewise possessed literary talents and served the President in a similar manner. There were also two editors, Duff Green and Isaac Hill, whose advice he frequently sought. To this group of "unconstitutional" advisers the President gave his full confidence; through them lay the shortest path to his favor, and upon their counsel he relied for assistance in shaping his public policies.

In his first message to Congress Jackson foreshadowed in a general way the future policy of his administration. He there gave notice that he would oppose the rechartering of the United States Bank, whose expediency and constitutionality he said "were ques-

[8] Sumner, "Life of Jackson," p. 147.
[9] *Ibid.*, p. 142.

tioned by a large portion of our fellow citizens " in spite of the decisions of the Supreme Court to the contrary; he gave the Cherokee Indians to understand that their attempt to set up an independent sovereignty within the State of Georgia would not be tolerated, and recommended Congress to set apart a district of territory west of the Mississippi for the permanent occupancy of such tribes as could be induced to emigrate thereto; declared that with regard to foreign affairs he should ask for nothing that was not right, and submit to nothing that was wrong; sounded a note of opposition to the policy of internal improvements under Federal auspices, chiefly on constitutional grounds; recommended that the surplus revenues in the national treasury be distributed among the States, and advised an amendment to the Constitution permitting popular election of the President.   " Since circumstances," he said, referring to Clay's part in the election of Adams, " may give the power of deciding the election to a single individual, may he not be tempted to name his reward? " [10]   His utterances upon the tariff were conveniently vague and ambiguous.   The late tariff, he said, had neither injured agriculture and commerce nor benefited manufactures as had been anticipated; but " some modifications " were desirable and should be considered in a non-partisan spirit.

The controversy between Georgia and the United States with regard to the Creek Indians occupied, as has already been mentioned, the attention of the Adams administration during a considerable part of the presidential term, ending in the virtual triumph of Georgia.   Emboldened by its success with regard to the Creeks, the State now undertook, December, 1828, by act of legislature, to extend its jurisdiction over a part of the Cherokee nation which occupied a large and fertile region in the northwestern part of the State, and demanded in strong terms that the national government should extinguish the title to all lands held by the Cherokees in the State.   The act furthermore divided up the Cherokee lands into counties, and excluded Indian testimony from the courts in all cases involving the interests of white men.   The people of Georgia very naturally regarded the Indian occupancy of this region, constituting as it did a semi-independent community within their borders, as an encumbrance upon their own sovereignty and an obstacle to the development of the State.   The Indians had appealed to President Adams during the last days of his administra-

[10] Richardson, " Messages and Papers of the Presidents," vol. ii. p. 447.

tion for protection against the encroachments of the Georgia authorities, but he resolved not to embarrass his successor, and accordingly allowed the matter to go over to the next administration. The Georgia authorities had undoubtedly calculated that Jackson's well-known sympathy with them in their Indian policy could be turned to good advantage, and they showed their confidence in him by voting unanimously for him at the late election. In the month following his inauguration he informed the Indians that their attempt to establish an independent government within the limits of Georgia would not be countenanced by the executive of the United States, and advised them to emigrate beyond the Mississippi or submit to the laws of the State. He furthermore withdrew the Federal troops which had been sent to Georgia to protect the Indians, and allowed the Georgia militia to take charge.

The Indians having failed to secure the aid of the executive, now resorted to the courts; but with no better success. When the State courts took jurisdiction of a case of murder against a Cherokee named Tassels the Chief Justice of the United States Supreme Court undertook to have the case removed to that body on a writ of error, but the State authorities defied the Federal writ, and on December 28, 1830, Tassels was hanged by direction of Governor Troup. The Indians now filed a bill in the Supreme Court, praying for a writ of injunction to restrain the State from interfering with their treaty rights, but the court decided, in January, 1831, that the Cherokee nation was not a State, and could not, therefore, be a party to a suit in the courts of the United States; in other words, that the remedy was political and not judicial in its nature.[11] In the case of Worcester against Georgia, decided in the following year, the court gave a decision in favor of the Indians on the ground that the Georgia statutes which sought to extend the jurisdiction of the State over the Cherokee lands contravened Federal treaties, and ordered the release of the accused,[12] but the President never executed it and is said to have declared that he would leave its enforcement to the Chief Justice who made the decision, and at the same time leave it to the people to decide at the approaching Presidential election whether his conduct was proper or not.[13] This was but another evidence of the character of the

[11] Peters U. S. Reports, p. 1.
[12] *Ibid.*, p. 515.
[13] Greeley, "The American Conflict," vol. i. p. 106.

new democracy which was in control of the government, and was symptomatic of the crude views of constitutional law then prevailing, even in the highest circles. The vexatious Indian question was finally settled by an act of Congress of 1834, creating an Indian territory beyond the Mississippi, to which the Cherokees and the Creeks were to be removed as soon as practicable. By treaties made with the Choctaws and Chickasaws of Mississippi in 1830 and 1832, these two tribes, in consideration of the payment of stipulated sums, agreed to remove to the new territory. To these four tribes were presently added the Seminoles of Florida. Before Jackson retired from office, therefore, most of the Southern Indians had been removed from the States in which they had been regarded as an encumbrance, to the Indian Territory, where their descendants, known as the five civilized tribes, live to this day undisturbed by the encroachments of the whites.

As Jackson leaned toward the States rights view in regard to the Indian question, so in regard to the policy of internal improvements under national auspices he was inclined to the narrower view adopted by Madison and Monroe that the general government had no constitutional authority for the practice which it had followed in this respect. He proposed that the surplus revenues of the government be distributed among the States, in order that they might make, under their own direction, such improvements as to them seemed expedient. The Congress, however, did not take this view of the matter, but proceeded to pass an act which pledged the aid of the government in the construction of a turnpike running from Maysville, Kentucky, to Lexington, a distance of some sixty miles. The President, true to his convictions, promptly vetoed the measure, on the ground that the Maysville road was not a truly national enterprise, and therefore not an object for national aid.[14] The friends of the measure were unable to secure a two-thirds majority to pass it over the executive veto, and hence it failed. Several other measures of the kind were passed during Jackson's term, but they were either vetoed, " pocketed " or returned at the next session unsigned. In his message of 1832 he recommended the sale of all the stocks held by the United States in canals, turnpikes, and similar enterprises.[15] The great difficulty then, as now, in determining whether a projected improvement was national or

[14] " Statesman's Manual," vol. i. p. 727.
[15] Richardson, " Messages and Papers of the Presidents," vol. ii. p. 602.

local opened the way for the application of the national funds for local purposes with its resulting abuses. Thus Jackson taught his party the evils of special legislation.[16]

Closely connected with the question of internal improvements was the disposition of the public lands. During Jackson's first term a memorable debate on the land question occurred in the United States Senate, which had the effect of bringing into prominence the growing sectional divergence, and the opposing views concerning the nature of the Union. The occasion for this forensic display was the introduction by Senator Foote of Connecticut, of a resolution proposing to institute an inquiry as to whether it was desirable or not to suspend for a period the sale of public lands, except such as were already surveyed, and for abolishing the office of surveyor-general. This resolution was immediately interpreted by the South and the West as additional evidence of the traditional neglect and jealousy of the East, and of her opposition to the erection of States in these regions. It was the view of the new democracy that the public lands should be given away to settlers at a price sufficient only to cover the actual cost of surveying and preparation for sale, and that by this means the West would become rapidly settled and her weight in the Union correspondingly increased. But the erection of States in the West was not looked upon with favor by the East, since it meant a draining away of population, a shifting of the balance of power from that section and a consequent loss of its former predominance in the Union. Senator Hayne of South Carolina, a man of real oratorical gifts, on January 19, 1830, made Foote's resolution the occasion of a general attack upon New England and an exposition of the doctrine of nullification. He accused the New England States of a desire to check the growth of other sections, and charged them with pusillanimous conduct in the late war with Great Britain.

The speech was replied to on the following day by Daniel Webster, who had already risen to the position of the foremost orator of the Union. In this first speech Webster confined his remarks mainly to the denial of the charge of Eastern hostility to the growth of the West, and did not enter upon a discussion of the nature of the Union under the Constitution. Colonel Hayne soon returned to the attack with a brilliant and lengthy speech, which the Southern members loudly applauded, and which even Webster's

[16] Sumner, "Life of Jackson," p. 194.

friends feared could not be successfully answered. In this speech Hayne, after assailing Webster personally, and attacking the patriotism of Massachusetts, made a full exposition of the doctrine of nullification. After a night of careful thought and preparation Webster rose to reply, January 26, 1830. It was a great historical occasion, the first notable forensic encounter between the North and the South. The speech which Webster delivered on that day to a crowded chamber will long remain one of the most memorable orations ever delivered in the Senate, and is surpassed by none in the annals of American oratory. Webster himself never equalled it in any subsequent speech.[17]

Hayne had taken the stand that the Constitution of the Union was a mere compact between the States composing it; that the national government was the agent of the States for certain specified purposes; that it could not be made the judge of the extent of its powers, for that would leave the States at the mercy of the general government, and would lead to the destruction of the federal character of the Republic. Finally Hayne contended that the States, the real principals, were the judges in cases of deliberate and palpable infractions of the Constitution by the national government, and could interpose to arrest such violations. The decision of this question could not be left to the national judiciary, because that would be vesting the agent with power to judge of the extent and nature of its own powers.

In reply to this course of reasoning Webster showed that the Constitution was not a compact, nor the Union a mere league dissoluble at the will of the States composing it, and that it was not the mere creature and agent of the States, but a supreme national government, clothed with adequate powers, the extent of which was a matter for the determination of the national judiciary and not for the States. He denied that each State had the power to interpret the Constitution according to its interests, and showed with great power that Hayne's doctrine of nullification would lead to the destruction of the Union, an object which the fathers could never have intended to bring about. The closing words of his oration, " Liberty and union, now and forever, one and inseparable," are familiar to every American schoolboy. This remarkable debate was the opening gun in the long controversy between the sections and made a profound impression upon the people through-

[17] Lodge, " Life of Webster," p. 174.

out the Union. It was the first clear statement by the leading statesmen of the two sections of the two opposing views of the nature of the Union as it had developed under the Constitution,[18] and it may be said that from this time forward the North, which had once wavered, became largely nationalist, while the South went over to the other side. It was thus, in a way, the turning point in the constitutional development of the country from the adoption of the Constitution to the outbreak of the Civil War.

As to the merits of the question it has been well said, that the ground which Webster took was new ground, while that which Hayne occupied was old ground; that Webster's position was one toward which the greater part of the nation was steadily advancing, while Hayne's was one upon which the South was presently to stand quite alone.[19] It is certainly true that in the early days of the Republic Hayne's view of the nature of the Union was quite generally accepted in the North as well as in the South; but by the beginning of the fourth decade of the century the North was slowly coming over to the national view, and the hastening of this change was the chief result of the debate between Hayne and Webster.

The theory of nullification which Hayne had championed in the Senate was soon to be put into practice, but without success, in the State he represented. It was not the question of the public lands or of the Indians this time, but the tariff, which was to furnish the occasion, and it was not Hayne, but John C. Calhoun, who was to be most conspicuous in the movement to carry it into effect. As we have already pointed out in another connection, Calhoun, after the enactment of the "monstrous" Tariff Act of 1828, prepared an elaborate statement of the theory of nullification for the use of the legislature of his State, which was officially promulgated as the "South Carolina Exposition."[20] In this manifesto he pointed out the dissimilarity in the economic interests of the North and South, showed that the recent high protective tariff legislation of Congress was operating to the detriment of the South, since the industries of that section were primarily agricultural in character, and asserted that if Congress should persist in its oppressive and unconstitutional legislation the only alternative left to an in-

---

[18] Lodge, "Life of Webster," p. 180.
[19] Wilson, "Division and Reunion," p. 47.
[20] Von Holst, "Life of John C. Calhoun," p. 76.

jured State was to interpose a suspensory veto upon such legislation so far as that particular State was concerned, until a constitutional amendment could be adopted expressly conferring upon Congress the power in question. Calhoun did not advocate immediate resort to this method, but proposed to wait for a returning sense of justice which it was believed would follow the election of General Jackson. He doubtless believed also that General Jackson's States rights sympathies would lead him, if not into approval, at least into acquiescence in the schemes of the nullifiers. But in this supposition the nullifiers were doomed to disappointment. At a notable Democratic banquet at Washington on April 13, 1830, the anniversary of Jefferson's birth, various toasts were proposed, all of which were permeated with the aroma of State sovereignty, and the responses were all that the nullifiers could wish for until the turn of the President came. With his characteristic directness he proposed to toast " Our Federal Union, it must be preserved." [21]

This was like throwing a firebrand into the camp of the nullifiers; it greatly disconcerted them, and convinced them that in counting on the aid of the chief executive they had reckoned without their host.[22] Although a strict constructionist in his constitutional law, Jackson had a high sense of the value of the Union, and as its chief magistrate his duty to do all in his power to insure its preservation seemed as clear as day to him. He is reported to have sent word to his friends in South Carolina that if a drop of blood was shed in that State in opposition to the laws of the United States he would promptly hang as a traitor the first one guilty of such conduct upon whom he could lay hands. His opposition to the nullification movement in South Carolina was doubtless further increased by the refusal of the State to cast its electoral vote for him, and by a personal breach between him and Calhoun. The breach grew out of Jackson's discovery about this time that Calhoun, as Secretary of War in Monroe's Cabinet, had proposed to censure him for his conduct in invading Spanish West Florida during the Seminole war, whereas Jackson had believed all along that Calhoun alone of the Cabinet members was his friend and that Adams was his chief enemy, when in reality Adams, almost alone of the Cabinet, had defended him. It was a principle of Jackson's ethics that no man, whether in his official or private character,

[21] Benton, " Thirty Years' View," vol. i. p. 148.
[22] Parton, " Life of Jackson," vol. iii. p. 286.

should censure him and still remain his friend. No explanation which Calhoun could offer was acceptable to Jackson, and from that time forward a state of unceasing hostility existed between the two men. It was now certain that Calhoun could no longer count upon the aid of the chief executive in his proposed nullification of the obnoxious tariff law. He thereupon published an " Address to the People of South Carolina," under the date of July 26, 1831, in which he reënforced the arguments of the " Exposition," and again elaborated his scheme of nullification. Once more his main contention was that with the great dissimilarity of interests in the country the only safe foundation for the Union lay in the sovereignty of the States, which enabled each to defend itself against usurpations.[23]

Meantime Congress was again tampering with the tariff, and in July, 1832, a new measure was passed which removed the most obnoxious features of the act of 1828, but still retained the principle of protection. It now looked as if the majority had no intention of abandoning what appeared to the South to be a policy ruinous to the interests of that section; indeed, there was reason to believe that it was intended to be a permanent part of the economic policy of the government. In South Carolina, where the opposition to the tariff was the strongest, preparations were now entered upon to free the State by extraordinary measures from the burdens of an obnoxious law against which the people had petitioned in vain. This was to be accomplished by the nullification of the law in accordance with the scheme worked out by Calhoun. Accordingly, in October, 1832, the governor called the legislature together in extraordinary session and it promptly issued a call for a State convention to meet at Columbia on November 19. On the 24th, with all the solemnity befitting the occasion, the convention adopted the famous Ordinance of Nullification, declaring the Tariff Act null and void so far as its operation within the jurisdiction of South Carolina was concerned. It further forbade the payment of all duties after February 1, 1833, on goods imported into the State, prohibiting appeals arising under the act from being taken to the United States courts, and declared that in the event of Congress attempting to reduce the State to obedience, South Carolina would regard her connection with the Union as dissolved. Before adjourning the convention issued two addresses, one to the people of

[23] Von Holst, "Life of Calhoun," p. 97.

South Carolina, calling upon them to give their unqualified obedience to the ordinance, and one to the people of the other States, reciting the reasons which had impelled South Carolina to nullify the law and justifying, on constitutional grounds, the course which the convention had taken.

The ordinance was then laid before the legislature and that body promptly passed the necessary measures to carry it into execution. The first of them was an act allowing consignees of merchandise held for non-payment of customs to recover the same by a writ of replevin, besides throwing various other obstacles in the way of Federal officers who should attempt to collect the duties. Another act provided for placing the State on a war footing for the purpose of resisting the authority of the United States, should an attempt be made to employ force in the execution of the nullified act. A final act, the most obnoxious of all, provided a test oath for all officers of the State as a means of excluding Union men from holding positions of honor or trust under the State.[24]

In the meantime the President had instructed the officials at Charleston to collect the duties, even if the employment of force should be necessary, and to that end dispatched troops to Fort Moultrie with orders to aid the collector and defend the property of the United States at all hazards. Finally, on December 10, the President issued an eloquent proclamation addressed to the people of South Carolina, in which he declared that the attempt of a State to nullify a law of the United States was rebellion pure and simple and wholly without constitutional justification. He denied the right of a State to pass upon the validity of a Congressional statute, and affirmed that the Federal judiciary had been created for the settlement of questions of this character. " I consider," he said, " the power to annul a law of the United States assumed by one State incompatible with the existence of the Union, contradicted expressly by the letter of the Constitution, unauthorized by its spirit, inconsistent with every principle on which it was founded, and destructive of the great object for which it was formed." With regard to his own duty in the premises the President said: " The laws of the United States must be executed. I have no discretionary power on the subject — my duty is emphatically pronounced in the Constitution. Those who told you that you might

[24] Burgess, " The Middle Period," pp. 224–226; Houston, " Nullification in South Carolina," pp. III–II4.

peacefully prevent their execution deceived you. Their object is disunion, and disunion by armed force is treason." [25] Every line of the proclamation rang with patriotism and good sense, and it closed with a strong appeal to the people of his native section to abandon their opposition to the Tariff Act and abide by the will of the majority. "It reads," says Parton, "more like the last appeal of a sorrowing but resolute father to wayward, misguided sons. It was clear in statement, forcible in argument, vigorous in style and glowing with the fire of a genuine and enlightened patriotism." [26] The firm stand of the President was supported with great unanimity by the people of the North, and in later years, when the secession movement was on the eve of culmination, Jackson's course was pointed to as one worthy of emulation by his successor. State after State from Maine to Mississippi promptly gave formal expression of their approval of the President's sentiments, and of their determination to support him in the exercise of his legitimate powers. In the South there was naturally more or less sympathy with the nullificationists, but outside the Gulf States it can hardly be said to have been enthusiastic, and in some of these it was of the feeblest sort. In fact, most of their State legislatures passed resolutions pronouncing South Carolina's action both unjustifiable and unwarranted, and warmly supporting the President and denouncing the doctrine of nullification.[27] Even in South Carolina there was a strong Union party and they held a convention at Charleston and adopted resolutions condemning the action of the nullifiers.

But the President's proclamation did not seem to have any marked effect upon the course of the nullifiers. Apparently they were as determined in their course as the President was in his, and refused to be deterred by his threats. Colonel Hayne, the recently elected governor, issued a counter-proclamation denouncing the attitude of the President, warning the good people of the State against his attempt " to seduce them from their allegiance," and calling upon them to stand firm in their opposition to the obnoxious tariff law; and the legislature of the State joined in the denunciation of Jackson and promised the governor its support. At this stage of the conflict Congress met, and it remained to see if that

[25] Richardson, "Messages and Papers of the Presidents," vol. ii. p. 652.
[26] Parton, "Life of Jackson," vol. iii. p. 469.
[27] Houston, "Nullification in South Carolina," p. 119.

body would support the President in his stand and enact whatever legislation might be necessary to enforce the execution of the obnoxious law in South Carolina. To the delight of the nullifiers the first move was in the direction of compromise, for on December 7, 1832, the Ways and Means Committee brought in a bill providing for a substantial reduction of the duties. This appeared to Jackson too much like abandoning the fight and leaving the authority of the government unvindicated. Accordingly he sent a message to Congress asking for authority to use the army and navy for the enforcement of the revenue laws, and to take such other steps as appeared to him to be necessary to uphold the dignity and authority of the United States. A measure dubbed by its enemies the " Force Bill," was promptly passed, and approved, on January 21, 1833, giving the courts of the United States jurisdiction of cases arising under the revenue laws, providing for the transfer of suits involving acts done under the authority of the United States or rights claimed thereunder from the State courts to the Federal courts, empowering the President to alter the customs districts and change the places of collection; and authorizing him to use the military and naval forces to resist interference with the collection of revenues.[28] The measure was variously attacked as arbitrary and destructive of the liberties of the people. It was no doubt severe, but in Jackson's opinion it was clearly demanded by the situation.

Meantime the proposal of the Ways and Means Committee to reduce the tariff duties was under discussion in Congress, and the result was the passage on February 26, 1833, of a compromise measure conceived by the pacific mind of Henry Clay. This act provided that all duties in excess of twenty per cent. should be gradually reduced until 1842, after which date there should be a uniform rate of twenty per cent.[29] This was acceptable to the nullifiers, and the prospect of its adoption by Congress, together with the failure of other States to join South Carolina, had already led to the suspension until the adjournment of Congress of the ordinance which was to have gone into effect February 1. The suspension was made, it will be noted, not by the convention which had proclaimed the act of nullification, but by an unofficial gathering of prominent citizens at Charleston, on January 21, 1833, the

[28] Burgess, " The Middle Period," p. 233.
[29] Taussig, " Tariff History of the United States," p. 110.

very day of the passage of the Force Bill. A week after the passage of the act for the lowering of the duties the convention reassembled and formally repealed the ordinance, but pronounced the Force Act null and void in South Carolina. This was the end of the controversy.

Whether the national principle or that of the nullificationists had triumphed is still a debatable question. The nation had asserted its right to enforce its commands in spite of the opposition of the people of a particular locality, and had passed a Force Bill as a means of overcoming resistance, and that measure had become a permanent statute. But on the other hand, the United States had yielded to the demands of the nullificationists by repealing the law which they had attempted to nullify. It could be said that a precedent had been created by which any State which disapproved of an act of Congress might threaten to resist it by nullification, and thus bring the national government to make the concessions demanded. But this was most improbable. The executive never retreated an inch from his position that nullification involved resistance to the authority of the United States, and had Congress seen fit not to repeal the objectionable tariff law, the President would doubtless have enforced it, though it would probably have required the employment of arms. Nullification, therefore, failed to make good its claim as a practicable and constitutional method of defense against the national government; it had, in fact, broken down at every point, and was never resorted to again. In this sense there was a distinct gain on the side of the national principle in our constitutional development. But the effect of the controversy was to alienate the people of South Carolina from the general government, and to create in their minds a disposition to look to secession as an ultimate necessity.[30]

III

JACKSON'S WAR AGAINST THE UNITED STATES BANK

In the midst of the excitement over the nullification controversy the presidential election had occurred and Jackson had been reëlected by an overwhelming electoral majority. Jackson's popularity had apparently lost little of its universality by reason of his

[30] Houston, "Nullification in South Carolina," p. 137.

inauguration of the spoils system, his attack upon the United States Bank, which was the real issue, and his firm stand against nullification; and consequently his reëlection had been a foregone conclusion. But it was not allowed to go uncontested. In the first place he was opposed by the new Anti-Masonic party, which had sprung into existence in consequence of the alleged abduction and murder, by order of the Masons in 1826, of one William Morgan, a bricklayer of Batavia, New York, charged with betraying the secrets of the Masonic order.[31] The leading principle of the new party was hostility to the Masonic order and the exclusion of its members from public office. At first confined to New York, the movement rapidly spread to a number of adjoining States. In 1831 a national convention of this party—the first national convention for the nomination of a presidential candidate in the history of the United States—was held at Baltimore and nominated the noted orator, William Wirt, of Virginia, for President, and Amos Ellmaker, of Pennsylvania, for Vice President. A little later in the same year a convention, representing the national wing of the Republicans, met at Baltimore likewise, and nominated Henry Clay of Kentucky for President, and John Sargent of Pennsylvania for Vice President.[32] In the spring of the following year a third convention, representing the young men of the country, was held at Washington to endorse the nomination of Clay.

The followers of Jackson, who were now beginning to be called the Democratic party, also held their national convention at Baltimore, and with practical unanimity renominated the general. On account of his quarrel with Calhoun, and the latter's activity in the nullification movement, it was decided not to renominate Calhoun for Vice President. Jackson's choice was Martin Van Buren, of New York, the leader of the Democrats in that State, and a successful politician of the true Jacksonian type. He had been nominated by Jackson as minister to England, but was rejected by the Senate and was forced to undergo the humiliation of returning home discredited and dishonored. Jackson therefore demanded the nomination of Van Buren as a personal endorsement of himself, believing that it would be a case of poetic justice to call Van Buren to the presidency of the body which had thought him unworthy to represent the United States at the Court of St. James.

[31] Hammond, "Political History of New York," vol. ii. p. 376.
[32] Sumner, "Life of Jackson," p. 255.

Van Buren had almost alone of the original Cabinet retained the confidence of Jackson.

Before the administration had advanced very far a disruption of the Cabinet took place in consequence of the refusal of the wives of the heads of departments to recognize socially the wife of the Secretary of War, Eaton. Tales affecting her character had been circulated, and Jackson, believing in her innocence, and remembering that the good name of his own wife had suffered from the aspersions of certain newspapers, gallantly made her cause his own, and sent out an order that Mrs. Eaton must receive the social recognition from the other Cabinet women to which her position entitled her. But the ladies refused to obey; whereupon Jackson ordered the members of the Cabinet who had wives to coerce them into obedience. Refusing to comply with the President's wishes, they were asked to resign, and they all did so. Throughout the whole controversy Van Buren, a widower, accorded due social recognition to the wife of the President's life-time friend and counsellor, and thereby retained his full confidence and respect.[33] Van Buren was nominated for Vice President, but with less unanimity than was Jackson.

While many of the voters did not approve of Jackson's measures, most of them admired his staunch patriotism and firmness of purpose, believing that his motives were always good and that whatever errors he had made were due to mistaken views of policy or to bad advice. He was, moreover, the representative of the new democracy, with its exaggerated conception of the rights and capacity of the people, which could not be said of the opposition candidates. The success of the administration candidates was, therefore, insured from the first. "My opinion is," said William Wirt, "that Jackson may be President for life if he chooses." [34] The electoral vote stood, Jackson, 219; Clay, 49; Wirt, 7. South Carolina and Kentucky alone of the Southern States repudiated Jackson, the South Carolina votes being thrown away upon John Floyd, of Virginia; those of Kentucky going to Clay. Vermont alone was carried by the Anti-Masons. Pennsylvania refused to support Van Buren and threw away her votes for Vice President on one of the United States senators from that State.[35]

[33] Parton, "Life of Jackson," vol. ii. p. 287.
[34] *Ibid.*, vol. iii. p. 432.
[35] Stanwood, "History of the Presidency," p. 164.

Jackson was quick to interpret the results of the election as an endorsement of his policy in every respect and as giving him *carte blanche* from the people to proceed with the measures which he had begun. Had he reflected, however, upon the proportion of the popular vote which he received, his opinion of the popular approbation must have been weakened. The fact is, the aggregate popular vote received by him was less than in 1828, and many of the States whose electoral votes were counted for him were carried by small majorities. It is by no means improbable that, had the opposition united on a strong candidate, he might have defeated Jackson in the electoral college.

Jackson's second term began in a political calm, but ended in a tempest. The greater part of it was taken up with the controversy over the United States Bank, an issue which overshadowed all others. It will be remembered that the second bank had been chartered in 1816 by a Democratic Congress for a term of twenty years, and hence its charter would expire in 1836. For reasons partly personal and partly for reasons of state, Jackson had formed an unfavorable opinion of the bank, and his opinion soon ripened into hostility. In his first message to Congress in 1829, seven years before the expiration of its charter, he expressed the opinion, which, he said, must be admitted by all, that the bank had failed in the great end of establishing a uniform and sound currency, and asserted that the constitutionality and expediency of the law creating the bank were questioned by a large portion of " our fellow citizens." The President further stated that he was moved to call the attention of Congress to the question of the renewal of the charter in order to avoid the " evils resulting from precipitancy," and suggested that a national bank, founded upon the credit of the government and its revenues, might be devised, which would avoid the constitutional objections raised, and at the same time secure all the advantages to the government which were expected to result from the old bank.[36]

Jackson also charged that the bank had used its influence in the recent election to defeat him, and this was no doubt the chief cause of his hostility. As no intimation had been given by the stockholders that application would be made during Jackson's term for a renewal of the charter, and as the charter still had seven years to run, considerable surprise was expressed that the President

[36] " Statesman's Manual," vol. ii. p. 713.

should have adverted to the subject at that time. Moreover, it was news to most of the people that the constitutionality of the bank was generally questioned, and that it had failed to supply a sound currency. As a matter of fact, the Supreme Court had decided in at least two cases, one of them being the famous case of Mc-Culloch v. Maryland, that the constitutionality of the bank was beyond question, while the currency issued by it was accepted equally with gold in every money center in the world. But it was a part of Jackson's constitutional law that the opinions of the judiciary had no binding force upon the other departments of the government, and consequently the decision in the McCulloch case did not, in his opinion, conclusively settle the question. The charge as to the unsoundness of the bank, along with other charges regarding mismanagement, favoritism, interference in elections, etc., were investigated by two congressional committees and both reported that the charges were without foundation.

But this did not convince Jackson nor deter him from his attacks upon the bank. They were, in fact, renewed each year in his message to Congress, and with increased hostility. A line of argument which had powerful influence in determining the attitude of the voters was Jackson's assertion that the bank was an " un-American monopoly," and that its special privileges were contrary to the spirit of republican institutions. In the rapidly developing West, where extreme democracy had its stronghold, more or less jealousy of the " Eastern money power " was naturally felt, and it was easy for a popular hero like General Jackson to turn that jealousy into hostility against an Eastern institution so highly endowed with privileges as was the United States Bank. The faith which the Democracy had in him made it certain that if the fate of the bank were to depend upon a plebiscite, its existence was doomed. Jackson believed that the Democracy was with him in this opposition to the bank, and after vainly appealing to Congress year after year to take action, he informed that body, in his message of December 6, 1831, that he had conscientiously discharged his duty in regard to the matter and would, therefore, leave the question to the " investigation of an enlightened people and their representatives." [37] He meant by this that the people at the approaching Presidential election would be asked to pass upon the question of recharter.

[7] " Statesman's Manual," vol. ii. p. 765.

Jackson's opponents, relying upon the great services of the bank to the government, accepted the challenge, and early in 1832 the bank presented to the Senate a petition for recharter. The petition was made the occasion of a severe attack upon the bank by Senator Benton, one of Jackson's lieutenants, who charged that the bank officials had been guilty of illegal practices.[38]   In spite of the opposition the bill for renewal passed the Senate on June 11, after prolonged discussion, by a vote of 28 to 20.   In the House strenuous efforts were made to postpone consideration of the bill, but it finally passed that body on June 30 by a vote of 107 to 85, and was sent to the President for his approval on July 4. On July 10 he sent in a message stating that he had vetoed the bill, mainly on the ground, (1) that some eight millions of the stock of the bank was held by foreigners, which he thought was a source of national danger to the Republic; (2) that the bank was operating to make the West tributary to the East; (3) that it was a monopoly in the enjoyment of special privileges, for which an inadequate sum was paid; and (4) that the bank was improperly constituted and vested with powers unduly large.[39]

The message has been described as one mainly devoted to proving that the bank was an " unnecessary, useless, expensive, unAmerican monopoly, always hostile to the interests of the people and possibly dangerous to the government as well."   After the reading of the message in the Senate, Mr. Webster moved the passage of the bill over Jackson's veto, but the friends of the bank were unable to muster the necessary two-thirds, and hence the bill was lost.   The veto message was, in some respects, an able document, but it contained a good deal of sophistry.   It was extensively circulated throughout the Union and had a decisive influence on the public mind in many communities where the bank was but little known.   In other localities, like Philadelphia, where the services of the bank were better understood and appreciated, large meetings were held and resolutions adopted condemning the action of the President.

At this stage of the controversy the Presidential election occurred, and the people pronounced their verdict by the reëlection of Jackson by a large electoral majority, which, as already said, he promptly construed as a commission from the electorate to proceed

38 See Benton, " Thirty Years' View," vol. i. pp. 191, 221.
39 " Statesman's Manual," vol. ii. p. 767.

with the work of putting an end to the bank. Its fate was now sealed, so far as the power of the executive could make it so. The next move of the President was to deprive the bank of the public deposits, for the use of which it had acted as the fiscal agent of the government. By the act creating the bank the public moneys, however, could be removed only by order of the Secretary of the Treasury, and he was required to lay his reasons before Congress immediately after taking such action. Jackson had already urged Congress to authorize the removal of the deposits, but that body refused to give the order, saying that they were safe in the bank. He now resolved to direct the Secretary of the Treasury to make the removal, and Mr. McLane, the secretary, being known to be opposed to such a course, was transferred to the State Department, and William J. Duane, of Pennsylvania, was appointed as his successor. But to the President's surprise Mr. Duane refused to make the removal, on the ground of insufficient reason, and protested strongly against the policy of removal. The President then asked him to resign and make way for one who would carry out his orders. This he refused to do; whereupon Jackson dismissed him from office and appointed the Attorney General, Roger B. Taney, of Maryland, as his successor.[40] The President had already informed the Cabinet in September that he had determined upon the removal of the deposits, that he would assume the responsibility himself, and had fixed upon October 1, 1833, as the date for the removal. The new Secretary promptly obeyed the orders of the President, and on the day appointed issued an order directing that the public moneys in the bank, amounting to $9,868,435, should be gradually drawn out to meet the current expenses of the government, and that no more should be deposited. Within a period of nine months the government deposits had all been withdrawn, making so severe a drain upon the bank that it was compelled to call in its loans in order to be able to withstand the strain.

Nor was the bank itself the only one affected; commercial distress was widespread, private credit was unfavorably affected, and business derangement amounting almost to a panic immediately followed.[41] The excitement throughout the country was intense, and delegations representing various private and public bodies waited on the President and begged that he would recommend some meas-

[40] Parton, "Life of Jackson," vol. iii. p. 517.
[41] Sumner, "Life of Jackson," p. 304.

ure of relief. To all these, however, Jackson replied that the distress was due to the action of the bank and not to any action of the government, and that the government could afford no relief. Petitions of this character poured into both houses of Congress and were favorably received in the Senate, where the opposition was in the majority; but in the House of Representatives, where Jackson's friends were in the ascendency, they met with little favor. The President informed Congress, in December, of his action, and gave the reasons therefor; saying that he had indisputable evidence that the bank had interfered in politics and had spent money to secure his defeat at the last election.[42]   His explanation was satisfactory to the House, but not to the Senate.   The latter body, upon the motion of Mr. Clay, adopted a resolution censuring the President for his action in removing the deposits and declared that he had " assumed authority and power not conferred by the Constitution and laws, but in derogation of both." [43]

Jackson refused to allow the censure to go unchallenged and sent to the Senate an elaborate protest against the right of that body to censure the action of a coördinate department of the government, and demanded that it be placed upon the records of the Senate.   It was an able State paper, and with the bank veto message contains a full exposition of the Jacksonian theory of government.[44]   But it did not convince the Senate, and by a substantial majority it was refused a place on the records.   The Senate furthermore adopted two joint resolutions declaring that the reasons given by the Secretary of the Treasury for the removal of the deposits were insufficient, and demanding that the public moneys be deposited in the United States Bank; but the House rejected both resolutions by a small majority.   By a somewhat larger majority it adopted a resolution declaring that the bank ought not to be rechartered.   The fate of the bank was now regarded as settled, and its friends abandoned all further hope of obtaining a new charter. Upon the expiration of the old charter in 1836 it took out a charter from the legislature of Pennsylvania and continued as a State bank with a capital of thirty-five million dollars.

After the withdrawal of the government deposits from the United States Bank the public moneys were deposited in certain

[42] "Statesman's Manual," vol. ii. p. 787.
[43] Parton, "Life of Jackson," vol. iii. p. 541.
[44] "Statesman's Manual," vol. ii. p. 843.

State banks, carefully selected with reference to party allegiance, and in the language of the day known as " pet banks." In order to obtain a share of the government funds, large numbers of such institutions, many of them of a "mushroom" character, sprang up in various parts of the country, especially in the South and West. As Whig banks were not in good standing with the administration, and not likely therefore to get a share of the public deposits, the new ones were mostly of the Democratic faith. Many of them issued circulating notes on fictitious capital, were poorly managed, and some disappeared as suddenly as they had come into existence, carrying with them government deposits and all.

The effect of distributing public moneys in large quantities throughout the West led to speculation, both legitimate and illegitimate, resulting in a general demoralization of business and involving disastrously many individuals and corporations.[45] This effect was heightened by an act of Congress passed in June, 1836, providing that the surplus revenues above $5,000,000 (the amount was about $40,000,000) should be deposited with the State governments in proportion to the representation of the States in Congress. Three quarterly installments, aggregating $28,000,000, were duly distributed, but by reason of the panic the fourth installment was not; in fact it had been swallowed up in the crash which followed. The amounts distributed among the States were declared to be of the nature of loans, but it was understood that they were not to be repaid. " They were," said Colonel Benton, " in name, a deposit; in form, a loan; in essence and design, a distribution." [46]

Finally, the derangement of business was further increased by the issue of the " specie circular " in July, 1836, directing the receivers of public moneys to accept nothing but gold and silver in payment of the public lands. This step was taken by the Treasury Department upon the direction of the President in consequence of a flood of State bank paper, much of it issued by irresponsible banking concerns, all of it depreciated, which was pouring into the Treasury as a result of the rapid sales of public lands in the West. Land speculators would organize a " bank " on Democratic lines, then secure a share of the government deposits, issue notes, borrow them and buy land; the notes were deposited, borrowed again, and so on indefinitely.[47] The President was alarmed at this condi-

[45] Sumner, "Life of Jackson," p. 323.
[46] Benton, "Thirty Years' View," vol. i. p. 556.
[47] Sumner, "Life of Jackson," p. 335.

tion of affairs and determined, against the advice of his Cabinet, that the government must require payment in specie. But as there were few or no specie paying banks, particularly in the West, a severe drain on the Eastern banks was necessary; they were unable to withstand the strain, a business crash followed, and one of the worst financial panics the country has even known set in. As in the case of the removal of deposits, Jackson assumed the entire responsibility for the order, and when petitions poured in upon him from all parts of the country, begging that the order be rescinded, he firmly refused to yield, and finally announced that he would not move a hair's breadth, even if a petition were presented containing the names of all the people in the land, including those on the gravestones. But the order had one salutary effect; it checked the tide of reckless speculation in public lands. A few days before the expiration of Jackson's term Congress passed a bill annulling the specie circular, but Jackson " pocketed " it on the ground that it was " obscure."

Another important financial measure of Jackson's administration was an act of Congress passed in 1834, changing the mint ratio between gold and silver from 15 to 1 to 16 to 1. Shortly after the enactment of the law of 1792, fixing the ratio at 15 to 1, it was found that gold had been undervalued; that is, in the markets of the world an ounce of gold was worth more than fifteen ounces of silver, and consequently the more valuable metal disappeared from circulation, either to be melted or exported. Gold being worth more as bullion than as coin, it was found unprofitable to coin it, but profitable to purchase silver and coin that, the amount of the profit being the difference between the mint and the market ratio. Instead of a double standard, therefore, we had only a single standard, and that of silver. The act of 1834 changed the mint ratio so as to make it correspond with the market ratio, but as the market ratio was a matter of supply and demand, the increased supply of gold, in consequence of the California discovery, soon disturbed the ratio and made another adjustment necessary.[48]

The domestic tranquillity of Jackson's administration was disturbed by two Indian wars, one in the Northwest in 1833, against the Sac and Fox tribes; the other in Florida, against the Seminoles in 1835. The former is commonly called the Black Hawk War,

[48] Laughlin, " Elements of Political Economy," p. 308.

from the name of the chief who stirred up the Indians to rebellion. After a brief campaign Black Hawk was captured and taken on a tour through the large cities of the East in order to impress him with the power and greatness of the United States. The second Seminole War grew out of the attempt of the President to remove these Indians to the Territory set apart for them west of the Mississippi River. Under their chief, Osceola, they rose in rebellion, committed various depredations and atrocities, and afterward retreated to the Everglades, where they were reached by the American troops with the greatest difficulty. It was not until after Jackson's retirement that the rebellious Indians were brought to terms.

In some directions Jackson's administration was an unqualified success. This was especially true of the conduct of foreign relations, notably with Great Britain concerning the West India trade, and with France concerning the payment of claims, amounting to some $5,000,000, for depredations upon American commerce during the Napoleonic wars. Ever since the Revolution Great Britain had imposed vexatious restrictions upon American trade with the British West Indies. Negotiations running through a long period had been undertaken for the removal of the restrictions, but nothing had resulted from the efforts. Jackson was greatly impressed with the importance to the United States of the West India trade, and informed the British Government that the United States was ready to treat on the basis of reciprocal privileges, and the offer was accepted. The result was an agreement by which both governments repealed the restrictions upon their colonial carrying trade, and the West India commerce was thrown open to the United States, while the ports of the United States were thrown open to the British colonies. As for the spoliation claims against France, Jackson pressed for a settlement with his characteristic energy and directness. In 1831 a convention was concluded by which France agreed to pay to the United States $5,000,000 in satisfaction of the said claims, and each high contracting party was to admit to its ports certain products of the other on favorable terms. The United States Congress promptly passed the law necessary to carry the treaty into effect, but the French Chambers neglected to make the appropriation called for in the treaty stipulation.[49] Finally, after waiting more than three years, Jackson lost patience and sent a message to Congress in December, 1834, sug-

[49] Foster, "Century of American Diplomacy," p. 279.

gesting the expediency of making reprisals upon French commerce.
The message caused great excitement in France. French journals
talked of war, and the king recalled his minister from the United
States. But in April, 1835, the French Chambers passed the appropriation with the condition that no money should be paid until
" satisfactory explanations " of the President's message should be
received. This condition the American Government refused to
comply with, and recalled its minister from Paris. Thus matters
stood until early in 1836, when the English Government interposed
its good offices and brought about a friendly understanding between the United States and France. The money was then
promptly paid to the American Government.[50] Besides the conventions with France and Great Britain, a number of commercial
treaties were concluded with other countries.

One of Jackson's last victories, one for which his friends had
labored both in and out of season, was the passage of a resolution
by the Senate expunging from the journal the censure which that
body had passed against him in 1834 for the removal of the deposits.
The general gave an elaborate dinner to those who voted for the
resolution, and to the end of his life held in the highest esteem the
" expungers," as they were called. Having issued a farewell address to his countrymen, summing up his political principles, and
warning the people against possible dangers as he foresaw them,
in imitation of Washington, Jackson retired to private life at the
Hermitage, near Nashville, where he spent the few remaining years
of his life.

The eight years of Jackson's Presidency formed an era of tremendous industrial development, of social transition, and of great
political change, marked by continuous agitation and excitement of
the public mind.[51] The influence of his administration upon the
country was probably unsurpassed by that of any of his predecessors. But historians are still divided in opinion whether the sum
of it was for good or evil. In favor of its beneficial influence may
be mentioned the firm and decided stand which he took in the
conduct of the foreign relations and in regard to nullification, the
positive and energetic character of his policies, the extinguishment
of the national debt, the concentration of public attention upon a

[50] Sumner, "Life of Jackson," p. 348; Parton, "Life of Jackson," vol.
iii. ch. xl.
[51] "Statesman's Manual," vol. ii. p. 1406.

specie currency, the settlement of the Indian question, and the check which he gave to speculation and extravagance through his opposition to internal improvements and inflated currency. On the other hand, General Jackson's critics contend that he is entitled to no credit for the liquidation of the public debt, as that rather belongs to his predecessors, who had adopted the policy of gradually reducing it, while the inauguration of the spoils system was enough to counteract every good feature of the administration. Besides, there was the President's arbitrary conduct, particularly with regard to the finances, which showed, or which seemed to show, a disregard of the Constitution and the laws, with its consequent evil influence as a precedent. His disposition to ignore constitutional restraints probably contributed something to the development of the spirit of lawlessness, although its share in this respect has perhaps been exaggerated by some historians. When all is said that may be said against Jackson's administration, it is still clear that in point of vigor, economy and preservation of the national honor and dignity abroad it deserves a favorable verdict.

IV

MARTIN VAN BUREN

Of the many personal victories which came to Jackson in the last years of his administration, none gave him such unalloyed pleasure as the choice of Van Buren to be his successor. Van Buren had been a faithful supporter in every issue which had been raised during the eight years of Jackson's rule. The rejection by the Senate of his nomination as minister to England Jackson interpreted as a personal rebuke to himself. Of all the politicians who had served him there was none to whom he desired so much to bequeath the Presidency as to the "little magician" of New York. With his enormous influence, therefore, he easily procured Van Buren's unanimous nomination by the party which he had himself built up and ruled with a master hand for eight years. The convention that nominated Van Buren — the second national convention of the party — met in an old Presbyterian church at Baltimore, in June, 1835, nearly a year and a half before the election. There were present over 500 delegates from twenty-three States, South Carolina, Alabama and Illinois not being represented. The rule requiring two-thirds of the whole number of votes for a nomination was adopted, because "it would have a more imposing effect," although nearly half the convention did not believe such a rule was in conformity with good Democratic principles.[52] Richard M. Johnson of Kentucky was nominated for the Vice Presidency against the strong protests of the Virginia delegates, who announced that they would not support Johnson. No platform was adopted, but a committee was appointed to prepare an address to the people.

The opposition, now called Whigs in imitation of the English party of the same name, and, like it, founded on hostility to executive prerogative, put forward General William Henry Harrison of Indiana. Judge Hugh L. White, of Tennessee, was nominated by the legislatures of Alabama, Illinois and Tennessee, and was supported by some of the Southern Whigs. A disorderly campaign now ensued. In response to a request from an obscure Western voter, the three candidates wrote letters defining their positions on the important questions of the day. Van Buren's letter was skillfully worded, evasive, non-committal; altogether one of the most remarkable letters ever written by a Presidential candidate. The party discipline which Jackson had organized was effective and Van Buren was elected, but with a majority far less than that of his master and predecessor, for he received 170 electoral votes, as against 124 for his opponents, making a majority of but 46; whereas Jackson had been elected four years previously by a majority of 159 electoral votes. Van Buren's popular majority was only about 25,000, as against Jackson's majority of 157,000 at the last election.[53] Massachusetts cast her vote for Daniel Webster, while South Carolina gave hers to Willie P. Mangum, of North Carolina. Georgia and Tennessee, which had voted almost unanimously for Jackson at the last election, now went for White, while Mississippi and Louisiana gave Van Buren majorities of but three hundred each. Thus Van Buren came to the Presidency supported by the great Middle States and New England, against the West, with the South divided. Omitting the uncontested election of Monroe in 1820, he was the first candidate for the Presidency who had carried New England since 1804. Richard M. Johnson, the Democratic candidate for Vice President, lacked one vote of receiv-

[52] Shepard, "Life of Martin Van Buren," p. 222.
[53] "Statesman's Manual," vol. iii. p. 1024.

ing the electoral majority required, in consequence of the refusal of many Southern electors on the Democratic ticket to vote for him, and in accordance with the Constitution the election devolved upon the Senate. Johnson was promptly chosen, receiving thirty-three votes, as against sixteen for Francis Granger, the Whig candidate.

The eighth President of the United States was the first of our chief magistrates to be born after the Revolution, and unlike all his predecessors, belonged by descent to a race stock other than those which had come from the British Isles. His ancestors had immigrated to New Netherlands from Holland and settled in the ancient town of Kinderhook, Columbia County, where the future President was born in 1782. At an early age Martin developed a love of politics and soon became a local leader of the Democratic-Republican party. He studied law with William P. Van Ness, an eminent attorney in the city of New York, and in due course was admitted to the bar. He served for a time in the State Senate of New York, was also Attorney General of the State, and in 1821 was elected to the United States Senate. Meantime, chiefly through his efforts, the " Albany regency " was formed, which controlled the Democratic politics of New York for many years. During this period Van Buren was its leader and his skill as a politician soon gave him a national reputation. He was a clever, shrewd political manager, but his methods were unusually honorable. In personality he was small in stature, and had keen, searching eyes. In manner he was courteous, extremely diplomatic in conversation and possessed far greater ability than some historians have given him credit for. In 1828 he was elected Governor of New York, but after a year's service was appointed Secretary of State by Jackson, and filled the office with fair ability. After the disruption of the Cabinet on account of the refusal of the Cabinet women to socially recognize Mrs. Eaton, wife of the Secretary of War, Van Buren was nominated minister to Great Britain, but the appointment was rejected by the Senate, as we have seen.

Van Buren's inauguration took place on the east portico of the Capitol, March 4, 1837, in the presence of twenty thousand spectators. With his predecessor and patron he rode to the Capitol in a " beautiful phaeton " built of wood taken from the old frigate *Constitution,* and presented to General Jackson by the loyal Democrats of New York.[54] Jackson was the third President — and so

[54] Shepard, "Life of Van Buren," p. 242.

far he has been the last — to serve through his term and then leave office amid demonstrations of enthusiasm equal to those that ushered him in.   After bidding Van Buren farewell, the Old Hero returned to Nashville, where he spent his eight remaining years, by far the most popular man in the country, still courted by politicians, consulted by statesmen, pursued by office seekers, and idolized by the great majority of his countrymen.[55]

President Van Buren inherited the greater part of Jackson's Cabinet as he did the office, but with them he also fell heir to one of the most widespread financial panics within the history of the country.   Jackson, with his unwise and violent financial policy, sowed the wind and his successor reaped the conventional crop. The derangement caused by the destruction of the United States Bank, the distribution of the government funds among the State banks and of the surplus among the States, the issue of the specie circular requiring payment for public lands to be made in specie, the mania for speculation, particularly in Western lands, the general spirit of extravagance as shown by the large importations of merchandise for which there was no legitimate demand, and the inflation of prices, all contributed to the disturbance of business and the confusion of the finances of the government.   During the last years of Jackson's administration these conditions had been slowly gathering, and the storm burst forth with a crash just at the time Van Buren assumed the reins of government.   Even before Jackson had retired the banks had begun to call in their loans, and in May, 1837, scarcely two months after Van Buren's inauguration, all the banks of New York city suspended specie payments, and were followed shortly afterward by those of the other principal cities of the country.[56]   Simultaneously with the suspension of specie payments by the banks came a large number of failures of mercantile establishments throughout the country.   In New York City alone over three hundred failures occurred, involving many millions of dollars, and in Boston the number exceeded one hundred and sixty.   Credit was almost paralyzed, the government deposits in the " Pet Banks " were lost, the surplus was transformed into a deficit, prices suffered a tremendous decline, large numbers of employees were discharged, and the domestic tranquillity was disturbed by bread riots in some communities, notably in New York City,

[55] Parton, " Life of Jackson," vol. iii. ch. xliv.
[56] Shepard, " Life of Van Buren," p. 274.

where 500 barrels of flour and a quantity of wheat were destroyed by a hungry mob, and the militia had to be called out to restore order.[57]

Petitions and memorials from various financial and commercial bodies poured in upon the President praying for a special session of Congress and the enactment of measures for the relief of the money market. The Whig journals everywhere fell to abusing the President for refusing to do something to relieve the commercial distress. Abbot Lawrence, a Boston millionaire, told a great meeting that " there was no other people on the face of God's earth that were so abused, cheated, plundered, and trampled upon by their rulers," and suggested that the time might come when " the crew must seize the ship." Great meetings were held in New York, Philadelphia, Baltimore and other large cities, and resolutions were adopted requesting the President to summon Congress in special session.

After some hesitation he yielded and summoned Congress to meet on the first Monday in September. The President's message to the Congress contained little which promised relief to the country; but, says his biographer, it is one of the greatest of American State papers and marks the zenith of his political wisdom.[58] He asserted that there was little or nothing which the government could do in the way of relief. He declared that the financial and business depression of the country had been caused by reckless speculation and bad management rather than by the policy of the government, and that it was not the province of the government to correct evils resulting therefrom.[59]

To reëstablish the national bank, he said, would be to disregard the popular will twice solemnly and unequivocally expressed. Turning to the State banks, which had held the government deposits, he inquired whether the evils inherent in any connection between the government and the banks of issue were not such as to require a divorce. Ought the public moneys be placed in such institutions for the benefit of private persons? He therefore recommended the establishment of sub-treasuries in which the funds of the government were to be kept in absolute divorce from the banks. This was poor comfort to those Whigs who were praying for a re-

[57] Sumner, "Life of Jackson," p. 383.
[58] Shepard, "Life of Van Buren," p. 279.
[59] See his Message in the " Statesman's Manual," vol. iii. p. 1051 *et seq.*

establishment of a national bank, and who, like Webster, believed that all the ills of the country were due to "the measures of the general government in relation to the currency." The proposed measure was criticised as only an administrative arrangement for the protection of the government, and not for the relief of the people. Congress, however, was impressed with the importance of the measure and the Senate promptly passed a bill embodying the President's recommendations, but it failed in the House. Tentative measures of relief adopted at the extra session were acts authorizing the issue of $10,000,000 in treasury notes, the postponement of the surplus distribution among the States, and a law permitting indulgence of payment to importers upon custom house bonds. By this time much of the distress had disappeared, and the excitement had abated, although there were bitter and deep-seated wounds still unhealed.

On October 10 the special session of Congress adjourned. At the next session the Independent Treasury Bill again passed the Senate and was again rejected by the House. This was repeated at each session of Congress until the last year of Van Buren's term, when the measure finally passed both houses and became a law. It was the most important legislative act of his term and stands as the chief monument of Van Buren's administration. Repealed for a short period upon the ascendency of the Whigs in 1841, it was reënacted in 1846 after the return of the Democrats to power, and became a permanent institution of the government. As finally passed it provided for the establishment of suitable vaults, safes, and the like for the keeping of the public moneys, provided for receivers-general in a number of the larger cities, required that the custodians of the public money should give bonds for the safe keeping of all funds entrusted to them, and enacted that all financial transactions with the United States should be exclusively on a gold and silver basis.[60]

Incidents in the foreign relations of the United States during Van Buren's term were an irritating dispute with Great Britain concerning the boundary between the State of Maine and the British possessions of New Brunswick, and the attempt of many citizens of the United States to take part in an insurrection in Canada. As a result of the boundary controversy the inhabitants of northeastern Maine and New Brunswick actually came to blows over the dis-

[60] Read Kinley, "The Independent Treasury." pp. 82-95.

puted territory. For a time a state of smoldering war existed in this region, and all efforts to reach an amicable settlement during Van Buren's term were unavailing. Congress authorized the President to call out 50,000 volunteers, and placed at his disposal $10,-000,000 with which to defend the claims of the United States; but before anything could be done his term expired. The Canadian insurrection grew out of the widespread discontent of the inhabitants of lower Canada on account of the alleged oppression of the British Government. With this discontent a large number of Americans, especially in New York, warmly sympathized. Many of the insurgent refugees from Canada flocked to New York, where they received an enthusiastic welcome. One of the refugees, McKenzie, the leader of the insurrection, raised a body of volunteers in Buffalo, and with their aid seized Navy Island in the Niagara River, belonging to Canada. Here he established a provincial government, and gathered about him a collection of arms, stores and men.

On the night of December 29, 1837, a party of Canadian militia crossed the Niagara and seized the *Caroline,* a vessel in the service of the insurgents, but on the American side of the river. The *Caroline* was then fired and sent over the falls a wreck. This infringement of neutrality caused intense excitement, not to say indignation, in the United States. The President issued a proclamation declaring that the neutrality laws must be rigidly enforced and all offenders punished. At the same time General Winfield Scott was sent to the border to enforce American neutrality, and the New York militia were called out and placed under his command. Finally, the insurgents abandoned Navy Island in January, 1838, and the insurrection came to an end, although several incursions from the United States were afterwards made into Canadian territory. Likewise with regard to Mexico, which had just lost Texas by revolution, the President maintained an attitude of neutrality, and when the new republic made overtures for annexation to the United States they were firmly declined. During his term, also, the second war with the Seminole Indians of Florida, to which reference has been made above, was brought to a close after years of hostility and the expenditure of over $15,000,000. Osceola was finally captured by General Jessup and sent to Fort Moultrie in Charleston harbor, where he was kept in prison until his death. The Seminoles were now transferred to the new Indian Territory west of the

Mississippi, and to-day constitute one of the civilized tribes of the State of Oklahoma.

With the expiration of Van Buren's term the Jacksonian epoch, so called, came to a close. The administration of Van Buren probably deserves more credit from historians than it has received. No suggestion was ever breathed against his integrity; he possessed strong moral courage, and he reached the Presidency by political abilities and public services of the first order. Less popular than Jackson he yet possessed far greater ability as a statesman, and had not his predecessor bequeathed to him a great business panic, which destroyed the confidence of the people, he might have left the record of a brilliant administration.[61]

[61] Sumner, "Life of Jackson," p. 384.